A study book for the

NEBOSH National Certificate in Construction

Health and Safety

RMS Publishing Limited
Victoria House, Lower High Street, Stourbridge DY8 1TA

© ACT Associates Limited.
Second Edition October 2007.

All rights reserved. No part of this publication may be stored in a retrieval system, reproduced, or transmitted in any form or by any means, electronic, mechanical, photocopying, recording or otherwise without either the prior written permission of the Publishers.

This book may not be lent, resold, hired out or otherwise disposed of by way of trade in any form or binding or cover other than that in which it is published, without the prior consent of the Publishers.

Whilst every effort is made to ensure the completeness and accuracy of the information contained herein, RMS/ACT can bear no liability for any omission or error. Please visit www.rmspublishing.co.uk for relevant updates to this edition.

Cover design by Graham Scriven
Printed and bound in Great Britain by CPI Antony Rowe.

ISBN-13: 978-1-900420-89-1

Foreword

EDITOR: JOHN LACEY

With the continued poor record of the construction industry in regards to Health and Safety, it is of the utmost importance to make those within the industry aware of procedures to change both standards and culture.

This study book compliments training with a structured approach to give students the tools to allow positive safety management within the construction industry.

After many years within the industry, I have seen major improvements but there is always a need for step-change action. The NEBOSH Certificate in Construction will assist construction personnel in achieving such a step-change.

John Lacey, C.F.I.O.S.H., F.S.I.A.. H.F.A.P.S, M.A.S.S.E
Chair of IOSH Construction Specialist Group and past president of IOSH.
Has been involved in and led by example construction health and safety,
in both the UK and other areas of the world for over 30 years.

Editor's Notes

Diagrams and photographs

A number of the diagrams included in the Study Book for the NEBOSH Certificate in Construction Safety and Health have been produced in hand-drawn format. In particular these are diagrams that students studying for NEBOSH examinations may be required, or find it helpful, to produce by hand at the time of examination. They are provided to help the student get an impression of how to do similar drawings of their own. I hope that these diagrams show that such drawings are achievable by hand and also assist in illustrating a standard that might be expected in examination.

We have taken particular care to support the text with a significant number of photographs. They are illustrative of both good and bad working practices and should always be considered in context with supporting text. I am sure that students will find this a useful aid when trying to relate their background and experience to the broad based NEBOSH Certificate in Construction Health and Safety syllabus. They will give an insight into some of the technical areas of the syllabus that people have difficulty relating to when they do not have a strong technical background.

Where diagrams/text extracts are known to be drawn from other publications, a clear source reference is shown and RMS/ACT wish to emphasise that reproduction of such diagrams/text extracts within the Study Book is for educational purposes only and the original copyright has not been infringed.

Legal requirements

The Study Book has at its heart the fact that health and safety should be managed as a risk. However as one of the risks to a business is the risk of prosecution care has been taken to relate topics to current legislation. The level of treatment is targeted to cover the interests of the Certificate in Construction student. Legislation is referred to in context in the various elements that comprise the Study Book and reflects the syllabus of the NEBOSH Certificate in Construction Health and Safety. In addition the book has an element dedicated to legislation entitled relevant statutory provisions, and here the student will find a useful summary of the legislation required by the NEBOSH Certificate in Construction Health and Safety.

The NEBOSH Certificate in Construction Health and Safety does not examine the student's knowledge of Regulation numbers. These are referred to in the Study Book in order to differentiate different components of the law and to aid the student in referencing legislation in the workplace, if required by their work.

Syllabus

Each element of the Study Book has an element overview that sets out the learning outcomes of the element, the content and any connected sources of reference. The Study Book reflects the order and content of the NEBOSH Certificate in Construction Health and Safety syllabus and in this way the student can be confident that the Study Book reflects the themes of the syllabus. In addition, the syllabus is structured in a very useful way, focusing on hazards, control and core management of health and safety principles.

Structure

The NEBOSH National Certificate in Construction award consists of three Units: NGC1, NCC1 and NCC2. This publication is designed to fulfil the learning requirements of Units NCC1 and NCC2. Where necessary, students should refer to the RMS study book for the NEBOSH National General Certificate, Unit NGC1.

Acknowledgements

Managing Editor: Ian Coombes CMIOSH – Managing Director, ACT; NEBOSH Advisory Committee and Past Board member, IOSH Professional Affairs Committee member.

RMS Publishing and ACT Associates Ltd wish to acknowledge the following contributors and thank them for their assistance in the preparation of the Certificate in Construction study book: Nick Attwood, Roger Chance, Andrew Hayes, Dean Johnson, Geoff Littley, Barrie Newell, Richard Sherwood and Julie Skett.

NEBOSH Study Books also available from RMS:

Publication	Edition	10-digit ISBN	13-digit ISBN	EAN
The Study Book for the NEBOSH National General Certificate	Fourth	1 900420 87 2	978-1-900420-87-7	9781900420877
The Study Book for the NEBOSH International General Certificate	First	1 900420 90 2	978-1-900420-90-7	9781900420907
The Study Book for the NEBOSH Certificate in Fire Safety and Risk Management	Second	1 900420 88 0	978-1-900420-88-4	9781900420884
The Study Books for the NEBOSH National Diploma in Occupational Safety and Health:				
■ (Unit A) Managing Health and Safety	Second	1 900420 77 5	978-1-900420-77-8	9781900420778
■ (Unit B) Hazardous Agents in the Workplace	Second	1 900420 78 3	978-1-900420-78-5	9781900420785
■ (Unit C) Workplace and Work Equipment	Second Revised & Updated	1 900420 91 0	978-1-900420-91-4	9781900420914

rms

Contents

ELEMENT	TITLE	PAGE NO.

UNIT NCC1 - MANAGING AND CONTROLLING HAZARDS IN CONSTRUCTION ACTIVITIES

Element 1:	Construction law and management	01
Element 2:	Construction site - hazards and control	13
Element 3:	Movement of people and vehicles - hazards and control	25
Element 4:	Manual and mechanical handling - hazards and control	43
Element 5:	Work equipment - hazards and control	63
Element 6:	Electrical - hazards and control	89
Element 7:	Fire - hazards and control	105
Element 8:	Chemical and biological health - hazards and control	125
Element 9:	Physical and psychological health - hazards and control	157
Element 10:	Working at height - hazards and control	177
Element 11:	Excavation work and confined spaces - hazards and control	197
Element 12:	Demolition - hazards and control	211
	Relevant statutory provisions	221
	Assessment	279
	Index	303

Figure List (including tables and quotes)

Figure Ref	Title and Source	Page No.

Element 1
1-1	Assessing the competence of individual CDM co-ordinators. *Source: CDM 2007 ACOP, Regulation 4.*	8

Element 2
2-1	Site assessment - previous use. *Source: ACT.*	15
2-2	Site assessment - general. *Source: ACT.*	15
2-3	Roads. *Source: ACT.*	16
2-4	Footpaths. *Source: ACT.*	16
2-5	Railways. *Source: Welsh Highland Railway.*	16
2-6	Waterways. *Source: ACT.*	16
2-7	Commercial properties. *Source: ACT.*	17
2-8	Industrial properties. *Source: ACT.*	17
2-9	Means of access. *Source: ACT.*	17
2-10	Safe distance barriers for overhead services. *Source: HSG144.*	17
2-11	Site access. *Source: ACT.*	18
2-12	Site controls - access and roadways. *Source: ACT.*	18
2-13	Misuse of storage. *Source: ACT.*	19
2-14	Loading / unloading. *Source: ACT.*	19
2-15	Site signs. *Source: ACT.*	20
2-16	Steelworks. *Source: ACT.*	20
2-17	Unauthorised access. *Source: ACT.*	20
2-18	Perimeter fencing and signs. *Source: ACT.*	20
2-19	Protection of others. *Source: ACT.*	21
2-20	Sanitary conveniences. *Source: ACT.*	21
2-21	Washing facilities. *Source: ACT.*	22
2-22	Temporary showers. *Source: ACT.*	22
2-23	Accommodation for clothing. *Source: ACT.*	23
2-24	Rest and eating facilities. *Source: ACT.*	23

Element 3
3-1	Slips and trips. *Source: Lincsafe.*	27
3-2	Trip hazards. *Source: Lincsafe.*	27
3-3	Collision with moving vehicles. *Source: ACT.*	27
3-4	Falling materials. *Source: Lincsafe.*	27
3-5	Obstructions. *Source: Lincsafe.*	28
3-6	Public highway works. *Source: ACT.*	28
3-7	Slip resistant surfaces. *Source: ACT.*	29
3-8	Outer fencing and inner guarding. *Source: ACT.*	30
3-9	Protection of pedestrians. *Source: ACT.*	30
3-10	Correct clothing & footwear. *Source: ACT.*	31
3-11	Vision panels in fire doors. *Source: ACT.*	31
3-12	Temperature and weather protection. *Source: CDM 2007 Regulation 43.*	32
3-13	Temperature and weather protection. *Source: CDM 2007 Regulation 43.*	32
3-14	Vehicle overturned. *Source: Lincsafe.*	33
3-15	Collision with fixed objects. *Source: ACT.*	34
3-16	Road surface. *Source: ACT.*	34
3-17	Site layout. *Source: ACT.*	34
3-18	Public vehicle hazards. *Source: ACT.*	35
3-19	Roll bar and seat restraint. *Source: ACT.*	37
3-20	Suitability and protection. *Source: ACT.*	37
3-21	Organisation of pedestrians and vehicles. *Source: WHSWR 1992 Regulation 17(1).*	37
3-22	Traffic routes. *Source: CDM 2007 Regulation 36.*	38
3-23	Segregating pedestrians and vehicles. *Source: ACT.*	38
3-24	No segregation. *Source: ACT.*	38
3-25	Control of vehicle movement. *Source: ACT.*	38
3-26	Fencing and barriers at a distance. *Source: ACT.*	39
3-27	Visual warning on a dumper truck. *Source: ACT.*	39
3-28	Public highway works safety measures. *Source: ACT.*	41

Element 4
4-1	Manual handling - spine. *Source: ACT.*	45
4-2	Manual handling risk assessment. *Source: HSE Manual handling (Manual Handling Operations Regulations 1992) Guidance L23.*	45
4-3	Manual handling. *Source: ACT.*	46
4-4	Guideline figures. *Source: HSE Manual Handling (Manual Handling Operations Regs 1992) Guidance L23.*	47
4-5	Handling while seated. *Source: HSE Guidance L23.*	47
4-6	Twisting. *Source: HSE Guidance L23.*	47
4-7	Mechanical assistance. *Source: ACT.*	48
4-8	Basic lifting principles. *Source: Ambiguous.*	49
4-9	Telehandler. *Source: HSG6, HSE books.*	51
4-10	Dumper truck. *Source: ACT.*	51
4-11	Excavator hazards. *Source: ACT.*	51
4-12	Excavator. *Source: ACT.*	51
4-13	Width of traffic route. *Source: ACT.*	52

© ACT

4-14	Warning of traffic. *Source: ACT.*	52
4-15	Wheelbarrow. *Source: ACT.*	52
4-16	Sack truck. *Source: ACT.*	52
4-17	Diagrammatic layout of belt conveyor showing in-running nips. *Source: J Ridley; Safety at Work; Fourth Edition.*	53
4-18	Preventing free running roller trap. *Source: J Ridley; Safety at Work; Fourth Edition - Courtesy HSE.*	53
4-19	Guards between alternative drive-rollers. *Source: J Ridley; Safety at Work; Fourth Edition - Courtesy HSE.*	53
4-20	Roller conveyor. *Source: ACT.*	54
4-21	Belt conveyor guard. *Source: ACT.*	54
4-22	Nip points on roller conveyor with belts. *Source: J Ridley; Safety at Work; Fourth Edition - Courtesy HSE.*	54
4-23	Screw conveyor guarding. *Source: J Ridley; Safety at Work; Fourth Edition - Courtesy HSE.*	54
4-24	Safety latch on hook. *Source: Corel Clipart.*	54
4-25	Lift / hoist. *Source: HSG150, HSE books.*	56
4-26	Lifting operation. *Source: ACT.*	57
4-27	Lifting points on load. *Source: ACT.*	57
4-28	Accessories. *Source: Lincsafe.*	58
4-29	Accessories. *Source: ACT.*	58
4-30	Crane operation. *Source: ACT.*	59
4-31	Lifting operations. *Source: ACT.*	59
4-32	Lifting operations. *Source: ACT.*	59
4-33	Stability of cranes (hand drawn example). *Source: ACT.*	60
4-34	Danger zone - crane & fixed item. *Source: ACT.*	60
4-35	Siting and stability. *Source: ACT.*	61
4-36	Marking of accessories. *Source: ACT.*	62

Element 5

5-1	Air road breakers. *Source: Speedy Hire plc.*	65
5-2	Floor scabbler. *Source: Speedy Hire plc.*	65
5-3	Hand held scabbler. *Source: Speedy Hire plc.*	65
5-4	Lifting sling. *Source: ACT.*	65
5-5	Conveyor. *Source: ACT.*	68
5-6	Electrical isolator with hole for padlock. *Source: ACT.*	68
5-7	Inspection and examination. *Source: ACT.*	69
5-8	Air compressor. *Source: Speedy Hire plc.*	70
5-9	Controls and emergency stop. *Source: ACT.*	71
5-10	Controls. *Source: ACT.*	71
5-11	Eye injury & sparks. *Source: Speedy Hire plc.*	74
5-12	Impact injury. *Source: Speedy Hire plc.*	74
5-13	Auger drill - entanglement. *Source: STIHL.*	76
5-14	Abrasion. *Source: ACT.*	76
5-15	Chop saw - cutting. *Source: Speedy Hire plc.*	76
5-16	Shear. *Source: ACT.*	76
5-17	Stabbing & puncture. *Source: Speedy Hire plc.*	77
5-18	Impact. *Source: ACT.*	77
5-19	Crushing. *Source: ACT.*	77
5-20	Drawing-in. *Source: ACT.*	77
5-21	Disc saw - ejection. *Source: STIHL.*	77
5-22	Fluid injection. *Source: ACT.*	77
5-23	Examples of mechanical machinery hazards (Questions). *Source: ACT.*	78
5-24	Examples of mechanical machinery hazards (Answers). *Source: ACT.*	79
5-25	Abrasive wheel (grinder). *Source: ACT.*	80
5-26	Pedestal drill. *Source: ACT.*	80
5-27	Bench cross-cut circular saw. *Source: ACT.*	80
5-28	Cement mixer. *Source: ACT.*	80
5-29	Cement mixer. *Source: ACT.*	81
5-30	Ground consolidation equipment. *Source: ACT.*	81
5-31	Fixed guard (hand drawn example). *Source: ACT.*	83
5-32	Total enclosure fixed guard. *Source: BS EN ISO 12100.*	83
5-33	Fixed guard - panel removed. *Source: ACT.*	83
5-34	Fixed guard over fan - mesh too big. *Source: ACT.*	83
5-35	Open & closed interlock guard. *Source: BS EN ISO 12100.*	84
5-36	Power press - interlock guard. *Source: BS EN ISO 12100.*	84
5-37	Trip device. *Source: BS EN ISO 12100.*	84
5-38	Trip device on radial drill. *Source: ACT.*	84
5-39	Adjustable (fixed) guard. *Source: BS EN ISO 12100.*	85
5-40	Self adjusting (fixed) guard. *Source: ACT.*	85
5-41	Fixed guard. *Source: ACT.*	85
5-42	Fixed guard and push stick. *Source: Lincsafe.*	85
5-43	Information and instruction. *Source: ACT.*	86
5-44	PPE and supervision. *Source: ACT.*	86

Element 6

6-1	A basic electrical circuit. *Source: ACT.*	91
6-2	An electric circuit under fault conditions showing resistances in the path of a fault current. *Source: R. Gilmour.*	91
6-3	Effects of current flowing in the human body. *Source: ACT.*	93
6-4	Electrical equipment near water. *Source: ACT.*	93
6-5	Contact with high voltage buried cable. *Source: ACT.*	93
6-6	Risk of electric shock due to damage to cable. *Source: ACT.*	93
6-7	Work on live circuits. *Source: ACT.*	93
6-8	First aid sign. *Source: ACT.*	94
6-9	Used coiled up - risk of overheating. *Source: ACT.*	95
6-10	Max current capacity exceeded. *Source: ACT.*	95

6-11	Worn cable - risk of electrical fire. *Source: ACT.*	95
6-12	Evidence of overheating. *Source: ACT.*	95
6-13	Hazard - fuse wired out. *Source: ACT.*	96
6-14	Continued use of defective equipment. *Source: ACT.*	96
6-15	Hazard - damaged cable. *Source: ACT.*	96
6-16	Hazard - taped joints. *Source: ACT.*	96
6-17	Construction site generator. *Source: ACT.*	97
6-18	Construction site power supply panel. *Source: ACT.*	97
6-19	110v generator. *Source: ACT.*	98
6-20	110v extension lead. *Source: ACT.*	98
6-21	Power supply isolation. *Source: ACT.*	98
6-22	Plug-foil fuse no earth. *Source: ACT.*	99
6-23	Earthing. *Source: ACT.*	99
6-24	110v centre tapped earth transformer. *Source: ACT.*	100
6-25	Battery powered drill - 12V. *Source: ACT.*	100
6-26	110V powered drill. *Source: ACT.*	100
6-27	110V powered drill. *Source: ACT.*	100
6-28	Residual current device. *Source: ACT.*	100
6-29	Plug-in residual current device. *Source: ACT.*	100
6-30	Double insulated 240V drill. *Source: ACT.*	101
6-31	Double insulation symbol. *Source: HSG107.*	101
6-32	PAT labels. *Source: ACT.*	103
6-33	Working near power lines. *Source: HSG144.*	104
6-34	Overhead power lines. *Source: Lincsafe.*	104

Element 7

7-1	Fire triangle. *Source: Corel.*	107
7-2	Welding. *Source: Speedy Hire Plc.*	107
7-3	Combustible materials. *Source: ACT.*	107
7-4	Careless action. *Source: ACT.*	109
7-5	Misusing equipment. *Source: ACT.*	109
7-6	Defective electrical equipment. *Source: ACT.*	109
7-7	Deliberate ignition of materials. *Source: ACT.*	109
7-8	Not knowing the sound of an alarm. *Source: ACT.*	110
7-9	Compartment undermined-holes cut. *Source: ACT.*	110
7-10	Fire door held open. *Source: ACT.*	110
7-11	Materials inappropriately stored. *Source: ACT.*	110
7-12	Materials in escape route. *Source: Lincsafe.*	113
7-13	Control arson by external security. *Source: ACT.*	114
7-14	Control arson by housekeeping. *Source: ACT.*	114
7-15	Hot work. *Source: Speedy Hire Plc.*	115
7-16	Gas cylinders for huts. *Source: ACT.*	116
7-17	Poor storage of flammable liquids. *Source: ACT.*	118
7-18	Storage of flammable materials. *Source: ACT.*	118
7-19	Easy operation alarm call point. *Source: ACT.*	119
7-20	Alarm point identified & well located. *Source: ACT.*	119
7-21	Colour coding by label and sign. *Source: ACT.*	120
7-22	Fire escape - hazard. *Source: ACT.*	122
7-23	Assembly point. *Source: ACT.*	123
7-24	Fire instruction notice. *Source: ACT.*	124

Element 8

8-1	Harmful, toxic. *Source: ACT.*	128
8-2	Skin burns from wet cement. *Source: SHP (August 03).*	130
8-3	Respiratory system. *Source: BBC.*	131
8-4	Hand drawn respiratory system. *Source: ACT.*	131
8-5	Digestive system. *Source: STEM.*	131
8-6	Hand drawn digestive system. *Source: ACT.*	131
8-7	Skin layer. *Source: SHP.*	132
8-8	Hand drawn skin layer. *Source: ACT.*	132
8-9	Dermatitis. *Source: SHP.*	132
8-10	Product labels. *Source: Stocksigns.*	133
8-11	Detector tube example (hand drawn). *Source: ACT.*	135
8-12	Gas detector pump. *Source: Drager.*	135
8-13	Personal sampling equipment. *Source: ROSPA OS&H Apr 98.*	136
8-14	Stain tube detector operating instructions. *Source: Reproduced by kind permission of Drager.*	137
8-15	Reduced exposure - bulk supply. *Source: ACT.*	140
8-16	Captor system on circular saw. Clearly shows the fixed captor hood, flexible hose and rigid duct. *Source: ACT.*	141
8-17	Shows the size of fan and motor required for industrial scale LEV. *Source: ACT.*	141
8-18	Flexible hose showing how captor hood can be repositioned to suit the work activity. *Source: ACT.*	141
8-19	Self contained unit which can be moved around the workplace. *Source: ACT.*	141
8-20	Components of a basic system (hand drawn). *Source: ACT.*	141
8-21	Paper filter respirator. *Source: Haxton Safety.*	142
8-22	3M disposable respirator. *Source: ACT.*	143
8-23	Full face canister respirator. *Source: Haxton Safety.*	143
8-24	Breathing apparatus. *Source: Haxton Safety.*	143
8-25	Mis-use of respirator. *Source: ACT.*	143
8-26	Eye and ear protection. *Source: Speedy Hire plc.*	144
8-27	Arc welding visor - UV reactive. *Source: ACT.*	144
8-28	Gloves. *Source: Speedy Hire plc.*	145
8-29	Protective clothing. *Source: ACT.*	145

© ACT

8-30	Personal protective equipment. *Source: ACT.*	145
8-31	Schedule 6 medical surveillance. *Source: COSHH AcoP.*	146
8-32	Asbestos label. *Source: Scaftag.*	148
8-33	Asbestos cement sheets. *Source: www.risk-it.co.uk.*	149
8-34	Asbestos pipe lagging. *Source: www.risk-it.co.uk.*	149
8-35	Hazard label - environment. *Source: ACT.*	153
8-36	Environmental hazard. *Source: ACT.*	153
8-37	Measures to control pollution. *Source: ACT.*	153
8-38	Measures to control pollution. *Source: ACT.*	153

Element 9

9-1	Posture. *Source: Speedy Hire Plc.*	160
9-2	Working area. *Source: ACT.*	161
9-3	Inner ear diagram. *Source: www.echalk.co.uk.*	161
9-4	The ear (hand drawn). *Source: ACT.*	161
9-5	Rms and peak levels of a sound wave. *Source: ACT.*	162
9-6	Noise hazard sign. *Source: ACT.*	163
9-7	Mandatory signs. *Source: Stocksigns.*	163
9-8	Basic layout of the main control methods. *Source: ACT.*	164
9-9	Silenced diesel welder. *Source: Speedy Hire Plc.*	165
9-10	Ear defenders. *Source: ACT.*	166
9-11	Disposable ear plugs. *Source: ACT.*	166
9-12	Use of road drill - vibration. *Source: ACT.*	167
9-13	Dumper truck seat. *Source: ACT.*	167
9-14	Workplace temperature. *Source: ACT.*	169
9-15	Ionising radiation. *Source: ACT.*	170
9-16	UV - from welding. *Source: Speedy Hire Plc.*	171
9-17	Radio mast. *Source: ACT.*	171
9-18	Personal dose monitor. *Source: ACT.*	173
9-19	Contamination monitoring. *Source: ACT.*	173
9-20	Definition of work related violence. *Source: HSE.*	

Element 10

10-1	Working above ground level. *Source: ACT.*	180
10-2	Independent tied scaffold. *Source: ACT.*	182
10-3	Independent tied scaffold. *Source: HSG150 Safety in Construction.*	183
10-4	Independent tied scaffold (hand drawn example). *Source: ACT.*	183
10-5	Independent tied scaffold. *Source: ACT.*	183
10-6	Tie through window. *Source: ACT.*	183
10-7	Putlog scaffold. *Source: HSG150 Safety in Construction.*	184
10-8	Putlog (hand drawn example). *Source: ACT.*	184
10-9	Putlog scaffold. *Source: ACT.*	184
10-10	Putlog scaffold. *Source: ACT.*	184
10-11	Fans. *Source: ACT.*	185
10-12	Wheels with brakes. *Source: ACT.*	185
10-13	Mobile tower scaffold. *Source: ACT.*	185
10-14	Mobile tower scaffold. *Source: ACT.*	185
10-15	Base plates and sole boards. *Source: Lincsafe.*	186
10-16	Base plate and protection. *Source: ACT.*	186
10-17	Scaffold boards - some defective. *Source: ACT.*	186
10-18	Ladder access. *Source: ACT.*	186
10-19	Brick guards. *Source: HSG150 Safety in Construction.*	187
10-20	Nets and sheets. *Source: ACT.*	187
10-21	Nets. *Source: ACT.*	187
10-22	'Scaftag'. *Source: ACT.*	189
10-23	Lighting. *Source: ACT.*	189
10-24	Mobile elevated work platform (MEWPs). *Source: ACT.*	189
10-25	Use of harness with a MEWP. *Source: HSG150.*	190
10-26	Mobile elevated work platform (MEWPs). *Source: ACT.*	190
10-27	Scissor lift. *Source: HSG150, HSE.*	190
10-28	Scissor lift. *Source: ACT.*	190
10-29	Ladder as access and workplace. *Source: ACT.*	191
10-30	Improper use. *Source: ACT.*	191
10-31	Poor storage. *Source: Lincsafe.*	191
10-32	Use of roof ladders. *Source: HSG150, HSE.*	191
10-33	Stepladder. *Source: ACT.*	192
10-34	Personal suspension equipment. *Source: ACT.*	193
10-35	Safety nets. *Source: ACT.*	194
10-36	Edge protection and boards. *Source: ACT.*	194
10-37	Nets / sheeting. *Source: ACT.*	195
10-38	Marking. *Source: ACT.*	195

Element 11

11-1	Buried services. *Source: ACT.*	201
11-2	Excavation hazards. *Source: ACT.*	201
11-3	Water in excavation. *Source: ACT.*	202
11-4	Marking of services. *Source: ACT.*	203
11-5	Permit to dig. *Source: Reproduced by kind permission of Lincsafe.*	204
11-6	Battering. *Source: ACT.*	205
11-7	Trench box - for shoring. *Source: ACT.*	205
11-8	Close boarded excavation. *Source: BS6031.*	205

© ACT

11-9	Open sheeting. *Source: BS6031.*	205
11-10	Close sheeting. *Source: ACT.*	206
11-11	Open sheeting. *Source: ACT.*	206
11-12	Materials storage. *Source: ACT.*	206
11-13	Preventing water ingress. *Source: ACT.*	206
11-14	Confined space - chamber. *Source: ACT.*	209
11-15	Confined space - sewer. *Source: ACT.*	209
11-16	Confined space - Cement Silo. *Source: ACT.*	209
11-17	Confined space - open tank. *Source: ACT.*	209
11-18	Entrance to a confined space. *Source: ACT.*	212
11-19	Confined space. *Source: HSG150, HSE.*	212

Element 12

12-1	Risk of falling or premature collapse. *Source: ACT.*	215
12-2	Falling materials. *Source: ACT.*	215
12-3	Noise and dust. *Source: Rollaston Council.*	216
12-4	Siting of plant. *Source: ACT.*	216
12-5	Doubtful competence of workers. *Source: Lincsafe.*	218
12-6	Use of demolition equipment. *Source: ACT.*	218
12-7	Building structure. *Source: ACT.*	219
12-8	Structural condition and substances. *Source: ACT.*	219
12-9	Hazardous substances. *Source: Stocksigns.*	219
12-10	Proximity of other structures. *Source: D Hitchen.*	219
12-11	Hydraulic demolition jaws. *Source: ACT.*	220
12-12	Hydraulic demolition grapple. *Source: ACT.*	220
12-13	Protection of public. *Source: ACT.*	221
12-14	Disposal of waste. *Source: ACT.*	221

List of abbreviations

LEGISLATION

CHIP 3	Chemicals (Hazard Information and Packaging for Supply) Regulations 2002
CSR	Confined Spaces Regulations 1997
CDM	Construction (Design and Management) Regulations 2007
CHPR	Construction (Head Protection) Regulations 1989
CAR	Control of Asbestos Regulations 2006
CNWR	Control of Noise at Work Regulations 2005
COSHH	Control of Substances Hazardous to Health Regulations 2002
CVWR	Control of Vibration at Work Regulations 2005
DSEAR	Dangerous Substances and Explosive Atmospheres Regulations 2002
EWR	Electricity at Work Regulations 1989
EPA	Environmental Protection Act 1990
HWR	Hazardous Waste Regulations 2005
FAR	Health and Safety (First-Aid) Regulations 1981
HASAWA	Health and Safety at Work etc Act 1974
IRR	Ionising Radiations Regulations 1999
LOLER	Lifting Operations and Lifting Equipment Regulations 1998
MHSWR	Management of Health and Safety at Work Regulations 1999
MHOR	Manual Handling Operations Regulations 1992
NRSWA	New Roads and Street Works Act 1991
PPER	Personal Protective Equipment at Work Regulations 1992
PUWER	Provision and Use of Work Equipment Regulations 1998
RRFSO	Regulatory Reform (Fire Safety) Order (RRFSO) 2005
RIDDOR	Reporting of Injuries, Diseases and Dangerous Occurrences Regulations 1995
SMSR	Supply of Machinery (Safety) Regulations 1992
SSSR	Health and Safety (Safety Signs and Signals) Regulations 1996
WAH	Work at Height Regulations 2005

GENERAL

AC	Alternating Current
ACOP	Approved Code of Practice
ACTS	Advisory Committee on Toxic Substances
AIDS	Acquired Immune Deficiency Syndrome
APF	Assigned Protection Factor
BMGV	Biological Monitoring Value
BSI	British Standards Institution
CAT	Cable Avoidance Tool
CCTV	Closed Circuit Television
CEN	European Standards
CIRIA	Construction Industry Research and Information Association
CPR	Cardio Pulmonary Resuscitation
CTS	Carpel Tunnel Syndrome
DC	Direct Current
EPA	Environment Protection Agency
EU	European Union
FGD	Flue Gas Desulphurisation
FLT	Forklift Truck
FRA	Fire Risk Assessment
HAVS	Hand-arm Vibration Syndrome
HEPA	High Efficiency Particulate Air
HGV	Heavy Goods Vehicle
HIV	Human Immunodeficiency Virus
HML	High, Medium and Low
HSC	Health and Safety Commission
HSE	Health and Safety Executive
IT	Information Technology
IEE	Institute of Electrical Engineers
IPC	Integrated Pollution Act
LAAPC	Air Pollution Control by Local Authorities
LEV	Local Exhaust Ventilation
LPG	Liquefied Petroleum Gas
LTEL	Long Term Exposure Limit
MDHS	Methods for the Determination of Hazardous Substances
MDI	Methylene Bisphenyl Di-isocyanate
MEWP	Mobile Elevated Work Platform
MSDS	Material Safety Data Sheet
MSW	Municipal Solid Wastes
NEBOSH	National Examination Board in Occupational Safety and Health
NVQ	National Vocational Qualification

© ACT

OPSI	Office of Public Sector Information
PAT	Portable Appliance Testing
PPE	Personal Protective Equipment
RCD	Residual Current Device
RMS	Root Mean Square
RPA	Radiation Protection Adviser
RPE	Respiratory Protective Equipment
RTFLT	Rough Terrain Fork Lift Truck
SNR	Single Number Rating
STEL	Short Term Exposure Limit
SWL	Safe Working Load
TDI	Toluene Di-isocyanate
TWA	Time Weighted Average
UV	Ultra Violet
VCM	Vinyl Chloride Monomer
VWF	Vibration White Finger
WATCH	Working on Action to Control Chemicals
WBV	Whole Body Vibration
WEL	Workplace Exposure Limit
WRULD	Work Related Upper Limb Disorder

Element 1

Construction law and management

Learning outcomes

On completion of this element, candidates should be able to demonstrate understanding of the content through the application of knowledge to familiar and unfamiliar situations. In particular they should be able to:

1.1 Identify the scope, definition and nature of construction activities.

1.2 Outline the legal, moral and financial consequences of failing to manage health and safety within the construction industry.

1.3 Identify the scope and application of the Construction (Design and Management) Regulations 2007.

1.4 Identify the nature and main sources of external construction health and safety information.

Content

1.1 - Scope, definition and nature of construction activities 3
    Types of work...3
    Range of activities 3
    Particular construction issues 4
1.2 - The legal, moral and financial consequences of failing to manage health and safety within the construction industry..5
    General argument..5
    The size of the construction health and safety 'problem' in terms of numbers of work related fatalities and incidents of ill health 5
    Prime concerns, priorities and targets of the regulator...5
1.3 - Scope and application of the Construction (Design and Management) Regulations 2007 6
    The particular duties under the Construction (Design and Management) Regulations (CDM) 2007 6
    Appointment and competence required of relevant parties 8
    Notification of projects 8
    Preparation of the health and safety plan..8
    Provision of information 10
    Preparation of the health and safety file 10
1.4 - Sources of information on health and safety... 11
    External to the organisation 11

Sources of reference

Managing Health and Safety in Construction (ACoP) (L144), HSE Books ISBN 0-7176-6223-4
Successful Health and Safety Management (HSG65), HSE Books ISBN 0-7176-1276-7
The Management of Health and Safety at Work (ACoP) (L21), HSE Books ISBN 0-7176-2488-9

Relevant statutory provisions

The Construction (Design and Management) Regulations (CDM) 2007
The Health and Safety at Work etc Act (HASAWA) 1974-Sections 2, 20-25, 33 and 39-40
The Management of Health and Safety at Work Regulations (MHSWR) 1999-regulation 5

1.1 - Scope, definition and nature of construction activities

Types of work

BUILDING WORKS

Building works involve most trades within the construction industry such as ground workers, steel erectors, brick layers, carpenters, plasterers, etc all working closely together with the common goal of creating a new finished building or structure.

RENOVATION, ALTERATION AND MAINTENANCE OF EXISTING PREMISES

Renovation

Renovation work involves restoring an existing building or structure to a condition that is representative of its original condition or improved by repair and modernisation using more up-to-date materials and practices. As with new building works, this also involves most of the common trades normally used within the construction industry.

Alteration

Alteration works are required when the layout of an existing building, structure or premises no longer suits the use for which it was originally intended. This can include elements of both new building works and renovation works. Alterations can comprise of 'an extension to an existing structure or demolition and removal of sections of the internal structure to make premises more spacious. Alternatively, an alteration may involve dividing the existing structure into smaller, separate sections by the introduction of partition walls of various materials (block-work, brick-work or studding and plasterboard).

Maintenance of existing premises

Maintenance work is an essential element to ensure that the condition of an existing building, premises or structure does not deteriorate and that it remains in as good a condition as is possible. Work is normally carried out on a regular scheduled basis to deal with issues of wear and tear, but can also be required when a problem suddenly occurs that requires urgent attention e.g. loss of roofing materials following a storm. Maintenance can be carried out on all components of existing premises, including the building, services, and any final building finish and furnishing. Careful planning of maintenance work should be given if the building or premises are occupied. Hazards from paint, dust, falling masonry and excavations should be considered, suitable and sufficient risk assessments should be made and controls implemented. Unoccupied premises/buildings can pose other hazards, with unstable groundwork, footings, walls, beams supporting floors and roofing. In addition unoccupied buildings are likely to be infested with vermin or suffer intrusion by pigeons in rafters where roof integrity may have failed, preening the risks of biological hazards. Again these hazards should be highlighted, suitable risk assessments should be made and controls implemented.

CIVIL ENGINEERING AND WORKS OF ENGINEERING CONSTRUCTION

Civil engineering and engineering works normally relate to heavy construction activities requiring large items of plant and equipment such as cranes and excavators. This work will require specialist knowledge and experience in order to undertake activities such as highway construction, bridge construction, piling works, large foundations, large concrete structures, excavations and utility projects.

DEMOLITION

The term demolition refers to 'breaking down' or 'removing'. In construction this is applied to buildings and structures that are no longer required or are possibly derelict and unsafe. Demolition must be carried out in a well-planned and controlled manner in compliance with a safe system of work. Account needs to be taken of potential hazards that may arise from demolition (asbestos dust and falling debris). Any project that involves any element of demolition (full or part demolition) falls under the control of the Construction (Design and Management) Regulations (CDM) 2007.

Range of activities

SITE CLEARANCE

Site clearance consists of preparing the site prior to the works being undertaken. This may involve removal of hazardous waste, obstructive trees, unwanted scrub and landscaping. Demolition activities may also be required as part of site clearance prior to construction works beginning. Where there are high levels of contaminants it may also be necessary for ground remediation.

Following completion of construction works site clearance will involve removal of all waste associated with the construction activities (e.g. brick and timber off-cuts, packaging, spoil) to a licensed waste disposal site. It will also include the removal of all plant and equipment used on the construction with the aim of leaving the site in a clean and tidy state ready for its intended use.

DEMOLITION AND DISMANTLING

Demolition / deconstruction / dismantling activities will generally also include a survey of the structure to be demolished in order to identify any potential contamination hazards that are concealed and are not obvious (asbestos dust, lead, chemicals, live utility services). Various techniques will be employed to carry out demolition, including 'piece meal'-large sections are demolished at a time by machines or demolition by hand - where items are broken into their individual parts to be reclaimed or reused. Where material recovery is not important long reach crane with demolition ball, long reach mechanical pincer jaw and explosive charges may be used in some cases. Protection should be ensured for all workers involved through controlled access to the area. The danger area should be defined and suitably fenced with controlled access only to authorised personnel. Demolition must be carried out in a structured sequence to prevent any premature collapse of the structure. Falling debris must not be allowed to fall onto any surrounding area or buildings.

UNIT NCC1 - ELEMENT 1 - CONSTRUCTION LAW AND MANAGEMENT

EXCAVATION

The interpretation according to the Construction (Design and Management) Regulations (CDM) 2007 of "excavation" includes any earthwork, trench, well, shaft, tunnel or underground working.

Excavation consists of digging below ground level to various depths in order to create a cavity that can be used for exposure of buried utility services, trenching for installation of utility services, casting building foundations or ground investigations. Methods of digging used for excavation work include the use of hand tools (pick, fork, shovel), and also by using a mechanical excavator. Major excavations for basements, sub-structures etc, remain as a permanent part in the construction operation.

LOADING, UNLOADING AND STORAGE OF MATERIALS

Construction sites use a host of different materials in the construction process that will require loading or unloading by mechanical or manual means. These can be broken down into materials that are used or removed immediately at site (i.e. excavation spoil, concrete mix, mortar mix) and materials that are stored at site and used or removed at regular intervals as required (bricks, cement, sand, timber, sundries, waste disposal skips). Loading and unloading should be undertaken using the correct procedures that comply with site safe systems of work and wherever possible avoiding the need for manual handling. Storage requirements should be identified and planned for the whole project. This will need to consider security, safe position and suitable ground condition; protection from adverse weather and potential for falls from a height or into an excavation.

SITE MOVEMENTS

Construction sites contain various types of heavy mobile plant and equipment and large numbers of site workers. Construction sites projects should be well planned to take into account vehicles moving around the site. In particular consideration to safe access and egress would include issues of adequacy of space for manoeuvring and ensuring operator visibility. Routes for both vehicles and pedestrians should be provided and be suitably surfaced, clearly defined and separated.

FABRICATION

Fabrication at site can include steel erecting, welding and form-working. Quite often it can involve working at height (where specialist work platforms and fall arrest equipment should be used) and adequate control is essential to prevent the falling of materials and tools. A variety of specialist equipment may be required; e.g. welding machine, bolt gun, or nail gun, and such equipment should only be used by competent persons.

DECORATION

Decoration consists of applying various coatings, e.g. paints, wallpaper, and artex, necessary to create the final finished appearance to a building or structure. The tools involved with decoration are often handheld and not powered. Various access systems including mobile platforms are required for this type of work. .

CLEANING

Cleaning involves applying water, steam or various abrasive or chemical agents to the surfaces to be treated, e.g. walls, windows, floors, fabric. The method of application can require the use of various types of equipment ranging from vacuum cleaners, floor polisher through to high pressure jets. Consideration should be given to the correct disposal of waste materials.

INSTALLATION, REMOVAL AND MAINTENANCE OF SERVICES

Various utility services (e.g. electricity and water) are required on both existing and new construction sites, and are usually buried underground. In new installations this involves a great deal of liaison with the planning authority, utility companies and designer concerning the route the services will take and will involve excavation with heavy plant, loading and unloading of materials. New services are often connected to their source at a location that is situated outside the construction site boundary. Where this occurs, the additional hazard to the general public presents itself and suitable means of traffic control (e.g. signing and lighting), guarding and protection of the public (barriers and warning signs) will need to be employed. Removing or maintaining utilities can present other hazards, and these should be isolated correctly prior to any work commencing. This may require involving the utility companies, so proactive planning is essential.

LANDSCAPING

Landscaping usually takes place during the final stages of the construction phase, when there is little or no construction plant travelling around the site. Landscaping may include altering site levels and the introduction of trees, shrubs, grass turf / seed etc. The works generally consist of loading and unloading of materials, manual handling, and cleaning work (footways and roads). Note that care should be taken to avoid planting trees close to underground services or near to building footings.

Particular construction issues

TRANSITORY NATURE OF WORKERS

The building and construction industry is characterised by its intermittent, temporary, transitory nature. Generally, building and construction contractors hire a work force on a project basis. Thus, workers in the building and construction industry are accustomed to travelling from areas where work is not plentiful to fill short-term labour shortages created by expansion and contraction of local construction activity.

TEMPORARY NATURE OF CONSTRUCTION ACTIVITIES AND THE CONSTANTLY CHANGING WORKPLACE

Construction sites constantly change through the build phase, as the trades that are associated with the construction vary greatly at each stage. Consideration needs to be given to site induction for new workers as appropriate. The safe systems of work, risk assessments, site safety procedures and site inductions will need to be updated regularly to suit the most current situation. A construction site will always be an unfamiliar workplace with new hazards and dangers posed as each phase moves to the next.

TIME PRESSURES FROM CLIENTS

Clients have one of the biggest influences on the health and safety of those working on a construction project. Their decisions have substantial influence on the time, money and other resources available for the project. Because of this, the Construction (Design and Management) Regulations (CDM) 2007 make them accountable for the impact their decisions have on health and safety.

WEATHER CONDITIONS

For those working outdoors, adverse weather can create numerous problems. Short term exposure to the sun can cause excessive sweating, dehydration and fatigue. There are fears that prolonged exposure can cause skin cancer. Strong wind increases risk when working at height and can cause unexpected movement of loads suspended on cranes. Heavy rain may cause soft ground conditions which can increase problems with site traffic and undermine the stability of scaffolds and excavations. Extreme cold leads to snow and ice which increases the likelihood of slips and falls. It may also increase the risk of brittle failure of equipment.

POOR LEVELS OF NUMERACY AND LITERACY OF WORKERS

Poor levels of literacy and numeracy can significantly impede the progress of workers at a workplace. The level of understanding and critical information retention required, for example, when attending a health and safety induction, can be significantly reduced. Where numbers and the written word are utilised instead of a pictographic approach, then the meaning can be marred regarding written critical safety instructions or directions that may need to be followed could be unintentionally ignored. Weights and measures, dates and times critical to processes could also be misconstrued or overlooked if workers are innumerate.

NON-ENGLISH SPEAKING WORKERS

Employers need to consider the following with reference to their non-English speaking employees:

- Can they speak and understand enough English for their role?
- Can they read and understand working instructions and health and safety related notices and warnings? Employers have a legal duty to ensure the employee understands notices, symbols etc. related to health and safety. If the employee does not understand or can't read English, these have to be translated into the employee's language.
- Are there other members of staff who can speak the employee's native language? They could help the employee understand the working culture and environment in the UK.
- What is the employee's job history? This shows whether he/she has relevant experience to work in this job.

1.2 - The legal, moral and financial consequences of failing to manage health and safety within the construction industry

General argument

There are three good reasons for preventing accidents in the work place:

1) *Moral*

   Injury accidents result in pain and suffering for those affected. Construction activities in the UK resulted in an average of two fatalities for each three week period during 2004. Clearly, it is important that employers and employees do everything that they can to avoid this.

2) *Legal*

   It is a legal requirement to safeguard the health and safety of employees and others that might be affected by an organisation's operations.

3) *Financial*

   Accidents at work cost a great deal of money, especially when damage is added. Accidents (particularly when they interrupt production, downgrade the quality of products or impair the environment). Costs can be enormous - and can be many times larger than could initially be perceived.

The size of the construction health and safety 'problem' in terms of numbers of work related fatalities and incidents of ill health

Every working day in Great Britain at least one person is killed and over 6,000 are injured at work.

Health and Safety Executive (HSE) statistics reveal that 59 workers were killed in the construction industry during the year 2005/06. A breakdown of these 59 fatal injuries that occurred in 2005/06 indicates that falls from height remain the single biggest cause of death (41 per cent). This is followed by being struck by an object - other than a vehicle (14 per cent), electricity (10 per cent), transport (7 per cent), collapse (7 per cent) and other kinds (10 per cent). This breakdown of type of injury is consistent with previous years, although there has been a slight rise in the number of electrical accidents.

Every year three-quarters of a million people take time off work because of what they regard as work-related illness. About 30 million workdays are lost as a result.

Accidents and ill health are costly to workers and their families. They can also impact significantly on organisations because, in addition to costs of personal injuries, they may incur far greater costs from damage to property or equipment, and lost production.

Prime concerns, priorities and targets of the regulator

The government and Health and Safety Commission (HSC) have a prime *concern* that in Great Britain in 2000 the same proportion of people had been injured at work since the early 1990s. A 10-year strategy to improve health and safety at work was launched jointly by the Government and HSC on 7 June 2000 and was called Revitalising Health and Safety. It sets out targets and priorities in order to meet the targets. The Health and Safety Executive implement this strategy, which is designed to inject new impetus into better health and safety in all workplaces.

The revitalising health and safety **targets** are:

- Reduce the number of working days lost per 100, 000 workers from work-related injury and ill health by 30% by 2010.
- Reduce the incidence rate of fatal and major injury accidents by 10% by 2010.
- Reduce the incidence rate of cases of work-related ill health by 20% by 2010.

The **priorities** of the strategy are to focus on three specific industry sectors which have a large number of people employed in them and a high incidence of injury and ill health. These are the agriculture sector, construction sector and health services sector. In addition the priorities focus on specific issues that cause harm in these and other industries:

- Falls from height.
- Musculoskeletal disorders.
- Slips and trips.
- Work-related stress.
- Workplace transport.

These priorities are supported by an additional priority – "Government setting an example" – this is part of the commitment to improving health and safety in the public sector.

Source: hse.gov.uk.

1.3 - Scope and application of the Construction (Design and Management) Regulations 2007

The scope of the CDM Regulations 2007 extends to "construction work" on a "structure". These terms are defined in detail in the ACOP that accompanies the regulations. Also there is additional detail in the relevant statutory provisions within this publication. The definitions are far too lengthy to repeat in full. However, the following is a brief extract from the Regulations:

"Construction work" means the carrying out of any building, civil engineering or engineering construction work and includes:

- The construction, alteration, conversion, fitting out, commissioning, renovation, repair, upkeep, redecoration or other maintenance (including cleaning which involves the use of water or an abrasive at high pressure or the use of corrosive or toxic substances), de-commissioning, demolition or dismantling of a structure.
- The preparation for an intended structure, including site clearance, exploration, investigation (but not site survey) and excavation, and the clearance or preparation of the site or structure for use or occupation at its conclusion.
- The assembly on site of prefabricated elements to form a structure or the disassembly on site of prefabricated elements which, immediately before such disassembly, formed a structure.
- The removal of a structure or of any product or waste resulting from demolition or dismantling of a structure or from disassembly of prefabricated elements which immediately before such disassembly formed such a structure.
- The installation, commissioning, maintenance, repair or removal of mechanical, electrical, gas, compressed air, hydraulic, telecommunications, computer or similar services which are normally fixed within or to a structure, but does not include the exploration for or extraction of mineral resources or activities preparatory there to carried out at a place where such exploration or extraction is carried out.

"Structure" means: any building, timber, masonry, metal or reinforced concrete structure, railway line or siding, tramway line, dock, harbour, inland navigation, tunnel, shaft, bridge, viaduct, waterworks, reservoir, pipe or pipe-line, cable, aqueduct, sewer, sewage works, gasholder, road, airfield, sea defence works, river works, drainage works, earthworks, lagoon, dam, wall, caisson, mast, tower, pylon, underground tank, earth retaining structure or structure designed to preserve or alter any natural feature, fixed plant and any structure similar to the foregoing; or any formwork, falsework, scaffold or other structure designed or used to provide support or means of access during construction work, and any reference to a structure includes a part of a structure.

The particular duties under the Construction (Design and Management) Regulations (CDM) 2007

WHO IS THE CLIENT?

The client is an organisation or individual for whom a construction project is undertaken. Clients only have duties when the project is associated with a business or other undertaking (whether for profit or not). An organisation or individual can be, for example, a local authority, school governors, insurance companies and project originators on private finance initiative projects. Domestic clients are people who have work done on their own home or the home of a family member that does not relate to trade or business, whether for profit or not. Domestic clients are a special case and do not have duties under CDM 2007.

CLIENT DUTIES

- For **all** projects, ensure that:
  - Work can be carried out safely.
  - Adequate welfare facilities are provided.
  - Any workplace complies with the Workplace (Health, Safety and Welfare) Regulations (WHSWR) 1992.
  - Make relevant pre-construction health and safety information available.
- Where a project is notifiable, the client shall:
  - As soon as practicable appoint a competent CDM co-ordinator.
  - Then appoint a competent principal contractor.
  - Promptly provide the CDM co-ordinator and principal contractor with pre-construction information.
  - Not allow work to start until the construction phase plan and adequate welfare facilities are in place.

- Provide the CDM co-ordinator with information for inclusion in the health and safety file.
- Keep health and safety file available for inspection and revised as necessary.

WHO IS THE DESIGNER?

Designers are those who have a trade or business which involves those preparing designs for construction work and variations. They can prepare drawings, design details, specifications, bills of quantities, specification (or prohibition) of articles and substances, as well as the related analysis, calculations and preparatory work or the arranging for their employees or others under their control to prepare designs relating to a structure or part of a structure. A designer could be an architect, structural engineer, building surveyor, landscape architect, other consultants or manufacturing and design practices contributing to or having overall responsibility of any part of a design.

DESIGNER DUTIES

- For *all* projects, ensure that:
  - The client is aware of their duties.
  - Take account of other design considerations.
  - Design to avoid foreseeable risk during construction, use and maintenance of the building.
  - Give priority to collective measures over individual measures.
  - Ensure where it is not possible to avoid risks that they are minimised.
  - Provide adequate information about materials used in the design that could affect the health and safety of persons carrying out construction work.
- Where a project is notifiable:
  - Shall not commence until a CDM co-ordinator has been appointed.
  - Provide the CDM co-ordinator with information for inclusion in the health and safety file.

WHO IS THE CDM CO-ORDINATOR?

The CDM Co-ordinator is appointed by and assists the client with health and safety risk management matters and the appointment of competent contractors. Another key feature of the CDM Co-ordinator is to advise on the adequacy of management arrangements of the health and safety provisions, facilitate good communication and cooperation between project team members and preparation of the health and safety file.

CDM CO-ORDINATORS DUTIES

CDM Co-ordinators should:

- Be in a position to give advice to clients.
- Ensure co-operation between persons involved in the project.
- Ensure that designers include among the design considerations the principles of prevention.
- Liaise with principal contractor regarding information for the health and safety plan and health and safety file.
- Identify and collect pre-construction information.
- Ensure that designers comply with their duties.
- Ensure co-operation between designers and principal contractor in relation to any design change.
- Prepare a health and safety file.
- Ensure that a health and safety file is delivered to the client.
- Notify the HSE.

WHO IS THE PRINCIPAL CONTRACTOR?

The principal contractor is the lead or main managing contractor responsible for properly planning, managing and coordinating work during the construction phase, in order to ensure that the risks on site are properly controlled, which allows the management of health and safety to be incorporated into the project.

PRINCIPAL CONTRACTORS DUTIES

The principal contractor should:
- Plan, manage and monitor the construction phase to ensure that it is carried out without risk.
- Liaise with the CDM co-ordinator.
- Ensure adequate welfare facilities are provided.
- Draw up site rules.
- Ensure that every contractor is:
  - Informed of the minimum amount of time allocated for planning and preparation.
  - If necessary, consulted about the health and safety plan.
  - Given access to the health and safety plan.
  - Given any relevant information.
  - Informed about the information that may be required for inclusion in the health and safety file.
- Display the notification details.
- Prevent unauthorised access to the site.
- Ensure that every worker is provided with:
  - Site induction.
  - Information that has to be provided by a contractor (see below).
  - Any further information that might be necessary.

WHO ARE CONTRACTORS AND THE SELF EMPLOYED?

The contractors and the self employed are workers who are engaged in the project but have a duty to co-operate with principal contractor, in planning and managing the work to ensure that risks are properly controlled. Contractors can be engaged to conduct specialist work such as utility provision and special trades.

CONTRACTORS DUTIES

- For *all* projects, ensure that:
  - They do not start work unless they are aware of their duties.
  - Plan, manage and monitor work to ensue that it is carried out without risk.
  - Every contractor that the contractor appoints is provided with relevant information.
  - Every worker under the contractors control is given information and training which should include:
    - Site induction (if not provided by the principal contractor).
    - Results of risk assessments and control measures.
    - Site rules.
    - Emergency procedures and the persons involved in implementing the procedures.
  - They do not commence work until unauthorised access to the site has been prevented.
  - Ensure that adequate welfare facilities are provided.
- Where a project is notifiable the contractor shall:
  - Not start work unless the contractor knows the names of the CDM co-ordinator and principal contractor, has been given access to the health and safety plan and the project has been notified to the HSE.
  - Provide relevant information to the principal contractor on the health and safety risks created by their works and how they will be controlled.
  - Identify any contractors they have appointed to the principal contractor.
  - Comply with directions given by the principal contractor and any rules in the health and safety plan.
  - Provide the principal contractor with any Reporting of Injuries, Diseases and Dangerous Occurrences Regulations (RIDDOR) 1995 reports.

Appointment and competence required of relevant parties

Where a project is notifiable, the client shall appoint a CDM Co-ordinator and a principal contractor as soon as is practicable after initial design work or other preparation for construction work has begun.

No person on whom these Regulations place a duty shall:

(a) Appoint or engage a CDM co-ordinator, designer, principal contractor or contractor unless the person to be engaged is competent

(b) Accept such an appointment unless the CDM Co-ordinator is competent

(c) Instruct a worker to carry out or manage design or construction work unless the worker is:
- Competent.
- Under the supervision of a competent person.

To be competent an organisation or individual must have knowledge of specific tasks and the risks that may arise.

> "An appropriate health and safety qualification such as the NEBOSH construction certificate will demonstrate that the person has adequate knowledge of health and safety, but this will need to be coupled with a **Stage 2** assessment to demonstrate that they have experience in applying this knowledge in the construction environment"."

Figure 1-1: Assessing the competence of individual CDM co-ordinators.　　　　*Source: CDM 2007 ACOP, Regulation 4.*

Notification of projects

CDM applies to all construction projects. However, construction projects with a construction phase longer than 30 days or involving more than 500 person days of construction work are notifiable to the Health and Safety Executive (HSE). Notification by the CDM Co-ordinator must be in writing and can be made using the form F10 (rev).

Preparation of the health and safety plan

Pre-construction information

Pre-construction information is essentially a collection of information about the significant health and safety risks of the construction project which the principal contractor will have to manage during the construction phase. The pre-construction information will mainly come from:

- **The client** - who has to provide information relevant to health and safety to the CDM co-ordinator. This could include existing drawings, surveys of the site or premises, information on the location of services, etc.
- **Designers** - who have to provide information about the risks which cannot be avoided and will have to be controlled by the principal contractor and other contractors. Typically this information may be provided on drawings, in written specifications or in outline method statements.

The pre-construction information serves three main purposes:

- During its development the plan can provide a focus at which the health and safety considerations of design are brought together under the control of the CDM co-ordinator.
- Secondly, the plan plays a vital role in the tender documentation. It enables prospective principal contractors to be fully aware of the project's health, safety and welfare requirements. This will allow prospective principal contractors to have a level playing field as far as health and safety is concerned on which to provide tender submissions.

- Thirdly, the plan provides a template against which different tender submissions can be measured. This helps the CDM co-ordinator to advise the client on the provision of resources for health and safety and to assess the competence of prospective principal contractors.

The CDM co-ordinator is responsible for ensuring that the pre-construction information is prepared. This does not mean that the CDM co-ordinator must produce the plan directly, but the CDM co-ordinator must ensure that it is prepared.

Content of the pre-construction information pack

The contents of the pre-construction information will depend on the nature of the project itself. However, the following areas should be considered:

- Project description and programme details.
- Details of client, designers, CDM co-ordinator and other consultants.
- Extent and location of existing records and plans.
- Client's considerations and management requirements.
- Structure and organisation.
- Safety goals for the project and arrangements for monitoring and review.
- Permits and authorisation requirements.
- Emergency procedures.
- Site rules and other restrictions on contractors, suppliers and others e.g. access arrangements to those parts of the site which continue to be used by the client.
- Activities on or adjacent to the site during the works.
- Arrangements for liaison between parties.
- Security arrangements.
- Environmental restrictions and existing on-site risks.
- Hazards.

a. Safety hazards, including:
   - Boundaries and access, including temporary access.
   - Adjacent land uses.
   - Existing storage of hazardous materials.
   - Location of existing services - water, electricity, gas, etc.
   - Ground conditions.
   - Existing structures - stability, or fragile materials.

b. Health hazards, including:
   - Asbestos, including results of any surveys.
   - Existing storage of hazardous materials.
   - Contaminated land, including results of surveys.
   - Existing structure's hazardous materials.
   - Health risks arising from client's activities.
   - Significant design and construction hazards.
   - Design assumptions and control measures.
   - Arrangements for co-ordination of on-going design work and handling design changes.
   - Information on significant risks identified during design (health and safety risks).
   - Materials requiring particular precautions.

Format of the pre-construction information pack

If the pre-construction information is to be effective in helping to select a principal contractor, the CDM co-ordinator and any other professional advisers who put together the tender documentation will need to determine what the most suitable format for the plan is. Clearly the way the pre-construction information is included in the tender documentation and is structured is essential if responses on health and safety are to be made by prospective principal contractors. The pre-construction information does not have to be a separate document. If the project is a large and complex one, a separate document which ensures that the key information is highlighted, makes sense. However, on small projects, some of the information outlined will already be in existing tender documentation. In this case, the key information can be highlighted in a covering letter or by use of an index pointing to which information should be considered.

Source: HSE Construction Information Sheet No. 42.

The construction phase health and safety plan

The plan is developed by the principal contractor and is the foundation on which the health and safety management of the construction work is based. The contents of the construction phase health and safety plan will depend on the nature of the project itself. However, the health and safety plan can usefully open with:

- A description of the project. This will include details of key dates, details of other parties and the extent and location of existing records and plans.
- The management structure and responsibilities of the various members of the project team, whether based at site or elsewhere.
- The health and safety standards to which the project will be carried out. These may be set in terms of statutory requirements or high standards that the client may require in particular circumstances.
- Means for informing contractors about risks to their health and safety arising from the environment in which the project is to be carried out and the construction work itself.

- All contractors, the self employed and designers to be appointed by the principal contractor are properly selected (i.e. they are competent and will make adequate provision for health and safety).
- Means for communicating and passing information between the project team (including the client and any client's representatives) the designers, the CDM co-ordinator, the principal contractor, other contractors, workers on site and others whose health and safety may be affected.
- Arrangements for the identification and effective management of activities with risks to health and safety, by carrying out risk assessments, incorporating those prepared by other contractors, and also safety method statements which result. These activities may be specific to a particular trade or to site-wide issues.
- Emergency arrangements for dealing with and minimising the effects of injuries, fire and other dangerous occurrences.
- Arrangements for passing information to the principal contractor about accidents, ill health and dangerous occurrences that require to be notified to the health and safety executive (HSE) under RIDDOR 1995.
- Arrangements for the provision and maintenance of welfare facilities.
- Arrangements to ensure the principal contractor checks that people on site have been provided with health and safety information and safety training.
- Arrangements that have been made for consulting and co-ordinating the views of workers or their representatives.
- Arrangements for making site rules and for bringing them to the attention of those affected.
- Arrangements for passing on information to the CDM co-ordinator for the preparation of the health and safety file.
- Arrangements should be set out for the monitoring systems to achieve compliance with legal requirements; and the health and safety rules developed by the principal contractor.

Provision of information

To ensure the health and safety of persons affected by the project, and, to assist the persons to whom information is provided under this regulation. In order to perform their duties under these Regulations, every client shall ensure that:

- Every person designing the structure who may be bidding for the work (or who intend to engage), with the project-specific health and safety information needed to identify hazards and risks associated with the design and construction work.
- Every contractor who has been or may be appointed by the client is promptly provided with pre-construction information in accordance with the (CDM) 2007 regulations.

The pre-construction information shall consist of all the information in the client's possession (or which is reasonably obtainable), including:

- Any information about or affecting the site or the construction work.
- Any information concerning the proposed use of the structure as a workplace.
- The minimum amount of time before the construction phase which will be allowed to the contractors appointed by the client for planning and preparation for construction work.
- Any information in any existing health and safety file.

Preparation of the health and safety file

The CDM co-ordinator is responsible for ensuring the health and safety file is prepared. Putting together the health and safety file is a task which should ideally be a continual process throughout the project and not left until the construction work is completed. Early on in the construction project the CDM co-ordinator may find it useful to discuss the health and safety file with the client. This will help determine what information the client requires and how the client wishes the information to be stored and recorded.

When the client's requirements are known, procedures may need to be drawn up by the CDM co-ordinator so that all those who will be contributing to the health and safety file (e.g. designers and contractors) are aware of:

- What information is to be collected.
- How the information is to be collected, presented and stored.

The CDM co-ordinator may find it useful to detail in the pre-tender stage health and safety plan requirements on how and when the information for the health and safety file is to be prepared and passed on. The principal contractor may also find it useful to include similar procedures in the health and safety plan for the construction phase.

Throughout the project those who carry out design work (including contractors) will need to ensure so far as is reasonably practicable that information about any feature of the structure which will involve significant risks to health and safety during the structure's lifetime are passed to either the CDM co-ordinator or to the principal contractor.

Providing this information on drawings will allow for amendments if any variations arise during construction. It will also allow health and safety information to be stored on one document, therefore reducing the paperwork. The principal contractor may need to obtain details of services, plant and equipment which are part of the structure from specialist suppliers and installers, e.g. mechanical and electrical contractors and pass this information on.

Contractors have a specific duty in the CDM Regulations 2007 to pass information for the health and safety file to the principal contractor, who in turn has to pass it to the CDM co-ordinator. This information could include 'as built' and 'as installed' drawings as well as operation and maintenance manuals.

At the end of the project the CDM co-ordinator has to hand over the health and safety file to the client. In some cases it might not be possible for a fully developed file to be handed over on completion of the project. This may happen because the construction work was finished rapidly to meet a tight deadline and completion of the health and safety file was impossible. Clearly a common sense approach is needed so that the health and safety file is handed over as soon as practical after a completion certificate or similar document has been issued.

1.4 - Sources of information on health and safety

External to the organisation

MANUFACTURERS' DATA

Section 6 of the Health and Safety at Work Act (HASAWA) 1974 requires manufacturers to provide information. There are a wide variety of regulations for example such as Control of Substances Hazardous to Health (COSHH) 2002 and the Supply of Machinery (Safety) Regulations (SMSR) 1992 which assist and reinforce this requirement. Where products are delivered to site there should be information readily available related to weight, specialist handling, storage, preservation, where applicable, along with other identified hazardous properties.

LEGISLATION

Details of Acts and Regulations are available from the website of the Office of Public Sector Information (OPSI). New statutory instruments are published on the internet within 15 days of the printed publication (http://www.opsi.gov.uk/legislation/about_legislation.htm). Acts and Regulations are prime sources of information, they give the precise legal requirements that are to be complied with. They can, however, be difficult to read without some legal understanding. It is also easy to miss changes and amendments unless an updating service is used.

HSE AND HSC PUBLICATIONS

HSE Books publishes both HSC approved codes of practice (ACOPs) and HSE guidance notes. While failure to follow an ACOP is not in itself an offence, a defendant would have to show that the steps they took were equally effective thus transferring the burden of proof onto the defendant. This makes ACOPs a particularly important source of information. Guidance notes, and other advisory literature, are persuasive in a law court; however they can set standards higher than the basic legal minimum. Lists of both priced and free publications are available from HSE Books (http://www.hsebooks.com).

The HSE also provides a free "newsfeed" and email newsletter / bulletin service, available from its web site (http://www.hse.gov.uk).

TRADE ORGANISATIONS

The **CITB-Construction Skills** is the sector skills council for construction. It provides initiatives and programmes relating to its sector skills role, providing support and guidance to the construction industry. Organisations such as the CITB-Construction Skills provide publications, videos/DVDs and CDs to help deliver effective training and development across most subjects within the construction industry.

The Construction Industry Research and Information Association was founded in 1960. In recent times the organisation's name was shortened to **CIRIA.** Today, CIRIA is now known solely by its abbreviated name. CIRIA's mission is to improve the performance of those in the construction and related industries.

CIRIA works with the construction industry, Government and academia to provide performance improvement products and services in the construction and related industries and currently engages with around 700 subscribing organisations. Activities include collaborative projects, networking, publishing, workshops, seminars and conferences. Each year CIRIA runs about 40 projects, holds over 90 events and publishes 25 best practice guides.

INTERNATIONAL / EUROPEAN / BRITISH STANDARDS

The British Standards Institute (BSI) provides some high quality advice which is usually above the legal minimum standard. There is a distinct trend towards linking British Standards with legislation, for example, with the Health and Safety (Safety Signs and Signals) Regulations (SSSR) 1996 and BS 5378 as described in the communications module. There is also progressive harmonisation to European Standards (CEN) and the use of CE Marking. The BSI has introduced a health and safety management system standard called "Occupational health and safety management systems BS OHSAS 18001:2007".

IT SOURCES

There are many Information technology sources of information. These include a variety of websites, manufacturer's software and BSI standards. Information via IT is widely available from utility companies, Government Agencies (HSE, EA, etc.), the International Labour Organisation, Local Authorities and the Department of Trade and Industry.

This page is intentionally blank

Element 2

Construction site - hazards and controls

Learning Outcomes

On completion of this element, candidates should be able to demonstrate understanding of the content through the application of knowledge to familiar and unfamiliar situations. In particular they should be able to:

2.1 Describe the factors which should be considered when carrying out an initial assessment of a site to identify significant hazards and their risks.

2.2 Identify the general site appropriate control measures needed in setting up and organising a site.

2.3 Identify the welfare facilities required on construction sites.

Content

2.1 - Initial site assessment	15
Factors to consider in site assessments	15
2.2 - Site appropriate control measures and facilities	18
Site planning	18
Site preparation for specialist activities	19
Site security and means of protecting the public	20
Arrangements with client/occupier of premises	21
Arrangements for site inductions	22
2.3 - Welfare facilities	22
Provision of welfare facilities	22

Sources of Reference

Essentials of Health and Safety at Work, HSE Books ISBN 0-7176-0716-X
Health and Safety in Construction (Guidance) (HSG150rev), HSE Books ISBN 0-7176-0716-X
Health and Safety in Construction (HSG 150), HSE Books ISBN 0-7176-2106-5
Managing Health and Safety in Construction (ACOP) (HSG224), HSE Books ISBN 0-7176-2139-1
Safe Use of Work Equipment (ACOP) (L22), HSE Books ISBN 0-7176-1626-6
Work at Height Regulations 2005 - A Brief Guide, HSE Books (INDG 401) 0-7176-2976-7

Relevant Statutory Provisions

The Construction (Design and Management) Regulations (CDM) 2007
The Construction (Head Protection) Regulations (CHPR) 1989
The Health and Safety (First Aid) Regulations (FAR) 1981
The Health and Safety (Safety Signs and Signals) Regulations (SSSR) 1996
The Personal Protective Equipment at Work Regulations (PPER) 1992
The Provision and Use of Work Equipment Regulations (PUWER) 1998
The Work at Height Regulations (WAH) 2005

2.1 - Initial site assessment

Factors to consider in site assessments

PREVIOUS/CURRENT USE

The previous and / or current use of a site may present many hazards that need to be identified in an initial assessment before construction work starts. If for example it is a "green field" (undeveloped) site, it may provide public access / right of way to members of the public or a recreation area for children. The site could be private and used for agriculture or grazing of livestock. If a "brown field" (previously used, developed) site, it could contain occupied or unoccupied buildings/ premises. Occupied premises will mean regular traffic on the site whilst unoccupied premises may be in a state of disrepair and dereliction. Any existing premises that are either occupied or unoccupied will, more than likely, be or have been connected to various below ground or overhead services that may require further investigation.

Figure 2-1: Site assessment - previous use.   *Source: ACT.*

Figure 2-2: Site assessment - general.   *Source: ACT.*

HISTORY OF SITE

It is important to take into account the history of a site, as the site may present hazards in the form of asbestos or chemical contamination which requires specialist land reclamation services. There may be mineshafts present or other types of underground voids such as abandoned cellars, manhole chambers or large diameter drains. Action should be taken to make site surveys and obtain current and / or historic plans that may identify any or all of the above circumstances.

AREA OF SITE AND RESTRICTIONS

The location or area of the site should be considered and any possible restrictions noted, e.g. there may be trees that are protected and unable to be felled or other natural obstacles that could cause problems to the works. If, for example, a site is bounded by a main railway line then the available space (headroom) for any construction related plant and equipment to operate, or be stored around the construction site, may be restricted once work begins.

TOPOGRAPHY AND GROUND CONDITIONS

Topography relates to the physical surface conditions of the site and is an important factor to be considered along with the ground conditions below the surface. The landscape may be flat and even or is it made up of banks, dips and hills therefore making any operations on site far more difficult to carry out. The ground conditions may be soft soil, clay or rock, each condition presenting its own individual problems and hazards. The site could have a high water table or be susceptible to becoming flooded or waterlogged.

Contaminated ground conditions

Site preparation work which involves the removal of topsoil from land known to be contaminated with heavy metals will require specific arrangements in relation to personal protective equipment required and practices to be carried out. The work is likely to require the provision of gloves, overalls, eye protection and respirators. Additionally, the work will require campaigns of awareness training to ensure good levels of personal hygiene are maintained, with emphasis on ensuring that open cuts are covered with waterproof dressings whenever required. Consideration will need to be given to specific welfare facilities provision, for example a decontamination unit may be needed which has a dirty area where contaminated clothing can be removed after work, an area with a shower or other means of washing and a clean area where normal clothes could be kept while employees are working on site. There should be arrangements in place in order to prevent contamination when eating and smoking. First-aid and emergency decontamination facilities should be made available located near to the place of work.

OTHER (NON CONSTRUCTION) ACTIVITIES ON SITE

When a site is acquired, it may be necessary for other non-construction activities to be carried out prior to any construction works being authorised to begin. This could be site reclamation and clearance, installation of security fencing, lighting and signs, ground investigations, piling operation, site surveys and installation of essential utilities (power, water and gas). Other non-construction activities usually continue when construction has started, consisting of delivery of plant, equipment or materials, site security and development of utility network around the site.

NATURE OF SURROUNDINGS

The nature of site surroundings and their proximity can have detrimental effects even if not directly associated to the site being operated.

UNIT NCC1 - ELEMENT 2 - CONSTRUCTION SITE - HAZARDS AND CONTROLS

Roads

Roads and highways that surround a site boundary can be a significant source of additional hazard and are a main area for consideration as access to any site is primarily via some form of roadway. Factors such as the type of road (dual carriageway, main road, one-way system, country lane), road speed encountered, volume of traffic (high all day, cyclical, rush hour), type of traffic using the road (agricultural plant, cars, heavy goods vehicles (HGV's), well lit or unlit, capacity of road (weight, height or width restrictions). It may be that special requests or notifications are to be made with the local authority regarding access and site traffic proposals. If the site is within a residential area or in close proximity to a school, permissions or restrictions may be enforced regarding when or if surrounding roadways may or may not be used. In any of the above situations, there is a potential for danger.

Figure 2-3: Roads.   *Source: ACT.*

Figure 2-4: Footpaths.   *Source: ACT.*

Footpaths

Footpaths are a means of providing pedestrians with a safe means of travelling by foot usually alongside a highway. It should be identified how the footpath is used (e.g. for a school journey by children or by people queuing for a bus). The risk of injury may be increased at the entrance to a construction site where pedestrians cross the access opening and might encounter heavy site mobile plant or goods vehicles delivering materials to site. Footpaths may also skirt the construction site boundary, where pedestrians may also become at risk due to the activities within the site (e.g. falling objects from a scaffold structure, flying objects from cutting, drilling or hammering operations, fumes, dust, chemicals).

Railways

Railways present the hazard of heavy, high speed trains (up to and in excess of 125 mph) that do not have the ability to respond to dangerous circumstances that may arise as other transport modes are able to, i.e. quick emergency stopping, avoidance by changing direction. In addition to these hazards, there may be overhead cables carrying 25,000 volts or rails carrying 750 volts. Work near to railways requires suitable planning, as any clash between a travelling train and site equipment, plant or vehicles could, and most likely would, lead to disastrous consequences. Rail authorities have laid down strict procedures that are to be followed and any party working on railways should be in possession of a 'Personal Track Safety' certificate. High visibility clothing that is worn on or near to a railway line should be of the correct standard and colour (high visibility orange). Restrictions on colours worn on or near to a railway should be strictly followed and nothing that is red or green be worn due to the fact that it may be mistaken as a signal by a train driver. Communications should be maintained with the rail authority and notification given of any works being carried out on or near to the railway in order that all issues can be complied with correctly.

Figure 2-5: Railways.   *Source: Welsh Highland Railway.*

Figure 2-6: Waterways.   *Source: ACT.*

Waterways

Waterways located on or near construction sites present a risk of drowning; the water does not have to be fast flowing to cause a worker to get into difficulty. Other factors to consider if waterways are in close proximity to a construction site are: the likelihood of floods occurring, environmental pollution of the waterway, damage to associated wildlife by site activities. Conversely, it is necessary to consider exposure of site staff to hygiene hazards through contaminants or disease (chemical pollutants, Weils disease) within the waterway. Waterways are used by a considerable number of boat operators that may be affected by the activities on site (e.g. falling objects from a scaffold structure, flying objects from cutting, drilling or hammering operations, fumes, dust, chemicals). Boat operators may equally affect site safety (e.g. collision of the boat with a scaffold structure, possibly noise or pollution associated with their work).

Residential/commercial/industrial properties

Construction can take place in local or immediate proximity of residential, industrial or commercial property that may be either unoccupied or occupied and fully operational. The range of hazards is wide and each concerns members of the public or others (staff, contractors). Residential property areas are usually busy areas and can include regular traffic flow, children, the elderly and animals. Commercial property areas (shops, offices) are also busy areas that include members of the public and members of staff carrying out their own duties within the work area. Industrial property areas (factories, workshops) involve people at work and present additional hazards of machinery, plant, equipment, chemicals, etc. being used that construction workers may not ordinarily be familiar with.

Figure 2-7: Commercial properties.   Source: ACT.

Figure 2-8: Industrial properties.   Source: ACT.

Schools

Schools are very busy areas and accommodate children of various ages that may have no or little perception of danger or risk and by their nature are often very inquisitive of their surroundings. In addition to children, parents or carers that deliver children to and collect children from the school create pedestrian and vehicular traffic hazards around the immediate area. Children are frequently tempted to try to gain access to construction sites and normally achieve this when site security is poor and consideration has not been given to access through small openings. Sites often underestimate the size of openings, which some small children are able to fit through, particularly when compared with that which is required to restrict adult access.

MEANS OF ACCESS

Access to a construction site should be through a controlled point and requires adequate planning to take into account the surrounding area. Restrictions and hazards relating to safe access to a construction site may include the conditions of the highway from which access is being gained (size, speed, use). The traffic that will operate on the site needs to be considered (size, type, frequency, volume).

Figure 2-9: Means of access.   Source: ACT.

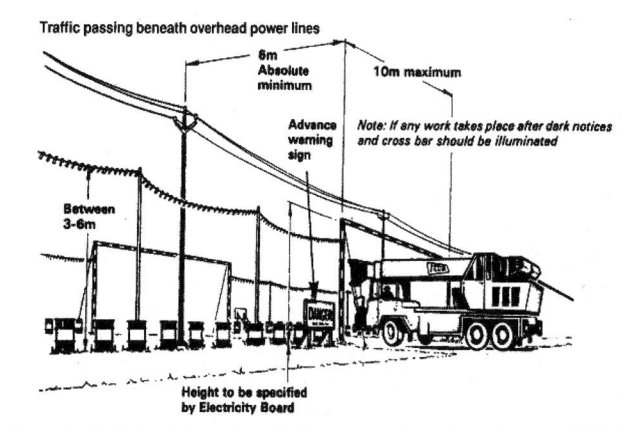

Figure 2-10: Safe distance barriers for overhead services. Source: HSG144.

PRESENCE OF OVERHEAD AND BURIED SERVICES

Overhead services in the form of electricity cables present the obvious risk of electrocution through either making direct contact with the electricity cable or where arcing (discharge by spark 'jumping' to a near earth point) occurs. Overhead cables should be identified prior to site works and the risk factors determined. Construction sites may involve the use of various pieces of large, mobile plant and equipment (cranes, excavators, etc) and steel scaffold systems near to power supplies. If such equipment is allowed to come too close to an overhead cable it may provide a sufficient level of earth for the power to 'leap', making the particular item of plant live. If this occurs, subsequent 'arcs' are possible to other people or plant within close proximity of the original earth point. In order to control this at points of risk the power may be isolated, cables covered or, if none of these is practicable, contact may be prevented by using barriers to set a safe distance from overhead services.

Buried services (electricity, gas, water, etc) are not obvious and the likelihood of striking a service when excavating, drilling or piling is thus increased without a site survey to identify any service present. The results of striking an underground service are varied, and the potential to cause injury or fatality is high. As with overhead power lines, any underground service should be treated as live until confirmed and documented otherwise by an authorised source. Incidents can include shock, electrocution, explosion and burns from power cables, explosion, burns or unconsciousness from gas or power cables, impact injury from dislodged stones / flooding from ruptured water mains.

2.2 - Site appropriate control measures and facilities

Site planning

Following an initial site assessment that has identified hazards and risks associated with the works, control measures should be implemented to ensure the safety and well being of all those who are affected by the construction site and its activities. A plan must be assembled to take into consideration the following factors.

ARRANGEMENTS FOR SITE ACCESS

Access to a construction site must be planned to minimise any hazards identified during the initial assessment. When a suitable location for site access has been identified, this must be controlled at a point or points that are designated as authorised access point/s and the remainder of the construction site boundary must be secure against unauthorised access. Site safety information should be displayed at access points to inform all attendees of contact names, rules and emergency procedures. Barrier systems are normal on complex undertakings, accompanied by procedures for admittance and exit of people and plant. Special rules for site safety induction and issue of any site security identification are often used to maintain control.

Figure 2-11: Site access. *Source: ACT.*

Figure 2-12: Site controls - access and roadways. *Source: ACT.*

ROADWAYS

Public roadways often extend or continue into construction sites and are subject to pedestrian and vehicular traffic. Construction site roads should be subject to site safety rules such as speed limits, safety restraints (seat belts), direction of flow (one way systems where possible), and there should be segregation of pedestrian and vehicular traffic similar to that used on the public highway. Adequate space should be provided for parking and to allow vehicles and plant to manoeuvre safely and the area should be well lit as required. Vehicles and mobile plant should never be allowed to block roadways or access points as this may prevent emergency vehicles and crews gaining access in the event of a major incident. Site slurry / mud on the road surface that can create skid hazards for site plant and vehicles should not be allowed to accumulate and there should be a system for inspection and cleaning of the surface and vehicles' wheels.

STORAGE

The storage requirements are dependent on the type of material to be stored. Different material types should be stored separately, to avoid cross contamination and the potential for a harmful adverse chemical reaction. If combined storage is permitted, it is advisable that different materials be kept separated for easy identification and retrieval. In addition to authorised access of site operatives, the storage area should be designed to allow safe access by forklift trucks and for the use of suitable mechanical lifting aids to eliminate the need for manual handling where possible. House keeping should be of a good standard and kept clean and tidy with suitable lighting and ventilation. There should be appropriate fire precautions and provision of correct fire extinguishers. Storage areas should be restricted areas to authorised site staff only and have the correct safety information signs that warn of any dangers or mandatory signs enforcing the wearing of PPE. They should be used for solely that purpose and must not be used for any other purposes such as mixing operations or as a rest or smoking area.

Storage of flammable substances
Substances should be stored in such a way that they cannot

1) Escape and contaminate personnel or the environment   **2)** React with other substances causing explosion, fire or toxic fumes.

Requirements for storage:
- Store small quantities only in the workplace.
- Small quantities of flammables should be stored in clearly marked flameproof metal containers.
- Non-compatible chemicals should be stored apart.
- Chemicals giving off fumes should be stored and used only with suitable respiratory protection.
- Chemicals should be stored away from sources of heat, possibly refrigerated.
- Bulk storage should be outside away from other buildings and sources of heat, including sunlight.

Features of a bulk flammable substance store
- Single storey, light construction in non-combustible materials.
- Flame proof electrical equipment.
- Door sill and perimeter bunding for containment of up to 110% of the maximum storage container of the chemical. If more than one container is stored, the system must be capable of storing 110% of the biggest container capacity or 25% of the total tank capacity within the bund. Whichever is the greater must be adopted.
- Interceptor pits for spillage.

Figure 2-13: Misuse of storage.   Source: ACT.

Figure 2-14: Loading / unloading.   Source: ACT.

LOADING/UNLOADING

Construction sites are constantly changing with a variety of tasks all happening at once, including continuous staff, vehicles and material movements around the site. With this in mind, it is very important that any loading and unloading of materials used on the construction site is carried out in its own dedicated area/ zone under competent supervision. The delivery of materials or equipment to a construction site should be scheduled and planned to minimise the volume of traffic at site at any one time, and drivers / operators of delivery vehicles given a site specific induction to ensure an awareness of hazards, site safety rules and procedures.

Loading and unloading of materials or equipment should be planned and organised. Materials should not be allowed to be placed too high or to lean over creating a potential risk of collapse with the possible result of major injury or a fatality. A number of people have been killed on construction sites due to carelessness in handling. Generally, loads should be kept small with goods on pallets that are in good repair. Lightweight boxes that offer no strength and can be crushed or bags of free-flowing solid (gravel) should always be palletised and never be stacked on top of each other. Different types of container should be stacked separately.

Loads should not block or be placed near emergency exits, fire points / extinguishers, vehicle routes or block light or visibility. They should be placed on firm, solid ground or floors that are strong enough to provide adequate support. Workers should be trained in the correct way to handle loads and also in the dangers associated with unsafe practices / or incorrect loading methods. Site staff should be instructed never to climb up or stand on top of racking or palletized material.

OFFICES

There should be an office available on site to house first aid facilities and equipment, emergency procedures, health and safety information, site induction documentation, health and safety plan (if the Construction (Design and Management) Regulations (CDM) 2007 apply), construction drawings and specifications. General site office equipment and records (telephone, fax, training records, visitor personal protective equipment and filing facility) are also stored in the site office.

LIGHTING

Adequate lighting should be provided that allows safe access and egress into and around the construction site along roadways, vehicle and pedestrian routes. Special consideration should be made to areas such as scaffold structures, excavations, flammable stores or fuel bunkers / tanks. Signs warning of dangers at site should be clearly lit to allow approaching people advance notice.

SIGNS

The provision of suitable signs is an important factor in making people aware of the hazards and precautions that relate to construction work. The entrance to a construction site should have an information board that provides details of the client, architect, supervisor, contractor and any other important parties. It will also include mandatory health and safety signs such as those requiring the use of hard hats or ear protection. Other information could include a basic site layout plan and details of where to report upon arrival at the site.

Site preparation for specialist activities

LIFTING

Lifting operations on construction sites can vary widely dependent upon the size and weight of the load required to be lifted and the lifting equipment required to carry out the lift. Specialist lifting equipment on construction sites is usually either mobile crane or tower crane type. Prior to undertaking lifting operations with any piece of lifting equipment, vital preparation is required to ensure the safety of all those affected. This includes thorough planning of the lift to include a safe system of work, method statements, risk assessments, permits to work (if required) and competent authorised persons assigned to manage the lifting operation. The ground on which the lifting equipment is to be situated should be firm and level and suitable load spreading decking provided to ensure stability. Consideration should also be given to surrounding structures and overhead power cables, ensuring the minimum safe working distances from them. Access to the area below the lifting area should be controlled or restricted to protect people at site from items falling during the lift. The equipment used for the lift must be inspected prior to use and regularly as per the specified frequencies and all test certificates made available. The Lifting Equipment and Lifting Operation Regulations (LOLER) 1998 are specifically related to mechanical lifting and associated equipment.

PILING

Piling is a method of creating long, straight underground cavities that are used for providing foundations for a building or structure. This is performed by either using drilling or by compacting force. The most common method of piling involves the use of a guide 'tube' in which a heavy solid 'driving piece' supported by lifting equipment is released down the guide tube causing the material it strikes to displace upon impact and thus create a cavity when withdrawn. This operation is repeated until the required depth of bore is achieved. Another method involves a steel liner being mechanically 'hammered' into the ground to the required depth. Preparations for piling works may include identifying buried services, hidden voids, the density of the material being piled and ground stability for equipment, water table levels and any local buildings or structures that may be affected by vibrations. Piling is a very noisy operation and consideration should be given to surrounding areas.

Figure 2-15: Site signs.   *Source: ACT.*

Figure 2-16: Steelworks.   *Source: ACT.*

STEELWORKS

Steelwork is often used to form the basic 'skeleton' on which a structure is built. The majority of steelwork is designed and manufactured off site and is then assembled using the various pre-fabricated sections and steel beams during the build. Associated activities usually involve working at height with materials that are very heavy and difficult to manoeuvre. Site preparation involves thorough planning to include safe systems of work, risk assessments, method statements and permits to work where required. Where practicable, risks should be eliminated or reduced to the minimum possible level by combating hazards at source (e.g. use of mobile elevated work platform for access, cranes for lifting). Any lifting equipment or access equipment should only be used on firm and level ground.

Site security and means of protecting the public

PERIMETER FENCING

Construction sites must be contained within a perimeter fence. The main purpose of fencing is to keep out unauthorised persons (e.g. members of the public and children) and to prevent injury or death. Perimeter fencing also provides security against theft of materials, plant or equipment from the site. Fences should be adequate and suitable and installed at a reasonable distance from the structure to allow unrestricted movement on site of people and mobile plant, and prevent any activities being undertaken affecting the environment outside the fence. The fence should be regularly inspected to ensure there is no damage, breaks or gaps to allow unauthorised entry. When one piece of fencing or barrier is fixed to another, the fixing should face into the protected site, where possible, so as to impede tampering and removal of such barriers or fences by unauthorised persons.

Figure 2-17: Unauthorised access.   *Source: ACT.*

Figure 2-18: Perimeter fencing and signs.   *Source: ACT.*

SIGNS

Signs should be fixed at regular intervals on the perimeter fence to warn of the dangers within the site and instruct people to 'keep out'. Quite often, the name of the security company that is responsible for 'out of hours' security will also be displayed with a telephone number for emergency contact or to report any trespass.

SAFE VIEWING POINTS

Members of the public are quite often intrigued by construction sites and can be attracted to the perimeter fence to see for themselves what is going on. This may result in injury from flying particles, dust, fumes or splashes, even though the person is outside the perimeter fence. This can be avoided by arranging for a pre-planned viewing point that consists of a wire mesh panel integrated into the fence that allows members of the public to view the site's activities. The viewing point will be planned and situated in an area that is not exposed to hazards.

MEANS OF SECURING PLANT, CHEMICALS, ETC

Plant, equipment, materials or chemicals should be suitably secured to prevent injury by unauthorised access. Plant should be locked up at all times when not in use and keys held in a secure location (site office, safe). It may be practical to house plant in an additional internal site compound. In order to improve security certain items of heavy mobile plant are provided with steel sheets or shutters fitted around the cab and padlocked in position.

MEANS OF CONTROLLING ENVIRONMENTAL DANGERS ON PUBLIC HIGHWAYS

Areas that surround a construction site are subject to mud and debris from the tyres and chassis of vehicles that frequent the site, which creates additional hazards to other road users as highway surfaces become slippery and create skid hazards. This can be controlled by the implementation of regular highway cleaning with road sweeper vehicles. Action can also be taken at site exits prior to vehicles leaving the site by routing site traffic through a tyre and undercarriage cleaning system, which assists in preventing mud and debris leaving the site.

Arrangements with client/occupier of premises

SITE RULES

Site rules will vary at different sites or premises due to the wide range of activities that may be undertaken. Site rules provide instructions that must be followed by permanent site staff and visitors and also other important information relating to site / location specific hazards. Occupiers of premises or clients may have different standards of site rules and some may enforce them more stringently than others. Contractors should always enforce their own site rules in addition to client / occupier rules.

CO-OPERATION

Co-operation between client and occupier is a very important factor. The occupier of a premises or site will have a detailed knowledge of any site specific hazards that may or may not be obvious to a contractor undertaking construction works and this may impact upon the works. In addition, the client or occupier has the authority to place controls and restrictions on the site. The contractor should be experienced in the activities that will be carried out and will have assessed any hazards related to the activities that are to be carried out at site. It is vital that all parties co-operate and communicate in order that this knowledge and information can be assessed to determine any new hazards that may arise and to enable appropriate information to be cascaded to other people at risk on the site. Co-operation will also be required where site activities need to be controlled or access restricted or where a shared knowledge is required to undertake a task e.g. decommissioning or removal of machinery.

SHARED FACILITIES

Occupied premises will quite often have various facilities available for existing staff / occupiers (hot & cold water, toilets, communications, restroom) depending upon the type of property it is. It may be acceptable upon agreements with the party in control of the premises and its facilities for these to be shared for mutual benefit.

Figure 2-19: Protection of others.   *Source: ACT.*

Figure 2-20: Sanitary conveniences.   *Source: ACT.*

First Aid

It is the duty of the employer (this could be the main contractor) to provide under the Health and Safety (First-Aid) Regulations (FAR) 1981, first-aid provisions and to inform the employees of these arrangements. These facilities should be in a clean environment, probably sited in a separate site office or portacabin. Reporting of Diseases and Dangerous Occurrences (RIDDOR) 1995 regulations require an accident book to be kept on site. All reportable accidents/dangerous occurrences must be recorded with deaths being reported immediately, by telephone, directly to the HSE.

Protection of other employees/ visitors

Construction related activities that are carried out in addition to those normally undertaken at the premises must take into account a lack of knowledge of other parties using the premises. Consideration must be paid to protecting not only those staff directly involved in the works, but also to any other person that may encounter the works including permanent site staff and / or visitors attending the site. This may require site rules to be amended, and be supported by induction, personal protective equipment issue, signs, barriers, lighting or verbal instruction.

Arrangements for site inductions

All new or transferred employees, sub-contractors, including utility suppliers, architects' and surveyors should receive a site induction. This should be tailored to the site concerned and follow a formal structure, with documentation signed and logged. The following subjects should be covered (as a minimum):

- Welfare provisions (toilets, showers, rest areas).
- Site rules
- Access and egress, e.g. signing in and out
- Fire fighting equipment and assembly points.
- Use of personal protective equipment (PPE) and any training requirements.
- First-aid provision.
- Permits to work; any specific work restrictions.
- Traffic management plans.
- Work procedures
- Method statements
- Emergency procedures
- Reporting procedures, i.e. incidents, accidents, unsafe conditions

Specific hazards and controls:
- Electrical
- Plant and equipment
- Hazardous substances
- Manual handling

2.3 - Welfare facilities

Provision of welfare facilities

SANITARY CONVENIENCES

Suitable and sufficient sanitary conveniences should be made available at readily accessible places. Rooms containing sanitary conveniences should be adequately ventilated and well lit. Men and women may use the same room provided as long as it is lockable from the inside. Provision should be made for regular cleaning and replenishment of consumable toilet items.

WASHING FACILITIES

On all sites, a suitable number of wash basins big enough to allow a person to wash their hands, face and forearms should be available. All basins should have a supply of hot and cold water (warm water as a minimum). A means of drying must also be provided. Where work is particularly dirty or workers are exposed to toxic or corrosive substances, showers may also be necessary.

Figure 2-21: Washing facilities.   Source: ACT.

Figure 2-22: Temporary showers.   Source: ACT.

DRINKING WATER

An adequate supply of wholesome drinking water must be made available at suitable and readily accessible places. Drinking water supplies should be clearly marked to distinguish them from those that are not fit for human consumption. Unless the supply is in the form of a fountain, cups or other drinking vessels must be available.

CHANGING AREAS

Where a person has to wear special clothing for work, suitable facilities - separate for men and women - must be provided. Changing areas must be big enough, sufficiently warm and secure.

ACCOMMODATION FOR CLOTHING

There must be arrangements for storage and segregation of clothing not worn on site from protective clothing needed for site work. There should be somewhere to dry wet clothing and separate storage for contaminated clothes. Storage areas must be secure.

REST, FOOD / DRINK PREPARATION AND EATING FACILITIES

Readily accessible, suitable and sufficient rest facilities must be provided. Suitable rest facilities must also be provided for pregnant women and nursing mothers.

Where meals are regularly eaten in the workplace suitable and sufficient facilities must be provided for their consumption. Eating facilities should include a facility for preparing or obtaining a hot drink, and where hot food cannot be readily obtained, means should be provided to enable workers to heat their own food.

Figure 2-23: Accommodation for clothing.   *Source: ACT.*

Figure 2-24: Rest and eating facilities.   *Source: ACT.*

VENTILATION, HEATING AND LIGHTING OF FACILITIES

All of the facilities mentioned above shall be kept clean, warm, properly ventilated and well lit.

FIRST AID FACILITIES

First aid facilities should contain essential first aid provision and equipment:

- Sink with hot and cold running water.
- Drinking water and disposable cups.
- Soap and paper towels.
- A store for first aid materials.
- Foot-operated refuse containers, lined with disposable yellow clinical waste bags or a container for the safe disposal of clinical waste.
- A couch with waterproof protection.
- Clean pillows and blankets.
- A chair.
- A telephone or other communication equipment.
- A record book for recording incidents where first aid has been given.

This page is intentionally blank

Element 3

Movement of people and vehicles - hazards and control

Learning outcomes

On completion of this element, candidates should be able to demonstrate understanding of the content through the application of knowledge to familiar and unfamiliar situations. In particular they should be able to:

3.1 Identify the hazards that may cause injuries to pedestrians in the workplace, including when using public highways as a workplace.

3.2 Outline the appropriate control measures to reduce the risk of injuries to pedestrians.

3.3 Identify the hazards presented by the movement of vehicles in the workplace, including when using public highways as a workplace.

3.4 Outline the appropriate control measures to reduce the risks that movement of vehicles present.

Content

3.1 - Movement of people	27
Hazards to pedestrians	27
3.2 - Control measures for pedestrian hazards	29
Risk assessment	29
Slip resistant surfaces	29
Spillage control and drainage	29
Designated walkways	30
Fencing and guarding	30
Use of signs and personal protective equipment	30
Information, instruction, training and supervision	31
Maintenance of a safe workplace	31
Particular measures to protect members of the public who may be affected by construction activities on public highways	33
3.3 - Hazards in vehicle operations	33
Typical hazards causing loss of control and overturning of site vehicles	33
Collisions with other vehicles, pedestrians and fixed objects	33
Site layout	34
Road surfaces	34
Gradients	34
Excavations	35
Scaffolding and false work	35
Refuelling	35
The hazard presented by, and caused to, public vehicles during public highway works	35
Conditions and environments in which each hazard may arise	35
3.4 - Control measures for safe vehicle operations	36
General site strategies	36
Risk assessment	36
Suitability and sufficiency of traffic routes	36
Management of vehicle movements	36
Environmental considerations	36
Driver protection and restraint systems	37
Suitability and maintenance of vehicles	37
Means of segregating pedestrians and vehicles	37
Protective measures for people and structures	39
Site rules	40
Selection and training of drivers	40
Management systems for assuring driver competence including local codes of practice	41
Traffic safety measures and signs used when conducting construction activities on public highways	41

Sources of reference

Essentials of health and safety at work, HSE Books ISBN 0-7176-6179-2

Lighting at work (HSG38), HSE Books ISBN 0-7176-1232-5

Safety at streetworks and roadworks (Code of Practice), HMSO ISBN 0-1155-1958-0

Safe use of vehicles on construction sites (HSG144), HSE Books ISBN 0-7176-1610-X

Safe use of work equipment (ACoP) (L22), HSE Books ISBN 0-7176-1626-6

The Health and Safety (Safety Signs and Signals) Regulations 1996. Guidance on Regulations (L64), HSE Books ISBN 0-7176-0870-0

The Traffic Signs Manual (Chapter 8: The Traffic Safety Measures and Signs for Roadworks and Temporary Situations), Department for Transport ISBN 0-1155-2738-9

Relevant statutory provisions

The Construction (Design and Management) Regulations (CDM) 2007 - Part 4 in particular

The Health and Safety (Safety Signs and Signals) Regulations (SSSR) 1996

The New Roads and Street Works Act (NRSWA) 1991

The Provision and Use of Work Equipment Regulations (PUWER) 1998 - Part III in particular

The Work at Height Regulations (WAH) 2005

3.1 - Movement of people

Hazards to pedestrians

TYPICAL CONSTRUCTION HAZARDS

Slips, trips and falls on the same level

Slips, trips and falls on the same level are the most common causes of major injuries reported to the Health and Safety Executive (HSE) under the Reporting of Injuries, Diseases and Dangerous Occurrences Regulations (RIDDOR) 1995. Broken bones are the usual result when the following conditions are present.

- Poorly maintained surfaces - e.g. potholes in roads, site debris, excavations and poor reinstatements of roads or walk ways.
- Changes in level caused by temporary road surfaces or reinstatements, excavation covers, heavy plant tracks, ramps, kerbs, or chamber lids not clearly marked.
- Slippery surfaces caused by water, oils, fuels, silt, mud, or mixed compounds - e.g. mortar, plaster, render.
- Inappropriate footwear.
- Sites rules not followed - e.g. running or not taking care when walking on site.
- General obstructions in walkways such as trailing cables, pipes and air hoses.

Figure 3-1: Slips and trips.   *Source: Lincsafe.*

Figure 3-2: Trip hazards.   *Source: Lincsafe.*

Falls from a height

Commonly caused by:

- Fragile roofs.
- Inadequate access to and from the workplace.
- Inadequate barriers e.g. hand rails, edge protection boards.
- Trenches - absence of or ineffective barriers / fences.

Figure 3-3: Collision with moving vehicles.   *Source: ACT.*

Figure 3-4: Falling materials.   *Source: Lincsafe.*

Collisions with moving vehicles

- Restricted space to allow for manoeuvring and passing - e.g. where there is a high volume of mobile plant and materials.
- Undefined routes to segregate site traffic - e.g. people with heavy goods vehicles, excavators, dump trucks and vans.
- Poor ground conditions - e.g. loose surface, slippery. Poor grip.
- Disregard for site rules concerning site vehicles - e.g. speed restrictions, competent operators.
- No or insufficient warning devices fitted to vehicles and a general lack of maintenance.
- Unstable ground conditions.

Striking by moving, flying or falling objects

When working above ground such as on a scaffold, it is easy to concentrate on protecting people from falling. However, it is also important to consider precautions to prevent falling objects. Situations that increase the likelihood of falling objects are:

- Overloading of materials on scaffolds, roofs or mobile elevated work platforms.
- Lack of use of barriers or mesh screens to prevent materials falling from height or being blown off.
- Faulty or inappropriate means of lifting or lowering materials to the workplace.
- Unstable loads on vehicles - e.g. not correctly supported, tied or secured.
- Unstable workplace structure - e.g. insufficient number of scaffold tie points or uneven ground.

Striking against fixed or stationary objects

Whilst bumps and bruises are considered by many as "minor" injuries, they are painful and can be distressing for the sufferer. Therefore, the following situations should be avoided.

- Low level or protruding scaffold tubing not correctly protected or highlighted with hi-visibility warning tape.
- Insufficient space for storing tools and materials causing poor access in and out.
- Poor lighting / work in enclosed areas.
- Cranes or lifting devices with hanging hooks / slings.

Treading on sharp items

Sharp objects represent a hazard to pedestrians. Construction sites have a large amount of materials moved onto and around them. Sometimes materials such as sections of trunking are cut to length and off cuts may fall to the ground and be left there. Similarly, material can arrive on site with wire binding and when the binding is removed the off cuts are often left on the ground. In addition, nailed together timber is sometimes used for improvised tasks, and when it is finished with it may be broken apart and discarded, leaving nails protruding. This can also be the case with broken pallets.

HAZARDS TO THE GENERAL PUBLIC CAUSED BY CONSTRUCTION ACTIVITIES, INCLUDING PUBLIC HIGHWAYS

The majority of the general public are attracted to construction activities, including construction activities on public highways, usually out of curiosity for the project underway. The hazards and dangers present at the site are often significantly magnified due to the public's lack of knowledge or awareness of site issues of health and safety.

Construction activities on public highways may pose a higher risk due to activities being carried out actually within the public area resulting in an increased level of public curiosity. Due to the temporary nature of the majority of construction activities on public highways the working area is often within less secure barrier systems and security is reduced to the vigilance of staff working in the area providing enforcement of site access rules. Items of heavy plant or material deliveries often operate outside the barrier systems that are set up, thus creating increased risk to the public. Works involving scaffold structures on the highway pose an obstruction to members of the public. The risk of impact with scaffold bars must be controlled by installing horizontal tubes high enough to avoid head injury and also cladding the bars with protective foam and high visibility tape.

Consideration also has to be given to those who may gain unauthorised access outside the core working hours undertaken at the site or project. Adequate means of preventing access should be implemented and any hazards made suitably safe after work, e.g. excavations guarded, covered and lit; ladders secured and plant locked up.

Figure 3-5: Obstructions.   Source: Lincsafe.   Figure 3-6: Public highway works.   Source: ACT.

CONDITIONS AND ENVIRONMENTS IN WHICH HAZARDS MAY ARISE

- Poor standards of housekeeping in the workplace. Allowing rubbish to accumulate also increases the risk of fire, and biological hazards from vermin.
- Adverse weather conditions - e.g. high winds, rain, and snow.
- Outdoor working - warehouses where vehicles operate alongside people or poorly laid out offices.
- Typical high risk work - maintenance, construction, demolition and excavating.
- Distribution centres, commercial vehicle depots, loading yards where fork lift trucks are used, freight and bus terminals.

Why accidents may occur on staircases
- Poor design of the staircase.
- Not using handrail (e.g. carrying).
- Slippery condition of the stairs (e.g. due to polish or ice/water).
- Inadequate maintenance (e.g. worn or damaged stairs, tiles, carpets).
- Obstructions on the stairs (e.g. boxes of photocopy paper).
- Inadequate standards of lighting.
- Bad practice (carrying loads, inappropriate footwear, non-use of handrails or rushing).
- Too narrow for volume of people using it.

3.2 - Control measures for pedestrian hazards

Risk assessment

Some or all of the following issues might affect the hazards faced by pedestrians and should be considered when carrying out a risk assessment:
- Weather conditions - particularly snow and ice.
- Lighting - especially at night.
- Surfaces - the presence of holes to the floor or the presence of mud.
- Unusually high numbers of people. Consider, for example, busy periods such as holiday sales in department stores causing large numbers of the public to be near construction activities on public highways and fluctuations in workloads which could lead to an influx of temporary workers.
- The effectiveness of existing controls - such as barriers.
- Unexpected movements of people - such as shortcuts, entry into restricted areas, emergency evacuation.
- Special needs for certain groups of people - such as people in wheel chairs, pregnant women and elderly people.

Slip resistant surfaces

How slip and trip hazards in the workplace might be controlled:
- Improved work layout with designated walkways.
- Using high grip surface coating.
- Highlighting changes in level with hazard warning strips.
- Providing good lighting.
- Introducing procedures for reporting defects and for dealing with spillage.
- Ensuring high standards of housekeeping to keep floors clear of obstructions, debris or spillage.
- Roughened non-slip concrete walkways on site.
- High grip grit sheets on the edge of steps and stairs.
- Mats at entrance to buildings and cabins.

Design features and/or safe practices intended to reduce the risk of accidents on staircases used as internal pedestrian routes within work premises:
- The removal of obstructions, paying particular attention to escape routes.
- The provision of non-slip surfaces, together with reflective edging.
- Adequate lighting and effective maintenance.

Figure 3-7: Slip resistant surfaces. *Source: ACT.*

Important design features of a staircase (which are to a large extent defined by building standards) are its width, the provision of handrails, the dimensions of treads and risers, and the provision of landings. Thought should be given to special provision for disabled persons and to the possibility of using a lift as an alternative. Avoid the need to carry large or heavy items up or down stairs. Site rules should address such issues as well as defining appropriate footwear.

Spillage control and drainage

A PROCEDURE FOR SPILLAGE RESPONSE FOR HAZARDOUS LIQUIDS SHOULD INCLUDE:
- Raise the alarm and inform emergency services and relevant authorities (e.g. fire service, water authority).
- Evacuate all personnel, seal off access from danger area.
- Quickly assess the nature and extent (if possible) of the incident.
- Do not approach the liquid if you do not know what it is.
- Raise first aid treatment for those who might have been affected.
- Keep people away.
- Isolate any ignition sources.
- Issue appropriate personal protective equipment to those involved and competent in carrying out the procedure.
- Provide bunding or some other form of spillage containment such as sand or special granules to contain the spillage.
- For internal spills with no fire risk, if safe to do so, ventilate by opening windows and closing doors, that is, ventilate the area but isolate the material.
- For external spills, cover drains to prevent the material going into drains and watercourses. Do not wash spillage into drains.
- Ensure safe disposal of the spilled substance and any absorbent material used.

Designated walkways

An important consideration when considering traffic systems is the safety interface between pedestrians and traffic. The routes that people use should be clearly defined and marked via fencing, barriers, crossing points and in the paper format via traffic management plans which are posted in relevant areas and signing in points. It is a requirement of the Construction (Design and Management) Regulations (CDM) 2007 regulation 36 that every construction site shall be organised in such a way that, so far as is reasonably practicable, pedestrians and vehicles can move safely and without risks to health, and that traffic routes shall be suitable for the persons or vehicles using them, sufficient in number, in suitable positions and of sufficient size.

Good site planning should ensure the provision of designated walkways as part of the site layout. For sites that will be used by a significant number of people over a period of time consideration should be made to laying formal concrete walkways for workers, particularly at parts of the site where there will be a high amount of pedestrian traffic - such as entrances, rest facilities and routes through the site. Effort should be made to segregate pedestrians from site traffic, particularly on approach roads and where vehicles manoeuvre. When arrangements are being made for designated walkways the need for emergency routes and exits need to be considered also. Routes must be clearly indicated and be adequate for the people and hazards present on site.

The Workplace (Health, Safety and Welfare) Regulations (WHSWR) 1992 Regulation 12 requires that floors and traffic route surfaces must be constructed so that they are suitable for the purpose for which they are used. This means such things as having no holes or being slippery or uneven. Measures to control hazards related to floors and gangways may include:

- Kept clean and free from obstructions that may hinder passage.
- Good drainage in wet processes areas or wet weather conditions.
- Suitable footwear or working platforms provided where necessary.
- Ramps kept dry and with non-skid surfaces.
- Level, even ground without holes or broken boards.
- Floor load capacities posted in lofts and storage areas.
- Salting/sanding and sweeping of outdoor routes during icy or frosty conditions.
- Steps, corners and fixed obstacles clearly marked.
- Excavations and chambers kept covered when not in use and the edges clearly marked.

Fencing and guarding

Particular attention should be taken to control hazards through the use of fencing and guarding. Fencing of the outer area of a work site, at a suitable distance, will assist in the control of movement of people and vehicles. In addition, workers and vehicles in the site need protection and in this case inner guarding using barriers may be necessary, for example to protect the edge of an excavation. It is essential that any fences or guarding (barriers) provided are stable to ensure proper protection is achieved.

> "Suitable and sufficient steps shall be taken to prevent, so far as is reasonably practicable, any person falling" and
>
> "Where necessary to prevent danger to any person, suitable and sufficient steps shall be taken to prevent, as far as is reasonably practicable, the fall of any material or object"
>
> In any case where the steps identified above include the provision of any guard rail, toe board, barrier or other similar means of protection; or working platform, these shall comply with the provisions of schedules 2 of the Work at Heights Regulations 2005, regulation 8.

Physical barriers should be erected to ensure that there is adequate protection for pedestrians who may be exposed to falls, falling objects and being struck by a moving object such as a vehicle. In addition, where pedestrians may walk into or strike an object, such as a protruding scaffold pole or a ladder the area around the objects should be guarded by means of a barrier.

Figures 3-8: Outer fencing and inner guarding.   *Source: ACT.*

Figure 3-9: Protection of pedestrians.   *Source: ACT.*

Use of signs and personal protective equipment

Signs must conform to the standards specified in the Health and Safety (Safety Signs and Signals) Regulations (SSSR) 1996. They must be clearly visible and be easily understood.

Safety signs should indicate the need to use personal protective equipment, such as hard hats, protective footwear or high visibility clothing, when entering certain work areas even if people are just visiting or passing quickly through.

Signs to indicate the presence of a temporary hazard should be used to warn people who might be affected to keep clear of that area. Hazard signs might be used where excavations are present, a change in height occurs or for the demarcation of a hazard area to assist with the provision of diversionary routes - for example, a vehicle unloading area where pedestrians are prohibited.

Edges of steps, overhead obstructions and cables or pipes laid temporarily across walkways should also be clearly identified with hazard markings.

The Construction (Head Protection) Regulations (CHPR) 1989 require employees and self-employed persons to wear suitable head protection when required to do so by rules made, or directions given, under regulation 5. In the absence of rules or directions there is no requirement under the regulations for employees or self-employed persons working under the control of another person to wear head protection.

Where there is a significant risk present to cause a head injury, site rules should include the mandatory provision and wearing of head protection.

Suitable footwear is important to avoid slips or trips or puncture wounds in the workplace. The risk assessment process should consider the possibility of slips, trips and sharp material hazards, and where the decided control of this hazard includes the use of specific footwear this should be arranged.

If the footwear has particular properties, such as anti-slip soles or steel mid-plates, this would fall under the requirements of the Personal Protective Equipment Regulations (PPER) 1992 and as such the employer should provide them to employees without charge.

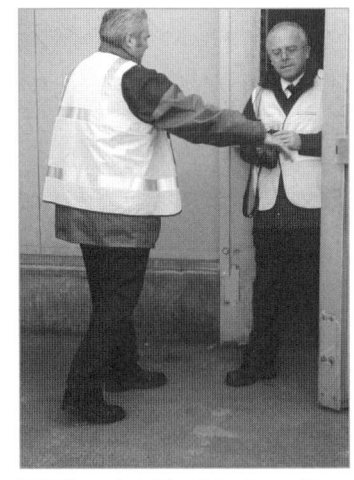

Figure 3-10: Correct clothing & footwear. *Source: ACT.*

Where specific personal protective footwear is not required but employees need to wear suitable personal shoes to work, this should be specified and would not normally be subject to the PPER 1992. In addition, footwear with a protective toe cap is necessary for those that may work in close proximity to vehicles.

On sites where vehicles operate and for construction activities on public highways it is essential that workers are able to be seen, therefore it is essential that high visibility clothing be used. Though this is not a substitute for the separation of vehicles from people, for the many situations where workers work in close proximity to vehicles it will provide valuable assistance in preventing contact.

Information, instruction, training and supervision

The employer, through management, should ensure that rules, policies and procedures are followed and that people do not act irresponsibly. Certain circumstances may require specific information, instruction and training, for example, procedures for climbing ladders or wearing appropriate clothing (e.g. high visibility jackets).

The Health and Safety at Work Act etc 1974 (HASAWA) section 2 (2) (c) states "the provision of such information, instruction, training and supervision as is necessary to ensure, so far as is reasonably practicable, the health and safety at work of his employees;requires." This means that the employer must actively supervise the workplace and the work conducted in it, for example, if high visibility clothing is required or walkways are to be kept clear this must be supervised. The concept requires the supervisor to increase the level of supervision on a needs basis, for example, the higher the risk related to the work or workplace hazard or the more persistent the problem, the greater is the supervision necessary. If a large number of the public are to use a route after it has been cleaned the supervisor should make a special effort to ensure that it is safe. If an obstruction of a walk route keeps returning, the supervisor will need to put in extra effort to bring it under control.

Maintenance of a safe workplace

CLEANING AND HOUSEKEEPING REQUIREMENTS

Maintenance of a safe workplace may be achieved through the development of a housekeeping procedure. Good housekeeping implies "a place for everything and everything in its place". Laid down procedures are necessary for preventing the spread of contamination, reducing the likelihood of accidents resulting in slips, trips, and falls and reducing the chances of unwanted fire caused by careless storage of flammable waste.

ACCESS AND EGRESS
- Adequate space for easy movement, and safe plant or equipment use.
- No tripping hazards, e.g. trailing cables or pipes.
- Handholds or guardrails where people might fall from floor edges.
- Emergency provision, e.g. life belts/jackets for work near water or means of escape from confined spaces.
- Neat and tidy storage of tools, plant and equipment so that they do not present a hazard to passers-by.
- Identify storage areas.
- Mark areas to be kept clear.
- Pay particular attention to emergency routes.
- Vision panels in doors to avoid contact injuries.
- Emergency provision e.g. life belts/jackets for work near water; means of escape from freezer rooms.

Figure 3-11: Vision panels in fire doors. *Source: ACT.*

UNIT NCC1 - ELEMENT 3 - MOVEMENT OF PEOPLE AND VEHICLES - HAZARDS AND CONTROL

ENVIRONMENTAL CONSIDERATIONS

Heating

"Suitable and sufficient steps shall be taken to ensure, so far as is reasonably practicable, that during working hours the temperature at any indoor place of work is reasonable having regard to the purpose to which the place is used"

Figure 3-12: Temperature and weather protection. *Source: CDM 2007 Regulation 43.*

The approved code of practice (ACOP) which accompanies WHSWR 1992 states that a temperature of 16^0C should be maintained for sedentary (low activity mainly sitting) work, for example in site offices, and a temperature of 13^0C for work that requires physical effort. Because these figures are stated in the WHSWR 1992 ACOP, they should be regarded as minimum figures. Construction workers can be exposed to a varying degree of conditions and resultant temperatures. The effects of excessive cold or heat can have harmful effects on their health and accidents can result due to fatigue or thermal stress. When work in hot environments or in controlled systems is required, it will be necessary for workers to be acclimatised. Drinks and the provision of refuge from heat may be necessary to reduce body temperatures.

"Every place of work outdoors shall, where necessary to ensure the health and safety of persons at work there, be so arranged that, so far as is reasonably practicable and having regard to the purpose for which that place is used and any protective clothing or work equipment provided for the use of any person at work there, it provides protection from adverse weather."

Figure 3-13: Temperature and weather protection. *Source: CDM 2007 Regulation 43.*

Where the temperatures cannot be maintained, for example, when working outside, areas should be provided to enable workers who work in cold environments to warm themselves. Practical measures and adequate protection must be provided against adverse conditions, for example, workers may be provided with a sheeted area to work in order to protect them from the rain and wind.

Lighting

Lighting plays an important part in health and safety. Factors to consider include:

- Good general illumination with no glare, especially where there are vehicle movements.
- Regular cleaning and maintenance of lights and windows.
- Local lighting for dangerous processes and to reduce eye strain and fatigue.
- No flickering from fluorescent tubes (it can be dangerous with some rotating machinery).
- Adequate emergency lighting which is regularly tested and maintained.
- Specially constructed fittings for flammable or explosive atmospheres e.g. where paint spraying is carried out.
- Outside areas satisfactorily lit for work and access during hours of darkness - for security as well as safety.
- Light coloured wall finishes improving brightness, or darker colours to reduce glare. For example, arc welding flash.

Care should be taken, in particular where temporary lighting is rigged, to ensure that glare and shadows are minimised. Particular attention should be paid to changes in level, corners and where workers pass between the outside and inside of buildings when darkness occurs.

Noise

Noise can produce a number of types of damage to the ear. Noise levels should be assessed and appropriate controls established. Noise can cause an environmental nuisance to surrounding areas, and can have negative effects on communities in general and wildlife. Controls implemented may include barriers and screens around site boundaries to contain noise produced, the use of equipment that produces lower noise levels and restrictions on operating times to reduce the nuisance dependant upon the sensitivity of the area. *See also - Unit NCC1 - Element 9 - Physical and psychological health - hazards and controls.*

Dust

General strategies for dust

Dust is a common hazard on construction sites and because it enters the atmosphere can easily escape past site boundaries and then have adverse effects on the environment. The health hazards associated with dusts can vary but usually result in an attack on the respiratory system on humans and other living creatures. Dust can also present significant risk of eye injury and general discomfort. Other problems are layers of dust settling within the environment, causing damage to vegetation, wildlife habitats and private property. Activities creating dust include external cleaning of buildings, cutting and chasing of masonry and sanding operations.

The area where dust may be created can be watered down to minimise dust transfer into neighbouring premises. Stockpiles of material should be damped down or otherwise suitably treated to prevent the emission of dust from the site. Stockpiles should be planned and sited to minimise the potential for dust generation. The handling of material should be kept to a minimum and when deposited onto a stockpile it should be from the minimum possible height. Dust pollution shall be minimised during demolition by:

- The complete screening, if practicable, of the building or structure to be demolished with debris screens or sheets.
- Control of cutting or grinding of materials on the site.
- Mixing of large quantities of concrete or bentonite slurries in enclosed/shielded areas.

Skips and removal vehicles shall be properly covered when leaving the site. Materials should be handled in such a way that they do not give rise to excessive dust. Watering of rubble chutes shall be undertaken where necessary to prevent dust emission.

Ensure that the area around the site, including the public highway, is regularly and adequately swept to prevent any accumulation of dust and dirt. The use of wheel cleaning facilities and road sweeping equipment may be required.

Any plant used for the crushing of materials must be authorised by a local authority under the Environmental Protection Act Part 1 (Prescribed Processes). All works shall be carried out in accordance with the conditions of such an authorisation. Where plant is used to recycle materials, the appropriate licence from the Environment Agency shall be obtained. The process operator should notify the local authority prior to the movement of the plant on to the site.

Sandblasting
- The work area shall be close-sheeted to reduce dust nuisance from grit. Routine checking is required to ensure that the sheeting remains sound and sealed during sandblasting activities.
- Particular attention shall also be given to the working platform to ensure that it is properly sheeted or sealed to contain dust.
- Non-siliceous grit shall be used to avoid long term irreversible lung damage from silica dust.
- Proper protection shall be provided for any structure painted with lead-based paint.
- In cases where water is used for large scale cleaning and blasting the requirements of the Environment Agency should be followed.
- All grit must be prevented from falling into water courses.

Particular measures to protect members of the public who may be affected by construction activities on public highways

Between 1986 and 1996, construction activities killed 88 members of the public, including 27 children. More than 1,250 were seriously injured, of which over 450 were children. The importance of protecting such people cannot be emphasised enough, especially as almost all of these accidents could have been prevented.

Adopting a proper health and safety culture and providing suitable protection for those carrying out construction work will often go some way towards protecting others who may be affected by it, such as members of the public.

But the precautions which need to be taken to adequately protect the public and visitors may differ from those taken to protect those working on the site.

The main measures used to protect the public include the provision of a perimeter fence with controlled access. Protection is provided by sheeting dusty operations and protection from falling materials by means of debris nets, brick guards and fans. Where ever possible the public should be placed at a suitable distance from the work activity by the use of barriers and in some cases diversions away from the work by, for example, crossing the road. The public should be protected from inadvertently coming into contact with the work or barriers around it; they should be supplemented by warning signs and lighting to prevent contact.

3.3 - Hazards in vehicle operations

Over 100 people die each year because of works transport related accidents. There is also a high incidence of accidents causing serious injury, e.g. spinal damage, amputation and crush injuries. Very few accidents involving traffic result in minor injury. In addition, transport accidents cause damage to plant, infrastructure and vehicles.

Typical hazards causing loss of control and overturning of site vehicles

Various circumstances that may cause such a vehicle to overturn are insecure and unstable loads, manoeuvring with the load elevated, colliding with kerbs and other obstructions, cornering at speed, braking harshly, driving on uneven or soft ground, and mechanical failure.

POSSIBLE CAUSES OF A DUMPER TRUCK OVERTURNING
- Overloading or uneven loading of the bucket.
- Cornering at excessive speed.
- Hitting obstructions.
- Driving too close to the edges of embankments or excavations.
- Mechanical defects.
- Inappropriate tyre pressures.
- Driving across slopes.

POSSIBLE CAUSES OF A FORK LIFT TRUCK OVERTURNING
- Driving too fast.
- Sudden braking.
- Driving on slopes.
- Driving over debris.
- Under-inflated tyres.
- Driving over holes in floor, such as drains.
- Driving with load elevated.
- Overloading - exceeding maximum capacity.
- Collisions with buildings or other vehicles.

Figure 3-14: Vehicle overturned. Source: Lincsafe.

Collisions with other vehicles, pedestrians and fixed objects

Because construction work involves progressive change by building, altering or demolishing things there is an increased risk of vehicles colliding with other vehicles, pedestrians and fixed objects. A scaffolding or staging may be erected that a driver is not aware of or an excavation appear in a previous route. The risk of collision is increased by the fact that scaffolds may overhang a vehicle route or power cables may run across the site. People may unexpectedly appear from a part built or demolished structure or workers intent on the work they are doing may step away from where they are working to collect materials or tools. Other factors are:

- Inadequate lighting.
- Inadequate direction signs.
- Inadequate signs or signals to identify the presence of vehicles.
- Drivers unfamiliar with site.
- Need to reverse.
- Poor visibility e.g. sharp bends, mirror / windscreen misted up.
- Poor identification of fixed objects e.g. overhead pipes, doorways, storage tanks, corners of buildings.
- Lack of separation of pedestrians and vehicles.
- Lack of safe crossing points on roads and vehicle routes.
- Lack of separate entrance / exit for vehicles and pedestrians.
- Pedestrians using doors provided for sole vehicle use.
- Lack of barriers to prevent pedestrians suddenly stepping from an exit/entrance into a vehicle's path.
- Poor maintenance of vehicles e.g. tyres or brakes.
- Excessive speed of vehicles.
- Lack of vehicle management e.g. use of traffic control, 'banksman'.
- Environmental conditions e.g. poor lighting, rain, snow or ice.

Figure 3-15: Collision with fixed objects. Source: ACT.

Site layout

Construction sites are unfamiliar places due to the fact that constant development results in a dynamically changing environment on site until the project is complete. Materials, plant and operatives are concentrated in different areas of the site that also change depending upon the phase of the construction. Quite often there are no defined boundaries, roadways, or plot layouts and unless adequately controlled, traffic around a construction site can be uncoordinated and haphazard. It is important to recognise that delivery drivers of plant and materials will not be familiar with the site and that controls should be in place to guide them safely to their destination. In the first instance this can mean controlled access to the site with security staff checking where they need to go. In some larger more complicated sites this can mean controlling, directing or supervising drivers along prescribed routes that suit the vehicle and the load. Good signage will also assist in clarifying correct routes, and colour coding and naming routes helps to maintain driver orientation. Remember signs are often positioned for drivers to find their way in to sites and are poorly positioned to enable smooth exit. This can result in a good driver taking a wrong turn and causing a lot of damage, injury or delay.

Road surfaces

The state and condition of road surfaces within or around construction sites can vary greatly. Poor soil surfaces can rapidly deteriorate as rain turns it to mud. Some site vehicles may be well adapted to this but visiting vehicles may fare less well, resulting in them getting bogged down or failing to stop effectively, causing a collision with people or structures. Commonly, during the construction phase, the subsurface is all that provides any definition of a roadway (roadstone / hardcore). This surface offers very little grip for vehicles due to its loose nature and may be driven into the shape of ramps and dips, and this may cause a site vehicle or piece of plant to lose control. Additionally, where the final surface has not been applied, manhole access lids or stop tap boxes may be exposed which are not secured and can result in vehicle wheels falling into the opening beneath. Where a tarmac top coat has been applied, this can become wet, covered in site mud /slurry and debris and become slippery which can also result in site plant and vehicles skidding out of control.

Figure 3-16: Road surface. Source: ACT.

Figure 3-17: Site layout. Source: ACT.

Gradients

Gradients or slopes on a construction site can magnify the hazards already presented by the road surfaces. Extra effort is required when engaging gradients which can increase the risk of loss of control. When going down a gradient more effort is required in controlling, slowing down and stopping which can increase the risk of skidding. This may mean driving forward up a gradient and reversing downwards, particularly the case with plant such as fork lift trucks. When approaching gradients it is important that the correct method be adopted. In most circumstances and especially when carrying loads, gradients should not be engaged in a sideways manner as the centre of gravity of the vehicle may shift outside the stability base of the vehicle. This can add to the risk of material falling off or cause the plant or vehicle to overturn.

Excavations

Excavations pose the hazard of collapse if vehicles operate too close. This can result in plant or vehicles tipping into the excavation which could cause:

- Trapping or crushing workers.
- Trapping the driver.
- Damage to exposed buried services.
- Toppling loads may create a further crush hazard.
- Environmental hazards such as release of oils or fuels.

In addition, there is a risk of vehicles simply driving into them, for example, when a dumper truck is back filling an excavation or where the edge is not protected or well identified in poor lighting. Even when excavations are filled in they remain a risk for a considerable time as the material is not well compacted and the additional weight of the vehicle, for example, a mobile crane, may cause the soil to compact and the vehicle to overturn. For each of these reasons it is essential that excavations on site be well protected by barriers, fencing and lighting.

Scaffolding and false work

Scaffolding and false work are temporary fabrications that are used in the construction of structures. Scaffolding provides the means to access and carry out work activities at height via a system of tubes and work platforms. False work provides a temporary means of support whilst casting concrete structures until the structure can support itself and is then removed. Hazards are impact from plant or vehicles that operate too close to the fabrication. Any damage sustained from an impact can result in a knock-on effect causing the entire fabrication to fail. This can lead to operatives, materials or equipment falling from a height on a scaffold or heavy pieces of support materials falling from a height in a false work with the additional risk of the structure that is being formed collapsing.

Refuelling

Dependant upon the size and number of pieces of plant operating on construction sites, there may be facilities for the storage of fuel in bulk or smaller quantities. Even the smallest, most simple sites may have refuelling activities carried out via means of a suitable fuel container having its contents transferred into the fuel tank of, for example, a small generator. Hazards quite often include lack of enforcement of stringent rules and procedures that are commonplace in public fuel stations. Inexperienced operatives may be involved in refuelling processes and this may lead to various dangerous activities that may ultimately lead to fire and explosion, for example due to:

- Refuelling whilst engines are running.
- Smoking in the vicinity of fuel or refuelling activities.
- Impact from vehicles leading to leak and pollution incidents.
- Poorly maintained fuel containment, pipes, and valves.
- Inappropriately positioned / segregated fuel storage.
- Poor security attracting theft / damage / vandalism.

The hazards presented by, and caused to, public vehicles during public highway works

Public highway works usually involve surface removal and renewal, line painting, excavation for exposure, renewal or installation of buried services or cleaning activities (gutters, gullies). When these operations take place, precautions often include signing, lighting and guarding the area as required by The New Roads and Street Works Act (NRSWA) 1991.

The primary hazard associated with public highways works is fast moving vehicles travelling along the highway with a large percentage of vehicle drivers possibly unaware that works are present. When within the vicinity the various hazards include:

- Lane closure causing diversionary manoeuvres often into opposing traffic flows.
- Open excavations.
- Ramps and poor road surfaces.
- Operatives involved in the public highway works.

Figure 3-18: Public vehicle hazards.   Source: ACT.

- Diversionary measures placed on pedestrians or members of the public forcing them to cross the highway.
- Heavy plant incorporating swinging bodies / jibs (360^0 excavators, restricted swing excavators, cranes).

Conditions and environments in which each hazard may arise

- Poor lighting.
- Poor direction signs.
- Inadequate signs or signals to identify the presence of vehicles.
- Drivers unfamiliar with site.
- Need to reverse.
- Poor visibility e.g. sharp bends, mirror / windscreen misted up.
- Poor identification of fixed objects e.g. overhead pipes, doorways, storage tanks, corners of buildings.
- Lack of separation of pedestrians and vehicles.
- Lack of safe crossing points on roads and vehicle routes.
- Lack of separate entrance / exit for vehicles and pedestrians.
- Pedestrians' misuse of doors provided for vehicle use.
- Lack of barriers to prevent pedestrians suddenly stepping from an exit/entrance into a vehicle's path.
- Poor maintenance of vehicles e.g. tyres or brakes.
- Excessive speed of vehicles.
- Lack of vehicle management e.g. use of traffic control, 'banksman' / 'signallers'.
- Environmental conditions e.g. poor lighting, rain, snow or ice.

3.4 - Control measures for safe vehicle operations

General site strategies

Design features of the vehicle intended to minimise the consequences of an overturn include rollover protection and seat belts. In addition, features designed to prevent overturning include the width of the wheelbase and the position of the centre of gravity of the vehicles.

Risk assessment

The employer, through management, needs to consider the safe movement of vehicles and their loads as part of the overall safety policy. This includes the use of vehicles such as dumper trucks, lift trucks, and those used for delivery. Consideration should be given to the following.

Suitability and sufficiency of traffic routes

- Clearly marked and signed. These should incorporate speed limits, one way systems, priorities and other factors normal to public roads. Vehicles which are visiting the premises should be made aware of any local rules and conditions.
- Consideration should be given to adequate lighting on routes and particularly in loading/unloading and operating areas.
- Separate routes, designated crossing places and suitable barriers at recognised danger spots. As far as is practicable pedestrians should be kept clear of vehicle operating areas and/or a notice displayed warning pedestrians that they are entering an operating area.
- Clear direction signs and marking of storage areas and buildings can help to avoid unnecessary movement, such as reversing.
- Sharp bends and overhead obstructions should be avoided where possible. Hazards that cannot be removed should be clearly marked with black and yellow diagonal stripes i.e. loading bay edges, stacks, pits etc. If reasonably practicable barriers should be installed.
- Consideration to vehicle weight and height restriction on routes - signs, barriers and weight checks may be necessary.

FACTORS WHEN PLANNING TRAFFIC ROUTES FOR CONSTRUCTION TRANSPORT

- The purpose of the routes.
- The types of vehicle using the routes.
- The likely volume of traffic.
- The layout of the area.
- The possible need for one-way systems.
- Speed limits and markings.
- Crossing points and signs.
- Separating pedestrians and vehicles - physical barriers.
- Suitability of the road structure.
- Environmental issues such as lighting levels, silting of drains and drain protection, land contamination and waste.

Management of vehicle movements

Many sites are complex in nature and require the careful management of vehicles in order to ensure that they are brought onto, move around and leave the site safely. This can start at the project planning stage as it can cause many problems when a vehicle is brought onto site too early when the site is at an earlier phase and is not ready for it. Conversely if it is brought in part way through the project it may be difficult to get it to where it is needed and it may be better to get it to site early. Where materials are brought to site it may be necessary to manage deliveries so that too many vehicles do not arrive at the site at the same time causing them to back up into the public highway. Site security arrangements play a significant part in the management of vehicles on site and will assist with controlling vehicles so that they are routed correctly and safely. It is not uncommon for vehicles to be sent to a site that are too big or too heavy to access the roadways. Site security staff should be trained to identify these to prevent them accessing the site and causing harm. Major vehicle movements, such as a heavy crane may be timed so that the minimum of workers are on site and that it can be conducted easily in a controlled manner.

Banksmen or signallers as they are also known are used to control vehicle movements i.e. reversing and lifting operations. Due to the amount of serious or fatal injuries every year, it is important that they are fully trained and competent. A safe system of work should be adopted with all drivers using standard signals that are easily understood. Drivers should know to stop their vehicle immediately if the banksman disappears from sight. The standard signals are given in the Health and Safety (Safety Signs and Signals) Regulations (SSSR) 1996.

SAFE OPERATION

- Appoint someone on site to be responsible for transport.
- Drivers properly trained.
- Ensure unauthorised people are not allowed to drive.
- Make sure visiting drivers are aware of site rules.
- Check vehicles daily and have faults rectified promptly.
- Keep keys secure when vehicles are not in use.
- Ensure safe movements - particularly when reversing.
- Keep roadways/gangways properly maintained and lit.
- Separate vehicles and pedestrians where practicable.
- Use of horns before entering doorways or at blind corners.

Environmental considerations

Where vehicles operate, environmental conditions such as lighting and adverse weather will make a significant impact on their safe operation by affecting **visibility**. Where reasonably practicable a suitable standard of lighting must be maintained so that operators of vehicles can see to operate their vehicle and can be seen by others. It is important to avoid areas of glare or shadow that could mask the presence of a person or vehicle. Similarly if vehicles travel from within buildings to the outside it is important that the light level is maintained at a roughly even level in order to give the driver's eyes time to adjust to the change in light. Fixed structure hazards should be made as visible as possible with additional lighting and/or reflective strips.

Roads, gangways and aisles should have sufficient width and overhead clearance for the largest vehicle. Attention should be paid to areas where they might meet other traffic, e.g. the entrance to the site. If ramps (speed bumps) are used a by-pass for trolleys and shallow draft vehicles should be provided. A one-way traffic system should be considered to reduce the risk of collision.

Gradients and changes in ground level, such as ramps, represent a specific hazard to plant and vehicle operation. Vehicles have a limit of stability dependent on loading and their wheelbase. These conditions could put them at risk of overturning or cause damage to articulated vehicle couplings. Any gradient in a vehicle operating area should be kept as gentle as possible.

Where *changes in level* are at an edge that a vehicle might approach, and there is risk of falling, it must be provided with a robust barrier or similar means to demarcate the edge. Particular care must be taken at points where loading and unloading is conducted.

In some workplaces, such as factories or chemical plants, process products may contaminate the *surface condition* of the road making it difficult for vehicles to brake effectively.

It is important to have a programme that anticipates this with regular cleaning or scarifying of the surface as well as means of dealing with spills. The floor surface should be in good condition, free of litter and obstructions.

Excessive ambient noise levels can mask the sound of vehicles working in the area; additional visual warning e.g. flashing lights should be used. Sufficient and suitable parking areas should be provided away from the main work area and located where the risk of unauthorised use of the vehicles will be reduced.

Driver protection and restraint systems

ROLL OVER

In many work vehicle accidents the driver is injured because the vehicle does not offer protection when it rolls over or it does not restrain the driver to prevent them falling out of the vehicle and being injured by the fall or the vehicle falling on them. Vehicles such as dumper trucks, road rollers and forklift trucks are examples of equipment that may present this risk. The Provision and Use of Work Equipment Regulations 1998 regulation 26 Part 3 recognises the importance of this and now set out requirements for equipment to be adapted, where practicable, to provide this protection. New equipment must now be provided with protection and restraint systems, where relevant.

Figure 3-19: Roll bar and seat restraint.   *Source: ACT.*

Figure 3-20: Suitability and protection.   *Source: ACT.*

PROTECTION FROM FALLING MATERIALS

There is a risk of material falling on a vehicle driver where the vehicle is used to provide materials at a height or to remove materials from delivery vehicles. It is important that suitable protection of the driver be provided by the structure of the vehicle. Protection should also be provided where vehicles work in close proximity to areas where there is a risk from falling materials. This may be by the provision of a frame and mesh above it or by the provision of a totally enclosing cab. Safety helmets alone are unlikely to provide sufficient protection but may be a useful addition where a mesh structure is provided.

WEATHER CONDITIONS

It is important to review risk assessments and planned methods of work where the work place has been significantly altered and may pose a further or additional risk to the health and safety of anyone who might be affected by the intended work. Consideration should be given to extreme heat, cold conditions, high winds and lightning. Working conditions and work place environments can generate high risks and would therefore require as much advanced forethought and planning, especially on long protracted projects or sites. I.e. slippery conditions and cold in winter should be considered as a possible risk in advance of project or site commencement.

Suitability and maintenance of vehicles

All vehicles should be well maintained and 'roadworthy' with a formal system of checks and maintenance in place. A vehicle, such as one used for moving trailers in a transport yard, that does not usually go outside the site would be expected to be kept to the same good standard as one that was used on public roads for such critical items as tyres and brakes. Vehicle maintenance should be planned for at regular intervals and vehicles taken out of use if critical items are not at an acceptable standard. In addition, it is important to conduct a pre-use check of the vehicle. This is usually done by the driver as part of their taking it over for a period of use such as a work shift or day. This would identify the condition of critical items and provide a formal system to identify and consider problems that may affect the safety of the vehicle. If there is no nominated driver and the vehicle is for general use someone should be nominated to make these checks. A record book or card would usually be used to record the checks and the findings.

Means of segregating pedestrians and vehicles

"Every workplace shall be organised in such a way that pedestrians and vehicles can circulate in a safe manner".

Figure 3-21: Organisation of pedestrians and vehicles.   *Source: WHSWR 1992 Regulation 17(1).*

"Every construction site shall be organised in such a way that, so far as is reasonably practicable, pedestrians and vehicles can move safely and without risks to health."

"Traffic routes shall be suitable for the persons or vehicles using them, sufficient in number, in suitable positions and of sufficient size."

Figure 3-22: Traffic routes. *Source: CDM 2007 Regulation 36.*

Clearly defined and marked routes should be provided for people going about their business at work. These should be provided for access and egress points to the workplace, car parks, and vehicle delivery routes. Safe crossing places should be provided where people have to cross main traffic routes. In buildings where vehicles operate, separate doors and walkways should be provided for pedestrians to get from building to building. Meshed handrails can be used to channel people into the pedestrian route. Where it is not possible to have a pedestrian route with a safe clearance from vehicle movement, because of building and plant design, then a raised pedestrian walkway could be considered to help in segregation.

- Accidents can be caused where vehicles are unsafely parked as they can be an obstruction and restrict visibility. There should be clear entrance and exit routes in parking areas and designated parking areas to allow the load and sheeting of outgoing transport to be checked safely before leaving the site.

Figure 3-23: Segregating pedestrians and vehicles. *Source: ACT.*

- There should be clear, well-marked and signposted vehicle traffic routes, which avoid steep gradients where possible, especially where fork lift trucks operate. It is important to have speed limits that are practicable and effective. Speed limit signs should be posted and traffic slowing measures such as speed bumps and ramps may be necessary in certain situations. Monitoring speed limit compliance is necessary, along with some kind of action against persistent offenders.
- Speed limits of 10 or 15 mph are usually considered appropriate, although 5 mph may be necessary in certain situations.
- Transport requires clear routes to be designated, marked with painted lines and preferably fenced off from pedestrians. Accidents can occur when plant and people collide: the pedestrian may be injured by contact and the driver injured if the vehicle overturns.
- Separate gates/doorways should be provided for vehicles' entry, and blind spots (where vision of the driver / pedestrian is restricted) should be dealt with by the careful positioning of mirrors on walls, plant or storage. Routes should be wide enough to allow manoeuvrability and passing.
- Where it is unavoidable that pedestrians will come into proximity with transport, people should be reminded of the hazards by briefings, site induction and signs, so they are aware at all times.

Any traffic route which is used by both pedestrians and vehicles should be wide enough to enable any vehicle likely to use the route to pass pedestrians safely. On traffic routes in existence before 1 January 1993, where it is not practical to make the route wide enough, passing places or traffic management systems should be provided as necessary. In buildings, lines should be drawn on the floor to indicate routes followed by vehicles such as fork lift trucks.

MEASURES TO BE TAKEN WHEN SEGREGATION IS NOT PRACTICABLE

Where pedestrians and vehicle routes cross, appropriate crossing points should be provided and used. Where necessary, barriers or rails should be provided to prevent pedestrians crossing at particularly dangerous points and to guide them to designated crossing places. At crossing places where volumes of traffic are particularly heavy, the provision of suitable bridges or subways should be considered. At crossing points there should be adequate visibility and open space for the pedestrian where the pedestrian route joins the vehicle route.

Figure 3-24: No segregation. *Source: ACT.*

Figure 3-25: Control of vehicle movement. *Source: ACT.*

Where segregation is not practicable and vehicles share the same workplace as pedestrians it is important to mark the work areas as being separate from vehicle routes to warn drivers to adjust their approach and be more aware of pedestrians. Audible and visual warnings of the presence of the vehicle would also assist. Where vehicles are dominant but pedestrians need to access, similar means may be used but for the opposite reason. In this situation the added use of personal protective equipment that increases the ability to see the pedestrian, and safety footwear, are usually needed. High visibility clothing is mandatory on the majority of construction projects. The reversing of large vehicles that have a restricted view should be controlled by the use of a banksman / signaller to guide them.

SUMMARY OF MEASURES FOR SAFE MOVEMENT OF PEOPLE AND VEHICLES

- Use of barriers.
- Defined traffic routes.
- One-way systems.
- Provision of refuges.
- Speed control.
- Mirrors / cameras.
- Good lighting.
- High visibility clothing.
- A good standard of housekeeping.
- Audible warnings on vehicles.
- Training and supervision of drivers.
- Drawing up and enforcement of site rules.

Protective measures for people and structures

It is important to anticipate that drivers of vehicles might misjudge a situation and collide with structures whilst operating. For this reason vulnerable plant and parts of the building should be provided with barriers that continuously surround the plant or alternatively posts can be provided at key positions. Clearly, important plant and structures that are at the same level of the vehicle should be protected. Care should also be taken of structures at a height, such as a pipe bridge, roof truss or door lintel. All of these could be damaged by tall vehicles or those that have tipping mechanisms that raise their effective height. Though it may not always be possible to protect all structures, such as a doorway, it is important to apply *markings* to make them more visible. In addition, *signs* warning of overhead structures or the presence of vehicles in the area will help increase awareness and avoid collisions. There is a need to alert people to the hazard when working in or near a vehicle operating area. Signs might help and these can be supplemented by *visual and audible warning systems* that confirm the presence of the vehicle. These may be operated by the driver, such as a horn on a dumper truck or automatically, such as an audible reversing signal on a large road vehicle. Visibility can be improved by mounting mirrors at strategic points. Consideration should be given to the provision of protective clothing - boots, helmets and high visibility clothing - for personnel working within areas where vehicles operate.

BARRIERS

Moving vehicles, and in particular large plant, have high impact energy when they are in contact with structures or people. A glancing blow from a large vehicle may be sufficient to bring down a large section of scaffolding. It is essential that vehicles be separated from vulnerable people and structures. Because of the high energy involved the barrier used must reflect the type of thing in contact with it. If it is only people that might contact it a simple portable barrier may be adequate, but if it is heavy plant robust barriers including concrete structures may need to be considered. It is important to identify vulnerable locations that warrant protection, for example the corner of a scaffold that vehicles need to manoeuvre around, excavations where articulated vehicles may lose a trailer wheel into a hole as it corners or high risk equipment such as electrical supplies units.

MARKINGS

Any structure that represents a height or width restriction should be readily identified for people and vehicle drivers. This will include low beams or doorways, pipe bridges and protruding scaffolds and edges where a risk of falling exists. These markings may be by means of attaching hazard tape or painting the structure to highlight the hazard.

SIGNS

Signs should be used to provide information, such as height restrictions, and to warn of hazards on site. Signs may direct vehicles around workers at a safe distance.

Figure 3-26: Fencing and barriers at a distance. *Source: ACT.*

Figure 3-27: Visual warning on a dumper truck. *Source: ACT.*

WARNINGS ON VEHICLES

Warnings may be audible or visual or a combination of each. They are used to warn that the vehicle is operating in the area, such as a flashing light on the top of a dumper truck or to warn of a specific movement, such as an audible warning that a large vehicle is reversing. These are designed to alert people in the area in order that they can place themselves in a position of safety. They do not provide the driver with authority to reverse the vehicle or to proceed in a work area without caution.

Measures to prevent accidents when pedestrians work in vehicle manoeuvring areas
- Segregated systems for vehicular and pedestrian traffic (barriers, separate doors).
- Maintaining good visibility (mirrors, transparent doors, provision of lighting, vehicle reversing cameras).
- Signs indicating where vehicles operate in this area.
- Audible warnings on vehicles and sometimes flashing lights on vehicles.
- Establish and enforcement of site rules.
- The provision of refuges.
- The wearing of high-visibility clothing.
- A good standard of housekeeping.
- Training for, and supervision of, all concerned, competency certificates, refresher training, trained banksmen / signallers to direct cranes.
- Provision of parking areas.
- Provision of suitable battery charging or refuelling areas if necessary.
- Careful design of traffic routes.
- Maintenance of traffic routes.
- Traffic control e.g. identification of "no go" areas.

Precautionary measures for reversing vehicles within a workplace
- Separation of vehicles and pedestrians.
- Warning signs.
- Audible alarms / vehicle cameras.
- Space to allow good visibility / mirrors / refuges / lighting.
- Appropriate site rules adequately enforced.
- Procedural measures such as the use of trained banksmen.
- Avoiding the need for vehicles to reverse (by the use of one-way and 'drive-through' systems or turning circles).

Site rules

It is important to establish clear and well understood site rules regarding vehicle operations. These may have to be communicated to drivers by security staff at the time they visit the site. They would often stipulate where the driver should be whilst vehicles are being loaded, where the keys to the vehicle should be, not reversing without permission and what access they have to areas of the site for such things as refreshment. Pedestrians should also know what the site rules are in order to keep themselves safe. Site rules for pedestrians might include such things as using pedestrian exits/entrances or crossing points, not entering hazardous areas or the need to wear personal protective equipment in hazardous areas, and not walking behind a reversing vehicle. Where sites are made up of or join a highway, such as carriageway repairs on a motorway, it is important to identify who has priority - the vehicle or the worker. Site rules may clarify that once the site boundary is crossed the worker has priority - this has to be clear. The site rules may be reinforced by the provision of additional signs to clarify a speed limit and the nature of the priority of workers.

Selection and training of drivers

Only authorised persons should be permitted to operate plant or vehicles after they have been selected, trained and authorised to do so, or are undergoing properly organised formal training, under supervision.

SELECTION

The safe usage of plant and vehicles calls for reasonable physical and mental fitness. The selection procedure should be devised to identify people who have been shown to be reliable and mature enough to perform their work responsibly and carefully. To avoid wasteful training for workers who lack co-ordination and ability to learn, selection tests should be used.

Consideration must be given to any legal age restrictions that apply to vehicles that operate on the public road. A similar approach may be adopted for similar vehicles used on site though the law may not be specific on age limitations in such cases.

Potential operators should be medically examined prior to employment/training in order to assess the individual's physical ability to cope with this type of work. They should also be examined every five years in middle age and after sickness or accident.
Points to be considered are:

a) General - Normal agility, having full movement of trunk, neck and limbs.

b) Vision - Good eyesight is important, as operators are required to have good judgement of space and distance.

c) Hearing - The ability to hear instructions and warning signals with each ear is important.

TRAINING

It is essential that immediate supervisors receive training in the safe operation of plant and vehicles and that senior management appreciates the risks resulting from the interaction of vehicles and the workplace.

For the operator/driver, safety must constitute an integral part of the skill-training programme and not be treated as a separate subject. The operator/driver should be trained to a level consistent with efficient operation and care for the safety of themselves and other persons. On completion of training they should be issued with a company authority to drive and a record of all basic training, refresher training and tests maintained in the individual's personal documents file. Certification of training by other organisations must be checked.

Management systems for assuring driver competence including local codes of practice

THE TRAINED OPERATOR/DRIVER

It should not be assumed that employees who join as trained operators/drivers have received adequate training to operate safely in their new company. The management must ensure that they have the basic skills and receive training in company methods and procedures for the type of work they are to undertake. They should be examined and tested before issue of company driving authority.

TESTING

On completion of training, the operator/driver should be examined and tested to ensure that he/she has achieved the required standard. It is recommended that at set intervals or when there is indication of the operator/driver not working to required standards, or following an accident, formal check tests be introduced.

REFRESHER TRAINING

If high standards are to be maintained, periodic refresher training and testing should be considered.

A vigorous management policy covering operator training, plant maintenance and sound systems of work, supported by good supervision will reduce personal injury and damage to equipment and materials. This in turn will lead to better vehicle utilisation and increased materials handling efficiency.

OPERATOR/DRIVER IDENTIFICATION

Many organisations operate local codes of practice and take great care to evidence the authority they have given to operators/drivers by the provision of a licence for that vehicle and sometimes a visible badge to confirm this. Access to vehicles is supervised and authority checked carefully to confirm that the actual class of vehicle is within the authority given. This is important with such things as rough terrain lift trucks that operate differently to a standard counterbalance truck. *See also - Unit NCC1 - Element 4 - Manual and mechanical handling - hazards and control.* It is essential that access to keys for vehicles is restricted to those that are competent to operate/drive them; this is not just a practical point but enables compliance with Provision and Use of Work Equipment Regulations 1998.

Traffic safety measures and signs used when conducting construction activities on public highways

It is the responsibility of whoever is in control of construction activities on public highways to sign, guard light and maintain the works safely. This will require a certain amount of planning to ascertain what procedures need to be implemented and what equipment is required to ensure safety.

Measures to be taken can be found in the document, "Safety at Street Works and Road Works" that has statutory backing as a code of practice for the New Roads and Street Works Act (NRSWA) 1991 and the Street Works (Northern Ireland) Order. This code of practice will help you to safely carry out temporary signing, lighting and guarding of construction activities on public highways. Failure to comply with the code of practice may lead to criminal prosecution in addition to any civil proceedings. Further recommendations regarding safety measures at road works can be found in Chapter 8 of the "Traffic Signs Manual".

Prior to any works starting, and in order to ensure compliance with current health and safety legislation, an on-site risk assessment must be carried out to ensure a safe system of working is derived in respect of signing, lighting and guarding is in place at all times.

Any signs, lights or guarding equipment must be secured against being blown over or out of position by wind or passing traffic. This is usually done by the use of sand bags; hard items should not be used as these can be hazardous if struck by traffic. Signs should be placed sufficiently away from the works in order to provide drivers with adequate prior warning of the works and not present a hazard to pedestrians if placed in footpaths. Signs should also be of a reflective nature and be monitored to ensure they remain clean and visible. Any permanent signs or signals that become overridden by the temporary signing, lighting and guarding may require covering over. Consent for this will need to be received from the highway authority.

The placing of signs must consider traffic approaching from all directions, whether it is by two-way traffic or traffic at road junctions. The working area must also be demarcated with an allowance made for a safety zone (between 0.5m to 1.2m) surrounding the works, and also marked off with cones and lighting as necessary. The safety zone must never be used as a work area or for storing plant, equipment or vehicles.

Figure 3-28: Public highway works safety measures. *Source: ACT.*

When the site is not in use, but signing, lighting and guarding are in place, then arrangements must be in place to ensure regular inspections and any damaged or displaced equipment remedied immediately. Site vehicles at the works should always operate roof mounted amber beacons if fitted to the vehicles. Hazard warning indicators should not be used at road works as these confuse other road users.

Following completion of a project, all plant, equipment, materials, signs, lights and guarding should be removed immediately.

This page is intentionally blank

Element 4

Manual and mechanical handling - hazards and control

Learning outcomes

On completion of this element, candidates should be able to demonstrate understanding of the content through the application of knowledge to familiar and unfamiliar situations. In particular they should be able to:

4.1 Describe the hazards and the risk factors which should be considered when assessing risks from manual handling activities.

4.2 Suggest ways of minimising manual handling risk.

4.3 Identify the hazards in the use of lifting and moving equipment.

4.4 Explain the precautions and procedures to ensure safety in the use of lifting and moving equipment.

Content

4.1 - Manual handling hazards and risks	45
Common types of manual handling hazard and injury	45
The assessment of manual handling risks	45
4.2 - Minimising manual handling risks	48
Means of minimising the risks from manual handling in construction activities	48
Recognised techniques for manually lifting loads	49
4.3 - Hazards of lifting and moving equipment operations	50
Associated hazards	50
4.4 - Control measures for lifting and moving equipment operations	55
Safe use and maintenance	55
Requirements for lifting operations	59
Requirements for the inspection and examination of lifting equipment	62

Sources of reference

Backs for the future: Safe manual handling in construction (HSG149), HSE Books ISBN 0-7176-1122-1
British Standard Code of practice for safe use of cranes (BS 7121), British Standards Institution
Getting to grips with manual handling (INDG143rev2), ISBN 0-7176-2828-0
Manual handling. Manual Handling Operations Regulations 1992. Guidance on Regulations (L23), HSE Books ISBN 0-7176-2823-X
Rider-operated lift trucks. Operator training. (ACoP and Guidance) (L117), HSE Books ISBN 0-7176-2455-2
Safe use of lifting equipment (L113), HSE Books ISBN 0-7176-1628-2
Safe use of work equipment (ACoP) (L22), HSE Books ISBN 0-7176-1626-6
Safety in working with lift trucks (HSG6), HSE Books ISBN 0-7176-1781-6

Relevant statutory provisions

The Lifting Operations and Lifting Equipment Regulations (LOLER) 1998
The Manual Handling Operations Regulations (MHOR) 1992
The Provision and Use of Work Equipment Regulations (PUWER) 1998

4.1 - Manual handling hazards and risks

Common types of manual handling hazard and injury

Around 25% of all injuries reported to the appropriate enforcing authority have been attributed to the manual lifting and handling of loads. The injuries arise from such *hazards* as stooping while lifting, holding the load away from the body, twisting movements, frequent or prolonged effort, heavy / bulky / unwieldy / unstable loads, sharp / hot / slippery surfaces of loads, space constraints, and lack of capability of the individual.

Manual handling operations can cause many types of *injury*. The most common injuries are:

- Rupture of intervertebral discs ('slipped disc') in the lower spine.
- Muscle strain and sprain.
- Tendons and ligaments can also be over-stretched and torn.
- Rupture of a section of the abdominal wall can cause a hernia.
- Loads with sharp edges can cause cuts.
- Dropped loads can result in bruises, fractures and crushing injuries.

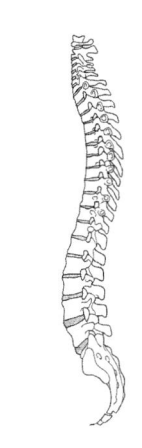

Figure 4-1: Manual handling - spine. *Source: ACT.*

The assessment of manual handling risks

FACTORS TO CONSIDER

The Manual Handling Operations Regulations (MHOR) 1992 specify that the four factors to which the employer must have regard, and questions he must consider, when making an assessment of manual handling operations are:

- *L* oad.
- *I* ndividual Capability.
- *T* ask.
- *E* nvironment.

Each factor in turn should be assessed to determine whether there is a risk of injury. When this has been completed the information can then be processed giving a *total* risk assessment.

FACTORS	QUESTIONS	Level of Risk: High	Med	Low
Load	Is it: ■ Heavy? ■ Bulky or Unwieldy? ■ Difficult to grasp? ■ Unstable, or with contents likely to shift? ■ Sharp, hot or otherwise potentially damaging?			
Individual Capability	Does the job: ■ Require unusual strength, height, etc? ■ Create a hazard to those who have a health problem? ■ Require special knowledge or training for its safe performance?			
Task	Does it involve: ■ Holding load at distance from trunk? ■ Unsatisfactory bodily movement or posture? • Twisting the trunk. • Stooping. ■ Excessive movement of load? • Excessive lifting or lowering distances. • Excessive pushing or pulling distances. • Risk of sudden movement of load. • Frequent or prolonged physical effort. • Insufficient rest or recovery periods.			
Working Environment	Are there: ■ Space constraints preventing good posture? ■ Uneven, slippery or unstable floors? ■ Variations in level of floors or work surfaces? ■ Extremes of temperature, humidity or air movement? ■ Poor lighting conditions?			

Figure 4-2: Manual handling risk assessment. *Source: HSE Manual handling (Manual Handling Operations Regulations 1992) Guidance L23.*

The detailed consideration of each factor is necessary to achieve a suitable and sufficient risk assessment. The process of risk assessing includes observing the task as it is actually done; recording the factors that contribute to risk; assessing the level of risk that each factor represents (taking account of the circumstances and controls in place); and considering if the risks are different at different times and for different people. The following considerations are offered to assist in making a risk assessment.

The Load

- Consideration should be given to reducing the weight although this may mean increasing the frequency of handling.
- If there is a great variety of weight to be handled it may be possible to sort the loads into weight categories so that precautions can be applied selectively.
- Where the size, surface texture or nature of a load makes it difficult to grasp, consideration should be given to the provision of handles, hand grips, indents etc. to improve the grasp.
- Loads in packages should be such that they cannot shift unexpectedly while being handled.
- Any loads to be handled should not have sharp corners, jagged edges, rough surfaces and the like.

Figure 4-3: Manual handling. *Source: ACT.*

Individual capability

- The individual's state of health, fitness and strength can significantly affect the ability to perform a task safely.
- An individual's physical capacity can also be age-related, typically climbing until the early 20's and declining gradually from the mid 40's.
- It is clear then that an individual's condition and age could significantly affect the ability to perform a task safely.

The Task

- Ensure work and components in regular use are stored at waist height. Storage above or below this height should be used for lighter or less frequently used items.
- Layout changes should avoid the necessity for frequent bending, twisting, reaching, etc. and the lessening of any travel distances.
- Pay attention to the work routine i.e. fixed postures dictated by sustained holding or supporting loads, frequency of handling loads, with particular emphasis on heavy and awkward loads.
- Fixed breaks are generally less effective than those taken voluntary within the constraints of the work organisation.
- Handling while seated also requires careful consideration. Use of the powerful leg muscles is precluded and the weight of the handler's body cannot be used as a counterbalance. For these reasons, the loads that can be handled in safety by a person who is seated are substantially less than can be dealt with while standing.
- Team handling could be a solution for some tasks that are beyond the capability of one person. However team handling can create additional problems. The proportion of the load carried by each member of the team will vary; therefore, the load that can be handled in safety will be less than the sum of the loads with which an individual could cope.

The Working Environment

- Adequate gangways, space and working area should be provided in order to allow room to manoeuvre during handling.
- Lack of headroom could cause stooping and constrictions caused by a poor workstation; adjacent machinery etc. should also be avoided.
- In many cases problems are simply caused by lack of attention to good housekeeping.
- Whenever possible all manual handling tasks should be carried out on a single level. If tasks are to be carried out on more than one level, access should preferably be by a gentle slope, or failing that, properly positioned and well maintained stairs/steps. Steep slopes should be avoided.
- Workbenches should be of a uniform height, thus reducing the need for raising or lowering loads.
- Finally, look at the general working environment. A comfortable working environment (e.g. heating, ventilating and lighting) will help to reduce the risk of injury.

REVIEWING ASSESSMENTS

The assessment should be kept up to date. It should be reviewed whenever there is a reason to suppose that it is no longer valid, for example, because the working conditions or the personnel carrying out the operations have changed. It should also be reviewed whenever there has been a significant change in the manual handling operations, for example, affecting the nature of the task or load.

GUIDELINES FOR ASSESSMENT OF MANUAL HANDLING OPERATIONS

Lifting

The MHOR 1992 set no specific requirements such as weight limits. The following guidelines set out an **approximate** boundary within which manual handling operations are unlikely to create a risk of injury sufficient to warrant assessment that is more detailed. This should enable assessment work to be concentrated where it is most needed.

The guideline figures are not weight or force limits. They may be exceeded where a more detailed assessment shows it is safe to do so. However, the guideline figures should not normally be exceeded by more than a factor of about two. The guideline figures for weight and force will give reasonable protection to nearly all men and between one half and two thirds of women.

Carrying

The guideline figures for manual handling operations involving carrying are similar to those given for lifting and lowering. It is assumed that the load is held against the body and is carried no further than about 10 metres without resting.

If the load is carried over a longer distance without resting the guideline figures may need to be reduced. Where the load can be carried securely on the shoulder without attendant lifting (e.g. unloading sacks from a lorry) a more detailed assessment may show that it is safe to exceed the guideline figure.

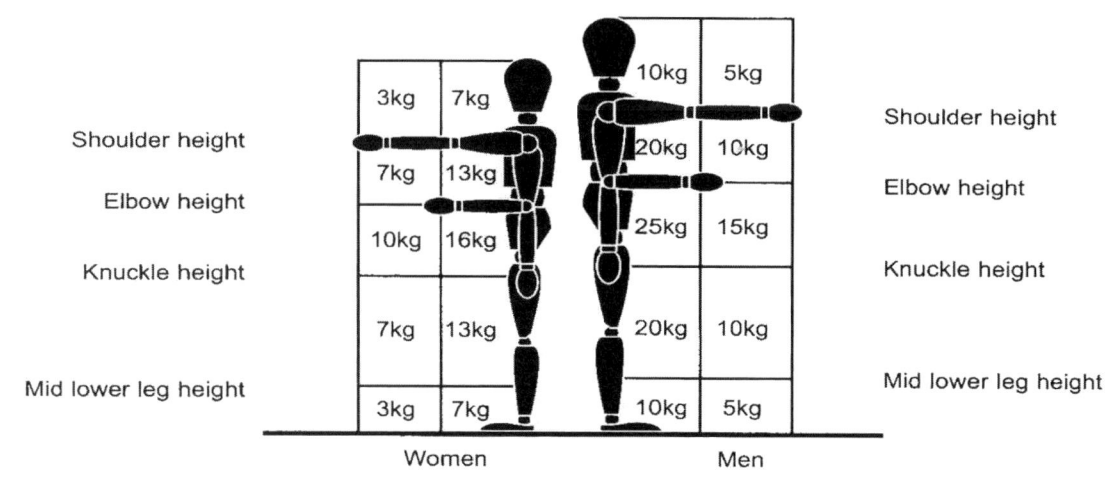

Figure 4-4: Guideline figures.   *Source: HSE Manual Handling (Manual Handling Operations Regs 1992) Guidance L23.*

Pushing and pulling

Guideline figures for manual handling operations involving pushing and pulling, whether the load is slid, rolled or supported on wheels, are as follows:

- The guideline figure for starting or stopping the load is a force of about 250 Newtons (i.e. a force of about 25 Kg as measured on a spring balance).
- The guideline figure for keeping the load in motion is a force of about 100 Newtons.
- No specific limit is intended as to the distances over which the load is pushed or pulled provided there are adequate opportunities for rest or recovery.

Handling while seated

The guideline figure for handling operations carried out while seated is given below and applies only when the hands are within the box zone indicated. If handling beyond the box zone is unavoidable, a more detailed assessment should be made.

Twisting

The basic guideline figures for lifting and lowering should be reduced if the handler twists to the side during the operation. As a rough guide, the figures should be reduced by about 10% where the handler twists through 45° and by about 20% where the handler twists through 90°.

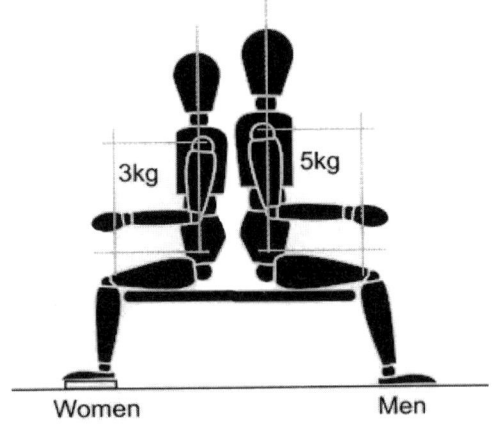

Figure 4-5: Handling while seated.   *Source: HSE Guidance L23.*   Figure 4-6: Twisting.   *Source: HSE Guidance L23.*

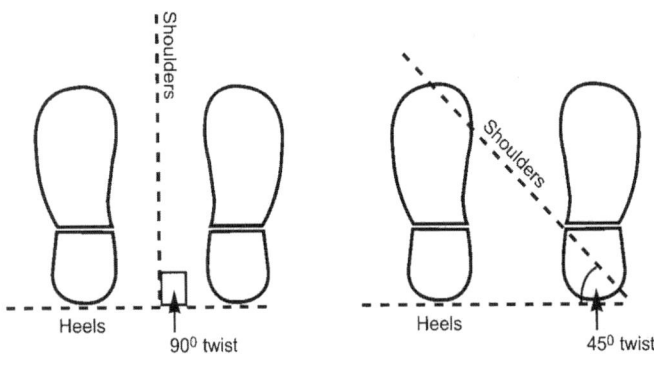

Assumptions

The guideline figures should not be regarded as precise recommendations and should be applied with caution, noting particularly that they are based on the following assumptions:

- The handler is standing or crouching in a stable body position with the back substantially upright.
- The trunk is not twisted during the operation.
- Both hands are used to grasp the load.
- The hands are not more than shoulder width apart.
- The load is positioned centrally in front of the body and is itself reasonably symmetrical.
- The load is stable and readily grasped.
- The work area does not restrict the handler's posture.
- The working environment (heat, cold, wet, condition of floor) and any personal protective equipment used do not interfere with performance of the task.

4.2 - Minimising manual handling risks

Means of minimising the risks from manual handling in construction activities

GENERAL APPROACH

Practical measures that can be taken to reduce the risk of injury can also be based on *LITE*. For example:

L oad	Changing the load by lightening, reducing in size, provision of handles, elimination of sharp edges etc.
I ndividual	Address the individual factors such as selection, provision of information and training, provision of appropriate protective equipment and clothing.
T ask	Redesign the task so that manual handling is eliminated or reduced by mechanisation, reducing carrying distances, team lifting, job rotation, etc.
E nvironment	Improving the working environment e.g. optimum heights of surfaces, improving floor conditions, increasing workspace, improving lighting, avoidance of changes in floor level etc.

MINIMISING THE RISK FROM MANUAL HANDLING

Each manual handling operation should be examined and appropriate steps taken to minimise the risk of injury to the lowest level reasonably practicable. Wherever reasonably practicable, manual handling should be replaced or reduced by using mechanical handling aids, examples of which are shown below.

Mechanical assistance

This involves the use of handling aids. Although this may retain some elements of manual handling, bodily forces are applied more efficiently.

Examples are:

Levers	Reduces bodily force to move a load. Can avoid trapping fingers.
Hoists	Can support weights, allowing handler to position load.
Trolley, sack truck, truck roller or hoist	Reduces effort to move loads horizontally.
Chutes	A way of using gravity to move loads from one place to another.
Handling devices	Hand-held hooks or suction pads can help when handling a load that is difficult to grasp.

Figure 4-7: Mechanical assistance. Source: ACT.

Information, instruction, training and supervision

It is important that employers recognise the need for training standards in manual handling. There is a legal requirement to ensure that those advising and training others in safer manual handling practice have the appropriate skills and knowledge.

The Manual Handling Operations Regulations (MHOR) 1992 (Regulation 4 (1)(b) (i), (ii), (iii), Regulation 5) do not specify training but this is implicit in some of its requirements. Employees should be given information on:

- Task, load, environment and individual capability.
- Recognition of risk.
- Safe working systems.
- Use of equipment.
- How to carry out safe manual handling, including good handling technique.
- Features of the working environments that contribute to safety.
- The importance of good housekeeping.
- Factors affecting individual capability.
- Good handling techniques.

It should always be remembered that training is not a "one off remedy". For training to be effective it should be on-going to reflect improved techniques developed by experienced workers and be supported by periodic refresher training and supervision.

Recognised techniques for manually lifting loads

LIFTING TECHNIQUES USING KINETIC HANDLING PRINCIPLES

In order to avoid musculoskeletal disorders due to lifting, poor posture and repetitive awkward loads it is important to use recognised techniques. Many of these techniques use a kinetic handling approach, which seeks to use the body's natural movement to the advantage of lifting.

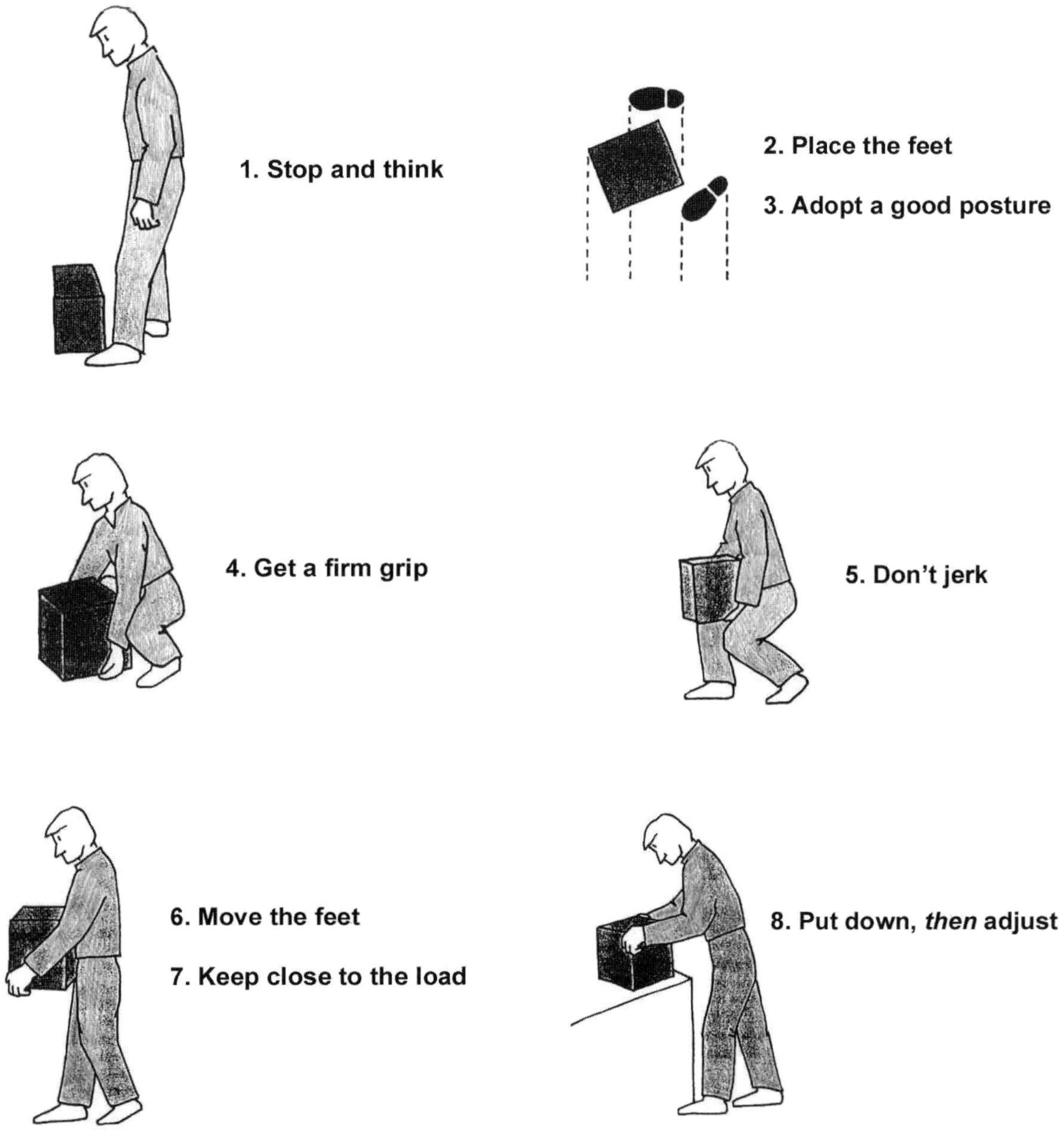

1. Stop and think
2. Place the feet
3. Adopt a good posture
4. Get a firm grip
5. Don't jerk
6. Move the feet
7. Keep close to the load
8. Put down, *then* adjust

Figure 4-8: Basic lifting principles. Source: Ambiguous.

Putting it all into practice

a) Begin with the **load between the feet**, the leading foot should be in line with the side of the load, pointing in the direction of movement.
b) Bend your knees, tuck your chin in **and keep your back straight** (not vertical).
c) Generally grip the load at the upper outer corner on the side of the leading foot, tilt it slightly and grip the opposite corner with the other hand. **(Ensure the palm, not fingers, take the weight).**
d) Keep your **arms close to your body**, move rear hand forward along the lower edge of the load. Stand up in one movement, keeping the load in contact with the body at all times.
e) To lower the load, reverse the procedure, **bending your knees** whilst tilting the load to avoid trapping fingers.

Always remember:
- Assess the load.
- Lift the load smoothly - do not jerk.
- Avoid twisting and stretching.

Poor posture

Injuries that are received as a result of carrying out activities that include manual handling operations need not necessarily arise solely from lifting large, awkward or heavy items. Poor posture can greatly increase the likelihood of suffering manual handling injuries. Examples of poor posture can include over-stretching, twisting, lifting with the spine (in bending position) or lifting whilst seated. Many construction tasks can encourage the worker to take up a poor posture so they are bent over for a period of time, for example laying a floor. Training should be given in correct manual handling techniques, adoption of the correct posture and ensuring that the 'kinetic' lifting method is used (feet slightly apart, straight back and use of the leg muscles to lift).

Guidance published by the Health & Safety Executive (HSE), indicates values of weights and ideal positions for these given weight values that should be adopted when manually handling *(see also - Figure 4-4: Guideline figures - earlier in this element)*. It can be seen from the guidance that the ideal position for manually handling is waist height whilst standing; also to be noted are the different values given for the male and female gender. These figures are not strict and are quoted as maximum under guidance only and allowances must be made for individual differences in capability.

Whilst standing is seen to give the more suitable posture for lifting, it should also be noted that movements made in the standing position can also reduce individual weight values and lifting zones significantly. A twisting motion of the spine of 45 degrees will result in a 10% reduction in lifting capability, whilst a twisting motion of 90 degrees will result in a 20% reduction.

Manually handling whilst seated also reduces individual weight values and lifting zones significantly, with guidance stating 5kg for a male and 3kg for a female as maximum weights whilst seated. Sitting, something done more frequently during work activities can result in back injuries. Research has found that pressure exerted on the spine and disc of the spine are increased by approximately 40% whilst seated; this pressure increases to 90% when leaning forward.

Repetitive movements

The aim of the regulations is to reduce the risk of injury from manual handling operations. One of the main methods used to reduce the load being manually lifted is to package smaller weights or break the bulk load down into smaller batches. This solution avoids the need to lift heavy items; however it will introduce increased frequency.

Injuries received from manual handling operations can either be immediate, resulting from over exertion and poor posture or also occur over time as a result of performing the manual handling task repeatedly, for example digging an excavation or laying bricks. Whilst acute, painful injuries are typically more immediately noticeable, long-term effects from cumulative muscle strain can prove equally detrimental to individual health.

Where frequency is increased, in addition to training in the correct lifting method, regular breaks or job rotation must be introduced in order to share the workload suitably throughout the workforce. Mechanical assistance may also be introduced to prevent twisting or bending under strain (rollers, conveyors, air suction devices, and waist height benches).

Awkward movements

Training should be given in the correct lifting method (the kinetic method), that if used correctly, should eliminate incorrect posture and provide a means for lifting safely in most positions (floor level, waist height, not stretching). Awkward movements that should be avoided include stretching, bending at the waist using the spine, twisting, lifting whilst seated, sudden movements, jerky movements, over exertion whilst pushing or pulling. It should be remembered that many construction tasks require a person to hold awkward positions for a period of time, for example the fitting of overhead lights or tiles. These awkward movements can lead to cumulative strain and it is important that there are sufficient rest periods or work rotation built into the work activity to allow relief of the muscles likely to be affected.

4.3 - Hazards of lifting and moving equipment operations

Associated hazards

FORKLIFT TRUCKS (INCLUDING ROUGH TERRAIN)

Although the forklift truck (FLT) is a very useful machine for moving materials in many industries, it features prominently in industrial accidents. Every year about 20 deaths and 5,000 injuries can be attributed to forklift trucks and these can be analysed as follows:

- Injuries to driver.   40%
- Injuries to assistant.   20%
- Injuries to pedestrians. 40%

- Fractures.   80%
- Injury to ankles and feet. 60%

Unless preventative action is taken these accidents are likely to increase as forklift trucks are increasingly used in industry.

As about 45% of the accidents can be wholly or partly attributed to operator error, the need for proper operator training is underlined. There are, however, many other causes of accident including inadequate premises, gangways, poor truck maintenance, lighting etc.

- Overturning:
  - Driving too fast.
  - Sudden braking.
  - Driving on slopes.
  - Driving with load elevated.
- Collisions:
  - With buildings.
  - With pedestrians.
  - With other vehicles.
- Loss of load:
  - Insecure load.
  - Poor floor surface.
  - Passengers should not be carried.
- Overloading:
  - Exceeding maximum capacity.
- Failure:
  - Load bearing part (e.g. chain).

TELEHANDLERS

Telehandlers are all-purpose machines that can be used for construction site preparation, material handling, scaffold erection, elevated work platforms and for final site cleanup. A telehandler consists of a heavy duty chassis, body and lifting gear on large diameter wheels and deep tread pneumatic traction tyres. Increased power required to cope with the demands of construction sites is transferred through larger drive shafts / wheels and generally larger and heavier duty mechanical ancillary items. In the case of a telehandler, hazards include moving large hydraulic rams that actuate the front forks or bucket with hydraulic hoses attached that are under high pressure. Materials handling is through various attachments fixed to a boom that enables vertical, horizontal and diagonal reach. Construction sites are finding various uses for telehandlers and, with the different attachments available, greater flexibility is provided for the variety of jobs that may be encountered.

Hazards include the generic hazards associated with all heavy plant. There are various mechanical hazards involved, such as impact, crush, trap, and shear. In addition to these there are non-mechanical hazards such as heat, fumes, chemicals and noise.

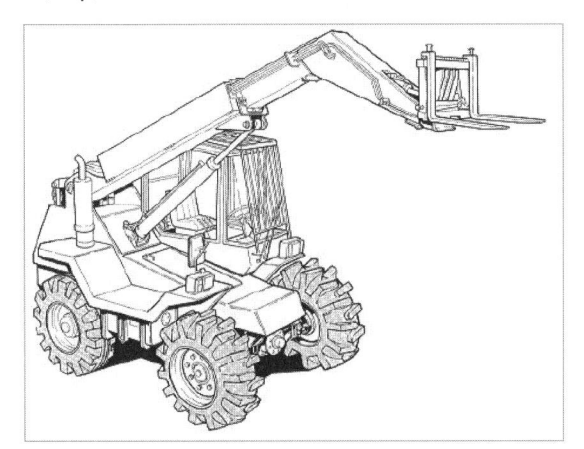

Figure 4-9: Telehandler. *Source: HSG6, HSE books.*

Figure 4-10: Dumper truck. *Source: ACT.*

DUMPER TRUCKS

A dumper truck is a general piece of plant consisting of a heavy-duty chassis, body and tipping bucket on large diameter wheels and deep tread, traction tyres, used for transporting materials around a construction site or street works. The equipment is generally used as a large mechanised wheelbarrow.

Hazards include the generic hazards associated with mobile equipment. Specific hazards associated with dumper trucks are impact with pedestrians or vehicles, trap and crush beneath the tipping bucket as it discharges its contents, falling items or objects from the bucket, high pressure hydraulic lines and tipping over on unstable ground or into excavations. Other hazards include noise, chemicals and fumes produced by the running of the machinery which may find their way into places like excavations.

EXCAVATORS

Consisting of a heavy duty chassis, fixed or rotating body and digging gear (jib arms & bucket) on large diameter wheels and deep tread, pneumatic traction tyres or caterpillar track system.

Figure 4-11: Excavator hazards. *Source: ACT.*

Figure 4-12: Excavator. *Source: ACT.*

Specific hazards associated with excavators are impact with pedestrians or vehicles by swinging jibs and booms, trap and crush beneath the excavator bucket as it digs into the ground or discharges its contents, falling items or objects from the bucket, high pressure hydraulic lines and tipping over on unstable ground or into excavations. Other hazards include noise, chemicals and fumes produced by the running of the equipment. Excavation equipment is generally adapted and used for a variety of different purposes that it may not specifically be designed for, including towing /shunting, lifting, loading / unloading / transport of articles and equipment. The fact that these are improvised activities increases the risk of injury.

Figure 4-13: Width of traffic route.　　Source: ACT.

Figure 4-14: Warning of traffic.　　Source: ACT.

MANUALLY OPERATED LOAD MOVING EQUIPMENT HAZARDS

Wheelbarrows

A wheelbarrow is a low-tech fabrication, generally consisting of a shallow hopper style bucket supported on a single wheel at the front and two legs at the rear with handle bars for grip and use when moving. In use, the load being carried is pivoted and supported over the front wheel. There is still a need to manually handle materials when loading and unloading the wheel barrow, with speed of operation and the capacity of the truck governed by the individual that uses the equipment.

Wheel barrows are typically manually driven pieces of equipment and the hazards arising from their use are generally of an ergonomic nature relating to posture and over exertion. Mechanical hazards are restricted to the single wheel of the barrow that only moves when moved by the operator. Other associated hazards are tripping and falling whilst using the equipment or ejecting the contents of the barrow.

Figure 4-15: Wheelbarrow.　　Source: ACT.

Figure 4-16: Sack truck.　　Source: ACT.

Sack truck

A sack truck is a simple, 'low-tech' fabrication fitted with two wheels on which the load is pivoted and supported when the truck is tilted back and pushed manually. A risk assessment must be made of manual handling operations associated with using equipment of this type. As with the wheelbarrow there is still a need to manually handle materials when using a sack truck.

Sack trucks are typically manually driven and like the wheelbarrow the hazards arising from their use are generally of an ergonomic nature relating to posture and over exertion through manual handling. Mechanical hazards are restricted to the wheels of the truck that only moves when moved by the operator. Other associated hazards are tripping and falling whilst using the equipment and manual handling back and strain injuries.

Pallet trucks

This truck has two elevating fingers for insertion below the top deck of a pallet. When the 'forks' are raised the load is moved clear of the ground to allow movement. This truck may be designed for pedestrian or rider control. It has no mast and cannot be used for stacking. Pallet trucks may be powered or non-powered.

Pallet trucks can be driven both manually or by quiet running electric motor. Hazards include crush from moving loads or momentum of the equipment when stopping, crush and trap in the forks of the equipment, manual handling strain injuries and electricity hazards from battery power points. In addition, some pallet trucks have a lifting mechanism to raise and lower the load.

LIFTS AND HOISTS

In general, the hazards associated with lifts and hoists are the same as with any other lifting equipment.

- The lift / hoist may overturn or collapse.
- The lift / hoist can strike persons, during normal operations, who may be near or under the platform or cage.
- The supporting ropes may fail and the platform/cage falls to the ground.
- The load or part of the load may fall.
- The lift / hoist may fail in a high position.
- Persons being lifted may become stranded if the lift or hoist fails.

CONVEYORS

- Typical hazards associated with conveyors are:
- Drawing in   -   Clothing or limbs being drawn in to in-running nips caused by moving parts.
- Contact   -   With moving parts (cut and abrasion).
- Entanglement   -   With rollers.
- Striking   -   Falling objects, especially from overhead conveyors.
- Manual Handling   -   Loading and unloading components / packages.
- Noise   -   From mechanical movement.

Types of conveyor

The three basic types of conveyor are belt, roller and screw.

Belt

Materials are transported on a moving belt. Trapping points are created between the belt and the rotating drum. The 'head and tails' pulleys create the main risks. Guards can be fitted enclosing the sides or at each drawing in point (in-running nip).

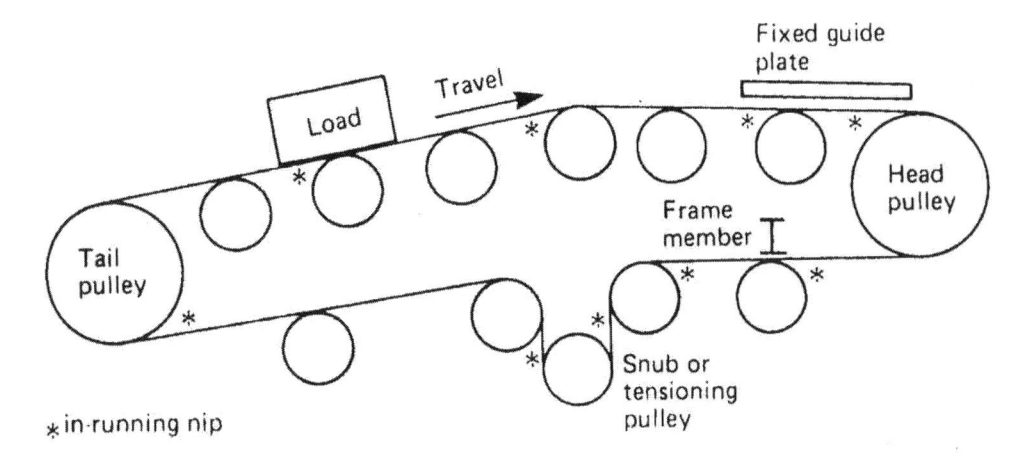

Figure 4-17: Diagrammatic layout of belt conveyor showing in-running nips.
Source: J Ridley; Safety at Work; Fourth Edition.

Roller

- Power driven rollers: guards are required on power drives and in-running nips.
- Powered and free running rollers: guards are required between each pair of powered and free running rollers.
- Free running rollers: no nips occur on these, but injuries can occur when people try to walk across them. Providing walkways can solve this problem.

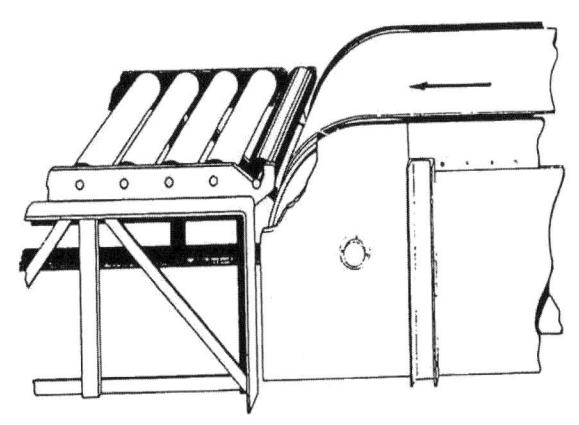

Figure 4-18: Preventing free running roller trap.
Source: J Ridley; Safety at Work; Fourth Edition - Courtesy HSE.

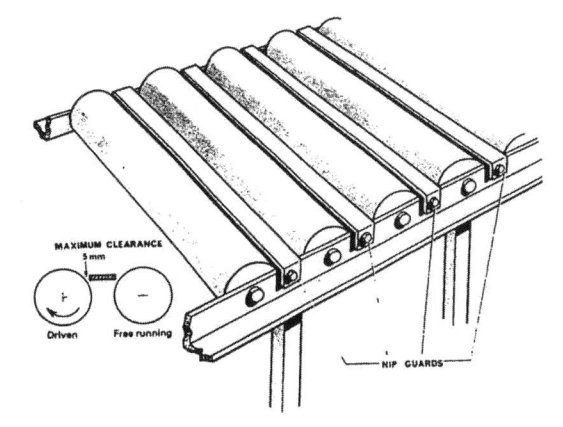

Figure 4-19: Guards between alternative drive-rollers.
Source: J Ridley; Safety at Work; Fourth Edition - Courtesy HSE.

Figure 4-20: Roller conveyor. *Source: ACT.*

Figure 4-21: Belt conveyor guard. *Source: ACT.*

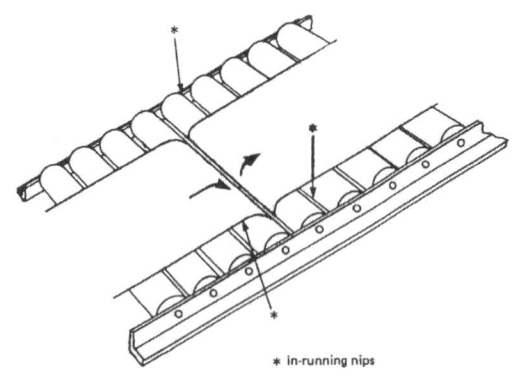

Figure 4-22: Nip points on roller conveyor with belts.
Source: J Ridley; Safety at Work; Fourth Edition - Courtesy HSE.

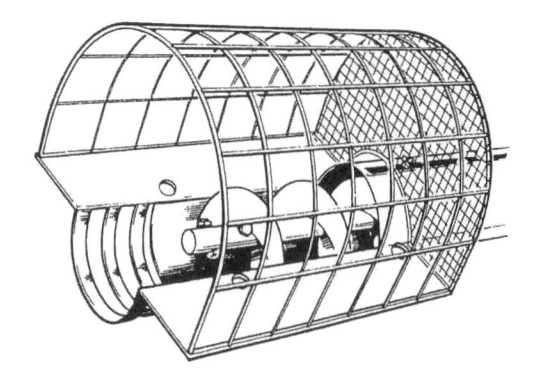

Figure 4-23: Screw conveyor guarding.
Source: J Ridley; Safety at Work; Fourth Edition - Courtesy HSE.

Screw

Materials are pushed forward by a rotating screw. Screw conveyors can cause terrible injuries and should be guarded or covered at all times. A locking-off system is required for maintenance and repairs.

MOBILE AND TOWER CRANES

The principal hazards associated with any lifting operation are:

- **Overturning** which can be caused by weak support, operating outside the capabilities of the machine and by striking obstructions.
- **Overloading** by exceeding the operating capacity or operating radii, or by failure of safety devices.
- **Collision** with other cranes, overhead cables or structures.
- **Failure of load bearing part** - placing over cellars and drains, outriggers not extended, made-up or not solid ground, or of structural components of the crane itself.
- **Loss of load** from failure of lifting tackle or slinging procedure.

No matter what the type of crane, the main issues are the same:

- The ground the crane stands on - is it capable of bearing the load? Is it level? Are there any underground caverns or cellars?
- The load bearing capacity of the crane - is it sufficient for the task?
- Positioning the crane - is there enough room for the lift? Are there any overhead power lines, nearby buildings or other cranes? Will there be personnel or members of the public nearby? Is the tower crane near an airport or in a flight path?
- Adverse weather conditions.
- Structural integrity of the crane - are there signs of corrosion?
- Erecting and dismantling the crane - will other cranes be used?

Figure 4-24: Safety latch on hook. *Source: Corel Clipart.*

4.4 - Control measures for lifting and moving equipment operations

Safe use and maintenance

FORKLIFT TRUCKS (INCLUDING ROUGH TERRAIN)

Selection of equipment

There are many types of truck available for a range of activities. There are many situations when specialist trucks such as reach trucks, overhead telescopic or rough terrain trucks are required. Many accidents happen due to the incorrect selection and/or use of forklift trucks.

When choosing the right truck for the job the following factors should be taken into account:

- Power source - the choice of battery or diesel will depend on whether the truck is to be used indoors or outdoors.
- Tyres - solid or pneumatic depending on the terrain.
- Size and capacity - dependent on the size and nature of loads to be moved.
- Height of the mast.
- Audible and/or visual warning systems fitted according to the proximity of pedestrians.
- Protection provided for the operator dependent on rough terrain which might increase the likelihood of overturning or the possibility of falling objects say from insecure racking.
- Training given to operators must be related specifically to the type of truck.

MECHANICAL HANDLING EQUIPMENT OPERATORS

No person should be permitted to drive a forklift truck or mobile plant unless they have been selected, trained and authorised to do so, or is undergoing properly organised formal training.

Selection of personnel

The safe use of forklift trucks calls for a reasonable degree of both physical and mental fitness and of intelligence. The selection procedure should be devised to identify people who have shown themselves reliable and mature during their early years at work.

Training

Training should consist of three stages, the last being the one in which the operator is introduced to his future work environment. This is illustrated by the stages of training of a fork lift truck operator.

Stage one - should contain the basic skills and knowledge required to operate the forklift truck safely, to understand the basic mechanics and balance of the machine, and to carry out routine daily checks.

Stage two - under strict training conditions closed to other personnel. This stage should include:

- Knowledge of the operating principles and controls.
- Use of the forklift truck in gangways, slopes, cold-stores, confined spaces and bad weather conditions etc.
- The work to be undertaken e.g. loading and unloading vehicles.

Stage three - after successfully completing the first two stages, the operator should be given further instruction in the place of work.

Testing - on completion of training, the operator should be examined and tested to ensure that he/she has achieved the required standard.

Refresher training - if high standards are to be maintained, periodic refresher training and testing is essential good practice.

Traffic routes

1) Separate routes, designated crossing places and suitable barriers at recognised danger spots.
2) Roads, gangways and aisles should have sufficient width and overhead clearance for the largest forklift truck.
3) Clear direction signs.
4) Sharp bends and overhead obstructions should be avoided.
5) The floor surface should be in good condition.
6) Any gradient in a forklift truck operating area should be kept as gentle as possible.

Parking areas

Sufficient and suitable parking areas should be provided away from the main work area.

Protection of personnel

There is a need to alert people to the hazard when working in or near a mechanical handling plant operating area. This is achieved by putting up signs and/or fitting audible warnings to vehicles.

Summary of controls

- Make someone responsible for transport.
- Select and train drivers thoroughly.
- Daily vehicle checks.
- Keep keys secure. ***Do not leave in the ignition.***
- Maintain and light gangways.
- Separate vehicles and pedestrians.

TELEHANDLERS

Control measures should include: use only by competent operators, barriers to segregate pedestrians from machinery to a safe distance, good visibility with the assistance of mirrors, high visibility clothing for those working nearby, seat restraints for the operator who should be enclosed in a protective cage that can also act as a guard against contact with moving machinery and the effects of overturning.

DUMPER TRUCKS

Control measures should include trained, authorised, operatives; maintenance and inspection; segregation of pedestrians to a safe distance by the provision of suitable barriers and signs advising of the dangers of operating plant; stop blocks for tipping into excavations; seat restraints and rollover protection for the operator.

EXCAVATORS

Control measures should include trained and authorised operatives; not overloading the bucket; maintenance and inspection; segregation of pedestrians to a safe distance by the provision of suitable barriers and signs advising of the dangers of operating plant; good visibility with the assistance of mirrors where necessary, high visibility clothing for those working nearby, seat restraints for the operator who should be enclosed in a protective cage that can also act as a guard against contact with moving machinery and the effects of overturning.

MANUALLY OPERATED LOAD MOVING EQUIPMENT

Wheelbarrows

Control measures include indicating a safe working load for the equipment and the provision of information / instruction in the safe loading and use of the equipment for the operator. A manual handling assessment may be required when using this equipment.

Sack trucks

Control measures include indicating a safe working load for the equipment and the provision of information / instruction in the safe loading and use of the equipment for the operator. A manual handling assessment may be required when using this equipment.

Pallet trucks

Control measures should include trained and authorised operatives; identification of safe working loads; inspection and maintenance; and designated areas for parking the equipment.

LIFTS AND HOISTS

Lifts and hoists for movement of goods require:

- Statutory safety devices.
- Holdback gears (for rope failure).
- Overrun tip systems.
- Guards on hoist machinery.
- Landing gates (securely closed down during operation).

In addition, passenger hoists require more sophisticated controls:

- Operating controls inside the cage.
- Electromagnetic interlocks on the cage doors.
- The enclosing shaft must be of fire-proof construction, if within a building.

Safe use of lifts and hoists depends on:

- Adequate design.
- Competent operation.
- Sound construction.
- Regular inspection.
- Correct selection.
- Adequate maintenance.
- Correct installation.

The legislation governing the construction, use and thorough examination of lifts and hoists, is the Lifting Operations and Lifting Equipment Regulations (LOLER) 1998.

For further details see later in this element and also - Relevant statutory provisions.

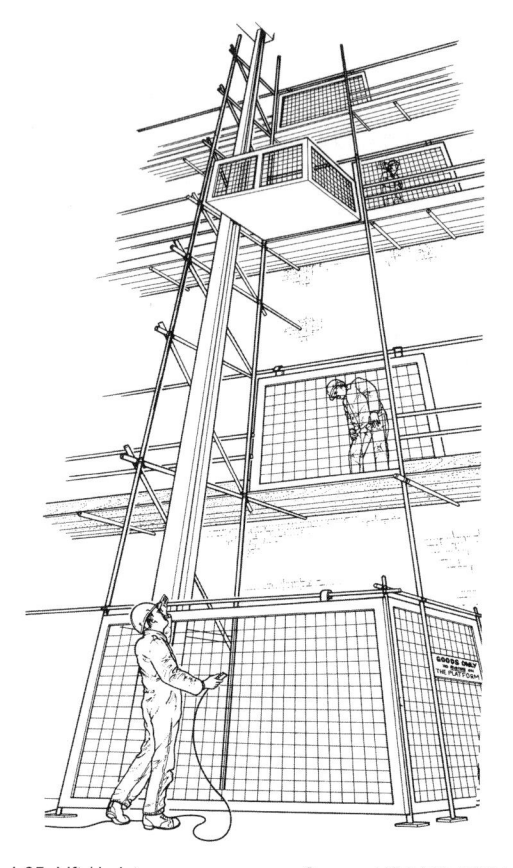

Figure 4-25: Lift / hoist. *Source: HSG150, HSE books.*

CONVEYORS

To ensure the safe use of conveyors:
- Fixed guards on drums.
- Enclosure of conveyed items by side guards.
- Trip wires, if necessary, along the full length of the conveyor.
- Emergency stop buttons.
- Safe access at regular intervals.
- Avoid loose clothing.
- Restrict access.
- Wearing bump caps.
- Regular maintenance by competent people.

MOBILE AND TOWER CRANES

Lifting operations must be properly planned by a competent person, appropriately supervised and carried out in a safe manner.

No matter what type of crane, there are a number of common measures for safe operation that apply, including crane identification and capacity marking safe working load (SWL), and maintenance (preventative maintenance, as well as statutory implications). The main safety measures that should be incorporated for the safe operation of a crane include:

- Pre-use check by operator.
- Lifting equipment must be of adequate strength and stability for the load. Stresses induced at mounting or fixing points must be taken into account. Similarly every part of a load, anything attached to it and used in lifting must be of adequate strength.
- The safe working load (SWL) must be clearly marked on lifting machinery, equipment and accessories in order to ensure safe use. Where the SWL depends on the configuration of the machinery, it must be clearly marked for each configuration used and kept with the machinery. Equipment which is not designed for lifting persons, but which might be used as such, must have appropriate markings to the effect that it is not to be used for passengers.
- Load indicators - two types - a requirement with jib cranes, but beneficial if fitted to all cranes.
  - ✓ Load/radius indicator - shows the radius the crane is working at and the safe load for that radius. Must be visible to the driver.
  - ✓ Automatic safe load indicator - providing visible warning when SWL is approached and audible warning when SWL is exceeded.
- Controls - should be clearly identified and of the "hold to run" type.
- Over travel switches - limit switches to prevent the hook or sheave block being wound up to the cable drum.
- Access - safe access should be provided for the operator and for use during inspection and maintenance/emergency.
- Operating position - should provide clear visibility of hook and load, with the controls easily reached.
- Passengers - should not be carried without authorisation, and never on lifting tackle.
- Lifting tackle - chains, slings, wire ropes, eyebolts and shackles should be tested / examined.

Figure 4-26: Lifting operation. *Source: ACT.*

Figure 4-27: Lifting points on load. *Source: ACT.*

Accessories

Lifting accessories include slings, hooks, chains eyes and cradles.

This equipment is designed with the aim of assisting in lifting items without the need for manual force because these accessories are in a constantly changing environment and are in and out of use. They need to be protected from damage, and a failure of any one item could have fatal effects. Wire ropes are commonly found on construction sites and are very often misused and become defective. Typical defects include kinking, broken wires ('needles'), ovalling caused by external wear or stretching, corrosion, damage to thimbles and ferrules, 'bird-caging' and the lack of any identification or indication of the sling's safe working load.

For example, lifting eyes need to be correctly fitted, slings have to be used with the correct technique and all equipment must be stored when not in use to prevent damage.

Accessories must be attached correctly and safely to the load by a competent person, and then the lifting equipment takes over the task of providing the necessary required power to perform the lift.

As with all lifting equipment, accessories must be regularly inspected and certificated and only used by trained authorised persons.

Figure 4-28: Accessories. *Source: Lincsafe.*

Figure 4-29: Accessories. *Source: ACT.*

Operator training and practices

Crane operators and slingers should be fit and strong enough for the work. Training should be provided for the safe operation of the particular equipment.

A safe system of work should be developed and communicated to all those involved. The planning should involve selecting competent persons including the mobile crane driver and appointed person who will supervise the lifting operation.

A number of safety rules are suggested as a basis of a code of practice for the safe operation of mobile cranes. Circumstances differ from site to site and additional rules should be inserted to cover individual cases and conditions.

For example, before taking over a mobile crane the driver must always check around the crane, and check the pressure of tyres, the engine for fuel, lubrication oil, water and the compressed air system. All controls, such as clutches, brakes and safe load indicator, should be tested to see that all ropes run smoothly and check limit switches, where fitted.

The driver of a *mobile crane* should carry out the following:

- Before travelling unladen, lower jib onto its rest (if fitted) or to the lowest operating position and point in the direction of travel, but beware of steep hills.
- Understand the signalling system and observe the signals of the appointed banksman.
- Do not permit unauthorised persons to travel on the crane.
- Do not use the crane to replace normal means of transport, or as a towing tractor.
- Before lifting, check that the crane is on firm and level ground, and that spring locks and out-riggers are properly in position.
- Keep a constant watch on the load radius indicator. Do not lift any suspected overload. Overloads are forbidden.
- Ensure movements are made with caution. Violent handling produces excess loading on the crane structure and machinery.
- Make allowances for adverse weather conditions.
- Do not attempt to drag loads or cause loads to swing. Always position the crane so that the pull on the hoist rope is vertical.
- Ensure that the load is properly slung. A load considered unsafe should not be lifted.
- Ensure that all persons are in a safe position before any movement is carried out.
- Make certain before hoisting that the hook is not attached to any anchored load or fixed object.
- Do not drag slings when travelling.
- If the crane is slewing, the jib, hook or load must be in a position to clear any obstruction, but the load must not be lifted unnecessarily high.
- Be on a constant lookout for overhead obstructions, particularly electric cables.
- Never tamper with or disconnect safe load indicators.
- If the hoist or jib ropes become slack or out of their grooves, stop the crane and report the condition.
- Report all defects to the supervisor and never attempt to use a crane with a suspected serious defect until rectified and certified by a competent person that it is not dangerous.
- When leaving a crane unattended, ensure that the power is off, the engine stopped, the load unhooked, and the hook is raised up to a safe position.
- Where using special devices; e.g. magnets, grabs, etc. ensure they are used only for the purpose intended and in accordance with the instruction given.
- Keep the crane clean and tidy.
- When parking a crane after use, remember to apply all brakes, slew locks, and secure rail clamps when fitted. Some cranes, however, particularly tower cranes, must be left to weather vane and the manufacturers instructions must be clearly adhered to. Park the crane where the weather vaning jib will not strike any object. Lock the cabin before leaving the crane.
- When it is necessary to make a report this must be done promptly through supervision.
- Drive smoothly - drive safely. Remember that cranes are safe only when they are used as recommended by the makers. This applies in particular to speciality cranes.

Rules for safe operation of a crane

Always	Ensure operators/slingers are trained and competent.
Always	Select the right appliance and tackle for the job.
Always	Ensure the appliance is stable when lifting - e.g. not outside lifting radius, firm, level ground, outriggers.
Always	Use correct slinging methods.
Always	Protect sling from sharp edges - pack out and lower onto spacers.

Always	Ensure the sling is securely attached to the hook.
Always	Ensure load is lifted to correct height and moved at an appropriate speed.
Always	Use standard signals - refer to the Health and Safety (Safety Signs & Signals) Regulations (SSSR) 1996.
Never	Use equipment if damaged (check before use) - e.g. stretched or not free movement, worn or corroded, outside inspection date.
Never	Exceed the safe working load.
Never	Lift with sling angles greater than 120^0.
Never	Lift a load over people.
Never	Drag a load or allow sudden shock loading.

Figure 4-30: Crane operation. Source: ACT.

Control of lifting operations

Under regulation 8 of the LOLER 1998 employers have a duty to ensure that every lifting operation involving lifting equipment for the purposes of lifting or lowering of a load is organised safely. This will include ensuring the following:

a) Lifting operations to be properly planned by a competent person.

b) Provision of appropriate supervision.

c) Work is to be carried out in a safe manner.

Figure 4-31: Lifting operations. Source: ACT.

Figure 4-32: Lifting operations. Source: ACT.

Requirements for lifting operations

STRONG, STABLE AND SUITABLE EQUIPMENT

Strength

Regulation 4 of LOLER 1998 requires every employer shall ensure that:

- Lifting equipment is of adequate strength and stability for each load, having regard in particular to the stress induced at its mounting or fixing point.
- Every part of a load and anything attached to it and used in lifting it is of adequate strength.

When assessing whether lifting equipment has adequate strength for the proposed use the combined weight of the load and lifting accessories should be taken into account. It is important to consider the load, task and environment in order to match the strength of the lifting equipment to the circumstances of use.

For example, if the environment is hot or cold this can affect the lifting capacity of the lifting equipment.

In order to counteract this effect equipment with a higher rated safe working load may be needed. If the load to be lifted is a person, equipment with a generous capacity above the person's weight may be selected in order to provide a higher factor of safety. If the load is likely to move unexpectedly, such as an animal or liquids in a container, this sudden movement can put additional forces on the equipment and may necessitate equipment with higher strength to be selected.

When conducting the lifting task the lifting accessories may be used in such a way that may reduce its lifting capacity below its stated safe working load, sharp corners on a load and 'back hooking' can have this effect. In these circumstances accessories with a higher rated safe working load may be required. It is essential to remember that in a lifting operation the equipment only has an overall lifting capacity equivalent to the item with the lowest strength.

For example, in a situation where a crane with a lifting capacity of 50 tonnes is used with a hook of 10 tonnes capacity and a wire rope sling of 5 tonnes capacity this would give an overall maximum lifting strength/capacity of 5 tonnes.

Stability

A number of factors can affect the stability of lifting equipment, for example wind conditions, slopes/cambers, stability of ground conditions and how the load is to be lifted.

Lifting equipment must be positioned and installed so that it does not tip over when in use. Anchoring can be achieved by securing with guy ropes, bolting the structure to a foundation, using ballast as counterweights or using outriggers to bring the centre of gravity down to the base area.

Mobile lifting equipment should be sited on firm ground with the wheels or outrigger feet having their weight distributed over a large surface area. Care should be taken that the equipment is not positioned over cellars, drains or underground cavities, or positioned near excavations.

Sloping ground should be avoided as this can shift the load radius out or in, away from the safe working position. In the uphill position, the greatest danger occurs when the load is set down. This can cause the mobile lifting equipment to tip over. In the downhill position, the load moves out of the radius and may cause the equipment to tip forwards.

Suitability

Lifting equipment, and any accessories used for lifting, are pieces of work equipment under the Provision and Use of Work Equipment Regulations (PUWER) 1998. Regulation 4 of PUWER 1998 states:

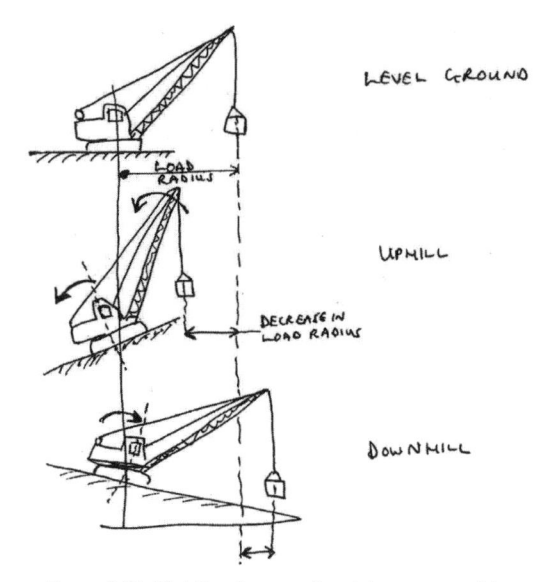

Figure 4-33: Stability of cranes (hand drawn example). *Source: ACT.*

'Every employer shall ensure that work equipment is used only for operations for which, and under conditions for which, it is suitable in order to avoid any reasonably foreseeable risk to the health and safety of any person'.

In order for lifting equipment to be suitable it must be of the correct type for the task, have a safe working load limit in excess of the load being lifted, and have the correct type and combination of lifting accessories attached.

Lifting equipment used within industry varies and includes mobile cranes, static tower cranes and overhead travelling cranes. The type of lifting equipment selected will depend on a number of factors including the weight of the load to be lifted, the radius of operation, the height of the lift, the time available, and the frequency of the lifting activities. This equipment is often very heavy, which means its weight can cause the ground underneath the equipment to sink or collapse. Other factors like height and size may have to be considered as there may be limitations in site roads that are located between structures or where overhead restrictions exist. Careful consideration of these factors must be made when selecting the correct crane. Selecting lifting equipment to carry out a lifting activity should be done at the planning stage, where the most suitable equipment can be identified that is able to meet all of the lifting requirements and the limitations of the location.

POSITIONED AND INSTALLED CORRECTLY

Lifting equipment must be positioned or installed so that the risk of the equipment striking a person is as low as is reasonably practicable. Similarly, the risk of a load drifting, falling freely or being unintentionally released must also be considered and equipment positioned to take account of this.

All nearby hazards, including overhead cables and uninsulated power supply conductors, should be identified and removed or covered by safe working procedures such as locking-off and permit systems. The possibility of striking other lifting equipment or structures should also be examined.

Detailed consideration must be given to the location of any heavy piece of lifting equipment due to the fact that additional weight is distributed to the ground through the loading of the equipment when performing a lift.

Surveys must be carried out to determine the nature of the ground, whether soft or firm, and what underground hazards are present such as buried services or hollow voids.

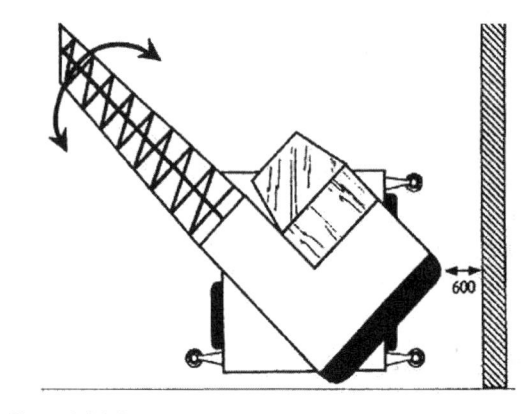

Figure 4-34: Danger zone - crane & fixed item. *Source: ACT.*

If the ground proves to be soft, then this can be covered in timber, digger mats or hard core to prevent the equipment or its outriggers sinking when under load. The surrounding environment must also be taken into consideration and factors may include highways, railways, electricity cables, areas of public interest. The area around where lifting equipment is sited should be securely fenced, including the extremes of the lift radius, with an additional factor of safety to allow for emergency arrangements such as emergency vehicle access or safety in the event of a collapse or fall.

Where practicable, lifting equipment should be positioned and installed such that loads are not carried or suspended over areas occupied by people. Where this is necessary appropriate systems of work should be used to ensure it is done safely.

If the operator cannot observe the full path of the load an appointed person (and assistants as appropriate) should be used to communicate the position of the load and provide directions to avoid striking anything or anyone.

VISIBLY MARKED (SWL)

The safe working load (SWL) must be clearly marked on lifting machinery, equipment and accessories in order to ensure safe use. Where the SWL depends on the configuration of the machinery, it must be clearly marked for each configuration used and kept with the machinery. Accessories must be marked with supplementary information that indicates the characteristics for its safe use, for example safe angles of lift.

Equipment designed for lifting people must be clearly marked as such and equipment which is not designed for lifting persons, but which might be used as such, must have appropriate markings to the effect that it is not to be used for lifting people.

LIFTING OPERATIONS PLANNED, SUPERVISED AND CARRIED OUT IN SAFE MANNER BY COMPETENT PEOPLE

Regulation 8 of LOLER 1998 requires that every employer shall ensure that every lifting operation involving lifting equipment is:

- Properly planned by a competent person.
- Appropriately supervised.
- Carried out in a safe manner.

The type of lifting equipment that is to be used and the complexity of the lifting operations will dictate the degree of planning required for the lifting operation.

Planning combines two parts:

1) Initial planning to ensure that lifting equipment is provided which is suitable for the range of tasks that it will have to carry out.

2) Planning of individual lifting operations so that they can be carried out safely with the lifting equipment provided.

Factors that should be considered when formulating a plan include:

- The load that is being lifted - weight, shape, centres of gravity, surface condition, lifting points.
- The equipment and accessories being used for the operation and suitability - certification validity.
- The proposed route that the load will take including the destination and checks for obstructions.
- The team required to carry out the lift - competencies and numbers required.
- Production of a safe system of work, risk assessments, permits to work.
- The environment in which the lift will take place - ground conditions, weather, local population.
- Securing areas below the lift - information, restrictions, demarcation and barriers.
- A suitable trial to determine the reaction of the lifting equipment prior to full lift.
- Completion of the operation and any dismantling required.

Figure 4-35: Siting and stability. Source: ACT.

It is important that someone takes supervisory control of lifting operations at the time they are being conducted. Though the operator may be skilled in lifting techniques this may not be enough to ensure safety as other factors may influence whether the overall operation is conducted safely, for example people may stray into the area. The supervisor of the lifting operation must remain in control and stop the operation if it is not carried out satisfactorily. Lifting equipment and accessories should be subject to a pre-use check in order to determine their condition and suitability. In addition, care should be taken to ensure the lifting accessories used are compatible with the task and that the load is protected or supported such that it does not disintegrate when lifted.

Lifting operations should not be carried on where adverse weather conditions occur, such as fog, poor lightning, strong wind or where heavy rainfall makes ground conditions unstable. It is important that measures be used to prevent lifting equipment overturning and that there is sufficient room for it to operate without contacting other objects. Lifting equipment should not be used to drag loads and should not be overloaded. Special arrangements need to be in place when lifting equipment not normally used for lifting people is used for that purpose, for example de-rating the working load limit, ensuring communication is in place between the people being lifted and the operator, and ensuring the operation controls are manned at all times.

The Health and Safety at Work etc Act (HASAWA) 1974 places a duty on employers to their employees for the provision of information, instruction, training and supervision as is necessary to ensure, so far as is reasonably practicable, the health and safety at work of the employees. In addition to this general duty, a further duty exists under The Provision and Use of Work Equipment Regulations (PUWER) 1998. Employers must ensure that any person who uses a piece of work equipment has received adequate training for purposes of health and safety, including training in the methods which may be adopted when using work equipment, any risks which such use may entail and precautions to be taken.

Drivers / operators of cranes and other lifting appliances, including others involved in lifting operations (e.g. those that direct the movement of the load), must be adequately trained, experienced and aged 18 years or over. The only exception is when under the direct supervision of a competent person for training requirements.

There are various appointments with specified responsibilities in order to ensure the safety of lifting operations on site, these are as follows.

- Competent person   -   Appointed to plan the operation.
- Load handler   -   Attaches and detaches the load.
- Authorised person   -   Ensures the load safely attached.
- Operator   -   Appointed to operate the equipment.
- Responsible person   -   Appointed to communicate the position of the load (banksman).
- Assistants   -   Appointed to relay communications.

SPECIAL REQUIREMENTS FOR LIFTING EQUIPMENT FOR LIFTING PERSONS

Regulation 5 of PUWER 1998 requires every employer to ensure that lifting equipment for lifting persons:

- Is such as to prevent a person using it being crushed, trapped or struck or falling from the carrier.
- Is such as to prevent so far as is reasonably practicable a person using it, while carrying out activities from the carrier, being crushed, trapped or struck or falling from the carrier.
- Has suitable devices to prevent the risk of a carrier falling.
- Is such that a person trapped in any carrier is not thereby exposed to danger and can be freed.

In addition, every employer shall ensure that if the risk described above cannot be prevented for reasons inherent in the site and height differences the following requirements are met:

- The carrier has an enhanced safety coefficient suspension rope or chain.
- The rope or chain is inspected by a competent person every working day.

Special arrangements need to be in place when lifting equipment not normally used for people is used for that purpose, e.g. de-rating the working load limit, ensuring communication is in place between the people and operator, and ensuring the operation controls are manned at all times. Lifting equipment for lifting people is subject to specific requirements for statutory examination - see below for details.

Requirements for the inspection and examination of lifting equipment

Statutory requirements are set out in Regulation 9 of the LOLER 1998.

Used lifting equipment must be thoroughly examined before being put into service for the first time by a new user. This does not apply to new lifting equipment (unless its safety depends on installation conditions) or equipment that conforms to European Community requirements and has been certified as being examined within the previous 12 months. Suppliers of used lifting equipment are obliged to certify that a thorough examination has been carried out.

Where the safety of lifting equipment depends on the installation conditions it must be thoroughly examined prior to first use, after assembly and on change of location in order to ensure that it has been installed correctly and is safe to operate.

Lifting equipment exposed to conditions causing deterioration that is liable to result in dangerous situations is to be thoroughly examined by a competent person:

a) At least every 6 months - lifting equipment for lifting persons and lifting accessories.

b) At least every 12 months - other lifting equipment.

c) In either case, in accordance with an examination scheme.

d) On each occurrence of exceptional circumstances liable to jeopardise the safety of the lifting equipment.

Figure 4-36: Marking of accessories. *Source: ACT.*

Regulation 10 of LOLER 1998 requires those persons carrying out the thorough examination as specified under regulation 9 to, as soon as is practicable, make a written report of the results of the examination. This is to be signed by the competent person carrying out this task.

Regulation 11 of LOLER 1998 concerns the keeping of information in relation to examinations and specifies that any report written by a competent person, following an examination, must be kept available for inspection for the period of validity of the report.

Where appropriate to ensure health and safety, inspections must be carried out at suitable intervals between thorough examinations. Examinations and inspections must ensure that the good condition of equipment is maintained and that any deterioration can be detected and remedied in good time.

Element 5

Work equipment - hazards and control

Learning outcomes

On completion of this element, candidates should be able to demonstrate understanding of the content through the application of knowledge to familiar and unfamiliar situations. In particular they should be able to:

5.1 Outline general requirements for work equipment.

5.2 Outline the hazards and controls for hand-held tools, both powered and non-powered.

5.3 Describe the main mechanical and non-mechanical hazards of machinery.

5.4 Describe the main appropriate control measures for machinery hazards.

Content

5.1 - General requirements for work equipment 65
    Scope of work equipment 65
    Suitability as it relates to provision of equipment..65
    Requirement to restrict the use and maintenance of equipment with specific risks.....................................67
    Information, instruction and training 67
    Requirement for equipment to be maintained and maintenance to be conducted safely 67
    Importance of operation and emergency controls 70
    Responsibilities of users 73
5.2 - Hand-held tools...73
    Hazards and misuse of hand tools 73
    Appropriate control measures for safe use...73
    Hazards of portable power tools 73
    Suitability for location 75
    Procedures for defective equipment..75
5.3 - Machinery hazards..76
    Main mechanical and non-mechanical hazards 76
    Hazards presented by a range of equipment 80
5.4 - Appropriate control measures for machinery hazards..82
    The principles, merits and limitations of protection methods...83
    Application of protection methods to a range of equipment listed...87
    Basic requirements for guards and safety devices..88

Sources of reference

Chainsaws at work, HSE Books ISBN 0-7176-6187-3
BS EN ISO 12100 (formerly BS EN 292), British Standards Institution ISBN 0-5804-2922-9
Safe use of woodworking machinery (L144), HSE Books ISBN 0-7176-1630-4

Relevant statutory provisions

The Personal Protective Equipment at Work Regulations (PPER) 1992
The Provision and Use of Work Equipment Regulations (PUWER) 1998 - Part II
The Supply of Machinery (Safety) Regulations (SMSR) 1992 - scope and application, and relationship to CE marking

5.1 - General requirements for work equipment

Scope of work equipment

The Provision and Use of Work Equipment Regulations (PUWER) 1998 are concerned with most aspects relating to work equipment. The Regulations define work equipment as any machinery, appliance, apparatus, tool or assembly of components which are arranged so that they function as a whole. Clearly the term embraces many hand tools, power tools and machinery.

Examples of work equipment commonly used in the construction industry include:

- Air compressor.
- Air road breakers.
- Floor saws.
- Piling hammers.
- Drill rigs.
- Nail guns.
- Road breakers.
- Scabblers.
- Mobile elevating work platforms (MEWP's).
- Lifting sling.
- Mobile access platform.
- Hand-held tools.
- Power tools, drills, jig saws etc.
- Rough terrain fork lift truck (RTFLT).

Not work equipment:

- Livestock.
- Substances.
- Structural items (buildings).
- Private car.

Figure 5-1: Air road breakers. *Source: Speedy Hire plc.*

Figure 5-2: Floor scabbler. *Source: Speedy Hire plc.*

Figure 5-3: Hand held scabbler. *Source: Speedy Hire plc.*

Figure 5-4: Lifting sling. *Source: ACT.*

Suitability as it relates to provision of equipment

PROVISION OF WORK EQUIPMENT REGULATIONS [PUWER] 1998

PUWER Regulation 4 - Suitability of work equipment

(1) Every employer shall ensure that work equipment is so constructed or adapted as to be suitable for the purpose for which it is used or provided.

(2) In selecting work equipment, every employer shall have regard to the working conditions and to the risks to the health and safety of persons which exist in the premises or undertaking in which that work equipment is to be used and any additional risk posed by the use of that work equipment.

(3) Every employer shall ensure that work equipment is used only for operations for which, and under conditions for which, it is suitable.

(4) In this regulation "suitable" means suitable in any respect which it is reasonably foreseeable will affect the health or safety of any person.

Suitability should consider:

- Its initial integrity.
- The place where it will be used.
- The purpose for which it will be used.

Integrity - is equipment safe through its design, construction or adaptation? - sharp edges removed from equipment casings, tools modified or made by workers to enable them to do their tasks, equipment adapted to do a specific task.

Place - is equipment suitable for different environments (risks)? - wet or explosive. Account must be taken of the equipment causing a problem - a petrol generator used in a confined space, a hydraulic access platform used in a location with a low roof.

Use - is equipment suitable for the specific task? - a hacksaw being used to cut metal straps used to secure goods to a pallet (instead of a purpose designed tool); the use of a ladder to do work at a height (instead of a scaffold or other access platform); exceeding the safe working load of a crane or fork lift truck, a swivel chair used as a means of access to a shelf.

CONFORMITY WITH RELEVANT STANDARDS, CE MARKING AND ITS LIMITATIONS

Section 6 of The Health and Safety at Work Act (HASAWA) 1974 requires those involved in the supply (including design and manufacture) of equipment to ensure that it is safe and healthy, so far as is reasonably practicable. This will require them to take account of all relevant standards.

PUWER Regulation 10 - Conformity with community requirements

1. Every employer shall ensure that an item of work equipment has been designed and constructed in compliance with any essential requirements, that is to say requirements relating to its design or construction in any of the instruments listed in Schedule 1 (being instruments which give effect to Community directives concerning the safety of products).

2. Where an essential requirement applied to the design or construction of an item of work equipment, the requirements of regulations 11 to 19 and 22 to 29 shall apply in respect of that item only to the extent that the essential requirement did not apply to it.

3. This regulation applies to items of work equipment provided for use in the premises or undertaking of the employer for the first time after 31st December 1992.

Work equipment provided for use after 31 December 1992 must conform with legislation made in the UK in response to EC directives relating to work equipment. Only those directives listed in schedule 1 of PUWER 1998 are to be considered and then only those that have been translated to UK law. Examples relate to:

- The amount of noise emitted from a variety of equipment (e.g. construction equipment or lawn mowers).
- Electro-medical equipment.
- Simple pressure vessels.
- Machinery safety.
- Personal protective equipment.

Directives, and in turn UK Regulations, tend to contain details of 'essential health and safety requirements' and a system whereby compliance may be demonstrated. Compliance is usually demonstrated by the attachment of a CE mark and the manufacturer/supplier holding an EC declaration of conformity. This declaration may, in the early days of the legislation, be a self declaration or a third party declaration.

FIT FOR PURPOSE

Equipment used for any activity must be suitable to fulfil the exact requirements of the task. This means considering the ergonomic requirements *(see paragraph below)*, strength, durability, power source, portability, protection against the environment, range of tasks to be carried out and the frequency and duration of use. Equipment that is designed to perform a specific task must only be used for that task and not adapted for other tasks not considered in the manufacturer's design and instructions. An example of this is where a portable battery operated drill is rotated by hand or the back / butt of the drill is used as a hammer, clearly a task not meant for this equipment. Equipment used in these types of situation identifies a lack of forethought in the planning stage of a project when the correct equipment should have been sought and used.

The equipment may be used indoors or outdoors where consideration must be given to the dangers of damp, water and electricity or explosive atmospheres within confined spaces. The grade of equipment should be industrial or commercial type for work activities and not the type of equipment designed for use at home. Whenever equipment is required, the full capacity and limitation requirements should be identified and it should be confirmed that the equipment provided can cope with the demands/limitations placed upon it. For example, construction sites use 110 volt supply and it is important that workers only use equipment that suits this power supply.

ERGONOMIC CONSIDERATIONS

Ergonomic considerations involve the study of person-equipment interface, with an emphasis on adjustability of the machinery and equipment. The aim is to suit a variety of individual sizes and positions in order to provide the most comfortable position possible. In considering the ergonomic factors of a task that requires equipment to be used, it is essential to include the operator's individual attributes, and how they affect and may be affected by the process. Factors might include posture when seated or standing, height of the work station, how the equipment may be adjusted and frequency of the task being performed. It is essential that ergonomic considerations form an active part at the planning stage of a process to ensure the correct equipment is obtained and the reactive effects of poor ergonomics eliminated.

Requirement to restrict the use and maintenance of equipment with specific risks

STATUTORY RESTRICTIONS ON USE OF WORK EQUIPMENT

PUWER Regulation 7 - Specific risks

1) Where the use of work equipment is likely to involve a specific risk to health or safety, every employer shall ensure that:
    a) The use of that work equipment is restricted to those persons given the task of using it; and
    b) Repairs, modifications, maintenance or servicing of that work equipment is restricted to those persons who have been specifically designated to perform operations of that description (whether or not also authorised to perform other operations).

2) The employer shall ensure that the persons designated for the purposes of sub-paragraph (b) of paragraph (1) have received adequate training related to any operations in respect of which they have been so designated.

For example, in view of the specific risks, it would be appropriate to restrict the use of a nail gun, circular saw or mobile elevated work platform to those competent and authorised to use it. In the same way maintenance (replacement of a grinding wheel) of an abrasive wheel or (replacement of load bearing components) of a rough terrain fork lift truck should be restricted.

Information, instruction and training

INFORMATION AND INSTRUCTION

Whenever equipment is provided and used in the workplace there is a requirement to ensure that all operators are given adequate information and instruction in order that they can use the equipment safely. The issues covered should include the safe operation of the equipment and also the capacities ands limitations of the equipment. Specific information must be given on the particular hazards of equipment and instruction and training given on how to implement, use and maintain control measures correctly.

PUWER Regulation 8 - Information and instruction

"Every employer shall ensure that all persons who use work equipment have available to them adequate health and safety information and, where appropriate, written instructions pertaining to the use of the work equipment.

Every employer shall ensure that any of his employees who supervises or manages the use of work equipment has available to him adequate health and safety information and, where appropriate, written instructions pertaining to the use of the work equipment, information and, where appropriate, written instructions on -

a) The conditions in which and the methods by which the work equipment may be used.
b) Foreseeable abnormal situations and the action to be taken if such a situation were to occur.
c) Any conclusions to be drawn from experience in using the work equipment."

TRAINING

PUWER Regulation 9 - Training

"Every employer shall ensure that all persons who use work equipment have received adequate training for purposes of health and safety, including training in the methods which may be adopted when using the work equipment, any risks which such use may entail and precautions to be taken.

Every employer shall ensure that any of his employees who supervises or manages the use of work equipment has received adequate training for purposes of health and safety, including training in the methods which may be adopted when using the work equipment, any risks which such use may entail and precautions to be taken."

Training may be needed for existing staff as well as inexperienced staff or new starters (do not forget temporary staff), particularly if they have to use powered machinery. The greater the danger, the better the training needs to be. For some high risk work such as driving forklift trucks, using a chainsaw and operating a crane, training should be carried out by specialist instructors. Remember that younger people can be quite skilful when moving and handling powered equipment, but they may lack experience and judgment and may require closer supervision to begin with.

Examples:

Users - How to carry out pre-use checks, report defects, only to use equipment for the purpose designed.

Maintenance - Safe isolation, recommended spares and adjustments in accordance with manufacturer's manuals.

Managers - Be aware of the hazards and controls and maintain effective supervision.

Requirement for equipment to be maintained and maintenance to be conducted safely

EQUIPMENT TO BE MAINTAINED

PUWER Regulation 5 - Maintenance

Equipment must be maintained in efficient working order and good repair. In order to achieve this, a system of maintenance should be in place which involves regular inspection, adjustment and testing. Maintenance logs, where they exist, must be kept up to date.

UNIT NCC1 - ELEMENT 5 - WORK EQUIPMENT - HAZARDS AND CONTROL

MAINTENANCE TO BE CONDUCTED SAFELY

PUWER Regulation 22 - Maintenance

No one should be exposed to undue risk during maintenance operations. In order to achieve this equipment should be stopped and isolated as appropriate before work starts. If it is necessary to keep equipment running then the risks must be adequately controlled. This may take the form of controlling running speed, range of movement or providing temporary guards. Consideration must be given to other legislation such as Electricity at Work Regulations (EWR) 1989 during the assessment.

Maintenance hazards

The principal sources of hazards are associated with maintenance work on:

- Heavy plant.
- Crushers.
- Cranes.
- Concrete pumps.
- Storage tanks.
- Batching plant.

Typical hazards associated with maintenance operations

Mechanical	-	Entanglement, machinery traps, contact; shearing traps, in-running nips, ejection, unexpected start up.
Electrical	-	Electrocution, shock, burns.
Pressure	-	Unexpected pressure releases, explosion.
Physical	-	Extremes of temperature, noise, vibration, dust.
Chemical	-	Gases, vapours, mists, fumes, etc.
Structural	-	Obstructions and floor openings.
Access	-	Work at heights, confined spaces.

Typical accidents

- Crushing by moving machinery.
- Falls.
- Burns.
- Asphyxiation.
- Electrocution.

One or more of the following factors causes maintenance accidents:

- Lack of perception of risk by managers/supervisors, often because of lack of necessary training.
- Unsafe or no system of work devised, for example, no permit-to-work system in operation, no facility to lock off machinery and electricity supply before work starts and until work has finished.
- No co-ordination between workers.
- Insufficient communication with other workers, supervisors or managers.
- Lack of perception of risk by workers, including failure to wear protective clothing or equipment.
- Inadequacy of design, installation, siting of plant and equipment.
- Use of contractors with no health and safety systems or who are inadequately briefed on health and safety aspects.

Figure 5-5: Conveyor. *Source: ACT.*

Figure 5-6: Electrical isolator with hole for padlock. *Source: ACT.*

Maintenance control measures

Isolation

This does not simply mean switching off the equipment using the stop button. It includes switching the equipment off at the start button and switching off the isolator for the equipment

In new workplaces, individual isolators should be used, i.e. each piece of equipment has its own isolator near to it. In the past, one isolator often governed several items of equipment making it impossible to isolate a single piece of equipment on its own.

Lock out & tag out

Isolation alone does not afford adequate protection because there is nothing to prevent the isolator being switched back on, or fuses being replaced inadvertently, while the person who isolated the item in the first place is still working on the equipment (and still in danger).

To ensure that this does not happen, the isolator needs to be physically locked in the off position (typically using a padlock, the key to be held by the person in danger). Multiple lock out devices that can carry a number of padlocks for the different people working on the equipment, are also available. It is also a good idea to sign **"Do not switch on..."** or tag the equipment.

Summary of control measures
- Plan work in advance - provide safe access, support parts of equipment which could fail.
- Use written safe systems of work, method statements or permit to work systems as appropriate.
- Plan specific operations using method statements.
- Use physical means of isolating or locking off plant.
- Systems of working should incorporate two-man working for high risk operations.
- Integrate safety requirements in the planning of specific high risk tasks.
- Prevent unauthorised access to the work area by using barriers and signs.
- Ensure the competence of those carrying out the work.
- Ensure the availability and use of appropriate personal protective equipment (PPE) - gloves, eye protection.
- Prevent fire or explosion - thoroughly clean vessels that have contained flammable solids or liquids, gases or dusts and check them thoroughly before hot work is carried out.

Procedures for defective equipment

Under section 7 of the HASAWA 1974, employees have a duty and should notify any shortcomings in the health and safety arrangements, even when no immediate danger exists, so that employers can take remedial action if needed. The duties placed on employees do not reduce the responsibility of the employer to comply with his own duties.

Under Regulation 5 of the PUWER 1998, "every employer shall ensure that work equipment is maintained in an efficient state, in efficient working order and in good repair". Regulation 6 of PUWER 1998 lays down requirements for inspecting work equipment to ensure that health and safety conditions are maintained and that any deterioration can be detected and remedied in good time. With duties being placed upon both the employer and the employee to ensure the use of safe equipment, when identified in the workplace, faulty equipment should be isolated until such a time repaired by a competent party.

REQUIREMENT FOR INSPECTION AND STATUTORY REQUIREMENTS FOR EXAMINATION OF BOILERS AND AIR RECEIVERS

Inspection and examination

PUWER Regulation 6 - inspection

"Every employer shall ensure that work equipment exposed to conditions causing deterioration which is liable to result in dangerous situations is inspected:

a) At suitable intervals.
b) Each time that exceptional circumstances which are liable to jeopardise the safety of the work equipment have occurred, to ensure that health and safety conditions are maintained and that any deterioration can be detected and remedied in good time.

Every employer shall ensure that the result of an inspection made under this regulation is recorded and kept until the next inspection under this regulation is recorded."

Figure 5-7: Inspection and examination.   Source: ACT.

Equipment should be inspected on a regular basis in order to confirm the condition that it is in. The inspection required is more than a simple daily pre-use check carried out by the operator. The person using equipment, who should be confirmed as competent, should carry out operator checks prior to the use of any equipment. Operator checks should include guards, cables, casing integrity, cutting or machine parts and safety devices such as cut-outs. The inspection required under this regulation should be significant and address a list of identifiable health and safety critical parts. For example the main items for inspection on a *dumper truck* that should be the subject of periodic inspection, include: the provision and condition of roll over protection and driver restraints (e.g. seat belts); the condition of the bodywork and seats; the condition of the tyres; the effectiveness of the braking system, steering and warning devices; the performance of the bucket release and tilt mechanisms; the integrity of fuel, oil and hydraulic systems and the legibility of labels and signs.

Similarly, the main items for regular (e.g. weekly) inspection of a 360^0 wheeled *excavator* include: hydraulic systems; wheels and tyres; windscreens and other windows; brakes and steering; the condition of bodywork and seats (including any seat belts); lights and visual warning devices; the condition of mirrors and other rear view equipment and the proper functioning of the controls.

The purpose of an inspection sheet is to record deterioration of specific parts, abuse and misuse and also to ensure that all items are considered at the time of inspection, by serving as a reminder. The results of the inspection will confirm whether or not a piece of equipment is in a safe enough condition to use. Other regulations, such as the Lifting Operations and Lifting Equipment Regulations (LOLER) 1998 require and set certain statutory inspection requirements. Note also that Regulation 6(5) of PUWER 1998 has been amended by the Work at Height Regulations (WAH) 2005 to include 'work equipment to which regulation 12 of the WAH 2005 applies'.

See also - Relevant statutory provisions - The Work at Height Regulations (WAH) 2005.

Examination of pressure systems - boilers and air receivers

A pressure system is, as defined in the Pressure Systems Safety Regulations, as follows:

- A system comprising one or more pressure vessels of rigid construction, and any associated pipework and protective devices.
- The pipework with its protective devices to which a transportable gas container is or is intended to be connected.
- A pipeline and its protective devices.

A pressure vessel is generally considered one which operates at a pressure greater than atmospheric pressure, e.g. steam boilers, receivers and air receivers.

Competent persons

The Pressure Systems Safety Regulations 2000 define the term competent person as a competent individual person (other than an employee) or a competent body of persons. There are three distinct functions of the competent person:

Figure 5-8: Air compressor.   Source: Speedy Hire plc.

1) Advising the user on the scope of the written scheme of examination.
2) Drawing up or certifying schemes of examination.
3) Carrying out examinations under the scheme.

It is the responsibility of all users to select a competent person who is capable of carrying out his duties in a proper manner. The competent person should have relevant knowledge and experience of the system. For complex systems, the competent person may be a number of different people for different parts of the system.

The examinations should be impartial and objective with the safety considerations and use of the system in mind.

Schemes of examination

Examination means a careful and critical scrutiny of a pressure system or part of a pressure system, in or out of service as appropriate. It means using suitable techniques, including testing where appropriate, to assess its actual condition and whether, for the period up to the next examination, it will not cause danger when properly used if normal maintenance is carried out.

Normal maintenance means such maintenance as it is reasonable to expect the user (in the case of an installed system) or owner (in the case of a mobile system) to ensure is carried out independently of any advice from the competent person making the examination.

A written scheme of examination must be available before any system is used. This should be established up by a competent person and include:

- Pressure vessels.
- Pipe work and valves.
- Protective devices.
- Pumps and compressors.

Examination intervals should be specified, though these may be different for different parts of the system, so that, for example, deterioration can be detected before danger arises. An initial examination should be done before use. Any repairs or modifications should be controlled. Factors to be taken into account when deciding upon the frequency of examination will include:

- Previous intervals and system records.
- Standards of supervision and routine checks.
- Type and quality of fluids in the system.
- The likelihood of creep, fatigue, etc. failures.
- Corrosion potential and effect.
- Presence of heat sources etc.

The type of examination should also be specified.

Examinations should be carried out in accordance with the written scheme and the system adequately assessed for fitness for continued use. Appropriate preparations for and precautions during examination should be arranged for by the user. A report with any conditions or limitations on use should be prepared on completion of the examination.

Where the competent person's examination identifies imminent danger then a report must be made to the user who should ensure the system is not used further and a report is sent to the relevant enforcing authority.

Anyone operating a pressure system must be given adequate and suitable instructions for safe operation and emergency action. This instruction should form part of the operating instructions for the plant and should include information on start-up, shutdown, normal operation, functions of controls and emergency procedures. Doors providing routine access should be dealt with by specific instructions covering interlocking checks, opening and closing precautions and failure signs. Precautions must be taken to prevent unintentional pressurisation of parts of any system not designed for pressure.

Routine and regular maintenance should be carried out including periodic checks and inspections of critical parts or components.

Adequate records of examinations, repairs, modifications etc., should be kept at the premises where the system is used.

Importance of operation and emergency controls

OPERATION AND EMERGENCY CONTROLS

PUWER Regulation 14 - Controls for starting or making a significant change in operating conditions

(1) Every employer shall ensure that, where appropriate, work equipment is provided with one or more controls for the purposes of -

(a) Starting the work equipment (including re-starting after a stoppage for any reason).

(b) Controlling any change in the speed, pressure or other operating conditions of the work equipment where such conditions after the change result in risk to health and safety which is greater than or of a different nature from such risks before the change.

(2) Subject to paragraph (3), every employer shall ensure that where a control is required by paragraph (1), it shall not be possible to perform any operation mentioned in sub-paragraph (a) or (b) of that paragraph except by a deliberate action on such control.

Paragraph (1) Shall not apply to re-starting or changing operating conditions as a result of the normal operating cycle of an automatic device.

Any change in the operating conditions should only be possible by the use of a control, except if the change does not increase risk to health or safety. Examples of operating conditions include speed, pressure, temperature and power.

The controls provided should be designed and positioned so as to prevent, so far as possible, inadvertent or accidental operation. Buttons and levers should be of appropriate design, for example, including a shroud or locking facility. It should not be possible for the control to 'operate itself' such as due to the effects of gravity, vibration, or failure of a spring mechanism.

PUWER Regulation 15 - Stop controls

(1) Every employer shall ensure that, where appropriate, work equipment is provided with one or more readily accessible controls the operation of which will bring the work equipment to a safe condition in a safe manner.

(2) Any control required by paragraph (1) shall bring the work equipment to a complete stop where necessary for reasons of health and safety.

(3) Any control required by paragraph (1) shall, if necessary for reasons of health and safety, switch off all sources of energy after stopping the functioning of the work equipment.

(4) Any control required by paragraph (1) shall operate in priority to any control, which starts or changes the operating conditions of the work equipment.

The primary requirement of this Regulation is that the action of the control should bring the equipment to a safe condition in a safe manner. This acknowledges that it is not always desirable to bring all items of work equipment immediately to a complete or instantaneous stop, for example, to prevent the unsafe build-up of heat or pressure or to allow a controlled run-down of large rotating parts. Similarly, stopping the mixing mechanism of a reactor during certain chemical reactions could lead to a dangerous exothermic reaction.

The Regulation is qualified by 'where necessary for reasons of health and safety'. Therefore, accessible dangerous parts must be rendered stationary. However, parts of equipment which do not present a risk, such as suitably guarded cooling fans, do not need to be positively stopped and may be allowed to idle.

PUWER Regulation 16 - Emergency stop controls

(1) Every employer shall ensure that, where appropriate, work equipment is provided with one or more readily accessible emergency stop controls unless it is not necessary by reason of the nature of the hazards and the time taken for the work equipment to come to a complete stop as a result of the action of any control provided by virtue of regulation 15(1).

(2) Any control required by paragraph (1) shall operate in priority to any control required by regulation 15(1).

Emergency stops are intended to effect a rapid response to potentially dangerous situations and they should not be used as functional stops during normal operation.

Emergency stop controls should be easily reached and actuated. Common types are mushroom-headed buttons, bars, levers, kick plates, or pressure-sensitive cables.

Figure 5-9: Controls and emergency stop.　　Source: ACT.　　Figure 5-10: Controls.　　Source: ACT.

PUWER Regulation 17 - Controls

(1) Every employer shall ensure that all controls for work equipment shall be clearly visible and identifiable, including by appropriate marking where necessary.

(2) Except where necessary, the employer shall ensure that no control for work equipment is in a position where any person operating the control is exposed to a risk to his health or safety.

(3) Every employer shall ensure where appropriate:

(a) That, so far as is reasonably practicable, the operator of any control is able to ensure from the position of that control that no person is in a place where he would be exposed to any risk to his health or safety as a result of the operation of that control, but where or to the extent that it is not reasonably practicable.

UNIT NCC1 - ELEMENT 5 - WORK EQUIPMENT - HAZARDS AND CONTROL

(b) That, so far as is reasonably practicable, systems of work are effective to ensure that, when work equipment is about to start, no person is in a place where he would be exposed to a risk to his health or safety as a result of the work equipment starting, but where neither of these is reasonably practicable.

(c) That an audible, visible or other suitable warning is given by virtue of regulation 24 whenever work equipment is about to start.

(4) Every employer shall take appropriate measures to ensure that any person who is in a place where he would be exposed to a risk to his health or safety as a result of the starting or stopping of work equipment has sufficient time and suitable means to avoid that risk.

It should be possible to identify easily what each control does and on which equipment it takes effect. Both the controls and their markings should be clearly visible. As well as having legible wording or symbols, factors such as the colour, shape and position of controls are important.

Warnings given in accordance with regulation 17(3) (c) should be given sufficiently in advance of the equipment actually starting to give those at risk time to get clear. As well as time, suitable means of avoiding the risk should be provided. This may take the form of a device by means of which the person at risk can prevent start-up or warn the operator of his/her presence. Otherwise, there must be adequate provision to enable people at risk to withdraw, e.g. sufficient space or exits. Circumstances will affect the type of warning chosen.

PUWER Regulation 18 - Control systems

(1) Every employer shall -
(a) Ensure, so far as is reasonably practicable, that all control systems of work equipment are safe.
(b) Are chosen making due allowance for the failures, faults and constraints to be expected in the planned circumstances of use.
(2) Without prejudice to the generality of paragraph (1), a control system shall not be safe unless -
(a) Its operation does not create any increased risk to health or safety.
(b) It ensures, so far as is reasonably practicable, that any fault in or damage to any part of the control system or the loss of supply of any source of energy used by the work equipment cannot result in additional or increased risk to health or safety; (c) It does not impede the operation of any control required by regulation 15 or 16.

Failure of any part of the control system or its power supply should lead to a 'fail-safe' condition (more correctly and realistically called 'minimised failure to danger'), and not impede the operation of the 'stop' or 'emergency stop' controls. The measures, which should be taken in the design and application of a control system to mitigate against the effects of failure, will need to be balanced against the consequences of any failure, and the greater the risk, the more resistant the control system should be to the effects of failure.

STABILITY

PUWER Regulation 20 - Stability

Every employer shall ensure that work equipment or any part of work equipment is stabilised by clamping or otherwise where necessary for purposes of health or safety.

Most machines used in a fixed position should be bolted or otherwise fastened down so that they do not move or rock during use. It has long been recognised that woodworking and other machines (except those specifically designed for portable use) should be bolted to the floor or similarly secured to prevent unexpected movement.

LIGHTING

PUWER Regulation 21 - Lighting

Every employer shall ensure that suitable and sufficient lighting, which takes account of the operations to be carried out, is provided at any place where a person uses work equipment.

Local lighting may be needed to give sufficient view of a dangerous process or to reduce visual fatigue.

MARKINGS AND WARNINGS

PUWER Regulation 23 - Markings

Every employer shall ensure that work equipment is marked in a clearly visible manner with any marking appropriate for reasons of health and safety

There are similarities between regulation 23 and 24 covering markings and warnings. Certain markings may also serve as a warning, e.g. the maximum working speed, maximum working load or the contents being a hazardous nature (e.g. colour coded gas bottles or service mains.

PUWER Regulation 24 - Warnings

Every employer shall ensure that work equipment incorporates any warnings or warning devices which are appropriate for reasons of health and safety

Warnings given by warning devices on work equipment shall not be appropriate unless they are unambiguous, easily perceived and easily understood.

Warnings and warning devices are introduced following the implementation of markings and other physical measures have been taken and an appropriate risk to health and safety remains. Warnings are usually in the form of a notice, sign or similar. Examples of warnings being positive instructions (hard hats MUST be worn), prohibitions (no smoking) and restrictions (do not heat above 60 degrees Celsius). Warning devices are active units that give out either an audible or visual signal, usually connected to the equipment in order that it operates only when a hazard exists.

CLEAR UNOBSTRUCTED WORKSPACE

Workplace (Health, Safety & Welfare) (WHSWR) Regulations 1992

Regulation 11 - Room dimensions and space

Every room where persons work shall have sufficient floor area, height and unoccupied space for purposes of health, safety and welfare.

Workrooms should have enough free space to allow people to get to and from workstations and to move within the room with ease. Workrooms should be of sufficient height (from floor to ceiling) over most of the room to enable safe access to workstations. In older buildings with obstructions such as low beams, the obstruction should be clearly marked.

The total volume of the room, when empty, divided by the number of people normally working in it, should be at least 11 cubic metres. In making this calculation a room or part of a room which is more than 3.0 m high should be counted as 3.0 m high. The figure of 11 cubic metres per person is a minimum and may be insufficient if, for example, much of the room is taken up by furniture.

Where work equipment, such as a circular saw, is used in a workplace care should be taken to ensure that adequate space is around the equipment to ensure it is not overcrowded and does not cause risk to operators and those passing by the equipment when it is operating.

Responsibilities of users

Management of Health and Safety at Work (MHSWR) Regulation 14 - Employees duties

Every employee shall use any machinery, equipment, dangerous substance, transport equipment, means of production or safety device provided to him by his employer in accordance both with any training in the use of the equipment concerned which has been received by him and the instructions respecting that use which have been provided to him by the said employer in compliance with the requirements and prohibitions imposed upon that employer by or under the relevant statutory provisions.

Employees have a duty under section 7 of the HASAWA 1974 to take reasonable care for their own health and safety, and for that of others who, may be affected by their acts or omissions and to co-operate with the employer to enable him to comply with statutory duties for health and safety. Employees should notify any shortcomings in the health and safety arrangements, even when no immediate danger exists, so that employers can take remedial action if needed. The duties placed on employees do not reduce the responsibility of the employer to comply with his own duties.

5.2 - Hand-held tools

Hazards and misuse of hand tools

Hand tools are tools powered manually, i.e. axes, hammers, screwdrivers; therefore the biggest hazard would arise from errors made by the user e.g. striking a finger whilst using a hammer or cuts from a saw.

Appropriate control measures for safe use

Hammers	Avoid split, broken or loose shafts (handles) and worn or chipped heads. Heads should be properly secured to the shafts.
Files	These should have a proper handle. Never use them as levers.
Chisels	The cutting edge should be sharpened to the correct angle. Do not allow the head of cold chisels to spread to a mushroom shape - grind off the sides regularly. Use a hand guard on the chisel.
Screwdrivers	Never use them as chisels, and never use hammers on them. Use the correct size and type of screwdriver for the screw. Split handles are dangerous.
Spanners	Avoid splayed jaws. Scrap any which show signs of slipping. Have enough spanners of the right size. Do not improvise by using pipes, etc., as extensions to the handle.

SUITABILITY FOR PURPOSE AND LOCATION

Use of alloy or bronze hammers or spanners to prevent sparks, and damping with water, in areas where there is a flammable atmosphere.

Hazards of portable power tools

PNEUMATIC DRILL / CHISEL

Pneumatic drills or chisels are used commonly where heavy duty tasks are performed such as penetrating tarmac or concrete surfaces. This equipment is usually very heavy and labour intensive, resulting in manual handling hazards and risks. The pneumatic energy is usually delivered through mobile industrial compressors that are capable of supplying adequate power.

The compressor is a separate piece of equipment that introduces its own specific hazards. Perhaps the most obvious hazard is the drill or chisel piece which, when operating presents a risk of impact injury to the operator's, and others nearby, feet. During normal operation, the drill or chisel tool produces high frequency and intensity noise from impact with the surface. Other noise includes the exhausting of the pneumatic pressure from the internal drive of the equipment as the tool operates. The noise sources are located very close to the operator's ears and are at a level that is damaging to the ear and requires the user to wear hearing protection. The operation of the chisel produces the hazard of flying debris in the form of dust and fragments that pose the risk of abrasion, cuts or eye damage. In order to control this risk the surface may be damped down and protective goggles worn by the user. The energy produced by the compressor is converted into vibration. Vibration introduces the risk of injuries such as hand arm vibration syndrome

(HAVS) with possible long term effects including damage to the nervous system beginning at the fingertips. Precautions for vibration include using well maintained equipment, using equipment with lower vibration levels, taking frequent breaks or job rotation, exercise to improve circulation and warm the hands and seeking suitable personal protective gloves. There are risks associated with high pressure air lines becoming broken or damaged resulting in pipes lashing freely. Equipment should always be inspected as safe to use with certification for pressure lines. Screens can be used as a final measure to protect others at the site of the works.

Figure 5-11: Eye injury & sparks.   *Source: Speedy Hire plc.*

Figure 5-12: Impact injury.   *Source: Speedy Hire plc.*

ELECTRIC DRILL

Electric drills are used for penetrating various materials and in construction are usually of a medium to heavy-duty nature. This equipment involves rotating shafts and tool bits, sharp tools, electricity and flying debris.

Hazards

Obvious hazards include shock and electrocution leading to possible fatalities - however this potential is reduced by using 110 volt or battery operated equipment. Other hazards include puncture, entanglement hazards, noise and dust.

Control

Control measures include using only equipment that is suitable for the task, ensuring equipment is tested and inspected as safe to use, suitable shut off and isolation measures, goggles, hearing protection. Care should be taken to ensure the drill bits are kept sharp as injuries can occur when the rotating drill bit gets stuck in material and the drill is caused to kick and rotate in the operator's hands.

DISC CUTTER

Disc cutters consist of a motor providing power to a circular cutting disc (made of stone or steel). Power is provided by petrol, diesel, electricity or pneumatic energy. This equipment is used for slicing materials into sections or cutting grooves into surfaces. Hazards include initially the power of the equipment which may result in shock and electrocution, fire, inhalation of fumes or absorption of hazardous substances. When in operation the disc of the cutter may spin at speeds ranging from 2900 revolutions per minute. Hazards arising from cutting operations or due to cutter discs exploding following misuse include flying debris, sparks and dust. Goggles must be worn when operating this equipment, due to the velocity of the flying debris they must be grade 1 impact resistant and totally enclose the eye region of the face. Dust masks must also be worn when using this equipment; however the area being cut into may be damped down to minimise the production of dust clouds into the atmosphere. Vacuum attachments are available that make these operation almost dust-less when working correctly. Sparks arising from cutting operations can result in a fire and in order to control this risk, good housekeeping practice is essential, sources of fuel must be removed from the work area. Misuse of this equipment includes using the side of the cutting disc, using over worn discs, using the incorrect disc for the material being cut, leaving the cutter with the disc still spinning and not wearing the appropriate personal protective equipment (PPE). The disc when spinning may provide cuts to cables, hands and legs; entanglement with rotating parts; noise and hearing damage.

CUT OFF SAW (CHOP SAW)

These saws are normally powered by electricity, however petrol motors are available. They consist of a motorised disc or saw blade, which has an enclosed guard. This is mounted on a counter sprung or a pneumatic arm which is operated by pulling down onto the materials to be cut. These are usually used to cut timber, aluminium and plastic into manageable lengths. Hazards associated with these saws are electric shock, fire, inhalation of fumes, dusts, metal shavings or small off-cuts. Only trained and competent workers should use this equipment due to the hazards, with a method of locking-off the equipment to prevent unauthorised use.

Goggles and protective clothing must be worn to prevent injuries from flying debris or dusts/fumes from harming the human body. The equipment should be isolated from the mains supply prior to changing any cutting discs or replacing saw blades.

SANDER

Hazards

Sanding equipment is available in a variety of sizes from hand held equipment to large industrial machines. Sanders are used to provide a smooth finished surface, using a mechanical abrasive action. Sanding operations are carried out on a wide variety of materials including wood, minerals such as marble and man-made fibres. The main hazards associated with the sanding process are vibration and noise. Also, harm can be caused by the inhalation of respirable particles from dust. Where organic materials such as wood are being processed, fire may result from overheated surfaces or explosion from dust by-products. Associated hazards may include electrocution if supply cables are damaged by hand held sanders, and particularly if the sander is placed on the ground whilst still rotating. Other risks include trips from training leads, cuts from sharp surfaces and strains or sprains from manual handling of process materials.

Control

When using sanding equipment, suitable personal respiratory protective equipment (RPE) is required to protect the user from the dust exposure. Where possible, local exhaust ventilation equipment should be used to minimise dust in the atmosphere. In order to protect against vibration injuries, the operator should be given regular breaks and the equipment maintained at intervals, including the renewal of sanding media to prevent the need for over exertion by the operator. Where hand held tools are used suitable hand protection will also reduce injuries from vibration, cuts and manual handling. Pre use inspections by the operator and regular thorough examinations should be carried out to identify potential electrical problems. Care should be taken to ensure that power leads do not create tripping hazards and they are positioned so that the likelihood of mechanical damage is minimised.

CARTRIDGE AND PNEUMATIC NAIL GUNS

Nail guns are used in many activities in construction including carpentry, steelwork, plastering and surveying. Power sources range from battery power, electrical low voltage, pneumatic and explosive cartridge. They are used for shooting nails or pins into or through materials in order to secure a section. The noise produced is high intensity impact noise which may be amplified by the material it is vibrating through. Personal hearing protection must be worn at all times due to the risk of hearing damage from the high intensity impact noise. Vibrations produced by the use of this equipment, which is grasped by hand, may risk possible effects of HAVS in sustained use. There is a significant risk of flying debris from nailing operations and impact injuries to eyes or flesh, in addition to the risk of puncture wounds from nails released incorrectly from the gun.

CHAINSAW

Chainsaws are potentially dangerous pieces of equipment which can cause major injuries and even death if not used correctly. The Approved Code of Practice supporting regulation 9 of the Provision and Use of Work Equipment Regulations 1998 (PUWER 98) 6 sets a minimum standard for competence of people using chainsaws in tree work. All employees should receive adequate and appropriate training and have obtained a relevant certificate of competence or a national competence award. Chainsaw operators should have regular refresher/update training to ensure they work to industry best practice and maintain their levels of competence. The suggested intervals for such training are: occasional users - every two to three years; full-time users - every five years. Maintenance schedules are essential for safe use and protection against ill health from excessive noise and vibration. The saw must be maintained in its manufactured condition with all the safety devices in efficient working order and all guards in place. It should be regularly serviced by someone who is competent to do the job. Operators should report any damage or excessive wear from daily checks. Suitable PPE is essential to protect the operator from hazards, this must comply with European standards for chainsaws (Protective clothing for hand held chain saw users BS381). Hazards associated with chainsaw use are noise, hand-arm vibration, falls, falling branches, sawdust and potential back problems.

Suitability for location

In explosive or flammable atmospheres only correctly rated anti-spark hand-held tools should be used. Electrical tools e.g. drills should be totally enclosed to prevent sparks from the motor igniting and causing explosions in flammable atmospheres. These tools are made from an alloy metal know commonly as 'gun metal' these do not cause sparks when in contact with other metals. A good example of this is fuel tanks on cars and petrol pumps.

Procedures for defective equipment

Under section 7 of the HASAWA, employees have a duty and should notify any shortcomings in the health and safety arrangements, even when no immediate danger exists, so that employers can take remedial action if needed. The duties placed on employees do not reduce the responsibility of the employer to comply with his own duties.

Under Regulation 5 of the PUWER, "every employer shall ensure that work equipment is maintained in an efficient state, in efficient working order and in good repair". Regulation 6 of PUWER lays down requirements for inspecting work equipment to ensure that health and safety conditions are maintained and that any deterioration can be detected and remedied in good time. With duties being placed upon both the employer and the employee to ensure the use of safe equipment, when identified in the workplace, faulty equipment should be isolated until such a time repaired by a competent party.

5.3 - Machinery hazards

Main mechanical and non-mechanical hazards

MECHANICAL HAZARDS

Entanglement

The mere fact that a machine part is revolving can in itself constitute a very real hazard. Loose clothing, jewellery, long hair, etc. increase the risk of entanglement. Examples of rotating action hazards include: couplings, drill chucks/ bits, flywheels, spindles and shafts (especially those with keys/bolts).

Figure 5-13: Auger drill - entanglement.   Source: STIHL.

Figure 5-14: Abrasion.   Source: ACT.

Friction and abrasion

Friction burns and encountering rough surfaces moving at high speed, e.g. sanding machine, grinding wheel etc., can cause abrasion injuries.

Figure 5-15: Chop saw - cutting.   Source: Speedy Hire plc.

Figure 5-16: Shear.   Source: ACT.

Cutting

Saw blades, knives and even rough edges, especially when moving at high speed, can result in serious cuts and even amputation injuries. The dangerous part can appear stationary! Examples of cutting action hazards include saws, slicing machines, abrasive cutting discs, chains (especially chainsaws) etc.

Shear

When two or more machine parts move towards/past, one another a "trap" is created. This can result in a crush injury or even an amputation. Examples of shearing/crushing action hazards include: scissor lifts, power presses, guillotines etc.

Stabbing and puncture

The body may be penetrated by sharp pieces of equipment, or material contained in the equipment, e.g. fixing materials such as nails fired into a part of the body, or a drill bit puncturing the hand.

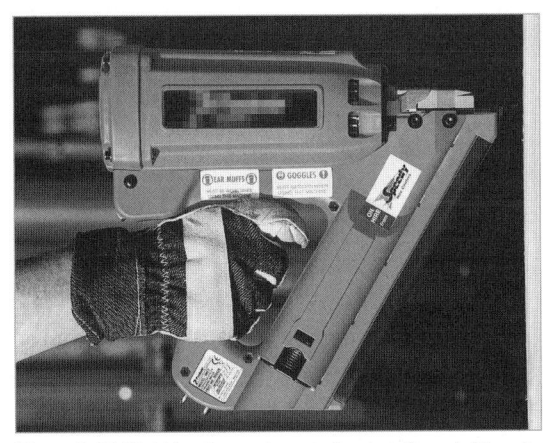

Figure 5-17: Stabbing & puncture.   Source: Speedy Hire plc.

Figure 5-18: Impact.   Source: ACT.

Impact

Impact is caused by objects that strike the body, but do not penetrate it. They may cause the person or part of the person to be moved, sometimes violently, resulting in injury e.g. struck by the jib of a crane/excavator or materials on a hoist or the moving platter of a machine like a surface grinder.

Figure 5-19: Crushing.   Source: ACT.

Figure 5-20: Drawing-in.   Source: ACT.

Crushing

Caused when part of the body is caught between either two moving parts of machinery or a moving part and a stationary object, e.g. the platform of hoist closing together with the ground or an overhead beam; moving parts of piling equipment or the callipers of a spot welding machine.

Drawing-in

When a belt runs round a roller an in-running nip is created between them (in the direction of travel); this inward movement draws in any part of the body presented to it. Examples of drawing-in (in-running / nip) hazards are V-belts - such as on the drive from a motor to the drum of a cement mixer, meshing gears and conveyors.

Figure 5-21: Disc saw - ejection.   Source: STIHL.

Figure 5-22: Fluid injection.   Source: ACT.

Ejection

When pieces of the material being worked on or components of the machinery are thrown or fired out of the equipment during operation they represent an ejection hazard. For example, parts of a shattered grinding wheel, sparks, swarf (waste metal trimmings) or a nail from a nail gun.

UNIT NCC1 - ELEMENT 5 - WORK EQUIPMENT - HAZARDS AND CONTROL

Injury by compressed air or high pressure fluid injection

Injection of fluids through the skin may lead to soft tissue injuries similar to crushing. Air entering the blood stream through the skin may be fatal. Examples are diesel injectors, spray painting, compressed air jets for blast cleaning the outside of a building and a high pressure lance for cutting concrete.

Check your understanding

Identify the mechanical hazards sketched in figure 5-23. Answers are given in figure 5-24.

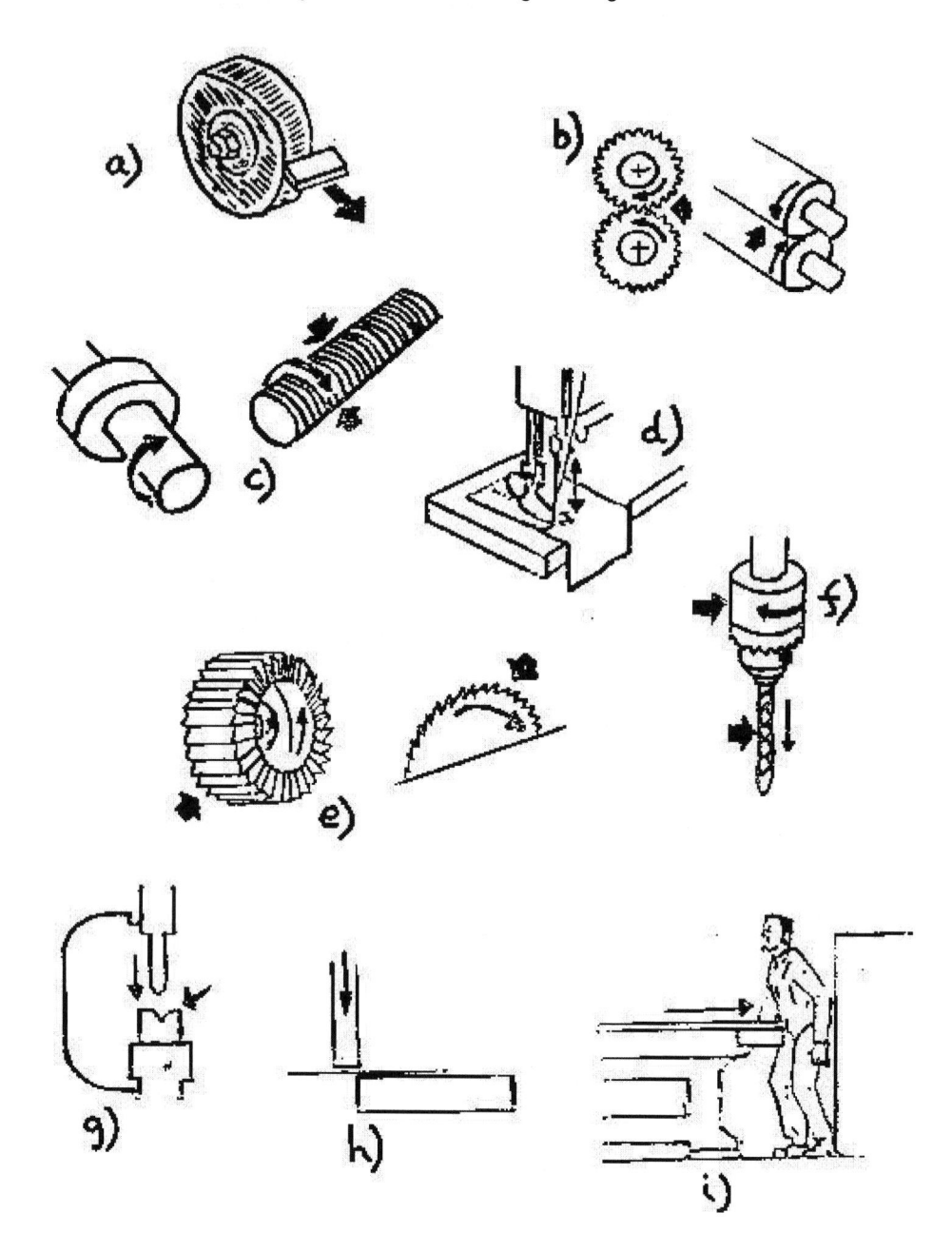

Figure 5-23: Examples of mechanical machinery hazards (Questions).
Source: ACT.

NON MECHANICAL HAZARDS

Machinery may also present other hazards. The nature of the hazard will determine the measures taken to protect people from them. The various sources of non-mechanical hazards include the following:

- Electricity - shock and burns.
- Hot surfaces / fire.
- Noise and vibration.
- Biological - viral and bacterial.
- High/low temperatures.
- Chemicals that are toxic, irritant, flammable, corrosive, explosive.
- Ionising and non ionising radiation.
- Access - slips, trips and falls; obstructions and projections.
- Manual handling.

SUMMARY - MACHINERY HAZARDS

Mechanical		**Non-mechanical**
Entanglement.	e.g. Auger drill, drilling machine.	Electricity.
Friction and abrasion.	e.g. Grinding wheel.	Hot surfaces / fire.
Cutting.	e.g. Sharp edges of circular saw.	Noise.
Shear.	e.g. Scissor lift mechanism.	Vibration.
Stabbing and Puncture.	e.g. Nail gun.	Extremes of temperature.
Impact.	e.g. Moving arm of an excavator.	Chemicals.
Crushing.	e.g. Platform of a hoist, ram of a forge hammer.	Radiation.
Drawing in.	e.g. Conveyor belt.	Access.
Injection.	e.g. High pressure hydraulic oil system.	Manual handling.
Ejection.	e.g. Grinding wheel - sparks.	

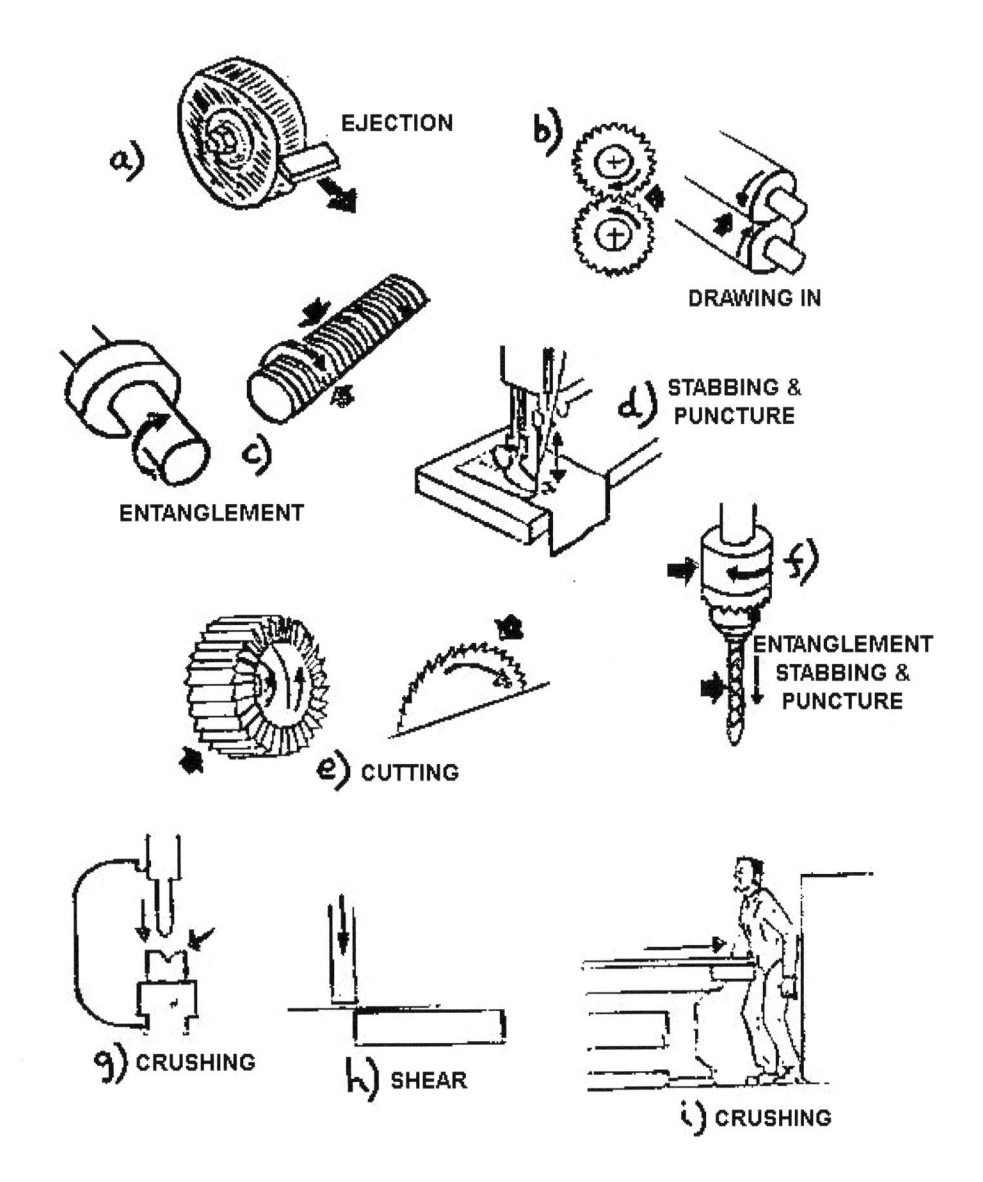

Figure 5-24: Examples of mechanical machinery hazards (Answers).

Source: ACT.

UNIT NCC1 - ELEMENT 5 - WORK EQUIPMENT - HAZARDS AND CONTROL

Hazards presented by a range of equipment

OFFICE MACHINERY

Photocopier
The hazards are drawing-in, hot surfaces, fumes, toner, electrical, manual handling, noise and glare.

Document shredder
The main hazards are drawing-in, cutting or crushing, and also cuts from paper handling and electrical dangers.

Figure 5-25: Abrasive wheel (grinder).   *Source: ACT.*

Figure 5-26: Pedestal drill.   *Source: ACT.*

WORKSHOP MACHINERY

Bench-top grinder
Bench top grinders are typically found in workshops (indoor use) and operators are required to be trained, competent and formally appointed in order to dress (re-surface) or change grinding wheels. Positioning of grinders should be at a suitable height to avoid poor posture whilst using them and they must be permanently fixed or bolted in position. Grinders may be used on construction sites when installed in a site mobile workshop. Tasks involve sharpening of tool bits (drills, chisels, blades), shaping steel, and de burring cut steel components lead to hazards including friction and abrasion from contact with the spinning wheel which can revolve at speeds in excess of 2,900 revolutions per minute, entanglement or drawing in (of fingers, gloves or other items being pulled between the rotating parts of the abrasive wheel and rest) and possible ejection when parts of the wheel or work piece break and sparks are thrown off. Other hazards are electricity, heat and noise.

Pedestal drill
Hazards in setting up the equipment include failure to remove chuck-key which may cause it to fly off in use and failure to secure guard to drive pulleys. Hazards when the equipment is in use include entanglement, puncture and flying swarf.

Bench-mounted circular saw
Cutting is the main hazard together with electricity, noise and sawdust.

Figure 5-27: Bench cross-cut circular saw.   *Source: ACT.*

Figure 5-28: Cement mixer.   *Source: ACT.*

Hand fed power planer
Hazards include noise, cuts and severs, dust, impact from flying debris, fire and electrocution.

Spindle moulding machine
Hazards include noise, cuts, entanglement and fire.

SITE MACHINERY

Compressor

Pneumatic compressors are a source of power for a variety of portable equipment used in construction activities. Tools that can source power from compressors include drills and chisels, saws, nail guns, mixing equipment and plasterer's surface scotchers. Whilst this list of tools is not exhaustive, the principle remains the same in that power is delivered through a high pressure air line to the tool and converted into mechanical power. Pneumatic compressors are typically large pieces of mobile plant that attach to the towing bar of a road going works vehicle. When at site, a compressor is free standing, only attached to the tool by the pressure air line.

Hazards arise from the fuelling of the plant (normally diesel) where contact with the skin can occur, splashes into eyes, inhalation of fumes and the possible risk of fire where hot temperatures are involved. In operation, the compressor produces exhaust gases from the motor which may, in addition to the fuel, require an assessment in compliance with the Control of Substances Hazardous to Health Regulations (COSHH) 2002. Noise and vibration at high levels may be produced from the compressor although these levels may vary dependant upon the effectiveness of the soundproofing material incorporated into the plant in addition to the condition of the equipment and frequency of maintenance programmes that may exist. This equipment also involves pressure lines that provide a trip hazard.

Cement mixer

Cement mixers are portable construction plant used for mixing a variety of aggregates and cement used in the construction process. The main benefit of this equipment is removing a significant volume of the manual labour aspect of the mixing process although a significant amount of labour intensive activities remain.

The equipment consists of a motor (electric, petrol or diesel) linked through a gear box and drive shaft to a rotating drum that incorporates internal mixing blades to aid the mixing process. The assembly may vary from a complete unit that pivots on a central bar or a two part system where the mixer is seated onto a plinth or stand and pivots forward to enable emptying of the drum when the mixture is complete.

Hazards arise from the source of power when electricity is combined with the water used in the mixing process.

In order to control this risk, a low voltage power supply should be used, with suitable heavy duty cable and cable covers when there is a risk of running over them with vehicles or plant. Used with a residual current protection device a good level of protection can be obtained. When the fuel source is diesel or petrol there is a risk of fire, which increases during refuelling operations when the exhaust system may still be hot or people may be smoking in the close vicinity of the equipment.

The rotating drum and drive shaft poses an entanglement risk with personal protective equipment and other tools. If covers are removed they can expose drive belts or gearing with the associated risk of drawing in. Operatives loading mixers should be warned of the dangers of shovels and trowels becoming caught in the mixer blades and snatching the hand tool out of the operatives hand with force, which may result in personal injury to limbs and muscles. Loading the mixer is a manual task which can result in injury from repetitive, twisting motion when emptying shovels or gauging buckets into the mixer. Job rotation should be planned. Assessments as required by the COSHH 2002 Regulations may be required for the fumes and dusts involved in the mixing process. Often the mixing activity is a slow process, operatives tend to leave the mixer running alone until the mix is ready. If the equipment is left running and unattended there is a risk of unauthorised access to the mixer and injuries to third parties. As the mixing process proceeds there is a likelihood of build up of materials on the floor, leading to a risk of slips and trips and a possibility of falling onto the moving equipment.

Figure 5-29: Cement mixer.   *Source: ACT.*

Figure 5-30: Ground consolidation equipment.   *Source: ACT.*

Plate compactor

Plate compactors are a simple machine used for consolidating aggregates or loose materials. They are also used for securing block paviors into position by applying a heavy downward force through a flat plate where the force is increased by the vibrating motion. They operate on the principle of a motor that rotates a cam through a drive belt which provides the vibration force. Upon first appearances from a distance, operators would appear to look as though they are operating a lawn mower as the equipment is walked up and down the surface to be compacted, with the vibration providing the drive, assisted by the operator. Hazards arise from the source of power, typically petrol, which has associated fire risks that are increased through refuelling operations when the exhaust system is still hot. This equipment, because of its purpose, has to be heavy which brings a risk of manual handling strain injuries when loading or unloading from a vehicle.

Ground consolidation equipment

Ground consolidation equipment serves the same purpose as a plate compactor. However, a plate compactor is generally for lighter duty than the large types of ground consolidation equipment such as man riding rollers or manual rollers. This heavy duty type of equipment requires competence and authorisation in order to use it on site. Ground consolidation equipment moves at a greater speed than lighter duty equipment and its power drives the equipment directly through the roller wheel. The potential harm from the drawing in / crush hazards are high, a crush sustained from a piece of this plant could more easily lead to a major injury or fatality.

Road-marking equipment

Road making equipment includes all of the previously described equipment in addition to heavy duty items such as road planers, excavators, piling equipment etc. Hazards posed from this type of equipment include impact and crush of pedestrians, impact and collision with other plant or site vehicles, contact with buried services, contact with or arc (electrical discharge) from overhead cables and possible collapse of the ground at excavations, voids or sewers. The equipment may have other forms of specific hazard, including - entanglement in drive shafts, impact from flying fragments, fumes and exhaust gases, shear or cutting risk and falls from the equipment.

5.4 - Appropriate control measures for machinery hazards

MACHINERY GUARDING

Objective of machinery guarding

- To prevent work people from coming into contact with dangerous parts of machinery.
- To prevent physical injury from power driven and manually operated machines.
- To enable machines to be operated safely without interference with production.

PUWER Regulation 11 - Dangerous parts of machinery

Every employer shall ensure that measures are taken in accordance with paragraph (2) which are effective - to prevent access to any dangerous part of machinery or to any rotating stock-bar; or

(b) To stop the movement of any dangerous part of machinery or rotating stock-bar before any part of a person enters a danger zone.

(2) The measures required by paragraph (1) shall consist of-

(a) the provision of fixed guards enclosing every dangerous part or rotating stock-bar where and to the extent that it is practicable to do so, but where or to the extent that it is not, then

(b) The provision of other guards or protection devices where and to the extent that it is practicable to do so, but where or to the extent that it is not, then

(c) The provision of jigs, holders, push-sticks or similar protection appliances used in conjunction with the machinery where and to the extent that it is practicable to do so, but where or to the extent that it is not, then

(d) The provision of information, instruction, training and supervision.

(3) All guards and protection devices provided under sub-paragraphs (a) or (b) of paragraph (2) shall -

(a) Be suitable for the purpose for which they are provided;

(b) Be of good construction, sound material and adequate strength;

(c) Be maintained in an efficient state, in efficient working order and in good repair;

(d) Not give rise to any increased risk to health or safety;

(e) Not be easily bypassed or disabled;

(f) Be situated at sufficient distance from the danger zone;

(g) Not unduly restrict the view of the operating cycle of the machinery, where such a view is necessary;

(h) Be so constructed or adapted that they allow operations necessary to fit or replace parts and for maintenance work, restricting access so that it is allowed only to the area where the work is to be carried out and, if possible, without having to dismantle the guard or protection device.

(4) All protection appliances provided under sub-paragraph c) of paragraph (2) shall comply with sub-paragraphs (a) to (d) and (g) of paragraph (3).

(5) In this regulation - "danger zone" means any zone in or around machinery in which a person is exposed to a risk to health or safety from contact with a dangerous part of machinery or a rotating stock-bar; "stock-bar" means any part of a stock-bar which projects beyond the headstock of a lathe.

Notes:

- Regulation 11(2) gives the measures that an employer should take to fulfil the duty under regulation 11(1). They have in the past been used pragmatically. A combination of measures may be necessary to satisfy regulation 11.
- When deciding on the appropriate level of safeguarding, risk assessment criteria i.e. likelihood of injury, potential severity of injury, numbers at risk, need to be considered both in relation to the normal operation of the machinery and also other operations such as maintenance, repair, setting, tuning, adjustment etc. Further information is given in machine-specific and sector-specific guidance.
- Regulation 11(2)(d) is particularly important where guards, protection devices and jigs are not effective in preventing access and a significant residual risk of injury remains. However, apart from supervision, there is duplication with the requirements in regulations 8 and 9.
- Regulation 11(3)(c) applies to the maintenance of guards and protection devices and will include those which are not attached to the machine itself, e.g. perimeter fences. However, regulation 5, which also covers maintenance, is particularly relevant to CE marked equipment.

The principles, merits and limitations of protection methods

HIERARCHY OF MEASURES FOR DANGEROUS PARTS OF MACHINERY
- Prevent access to dangerous parts by means of **F**ixed guard (preferably fully enclosing).
- When the above is not practicable protect by other guards (**I**nterlock, **A**utomatic) or safety devices (e.g. **T**rip device).
- When the above is not practicable protect by using safety appliances (e.g. push stick or jig).
- When the above is not practicable protect by information, instruction and training.
- The various guards and safety devices can be summarised as follows:

    F ixed

    I nterlock

    A utomatic

    T rip devices

FIXED GUARDS

A fixed guard/fence must be fitted such that it cannot be removed other than by the use of specialist tools which are not available to operators of the equipment. A fixed guard may be designed to enable access by authorised personnel for maintenance or inspection, but only when the dangerous parts of the machine have been isolated. A common example of a fixed guard is shown in figure 5-32. The holes in the mesh guard are of sufficient size to allow air circulation to cool the drive belt, but small enough to prevent the finger of the hand from penetrating the mesh and result in injury from the belt.

Distance (fixed) guard

Fixed guards do not completely cover the danger point but place it out of normal reach. The larger the opening (to feed in material) the greater must be the distance from the opening to the danger point. A tree shredding machine uses a fixed distance guard design to prevent operators reaching the dangerous part of a machine when in use.

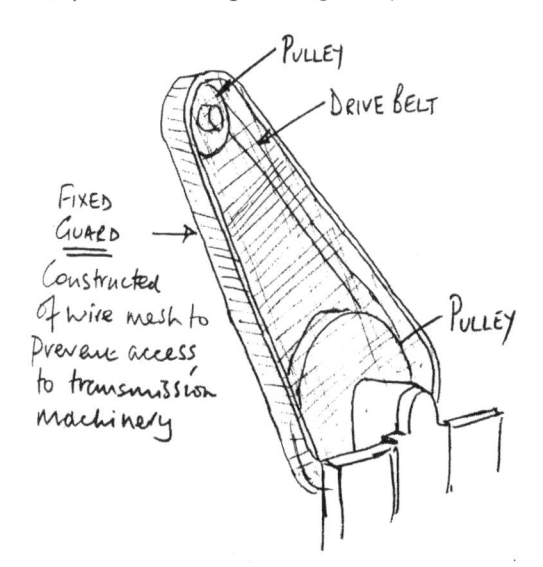

Figure 5-31: Fixed guard (hand drawn example). *Source: ACT.*

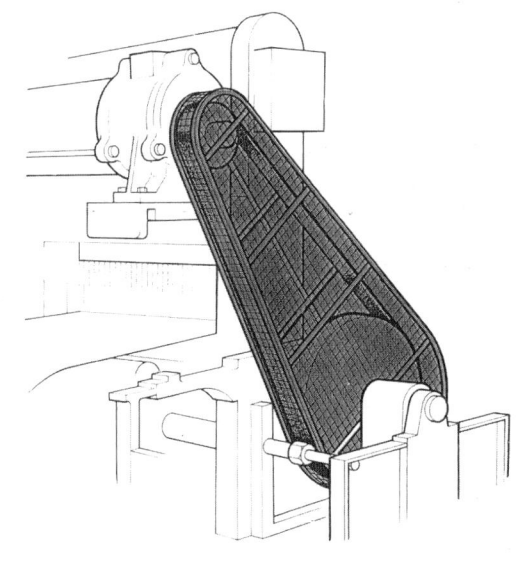

Figure 5-32: Total enclosure fixed guard. *Source: BS EN ISO 12100.*

Figure 5-33: Fixed guard - panel removed. *Source: ACT.*

Figure 5-34: Fixed guard over fan - mesh too big. *Source: ACT.*

Merits of fixed guards
- Create a physical barrier.
- Require a tool to remove.
- Can protect against non-mechanical hazards such as dust and fluids which may be ejected.
- No moving parts - therefore they require very little maintenance.

Limitations of fixed guards
- Do not disconnect power when not in place; therefore machine can still be operated without guard.

- May cause problems with visibility for inspection.
- If enclosed, may create problems with heat.

INTERLOCKED GUARDS

An interlocked guard is similar to a fixed guard, but has a movable (usually hinged) part, so connected to the machine controls that if the movable part is in the open/lifted position the dangerous moving part at the work point cannot operate. This can be arranged so that the act of closing the guard activates the working part (to speed up work efficiently), e.g. the front panel of a photocopier. Interlocked guards are useful if operators need regular access to the danger area.

Merits of interlocked guards
- Connected to power source; therefore machine cannot be operated with guard open.
- Allow regular access.

Limitations of interlocked guards
- Have moving parts therefore need regular maintenance.
- Can be over-ridden.
- If interlock is in the form of a gate, a person can step inside and close gate behind them (someone else could re-activate machine).
- Dangerous parts of machinery may not stop immediately the guard is opened. A delay timer or brake might need to be fitted as well, e.g. the drum on a spin drier does not stop instantly when the door is opened.

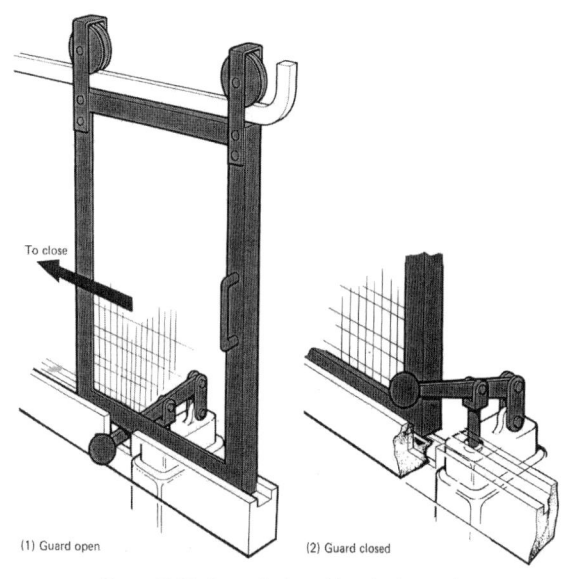

Figure 5-35: Open & closed interlock guard.
Source: BS EN ISO 12100.

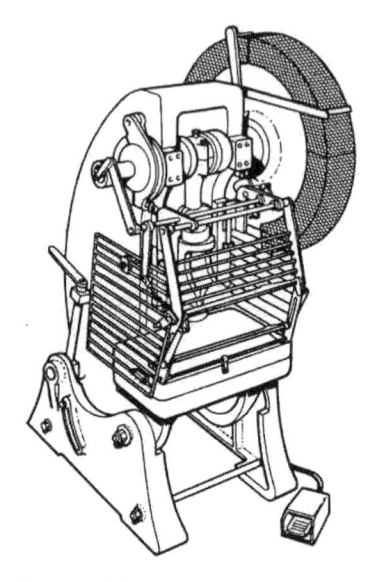

Figure 5-36: Power press - interlock guard.
Source: BS EN ISO 12100.

TRIP DEVICES

A sensitive rod, cable or other mechanism, which causes the device to activate a further mechanism which either stops or reverses the machine. It is important to note that this is not classed as a guard. A guard is something that physically prevents access to the hazard whereas a trip device detects the person in the danger zone and responds to this e.g. pressure sensitive mats.

Merits of trip devices
- Can be used as an additional risk control measure.
- Can minimise the severity of injury.

Limitations of trip devices
- Can be over-ridden.
- May not prevent harm from occurring.
- May cause production delays and increase stress in users with false 'trips'.

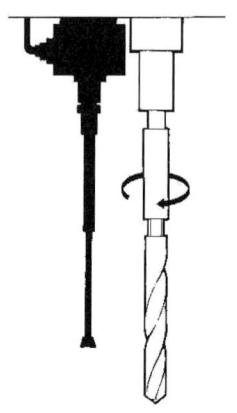

Figure 5-37: Trip device. *Source: BS EN ISO 12100.*

Figure 5-38: Trip device on radial drill. *Source: ACT.*

ADJUSTABLE GUARD

A fixed guard which incorporates an adjustable element (which remains fixed for the duration of a particular operation).

SELF ADJUSTING GUARD

Guards which prevent accidental access by the operator, but allow entry of the material to the machine in such a way that the material actually forms part of the guarding arrangement itself. For example, a hand held circular saw.

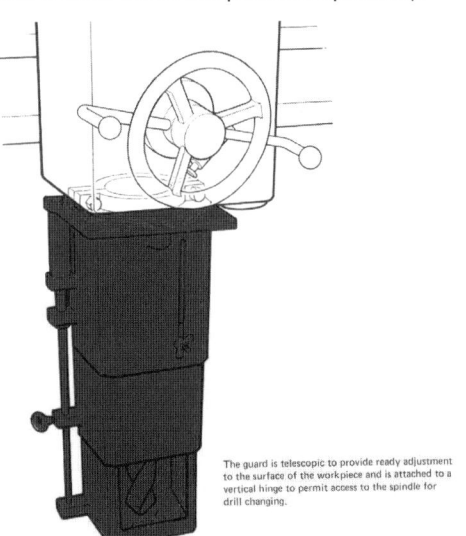

Figure 5-39: Adjustable (fixed) guard.   *Source: BS EN ISO 12100.*

Figure 5-40: Self adjusting (fixed) guard.   *Source: ACT.*

Merits of adjustable guards
- Can be adjusted by operator to provide protection.

Limitations of adjustable guards
- Are reliant on the operator to adjust to the correct position.
- May obscure visibility when in use.

TWO-HAND CONTROL (2HC) DEVICE

They provide a level of protection where other methods are not practicable, helping to ensure the operators' hands remain outside the danger area. A two handed control is a device that requires both hands to operate it. '2HC' devices protect only the operator of the equipment. This protection can be limited if the user gains assistance from someone else to activate one control leaving the other hand free to be moved into danger. Examples of equipment where two-hand control devices are used are hedge trimmers and garment presses.

Merits of two hand control devices
- Ensures both of the operator's hands are out of the danger area when the machine is operated.

Limitations of two hand control devices
- Only protects the operator from harm.
- May limit speed of operation, with delays if controls are not pressed at exactly same time.

Figure 5-41: Fixed guard.   *Source: ACT.*

Figure 5-42: Fixed guard and push stick.   *Source: Lincsafe.*

PROTECTIVE APPLIANCES

When the methods of safeguarding mentioned above are not practicable then protection appliances such as jigs, holders and push-sticks must be provided. They will help to keep the operator's hands at a safe distance from the danger area. There is no physical restraint to prevent the operator from placing their hands in danger.

Merits of protection appliances
- Provide distance between operator and hazard.

UNIT NCC1 - ELEMENT 5 - WORK EQUIPMENT - HAZARDS AND CONTROL

Limitations of protection appliances
- Harm may still occur from other non-mechanical hazards.
- Failure of protection appliance (e.g. breaking or kickback) may present additional hazard to operator.

EMERGENCY STOP CONTROLS

Emergency stops are intended to effect a rapid response to potentially dangerous situations and they should not be used as functional stops during normal operation.

Emergency stop controls should be easily reached and actuated. Common types are mushroom-headed buttons, bars, levers, kick plates, or pressure-sensitive cables.

Merits
- Removes power immediately.
- Equipment has to be reset after use.
- Prevents accidental restarting of the equipment.

Limitations
- Does not prevent access to the danger area.
- May be incorrectly positioned.

PERSONAL PROTECTIVE EQUIPMENT (PPE)

The Personal Protective Equipment at Work (PPER) Regulations 1992 governs the provision of PPE. PPE is a last resort and should only be relied upon when other controls do not adequately control risks. The use of machinery presents a number of mechanical hazards and care has to be taken that PPE is not used in situations where they present an increased risk of entanglement or drawing in to machinery, such as might happen with loose overalls and gloves.

Main examples are:

- Eye protection (safety spectacles / glasses, goggles and face shields) - protection for the eyes and face from flying particles, welding glare, dust, fumes and splashes.
- Head protection (safety helmets or scalp protectors i.e. bump caps) - protection from falling objects, or the head striking fixed objects.
- Protective clothing for the body (overalls) - protection from a wide range of hazards.
- Gloves (chain mail gloves and sleeves) - protection against cuts and abrasions when handling machined components, raw material or machinery cutters.
- Footwear (steel in-soles and toe-caps) - protection against sharp objects that might be stood on or objects dropped while handling them.
- Ear protection for noisy machine operations.

Merits
- Easy to see if it is being worn.
- Provides protection against a variety of hazards.

Limitations
- Only protects the user.
- May not give adequate protection.
- May pose additional hazards e.g. gloves becoming entangled.

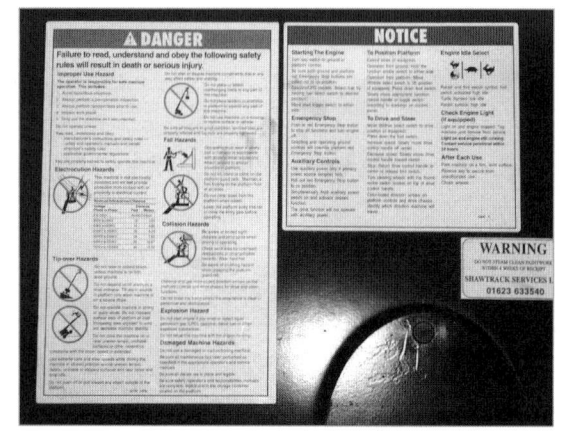

Figure 5-43: Information and instruction. Source: ACT.

Figure 5-44: PPE and supervision. Source: ACT.

INFORMATION, INSTRUCTION, TRAINING AND SUPERVISION

PUWER 1998 requires every employer to ensure that all persons who use work equipment and any of his employees who supervise or manage the use of work equipment have available to them adequate health and safety information and, where appropriate, written instructions pertaining to the use of the work equipment.

This includes information and, where appropriate, written instructions that are comprehensible to those concerned on:

- The conditions in which and the methods by which the work equipment may be used.
- Foreseeable abnormal situations and the action to be taken if such a situation were to occur.
- Any conclusions to be drawn from experience in using the work equipment.

Similarly PUWER 1998 requires employers to ensure that all persons who use work equipment and any of his employees who supervises or manages work equipment have received work equipment, any risks which such use may entail and precautions to be taken.

It is a requirement of the HASAWA 1974 that supervision be provided as necessary to ensure the health and safety of employees (and others).

Merits
- Easy to reach a wide audience on a variety of subjects.

Limitations
- Relies entirely on the person concerned to follow the instruction.
- May be misunderstood.

Application of protection methods to a range of equipment listed

Appropriate precautions (In addition to suitable instruction, information and training together with PPE).

OFFICE MACHINERY

Photocopier

Avoid loose clothing i.e. ties, signage for hot components, well ventilated / suitable extraction, gloves, isolate from power source, training in good practice when removing paper jams etc.

Document shredder

Interlocked guards and trip wires.

WORKSHOP MACHINERY

Bench-top grinder

Fixed and / or adjustable guards together with PPE.

Pedestal drill

Pre-use:
- Drive pulley entanglement prevented by isolation from power.
- Check that chuck key is removed before use.

During use:
- Prevent entanglement - close fitting clothing, control of long hair and removal of jewellery.
- Puncture prevented by jigs or clamping devices.
- Adjustable guard, face shield / goggles for protection from flying swarf.

Bench-mounted circular saw
- Guarding for crown and front of the saw, and for the part of the saw below the bench.
- Riving knife fitted at rear of the saw above the bench.
  Use of jigs/holders or push sticks where appropriate.
- Need for a table extension to ensure distance of at least 1.2m between edge of saw and end of table if an assistant is employed at the back of the bench.

Hand fed power planer
- Use of a suitable bridge guard, adjusted according to the operation being undertaken.
- Use clamps to secure to a stable platform.
- Keep tools sharp and clean.

Spindle moulding machine

No single type of guard or other safety device can deal adequately with the variety of work which can be done on a spindle moulding machine. Each job must be considered individually to provide the most effective protection. Comprehensive guidance is contained in the HSE Information Sheet (Woodworking Sheet No. 18) 'Safe Working Practices at Vertical Spindle Moulding Machines.'

SITE MACHINERY

Compressor
- Hose couplings fitted with pins or chains.
- Hoses, couplings inspected as part of daily plant inspection.
- Noise control equipment fitted to compressor.

Cement mixer

Interlocked and adjustable guards.

Plate compactor
- Use a remote-control rather than a hand-guided one to reduce risks from hand-arm vibration.
- Take regular breaks to reduce exposure or rotate use among several people.
- A safe system of work for handling this equipment may be required which could include; a hoist on site vehicles and a trolley to manoeuvre around the site.

Ground consolidation equipment

Control measures include segregation of pedestrians and plant using barriers, warning signs and close supervision.

Road-marking equipment

This equipment requires special training and authorisation for its safe use. Where this equipment is being used, barriers, warning signs and lighting is to be used, in addition to supervision.

When this equipment is being used it is normally a requirement to have refuelling facilities available on site. When this is the case suitable isolation from sources of heat should be ensured, with only authorised operatives allowed to carry out refuelling activities.

Basic requirements for guards and safety devices

PUWER REGULATION 11 PARAGRAPH 3 - EFFECTIVE GUARDS AND DEVICES

All guards and protection devices provided under sub-paragraphs (a) or (b) of paragraph (2) shall:

a) Be *suitable* for the purpose for which they are provided.
b) Be of *good construction*, sound material and adequate strength.
c) Be *maintained* in an efficient state, in efficient working order and in good repair.
d) Not give rise to any *increased risk* to health or safety.
e) Not be *easily bypassed* or disabled.
f) Be situated at *sufficient distance* from the danger zone.
g) Not unduly *restrict the view* of the operating cycle of the machinery, where such a view is necessary.
h) Be so constructed or adapted that they allow operations necessary to fit or replace parts and for maintenance work, restricting access so that it is allowed only to the area where the work is to be carried out and, if possible, without having to dismantle the guard or protection device.

COMPATIBLE WITH PROCESS

Compatibility with the material being processed - this is particularly important in the food processing industry where the guard material should not constitute a source of contamination of the product. Its ability to maintain its physical and mechanical properties after coming into contact with potential contaminants such as cutting fluids used in machining operations or cleaning and sterilising agents used in food processing machinery is also very important. In selecting an appropriate safeguard for a particular type of machinery or danger area, it should be borne in mind that a fixed guard is simple, and should be used where access to the danger area is not required during operation of the machinery or for cleaning, setting or other activities. As the need for access arises and increases in frequency, the importance of safety procedures for removal of a fixed guard increases until the frequency is such that interlocking should be used.

ADEQUATE STRENGTH

Guard mounting should be compatible with the strength and duty of the guard. In selecting the material to be used for the construction of a guard, consideration should be given to the following:

- Its ability to withstand the force of ejection of parts of the machinery or material being processed, where this is a foreseeable danger.
- Its ability to provide protection against hazards identified. In many cases, the guard may fulfil a combination of functions such as prevention of access and containment of hazards. This may apply where the hazards include ejected particles, liquids, dust, fumes, radiation, noise, etc. and one or more of these considerations may govern the selection of guard materials.

MAINTAINED

All guards must be maintained in effective order to perform their function. This will require a planned approach to checks on guards and work such as checking the security of fixed guards.

ALLOW MAINTENANCE WITHOUT REMOVAL

Its weight and size are factors to be considered in relation to the need to remove and replace it for routine maintenance.

NOT INCREASE RISK OR RESTRICT VIEW

Any guard selected should not itself present a hazard such as trapping or shear points, rough or sharp edges or other hazards likely to cause injury.

Power operated guards should be designed and constructed so that a hazard is not created.

NOT EASILY BY-PASSED

Guards or their components must not be easily by-passed, in particular by operators. There is always a temptation to do so when under production or similar pressures. When siting such things as interlock switches it is best to locate them away from the operator and preferably within the guard.

Element 6

Electrical - hazards and control

Learning outcomes

On completion of this element, candidates should be able to demonstrate understanding of the content through the application of knowledge to familiar and unfamiliar situations. In particular they should be able to:

6.1 Identify the hazards and evaluate the risks from the use of electricity in the workplace.

6.2 Describe the appropriate control measures that should be taken when working with electrical systems or using electrical equipment.

6.3 Outline the appropriate control measures to be taken when working near or underneath overhead power lines.

Content

6.1 - Hazards and risks associated with electricity at work 91
    Principles of electricity 91
    Hazards and risks of electricity 92
    Portable electrical equipment 95
6.2 - Appropriate control measures 96
    Selection and suitability of equipment 96
    Emergency procedures following an electrical incident 97
    Proper planning and installation of a progressively extending electrical system on site 97
    Advantages and limitations of protective systems 98
    Inspection and maintenance strategies 101
6.3 - Appropriate control measures for overhead power line hazards 103
    Avoidance where possible 103
    Pre-planning and consultation with service provider 103
    Ground level barriers 104
    Restriction of equipment/vehicle reach 104

Sources of reference

Electrical safety on construction sites (HSG141), HSE Books ISBN 0-7176-1000-4
Electricity at work - safe working practices (HSG85), HSE Books ISBN 0-7176-2164-2
Maintaining portable and transportable electrical equipment (HSG107), HSE Books ISBN 0-7176-2805-1
Memorandum of guidance on the Electricity at Work Regulations 1989 (HSR25), HSE Books ISBN 0-7176-1602-9

Relevant statutory provisions

The Electricity at Work Regulations (EWR) 1989
The Health and Safety (First-Aid) Regulations (FAR) 1981
The Reporting of Injuries, Diseases and Dangerous Occurrences Regulations (RIDDOR) 1995

6.1 - Hazards and risks associated with electricity at work

Principles of electricity

Electricity is a facility that we have all come to take for granted, whether for lighting, heating, as a source of motive power or as the driving force behind the computer. Used properly it can be of great benefit to us, but misused it can be very dangerous and often fatal.

Electricity is used in most industries, offices and homes and our modern society could now not easily function without it. Despite its convenience to the user, it has a major danger. The normal senses of sight, hearing and smell will not detect electricity, making contact with exposed conductors at the supply voltage of 240V potentially lethal.

Unlike many other workplace accidents, the actual number of electrical notifiable accidents is small. However, with a reported 10-20 fatalities each year, the severity is high. Accidents are often caused by complacency, not just by the normally assumed ignorance. It must be recognised by everyone working with electricity that over half of all electrical fatal accidents are to skilled/competent persons. In order to avoid the causes of electric injury, it is necessary to understand the basic principles of electricity, what it does to the body and what controls are necessary.

BASIC CIRCUITRY

The flow of electrons through a conductor is known as a current. Electric current flows due to differences in electrical "pressure" (or potential difference as it is often known), just as water flows through a pipe because of the pressure behind it. Differences in electrical potential are measured in V.

In some systems the current flows continually in the same direction. This is known as direct current (DC). However the current may also constantly reverse its direction of flow. This is known as alternating current (AC). Most public electricity supplies are AC. The UK system reverses its direction 50 times per second and it is said to have a frequency of 50 cycles per second or 50 Hertz (50Hz). DC is little used in standard distribution systems but is sometimes used in industry for specialist applications. Although there are slight differences in the effects under fault and shock conditions between AC and DC it is a safe approach to apply the same rules of safety for the treatment and prevention of electric shock.

As a current passes round a circuit under the action of an applied voltage it is impeded in its flow. This may be due to the presence in the circuit of resistance, inductance or capacitance, the combined effect of which is called impedance and is measured in ohms.

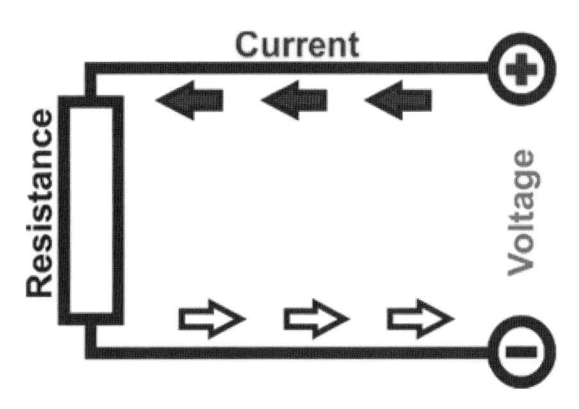

Figure 6-1: A basic electrical circuit.   Source: ACT.

RELATIONSHIP BETWEEN VOLTAGE, CURRENT AND RESISTANCE

There is a simple relationship between electrical pressure (V), current (measured in Amperes or milliamperes) and resistance (measured in Ohms) represented by Ohm's Law:

Voltage **(V)** = current **(I)** multiplied by the circuit resistance **(R)**. $V = I \times R$ or $I = \dfrac{V}{R}$

Hence, given any two values the third can be calculated. Also, if one value changes the other two values will change accordingly.

This basic electrical equation can be used to calculate the current that flows in a circuit of a given resistance.

This will need to be done to determine, for example, the fuse or cable rating needed for a particular circuit. Similarly, the current that will flow through a person who touches a live conductor can be calculated.

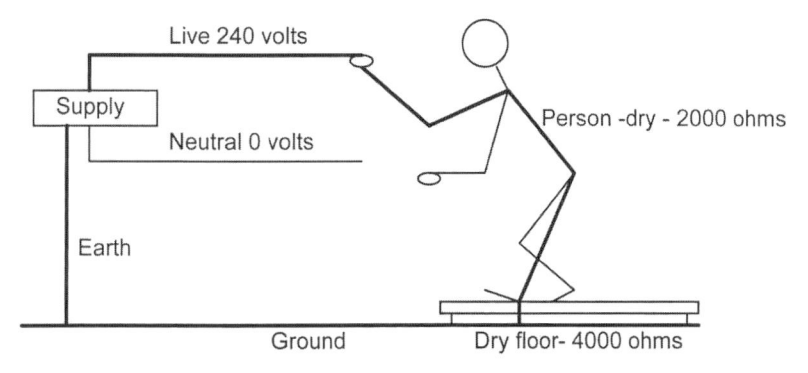

Figure 6-2: An electric circuit under fault conditions showing resistances in the path of a fault current.   Source: R. Gilmour.

By Ohm's law:

Current = $\dfrac{\text{Voltage}}{\text{Resistance}}$ or $I = \dfrac{V}{R}$

Resistance in a circuit is dependent on many factors. Most metals, particularly precious metals (silver, gold, platinum), allow current to pass very easily. These have a low resistance and are used as conductors. Other materials such as plastics, rubber and textiles have a high resistance and are used as insulators.

If the person is on, say, a dry concrete floor, resistance in the body will only be about 2,000 Ohms and the resistance in the floor about 4,000 Ohms; therefore the combined resistance would be 6,000 Ohms. Presuming the person is in contact with a live electrical supply at 240V the current flowing through the person in this fault condition can be calculated.

$$I = \frac{V}{R} = \frac{240 \text{ Volts}}{2,000 + 4,000 \text{ Ohms}} = 0.04 \text{ Amperes}$$

The current flowing through the operator will be about 0.04 Amperes or 40mA (40 milliAmperes). This could result in a fatal shock.

Hazards and risks of electricity

The consequences of contact with electricity are:

- *Shock* - resulting from the current flowing through the body interfering with muscle and central nervous system functions.
- *Electrical burns* - resulting from the heating effect of the current which burns the body tissue.
- *Electrical fires* - caused by overheating or arcing apparatus in contact with a fuel.
- *Explosions* - from sparks in a flammable atmosphere.
- *Secondary injuries* - falling from a ladder.

ELECTRIC SHOCK AND ITS EFFECT ON THE BODY

Factors influencing severity

The severity of electric shock or the amount of current which flows for a given voltage will depend on the frequency of the supply voltage, on the level of the voltage which is applied and on the state of the point of contact with the body, particularly the moisture condition.

Current

The current that flows through the body provides the energy to do the harm, the more current flowing the more harm likely to be done. The body can tolerate small levels of current flowing through it, but as the level increases the current is able to have a greater effect on the body, in particular the muscles. As such, low currents tend to influence only the smaller muscles and the larger muscles need a larger current to influence them. The effects on the muscle will be to cause it to spasm; therefore small muscles in the hand may contract causing the hand to close or at higher current flow larger muscles in the chest may contract restricting breathing. When the heart is affected by the current flow its normal beat may be disrupted and it attempts to beat in a discordant manner, this effect is known as fibrillation. It should be remembered that the level of current necessary to cause harm to the body is much less than that required to run most equipment and is in mA rather than Amperes.

Voltage

Voltage is the driving force behind the flow of electricity, somewhat like pressure in a water pipe. The correct name for this term is potential difference as a voltage is the measure of the difference in electrical energy between two points. Any electrical charge that is free to move about will move from the higher energy to the lower one, taking a bit of that energy difference with it.

Frequency

The frequency of current flow in an alternating current supply, such as the mains supply in an office block, operates at 50 cycles per second. This frequency is close to that of the heart when functioning normally. It can have the effect of disrupting the operation of the heart causing it to beat in a discordant manner, to fibrillate.

Duration

For an electric shock to have an effect a person needs to be in contact with the current for sufficient time. At low current levels the body tolerates the current so the time is not material, however at higher current levels, e.g. 50mA, the person has to remain in contact for sufficient time to affect the heart, in the order of milliseconds. In general, the longer a person is in contact with the current the more harm may be caused.

Resistance

The amount of resistance in a circuit influences the amount of current that is allowed to flow, as explained above by Ohm's law. It is possible for a person to be in contact with a circuit and to present sufficiently high resistance, that very little current is allowed to flow through their body. The example shown above illustrates this. It should be noted that the level of current is also dependent on the voltage; at high voltages an enormous amount of resistance is needed to ensure current flow will remain at a safe level. The human body contributes part of the resistance of a circuit, the amount it contributes depends on the current path taken and other factors such as personal chemical make-up (a large portion of the body is water), dryness and thickness of skin, and any clothing that is being worn, such as shoes and gloves.

Current path

The effect of an electric shock on a body is particularly dependent on the current path through the body. Current has to flow through from one point to another as part of a circuit. If the flow was between two points on a finger the effect on the body would be concentrated between the two points. If the current path is between one hand and another across the chest this means the flow will pass through major parts of the body, such as the heart, and may have a specific effect on it. In a similar way a contact between hand and foot (feet) can have serious effects on a great many parts of the body, including the heart. These latter current paths tend to be the ones leading to fatal injuries. Workers should be reminded that, although many may experience shock from 240V this may not be fatal if they were, for example, standing on or wearing some insulating material. This may be a matter of fortune and should not be relied on.

Effects of current flowing in the human body

Current (mA)	Length of time	Likely effects [mA = milliAmperes mS = milliseconds]
0-1	Not Critical.	Threshold of feeling. Undetected by person.
1-15	Not Critical.	Threshold of cramp. Independent loosening of the hands no longer possible.
15-30	Minutes.	Cramp-like pulling together of the arms, breathing difficult. Limit of tolerance.
30-50	Seconds to minutes.	Strong cramp-like effects, loss of consciousness due to restricted breathing. Longer time may lead to fibrillation.
50-500	Less than one heart period (70 mS).	No fibrillation. Strong shock effects.
	Greater than one heart period.	Fibrillation. Loss of consciousness. Burn marks.
Over 500	Less than one heart period.	Fibrillation. Loss of consciousness. Burn marks.

Figure 6-3: Effects of current flowing in the human body.   *Source: ACT.*

Causes of electric shock

Direct shock. Contact with a charged or energised conductor that is intended to be so charged or energised. In these circumstances the installation is operating in its normal or proper condition.

Indirect shock. Contact with a conductor or exposed conductive parts e.g. casing of the apparatus that is normally safe to touch but which, under fault conditions, could become dangerously live.

Common causes of electric shock

- Work on electrical circuits by unqualified persons.
- Work on live circuits.
- Replacement of fuses and light bulbs on supposedly dead circuits.
- Working on de-energised circuits that could accidentally be re-energised.

Figure 6-4: Electrical equipment near water.   *Source: ACT.*

Figure 6-5: Contact with high voltage buried cable. *Source: ACT.*

First aid treatment for electric shock

With electricity, of typically the reported accidents each year, 75 per year are thought to be fatal. The severity of accidents involving electricity therefore merits detailed study of their causes and development in order to prevent them. The first aid treatment points listed in this section are for guidance only and are not a substitute for a qualified first-aider with knowledge of the workplace.

Figure 6-6: Risk of electric shock due to damage to cable. *Source: ACT.*

Figure 6-7: Work on live circuits.   *Source: ACT.*

UNIT NCC1 - ELEMENT 6 - ELECTRICAL - HAZARDS AND CONTROL

In case of electrical shock:

Do

- Switch off or remove the plug.
- Check that there is no remaining connection to the supply and, if possible, prove that the system is discharged and dead.
- Assess the situation and any remaining danger to yourself or the casualty.
- Call for qualified support which may mean the 999 emergency services.
- If safe, check the casualty's response (What is the degree of consciousness?).

Check

A - Airway   -   Is it open?

B - Breathing   -   Is the casualty breathing normally?

C - Circulation   -   Does the casualty have a normal pulse?

Action

If airway obstructed by teeth, food etc., remove; if tongue tilt head back to clear, and then provide cardio pulmonary resuscitation (CPR).

If trained, place in the recovery position and/or apply resuscitation as required. Cool any burns with cold water.

Keep the casualty under observation for secondary effects until you hand over to a medically qualified person.

Do not

Do not go near the casualty until the electricity supply is proven to be off. This is especially important with overhead high voltage lines: keep yourself and others at least 18 metres away until the electricity supply company personnel advise otherwise.

Do not delay - after 3 minutes without blood circulation irreversible damage can be done to the casualty.

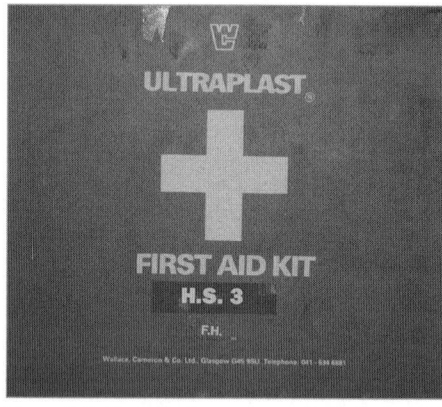

Figure 6-8: First aid sign.   Source: ACT.

Do not wait for an accident to happen - train in emergency procedures and first aid, plan procedures for an emergency (calling for help, from the emergency services, meeting ambulances and leading them to the casualty) as seconds saved may save a life. Hold emergency drills.

ELECTRICAL BURNS

Direct

There will be a heating effect along the route taken by electric current as it passes through body tissue. Whilst there are likely to be burn marks on the skin at the point of contact there may also be a deep seated burning within the body which is painful and slow to heal. As the outer layer of skin is burnt the resistance decreases and so the current will increase. The current flowing through the body can cause major injury to internal organs and bone marrow as it passes through them.

Indirect

If while working on live equipment the system is short-circuited by, for example, an un-insulated spanner touching live and neutral this will result in a large and sudden current flow through the spanner. This current will cause the spanner to melt and may throw molten metal out from the points of contact. When this molten metal contacts the parts of a person in the vicinity of the spanner, for example the hands or face, serious burns can take place as the molten metal hits and sticks to the person. With high voltages and the very low resistance of the spanner very large currents can flow. This rapid discharge of energy that follows contact with high voltages not only causes the rapid melting of the spanner but does so with such violent force that the molten particles of metal are thrown off with huge velocity. It is not necessary to have high voltages to melt a spanner in this way - it can also occur with batteries with sufficient stored energy, such as those on a fork lift truck. There are many experiences of people suffering injury in this way when servicing lift truck batteries as a spanner falls out of their overall top pocket.

ELECTRICAL FIRES

Common causes

Much electrical equipment generates heat or produces sparks and this equipment should not be placed where this could lead to the uncontrolled ignition of any substance.

The principal causes of electrical fires are:

- Wiring with defects such as insulation failure due to age or poor maintenance.
- Overheating of cables or other electrical equipment through overloading with currents above their design capacity.
- Incorrect fuse rating.
- Poor connections due to lack of maintenance or unskilled personnel.

Electrical equipment may itself explode or arc violently and it may also act as a source of ignition of flammable vapours, gases, liquids or dust through electric sparks, arcs or high surface temperatures of equipment. Other causes are heat created by poorly maintained or defective motors, heaters and lighting.

Figure 6-9: Used coiled up - risk of overheating. Source: ACT.

Figure 6-10: Max current capacity exceeded. Source: ACT.

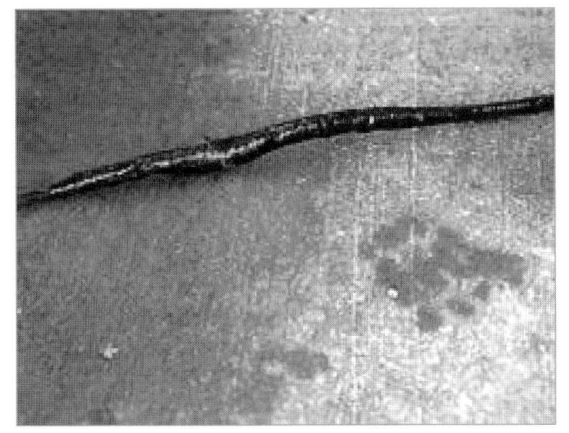

Figure 6-11: Worn cable - risk of electrical fire. Source: ACT.

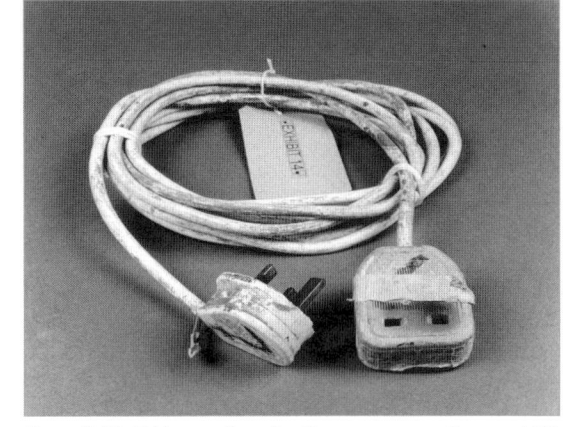

Figure 6-12: Evidence of overheating. Source: ACT.

SECONDARY HAZARDS (INCLUDING FALLS FROM HEIGHTS)

Secondary hazards occur where the injury results from the flow of electricity through the body's nerves, muscles and organs and causes abnormal function to occur. Muscular spasm may be severe, particularly if the leg muscles are affected, causing a person to be thrown several metres. Injuries may result from dislocation, impact with surrounding objects or fall from a height. In addition, a tool may be dropped causing such injuries as burns or impact injury to the user or others nearby.

Portable electrical equipment

Conditions and practices likely to lead to accidents

Unsuitable equipment
- Unsuitable apparatus for the duty or the conditions.
- Misuse.
- Failure to follow operating instructions.
- Wrong connection of system - supply phase, neutral or earth reversed.
- Wrong voltage or rating of equipment.

Inadequate maintenance
- Inadequate maintenance of the installation and the equipment.
- Wrong or broken connection to portable apparatus.
- Inadequate earthing.
- Poor maintenance and testing.
- No defect reporting system.

Use of defective apparatus
- Faulty cables, notably extension leads.
- Plugs and sockets.
- Damaged plug or socket.
- Protection devices, such as fuses or circuit breaker, incorrect rating, damaged or missing.
- Overloaded leading to damage or overheating.
- Short circuit leading to damage, overheating or movement.
- Isolation procedures or systems of work wrong.
- Bad circuit connections.

General
- Lack of competence.
- Poor access, lighting and emergency procedures.
- No work planning, e.g. permit-to-work.

Figure 6-13: Hazard - fuse wired out.   Source: ACT.

Figure 6-14: Continued use of defective equipment. Source: ACT

Figure 6-15: Hazard - damaged cable.   Source: ACT.

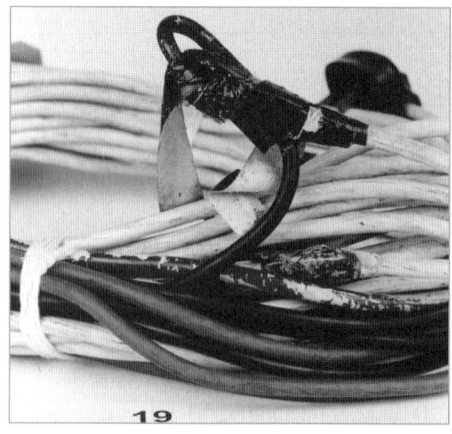

Figure 6-16: Hazard - taped joints.   Source: ACT.

6.2 - Appropriate control measures

Selection and suitability of equipment

The British Standard BS 7671, the Institute of Electrical Engineers (IEE) 16th edition requirements, Chapter 13 - 'Fundamental requirements for safety' - specifies the following needs. Good workmanship and proper materials shall be used. Construction, installation, inspection, testing and maintenance shall be such as to prevent danger. Equipment shall be suitable for the power demanded and the conditions in which it is installed. Additions and alterations to installations shall comply with regulations. Equipment, which requires operation or attention, shall be accessible.

The Low Voltage (Safety) Regulations place a duty on the supplier of equipment to ensure that equipment using between 50 and 100V AC is safe.

Construction, including flexible cables and cords, must be to European Union (EU) accepted good engineering practice standards. The Regulations are deemed satisfied if the equipment bears a recognised standard mark, certificate or other acceptable authorisation. Supply of unsafe equipment or components is prohibited.

It is important to ensure that all electrical equipment is suitable. For example, if it is to be used for outdoor work on a construction site in conditions that it might get wet, equipment providing protection from the ingress of water must be selected. Many tools are designed and provided for use in a domestic situation and they may not be suitable for use in the more arduous conditions of a construction site, for example, cable entry grips may be more secure and outer protection of cables thicker on equipment designed for construction work. Part of the selection process is to determine situations where low voltage, such as 110V systems, can be used in preference to 240V. HSG85 Electricity at Work-Safe Working Practices gives guidance on the frequency of inspection for such equipment.

CABLES AND LEADS

Insulation appropriate to the environment should be used to give resistance to abrasion, chemicals, heat and impact. The insulation must be in good condition. Flexible, multi-strand cables are required for portable tools and extension leads. Extension leads must be fused.

Cables must be secured by the outer sheath at their point of entry into the apparatus, including plugs. The individual conductor insulation should not show through the sheath and conductors certainly must not be exposed even through cuts may only be opened when the cable is bent. Temporary wiring should be used in compliance with standards and properly secured, supported and mechanically protected against damage. Attention to cables in offices is particularly important to avoid tripping hazards with phone, computer, calculator and kettle leads growing in number.

Taped joints in cables are not allowed and proper line connectors must be used to join cables. Connectors should be kept to a minimum to reduce earth path impedance.

Conductors across roads or pedestrian ways should be covered to protect them from damage. Where they are to cross a doorway this is usually best done by taking it around the door instead of trailing it across the floor.

Overhead cables likely to be hit by vehicles or persons carrying ladders, pipes etc. should be highlighted by the use of appropriate signs. Where necessary to protect them, cables should be protected in armoured sheath or run in protective conduit or trunking. Many cables are set up on a temporary basis but get left for a considerable time with improvised arrangements. Care should be taken to identify true short term temporary arrangements and those that warrant full longer term arrangements such as placing in trunking.

Regular examination should be made for deterioration, cuts, kinks or bend damage (particularly near to the point of entry into apparatus), exposed conductors, overheat or burn damage, trapping damage, insulation embrittling or corrosion.

Emergency procedures following an electrical incident

Following an incident the electricity supply should have been switched off, unplugged or isolated. Checks should be carried out by a competent person to ensure the electricity supply is dead. The casualty should have received suitable first-aid treatment; this could mean dialling 999 for the emergency services. A formal written incident report should be completed and recorded in the site or premises accident book. Risk assessments should be formally reviewed and updated, with any findings or recommendations communicated to all employees. Other sites run by the company should also have the new risk assessments provided. Additional training may be required to prevent any future occurrences. This should be scheduled with an approved training provider (if required).

Proper planning and installation of a progressively extending electrical system on site

Electricity in construction brings numerous hazards that require stringent planning and control systems. Prior to starting construction activities at the planning stage consideration must be given to factors including buried services, electricity sub-stations or proximity to overhead cables. A site may have existing buildings and tests must be made to determine whether existing services are live or dead. At the planning stage, a full site survey will include identifying the location of any electrical sources or conductors.

Planning also provides the ideal opportunity to ensure that where electricity is involved, the correct measures are implemented to control risk. This may include location of plant, planning cable runs or ducts, whether high or low voltage is required, control features when in use (switch panels, isolation, and lock off), protection devices (earthing arrangements, trip switches, residual current devices, panel housings, warnings and instructions). Maintenance should play a key part in the planning stage, with consideration given to access, isolation, lock-off and security.

When construction activities start heavy mechanical plant will be introduced that may operate in close proximity to sources of electricity. Safe systems should be introduced to include ensuring that sufficiently safe distances are maintained from overhead cables to prevent electrical 'arc' (discharge) from the uninsulated cables. Safe systems may include permits-to-work, 'goal post' type visual barriers, information for site workers and signs. There may be activities that involve explosive atmospheres that require intrinsically safe equipment to be used (e.g. work is sewers or chambers).

Most industrial installations work on high voltage systems due to increased consumption of electricity during the many different processes. Owing to economic advantages, industrial sites commonly include their own dedicated power sub-stations that operate at voltages typically in ranges of 11kV. This high voltage is then transformed down into values more commonly in the range of 415v. When working with high voltage circuitry, staff must be 'high voltage' trained and work under a permit to work system.

Figure 6-17: Construction site generator.   *Source: ACT.*

Figure 6-18: Construction site power supply panel.   *Source: ACT.*

It is essential that the planning and installation of electrical systems reflect not only the power needs but the lighting needs of the site as well. The plan should include anticipated needs or demand as the site changes, for example, extending provision as a structure is built or orderly withdrawal of provision as a structure is demolished. Planning should ensure power is available at key points as close to where work is carried out that requires it, thus minimising the need for extension cables to run for long distances. Planning should take account of where it is not practicable to provide a permanent system and where local power generation is more suitable. In this case the same planning is required to ensure the system provided is adequate for the demands. In some cases this will require the provision of a quantity of small generators to ensure the right amount of power is available where it is needed.

If work is to be conducted in someone else's building that is occupied and power is to be obtained by adapting the system within the building, consideration has to be given to the effects on the host's power supply of this additional demand. Care should be taken to ensure that power is drawn from agreed points and at agreed, safe voltages. Where practicable systems provided for construction work should run at 110V or lower and should be set into place at the earliest safe opportunity; in many cases this can be integrated into ground works that is planned for the site. If systems are to be left in place at the end of the work, and they do not form part of the system for the structure constructed, care should be taken to identify them on plans and if they are to be left 'dead' they should be checked to ensure this is the case.

Figure 6-19: 110v generator.   *Source: ACT.*

Figure 6-20: 110v extension lead.   *Source: ACT.*

PERMIT TO WORK PROCEDURES AND REQUIREMENTS

A permit to work is an official, documented safe system of work that is used for controlling high risk activities. Implementation is required prior to work beginning to ensure that all precautions are taken and are securely in place to prevent danger to the workforce. When managed correctly, a permit to work prevents any mistakes or deviations through poor communication; by stating the specific requirements of the task. For electrical systems, a permit to work is typically used for those rated at or in excess of 240v or where there is more than one point or means of isolation.

The authorised person issues the permit to work and will sign the document to declare that all isolations are made and remain in place throughout the duration of the task. In addition to this, the authorised person will make checks to ensure that all controls to be implemented by the acceptor are in place before work begins

The acceptor of the permit to work assumes responsibility for carrying out the work on the electrical system. The acceptor signs the document to declare that the terms and conditions of the permit to work are understood and will be complied with fully at all times by the entire work team. Compliance with a permit to work system includes ensuring the required safeguards are implemented and that the work will be restricted to only the equipment stated within the document.

Items included in the electrical permit to work are:

- Permit issue number.
- Authorised person identification.
- Points at which isolation is made.
- Test procedure and confirmation of dead circuitry.
- Warning information sign locations.
- Earth connection points.
- Details of the work to be carried out.
- Signature of authoriser.
- Signature of acceptor.
- Signature for works clearance / extension / handover.
- Signature for cancellation.
- Other precautions (risk assessments, method statements, and personal protective equipment).

Figure 6-21: Power supply isolation.   *Source: ACT.*

Advantages and limitations of protective systems

FUSE

This is a device designed to automatically cut off the power supply to a circuit within a given time when the current flow in that circuit exceeds a given value. A fuse may be a rewireable tinned copper wire in a suitable carrier or a wire or wires in an enclosed cartridge.

In effect it is a weak link in the circuit that melts when heat is created by too high a current passing through the thin wire in the fuse case. When this happens the circuit is broken and no more current flows. Fuses tend to have rating in the order of Amperes rather than mA which means it has *limited usefulness in protecting people from electric shock.* Fuses may also operate slowly if the current is just above the fuse rating. Using too high a fuse means that the circuit will remain intact and the equipment will draw power. This may cause it to overheat leading to a fire or if a fault exists the circuit will remain live and the fault current may pass through the user of the equipment when they touch or operate it.

The following formula should be used to calculate the correct rating for a fuse:

$$\text{Current (Amperes)} = \frac{\text{Power (watts)}}{\text{Voltage (volts)}}$$

For example, the correct fuse current rating for a 2-kilowatt kettle on a 240-volt supply would be:

$$\frac{2{,}000\ W}{240\ V} = 8.33A$$

Typical fuses for domestic supply voltages of 240V are 3,5,10 and 13 Ampere ratings.

The nearest fuse just above this current level is 10A.

	Typical examples of power ratings are:	Suitable fuses at 240 V:
Computer processor.	350 Watts.	3 Amperes.
Electric kettle.	1,850-2,200 Watts.	10 - 13 Amperes.
Dishwasher.	1,380 Watts.	10 Amperes.
Refrigerator.	90 Watts.	3 Amperes.

Summary

- A weak link in the circuit that melts slowly when heat is created by a fault condition. However, this usually happens too slowly to protect people.
- Easy to replace with wrong rating.
- Needs tools to replace.
- Easy to override by replacing a fuse with one of a higher rating or putting in an improvised 'fuse', such as a nail, that has a high rating.

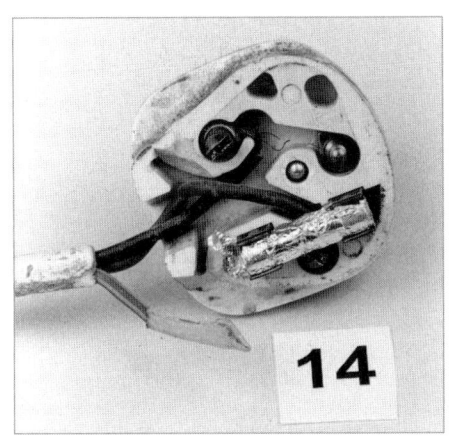

Figure 6-22: Plug-foil fuse no earth.   *Source: ACT.*

Figure 6-23: Earthing.   *Source: ACT.*

EARTHING

A conductor called an earth wire is fitted to the system; it is connected at one end to a plate buried in the ground and the other end connected to the metal casing of the equipment. If for any reason a conductor touches the casing so that the equipment casing becomes 'live' the current will flow to the point of lowest potential, the earth. The path to this point (earth) is made easier as the wire is designed to have very little resistance. This **may prevent electric shock** provided it is used in association with a correctly rated fuse, or better still a residual current device (RCD), and no one is in contact with the equipment at the time the fault occurs. It should be remembered that earthing is provided where the casing can become live. If the equipment is designed so that this cannot be the case, such as double insulated equipment where the user touches non-conducting surfaces, earthing of the equipment is no advantage. In summary, earthing provides a path of least resistance for "stray" current and provides protection against indirect shock.

ISOLATION

Isolation of an electrical system is an excellent way of achieving safety for those that need to work on or near the system; for example, isolation of a power supply into a building that is to be refurbished or isolation of plant that is to be maintained. In its simplest form it can mean switching off and unplugging a portable appliance at times it is not in use. Care must be taken to check that the isolation has been adequate and effective before work starts; this can include tests on the system. It is also important to ensure the isolation is secure; 'lock off' and 'tag out' systems will assist with this.

REDUCED LOW VOLTAGE SYSTEMS

One of the best ways to reduce the risk from electricity is to reduce the voltage. This is frequently achieved by the use of a transformer (step down) which will reduce the voltage. A common reduction is from the supply mains voltage of 240V to 110V. Normally, transformers that are used to reduce voltage are described as "centre tapped to earth". In practice this means that any voltage involved in an electrical shock will be 55V.

Using the earlier example of Ohms Law, if the voltage is 240V then:

$$I = \frac{V}{R} = \frac{240 \text{ Volts}}{2{,}000 + 4{,}000 \text{ Ohms}} = 0.04 \text{ Amperes or } 40 \text{ mA}$$

However, if a centre tapped to earth transformer is used then,

$$I = \frac{V}{R} = \frac{55 \text{ Volts}}{2{,}000 + 4{,}000 \text{ Ohms}} = 0.009 \text{ Amperes or } 9 \text{ mA}$$

Reference to figures 6-2 and 6-3 will clearly show how this **reduces the effects of electric shock** on the body.

An alternative to reduction in voltage by means of a transformer is to provide battery-powered equipment; this will commonly run on 12V-24V but voltages may be higher. The common method is to use a rechargeable battery to power the equipment which eliminates the need for a cable to feed power to the equipment and gives a greater flexibility of use for the user, e.g. for drills and power drivers.

UNIT NCC1 - ELEMENT 6 - ELECTRICAL - HAZARDS AND CONTROL

Figure 6-24: 110V centre tapped earth transformer. *Source: ACT.*

Figure 6-25: Battery powered drill - 12V. *Source: ACT.*

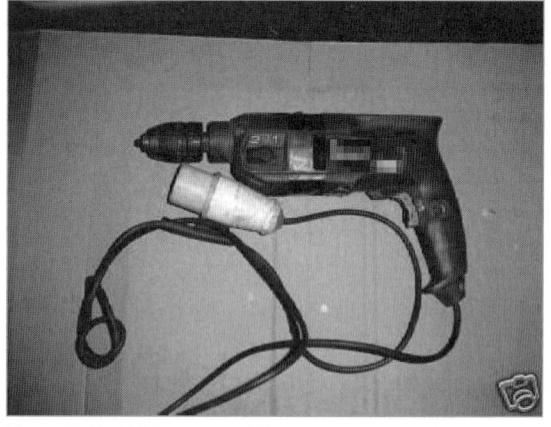

Figure 6-26: 110V powered drill. *Source: ACT.*

Figure 6-27: 110V powered drill. *Source: ACT.*

RESIDUAL CURRENT DEVICE (RCD)

An electro-mechanical switching device is used to automatically isolate the supply when there is a difference between the current flowing into a device and the current flowing from the device. Such a difference might result from a fault causing current leakage, with possible fire risks or the risk of shock current when a person touches a system and provides a path to earth for the current. RCDs can be designed to operate at low currents and fast response times (usually 30 mA and 30 mSeconds) and thus they *reduce the effect of an electric shock.* Though they do not prevent the person receiving an electric shock, they are very sensitive and operate very quickly and reduce some of the primary effects of the shock. It is still possible for a person to receive injury from the shock, not least some of the secondary injuries referred to earlier. But the use of this type of device means the fault current should be isolated before sustained shock, and therefore fibrillation, occurs. The equipment needs to be de-energised from time to time in order to be confident it will work properly when needed. This can easily be done by a simple test routine before use, as equipment is plugged into the RCD.

Summary
- Rapid and sensitive.
- Difficult to defeat.
- Easy and safe to test and reset.
- Does not prevent shock, but reduces the effect of a shock.

Figure 6-28: Residual current device. *Source: ACT.*

Figure 6-29: Plug-in residual current device. *Source: ACT.*

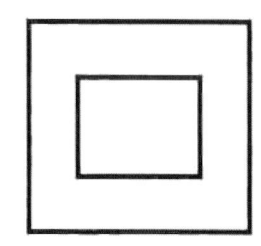

Figure 6-30: Double insulated 240V drill. Source: ACT.

Figure 6-31: Double insulation symbol. Source: HSG107.

DOUBLE INSULATION

This is a common protection device and consists of a layer of insulation around the live electrical parts of the equipment and a second layer of insulated material around this, commonly the casing of the equipment. Since the casing material is an insulator and does not conduct electricity, equipment having this type of protection does not normally have an earth wire.

Each layer of insulation must be sufficient in its own right to give adequate protection against shock.

Equipment, which is double insulated, will carry the symbol shown above.

Double insulated equipment has two layers of insulating material between the live parts of the equipment and the user. If a fault occurs with the live parts and a conductor touches the insulating material surrounding it no current can pass to the user, therefore *no shock occurs.*

Inspection and maintenance strategies

The legal duty for inspection and maintenance

The Electricity at Work Regulations (EWR) 1989, Regulation 4(2) requires that the owner shall 'as may be necessary to prevent danger, **maintain** all systems so as to prevent, so far as is reasonably practicable, such danger'. Danger is defined as the risk of injury from electric shock, electric burn, fire of electrical origin, electric arcing or explosion initiated or caused by electricity.

What is maintenance?

Guidance from the HSE (PM32) and in the IEE Code of Practice for In-Service Inspection and Testing of Electrical Equipment indicates that maintenance is a general term that in practice can include visual inspection, repair, testing and replacement. Maintenance will determine whether equipment is fully serviceable or needing repair. It further suggests that cost effective maintenance can be achieved by a combination of:

- Checks by the user.
- Visual inspections by a person appointed to do this.
- Combined inspection and tests by a competent person or by a contractor.

What needs maintenance?

The system. The Memorandum of Guidance on the EWR 1989 defines a system. In simple terms it will include any equipment which is, or may be, connected to a common source of electrical energy and includes the source and the equipment. Thus the distribution system in the plant and the apparatus connected to it are covered.

The IEE requirements apply similarly to the permanent installation in the building. It must be recognised that there is little benefit in having perfect portable apparatus if it is plugged into a defective socket which may be without proper insulation, with a switch that does not work properly, with the polarity reversed or with a high resistance earth connection.

Getting a maintenance programme started

In order to identify what systems will need maintenance, they should be listed. This same listing can be used as a checklist recording that the appropriate checks have been done. It may also include details of the type of the equipment, the checks and tests to be carried out.

USER CHECKS

The user of electrical equipment should be encouraged, after basic training, to look critically at apparatus and the source of power. If any defects are found, the apparatus should be marked and not be used again before examination by a competent person. Obviously, there must be a procedure by which the user brings faults to the attention of a supervisor and/or a competent person who might rectify the fault.

Checks by the user are the first line of defence but should never be the only line taken. Such inspections should be aimed at identifying the following:

- Damaged cable sheaths.
- Damaged plugs. Cracked casing or bent pins.
- Taped or other inadequate cable joints.
- Outer cable insulation not secured into plugs or equipment.
- Faulty or ineffective switches.

- Burn marks or discolouration.
- Damaged casing.
- Loose parts or screws.
- Wet or contaminated equipment.
- Loose or damaged sockets or switches.

FORMAL INSPECTON AND TESTS

Inspection

The maintenance system should always include formal visual inspection of all portable electrical equipment and electrical tests.

The frequency depends on the type of equipment and where it is used. The inspection can be done by a member of staff who has been trained in what to look for and has basic electrical knowledge. They should know enough to avoid danger to themselves or others. Visual inspections are likely to need to look for the same types of defects as user checks but should also include the following:

Opening plugs of portable equipment to check for:

- Use of correctly rated fuse.
- Effective cord grip.
- Secure and correct cable terminations.

Inspection of fixed installations for:

- Damaged or loose conduit, trunking or cabling.
- Missing broken or inadequately secured covers.
- Loose or faulty joints.
- Loose earth connections.
- Moisture, corrosion or contamination.
- Burn marks or discolouration.
- Open or inadequately secured panel doors.
- Ease of access to switches and isolators.
- Presence of temporary wiring.

User checks and a programme of formal visual inspections are found to pick up some 95% of faults.

Testing

Faults such as loss of earth or broken wires inside an installation or cable cannot be found by visual inspection, so some apparatus needs to have a combined inspection and test. This is particularly important for all earthed equipment and leads and plugs connected to hand held or hand operated equipment.

The system should be tested regularly in accordance with Institute of Electrical Engineers (IEE) requirements; tests may include earth continuity and impedance tests and tests of insulation material.

FREQUENCY OF INSPECTION AND TESTING

Question: "I have been told that I have to have my desk lamp tested every six months. Is this correct?"

Answer: No. The law requires it to be maintained. It does not require any elaborate or rigorous system of frequent electrical testing.

Source: HSE Note INDG 160L.

Deciding the frequency

Many approaches to establishing frequency suggest that they should be done regularly. As can be seen above, the word 'regularly' is not specified in terms of fixed time intervals for all systems; a management judgment must be made to specify an appropriate timetable. In effect, the frequency will depend on the condition the system is used in; for example, a test of office portable equipment may be sufficient if conducted every 3 years, whereas equipment used on a construction site may need to be tested every 3 months. The system as a whole rather that just portable equipment must also be tested periodically and again this will depend on the conditions of use and may vary from 10 years to 6 months. Factors to be considered when deciding the frequency include:

- Type of equipment.
- Whether it is hand held.
- Manufacturer's recommendations.
- Its initial integrity and soundness.
- Age.
- Working environment.
- Likelihood of mechanical damage.
- Frequency of use.
- Duration of use.
- Foreseeable use.
- Who uses it.
- Modifications or repairs.
- Past experience.

RECORDS OF INSPECTION AND TESTING

In order to identify what systems and equipment will need inspection and testing they should be listed. This same listing can be used as a checklist recording that the appropriate checks, inspections and tests have been done. It would be usual to include details of the type of the equipment, its location and its age. It is important that a cumulative record of equipment and its status is held available to those that are responsible for using the equipment as well as those that are conducting the inspection or test.

In addition, it is common practice to add a label to the system or part of the system (e.g. portable appliances) to indicate that an inspection and / or test has taken place and its status following this. Some labels show the date that this took place; others prefer to show the date of next inspection or test.

Figure 6-32: PAT labels. Source: ACT.

There is a growing trend, especially in offices, for employees to bring to work their own electrically powered equipment including calculators, radios, kettles and coffee makers. The number of electrical accidents has grown accordingly and fires from calculator chargers left on overnight are growing in number. All such equipment should be recorded, inspected and tested by a competent person before use and at regular intervals, as if it were company property.

ADVANTAGES AND LIMITATIONS OF PORTABLE APPLIANCE TESTING (PAT)

The purpose of portable appliance testing is to periodically confirm the critical aspects of the electrical integrity of portable appliances. Three levels of inspection should be included in a maintenance and inspection strategy for portable electrical appliances:

- The first level of inspection would be that carried out by the operator before the appliance is used and would consist of an informal check of the condition of the appliance and its cable and plug.
- The second check would be supplemented by a more formal visual inspection by an appointed person which would follow a set down procedure and include other matters such as the correctness of the rating of the fuses fitted, security of cable grips, earth continuity, impedance and insulation.
- The third strategy would include the periodic combined inspection and testing of the appliance by a competent person.

It is important to keep centralised records of the results of portable appliance testing within an organisation. Such records can then be used for setting the frequency for appliance testing, to verify whether unlabelled equipment had been tested or had merely lost its label and to provide a record of past faults on all appliances that had been recorded. This approach will demonstrate that the employer is in compliance with the regulations

The limitation with portable appliance testing is that people may have an over-reliance on the apparent assurance that the test indicates. They may be tempted to see it as a permanent assurance that the equipment is safe. This can lead to users not making their own pre-use checks of the appliance. In effect it is only a test, and therefore assurance, at a point in time. It does not assure that someone has not, for example, altered the fuse and put one in with an incorrect rating or that the cable grip has not come loose.

It must also be recognised that there is little benefit in having a perfect portable appliance if it is plugged into a defective socket which may be without proper insulation, with a switch that does not work properly, with the polarity reversed or with a high resistance earth connection.

6.3 - Appropriate control measures for overhead power line hazards

Avoidance where possible

It may be possible to have the overhead power lines diverted away from the site while work is carried out. Access routes to sites should be sited a safe distance away from overhead cables, if this is not possible then the adequate control measures should be adopted.

CONTROL MEASURES

Every year people are seriously hurt by coming into contact with overhead power lines, so it is important to identify the overhead cables and implement adequate control measures. Any lines found on a site should always be treated as live until they are proved to be otherwise. Control measures might include: diversion of the power lines; safe access points; restricted vehicle movements; barriers or fencing;

Pre-planning and consultation with service provider

Planning and consultation with service providers is essential and forms part of the safe system of work, as it may be necessary to isolate the supply in the event of an incident. Access routes should be established in consultation and these should be away from overhead cables. They should be clearly identified, signed and marked. Where this is not possible, then clear passing places with clear goal posts erected at both ends should be established, clearly signed, including clearance height and notice to driver to lower jibs. Lighting may be required if work is to take place after sunset.

ISOLATION OF SUPPLY

The supply may need to be isolated at some point in the event of heavy equipment movements on or around the site. Therefore it is essential that this has been adequately planned and a procedure has been adopted and approved with the electricity supplier.

Ground level barriers

If work is to be carried out near the lines then barriers should be used along with warning signs. The recommended distance for the position of the barriers is 6 metres (horizontally) from the nearest line. Some construction vehicles have jib's or telescopic arms that extend long distances, therefore the measurement should be taken with the reach of the jib (maximum outreach) measured (horizontally) from the position of the ground barrier. For very high voltages these distances may be increased significantly. Bunting may also be required to show drivers of these vehicles the position of the lines. The bunting should be placed at a height of 3 to 6 metres. The barriers should be sturdy enough so that they cannot be moved easily and should be coloured coded with red and white stripes. Types of barrier commonly used include: 40 gallon oil drums, filled with rubble or concrete; railway sleepers: a raised earth bank to 1 metre and marked by posts to prevent vehicle entry: a tension wire fence with flags attached (this should be earthed in consultation with the electricity supplier).

Restriction of equipment/vehicle reach

There may be a requirement to restrict certain equipment e.g. forklift trucks or cranes from working under power lines due to the jibs or forks coming into contact with or near enough to form an arc from the power lines. Safe working heights should be signed and posted on goal posts or barriers.

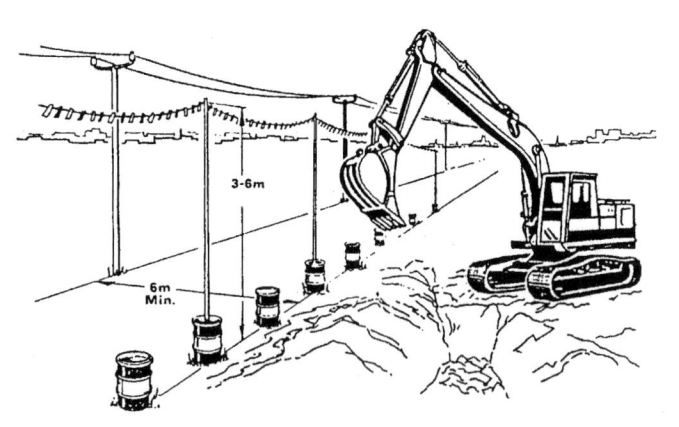

Figure 6-33: Working near power lines. Source: HSG144.

Figure 6-34: Overhead power lines. Source: Lincsafe.

Element 7

Fire - hazards and control

Learning outcomes

On completion of this element, candidates should be able to demonstrate understanding of the content through the application of knowledge to familiar and unfamiliar situations. In particular they should be able to:

7.1 Identify fire hazards and evaluate main fire risks in a construction workplace and the additional fire risks caused by construction activities in an existing workplace.

7.2 Explain the basic principles of fire prevention and the prevention of fire spread during construction activities.

7.3 Identify the appropriate fire alarm systems and fire-fighting equipment for construction activities.

7.4 Outline the requirements for an adequate and properly maintained means of escape in the construction workplace.

7.5 Outline the factors which should be considered when implementing a successful evacuation of a construction workplace in the event of a fire.

Content

7.1 - Basic fire principles, hazards and risks in the workplace	107
Definitions	107
Basic principles of fire	107
Classification of fires	108
Basic principles of heat transmission and fire spread	108
Common causes and consequences of fires during construction activities	108
Reasons why fires spread	109
Requirement for a fire risk assessment	110
7.2 - Fire prevention and prevention of fire spread	113
Appropriate control measures to minimise the risk of fire in a construction workplace	113
Small quantities of highly flammable or flammable liquids	117
Structural measures to prevent spread of fire and smoke	118
7.3 - Fire detection, fire alarm and fire fighting equipment	118
Common fire detection and alarm systems	118
Portable fire fighting equipment	119
Main extinguishing media	120
7.4 - Means of escape	122
Requirements for means of escape	122
7.5 - Evacuation of the workplace	123
Emergency evacuation procedures	123

Sources of reference

A short guide to making your premises safe from fire (05 FRSD 03546), DCLG Publications www.firesafetyguides.communities.gov.uk

Dangerous Substances and Explosives Atmospheres Regulations 2002 (ACoP) (L135), HSE Books 0-7176-2200-2

Fire safety in construction work (HSG168), HSE Books ISBN 0-7176-1332-1

Safe use and handling of flammable substances (HSG140), HSE Books ISBN 0-7176-0967-7

Storage of dangerous substances (ACoP) (L135), HSE Books ISBN 0-7176-2200-2

The storage of flammable liquids in containers (HSG51), HSE Books ISBN 0-7176-1471-0

Other sources of reference

Fire Safety: An Employer's Guide (HSE, Home Office, Scottish Executive, DoE Northern Ireland), The Stationery Office ISBN 0-1134-1229-0

Relevant statutory provisions

The Construction (Design and Management) Regulations (CDM) 2007

The Dangerous Substances and Explosives Atmospheres Regulations (DSEAR) 2002

The Fire (Scotland) Act (FSA) 2005

The Health and Safety (Safety Signs and Signals) Regulations (SSSR) 1996

The Management of Health and Safety at Work Regulations (MHSWR) 1999

The Regulatory Reform (Fire Safety) Order (RRFSO) 2005

7.1 - Basic fire principles, hazards and risks in the workplace

Definitions

FIRE PRECAUTIONS
The measures taken and the fire protection provided in a building to minimise the risk to occupants, contents and structure from an outbreak of fire.

FIRE PREVENTION
The concept of preventing outbreaks of fire or reducing the risk of fire spread and avoiding danger from fire to people or property.

FIRE PROTECTION
Design features, systems or equipment in a building provided to reduce the danger to persons and property by detecting, extinguishing or containing fires.

Basic principles of fire

THE FIRE TRIANGLE

In order for combustion to take place the three essential elements of a fire have to be brought together - fuel, oxygen and source of ignition (heat) - this is called the fire triangle.

In order to prevent fires these elements, particularly the fuel and ignition sources, are kept apart. When they are brought together in the right proportions combustion takes place. It should be noted that it is only the vapour from a fuel that burns. A solid or liquid must be heated to a temperature where the vapour given off can ignite before combustion takes place.

This principle is important when considering combustible dusts as this combustion process happens so quickly it becomes an explosion. This explosion can be caused by just a source of ignition, for example, a spark; similarly a small **dust explosion** can often disturb more dust and create bigger explosions.

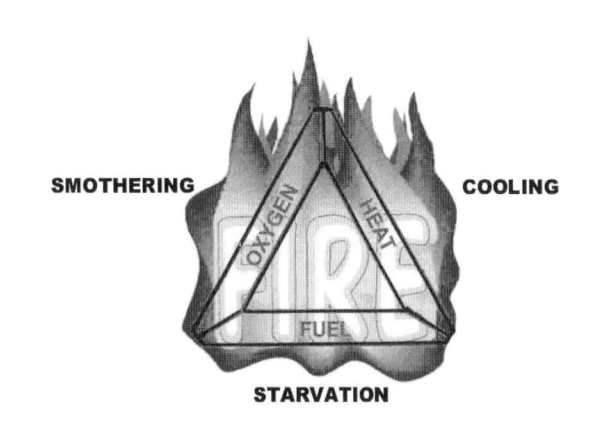

Figure 7-1: Fire triangle.   Source: Corel.

The other important aspect of this combustion principle is that if one or more of these elements of the fire is removed the fire will be extinguished.

This can be done by:

Cooling   -   the fire to remove the heat - by applying water to the fire.

Starving   -   the fire of fuel - by moving material from the area of a fire or closing off an area of combustible material from the fire.

Smothering   -   the fire by limiting its oxygen supply - by closing a lid on a metal bin that contained a fire, covering a fire with a fire blanket or applying an extinguishing medium such as foam.

SOURCES OF IGNITION

Any source of heat is a possible ignition source. Examples could be:

- Smokers' materials.
- Naked flames.
- Fixed or portable heaters.
- Hot processes e.g. welding.
- Cooking.
- Electrical equipment or machinery.
- Static electricity.

Figure 7-2: Welding.   Source: Speedy Hire Plc.

Figure 7-3: Combustible materials.   Source: ACT.

UNIT NCC1 - ELEMENT 7 - FIRE - HAZARDS AND CONTROL

SOURCES OF FUEL

Anything that burns is a fuel for a fire:

- Flammable liquids, e.g. petrol and diesel storage areas, refill containers.
- Flammable gases, e.g. butane LPG heater cylinder.
- Flammable chemicals, e.g. paints and solvents.
- Wood e.g. furniture, dust from manufacturing processes.
- Paper and card, e.g. stationery cupboards and waste paper bins.
- Plastics, rubber and foam, e.g. furniture.
- Insulating materials, e.g. wall and partition insulation.
- Waste materials, e.g. used waste chemicals, general waste, waste papers.

SOURCES OF OXYGEN

- Oxygen supplies e.g. cylinders or piped supply.
- Ventilation systems e.g. windows, doors, vents, air conditioning.
- Chemicals e.g. oxidising agents.

FIRE HAZARDS AND RISKS

The hazards relating to the radiant heat of a fire and contact with flames can give rise to the risk of heat stroke or burns. The degree of exposure to the heat or flames will influence greatly the effect on the body; which could quickly lead to shock, coma or death.

Both the hot gases and smoke involved in fires represent separate hazards to a person involved in a fire. The hot gases and smoke can present a direct effect on the lungs causing restriction in breathing. In addition, toxic gases may be liberated as part of a fire; these may include carbon monoxide, which if breathed in sufficient quantities can lead to asphyxiation. Other toxic products of combustion can include hydrogen cyanide and chlorine.

Furthermore, fires will cause the release of substances that can be harmful to the environment.

Classification of fires

A basic understanding of the classes of fire is needed because many fire extinguishers state the classes of fire on which they may be used.

Class A	-	Fire involving solids - wood, paper or plastics (usually material of an organic nature).
Class B	-	Fires involving liquids or liquefiable solids - petrol, oil, paint, fat or wax.
Class C	-	Fires involving gases - liquefied petroleum gas, natural gas or acetylene.
Class D	-	Fires involving metals - sodium, magnesium, aluminium and many metal powders.
Electrical Fires	-	There is not a class for electrical fires, but obviously we need to consider fires in electrical apparatus. In many cases, electricity is a source of heat.
Class F	-	Fires involving cooking oils and fats.

Basic principles of heat transmission and fire spread

There are four methods by which heat may be transmitted:

Convection	-	The movement of hotter gases up through the air (hot air rises).
		e.g. Smoke and hot gases rising up a staircase through an open door.
Control measure	-	Protection of openings by fire doors and the creation of fire resistant compartments in buildings.
Conduction	-	The movement of heat through a material (usually solid).
		e.g. A metal beam or pipe transmitting heat through a solid wall.
Control measure	-	Insulating the surface of a beam or pipe with heat resistant materials.
Radiation	-	Transfer of heat as invisible waves through the air (the air or gas is not heated but solids and liquids in contact with the heat are).
		e.g. Items or waste containers stored too near to a building may provide enough radiant heat to transfer the fire to the building if they are ignited.
Control measure	-	Separation distances or fire resistant barriers.
Direct Burning	-	Combustible materials in direct contact with naked flame.
		e.g. Curtains or carpet tiles may be consumed by combustion and enable fire to be transferred along them to other parts of a building.
Control measure	-	The use of fire retardant materials.

Common causes and consequences of fires during construction activities

CAUSES

Causes may be split into four main groups. These are:

Careless actions and accidents

e.g. hot works, discarded lighted cigarette end or match, smouldering waste, unattended burning or poor electrical connections.

Misusing equipment

e.g. overloading electrical circuits and using fuses of too high a rating, failure to follow servicing instructions, failure to repair faulty machinery/equipment promptly.

Defective machinery or equipment

e.g. electrical short circuits, electrical earth fault can cause local overheating and electrical insulation failure may occur when affected by heat, damp or chemicals.

Deliberate ignition

e.g. insurance fraud, aggrieved persons, concealment of another crime, political activists or vandalism.

Figure 7-4: Careless action. *Source: ACT.*

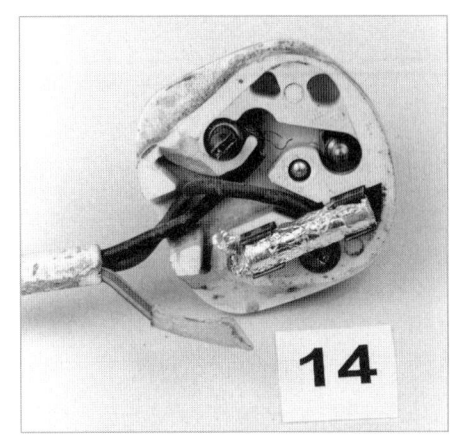

Figure 7-5: Misusing equipment. *Source: ACT.*

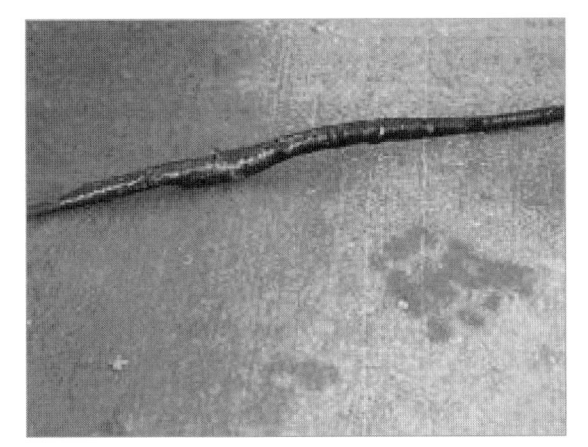

Figure 7-6: Defective electrical equipment. *Source: ACT.*

Figure 7-7: Deliberate ignition of materials. *Source: ACT.*

CONSEQUENCES

Consequences may be split into three main groups. These are:

Human harm

Each year some 500 people die due to fires in the UK and around 15,000 non-fatal casualties are caused. Though most of these do not occur in the workplace, fire has the potential for major loss of life in these circumstances due to direct contact with heat and flame or from the effects of smoke and toxic gases.

Economic effects

Commercial fire losses remain substantial, in the order of £672m in 2003, even though recent workplace injury and death has been low. When fires do occur in the workplace the business is usually so badly affected it does not resume business again.

Legal effects

There is a legal requirement under the Regulatory Reform (Fire Safety) Order (RRFSO) 2005 to prevent fire, protect employees and other relevant persons from the effects of fire and to mitigate the effect of fire on anyone in the vicinity of a premise on fire.

Reasons why fires spread

FAILURE OF EARLY DETECTION
- No detection system or patrols.
- No alarm system in place.
- People not knowing or confusing the sound of an alarm.
- Not promptly extinguished due to no hoses or extinguishers.
- Fire starts in unoccupied area.

- Fire starts out of normal work hours.
- Building material waste may be being burnt as a normal routine and smoke and other signs of fire may not be seen as unusual.
- Numerous hot working tasks conducted - therefore smells of burning ignored.
- Frequent occurrence of small, local fires caused by hot work, and not seen as significant.

ABSENCE OF COMPARTMENTS IN BUILDING STRUCTURE
- Open plan office.
- False ceilings.
- The structure under construction or alteration is incomplete and has reduced separation between levels and/or sections on a level.

Figure 7-8: Not knowing the sound of an alarm.   Source: ACT.

Figure 7-9: Compartment undermined-holes cut.   Source: ACT.

COMPARTMENTS UNDERMINED
- Fire doors wedged open.
- Poor maintenance of door structure.
- Holes may be designed to pass through compartments and are waiting fitment of services and subsequent sealing.
- Holes cut for ducts or doorways or to provide temporary access to locate/remove equipment.
- Compartments may be progressively created in buildings under alteration, thus increasing the risk of fire spread.

MATERIALS INAPPROPRIATELY STORED
- Flammable liquids not controlled - too much or in unsuitable containers.
- Boxes in corridors.
- Off cuts of wood and sawdust left in the areas where work has taken place.
- Packing materials used in the process, such as shredded paper, polystyrene, bubble wrap etc.
- Pallets and plastic covering left near to ignition sources.

Figure 7-10: Fire door held open.   Source: ACT.

Figure 7-11: Materials inappropriately stored.   Source: ACT.

Requirement for a fire risk assessment

The purpose of a fire risk assessment (FRA) is to identify where fire may start in the workplace, the people who would be put at risk, and to reduce the risk where possible.

Specific legal duties to conduct risk assessments are set out in the RRFSO 2005, which require the following.

Every 'Responsible Person' (Employer, Person in control or Owner) must make a suitable and sufficient assessment of:

- The risks to the health and safety of their **employees** to which they are exposed whilst they are at work.
- The risks to the health and safety of **persons not in their employment** (Relevant Persons) arising out of or in connection with the conduct by them of their undertaking.

Similarly every self-employed person must make a suitable and sufficient assessment of:

- The risks to their **own** health and safety to which they are exposed whilst at work.

- The risks to the health and safety of **persons not in his employment** (Relevant Persons), arising out of or in connection with the conduct by them of their undertaking.

The assessments must, at least, identify the measures needed to satisfy the 'General Fire Precautions' of the RRFSO 2005. This order requires fire and other emergency provisions to be in place; as such, risk assessments must be conducted to determine fire risks and the provisions necessary for the protection of people and the environment.

The measures would include:

- Reduction of the risk of fire.
- Prevention of fire spread.
- Adequate means of escape from fire.
- Maintenance measures to ensure means of escape available at all times.
- Means to fight fire.
- Means to detect and warn of fire.
- Fire actions / instructions and training.
- Actions to mitigate the effects of a fire.

Where the employer employs five or more employees they must record the significant findings of the assessment and any group of his employees identified by it as being especially at risk.

Assessments must be reviewed by the 'Responsible Person' if there is reason to suspect that it is no longer valid or there has been a significant change in the matters to which it relates.

CARRYING OUT A FIRE RISK ASSESSMENT

Step 1 - Identify fire hazards

- *Identify sources of ignition* - Smokers' materials, naked flames, heaters, hot processes, cooking, machinery, boilers, faulty or misused electrical equipment, lighting equipment, hot surfaces, blocked vents, friction, static electricity, metal impact and arson.
- *Identify sources of fuel* - Flammable liquids, flammable chemicals, wood, paper and card, plastics, foam, flammable gases, furniture, textiles, packaging materials, waste materials including shavings, off cuts and dust.
- *Identify sources of oxygen* - Natural ventilation, doors, windows, forced ventilation systems, air conditioning, oxidising materials, oxygen cylinders or piped oxygen systems.

Step 2 - Identify people at risk

- Consider people in the premises - staff, visitors, contractors, public, old, young, disabled, and their level of discipline and training.
- How could fire, heat or smoke spread to areas that people occupy - convection, conduction, radiation or direct burning.
- Who and where are the people that may be at risk? - people carrying out noisy tasks, placed high at the top of a building or in confined spaces conducting work, nearby workers or the public.
- Identify people who are especially at risk.
- How will people be warned of fire and could people be trapped by fire?

Step 3 - Evaluate, remove or reduce and protect from risk

Risk reduction by prevention

- *Reduce sources of ignition* - Remove unnecessary sources of heat or replace with safer alternatives, ensure electrical fuses etc are of the correct rating, ensure safe and correct use of electrical equipment, enforcing a 'hot work' permit system, safe smoking policy, arson reduction measures.
- *Minimise potential fuel for a fire* - Remove or reduce amount of flammable materials, replace materials with safer alternatives, ensure safe handling, storage and use of materials, safe separation distances between flammable materials, use of fire resisting storage, repair or replace damaged or unsuitable furniture, control and removal of flammable waste, care of external storage due to arson, good housekeeping.
- *Reduce sources of oxygen* - Close all doors and windows not required for ventilation particularly out of working hours, shutting down non essential ventilation systems, not storing oxidising materials near heat sources or flammable materials, controlling the use of oxygen cylinders and ensuring ventilation to areas where they are used.

Risk reduction by protection

Consider existing fire safety measures, risk reduction by protection (controls) in the workplace and consider possible improvements.

- Reducing unsatisfactory structural features.
    - Remove, cover or treat large areas of combustible wall and ceiling linings, improve fire resistance of workplace, install fire breaks into open voids.
- Fire detection and warning.
    - Can fire be detected quickly enough to allow people to escape?
    - Can means of warning be recognised and understood?
    - Do staff know how to operate the system?
    - Will staff know what to do if the alarm operates?
    - Are fire notices posted around workplace?
- Means of escape.
    - How long will it take for people to escape once they are aware of a fire?
    - Is this time reasonable?
    - Are there enough exits?
    - Are exits in the right places?

- Are there suitable means of escape for all people, including disabled?
- Could a fire happen that would affect all escape routes?
- Are escape routes easily identifiable?
- Are exit routes free from obstructions and blockages?
- Are exit routes suitably lit at all times?
- Have staff been trained in the use of the escape routes?
- Means of fighting fire.
    - Is the fire fighting equipment suitable for the risk?
    - Is it suitably located?
    - Is it signed where necessary?
    - Have people been trained to use equipment where necessary?
- Maintenance and testing.
    - Check all fire doors, escape routes, lighting and signs.
    - Check all fire fighting equipment.
    - Check all fire detectors and alarms.
    - Check any other equipment provided to help means of escape arrangements.
    - Are there relevant instructions to staff regarding maintenance and testing?
    - Are those who carry out maintenance and testing competent?
- Fire procedures and training.
    - Is there an emergency plan.
    - Does the emergency plan take account of all reasonably foreseeable circumstances?
    - Are all employees familiar with the plan, trained in its use, and involved in testing it?
    - Is the emergency plan made available to staff?
    - Are fire procedures clearly indicated throughout the workplace?
    - Have all people likely to be present, been considered?

Step 4 - Record, plan, inform, instruct and train

Where the employer employs five or more employees they must record the significant findings of the assessment and any group of his employees identified by it as being especially at risk.

A record must also be kept of measures that have been or will be taken by the responsible person. Suitable headings for a record would be:

Significant Hazard	People at risk	Existing control measures	Further action needed	Projected completion date	Responsible person

Emergency plans

Following completion of the fire risk assessment, an emergency plan should be devised. The plan should include the following:

- Action on discovery of fire.
- Action on hearing alarm.
- Details of the fire warning system.
- Details of the evacuation process.
- Means of escape - travel distances.
- Location of assembly points.
- Identification of escape routes - signs, emergency lighting.
- Details of fire fighting equipment.
- Specific staff duties.
- Safe evacuation of people who need assistance to escape.
- Safe working practices in high risk areas.
- Procedures for calling Fire Service.
- Staff training needs and arrangements for providing training.

Step 5 - Review and monitor

The fire risk assessment and the fire safety measures should be reviewed on a regular basis.

In addition a review should be done if:

- Changes to workplace are proposed, e.g. increased storage of flammable materials.
- Changes to work process / activity are proposed, e.g. introducing a new night shift.
- Changes to number or type of people present are proposed, e.g. public are invited on site to buy goods.
- A near miss or a fire occurs.

THE IMPLICATIONS OF CONSTRUCTION WORK WITH RESPECT TO A FIRE RISK ASSESSMENT IN EXISTING PREMISES AND TEMPORARY SITE ACCOMMODATION

Many serious fires occur in existing buildings during maintenance and construction work. Due to the increased fire risks during these periods of time, additional fire precautions may be needed.

Dependant upon the nature of the work to be carried out and the size and use of the workplace, it may be necessary to carry out a new fire risk assessment to include all the new hazards that will be created during the construction work. In some cases the increased risk will be due to the increase of sources of ignition or additional materials.

In other cases it will be due to the effect on the controls in place at the premises. Some work may require the isolation of smoke detectors or an alarm system. Normally well controlled escape routes may become cluttered by equipment, materials or workers.

Attention should be paid to :
- Accumulation of flammable waste and building materials.
- The obstruction or loss of exits and exit routes.
- Fire doors being propped open, wedged open or removed.
- Openings created in fire resisting structures.
- Isolation of fire detection, or fixed fire fighting systems.
- Introduction of additional electrical equipment, or other sources of ignition.
- Use of hot work process.
- Introduction of flammable products e.g. adhesives or flammable gases.
- The addition of new people to the premises that may be unfamiliar with fire arrangements e.g. alarm, routes, roll calls, assembly points.
- People working in unusual locations e.g. the roof, basement or duct areas.
- People working outside normal working hours.

Figure 7-12: Materials in escape route.   Source: Lincsafe.

7.2 - Fire prevention and prevention of fire spread

Appropriate control measures to minimise the risk of fire in a construction workplace

USE AND STORAGE OF FLAMMABLE AND COMBUSTIBLE MATERIALS

Where possible we should seek to *eliminate* the use of flammable materials in the workplace, for example, replacing adhesives that have a flammable content with those that are water based. Where this is not possible the amount used should be *reduced* and kept to the minimum. Quantities of material stored in the workplace must be in suitable containers and controlled to the minimum for immediate work needs. Flammable materials not in use should be removed to a purpose designed store in a well ventilated area, preferably outside the building but in a secure area. Lids should be kept on containers at all times when they are not in immediate use. Any waste containers, contaminated tools or materials should be treated in the same way and removed to a store in fresh air, until dealt with. Containers and contaminated materials need to be disposed of in a controlled manner so that they do not present a risk of fire.

Care has to be taken to control the delivery and therefore the storage of flammable and combustible materials to site. There is a temptation to have large quantities all delivered at the same time, but where possible deliveries should be staggered to reflect the rate of use in order to minimise the amount stored on site.

Terms used with flammable and combustible materials

Flashpoint

'Flashpoint' is defined as the lowest temperature at which, in a specific test apparatus, sufficient vapour is produced from a liquid sample for momentary or flash ignition to occur. It must not be confused with ignition temperature which can be considerably lower.

Flammable

Liquids with a flash point between 32°C and 55°C are classified as flammable.

Highly flammable

Liquids with a flash point below 32°C are classified as highly flammable.

General principles for storage and use of flammable liquids

When considering the storage or use of flammable liquids, the following safety principles should be applied:

V	Ventilation - plenty of fresh air.
I	Ignition - control of ignition sources.
C	Containment - suitable containers and spillage control.
E	Exchange - try to use a less flammable product to do task.
S	Separation - keep storage away from process areas, by distance or a physical barrier e.g. a wall or partition.

CONTROL OF IGNITION SOURCES

Welding
- Only use competent trained staff.
- Regulators should be of a recognised standard.
- Colour code hoses   - blue   - oxygen.
                                      - red   - acetylene.
                                      - orange - propane.
- Fit non-return valves at blowpipe/torch inlet on both gas lines.

UNIT NCC1 - ELEMENT 7 - FIRE - HAZARDS AND CONTROL

- Fit flashback arrestors incorporating cut-off valves and flame arrestors fitted to outlet of both gas regulators.
- Use crimped hose connections not jubilee clips.
- Do not let oil or grease contaminate oxygen supply due to explosion hazard.
- Check equipment visually before use, and check new connections with soapy water for leaks.
- Secure cylinders in upright position.
- Keep hose lengths to a minimum.
- Follow a permit to work system.

Hot work

Hot work has been responsible for causing many fires. One of the most tragic fires due to hot work was Dusseldorf Airport Fire in 1996. The fire was started by welding on an open roadway and resulted in damage in excess of £200 million, several hundred injuries and 17 deaths.

It is imperative that good safe working practices are utilised. Combustible materials must be removed from the area or covered up. Thought must be given to the effects of heat on the surrounding structure, and where sparks, flames, hot residue or heat will travel to. It is often necessary to have a fire watcher to spot any fires that may be started. Fire extinguishers need to be immediately available and operatives must know how to use them. The work area must be checked thoroughly for some time after the completion of work to ensure there are no smouldering fires. Strong consideration should be given to the use of hot work permits.

Smoking

On 2nd April 2007 the Smoke-free (Premises and Enforcement) Regulations 2006 came into force and from 1st July 2007 it has been unlawful to smoke within public buildings and the workplace. Prohibition notices should still be erected to enforce this new law. This has lead to some illicit smoking, especially on some construction sites and in response a number of construction companies have decided to set up dedicated smoking areas to try and combat this problem. Non-combustible receptacles for cigarette ends and other smoking material should be provided and emptied daily. Smoking should cease half an hour before closing down or shift change.

Arson

Simple but effective ways to deter the arsonist are by giving attention to security, both external and internal, which should encompass the following:

External security
- Control of people having access to the building/site.
- Use of patrol guards.
- Lighting the premises at night.
- Safety of keys.
- Structural protection.
- Siting of rubbish bins / skips at least 8m from buildings.

Internal security
- Good housekeeping.
- Inspections.
- Clear access routes.
- Visitor supervision.
- Control of sub-contractors.
- Audits.

Figure 7-13: Control arson by external security.   Source: ACT.

Figure 7-14: Control arson by housekeeping.   Source: ACT.

SYSTEMS OF WORK

Systems of work combine people, equipment, materials and the environment to produce the safest possible climate in which to work. In order to produce a safe system of work, it is essential to make an assessment of the area to determine where the hazards and risks arise and how best to control them.

The requirement to carry out a risk assessment should address the following:

- Identify potential fire hazards.
- Decide who may be in danger, and note their locations.
- Evaluate the risks and carry out any necessary improvement measures.
- Record findings and action taken.
- Keep assessment under review.

In addition to the risk assessment carried out, other measures may include implementing the following strategies.

1) A safe place

A safe place begins with ensuring that the fabric of the building is designed or planned in a way that will prevent ignition, suppress fire spread and allow for safe, speedy unobstructed evacuation with signs to direct people.

Factors to consider will include compartmentalisation, fire resistant materials, proper and suitable means of storage, means of detection, means of raising the alarm, good housekeeping and regular monitoring and review.

2) Safe person

A safe person begins with raising awareness to individuals of any risk of loss resulting from outbreak of fire. Information can be provided that will identify where to raise the alarm, what the alarm sounds like, how to evacuate and where to muster, responsibility for signing in and out of the site register, fire drill procedures, trained authorised fire appointed persons, use and storage of flammable materials, good housekeeping and use of equipment producing heat or ignition (including hot processes i.e. welding).

3) Safe materials

Safe materials begin with providing information and ensuring safe segregation and storage for materials and sources of ignition / heat. In addition, providing information on the correct way to handle materials and substances including a control of substances hazardous to health (COSHH) register that will detail methods of tackling a fire involving hazardous substances.

4) Safe equipment

Safe equipment begins with user information and maintenance to ensure good working and efficient order. Information should also provide the user with a safe method for use and the limitations of and risks from the equipment. Supervision may be necessary to ensure correct use and prevent misuse that may lead to short circuiting or overheating that could result in fire. Where work involves hot processes by nature (welding, grinding, casting, etc) then permit-to-work procedures may be necessary in order to tightly control the operations.

Other equipment required in relation to fire hazards and control may include smoke or heat detection equipment, alarm sounders / bells, alarm call points and appropriate fire extinguishing apparatus. It should be noted that in the event of a fire alarm, all the passenger lifts should not be used. Under normal circumstances the lift will drop to the ground floor and remain in that position with the doors locked in the open position. All equipment should be regularly tested to ensure its conformity and be accompanied with a suitable certificate of validity.

Safe systems must also include consideration for who is at risk, including those persons with special needs such as the young, elderly, infirm or disabled. There must be safe systems of work that meet the requirement to prevent smoking in the workplace. Safe systems may require the appointment of persons to take control of the situation and co-ordinate emergency responses in the event of an alarm. If the building relies solely on internal artificial lighting, then the requirement to install emergency back-up lighting will be needed. All systems must be regularly monitored in order to reflect changes to the environment and put remedies in place to ensure full preparedness in the event of a fire.

Permit to work procedures

A permit to work is an official, documented safe system of work that is used for controlling high risk activities. Implementation is required prior to work beginning to ensure that all precautions are taken and securely in place to prevent danger to the workforce. When managed correctly, a permit to work prevents any mistakes or deviations through poor verbal communication by stating the specific requirements of the project. For fire control, a permit to work is typically used where there is a requirement to use flammable materials or when hot work or processes are being carried out.

The authorised person shall issue the permit to work and will sign the document to declare that all isolations are made and remain in place throughout the duration of the project. In addition to this, the authorised person will make checks to ensure that all controls to be implemented by the acceptor are in place before work begins.

The acceptor of the permit to work shall assume responsibility for carrying out the works. The acceptor shall sign the document to declare that the terms and conditions of the permit to work are understood and will be complied with fully at all times by the entire work team. Compliance with a permit to work system includes ensuring the required safeguards are implemented and that the work will be restricted to the equipment only stated within the document.

Items included in a permit to work are:

- Permit issue number.
- Authorised person identification.
- Locations of fire fighting equipment.
- Locations of flammable materials.
- Warning information sign locations.
- Emergency muster points.
- Details of the work to be carried out.
- Signature of authoriser.
- Signature of acceptor.
- Signature for works clearance / extension / handover.
- Signature for cancellation.
- Other precautions (risk assessments, method statements, PPE).

Hot work permits

Hot work permits are formal management documents that control and implement a safe system of work whenever methods of work that utilise heat or flame systems are used. If the risk of fire is low, it may not be necessary to implement a hot work permit; however they should always be considered.

The hot work permit should be issued by an Authorised Person who ensures that the requirements stated in them are complied with before the permit is issued, and during duration of the work. Hot work permits should be issued for a specific time, for a specific place, for a specific task, and are issued to a designated competent person.

Figure 7-15: Hot work. *Source: Speedy Hire Plc.*

REQUIREMENTS FOR THE SAFE STORAGE, TRANSPORT AND USE OF LIQUEFIED PETROLEUM AND OTHER GASES IN CYLINDERS

Liquefied petroleum and other gases in cylinders

Liquefied Petroleum Gas (LPG) is a term that relates to gas stored in a liquefied state under pressure; common examples are propane and butane. LPG and other gas cylinders should be stored in line with the principles detailed below:

Storage
- Storage area should preferably be in clear open area outside.
- Stored in a secure compound - 2m high fence.
- Safe distance from toxic, corrosive, combustible materials, flammable liquids or general waste.
- Stored safe distance from any building.
- If stored inside building, keep away from exit routes, consider fire resisting storage.
- Well ventilated area - 2.5% of total floor and wall area as vents, high and low.
- Oxygen cylinders at least 3m away from flammable gas cylinders.
- Acetylene may be stored with LPG if quantity of LPG less than 50Kg.
- Control access to stores to prevent LPG etc being distributed all around site & keep locked.
- More than one exit (unlocked) may need to be available from any secure storage compound where distance to exit is greater than 12m.
- Lock storage compound to be locked when not in use.
- Protection from sunlight.
- Flameproof lighting.
- Empty containers stored separate from full.
- Fire extinguishers located nearby - consider powder and water types.

Transport
- Upright position.
- Secured to prevent falling over.
- Protection in event of accident e.g. position on vehicle.
- Transport in open vehicle preferably.
- Avoid overnight parking while loaded.
- Park in secure areas.
- 'Trem card' and warning signs.
- Driver training.
- Fire fighting equipment.

Use

General use
- Cylinder connected for use, should be stored in the workplace, additional cylinders should be kept in a purpose built store.
- Fixed position to prevent falling over, or on wheeled trolley - chained.
- Well ventilated area.
- Away from combustibles.
- Keep upright unless used on equipment specifically designed for horizontal use - e.g. gas powered lift truck.
- Handle carefully - don't drop.
- Allow to settle after transport and before use.
- Consider manual handling and injury prevention.
- Turn off cylinder before connecting, disconnecting equipment.
- Check equipment before use.
- Any smell of gas during use, turn off cylinder and investigate.
- Use correct gas regulator for equipment / task.
- Use equipment in line with manufacturers' instructions.

Use in huts
- Only allow cylinders in a hut if it is part of a heater (cabinet heater).
- Pipe into site huts from cylinder located outside where possible.
- If cylinder is outside the hut use the shortest connecting hose as possible.
- Hut to be adequately ventilated high and low.
- Heaters fitted with flame failure devices.
- Turn off heater and cylinder after use and overnight.
- Be aware of danger of leaks inside huts, especially overnight as a severe risk of fire or explosion may occur.
- Keep heaters away from clothing and other combustibles.

GOOD HOUSEKEEPING

Figure 7-16: Gas cylinders for huts. *Source: ACT.*

By 'housekeeping' we mean the general tidiness and order of the building. At first sight, this may seem a strange matter to discuss when considering fire safety, but as housekeeping affects so many different aspects of this subject, it cannot be ignored.

Housekeeping and its effect on fire safety

Fires need fuel. A build up of redundant combustible materials, rubbish and stacks of waste materials provide that fuel. We cannot eliminate all combustible materials, but we can control them. Any unnecessary build-up of rubbish and waste should be avoided. If a fire starts in a neatly stacked pile of timber pallets, around which there is a clear space, the fire may be spotted and extinguished before it can spread. However, if the same pile were strewn around in an untidy heap, along with adjacent rubbish, the likelihood is that fire would spread over a larger area and involve other combustible materials.

Bad housekeeping can also lead to
- Blocked fire exits.
- Obstructed escape routes.
- Difficult access to fire alarm call points / extinguishers / hose reels.
- Obstruction of vital signs and notices.
- A reduction in the effectiveness of automatic fire detectors and sprinklers.

Checklists

Fire Prevention is a matter of good routine and the checklists shown below are a guide as to what to look out for:

List A   Routine checks

Daily at the start of business - including:

- Doors which may be used for escape purposes - unlocked and escape routes unobstructed.
- Free access to hydrants, extinguishers and fire alarm call points.
- No deposits on electric motors.

List B   Routine checks

Daily at close-down - including:

- Inspection of whole area for which you are responsible - to detect any incipient smouldering fires.
- Fire doors and shutters closed.
- All plant and equipment safely shut down.
- Waste bins emptied.
- No accumulation of combustible process waste, packaging materials or dust deposits.
- Safe disposal of waste.
- Premises left secure from unauthorised access.

List C   Periodic inspection

During working hours - weekly/monthly/quarterly as decided:

- Goods neatly stored so as not to impede fire fighting.
- Clear spaces around stacks of stored materials.
- Gangways kept unobstructed.
- No non-essential storage in production areas.
- Materials clear of light fittings.
- Company smoking rules known and enforced.

Small quantities of highly flammable or flammable liquids

The objective in controlling the risk from these materials is to remove all unnecessary quantities from the workplace to a recognised storage area outside the building. This may be done as part of a close down routine at the end of the day. It is accepted that quantities of this material may need to be available in a workplace during normal working. This should not exceed 50 litres in any work area unless a full scale purpose constructed store is used. In other cases local small scale storage of up to **50 litres of highly flammable** or up to **250 litres of flammable** liquids may be kept within the workplace provided it is controlled and placed in a suitable store container. Highly flammable or flammable liquids removed from storage must be in suitable containers to prevent spills and loss of vapours.

Storage in the workplace
- In a suitable sealed container.
- In a suitable cabinet, bin or other store container.
- In a designated area of the workplace.
- Away from ignition sources, working or process areas.
- Capable of containing any spillage.
- It is a 30 min fire resistant structure.
- Provided with hazard warning signs to illustrate the flammability of the contents.
- Prohibition signs for smoking and naked flame.
- Not contain other substances or items.

Storage in open air
- Formal storage area on a concrete pad, with a sump for spills.
- Bunded all around to take content of largest drum plus an allowance of 10%.
- Away from other buildings.
- Secure fence and gate 2m high.
- Marked by signs warning of flammability.
- Signs prohibiting smoking or other naked flames.
- Protection from sunlight.
- If lighting is provided within store it must be flameproof.
- Provision for spill containment materials.
- Fire extinguishers located nearby - consider powder type.
- Full and empty containers separated.
- Clear identification of contents.

Figure 7-17: Poor storage of flammable liquids.   Source: ACT.

Figure 7-18: Storage of flammable materials.   Source: ACT.

Structural measures to prevent spread of fire and smoke

PROPERTIES OF COMMON BUILDING MATERIALS

Brickwork / blockwork

Both brickwork and blockwork perform well in fires. Dependent upon the materials, workmanship, thickness, and the load carried, fire resistance of 30 minutes to 2 hours may be achieved.

Steelwork

Steel and other metals are extensively used in modern building structures. Generally they can be affected by fire at relatively low temperatures unless they are protected from the effects of the fire by some form of fire retardant materials. This may be done by encasing in concrete, fire retardant boards or spray coatings.

Timber

Timber performs very well in fires as long as it is of sufficient size that, as its outer coat burns away, there is still sufficient strength to do its task. Generally timber does not fail rapidly in a fire, unlike steel.

Glass

Glass generally performs poorly in a fire unless it is fire resistant glass. At high temperatures glass will melt and sag, which is why the traditional fire resistant glass has wire within it.

PROTECTION OF OPENINGS AND VOIDS

Consideration should be given to the protection of openings and voids by the use of fire barriers such as fire shutters, cavity barriers and fire curtains. It is important that construction work be managed to minimise the effect on the structure being worked on to keep fire precautions intact as much as possible. This will involve planning for the prompt re-instatement of protection of openings and voids as soon after their breach to do work as is possible. The temptation to leave all breaches to the end of work and then re-instate them should be avoided - the longer that breaches are left open the higher the risk from fires. Where openings or voids are created as part of the construction process they should be considered as part of the fire risk assessment and consideration be given to the timeliness of their protection. If cavity barriers made from vulnerable or delicate material are to be used they may have to have temporary covering to protect them. This is a good example of the sort of thing that a designer should be considering and making arrangements for as part of the construction design.

7.3 - Fire detection, fire alarm and fire fighting equipment

Common fire detection and alarm systems

FIRE DETECTION

Heat detection

Sensors operate by the melting of a metal (fusion detectors) or expansion of a solid, liquid or gas (thermal expansion detectors).

Radiation detection

Photoelectric cells detect the emission of infra-red/ultra-violet radiation from the fire.

Smoke detection

Using ionising radiations, light scatter (smoke scatters beams of light), obscuration (smoke entering a detector prevents light from reaching a photoelectric cell).

Flammable gas detection

Measures the amount of flammable gas in the atmosphere and compares the value with a reference value.

ALARM SYSTEMS

The purpose of a fire alarm is to give an early warning of a fire in a building for two reasons:
- To increase the safety of occupants by encouraging them to escape to a place of safety.
- To increase the possibility of early extinction of the fire thus reducing the loss of or damage to the property.

Types of fire alarms

Voice	-	Simplest and most effective type but very limited because it is dependent upon the size of the workplace and background noise levels.
Manual alarms	-	Rotary gong, hand bell or triangle and sounder but limited by the scale of the building.
Call points with sounders	-	Standard system, operation of one call point sounds alarm throughout workplace.
Automatic system	-	System as above, with added fire detection to initiate the alarm.

Single-stage alarm

The alarm sounds throughout the whole of the building and calls for total evacuation.

Two-stage alarm

In certain large / high rise buildings it may be better to evacuate the areas of high risk first, usually those closest to the fire or immediately above it. In this case, an evacuation signal is given in the affected area, together with an alert signal in other areas. If this type of system is required, early consultation with the Fire Service is essential.

Staff alarms

In some premises, an immediate total evacuation may not be desirable, e.g. nightclubs, shops, theatres, cinemas. A controlled evacuation by the staff may be preferred, to prevent distress and panic to the occupants. If such a system is used, the alarm must be restricted to the staff and only used where there are sufficient members of staff and they have been fully trained in the action of what to do in case of fire.

Alarms must make a distinctive sound, audible in all parts of the workplace (sound levels should be 65 dB (A) or 5dB (A) above any other noise - which ever is the greater). The meaning of the alarm sound must be understood by all. They may be manually or automatically operated.

Figure 7-19: Easy operation alarm call point.   *Source: ACT.*

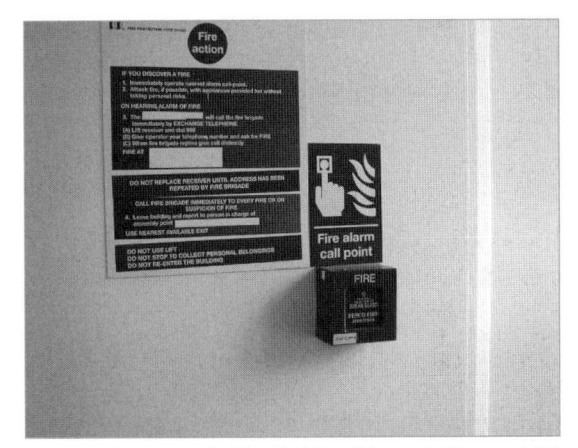

Figure 7-20: Alarm point identified & well located.   *Source: ACT.*

Portable fire fighting equipment

SITING

Portable fire extinguishers should always be sited:
- On the line of escape routes.
- Near, but not too near, to danger points.
- Near to room exits inside or outside according to occupancy and/or risk.
- In multi-storey buildings, at the same position on each floor e.g. top of stair flights or at corners in corridors.
- Where possible in groups forming fire points.
- So that no person need travel more than 30 metres to reach an extinguisher.
- With the carrying handle about one metre from the floor to facilitate ease of handling, removal from wall bracket, or on purpose designed floor stand.
- Away from excesses of heat or cold.

MAINTENANCE AND INSPECTION

The Regulations require that any fire fighting equipment provided must be properly maintained and subject to examination and test at intervals such that it remains effective.

Maintenance

This means service of the fire extinguisher by a competent person. It involves thorough examination of the extinguisher and is usually done annually.

UNIT NCC1 - ELEMENT 7 - FIRE - HAZARDS AND CONTROL

Inspection

A monthly check should be carried out to ensure that extinguishers are in their proper place and have not been discharged, lost pressure or suffered obvious damage. It may be necessary to increase the frequency of checks made for fire extinguishers on a construction site to a weekly basis, due to the less structured or controlled work environment that they are sited in. This could mean that there is a higher risk of them being damaged or used without notification.

TRAINING

The 'Responsible Person' must take measures for fire-fighting as necessary. They should nominate competent persons to implement these measures and provide training and equipment accordingly. It would be good practice to make sure that those that may need to take a lead in operating fire extinguishers can do this competently and for most people this would mean practising how to use them in a situation that reproduces the circumstances of a fire. Training should include:

- Understanding of principles of combustion and classification of fires.
- Identification of the various types of fire extinguisher available to them.
- Principles of use and limitations of extinguishers.
- Considerations for personal safety and the safety of others.
- How to identify if the extinguisher is appropriate to the fire and ready to use.
- How to attack fires with the appropriate extinguisher(s).
- Any specific considerations related to the environment the extinguishers are kept or used in.

Training has to clarify the general and specific rules for use of extinguishers:

General - aim at the seat of the fire and move the extinguisher across the fire to extinguish it - this is particularly appropriate for class A fires.

Specific - if using a foam extinguisher for class B fires the foam is allowed to drop onto the fire by aiming just above it. If this is for a flammable liquid fire contained in an open tank it is possible to get good results by this process or aiming it to the back of the tank and allowing the foam to float over the liquid. For other specific limitations or approaches to the use of individual types of extinguisher see section below.

Main extinguishing media

FIRE EXTINGUISHERS

Since January 1997 all types of certified fire extinguishers should have a red body. With up to 10% of the extinguisher casing in another colour in order to differentiate between extinguishers. British Standard (BS 7863) recommends that manufacturers affix different colour coded panels (for example labels or bands) using the old colour code scheme noted below when describing the different extinguishers.

Water (Colour code - Red)

Water extinguishers should only be used on Class A fires - those involving solids like paper and wood. Water works by cooling the burning material to below its ignition temperature, therefore removing the heat part of the fire triangle, and so the fire goes out. Water is the most common form of extinguishing media and can be used on the majority of fires involving solid materials.

Must not be used on liquid fires or in the vicinity of live electrical equipment.

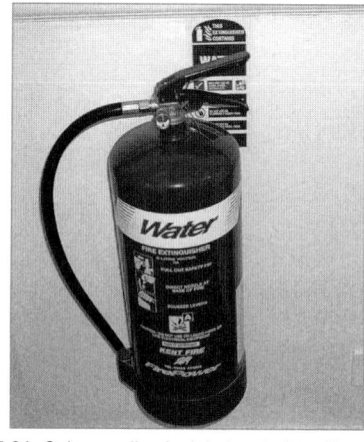

Figure 7-21: Colour coding by label and sign. *Source: ACT.*

Foam (Colour code - Cream)

Foam is especially useful for extinguishing Class B fires - those involving burning liquids and solids which melt and turn to liquids as they burn. Foam works in several ways to extinguish the fire, the main way being to smother the burning liquid, i.e. to stop the oxygen reaching the combustion zone. Foam can also be used to prevent flammable vapours escaping from spilled volatile liquids and also on Class A fires. It is worth noting that the modern spray foams are more efficient than water on a Class A fire.

Must not be used in the vicinity of live electrical equipment, unless electrically rated.

Dry powder (Colour code - Blue)

Designed for Class A, B and C fires but may only subdue Class A fires for a short while. One of the main ways in which powder works to extinguish a fire is the smothering effect, whereby it forms a thin film of powder on the burning liquid thus excluding air. The extinguisher is also excellent for the rapid knock down (flame suppression) of flammable liquid spills.

Powders generally provide extinction faster than foam, but there is a greater risk of re-ignition and this should always be borne in mind. If used indoors, a powder extinguisher can cause problems for the operator due to the inhalation of the powder and obscuration of vision. This type of extinguisher may be used on live electrical equipment.

Vaporising liquids (e.g. Halogenated Hydrocarbon or Halon) (Colour code - Green)

Note: Halons are no longer recommended, for environmental reasons.

Gaseous - Carbon Dioxide (CO_2) (Colour code - Black)

Carbon dioxide (CO2) extinguishers are safe and excellent for use on live electrical equipment. May also be used for small Class B fires in their early stages, indoors or outdoors with little air movement. CO2 replaces the oxygen in the atmosphere surrounding the fuel and the fire is extinguished.

As most carbon dioxide extinguishers last only a few seconds, only small fires should be tackled with this type of extinguisher. CO2 is an asphyxiant and should not be used in confined spaces. It does not remove the heat - therefore beware of the possibility of re-ignition. CO2 extinguishers are very noisy due to the rapid expansion of gas as it is released; this can surprise people when they operate the extinguisher. This expansion causes severe cooling around the discharge horn and can freeze the skin if the operator's hand is in contact with the horn.

Special fires

Class C fires

Except in very small occurrences, a Class C fire involving gas should not normally be extinguished. If a gas fire is to be extinguished, then isolation of the gas supply must also take place.

Class D fires

Class D metal fires are a specialist type of fire and they cannot be extinguished by the use of any of the traditional fire extinguishers. In fact, it may be dangerous to attempt to fight a metal fire with such an extinguisher as an explosion of the metal may take place or toxic fumes may be produced. Metal fires can be extinguished by smothering them with dry sand. However, the sand must be absolutely dry or an explosion may occur. Extinguishers specifically designed for metal fires are produced; the extinguishing agents used may be pyromet, graphite, talc or salt. All of these extinguishers basically operate by the smothering principle.

Class F fires

New style wet chemical extinguishers have been designed to specifically deal with Class F oil fires. This type of extinguisher congeals on top of the oil and excludes the oxygen. They may also be used on Class A fires depending upon the manufacturer's instructions.

SUMMARY MATRIX - FIRE EXTINGUISHERS

	METHOD	CLASS 'A'	CLASS 'B'	CLASS 'C'	CLASS 'D'	ELECTRIC	CLASS 'F'
WATER	Cools	Yes	No	No	No	No	No
SPRAY FOAM	Smothers	Yes	Yes	No	No	No	No
WET CHEMICAL	Chemical	No	No	No	No	No	Yes
DRY POWDER	Smothers & Chemical	Yes	Yes	Yes & Isolate	Special Powders	Yes - Low Voltage	No
HALON	Chemical & Smothers	ILLEGAL					
CARBON DIOXIDE	Smothers	No	Yes - Small Fires	No	No	Yes	No

HOSEREELS

Hosereels are designed for use on Class A - Carbonaceous fires. The hosereel acts as a replacement for water fire extinguishers and it is said that one hosereel equates to 4 x 9 litre water extinguishers. Modern hosereels have an adjustable nozzle and can be adjusted to give a jet of water, water spray or a combination of both. The water jet is normally used for its "striking power" in attacking the seat of a fire. The jet of water should be "played" across the fire surface and into the heart of the fire to extinguish embers etc. The water spray can be used if the burning material is easily disturbed with the possibility of spreading the fire. The spray pattern produced allows larger areas to be covered in one go than if the water jet has been used and, as it has less pressure behind it, it does not spread materials such as dusts or paper as easily.

Advantages

- Continuous supply of water - no time constraint.
- Greater quantity of water is delivered than from an extinguisher, and this has a better effect at extinguishing the fire.
- The person who is attempting to extinguish the fire does not need to get as close as when using extinguishers.
- A radical spray pattern can be produced to protect the user from radiated heat.

Disadvantages

- Considerable physical effort may be required to pull the hosereel to the fire, especially if the route is twisting and has lots of obstructions.
- Any doors through which the hosereel is pulled will become wedged open by the reel.
- The user may stay in the vicinity of the fire too long.
- The extended hosereel may create an additional tripping hazard.

Limitations

- Hosereels should be connected to a permanent water supply so they are not limited by discharge time factors as are extinguishers.
- The hosereel itself should comply with current standards which permit up to 30 metres of hosereel to be used. This does limit the use of a hosereel by virtue of the distance that it is located away from a fire.
- Considerable physical strength is required to pull 30 metres of hose, and for this reason consideration should be given to providing an increased number of hosereels with a shorter length of hose.
- A limiting factor is the likely route through which the hosereel will need to pass. If this route includes a lot of corners, turns or doors, then hosereels may not be the most suitable fire equipment to be provided.

7.4 - Means of escape

Requirements for means of escape

The RRFSO 2005 requires the responsible person to "make and give effect to such arrangements as are appropriate, having regard to the size of his undertaking and the nature of its activities, for the effective planning, organisation, control, monitoring and review of the preventive and protective measures". The RRFSO 2005 also sets out the type of requirements necessary with regard to emergency routes and exits. An adequate means of escape is essential for all premises. The following general factors should be taken into consideration when planning means of escape.

TRAVEL DISTANCES

Travel distance is a significant component of a successful means of escape plan. Travel distances are judged on the basis of distance to a place of safety in the open air and away from the building; the distance needs to be kept to the minimum. The distance includes travel around obstructions in the workplace and may be greatly affected by any work in progress on a construction site. If someone is outside on a scaffold it is unlikely to be considered as a place of safety and the distance would usually be taken as that to reach the ground away from the building (for example, at an assembly point).

- The route must be sufficiently wide and of sufficiently short distance to allow speedy and safe evacuation.
- There should normally be alternative routes leading in different directions.
- Everyone should be able to escape unaided (if able bodied).
- The distance between work stations and the nearest fire exit should be minimised.

STAIRS

Staircases form an integral part of the means of escape from fire in most buildings. If they are to be part of the escape route, the following points must be ensured:

Figure 7-22: Fire escape - hazard. *Source: ACT.*

- Fire resistant structure.
- Fitted with fire doors.
- Doors must not be wedged open.
- Wide enough to take the required number of people.
- Must lead direct to fresh air, or to two totally separate routes of escape.
- Non slip/trip and in good condition.
- No combustible storage within staircase.

PASSAGEWAYS

- The route should lead directly to the open air via a protected route (where necessary).
- Route to be kept unobstructed.

DOORS

- Exit doors are to open outwards easily (unless small numbers of people involved).
- Provide fire doors along the escape route.
- Fire doors along with fire resistant structures serve two purposes:
  - Prevent the spread of fire.
  - Ensure that there is means of escape for persons using the building.
- They should not be wedged open.
- Lead to open air - safety.

EMERGENCY LIGHTING

Emergency lighting should be considered if escape is likely to be required in dark conditions e.g. scaffolding. This could mean late afternoon in winter time, not just at night time.

EXIT AND DIRECTIONAL SIGNS

The escape route should be adequately signposted and easy to follow.

ASSEMBLY POINTS

The assembly point is a place of safety where staff wait whilst any incident is investigated, and where confirmation can be made that all persons have evacuated the premises. The main factors to consider are:

- Safe distance from building or site.
- Sited in a safe position.
- Not sited so that staff will be in the way of Fire Brigade.
- Must be able to walk away from assembly point and back to a public road.
- Clearly signed.
- More than one provided to suit numbers and groups of people.
- Communications should be provided between assembly points.
- Measures provided to decide if evacuation successful.
- Person must be in charge of assembly point and identified.
- Person to meet / brief the Fire Brigade clear and identified.

Figure 7-23: Assembly point. Source: ACT.

NEED FOR CONTINUAL REVIEW AS CONSTRUCTION ACTIVITY PROGRESSES

In all workplaces there is a need to actively review and revise the fire risk assessment, the fire safety measures that apply and the fire/emergency plans. This aspect of fire safety is absolutely vital in construction sites or any other workplace where layout changes are constantly taking place.

Dependant upon the state of the build, fire safety may need to be inspected on a weekly or even daily basis. Checks and assessment should be made to ensure that the fire plan for means of escape is still appropriate and that the following fire safety measures are not being compromised:

- Escape routes.
- Access to fire alarms.
- Audibility of fire alarm systems.
- Access and availability of fire fighting equipment.
- Suitability of fire safety signage.
- Need for and suitability of escape lighting.
- Fire protection / fire resistant structures within the building.
- Introduction of new fire hazards e.g. hot works.
- Correct storage / use of flammable materials.
- Site security / arson prevention.
- New staff and the need for 'fire induction'.

If, as a result of any works that need to be carried out, fire safety standards will be reduced then additional compensating factors may need to be introduced. For example, if detector heads need to be covered to prevent false alarms a fire watch system of patrols may be introduced to compensate. As can be seen, fire safety is a constantly changing factor which must be integral to the everyday management of site safety.

7.5 - Evacuation of the workplace

Emergency evacuation procedures

Article 15 of the RRFSO 2005 requires that the responsible person "establish and, where necessary, give effect to appropriate procedures, including safety drills, to be followed in the event of serious and imminent danger to relevant persons". Furthermore it sets out a requirement to "nominate a sufficient number of competent persons to implement those procedures in so far as they relate to the evacuation of relevant persons from the premises".

The danger which may threaten persons if an emergency occurs at work depends on many different factors; consequently it is not possible to construct one model procedure for action in the event of fire and emergency for all premises. Evacuation procedures need to reflect the type of emergency, the people affected and the premises involved. Many of the different issues to consider for different emergencies have common factors, for example, evacuation in an efficient / effective manner, an agreed assembly location (which may be different for different emergencies) and checks to ensure people are safe. These factors are considered below with regard to fire emergencies.

APPOINTMENT OF FIRE MARSHALS

In all premises a person should be nominated to be responsible for co-ordinating the fire evacuation plan. This may be the same person that organises fire instruction and training and drills and co-ordinates the evacuation at the time of the fire. They may appoint persons such as fire marshals to assist them in fulfilling the role. This involves the appointment of certain staff to act as fire marshals to assist with evacuation. The way in which they assist will vary between organisations; for example, some will check areas of the building in the event of a fire to ensure no person is still inside and others will lead the evacuation to show where to go. The fire marshals' appointment should be made known to workers and they should be clearly identifiable at the time of emergency so that those that are asked to evacuate understand the authority of the person requiring them to do so. The appointment of fire marshals contributes to an employer's compliance with the requirement to establish competent persons to assist with health and safety.

FIRE INSTRUCTION NOTICES

At conspicuous positions in all parts of the location, and adjacent to all fire alarm actuating points (e.g. break glass operated call points), printed notices should be exhibited stating, in concise terms, the essentials of the action to be taken upon discovering a fire and on hearing the fire alarm. It is usual to also state what someone must do when they discover a fire.

Fire action

The action in the event of a fire and upon discovery needs to be immediate, and a simple fire action plan should be put into effect. A good plan of action would include the following points.

On discovering a fire:

- Sound the fire alarm (to warn others).
- Call the fire service.
- Go to the assembly point.

On hearing the alarm:

- Leave the building by the nearest exit.
- Close doors behind you.
- Go to the assembly point.
- Get out of the building and stay out.

On evacuation:

- Do not take risks.
- Do not stop for personal belongings.
- Do not use lifts.
- Do not return to the building unless authorised to do so.
- Report to assembly point.

Figure 7-24: Fire instruction notice. Source: ACT.

Note: you must consider the wording on notices that are posted and ensure that workers are instructed and trained to do what is required.

FIRE TRAINING

Typical issues to be included in a fire training programme relating to emergency action are:

- Fire prevention.
- Recognition of fire alarms and the actions to be taken.
- Understanding the emergency signs.
- Location of fire escape routes and assembly points.
- Requirements for safe evacuation (e.g. non-use of lifts, do not run etc).
- Location and operation of call points and other means of raising the alarm.
- How the fire service is called.
- Location, use and limitations of fire fighting equipment.
- Consideration of people with special needs.
- Identity and role of fire marshals.

FIRE DRILLS

A fire drill is intended to ensure, by means of training and rehearsal, that in the event of fire:

- The people who may be in danger act in a calm, orderly and efficient manner.
- Those designated with specific duties carry them out in an organised and effective manner.
- The means of escape are used in accordance with a predetermined and practised plan.
- An opportunity for management leadership.

The fire drill enables all people involved in the evacuation to practice and learn under as near realistic circumstances as possible. This can identify what works well in the evacuation procedure and what does not. Practice in the form of a drill helps people to respond quickly to the alarm and, because they have done it before, to make their way efficiently to the assembly point. At least once a year a practice fire drill should normally be carried out simulating conditions in which one or more of the escape routes from the building are obstructed. This will assist in developing an awareness of the alternative exits that can be taken and assist in ensuring people understand the unpredictability of fires.

ROLL CALL

The traditional method of undertaking a roll call is by use of a checklist of names. Very few workplaces can now operate this system as they do not have such a static workforce as this system requires. Where they can operate they will provide a speedy and efficient means of identifying who has arrived at the assembly point and who has not. Where strict security control to a construction site is used, with signing in and out, this may make this process more viable. This requires people on site to report to their allocated assembly point and for someone (e.g. a Fire Marshal) to confirm that they have arrived safely and determine if anyone is missing.

If it is not known exactly who is in a building a system of Fire Marshals who can make a check of the building at the time of their own evacuation (without endangering their own safety) may be employed. This can assist with the process and may identify people that have not evacuated. However, this system may not be able to provide an absolute confirmation that everyone has evacuated as there may be limited opportunity for the Fire Marshal to check the whole of the area allocated to them. Any doubt or confirmed missing persons should be reported to the person nominated to report to the fire service, who in turn will provide a report to the fire service as soon as they arrive.

PROVISIONS FOR THE INFIRM AND DISABLED

When planning a fire evacuation system we need to consider who may be in the workplace, their abilities and capabilities. Any disability e.g. hearing, vision, mental or mobility impairment must be catered for. Some of the arrangements may be to provide the person with a nominated assistant(s) to support their speedy escape, for example, with the use of a specially designed evacuation chair to enable them to make their way out of a building down emergency exit stairs. Part of the provision is to make sure they are capable of knowing that an emergency exists. This may mean providing them with special alarm arrangements that cater for their disability, for example, a visual and or vibrating alert for the hearing impaired.

Element 8

Chemical and biological health - hazards and control

Learning outcomes

On completion of this element, candidates should be able to demonstrate understanding of the content through the application of knowledge to familiar and unfamiliar situations. In particular they should be able to:

8.1 Identify the forms of, and classification of, substances hazardous to health to be found on a construction site.

8.2 Explain the factors to be considered when undertaking an assessment of the health risks from substances commonly encountered in construction workplaces.

8.3 Describe the use and limitations of Workplace Exposure Limits including the purpose of long term and short term exposure limits.

8.4 Distinguish between acute and chronic health effects.

8.5 Outline appropriate control measures that should be used to reduce the risk of ill-health from exposure to hazardous substances.

8.6 Outline a strategy for the control of hazardous dusts in the construction workplace.

8.7 Outline the basic requirements related to disposal of waste and effluent (and the control of atmospheric pollution) from construction sites.

Content

8.1 - Forms and classification of hazardous substances	127
Forms of chemical agent	127
Forms of biological agents	127
Main classification of substances hazardous to health	127
The health risks of specific agents	129
8.2 - Risks associated with hazardous substances	130
Routes of entry	130
Use of the above to assess health risks	132
Sources of information	132
Limitations of information in assessing risks to health	134
Basic surveys for health risks	134
Basic monitoring equipment	134
8.3 - Workplace exposure limits	138
Basis for workplace exposure limits	138
Long-term and short-term exposure limits	138
Limitations of exposure limits	138
Principle of reducing exposure levels	138
8.4 - Acute and chronic health effects	139
Difference between acute and chronic health effects	139
8.5 - Appropriate control measures	139
Duty to prevent exposure or, where this is not reasonably practicable, adequately control it	139
Ensuring the workplace exposure limit is not exceeded	139
Methods of control	139
Further controls of substances that can cause cancer, asthma or damage to genes	146
8.6 - Control of hazardous dusts	147
Substances that can cause cancer, asthma or damage to genes that can be passed from one generation to another	147
Hazardous dusts	147
Asbestos	148
8.7 - Waste disposal and control of pollution	151
Basic environmental issues relating to waste disposal and effluent in the construction industry	151
The principal duties imposed by Parts I and II of the Environmental Protection Act 1990	151

Sources of reference

An introduction to local exhaust ventilation (HSG37), HSE Books ISBN 0-7176-1001-2
Asbestos essentials task manual (HSG210), HSE Books ISBN 0-7176-1887-0
Control of substances hazardous to health (ACOP) (L5), HSE Books ISBN 0-7176-2981-3
Health risks management: A guide to working with solvents (HSG188) HSE Books ISBN 0-7176-1664-9
Personal Protective Equipment at Work (Guidance) (L25), HSE Books ISBN 0-7176-6139-3
Respiratory protective equipment at work - A practical guide (HSG53), HSE Books ISBN 0-7176-2904-X
Step by step guide to COSHH assessment (HSG97), HSE Books ISBN 0-7176-2785-3
Occupational exposure limits (EH40), HSE Books (updated annually) ISBN 0-7176-2977-5
Working with asbestos cement (HSG189/2), HSE Books ISBN 0-7176-1667-3
Working with materials containing asbestos. Control of Asbestos Regulations 2006 (ACOP) (L143) HSE Books ISBN 0-7176-6206-3

Relevant statutory provisions

The Chemicals (Hazard Information and Packaging for Supply) Regulations (CHIP) 2002
The Control of Asbestos at Work Regulations (CAWR) 2006
The Control of Substances Hazardous to Health Regulations (COSHH) 2002
The Environmental Protection Act (EPA) 1990
The Hazardous Waste (England and Wales) Regulations (HWR) 2005
The Personal Protective Equipment at Work Regulations (PPER) 1992

8.1 - Forms and classification of hazardous substances

Forms of chemical agent

The form taken by a hazardous substance is a contributory factor to its potential for harm. Principally the form affects how easily a substance gains entry to the body, how it is absorbed into the body and how it reaches a susceptible site.

Chemical agents take many forms, the most common being as follows:

Dusts	These are solid airborne particles, often created by operations such as grinding, crushing, milling, sanding or demolition - e.g. silica.
Fibres	Dust may be created that is made up of tiny fibres e.g. mineral wool and asbestos.
Fumes	Are solid particles formed by condensation from the gaseous state - e.g. lead fume, welding fume.
Smoke	Particles that result from incomplete combustion. These can be either solid or liquid state.
Gases	Formless fluids usually produced by chemical processes involving combustion or by the interaction of chemical substance. A gas will normally seek to fill the space completely into which it is liberated - e.g. chlorine gas.
Mists and aerosols	Are finely dispersed liquid droplets suspended in air. Mists are mainly created by spraying, foaming, pickling and electro-plating - e.g. mist from a water pressure washer.
Vapour	Is the gaseous form of a material normally encountered in a liquid or solid state at normal room temperature and pressure; typical examples are solvents - e.g. trichloroethylene which releases vapours when the container is opened.
Liquids	Substances which are liquid at normal temperature and pressure.
Solids	Are materials which are solid at normal temperature and pressure.

Forms of biological agents

FUNGI

Fungi are a variety of organisms that act in a parasitic manner, feeding on organic matter. Most are either harmless or positively beneficial to health; however a number of them cause harm to humans and may be fatal. Examples of the fungi organism is the mould from rotten hay called aspergilla which causes aspergillosis (Farmer's Lung). Farmer's lung is an allergic reaction to the mould. This occurs deep in the lungs in the alveoli. It leads to shortness of breath, which gets progressively worse at each exposure. The resulting attack is similar to asthma. Aspergilla can also cause short-term effects of irritation to the eyes and nose and coughing. Moulds from the same family can cause Ringworm and Athlete's Foot.

BACTERIA

Bacteria are single cell organisms. Most bacteria are harmless to humans and many are beneficial. The bacteria that can cause disease are called pathogens. Examples of harmful bacteria are leptospira (causing Weil's disease), bacillus anthracis (causing anthrax), and legionella pneumophila (causing Legionnaires disease).

VIRUSES

Viruses are the smallest known type of infectious agent. They invade the cells of other organisms, which they take over and make copies of themselves and while not all cause disease many of them do. Examples of viruses are hepatitis which can cause liver damage and the Human Immunodeficiency Virus (HIV) which causes acquired immune deficiency syndrome (AIDS).

Main classification of substances hazardous to health

Indication of danger	Symbol (orange background)	Category of danger	Characteristic properties and body responses
Irritant	X	Irritant	A non-corrosive substance which, through immediate, prolonged or repeated contact with the skin or mucous membrane, can cause inflammation e.g. butyl ester, a severe irritant which can cause abdominal pain, vomiting and burning of the skin and eyes.
		Sensitising (by contact)	May cause an allergic skin reaction which will worsen on further exposures (allergic dermatitis), e.g. nickel or epoxy resin.

Indication of danger	Symbol (orange background)	Category of danger	Characteristic properties and body responses
Corrosive	☣	Corrosive	May destroy living tissues on contact e.g. sulphuric (battery) acid or sodium hydroxide (caustic soda).
Harmful	✕	Harmful	If inhaled or ingested or it penetrates the skin, has an adverse effect on health e.g. some solvents causing narcosis or central nervous system failure.
		Sensitising (by inhalation)	May cause an allergic respiratory reaction, which will progressively worsen on further exposures (asthma), e.g. flour dust, isocyanates.
		Mutagenic (category 3)	Evidence of mutation in Ames Test and possible somatic cell mutation.
		Toxic to reproduction (category 3)	Animal data, not necessarily relevant.
Toxic	☠	Toxic	If inhaled or ingested or it penetrates the skin, may involve serious acute or chronic health risks and even death e.g. arsenic, a systemic poison.
		Mutagenic (categories 1 & 2)	May cause genetic defects, e.g. 2-Ethoxyethanol may impair fertility.
		Toxic to reproduction (categories 1 & 2)	May cause harm to the unborn child, e.g. lead suspected of causing restricted development of the brain of the foetus.
Very Toxic	☠		If inhaled or ingested or it penetrates the skin, may involve extremely serious acute or chronic health risks and even death e.g. cyanide, a severe irritant and systemic poison.
			Source: The Chemicals (Hazard Information & Packaging for Supply) Regulations (CHIP 3) 2002.
Carcinogenic	☠	Carcinogenic (category 1)	Substances known to be carcinogenic to humans. There is sufficient medical evidence to establish a causal association between human exposure to the substance and the development of cancer.
	☠	Carcinogenic (category 2)	Substances that should be regarded as if they are carcinogenic to humans, for which there is sufficient evidence, based on long-term animal studies and other relevant information, to provide a strong presumption that human exposure may result in the development of cancer.
	✕	Carcinogenic (category 3)	Substances that cause concern owing to possible carcinogenic effects, but for which available information is not adequate to make satisfactory assessments. e.g. benzyl chloride.

Figure 8-1: Harmful, toxic. *Source: ACT.*

The health risks of specific agents

ORGANIC SOLVENTS

Include highly volatile / flammable cleaning agents such as acetone, organo chlorides such as trichloroethylene (used for commercial degreasing) or carbon tetrachloride used in dry cleaning processes. In the construction industry they may be encountered as residual contents of storage tanks or may be used as convenient cleaning substances to remove adhesives. Trichloroethylene is capable of absorption through the skin and it is a narcotic - classified "Harmful" by CHIP 2002 (as amended 2005). If the vapours are inhaled, it can cause drowsiness very quickly, depress the central nervous system and lead to liver failure and death if exposure is for prolonged periods.

CARBON DIOXIDE

A simple asphyxiant produced as a by-product of the brewing processes. As a simple asphyxiant it displaces oxygen in the air that we breathe and means insufficient oxygen goes to the brain, leading to collapse and death. Available commercially as a frozen solid 'dry ice' used as a refrigerant or to generate 'smoke' in theatre productions. Provides the constituent part of a carbon dioxide fire extinguisher and may be encountered in fixed fire fighting installations in buildings. It may be encountered in confined spaces, such as trenches, in areas with chalky soil as carbon dioxide is evolved naturally; it is heavier than air and tends to gather in low areas.

NITROGEN

Rapid release of nitrogen gas into an enclosed space can displace oxygen, and therefore represents an asphyxiation hazard. This may happen with very few warning symptoms or signs, since the human carotid body is a relatively slow and poor low-oxygen (hypoxia) sensing system.

Direct skin contact with liquid nitrogen causes severe frostbite (cryogenic burns) within moments to seconds, although not instantly on contact, depending on form of liquid nitrogen (liquid or mist) and surface area of the nitrogen-soaked material.

CARBON MONOXIDE

Is a chemical asphyxiant produced as a by-product of incomplete combustion of carbon fuels e.g. gas water heaters, compressors, pumps, dumper trucks or generators. It is a particular risk when operated in poorly ventilated confined areas where workers are forced to breathe it. Carbon monoxide has a great affinity (200 times that of oxygen) for the haemoglobin red blood cells which means it will inhibit oxygen uptake by red blood cells resulting in chemical asphyxiation, leading to collapse and death.

ISOCYANATES

Isocyanates are used in the manufacture of resins and urethane foams; common compounds are toluene di-isocyanate (TDI) and methylene bisphenyl di-isocyanate (MDI). TDI is an extremely volatile vapour and is evolved during the manufacture of foams. TDI and MDI are highly toxic in very small amounts (parts per billion) and inhalation will result in a severe respiratory reaction. Isocyanates are sensitising agents; in particular they sensitise the lungs.

LEAD

Lead poisoning results from the inhalation of fumes produced from the heating of lead, or certain solders containing lead, at temperatures above 5000C. In construction activities this will include exposure to lead by oxyacetylene cutting of metal coated with paint containing lead. In addition, lead poisoning may result from the inhalation of organic lead compounds e.g. tetraethyl lead. Chronic (cumulative) lead poisoning may result in anaemia, mental dullness and is often accompanied by the presence of a blue line around the gums. Acute lead poisoning is often fatal; symptoms include muscular twitch, hallucinations and violent behaviour.

SILICA

Silica exists naturally as crystalline minerals (tridymite, cristobalite). A common variety is quartz. Industrially silica is used in the morphous (after heating) form e.g. fumed silica, silica gel. In construction activities it may be encountered in stone work or work with quartz based tiles. Inhalation of silica can result in silicosis, a fibrosis of the lung. Nodular lesions are formed which ultimately destroy lung structure reducing the capacity of the lungs.

CEMENT DUST

Inhaling high levels of dust may occur when workers empty bags of cement. In the short term, such exposure irritates the nose and throat and causes choking and difficult breathing. Sanding, grinding, or cutting concrete can also release large amounts of dust containing high levels of crystalline silica. Prolonged or repeated exposure can lead to a disabling and often fatal lung disease called *silicosis*. Some studies also indicate a link between crystalline silica exposure and lung cancer.

WET CEMENT

The hazards of wet cement are due to its caustic, abrasive, and drying properties. Continuous contact between skin and wet concrete allows alkaline compounds to penetrate and burn the skin. When wet concrete or mortar is trapped against the skin for instance, by falling inside a worker's boots or gloves or by soaking through protective clothing the result may be first, second, or third degree burns or skin ulcers. These injuries can take several months to heal and may involve hospitalisation and skin grafts.

Ironically, severe cases often occur when personal protective clothing or equipment is worn. Wet concrete may get trapped inside rubber boots or gloves or gradually soak through coveralls. Concrete finishers kneeling on fresh concrete have had their knees severely burned. Moisture from sweat or wet clothing reacts with the cement dust to form a caustic solution.

WOOD DUST

Wood dust becomes a potential health problem when wood particles from processes such as sanding and cutting become airborne. Breathing these particles may cause allergic respiratory symptoms, mucosal and non-allergic respiratory symptoms, and cancer. The extent of these hazards and the associated wood types has not been clearly established.

LEPTOSPIRA

The bacteria Leptospira, spiral shaped bacteria, penetrates the skin and causes leptospirosis (Weil's disease). Rodents represent the most important reservoir of infections, especially rats (also gerbils, voles, and field mice). Other sources of infection are dogs, hedgehogs, foxes, pigs, and cattle.

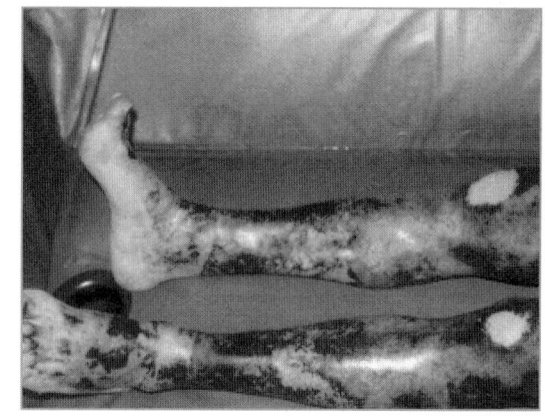

Figure 8-2: Skin burns from wet cement. *Source: SHP (August 03).*

These animals are not necessarily ill, but carry leptospires in their kidneys and excrete it in their urine. Infection can be transmitted directly via direct contact with blood, tissues, organs or urine of one of the host animals or indirectly by contaminated environment.

Infection enters through broken skin or mucous membrane. Symptoms vary but include flu-like illness, conjunctivitis, liver damage (including jaundice), kidney failure and meningitis. If untreated infection may be fatal.

Construction workers most at risk are those who work where rats prevail and will include water and sewage work, demolition or refurbishment of old unoccupied buildings, and those working on sites adjoining rivers and other watercourses. The bacteria's survival depends on protection from direct sunlight, so it survives well in water courses and ditches protected by vegetation.

LEGIONNELLOSIS / LEGIONNAIRES DISEASE

Legionnellosis / Legionnaires' disease is a type of pneumonia caused by Legionella Pneumophila, a bacterium. The organism is ubiquitous in water and frequently present in water cooling systems and domestic hot water systems. Large workplace buildings are therefore susceptible to infected water systems, especially hotels and hospitals.

The organism is widespread in the environment, but needs certain conditions to multiply, for example the presence of sludge, scale, algae, rust and organic material plus a temperature of 20 - 500°C. Transmission is from inhalation of the organism in contaminated aerosols. Smoking, age and alcohol may increase susceptibility. Symptoms are aching muscles, headaches and fever followed by a cough. Confusion, emotional disturbance and delirium may follow the acute phase. The fatality rate in the UK is about 12%.

Greatest risk areas are from showers, air conditioning sprays, water cooling towers and recirculating water cooling systems. The hazard can be controlled by proper design of water systems, disinfection/chlorination of water or heating water to 55-600°C.

HEPATITIS

Hepatitis is inflammation of the liver; there are a number of types of hepatitis the B variety being the most serious. Hepatitis is caused by a virus and is passed from human to human. Hepatitis A is spread by ingesting the virus from the faeces of an infected person, from food or water contaminated by the faeces of a contaminated person or from eating raw or undercooked shellfish harvested from contaminated water. The hepatitis B virus, which is very resilient in that it remains viable for weeks in the environment outside the human body, is resistant to common antiseptics and is not affected by boiling for less than thirty minutes.

Symptoms vary, but typically the sequence is: flu-like illness with aches and pains in the joints, general tiredness, anorexia, nausea and high fever, jaundice and the liver enlarged and tender.

Workers most at risk are: those in health care: hospital personnel, dentists, laboratory staff, domestic staff, teachers, prison officers, ambulance staff, police and customs officers. Intravenous drug abusers are also seriously at risk; therefore workers who are responsible for keeping streets, parks and toilets clean are at risk from discarded needles. Construction workers carrying out work on old derelict property and those clearing ground that may have been used by intravenous drug users are particularly at risk.

TETANUS

A life-threatening disease caused by toxins produced by the bacterium Clostridium tetani, which often grow at the site of a cut or wound while working, or even an animal bite. There is greater risk of developing tetanus if the wound is deep or if it gets dirty with soil or manure, but even small wounds such as a prick from a thorn can allow enough bacteria to get into the body to cause tetanus. Muscles first become stiff, then rigidly fixed (lockjaw). Vaccination against tetanus should be done every 10 years or at the time of injury.

8.2 - Risks associated with hazardous substances

Routes of entry

INHALATION

The most significant industrial entry route is inhalation. It has been estimated that at least 90% of industrial poisons are absorbed through the lungs. Harmful substances can directly attack the lung tissue causing a local effect or pass through to the blood system, to be carried round the body and affect target organs such as the liver.

Typical effects of entry are:

Local effect - Silicosis

Dust causes scarring of the lung leading to inelastic fibrous tissue to develop reducing lung capacity.

Systemic effect - Anoxia

Carbon monoxide replaces oxygen in the bloodstream affecting the nervous system.

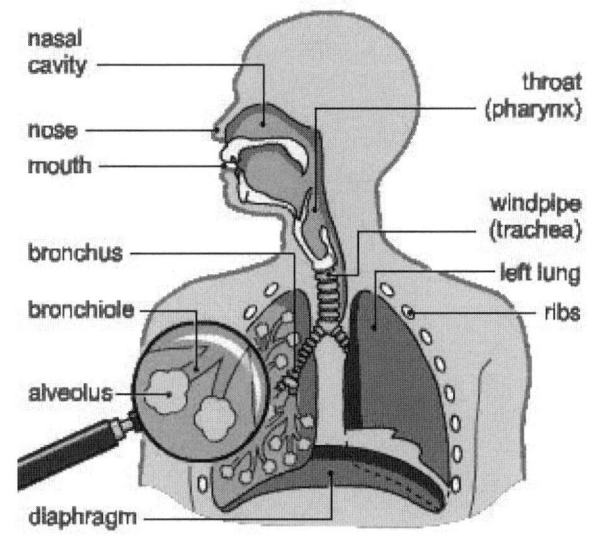

Figure 8-3: Respiratory system.   Source: BBC.

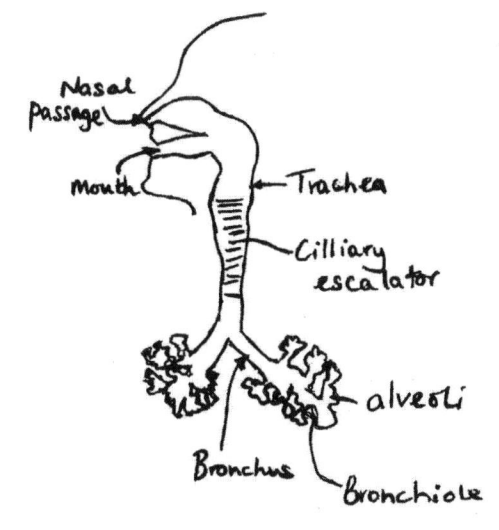

Figure 8-4: Hand drawn respiratory system.   Source: ACT.

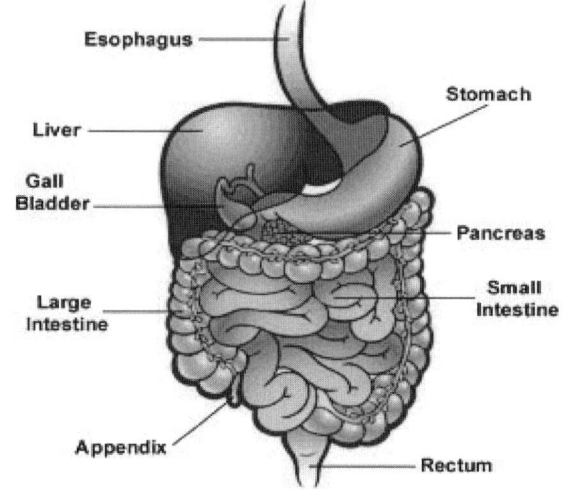

Figure 8-5: Digestive system.   Source: STEM.

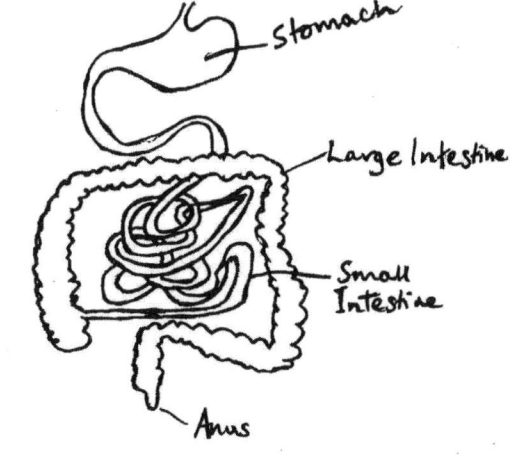

Figure 8-6: Hand drawn digestive system.   Source: ACT.

INGESTION

This route normally presents the least problem as it is unlikely that any significant quantity of harmful liquid or solid will be swallowed without deliberate intent. However, accidents will occur where small amounts of contaminant are transferred from the fingers to the mouth if eating, drinking or smoking in chemical areas is allowed or where a substance has been decanted into a container normally used for drinking. The sense of taste will often be a defence if chemicals are taken in through this route, causing the person to spit it out. If the substance is taken in, vomiting and/or excretion may mean the substance does not cause a systemic problem, though a direct effect, for example ingestion of an acid may destroy cells in the mouth, oesophagus or stomach.

ABSORPTION (SKIN CONTACT)

Substances can enter through the skin, cuts or abrasions and conjunctiva of the eye. Solvents such as organic solvents, e.g. toluene and trichloroethylene, can enter either accidentally or if used for washing. The substance may have a local effect, such as de-fatting of the skin resulting in inflammation and cracking of the horny layer, or pass through into the blood system causing damage to the brain, bone marrow and liver.

Contact dermatitis

Caused by contact with substances which interfere with normal skin physiology leading to inflammation of skin, usually on the hands, wrists and forearms. The skin turns red and in some cases may be itchy. Small blisters may occur and the condition may take the form of dry and cracked skin. There are many chemicals which may irritate the skin; including cement, soaps, detergents, industrial chemicals, some metals, cosmetics and plants. For babies, contact with urine causes nappy rash. Removal from exposure allows normal cell repair. A similar level of repeat exposure results in the same response. This class of dermatitis is called contact dermatitis.

Sensitisation dermatitis

A second form of dermatitis is called sensitisation dermatitis. In this case a person exposed to the substance develops dermatitis.

Tissue inflammation and cell damage. When taken away the dermatitis repairs, but the body gets ready for later exposures by preparing the body's defence mechanisms. A subsequent small exposure is enough to cause a major response by the immune system. The person will have become sensitised and will no longer be able to tolerate exposure to the substance without a reaction occurring.

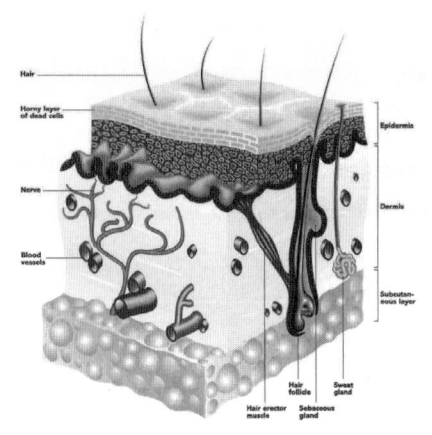

Figure 8-7: Skin layer.   *Source: SHP.*

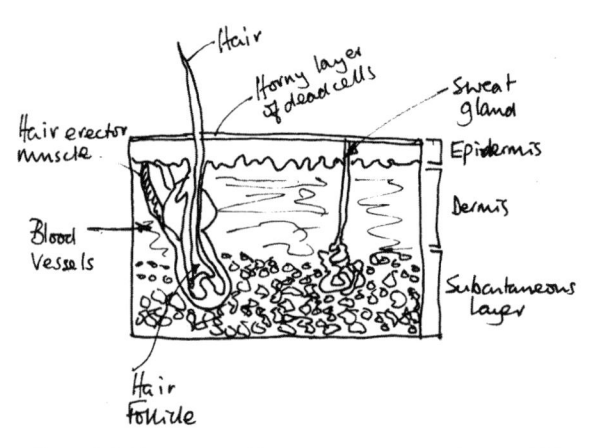

Figure 8-8: Hand drawn skin layer.   *Source: ACT.*

Dermatitis can be prevented by:
- Clean working conditions and properly planned work systems.
- Careful attention to skin hygiene principles.
- Prompt attention to cuts, abrasions and spillages onto the skin.
- Use of protective equipment.
- Barrier cream can help.
- Pre-employment screening for sensitive individuals.

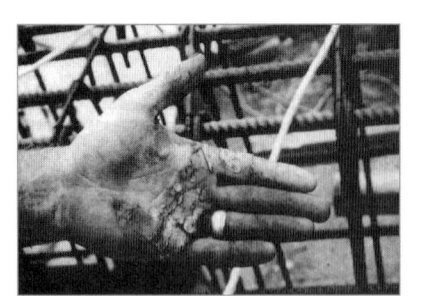

Figure 8-9: Dermatitis.   *Source: SHP.*

INJECTION

A forceful breach of the skin, perhaps as a result of injury, can carry harmful substances through the skin barrier; for example handling broken glass which cuts the skin and transfers a biological or chemical agent. On construction sites there are quite a few items that present a hazard of penetration, such as nails in broken up false work that might be trodden on and penetrate the foot presenting a risk of infection from tetanus. In addition, some land or buildings being worked on may have been used by intravenous drug users and their needles may present a risk of injection of a virus, such as hepatitis. The forced injection of an agent into the body provides an easy route past the skin, which usually acts as the body's defence mechanism and protects people from the effects of many agents that do not have the ability to penetrate.

Use of the above to assess health risks

In order to assess the risks to health it is necessary to know the following:
- The form the substance is in: solid, liquid, dust, gas, etc.
- The classification of the hazard: very toxic, toxic, corrosive, etc.
- How much of the substance will be present and its concentration.
- The routes of entry onto and into the body: inhalation, ingestion, skin, pervasion, absorption.
- Whether the substance has an acute or chronic affect or both.
- The extent to which the body's defences will deal with the substance.
- The first signs of damage or ill-health.
- The vulnerability of the people involved in the process: young persons, pregnant workers; anyone who has existing health problems, such as skin problems or bronchitis.
- The existing control measures.

Considering the above issues will help the assessor decide whether the risks to health are tolerable or acceptable or further controls are needed.

Sources of information

PRODUCT LABELS

All substances available for use in the workplace should be labelled in accordance with the Chemicals (Hazard Information Packaging for Supply) Regulations (CHIP) 2002 e.g. toxic, harmful, irritant, and corrosive.

Where a dangerous chemical is supplied in a package, the package must be labelled. Packaging must be safe and able to withstand the conditions. The label must state the hazards and precautions required.

More useful information to help ensure the safe use of dangerous substances comes in the form of risk phrases and safety phrases. These are often displayed either on the container label (if it is large enough) or in the safety data sheet. There are currently 122 risk phrases and 74 safety phrases, some examples are given below and detailed information can be found in the ACOP to CHIP 2002.

Risk Phrase		Safety Phrase	
R3	Extreme risk of explosion by shock, friction, fire or other sources of ignition.	S2	Keep out of reach of children.
R20	Harmful by inhalation.	S20	When using do not eat or drink.
R30	Can become highly flammable in use.	S25	Avoid contact with eyes.
R45	May cause cancer.	S36	Wear suitable protective clothing.
R47	May cause birth defects.	S41	In case of fire and/or explosion do not breathe fumes.

Absence of hazard symbols or risk and safety advice does not mean the item is harmless.

Figure 8-10: Product labels. *Source: Stocksigns.*

HSE GUIDANCE NOTE EH40

EH40, which is prepared and published annually by the Health and Safety Executive (HSE), contains the lists of Workplace Exposure Limits (WEL) for use with the Control of Substances Hazardous to Health Regulations (COSHH) 2002, a description of the limit setting process, technical definitions and explanatory notes. EH40 is mostly guidance but does contain sections of special legal status. Some sections have been approved by the Health and Safety Commission (HSC) and are statutory requirements that must be complied with.

MANUFACTURERS' HEALTH AND SAFETY DATA SHEETS

Section 6 of HASAWA 1974 requires manufacturers, importers and suppliers to provide information on substances for use at work; this is usually provided in the form of a material safety data sheet (MSDS). CHIP 2002 sets out the content of data sheets for substances, the content must include the following.

- Identification of the substance/preparation and the company.
- Composition/information on ingredients.
- Hazards identification.
- First-aid measures.
- Fire fighting measures.
- Accidental release measures.
- Handling and storage.
- Exposure controls/personal protection.
- Physical and chemical properties.
- Stability and reactivity.
- Toxicological information.
- Ecological information.
- Disposal considerations.
- Transport information.
- Regulatory information.

INFORMATION TO BE INCLUDED BY THE SUPPLIER

Providing hazard information

After deciding what the classification is, suppliers have to tell their customers about the hazards; and tell them, as far as possible, how their customers can use the supplier's chemicals safely.

Suppliers do this by a label and a material safety data sheet which is critical if the supplier's customers use their chemical at work. Other equally good measures may be used for consumers.

Labelling

If suppliers supply a dangerous chemical in a package, the package must be labelled. If the chemical is not supplied in a package (e.g. if the chemical is supplied from a tanker or down a pipeline), then the supplier does not have to provide a label since this would not be practical.

The aim of the label is to inform anyone handling the package or using the chemicals about its hazards, and give brief advice on what precautions are needed. Labels usually possess information such as the chemical's name and how packages should be labelled (e.g. the size of the label).

Material Safety Data Sheets (MSDS)

Material safety data sheets (MSDS) are needed if a chemical is not classified as dangerous, but contains small amounts of a dangerous substance.

If a supplier is selling to someone who is going to use the chemical for their work then a MSDS must be provided, but suppliers can use different (but equally good) methods for other customers, e.g. information on the package. The responsibility is placed on the supplier to ensure that the information provided is sufficient, i.e. enough to allow the user to decide how to protect:

- Workers at work.
- The environment.

This will usually include information on:
- The hazards of the chemical.
- Handling and storage.
- Its environmental effects.
- Exposure controls / personal protection.

Limitations of information in assessing risks to health

Information provided by manufacturers and contained within the HSE Guidance Note EH40 may be very technical and require a specialist to explain its relevance to a given activity. Some substances have good toxicological information, usually gained from past experience of harm; many others have a limited amount of useful toxicological information available to guide us as to the harm it may produce. This can lead to a reliance on data that is only our best understanding at the time and this may have to be revised as our knowledge on the substance changes. This is reflected in the use of WELs. Individual susceptibility of workers differs by, for example, age, gender or ethnic origin. Exposure history varies over the working life of an individual and current exposure may not indicate that the individual may suffer due to a cumulative effect from the earlier exposures. For example, an individual may have been or be engaged in a number of processes within a variety of workplaces or personal pastimes.

Basic surveys for health risks

As discussed in previous elements, the health effects of exposure to toxic substances can be acute or chronic. It will therefore be necessary to distinguish appropriate methods of measurement. When embarking upon a monitoring campaign to assess the risk to which an individual may be exposed, it is necessary to ask several questions.

1) What to sample?

This involves a review of the materials, processes and operating procedures being used within a plant, coupled with discussions with management and health and safety personnel. A brief 'walk-through' survey can also be useful as a guide to the extent of monitoring that may be necessary.

Hazard data sheets are also of use. When the background work has been completed it can then be decided what is to be measured.

2) On whom?

This depends on the size and diversity of the group that the survey relates to. From the group of workers being surveyed the sample to be monitored should be selected; this must be representative of the group and the work undertaken. Selecting the individual with the highest exposure can be a reasonable starting point. If the group is large then random sampling may have to be employed, but care has to be exercised with this approach. The group should also be aware of the reason for sampling.

3) How long do we sample for?

There are many considerations when answering this question: what are the control limits; is the hazard acute or chronic; what is our limit of detection; or simply what resources do we have at our disposal?

4) How do we monitor?

The particular sampling strategy, based on the hazard presented, is outlined in the following table:

Measurements to determine	Suitable types of measurement
Chronic hazard	Continuous personal dose measurement.
	Continuous measurements of average background levels.
	Short term readings of containment levels at selected positions and times.
Acute hazard	Continuous personal monitoring with rapid response.
	Continuous background monitoring with rapid response.
	Short term readings of background contaminant levels at selected positions and times.
Environmental control status	Continuous background monitoring.
	Short term readings of background contaminant levels at selected positions and times.
Whether area is safe to enter	Direct reading instruments.

Basic monitoring equipment

STAIN TUBE DETECTORS (MULTI-GAS/VAPOUR)

Simple devices for the measurement of contamination on the basis of a grab (short term) sample. It incorporates a glass detector tube, filled with inert material. The material is impregnated with a chemical reagent which changes colour ('stains') in proportion to the quantity of contaminant as a known quantity of air is drawn through the tube.

There are several different manufacturers of detector tubes including Dräger and Gastec.

It is important that the literature provided with the pumps and tubes is followed.

These provide a quick and easy way to detect the presence of a particular airborne contaminant. However they possess inherent inaccuracies and tube manufacturers claim a relative standard deviation of 20% or less (i.e. 1ppm in 5ppm).

Types of tube construction
- Commonest is the simple stain length tube, but it may contain filter layers, drying layers, or oxidation layers.
- Double tube or tube containing separate ampoules, avoids incompatibility or reaction during storage.
- Comparison tube.
- Narrow tube to achieve better resolution at low concentrations.

The above illustrates the main types of tubes; however there are more variations and therefore it can only be re-emphasised that the manufacturer's operating instructions must be read and fully understood before tubes are used.

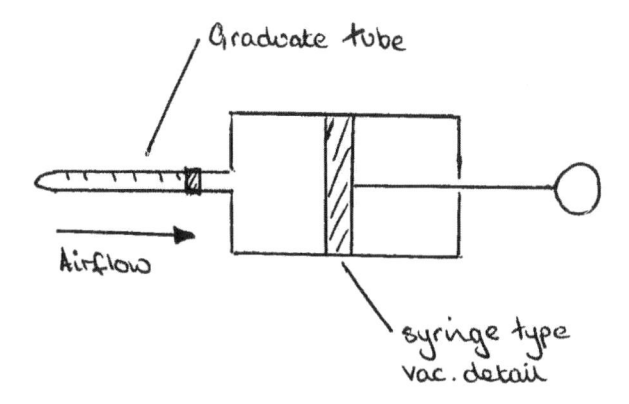

Figure 8-11: Detector tube example (hand drawn). Source: ACT.

Pumps
There are four types:
- Bellows pump.
- Piston pump.
- Ball pump.
- Battery operated pump.

Never mix pumps and tubes of different manufacturers.

How to use tubes
- Choose tube to measure material of interest and expected range.
- Check tubes are in date.
- Check leak tightness of pump.
- Read instructions to ensure there are no limitations due to temperature, pressure, humidity or interfering substances.
- Break off tips of tube, prepare tube if necessary and insert correctly into pump. Arrows normally indicate the direction of air flow.
- Draw the requisite number of strokes, to cause the given quantity of air to pass through the tube.
- Immediately, unless operating instructions say otherwise, evaluate the amount of contaminant by examining the stain and comparing it against the graduations on the tube. If there is any doubt when reading the tube, always err on the safe side.
- Remove tube and discard according to instructions.
- Purge pump to remove any contaminants from inside the pump.

Figure 8-12: Gas detector pump. Source: Drager.

Advantages of short term samplers:
- Quick and easy to use.
- Instant reading without further analysis.
- Does not require much expertise to use.
- Relatively inexpensive.

Disadvantages of short term samplers:
- Tubes can be cross sensitive to other contaminants.
- Accuracy varies - some are only useful as an indication of the presence of contaminants.
- Is only a grab sample.
- Relies on operator to accurately count pump strokes (manual versions).
- Only suitable for gases and vapours (not dusts).

PASSIVE PERSONAL SAMPLERS

Passive samplers are so described to illustrate the fact that they have no mechanism to draw in a sample of the contaminant but instead rely on passive means to sample. As such they take a time to perform this function, for example, acting as an absorber taking in contaminant vapours over a period of a working day. Some passive samplers, like gas badges, are generally fitted to the lapel and change colour to indicate contamination.

Active personal samplers

Filtration devices are used for dusts, mists and fumes. A known volume of air is pumped through a sampling head and the contaminant filtered out. By comparing the quantity of air with the amount of contaminant a measurement is made. The filter is either weighed or an actual count of particles is done to establish the amount, as with asbestos. The type of dust can be determined by further laboratory analysis. Active samplers are used in two forms, for personal sampling and for static sampling.

Figure 8-13: Personal sampling equipment. Source: ROSPA OS&H Apr 98.

Static sampling

These devices are stationed in the working area. They sample continuously over the length of a shift, or longer period if necessary. Mains or battery-operated pumps are used. Very small quantities of contaminant may be detected. The techniques employed include absorption, bubblers, and filtration; they are similar in principle to personal samplers, but the equipment is tailored to suit static use.

Advantages of long term samplers:
- Will monitor the workplace over a long period of time.
- Will accurately identify 8 hour time weighted average.

Disadvantages of long term samplers:
- Will not generally identify a specific type of contaminant.
- Will not identify multiple exposure i.e. more than one contaminant.
- Does not identify personal exposure.
- Unless very sophisticated, will not read peaks and troughs.

OXYGEN METERS

Oxygen depletion monitoring systems are installed to guard personnel who need to enter areas where either nitrogen or carbon dioxide might be present e.g. confined spaces, cellars, excavations. Oxygen should read 21% in normal atmospheres, a drop below 18% *should* issue a warning clearly visible to personnel accessing the area.

Personal gas detectors set to alarm at 18% are effective if the levels are dropping from 21% to 18% however a fixed gas sensor mounted inside the area connected back to a transmitter with a clear display will offer greater protection, preventing personnel entering the area where there are depleted levels of oxygen.

SMOKE TUBES

Smoke tubes are simple devices that generate a 'smoke' by means of a chemical reaction. A tube similar in type to those used in stain tube detectors is selected, its ends broken (which starts the chemical reaction) and it is inserted into a small hand bellows. By gently pumping the bellows smoke is emitted. By watching the smoke air flow can be studied. This can be used to survey extraction and ventilation arrangements to determine their extent of influence.

DUST MONITORING EQUIPMENT

Direct reading dust sampler (E.g. Tyndall lamp)

Simple methods are by direct observation of the effect of the dust on a strong beam of light e.g. using a Tyndall lamp. High levels of small particles of dust show up under this strong beam of light. Other ways are by means of a direct reading instrument. This establishes the level of dust by, for example, scattering of light. Some also collect the dust sample. The advantages and disadvantages are:

Advantages of direct reading dust samplers:
- Instant reading.
- Continuous monitoring.
- Can record electronically.
- Can be linked to an alarm.
- Suitable for clean room environments.

Disadvantages of direct reading dust samplers:
- Some direct reading instruments can be expensive.
- Does not differentiate between dusts of different types.
- Most effective on dusts of a spherical nature.

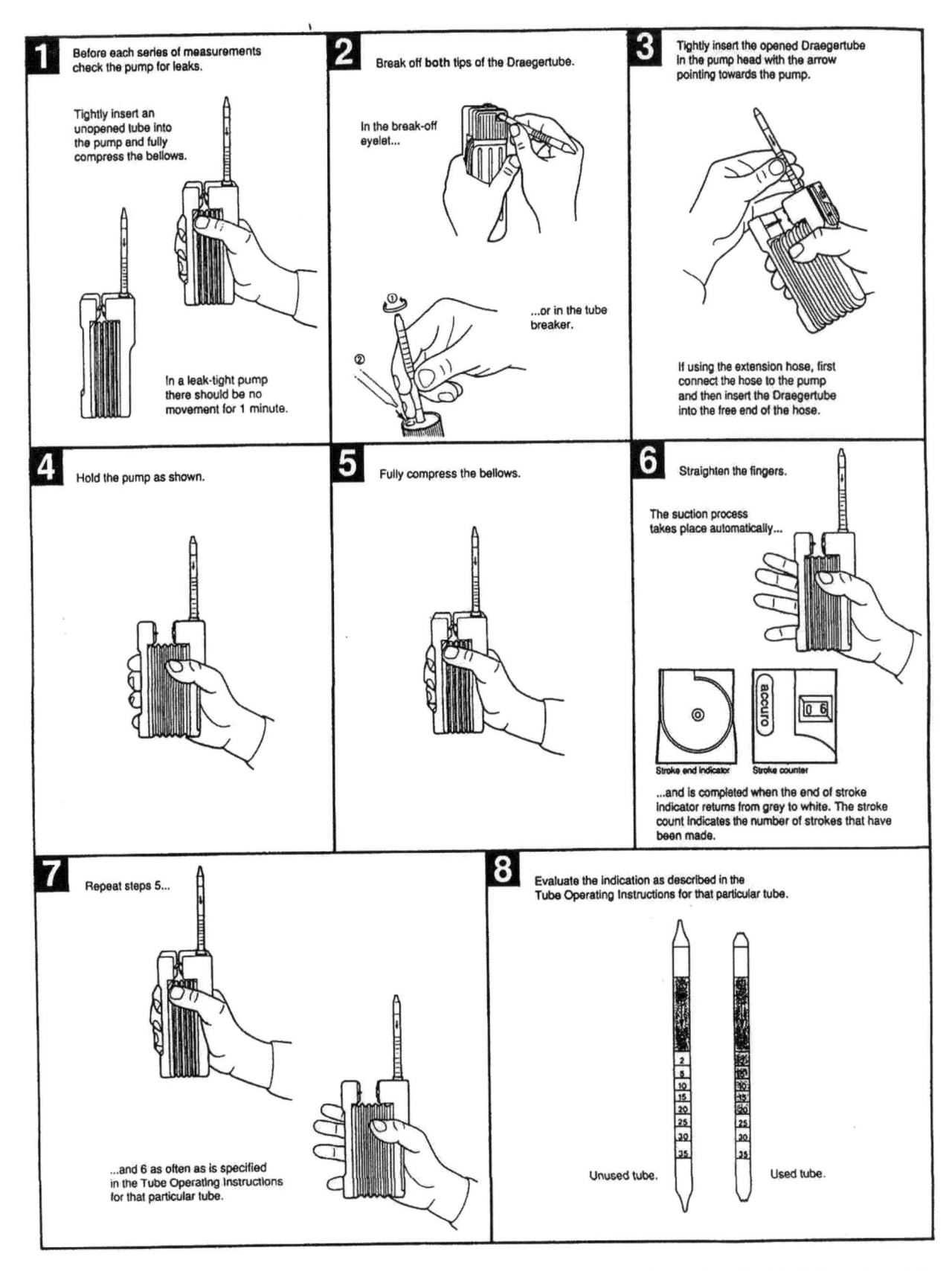

Figure 8-14: Stain tube detector operating instructions.

Source: Reproduced by kind permission of Drager.

8.3 - Workplace exposure limits

Basis for workplace exposure limits

Environmental hygiene guidance note 40 [EH40 WEL]

EH40, which is published annually, contains the lists of Workplace Exposure Limits (WEL) for use with The Control of Substances Hazardous to Health Regulations (COSHH) 2002 (as amended 2005).

SETTING WORKPLACE EXPOSURE LIMITS

ACTS and WATCH

Workplace Exposure Limits are set on the recommendation of the Advisory Committee on Toxic Substances (ACTS) following assessment, by the Working on Action to Control Chemicals (WATCH), of the toxicological, epidemiological and other data. The committees have to consider what concentration the limit should be set. Each substance is first reviewed by WATCH which considers what value should be recommended to ACTS. WATCH comes to a decision based on a scientific judgement of the available information on health effects and ACTS makes recommendations to the Health and Safety Commission (HSC).

Note: The **Working Group on Action to Control Chemicals** used to be called the Working Group on the Assessment of Toxic Chemicals and the acronym has remained as **WATCH**.

Workplace exposure limits

WELs are occupational exposure limits set under COSHH 2002 to protect the health of persons in the workplace. They are concentrations of airborne substances averaged over a period of time known as a Time Weighted Average (TWA). The two periods that are used are 8-hours and 15-minutes. The 8-hour TWA is known as an LTEL (long-term exposure limit), used to help protect against chronic ill-health effects. 15-minute STELs (short-term exposure limits) are to protect against acute ill-health effects such as eye irritation, which may happen in minutes or even seconds of exposure.

COSHH 2002 states that exposure to hazardous substances should be prevented where it is reasonably practicable. Where this cannot be done by, for example changing the process, substituting it for something safer or enclosing the process, exposure should be reduced by other methods.

Long-term and short-term exposure limits

Long-term exposure limits

LTEL   Concerned with the total intake averaged over a reference period (usually 8 hours) and is therefore appropriate for protecting against the effects of long term exposure (chronic effects).

Short-term exposure limits

STEL   Aimed primarily at avoiding the acute effects or at least reducing the risk of occurrence. They are averaged over a 15 minute reference period.

Limitations of exposure limits

There are many reasons why control of exposure should not be based solely on WELs:

- **Inhalation only.** Many substances (e.g. trichloroethylene) have the ability to absorb through the skin. WELs do not account for these compound routes of entry.
- **Personal susceptibility.** The majority of the work has been based on the average male physiology from the countries in which studies were conducted. Some work has been done where specific health related effects have been noted amongst females e.g. exposure to lead compounds.
- **Adopted from American TLV.** Work done to date has been based upon exposure to individuals in the developed countries e.g. Europe and USA.
- **Variations in control.**
- **Errors in monitoring.** Measuring microscopic amounts of contamination requires very accurate and sensitive equipment. Lack of maintenance and misuse can lead to inaccuracies in monitoring.
- **Synergistic effects.** The standards that are available relate to single substances and the effects of multiple substances in the workplace need to be considered.

Principle of reducing exposure levels

Though WELs may be set for substances the Health and Safety at Work Act (HASAWA) 1974 and COSHH 2002 require reduction to as low as is reasonably practicable. Existing data on exposure limits may not reflect the safe levels that should be achieved to ensure the health of people exposed to substances in the workplace. It is important to review work practices and control strategies to reduce levels of exposure whenever possible. Control strategies should be constantly reviewed to ensure the lowest levels of exposure are achieved. If the levels of exposure are to be maintained below the WEL, with confidence, it will be necessary to work below them sufficiently to account for changes in work situation. This is particularly important with those WELs that are set for substances that are carcinogens or sensitisers.

Regulation 7 (7) of COSHH 2002 states that control will be treated as adequate if:

(a) The principles of good practice for the control of exposure to substances hazardous to health set out in Schedule 2A are applied:

(b) Any workplace exposure limit approved for that substance is not exceeded; and

(c) For a substance:
  (i) Which carries the risk phrase R45, R46 or R49 (i.e. carcinogens), or for a substance or process that is listed in Schedule 1; or
  (ii) Which carries the risk phrase R42 or R42/43 (i.e. respiratory sensitisers), or which is listed in section C of HSE publication *"Asthmagen? Critical assessments of the evidence for agents implicated in occupational asthma"*, exposure is reduced to as low a level as is reasonably practicable.

8.4 - Acute and chronic health effects

Difference between acute and chronic health effects

ACUTE EFFECT

Is an immediate or rapidly produced, adverse effect, following a single or short term exposure to an offending agent, which is usually reversible (the obvious exception being death). Examples of acute effects are irritation, nausea, vomiting, headaches and narcosis.

CHRONIC EFFECT

Is an adverse health effect produced as a result of prolonged or repeated exposure, with a gradual or latent, and often irreversible, effect that may often go unrecognised for a number of years. Examples of chronic effects are cancers, asbestosis, mutagenic effects, atrophy (decrease in size of a bodily organ) and various respiratory problems such as emphysema.

8.5 - Appropriate control measures

Duty to prevent exposure or, where this is not reasonably practicable, adequately control it

The *eight* principles of good practice for the control of exposure to substances hazardous to health are set out in Schedule 2A of COSHH 2002 (as amended 2005) ACOP and guidance:

- Design and operate processes and activities to minimise emission, release and spread of substances hazardous to health.
- Take into account all relevant routes of exposure - inhalation, skin absorption and ingestion - when developing control measures.
- Control exposure by measures that are proportionate to the health risk.
- Choose the most effective and reliable control options which minimize the escape and spread of the substances hazardous to health.
- Where adequate control of exposure cannot be achieved by other means, provide, in combination with other control measures, suitable personable protective equipment.
- Check and review regularly all elements of control measures for their continuing effectiveness.
- Inform and train all employees on the hazards and risks from the substances with which they work and the use of control measures developed to minimize the risks.
- Ensure that the introduction of control measures does not increase the overall risk to health and safety.

Ensuring the workplace exposure limit is not exceeded

Correct application of the principles should ensure the control of exposure below any relevant Workplace Exposure Limit (WEL). Control by personal protective equipment should only be used when other measures are not reasonably practicable.

In the control of occupational health hazards many approaches are available, the use of which depends upon the severity and nature of the hazard. The principal control strategies are outlined below and follow the general strategy:

- Elimination or substitution.
- Process change.
- Reduced time exposure.
- Enclosure of hazards, process or people.
- Local exhaust ventilation.
- Dilution ventilation.
- Respiratory protective equipment.
- Other personal protective equipment.
- Personal hygiene.
- Health surveillance.

Methods of control

ELIMINATION OR SUBSTITUTION OF HAZARDOUS SUBSTANCES OR FORM OF SUBSTANCE

Elimination

This represents an extreme form of control and is appropriately used where high risk is present from such things as carcinogens. It is usually achieved through the prohibition of use of these substances. Care must be taken to ensure that all stock is safely disposed of and that controls are in place to prevent their re-entry, even as a sample or for research. If this level of control is not achievable then another must be selected.

Reduction

By substitution

The substitution of a less toxic substance in place of a more highly toxic one, e.g. toluene for benzene, glass fibre for asbestos, or water based adhesives for solvent based adhesives is a frequently used technique. It is also possible to substitute the form of the substance in that a substance that requires mixing from dry products, such as cement, may be ordered pre-prepared thus avoiding the additional contact with the substance in the mixing process and in the dry state where dust may be liberated. In the same way dust generated in a demolition process may be watered down so that the dust becomes liquid slurry.

Quantity

A useful approach is to reduce the actual quantity of the substance presenting the hazard. This may be achieved by limiting the amount used or stored. It may be possible to use a more dilute form than is presently being used, for example, with acids. In the case of disposal it is possible to reduce the quantity by neutralisation.

PROCESS CHANGES

The role of the occupational hygienist is to identify peaks in exposure to operators during their normal working day e.g. when charging or discharging process equipment - at this time higher than normal background levels of contamination may occur in the general work area.

Whenever process changes occur through plant failure or maintenance, consideration needs to be given to exposure to those affected at these times. It may be necessary to re-assess the process / maintenance arrangements to ensure adequacy of health controls.

Figure 8-15: Reduced exposure - bulk supply. Source: ACT.

REDUCED TIME EXPOSURE AND SIGNIFICANCE OF TIME WEIGHTED AVERAGES

There is a close relationship between exposure and time. At a fixed level of contamination the effect will be proportional to the time exposed. This is the basis of occupational exposure limits, i.e. long-term exposure limits (8 hours time weighted average value) and short-term exposure limits (15 minutes weighted average value). The strategy is also encompassed in the approach to control noise exposure whereby the total noise dose over an eight hour day, 5-day week, must not exceed 85 dB(A). It may be possible to organise work so that exposure to any one person is controlled by means of job/task rotation.

ENCLOSURE OF HAZARDS

In its simplest sense this can mean putting lids on substances that have volatile vapours, such as tins of solvent based products. In this way the strategy is to enclose the hazard so that vapours are not given off. In this case, this is best done when the substance is not in use, this does not just mean at the end of the day but at intervals when the substance is not actually in use. It makes a very simple and effective control of exposure to hazards.

SEGREGATION OF PROCESS

This strategy is based on the containment of an offending substance or agent to prevent its free movement in the working environment. It may take a number of forms, e.g. acoustic enclosures, pipelines, closed conveyors, laboratory fume cupboards. In construction situations this is used in processes such as asbestos removal where the work being done is enclosed in plastic sheeting in order to segregate the work from the surrounding areas. In a similar way this may be for building cleaning processes using shot or for spray protection being applied to a structure.

SEGREGATION OF PEOPLE

Segregation is a method of controlling the risks from toxic substances and physical hazards such as noise and radiation. It can take a number of forms:

By distance

This is a relatively simple method where a person is separated from a source of danger by distance. It can appropriately be used in the case of noise where the risk of occupational deafness decreases as the distance from the source increases.

By age

The protection of young workers in certain trades is still valid today, a good example being lead. In this case the CLAW 2002 Regulations exclude the employment of young persons in lead processes.

By time

This involves the restriction of certain hazardous operations to periods when the number of persons present is at its smallest, for instance at weekends. An example might be the radiation of an item for non-destructive test.

By gender

There remains the possibility of gender linked vulnerability to certain toxic substances such as lead; segregation affords a high level of control in these circumstances.

LOCAL EXHAUST VENTILATION

General applications and principles

Various local exhaust ventilation (LEV) systems are in use in the workplace, for example:

- Receptor hoods such as are used in fume cupboards and kilns.
- Captor hoods (used for welding and milling operations).
- High velocity low volume flow systems e.g. as used on a grinding tool.

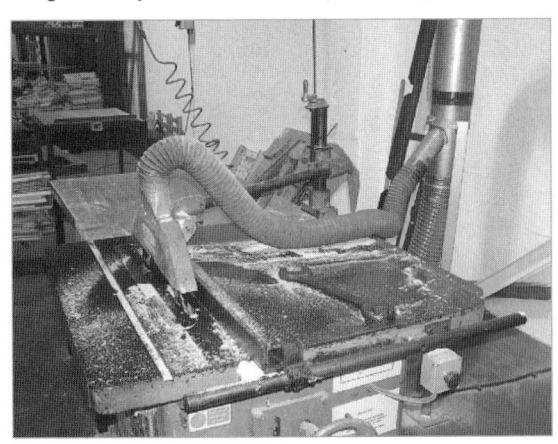

Figure 8-16: Captor system on circular saw. Clearly shows the fixed captor hood, flexible hose and rigid duct.   *Source: ACT.*

Figure 8-17: Shows the size of fan and motor required for industrial scale LEV.   *Source: ACT.*

Figure 8-18: Flexible hose showing how captor hood can be repositioned to suit the work activity.   *Source: ACT.*

Figure 8-19: Self contained unit which can be moved around the workplace.   *Source: ACT.*

COMPONENTS OF A BASIC SYSTEM

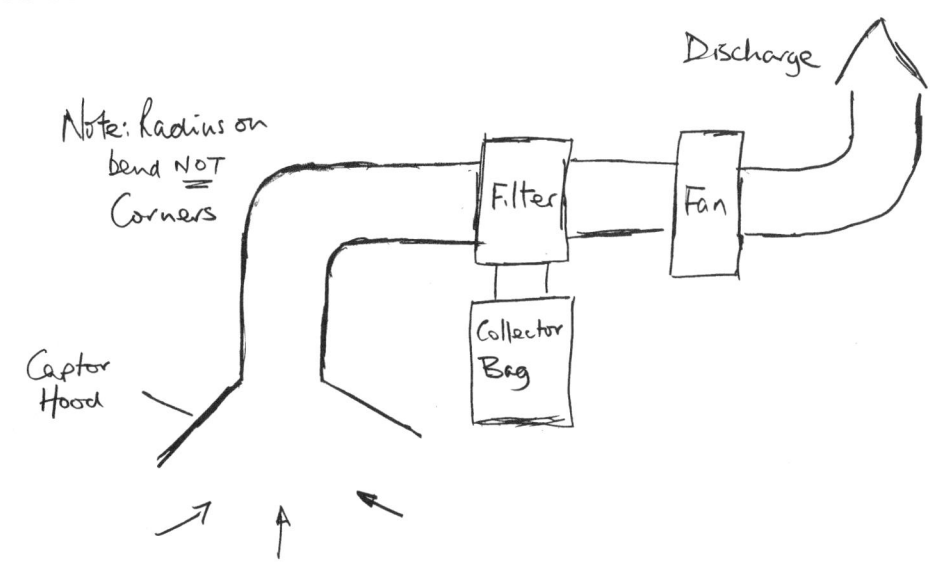

Figure 8-20: Components of a basic system (hand drawn).   *Source: ACT.*

FACTORS THAT REDUCE A LEV SYSTEM'S EFFECTIVENESS

The efficiency of LEV systems can be affected by many factors including the following:
- Damaged ducting.
- Unauthorised alterations.
- Process changes leading to overwhelming amounts of contamination.
- Incorrect hood location.
- Fan strength or incorrect adjustment of fan.

- Too many bends in ducts.
- Blocked or defective filters.
- Leaving too many ports open.
- The cost of heating make up air.

It is vital that the pre and post ventilation contamination levels are determined and the required reduction should be part of the commissioning contract.

LEV may also create environmental problems due to contamination being released into the atmosphere, odours and noise from the motors and fans.

REQUIREMENTS FOR INSPECTION

COSHH 2002 Regulation 9(2) and schedule 4 set out requirements for inspection of LEV systems. A thorough examination and test must take place once every 14 months (more frequently for those processes listed in schedule 4). Records must be kept available for at least 5 years from the date on which it was made.

The majority of ventilation systems, although effective in protecting workers' health from airborne contaminants, can create other hazards. One of the main hazards that need to be considered when designing LEV systems is that of noise. Even if it has been considered as a design feature when establishing LEV systems, it should be monitored on a periodic basis.

USE AND LIMITATIONS OF DILUTION VENTILATION

Dilution ventilation is a system designed to induce a general flow of clean air into a work area. This may be done by driving air into a work area, causing air flow around the work area, dilution of contaminants in the work area and then out of the work area through general leakage or through ventilation ducts to the open air.

A variation on this is where air may be forcibly removed from the work area, but not associated with a particular contaminant source, and air is allowed in through ventilation ducts to dilute the air in the work area. Sometimes a combination of these two approaches is used; an example may be general air conditioning provided into an office environment.

A particularly simple approach to providing dilution ventilation is to open a window and door and allow natural air flow to dilute the workplace air. This is not a reliable means of dealing with toxic contaminants and may be over relied on in the construction industry. On its own it may prove inadequate but supported by respiratory protection equipment it may be acceptable for some substances.

Because it does not target any specific source and it relies on dispersal and dilution instead of specific removal, it can only be used with nuisance contaminants that are themselves fairly mobile in air. Dilution ventilation systems will only deal with general contamination and will not prevent contaminants entering a person's breathing zone. Local exhaust ventilation is the preferred means of controlling a person's exposure to substances.

Dilution ventilation may only be used as the sole means of control in circumstances where there is:

- Non toxic contaminant or vapour (not dusts).
- Contaminant which is uniformly produced in small, known quantities.
- No discrete point of release.
- No other practical means of reducing levels.

RESPIRATORY PROTECTIVE EQUIPMENT

This equipment includes two main categories of respiratory protection:

1) Respirators.
2) Breathing apparatus.

Respirators

Respirators filter the air breathed but do not provide additional oxygen. There are a number of types of respirator that provide a variety of degrees of protection from dealing with nuisance dusts to high efficiency respirators for solvents or asbestos. Some respirators may be nominated as providing non-specific protection from contaminants whereas others will be designed to protect from a very specific contaminant such as solvent vapours.

There are five main types of respirators:

1) Filtering face piece.
2) Half mask respirator.
3) Full face respirator.
4) Powered air purifying respirator.
5) Powered visor respirator.

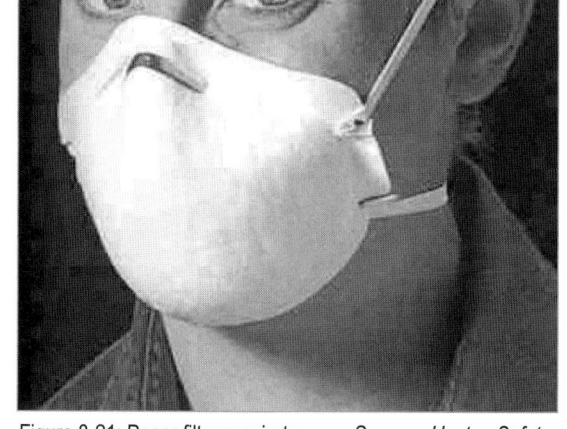

Figure 8-21: Paper filter respirator. *Source: Haxton Safety.*

Advantages

- Unrestricted movement.
- Often lightweight and comfortable.
- Can be worn for long periods.

Limitations

- Purify the air by drawing it through a filter to remove contaminants. Therefore, can only be used when there is sufficient oxygen in the atmosphere.
- Requires careful selection by a competent person.
- Requires regular maintenance.
- Knowing when a cartridge is at the end of its useful life.
- Requires correct storage facilities.
- Can give a 'closed in' / claustrophobic feeling.
- Relies on user for correct fit/use etc.
- Incompatible with other forms of personal protective equipment (PPE).
- Performance can be affected by beards and long hair.
- Interferes with other senses, e.g. sense of smell.

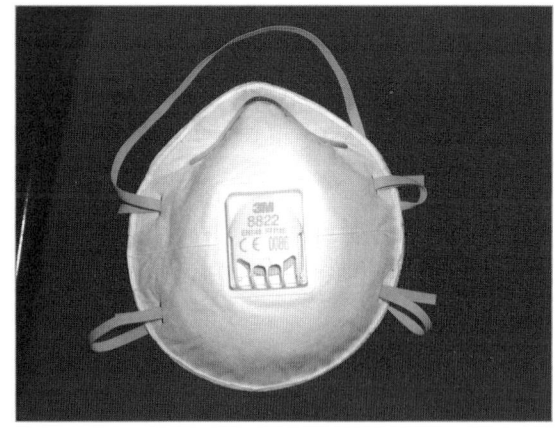

Figure 8-22: 3M disposable respirator.   Source: ACT.

Breathing apparatus

Breathing Apparatus provides a separate source of supply of air (including oxygen) to that which surrounds the person. Because of the self-contained nature of breathing apparatus it may be used to provide a high degree of protection from a variety of toxic contaminants and may be used in situations where the actual contaminant is not known or there is more than one contaminant.

There are three types of breathing apparatus:

1) Fresh air hose apparatus - clean air from uncontaminated source.
2) Compressed air line apparatus from compressed air source.
3) Self-contained breathing apparatus - from cylinder.

Figure 8-23: Full face canister respirator. *Source: Haxton Safety.*

Figure 8-24: Breathing apparatus. *Source: Haxton Safety.*

Advantages

- Supplies clean air from an uncontaminated source. Therefore, can be worn in oxygen deficient atmospheres.
- Has high **assigned protection factor** (APF). Therefore may be used in an atmosphere with high levels of toxic substance.
- Can be worn for long periods if connected to a permanent supply of air.

Limitations

- Can be heavy and cumbersome which restricts movement.
- Requires careful selection by competent person.
- Requires special training.
- Requires arrangements to monitor / supervise user and for emergencies.
- Requires regular maintenance.
- Requires correct storage facilities.
- Can give a 'closed in' / claustrophobic feeling.
- Relies on user for correct fit/use etc.
- Incompatible with other forms of PPE.
- Performance can be affected by e.g. long hair.
- Interferes with other senses, e.g. sense of smell.

Figure 8-25: Mis-use of respirator.   Source: ACT.

Selection

There are a number of issues to consider in the selection of respiratory protective equipment (RPE) not least the advantages and limitations shown above. A general approach must not only take account of the needs derived from the work to be done and the contaminant to be protected from, but must include suitability for the person.

This will include issues such as face fit and the ability of the person to use the equipment for a sustained period, if this is required. One of the important factors is to ensure that the equipment will provide the level of protection required. This is indicated by the assigned protection factor given to the equipment by the manufacturers - the higher the factor the more protection provided. With a little knowledge it is possible to work out what APF is needed using the following formula:

APF = $\dfrac{\text{Concentration of contaminant in the workplace}}{\text{Concentration of contaminant in the face-piece}}$

It is important to understand that this factor is only an indication of what the equipment will provide. Actual protection may be different due to fit and the task being conducted.

Use

Every employee must use any personal protective equipment provided in accordance with the training and instructions that they have received.

Maintenance

Where respiratory protective equipment (other than disposable respiratory protective equipment) is provided the employer must ensure that thorough examination and where appropriate testing, of that equipment is carried out at suitable intervals.

OTHER PROTECTIVE EQUIPMENT AND CLOTHING

Eye protection

When selecting suitable eye protection, some of the factors to be considered are:

Type and nature of hazard (impact, chemical, ultra violet (UV) light, etc.), type/standard/quality of protection, comfort and user acceptability issues, compatibility, maintenance requirements, training requirements and cost.

Figure 8-26: Eye and ear protection. *Source: Speedy Hire plc.*

Figure 8-27: Arc welding visor - UV reactive. *Source: ACT.*

Types	Advantages	Limitations
Spectacles	■ Lightweight, easy to wear. ■ Can incorporate prescription lenses. ■ Do not 'mist up'.	■ Do not give all round protection. ■ Relies on the wearer for use.
Goggles	■ Give all round protection. ■ Can be worn over prescription lenses. ■ Capable of high impact protection. ■ Can protect against other hazards e.g. dust, molten metal.	■ Tendency to 'mist up'. ■ Uncomfortable when worn for long periods. ■ Can affect peripheral vision.
Face shields (visors)	■ Gives full face protection against splashes. ■ Can incorporate a fan which creates air movement for comfort and protection against low level contaminants. ■ Can be integrated into other PPE e.g. head protection.	■ Require care in use, otherwise can become dirty and scratched. ■ Can affect peripheral vision. ■ Unless the visor is provided with extra sealing gusset around the visor, substances may go underneath the visor to the face.

Protective clothing

1) Head protection - safety helmets or scalp protectors (bump caps) - scalp protectors give limited protection and are unsuitable for confined spaces. Safety helmets have a useful life of three years and this can be shortened by prolonged exposure to ultra-violet light. There is specific legal requirement on construction sites where there is risk of injury from falling objects.

2) Protective outer clothing - normally PVC, often high visibility to alert traffic.

3) Protective inner clothing - overalls, aprons.

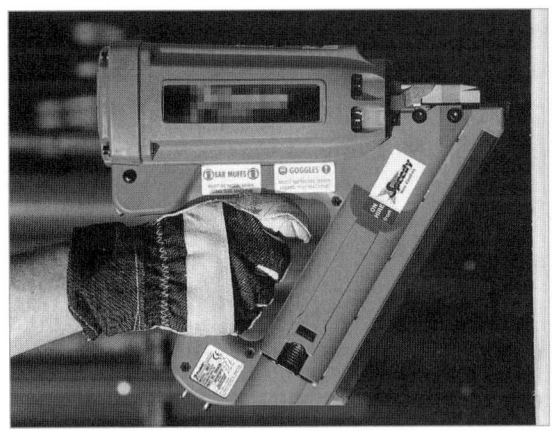

Figure 8-28: Gloves. *Source: Speedy Hire plc.*

Figure 8-29: Protective clothing. *Source: ACT.*

Hand / arm protection

This area of protection is vast. There are numerous types of glove and gauntlet available that offer protection from hazards:

- Chemical hazards such as acids, alkalis etc.
- Thermal hazards such as hot surfaces.
- Mechanical hazards in the form of splinters and sharp edges.

The materials used in the manufacture of these products are an essential feature to consider when making the selection. There are several types of rubber (latex, nitrile, PVC, butyl) all giving different levels of protection against aqueous chemicals; leather affords protection against heat, splinters and cuts; space age technology in the form of Kevlar (a tough, lightweight material) protects against cuts from knife blades and is used in the sleeves of jackets for those using chainsaws.

Footwear - safety boots / shoes

The importance of foot protection is illustrated by the fact that around 21,000 foot and ankle injuries were reported in 1996/97. Inadequate protection and a lack of discipline on the part of the wearer commonly cause these. There are many types of safety footwear on the market, many of them offering different types of protection. It is vital that the nature of the hazard is considered when selecting appropriate footwear. Here are some common examples:

- Falling objects - steel toe-caps.
- Sharp objects - steel in-soles.
- Flammable atmospheres - anti-static footwear.
- Spread of contamination - washable boots.
- Electricity - rubber soles.
- Wet environments - impermeable Wellington boots.
- Slippery surfaces - non-slip soles.
- Cold environments - thermally insulated soles.

Figure 8-30: Personal protective equipment. *Source: ACT.*

Ear protection

See also - Unit NCC1 - Element 9 - Physical and psychological health - hazards and control - for details of ear protection.

PERSONAL HYGIENE AND PROTECTION REGIMES

Personal hygiene and good housekeeping have an important role in the protection of the health and safety of the people at work. Laid down procedures and standards are necessary for preventing the spread of contamination. The provision of adequate washing / showering facilities is important to remove contamination from the body.

The provision of laundry facilities for overalls and PPE reduces the effect of contamination. Barrier creams and suitable hand protection are important considerations for chemical and biological risks.

Where personal hygiene is critical, for example, when stripping asbestos, a 'three room system' is employed. Workers enter the 'clean end' and put work clothes on, leaving by means of the 'dirty end'. When work has been completed they return by means of the 'dirty end', carry out personal hygiene and leave by means of the 'clean end'.

Vaccination

Certain occupations, such as water treatment / sewage workers, medical profession, have a higher than average risk from some biological hazards. Staff from these occupations may need to be immunised against common high risks e.g. hepatitis B. Whilst vaccination can be an effective way of preventing ill health as a result of exposure to biological agents, it is important that employers are aware of problems that can arise.

In the first instance, vaccination is intrusive. Employers need the permission of employees before adopting this method - this may not always be forthcoming. Secondly, it is possible that some people will suffer adverse effects from the vaccination. Finally, not all diseases are treatable by vaccination and, for those that are, vaccination might not be available.

UNIT NCC1 - ELEMENT 8 - CHEMICAL AND BIOLOGICAL HEALTH - HAZARDS AND CONTROL

HEALTH SURVEILLANCE

The Management of Health and Safety at Work Regulations (MHSWR) 1999, Regulation 6, deals with health surveillance and gives employers a duty to provide it where it is appropriate. Further details on health surveillance are contained in other Regulations e.g. COSHH 2002. Other than the cases stated in the COSHH 2002 schedule, surveillance may be appropriate where exposure to hazardous substances is such that an identifiable disease or adverse health effect may be linked to the exposure. There must be a reasonable likelihood that the disease or effect may occur under the particular conditions of work prevailing and that valid techniques exist to detect such conditions and effects.

The employer must keep records of surveillance in respect of each employee for at least 40 years. This requirement still applies where companies cease to trade, in which case the records must be offered to the HSE.

(Details can be found in the COSHH 2002 Approved Code of Practice schedule 6; extracts from the ACOP are given below).

Substances for which health surveillance is appropriate		Processes
Vinyl Chloride Monomer (VCM).		In manufacturing, production, reclamation, storage, discharge, transport, use or polymerization.
Nitro or amino derivatives of phenol and of benzene or its homologues.		In the manufacture of nitro or amino derivatives of phenol and of benzene or its homologues and the making of explosives with the use of any of these substances.
1-Napthylamine and its salts Orthotolidine and its salts.	Dianisidine and its salts Dichlorbenzidene and its salts.	In manufacture, formation or use of these substances.
Auramine.	Magenta.	In manufacture.
Carbon Disulphide Disulpher Dichloride Benzene, including benzol.	Carbon Tetrachloride Trichloroethylene.	Process in which these substances are used, or given off as a vapour, in the manufacture of indiarubber or of articles or goods made wholly or partially of indiarubber.
Pitch.		In manufacture of blocks of fuel consisting of coal, coal dust, coke or slurry with pitch as a binding substance.

Figure 8-31: Schedule 6 medical surveillance. *Source: COSHH AcoP.*

Biological monitoring guidance values

Biological monitoring may be particularly useful in circumstances where:

- There is likely to be significant skin absorption and/or gastrointestinal tract uptake following ingestion.
- Control of exposure depends on respiratory protective equipment.
- There is a reasonably well-defined relationship between biological monitoring and effect.
- It gives information on accumulated dose and target organ burden which is related to toxicity.

Biological Monitoring Values (BMGVs) are set where they are likely to be of practical value, suitable monitoring methods exist and there are sufficient data available.

BMGVs are non-statutory and any biological monitoring undertaken in association with a guidance value needs to be conducted on a voluntary basis (i.e. with the fully informed consent of all concerned). Where a BMG is exceeded it does not necessarily mean that any corresponding airborne standard has been exceeded nor that ill health will occur. It is intended that where they are exceeded this will give an indication that investigation into current control measures and work practices is necessary. Similarly a low BMGV should not suggest that there is no need to reduce workplace exposure further. Table 2 EH40/2005 lists BMGVs, a few examples of common substances are listed below:

Substance	Biological Monitoring Guidance Value	Sampling time
Butan-2-one.	µmol butan-2-one/L in urine.	Post shift.
Carbon monoxide.	30ppm carbon monoxide in end-tidal breath.	Post shift.
Lindane. (Organo chlorine pesticide).	35nmol/L(10µg/L of Lindane in whole blood (equivalent to 70nmol/Lidane in plasma).	Random.
Xylene, o-, m-, p- or mixed isomers.	650 mmol methyl hippuric acid/mol creainine in urine.	Post shift.

Source: EH40/2005 Workplace exposure limits.

Further controls of substances that can cause cancer, asthma or damage to genes

Carcinogens are substances that have been identified as having the ability to cause cancer. Examples of these include arsenic, hardwood dusts and used engine oils. Additionally, substances known as mutagens have been identified that cause changes to DNA, increasing the number of genetic mutations above natural background levels. These changes can lead to cancer in the individual affected or be passed to their offspring genetic material.

Due to the serious and irreversible nature of cancer and genetic changes, an employer's first objective must be to prevent exposure to carcinogens and mutagens. These substances should not be used or processes carried out with them, if a safer alternative less hazardous substance can be used instead.

Where this is not feasible suitable control measures should include:

- Totally enclosed systems.
- Where total enclosure is not possible, exposure to these substances must kept to as low level as possible through the use of appropriate plant and process control measures such as handling systems and local exhaust ventilation (these measures should not produce other risks in the workplace).
- Storage of carcinogens/mutagens must be kept to the minimum needed for the process, in closed, labelled containers with warning and hazard signs, including waste products until safe disposal.
- Areas where carcinogens/mutagens are present must be identified and segregated to prevent spread to other areas.
- The number of people exposed and the duration of exposure must be kept to the minimum necessary to do the work.
- Personal protective equipment is considered a secondary protection measure used in combination with other control measures.
- Measures should be in place for monitoring of workplace exposure and health surveillance for work involving carcinogens and mutagens.

Occupational asthma is caused by substances in the workplace that trigger a state of specific airway hyper-responsiveness in an individual, resulting in breathlessness, chest tightness or wheezing. These substances are known as asthmagens and respiratory sensitisers. Exposure to these substances should be prevented, and where that is not possible, kept as low as reasonably practicable. Control measures used should take account of long term time weighted averages and short term peak exposures to the substance. If an individual develops occupational asthma, their exposure must be controlled to prevent any further attacks. Employees who work with asthmagens must have regular health surveillance to detect any changes in respiratory function.

8.6 - Control of hazardous dusts

Substances that can cause cancer, asthma or damage to genes that can be passed from one generation to another

Mutagens are substances that cause heritable genetic changes (mutations). Most mutations are harmful and most mutagens are *carcinogens* and vice versa.

Substances that are known to impair fertility or to cause developmental toxicity in humans are defined as **toxic to reproduction**. This definition covers a broader range of health effects than the earlier **"teratogenic"** which applied only to substances that adversely affected the developing foetus.

As usual for hazardous materials, the first route of protection is to avoid exposure totally by using a safer alternative. If such an alternative is available and its use is "reasonably practicable" then this must be done. However, **carcinogenic** properties of possible chemical substitutes should be established and taken into account when considering changes. Synthetic routes should be chosen to avoid the use of carcinogenic materials and to avoid, as far as possible, the formation of by-products, intermediates, wastes or residual contaminants consisting of or containing carcinogenic substances.

Occupational **asthma** is an allergic reaction that can occur in some people when they are exposed to certain substances, for example isocyanates, latex, flour and wood dust in the workplace. These are called 'respiratory sensitisers' or asthmagens.

Employers should have a management system in place to identify asthmagens, assess the risk, and if exposure cannot be prevented then, adequately controlled. The employer should provide suitable and sufficient information, instruction and training. When employees are exposed to asthmagens then they should be under suitable health surveillance.

Hazardous dusts

LEAD

Because leaded dust is so small, it cannot be seen by the naked eye. Special cleaning methods are needed to make sure all harmful dust is removed.

All visible and invisible particles need to be removed. Lead dust is hard to remove with an ordinary household vacuum cleaner, particularly in poorly maintained buildings with rough and aging surfaces. An ordinary household vacuum will send lead dust through the work area because holes in between the filter are not small enough to filter the dust out. A HEPA (High Efficiency Particulate Air) vacuum is equipped with a special filter that removes lead dust particles from the vacuums exhaust air stream that would otherwise be sent throughout the workplace.

SILICA

First of all, try to get rid of silica dust from the work. Silica can be eliminated by substituting other materials, for instance, using non-silica grits for blasting. Where this is not practicable, it may be possible to get rid of or reduce the need for scabbling, cutting or drilling concrete through design.

If silica dust cannot be removed, exposure must be reduced. It is feasible to control respirable silica by dust suppression techniques or local exhaust ventilation. Exhaust ventilated tools which remove the dust at source, and tools fitted with a water supply for dust suppression, are widely available. Capturing or controlling the dust at source is nearly always better than attempting to control exposure by ventilating the whole area.

FIBRES

Man-made mineral fibres (including extruded fibres, wools, and ceramic fibres) e.g. insulation materials used in roofs and walls, and other fibres like synthetic organic fibres e.g. gypsum and calcium carbonate used within the construction industries are some of the more common fibres encountered. Exposure to these fibres must be controlled by the use of PPE e.g. suitable respiratory protective, eye protection, gloves and long sleeved overalls.

See also - section on asbestos later in this element.

ASBESTOS

Refer to Asbestos section later in this element.

CEMENT DUST

Work in a way which avoids dusty methods of work. For example, scabbling is often carried out to ensure an adequate bond between successive concrete pours and the amount of scabbling can be reduced by larger pours. The need to cut or break hardened concrete can be reduced by designing work so as to allow for tolerances, by not relying on perfect fit nor on cutting away to make things fit, by leaving positive gaps and specifying expanding grout, mastic or resilient materials as joint fillers.

Work in a way which minimises the amount of dust produced. So, open bags of cement with care, mix carefully etc. Handle dry material in a well-ventilated area.

Workers must be provided with and wear clothing to protect their skin from cement and cement mixtures, e.g.

- Gloves.
- Overalls with long sleeves and full-length trousers.
- Waterproof boots.

Clothing should be worn so as to avoid 'traps' for fresh mortar or concrete to fall in i.e. with sleeves over the gloves and trouser legs over the boots - not tucked inside. If 'trapping' does happen, steps should be taken immediately to clean the contaminated skin and protective clothing with copious amounts of clean water.

Suitable respiratory protective equipment should be work if dusty conditions cannot be avoided. Suitable eye protection must be worn when conditions give rise to a risk of eye injury (e.g. opening cement sacks, during mixing where splashing might occur).

Source: http://www.gov.im/lib/docs/dlge/enviro/cement.pdf

WOOD DUST

Because wood dust is an asthmagen, exposure must be reduced as low as is reasonably practicable. Therefore, the following steps should be considered:

- Provide dust extraction (also known as local exhaust ventilation or LEV) at woodworking machines to remove dust before it can get breathed in.
- Keep the extraction and collection system maintained to make sure it continues to work efficiently.
- It is a legal requirement to have dust extraction equipment examined by a competent person at least every 14 months.
- Use a vacuum system to clear up wood dust - either a free standing vacuum cleaner or preferably a vacuum pipe attached to your extraction system. Vacuum cleaners should be suitable and have a high efficiency particulate air (HEPA) filter.
- For particularly dusty tasks such as sanding use RPE as well as LEV.
- Don't use airlines or dry sweeping to clear dust away. Using airlines and dry sweeping of wood dust can cause high peaks of dust exposure and simply spread the dust around.

Carry out health checks:

- Because wood dust causes asthma, you need to make sure that any health affects are picked up early. This can be done using health surveillance.
- For most woods, a low level of health surveillance is sufficient.
- A higher level of health surveillance, including lung function testing, is needed for exposures to western red cedar which is a known asthmagen.

Source: http://www.hse.gov.uk/woodworking/dust.htm

Asbestos

Asbestos is a general term used to describe a range of mineral fibres (commonly referred to by colour i.e. white, brown and blue). Asbestos was mainly used as an insulating and fire resisting material. Asbestos fibres readily become air borne when disturbed and may enter the lungs, where they cause fibrosis (scarring and thickening) of the lung tissue, asbestosis or mesothelioma (thickening of the pleural lining). Asbestosis typically takes more than 10 years to develop. Research suggests that 50 per cent of asbestos sufferers will also develop cancer of the lung or bronchus.

ASBESTOS IDENTIFICATION

There are three main types of asbestos, which is a naturally occurring mineral. It can be amphibole asbestos which includes crocidolite (blue) and amosite (brown) asbestos, or serpentine asbestos which is chrysotile (white) asbestos. All three of these main types have been used in Great Britain at some time.

Figure 8-32: Asbestos label. *Source: Scaftag.*

Types of survey

Type 1 - Presumptive survey.

A visual inspection takes place where no samples are taken and any suspect material is assumed to be asbestos. Whilst this is a cheaper and quicker in the short term of complying with the regulations, in the long term you may well end up with an expensive management plan for unproven asbestos.

Type 2 - Visual with samples.

A representative number of samples are taken of any suspect materials and analysed in a laboratory, producing a far more accurate report. This survey takes longer and is more expensive to produce, and you only end up managing positive asbestos material and it is invariably a cheaper situation. Type 2 survey is the most widely used to comply with current legislation.

Type 3 - Fully intrusive with samples.

This type of survey is normally used prior to major refurbishment or demolition and is required to locate all asbestos within a building and therefore a more destructive inspection is carried out. Samples are taken in the same way as for type 2 surveys.

Who can undertake them

An independent expert/specialist organisation must:

- Have adequate training and be experienced in survey work.
- Able to demonstrate independence, impartiality and integrity.
- Have an adequate quality management system.
- Carry out any asbestos survey work in accordance with recommended guidance Methods for the Determination of Hazardous Substances (MDHS 100) Surveying sampling and assessment of asbestos-containing materials.

MDHS 100 states that organisations offering an asbestos survey service should be able to comply with the standard set out in EN45004: General criteria for the operation of various types of bodies' performance inspection.

Competence for Assessment

"Whoever carries out the assessment should:

- Have adequate knowledge, competence, training and expertise in understanding the risks from asbestos and be able to make informed decisions about the risks and precautions that are needed.
- Know how the work activity may disturb asbestos; be familiar with the asbestos regulations and understand the requirements of the ACOP *(Approved Code of Practice)*.
- Have the ability and the authority to collate all the necessary, relevant information.
- Be able to assess other non-asbestos risks on site".

Source: Work with materials containing asbestos.

Where it can be located

Asbestos has a number of valuable properties; these include physical strength, resistance to chemicals, non-combustibility and good thermal and electrical insulation. Asbestos is commonly mixed with other materials and is typically used in the following applications:

- As yarn or cloth - for protective clothing, etc.
- Insulation boards - for protection of buildings against fire.
- Asbestos cement products - for construction of buildings and pipes.
- Asbestos resins - for clutch faces and brake linings.
- Various other applications - in gaskets, filters, floor tiles and decorative plasterwork in old buildings.
- Asbestos spraying for thermal and acoustic insulation of buildings and plant, and for fire resistance in structural steelwork, is no longer carried out, although it is encountered as a problem when being removed.
- Atmospheric contamination of workplace and neighbourhoods may occur during building work involving asbestos products or during work to repair or remove such products. Slow disintegration of materials containing asbestos may also cause contamination. There is a hazard whenever airborne fibres are released.

It should be noted that uses of sprayed coating ceased in 1974 and asbestos lagging is unlikely to be found in buildings constructed after 1975.

Figure 8-33: Asbestos cement sheets. *Source: www.risk-it.co.uk.*

Figure 8-34: Asbestos pipe lagging. *Source: www.risk-it.co.uk.*

PROCEDURE FOR THE DISCOVERY OF ASBESTOS DURING CONSTRUCTION ACTIVITY

Employers must have prepared procedures which can be put into effect in the case an incident or emergency that could put people at risk should occur. Information and instruction should be made available to emergency services attending the incident so that they can adequately protect themselves.

REQUIREMENTS IF PERSONS ARE ACCIDENTALLY EXPOSED TO ASBESTOS MATERIALS

Regulation 15 of the Control of Asbestos Regulations (CAR) 2006 requires employers to have arrangements in place to deal with accidents, incidents and emergencies.

These procedures must include means of raising the alarm and means of evacuation. People not wearing personal protective equipment (PPE) must leave the work area. If people have been contaminated then arrangements must include means of decontaminating. (Contaminated PPE should be treated as contaminated waste). The contaminated area must be cleaned thoroughly by employees wearing PPE. Supervisors and managers must make sure that the work has been carried out.

REQUIREMENTS FOR REMOVAL

Un-licensed

Employers have a duty to avoid or, if not reasonably practicable, reduce exposure to hazards. This duty also applies to non-licensable asbestos. Work to remove non-licensable asbestos should be carried out in a way that reduces the likelihood of the release of fibres to a minimum. Avoiding the use of grinders, sanders and other inappropriate power tools is one example.

Licensed

If licensable work is to be carried out then the appropriate enforcing authority must be notified of details of the proposed work. Employers must carry out a risk assessment of the work. This assessment must be kept at the place where work is being carried out.

For licensable work, the plan of work *(see below)* should be site specific and contain the following information:

- The scope of work as identified in the risk assessment.
- Details of hygiene facilities, transit route, vacuum cleaners, air monitoring, protective clothing, respiratory protection equipment (RPE), communication between the inside and outside of the enclosure.
- Use of barriers and signs, location of enclosures and airlocks, location of skips, negative pressure units, cleaning and clearance certification, emergency procedures.

Notification and plan of work

If carrying out licensable work, it must be notified to the appropriate enforcing authority 14 days before work commences (the authority may allow a shorter period in an emergency if there is a serious risk to health).

For any work involving asbestos, the employer must draw up a written plan of work. The plan of work must include the following information:

- Nature and duration of the work.
- Number of persons involved.
- Address and location of the work.
- Methods used to prevent or reduce exposure.
- Type of equipment used to protect those carrying out the work and those present or near the worksite.

Work must not take place unless a copy of the plan is readily available on site.

RESPIRATORY EQUIPMENT

If, despite other control measures an employee's exposure is likely to exceed the control limit or exceed 0.6f/cm3 peak level measured over ten minutes, the employer must provide suitable RPE.

RPE must be matched to:

- The exposure concentrations (expected or measured).
- The job.
- The wearer.
- Factors related to the working environment.

Suitable RPE means:

- It provides adequate protection (i.e. reduces the wearer's exposure to asbestos fibres as low as is reasonably practicable, and anyway to below the control limits) during the job in hand and in the specified working environment (e.g. confined spaces).
- It provides clean air and the flow rate during the whole wear period at least conforms to the minimum recommended by the manufacturer.
- The face piece fits the wearer correctly.
- It is properly maintained.
- The chosen equipment does not introduce additional hazards that may put the wearer's health and safety.

PROTECTIVE CLOTHING

Protective clothing must be adequate and suitable. Cuffs, ankles and hoods should be elasticated and provide a tight fit at the face and neck. Pockets or other attachments which could trap dust should be avoided. Where disposable overalls are used they should be Type 5 (under BS EN ISO 13982-1).

TRAINING

Asbestos awareness training should be given to all employees who could foreseeably be exposed to asbestos. In particular, training should be given to employees whose work is likely to disturb the fabric of the building. The training should include the following topics:

- The properties of asbestos and its effects on health.
- The types, uses and likely occurrence of asbestos.
- Emergency procedures.
- How to avoid the risks from asbestos.

AIR MONITORING

Air testing is required for a number of reasons, such as to certify clearance after asbestos has been removed (a regulatory requirement in most cases), to ensure that leaks do not occur during asbestos treatment or removal and to provide reassurance that nobody has been placed at risk. Personal air monitoring is also necessary to ensure that RPE is providing the appropriate level of protection. Records must be kept for 5 years or, where employees are under health surveillance, for 40 years.

MEDICAL SURVEILLANCE

Regulation 22 of the Control of Asbestos Regulations (CAR) 2006 requires all employers to ensure that all employees who are exposed to asbestos are under adequate health surveillance.

The employer must keep health records for a minimum of 40 years after the last entry made in it. It is not a medical confidential record. It contains job exposure information and dates of previous medical examinations.

REQUIREMENTS FOR DISPOSAL

Licensed carrier

Since 2004 Health and Safety Executive (HSE) requirements on the licensed contractor has meant that each company must have in place an up to date standard operating procedure manual, which should contain all of the details relating to the safe removal and disposal of asbestos. This manual must also be sent to the local HSE inspector and constantly updated to reflect changes in guidance and legislation.

Waste carriers licence involves a simple application and anyone looking to transport waste asbestos will need to be a Registered Waste Carrier.

Notification

Employers must notify the appropriate enforcing authority 14 days before carrying out any licensable work. This can be done on form FOD ASB5.

Licensed disposal site

Any facility looking to accept waste asbestos has to apply to the Environment Agency for a site licence. This will set out the range and volumes of wastes that can be accepted on the site, the site control and management systems, engineering and infrastructure, manning and qualification requirements and reporting and monitoring regimes.

8.7 - Waste disposal and control of pollution

Basic environmental issues relating to waste disposal and effluent in the construction industry

Environmental pollution is a major issue today with the industrialised countries of the world concerned about the long term effects on Earth's resources and on plant, animal and human life. Major concerns on health are often blamed on pollution and there are many pressure groups that focus on environmental issues, particularly pollution.

The problem of pollution is not new; it has been with us since Roman times and the land around old lead mines is still contaminated with the heavy metal today. Since the industrial revolution industry has relied on the capacity of the environment to dilute and disperse pollutants by discharging them to the ground, water and air. This has left a legacy of polluted areas, land pollution being the most persistent, but the discharges to air and water are more global in their effect.

An example of an intentional release of pollution is the emission of sulphur dioxide (SO_2) and nitrogen oxides (NO_x) into the atmosphere by coal-fired power stations. This example also illustrates the global, as well as local, impact that such emissions have which, in this case, results in acid rain falling in Scandinavia, a country which emits very little sulphur dioxide itself. A further impact by the same power station is caused by the carbon dioxide emissions that lead to global warming.

The local effects of the emission of particulates and sulphur dioxide is illustrated by the London smog of the 1950s, and more recently by the increase in road traffic - many cities in Britain now have pollutants above recommended limits, especially in warm, still conditions.

Plant failure and accidents can lead to abnormal releases following higher than expected temperatures and pressures. This has led to a loss of process control with uncontrolled venting to the environment. Lack of control can lead to losses e.g. overfilling.

A definition of pollution

"The introduction into the environment of substance or energy liable to cause hazards to human health, harm to living resources and to ecological systems, damage to structures or amenity or interference with the legitimate use of the environment".

The principal duties imposed by Parts I and II of the Environmental Protection Act 1990

The Environmental Protection Act (EPA) 1990 is the primary legislation relating to environmental protection and management and the key parts are:

Part I: Integrated Pollution Control and Air Pollution Control

Part II: Waste on Land

The EPA was introduced in 1990 partially in response to European Union pressures but partly because of perceived needs in the UK to update the Control of Pollution Act 1974 (CPA) (much of which has never been implemented) and to introduce 'prior approval' together with a more integrated approach.

EPA Part I - Pollution control

The main features of the EPA 1990 affecting industry are:
- The introduction of Integrated Pollution Control (IPC) and Air Pollution Control by Local Authorities (LAAPC).

- The classification of Part A - EA and Part B - LAAPC processes, depending on the type of material being processed and size of facility.

Note:
The powers of the EA are affected by the following factors:
- Part B processes in regard to air pollution control being dealt with by local authorities.
- Their relationship with the HSE - there are potential problems over the COSHH Regulations 2002 and extracting workplace pollutants and venting to atmosphere directly.

EPA Part II - Waste on land
Please refer to later in this element under heading "Waste disposal".

AIR POLLUTION

The atmospheric system

The atmosphere of the planet is a complex fluid system of gases and suspended particles. Five gases - nitrogen, oxygen, argon, carbon dioxide and water vapour make up 99.9% of the total volume of the atmosphere. The balance is made up of suspended particles such as water droplets, dust and soot, and the minor gases. Into this system a range of pollutants are released.

Common sources of air pollutants

Many sources of air pollution are introduced to the atmosphere as a deliberate release from local exhaust extraction and ventilation stacks due to combustion and other industrial processes.

Sulphur dioxide. The major source of sulphur dioxide is the combustion of fossil fuels containing sulphur. These are predominantly coal and fuel oil, since natural gas, petrol and diesel fuels have relatively low sulphur content.

Suspended particulate matter. The main source of primary man-made particulate pollutants is combustion of fossil fuels, especially coal. Power stations use large tonnages of coal. There has been a massive decrease in urban concentrations of smoke. The main source of black smoke in urban air in the UK is diesel powered road vehicles.

Oxides of nitrogen. The most abundant nitrogen oxide in the atmosphere is nitrous oxide, N_2O, and this is formed by natural microbiological processes in the soil. It is not normally considered as a pollutant, although it does have an effect upon stratospheric ozone concentrations and there is concern that use of nitrogenous fertilisers may be increasing atmospheric levels of nitrous oxide. The main concerns are nitric oxide, NO, and nitrogen dioxide, N_2O, which together is called NOx. The major source of NOx is in high temperature combustion processes.

Carbon monoxide. The main source of this pollutant is petrol engine road vehicles. Car exhaust gases contain several per cent carbon monoxide under normal running conditions, and greater amounts when cold and choked.

Hydrocarbons. The major sources of hydrocarbons in air are the evaporation of solvents and fuels, and the partial combustion of fuels.

Carbon dioxide. Increasingly CO_2 is viewed as an air pollutant because of its importance as a "greenhouse gas". Its source lies in animal and plant respiration, and anoxic decomposition processes. It may be both absorbed and released by the oceans. Fossil fuel combustion receives a lot of attention but it is a minor source. However, a small imbalance in the CO_2 cycle is leading to a steady increase in atmospheric concentration.

Ozone. Ozone is a naturally occurring gas in the atmosphere and is important in the upper reaches because it forms a protective layer (the ozone layer) to filter out potentially harmful rays from the sun.

"Holes" in the ozone layer have been discovered at both North and South poles and severe thinning over large parts of North America and Europe - people living in these areas suffer from a greater risk of skin cancer due to increased ultra violet exposure. In addition plant and aquatic life can be affected with corresponding problems for the whole food chain. A range of chemicals containing chlorine or bromine primarily causes the ozone depletion. ***Chlorofluorocarbons (CFCs)*** are in this group and, when they react with radiation from the sun, release chlorine that reacts with and destroys ozone. However the chlorine is not destroyed and can go on to repeat the process up to 100,000 times. Other ozone depleting gases include halons and carbon tetrachloride.

WATER POLLUTION

Water is present on the planet in all three of its phases; that is, as a solid, liquid and gas. Most water vapour is found within the atmosphere; the oceans store most of the water in its liquid phase and the poles and high alpine regions store water in the form of ice. Water moves between each of these three states by processes such as evaporation, condensation, melting and freezing. Operating together these are known as the hydrological cycle and these processes make a major contribution to the weather of the planet. Over 97% of all water on Earth is salt water. Of the 3% that is fresh water 77.5% is locked up in the ice caps and glaciers. The atmosphere, rivers, lakes and underground stores hold less than 1%. The largest volumes of freshwater are held in the Great Lakes of North America.

In terms of water pollution it is the water in its liquid phase that is of most interest. This water appears in the oceans of the world, rivers, lakes, streams and lochs. Water is also stored in its liquid phase in the ground and is referred to as ***groundwater***. It is defined as water which occupies the earth's mantle and which forms the sub surface section of the hydrological cycle. An aquifer is a layer of permeable rock, sand or gravel that absorbs water and allows it free passage through the interstices of the rock.

Common sources of water pollution

One way of thinking about pollution is too much of something in the wrong place and therefore there are many potential water pollutants. This fact is recognised within the European Community by the listing of ***black*** and ***grey list*** materials, sometimes called List I and List II substances. Black List or List I substances are considered to be so toxic, persistent or bio accumulative in the environment that priority should be given to eliminating pollution by them. This includes waste substances such as organohalogens, organophosphorus, cyanide, cadmium and mercury and their compounds. Sheep-dip and solvents are included in this list. The Grey

List or List II covers those substances considered less harmful when discharged to water. Included here are metals such as zinc, nickel, chromium, lead, arsenic and copper. Also included are various biocides such as used in cooling towers or humidifiers and substances such as phosphorus and its compounds (detergents), and ammonia (present in sewage effluent).

Diffuse and point sources

A diffuse source of pollution is one which is spread over a wide area, an example of which is the use of fertilisers over wide areas. Nitrate pollution from fertilisers represents a significant pollutant to rivers, coastal areas and seas. A discharge from an industrial sewer represents an example of a point source. Pollution from diffuse sources is more significant than from point sources and is much more difficult to control.

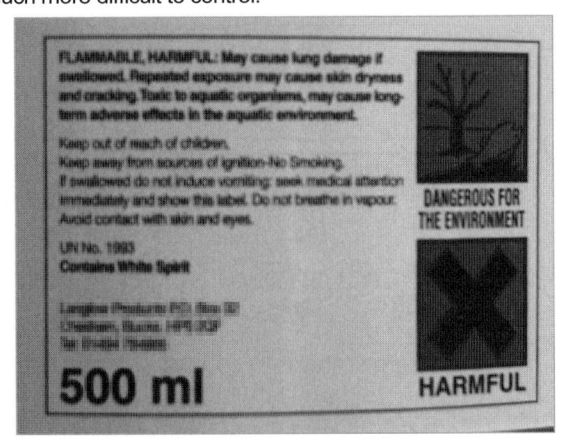

Figure 8-35: Hazard label - environment.   *Source: ACT.*

Figure 8-36: Environmental hazard.   *Source: ACT.*

Figure 8-37: Measures to control pollution.   *Source: ACT.*

Figure 8-38: Measures to control pollution.   *Source: ACT.*

Principles of protection against accidental release

Leaking and spillage can result from a number of sources: faulty valves or flanges to pipework; containers such as tins, drums or bags; loss from tanks (typically one tonne) of solids and liquids; road or rail freight containers; cargo vessels etc.

Typical techniques to contain spillage include: curbed areas for drum storage, tanker loading of liquids, bunded areas to contain sited tanks, drip trays at decanting points (piped systems and 45 gallon [205 litre] drums).

Portable tanks are available with two skins (a tank within a tank) to contain any spillage from the internal tank, often used where there is a need for portability such as with construction sites, to minimise the impact of spillage on the environment when storing materials such as fuel oils. Similarly cargo vessels may have double skinned tanks or hulls.

Bunding

A bund often consists of an area contained by a rectangular wall built upon a concrete slab. The bund floor and walls should be treated to be impervious to any spillage. Storage tanks are located within this confined area. It is necessary to consider the potential escape of any spillage beyond the bund area in the event of the tank developing a hole (known as jetting). The risk of this can be minimised by:

- Keeping the primary container as low as possible.
- Increasing the height of the bund wall.
- Leaving sufficient space between the tank and bund walls.
- Not sitting one tank above another.
- Providing screens or curtains.

The bund should be impermeable to the stored liquid and water which is likely to be present from rain fall and there should be no direct uncontrolled outlet:

- Connecting the bund to any drain, sewer or watercourse.
- Discharging onto a yard or unmade ground.

Ideally, pipework should not pass through the bund wall. If unavoidable, seal the pipe into the bund with a material that is resistant to attack by the substance stored to ensure the bund remains leak-proof.

The secondary containment system must provide storage of at least 110% of the tank's maximum capacity. If more than one container is stored, the system must be capable of storing 110% of the biggest container's capacity or 25% of the total tank capacity within the bund, whichever is the greater.

Source: Environment Agency: Above Ground Oil Storage Tanks.

WASTE DISPOSAL

The surface of the planet is made up of materials including rocks, gravels, sands, clays and soils, which are present in many combinations. Superimposed on these are the various ecosystems which combine to produce a complex system which is therefore not easy to characterise. Glacial action has formed the landscape as the ice age retreated. Rivers, floods, earthquakes, volcanoes, winds, and all forms of life shape the surface of the planet. Each country has unique forms and habitats which provide for the great diversity of life on the planet. Human life results in waste being generated and depending on how these are deposited pollution of the land can occur. As we have mainly populated the land masses, it is these that have traces of pollution dating back to ancient times. Some typical pollutants and their effects include the following:

Contaminant	Hazard pathway	Harmful effects
Heavy metals.	Ingestion.	May cause respiratory cancers, emphysema and other lung disorders, kidney dysfunction and birth defects (teratogenicity).
Zinc, copper, nickel.	Phytotoxicity.	Can stunt plant growth, cause discoloration, shallow root system and die back.
Sulphate and sulphides.	Contact with buildings.	Can corrode and accelerate the weathering of services and structural components.

EPA 1990 Part II - Waste and the duty of care

Waste is defined in the Act as:
- Scrap material.
- Effluent or unwanted substances.
- Something that is broken or worn out.
- Something contaminated or spoilt.
- Something discarded as if it is waste.

The Act introduces the common law concept of duty of care to waste management and applies it to anyone involved in producing, handling or disposing of waste.

Agents or 'brokers' who arrange for waste disposal also have a duty of care under the Act. The producer of the waste retains this duty of care until their waste loses its identity - e.g. it is mixed with other waste at a waste transfer station.

This duty does not apply to domestic producers. Their local authority assumes this responsibility.

The Act requires that the duty holder must:
- Store waste securely and prevent its escape.
- Ensure that waste is only transferred to a licensed carrier and eventually to a licensed site. This should involve the producer carrying out 'duty of care audits' on carriers and waste processors.
- Provide a description of the waste to anyone involved in handling it (Transfer Note). The Transfer Note should contain information including:
  - The identity of the waste.
  - The quantity.
  - The type of containers used.
  - Times and dates of transfer.
  - Names and addresses of producer, carrier etc.
  - Relevant license numbers.

Some *carriers* are exempt from the requirement for a waste carriers licence, such as charities and voluntary organisations. Some *businesses* are exempt from the need for a waste management licence, such as scrap metal recyclers or car dismantlers.

The penalty for a breach of the duty of care can be unlimited fines.

Hazardous waste

In July 2005, the Hazardous Waste Regulations (HWR) 2005 replaced the Special Waste Regulations 1996.

Under this regime:
- Waste Producers must register annually with the Environment Agency.
- Producers must issue a consignment note describing Hazardous Waste.
- The Waste Description must include a code obtained with reference to 14 hazardous properties described the *European Waste Catalogue*.

Non-hazardous waste

Non-hazardous waste does not have dangerous properties e.g. paper, wood, and which degrades without producing harmful decomposition products.

Controlled waste

This category covers the main waste streams from:
- *Household* - includes households, campsites, prisons, churches, schools.
- *Industrial* - includes factories, laboratories, workshops, bus depots, some hospital waste.
- *Commercial* - includes offices, showrooms, hotels, sports centres.

Consignment notes

When hazardous waste is moved from premises then consignment notes must be used. A consignment note must be completed prior to the movement and contains information on:

- Current location and destination.
- The waste producer.
- The waste description including process which gave rise to the waste.
- Chemical properties of the waste, including hazardous characteristics.

Registration of sites

Additional information required for the consignment is a unique reference number for the premises, the 'Hazardous Waste Generator Number'. This is obtained by registering with the Environment Agency.

The storage of incompatible materials and their segregation

In addition to general safe storage practices, segregated storage of incompatible materials is a must. As a minimum, wastes should be segregated according to similar hazards, such as flammability, corrosivity, sensitivity to water or air, and toxicity.

When establishing a storage scheme, the main consideration should be the flammability characteristics of the material. If the material will contribute significantly to a fire (i.e. oxidisers), it should be isolated from the flammables. If a fire were to occur, the response to the fire with water would exaggerate the situation.

Consider the toxicity of the material, with particular attention paid to regulated materials. In some cases, this may mean that certain wastes will be isolated within a storage area, for instance, a material that is an extreme poison but is also flammable, should be locked away in the flammable storage area to protect it against accidental release. There will always be some chemicals that will not fit neatly in one category or another, but with careful consideration of the hazards involved, most of these cases can be handled in a reasonable fashion. For the safety of all personnel and to protect the integrity of the facilities, hazardous materials must be segregated.

Minimising pollution from waste

Organisations should use the following hierarchy in reducing waste in their processes:

- Reduce the amount of raw materials and energy involved in their processes.
- Re-use materials or recover energy.
- Recycle materials - make a useful product from materials unusable in the original process.
- Convert waste to energy - by incineration and use of the heat for industrial heating or electricity generation.
- Dispose to landfill or land raising.

Physical and chemical waste treatment

The aim of physical and chemical treatment of wastes is to minimise the environmental impact. Physical treatment techniques include settling, sedimentation, filtration, flotation, evaporation and distillation (e.g. the separation of oil and water using settlement lagoons or the recovery of solvents by distillation). Chemical conversion processes, such as flue gas desulphurisation (FGD), change the chemical make-up of the substance making it more compatible with the environment. In this latter case, the conversion of sulphur dioxide into gypsum can render the waste inert with little or no environmental impact. Other techniques include:

- Making soluble wastes insoluble.
- Destroying toxicity (e.g. oxidation of cyanides).
- Neutralisation of acids and alkalis.

The majority of waste techniques of this type relate to waterborne contamination and particularly the Water Industry. It should be noted that treated wastes will still require final disposal of solid residues (e.g. water treatment residues).

Landfill and land raising sites

Landfill sites play a crucial role in waste management alongside other methods such as incineration, waste minimisation and recycling techniques. A landfill site is a complex engineering, technical and commercial project that requires thorough planning and high standards of management to ensure that it is successful throughout its lifetime, which may be up to 50 years or more. A land-raising site involves the filling of a natural geographical feature such as a flood plain. The raised site may then be used for industrial or domestic development. Land raising sites can have all the problems, which are discussed below, as can occur with a landfill site.

Legislation relating to landfill / land raising sites

Any person wishing to operate a site must comply with the relevant legislation and also obtain a waste management licence from the Environment Agency.

Sections 33, 35-43 and 54 of the EPA (Environment Protection Agency) 1990 provide for a new system of waste management licensing. The objective of the waste management licensing system is to ensure that waste management facilities do not cause pollution of the environment, do not cause harm to human health and do not become seriously detrimental to the amenities of the locality. The effect of this legislation has been to reduce dramatically the number of sites that will accept hazardous waste.

Incineration

Incineration falls under two main categories; the burning of:

1. Municipal solid wastes (MSW).
2. Hazardous wastes.

The principle of incineration of MSW is to reduce the volume of waste by burning it under controlled conditions in order to reduce volume/mass for final disposal. The heat produced can also be used as an energy source (as a fuel MSW wastes are about 30-40% that of industrial bituminous coal). Incineration is the only really secure environmental option for most pathogens, inflammable liquids and carcinogens such as PCBs or dioxins. Thus this option represents a suitable treatment/disposal for a waste stream if combustion or application of high temperature destroys or transforms it. Thus its potential as an environmental hazard is reduced. About 2% of controlled waste destined for disposal in the UK is incinerated. There are two main types of incinerator - thermal and catalytic.

Recycling or composting

The National Waste Strategy published in May 2006 sets a target of recovering 55% of municipal waste by 2020 and of recycling or composting 25% of household waste by 2006, rising to 30% by 2008. The EPA 1990 requires waste collection authorities to draw up plans for recycling household and commercial waste and empowers waste disposal authorities to pay recycling credits as a result of waste collected for recycling by waste collection authorities.

Element 9

Physical and psychological health - hazards and control

Learning outcomes

On completion of this element, candidates should be able to demonstrate understanding of the content through the application of knowledge to familiar and unfamiliar situations. In particular they should be able to:

9.1 Identify work processes and practices that may give rise to musculoskeletal health problems (in particular work-related upper limb disorders - WRULD) and suggest practical control measures.

9.2 Describe the health effects associated with exposure to noise and suggest appropriate control measures.

9.3 Describe the health effects associated with exposure to vibration and suggest appropriate control measures.

9.4 Describe the principal health effects associated with ionising and non-ionising radiation and outline basic protection techniques.

9.5 Explain the causes and effects of stress at work and suggest appropriate control actions.

9.6 Describe the causes and effects of violence, and effects of alcohol and drug misuse at work and suggest appropriate control actions.

Content

9.1 - Musculoskeletal health	159
The principles of ergonomics as applied to the workplace	159
The ill-health effects of poorly designed tasks and workstations	159
The factors giving rise to ill-health conditions	160
Examples of repetitive risk activities	160
Preventative and precautionary measures	161
9.2 - Noise	161
The effects on hearing of exposure to noise	161
Meaning of terms commonly used in the measurement of sound	162
Action and limit values	163
Simple noise measurement techniques	163
Basic noise control techniques	164
Health surveillance	166
9.3 - Vibration	166
The effects on the body of exposure to vibration	166
Assessment of exposure, including limit and action values	167
Basic vibration control measures	168
Health surveillance	169
9.4 - Heat and radiation	169
Temperature	169
Ionising and non-ionising radiation	170
Typical occupational sources of ionising and non-ionising radiation	172
The basic means of controlling exposures to ionising and non-ionising radiation	172
Basic radiation protection strategies	173
9.5 - Stress	173
Causes	174
Effects of stress	174
Prevention strategies	174
9.6 - Violence and drugs at work	175
Risk factors relating to violence at work	175
Effects on health and safety of alcohol and drugs	175

UNIT NCC1 - ELEMENT 9 - PHYSICAL AND PSYCHOLOGICAL HEALTH - HAZARDS AND CONTROL

Sources of reference

A pain in your workplace? Ergonomic problems and solutions (HSG121), HSE Books ISBN 0-7176-0668-6
Controlling noise at work (L108), HSE Books ISBN 0-7176-6164-4
Essentials of Health and Safety at Work, HSE Books ISBN 0-7176-0716-X
Hand-arm vibration - Control of Vibration at Work Regulations 2005 (L140), HSE Books ISBN 0-7176-6125-3
HSE stress management standards www.hse.gov.uk/stress/standards
Lighting at work (HSG38), HSE Books ISBN 0-7176-1232-5
Personal protective equipment at work (Guidance) (L25), HSE Books ISBN 0-7176-6139-3
Real solutions, real people: A managers guide to tackling work-related stress, HSE Books ISBN 0-7176-2767-5
Safe use of work equipment (ACoP) (L22), HSE Books ISBN 0-7176-1626-6
The law on VDUs - An easy guide (HSG90), HSE Books ISBN 07176-2602-4
The Workplace (Health, Safety and Welfare) Regulations 1992 (ACoP) (L24), HSE Books ISBN 0-7176-0413-6
Seating at work (HSG57), HSE Books ISBN 0717612317
Whole-body vibration - Control of Vibration at Work Regulations 2005 (L141), HSE Books ISBN 0-7176-6126-1
Work related upper limb disorders - A guide (HSG60), HSE Books ISBN 0-7176-1978-8
Work with display screen equipment (Guidance) (L26), HSE Books ISBN 0-7176-2582-6

Relevant statutory provisions

The Control of Noise at Work Regulations (CNWR) 2005
The Control of Vibration at Work Regulations (CVWR) 2005
The Construction (Design and Management) Regulations (CDM) 2007
The Health and Safety (Display Screen Equipment) Regulations (DSE) 1992
The Ionising Radiations Regulations (IRR) 1999
The Personal Protective Equipment at Work Regulations (PPER) 1992
The Provision and Use of Work Equipment Regulations (PUWER) 1998

9.1 - Musculoskeletal health

The principles of ergonomics as applied to the workplace

The study of ergonomics is essential to good job design. It can be defined as 'the study of the relationship between man, the equipment with which he works and the physical environment in which this man-machine system operates'.

It is a broad area of study that includes the disciplines of psychology, physiology, anatomy and design engineering. Ergonomics has the human being at the centre of the study where his capabilities and fallibilities are considered in order to, ultimately, eliminate the potential for human error. It is also the study of ways to prevent the so-called 'ergonomic illnesses' - work-related musculoskeletal disorders. These areas of ill health may lead to disability. They stem from poorly designed machines, tools, task and workplace. Research has shown that there are about one million cases of work-related musculoskeletal disorders annually in England and Wales.

Human beings work within certain boundaries which must be recognised for all situations. However, even when human beings work within their limitations, there will still be degradation in performance. Why, when and how degradation occurs needs to be understood in order to make allowances for or to remedy the situation.

The aims of ergonomics, therefore, are to design the equipment and the working environment to fit the needs and capabilities of the individual, i.e. fitting the task to the individual, and to ensure that the physical and mental well-being of the individual are being met. This involves a consideration of psychological and physical factors, including the work system, training, body dimensions, intelligence, noise, temperature and lighting.

The design of the human body is basically uniform, allowing for differences of gender. The spine, joints, tendons and muscles work in the same way and will suffer also the same abuse, although to a varying extent. Individuals, therefore, have different physical capabilities due to height, weight, age and levels of fitness. They also have different mental capabilities, memory retention and personalities.

The ill-health effects of poorly designed tasks and workstations

MUSCULOSKELETAL PROBLEMS INCLUDING WORK-RELATED UPPER LIMB DISORDERS [WRULD]

Were first defined in medical literature as long ago as the 19th century as a condition caused by forceful, frequent, twisting and repetitive movements. The body will be affected to a varying degree by tasks which involve bending, reaching, twisting, repetitive movements and poor posture. WRULD covers well-known conditions such as tennis elbow, flexor tenosynovitis and carpal tunnel syndrome. It is usually caused by the tasks and movements detailed above and aggravated by excessive workloads, inadequate rest periods and sustained or constrained postures. The result of which is pain, soreness or inflammatory conditions of muscles and the synovial lining of the tendon sheath. Present approaches to treatment are largely effective, provided the condition is treated in its early stages. Clinical signs and symptoms are local aching pain, tenderness, swelling, crepitus (a grating sensation in the joint).

Some common WRULDs are:

Carpel Tunnel Syndrome	CTS occurs when tendons or ligaments in the wrist become enlarged, often from inflammation, after being aggravated. The narrowed tunnel of bones and ligaments in the wrist pinches the nerves that reach the fingers and the muscles at the base of the thumb. The first symptoms usually appear at night. Symptoms range from a burning, tingling numbness in the fingers, especially the thumb and the index and middle fingers, to difficulty gripping or making a fist, to dropping things.
Tenosynovitis	An irritation of the tendon sheath. It occurs when the repetitive activity becomes excessive and the tendon sheath can no longer lubricate the tendon. As a result, the tendon sheath thickens and becomes aggravated.
Tendinitis	Tendinitis involves inflammation of a tendon, the fibrous cord that attaches muscle to bone. It usually affects only one part of the body at a time, and usually lasts a short time, unless involved tissues are continuously irritated. It can result from an injury, activity or exercise that repeats the same movement.
Peritendinitis	Inflammation of the area where the tendon joins the muscle.
Epicondylitis	Tennis Elbow or Lateral Epicondylitis is a condition when the outer part of the elbow becomes painful and tender, usually because of a specific strain, overuse, or a direct bang. Sometimes no specific cause is found. Tennis Elbow is similar to Golfer's Elbow (Medial Epicondolytis) which affects the other side of the elbow.

The aches, pains and fatigue suffered doing certain tasks will eventually impair the operator's ability and lead to degradation in performance. It is therefore essential to consider the task in order to match it to the individual so the level of general comfort is maximised. For example, when carrying out manual handling assessments it is important to look at the relationship between the individual, the task, the load and the environment.

HAND-ARM VIBRATION SYNDROME

Prolonged intense vibration transmitted to the hands and arms by vibrating tools and equipment can lead to a condition known as **hand-arm vibration syndrome (HAVs).** These are a range of conditions relating to long term damage to the circulatory system, nerves, soft tissues, bones and joints. Probably the best known of these conditions is known as vibration white finger (VWF). Here the fingers go white and numb (known as **Raynaud's phenomenon**), leading to 'pins and needles' and an often painful deep red flush. This seems to occur in response to a change in metabolic demand in the fingers induced, for example, by temperature change. It seems that the blood vessels are unable to dilate either at all or rapidly enough because of the thickened tissues that then become anoxic (lacking in oxygen).

The factors giving rise to ill-health conditions

TASKS

Tasks should be assessed to determine the health risk factors.

If the task is *repetitive* in nature, i.e. the same series of operations are repeated in a short period of time, such as ten or more times per minute, then injury may occur to the muscles and ligaments affected. Similarly, work of a *strenuous* nature, such as moving heavy or difficult shaped objects, perhaps in limited space or hot environments, will cause fatigue, strains and sprains.

ENVIRONMENT

Poor working environments. Working in *extremes of temperature* or handling hot or cold items will make simple work more strenuous. Long hours of work in cold conditions causes problems with blood circulation which, in turn, may increase the likelihood of hand arm vibration syndrome. Fatigue will also occur to the eyes if the *lighting* levels are low, typically below 100-200 lux. or bright, typically greater than 800 lux. Other lighting factors may need to be considered such as the stroboscopic effects associated with moving machinery, which may appear to be stationary when viewed under fluorescent light powered by alternating current.

The risk of injury increases with the *length of time* that a task is carried out. However, injury may occur over a short period if the work requires a lot of effort.

Working in *uncomfortable positions* such as working above head height or holding something in the same place for a long period of time increases the risk of injury. These factors will often be reduced if the worker is able to adjust the conditions to their personal needs.

There is robust scientific evidence of an association of increases in selected respiratory health effects with building dampness or visible mould. These health effects are asthma exacerbation in sensitized individuals, and cough, wheeze, and upper respiratory symptoms in otherwise healthy individuals.

Dampness in buildings is a concern because it often leads to growth of moulds and bacteria and to increased emissions of chemicals. In addition, dampness causes structural degradation on buildings. Building dampness problems have a number of causes. The report argues that the way to reduce these problems and the risk of associated health effects is to improve the design, construction, operation, and maintenance of buildings.

Poor posture. The position of the body and the way it has to move to carry out a particular function. This can be affected by such things as: badly designed work methods (e.g. the need for regular bending or twisting), and poor layout of the workplace (e.g. having to kneel or stretch to put articles in a cupboard).

Figure 9-1: Posture. Source: Speedy Hire Plc.

EQUIPMENT

All work factors that influence health issues should be under the influence of the operator as much as possible, such as the ability to adjust temperature and lighting, and the opportunity to take rest breaks. If this is not possible with continuous automated lines, such as with car assembly, then work should be designed to provide facilities for operators' work patterns to be rotated to reduce these effects. Consideration to automation should be given whenever possible.

Equipment design should take into account the ergonomic requirements of the operator and, where possible, allow the user to adjust any settings to suit his/her needs. Such things as workbench height and positioning of switches and buttons should be in the operator's control.

Examples of repetitive risk activities

KEYBOARD OPERATION

Some or all of the above factors may affect keyboard operators. In addition, over the years there has been some concern regarding conditions like:

- Common WRULDs associated with key board / mouse operation are:
  - Carpel Tunnel Syndrome - painful inflammation of the nerves and tendons passing through the carpal bone in the wrist area. Affects the whole hand.
  - Tenosynovitis - inflammation of the synovial lining of the tendon sheath.
- Radiation effects - extensive research has shown that exposure levels are well below any national and international exposure limits.
- Photosensitive epilepsy - a very rare form of epilepsy. Sufferers will usually know about the condition and not put themselves at risk.
- Facial dermatitis - evidence suggests that this condition is usually caused by other environmental factors such as low humidity.

ASSEMBLY OF SMALL COMPONENTS, BOLT FIXING, TIGHTENING OF NUTS AND SCREWS

Many repetitive light assembly tasks have a high risk of causing WRULDs. Typical tasks of this type would be inserting a spring into a car radiator cap using one's thumb, or operating a hand power press to insert ball bearings into a component. Each task should be reviewed to determine the best technique is used to reduce fatigue or strain. In the case of the radiator cap an example of a change following review would be - providing a tool to replace the use of the thumb.

Carpenters and steel workers are exposed to the repetitive movements involved with some work activities e.g. hammering, fixing bolts/screws.

Preventative and precautionary measures

PREVENTATIVE

Control measures
- Improved design or working areas.
- Provision of special tools.

PRECAUTIONARY

General
- Better training and supervision.
- Adjustment of workloads and rest periods.
- Health surveillance aimed at early detection.

Figure 9-2: Working area.   Source: ACT.

Information and training
(Regulations 6 and 7 - Health and Safety (Display Screen Equipment) Regulations)

Should include:
- Risks to health.
- How to recognise problems.
- Precautions in place (e.g. the need for regular breaks).
- How to report problems.

9.2 - Noise

The effects on hearing of exposure to noise

The ear senses **sound**, which is transmitted in the form of pressure waves travelling through a substance, e.g., air, water, metals etc. Unwanted sound is generally known as **noise.**

The ear has 3 basic regions **(see - Figure 9-3)**:

a) The **outer** ear channels the sound pressure waves through to the eardrum.

b) In the **middle** ear, the vibrations of the eardrum are transmitted through three small bones (hammer, anvil and stirrup) to the inner ear.

c) The cochlea in the **inner** ear is filled with fluid and contains tiny hairs (nerves) which respond to the sound. Signals are then sent to the brain via the acoustic nerve.

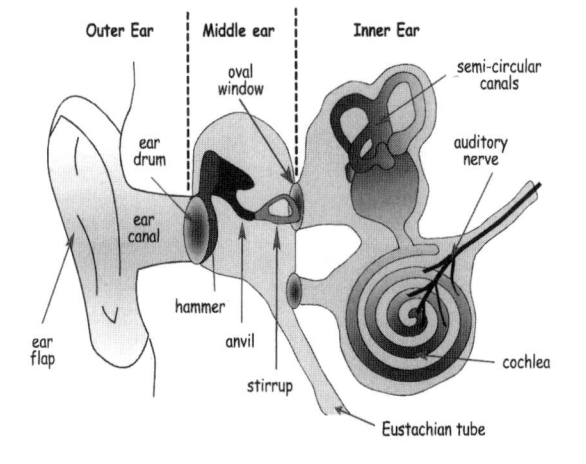

Figure 9-3: Inner ear diagram.   Source: www.echalk.co.uk. 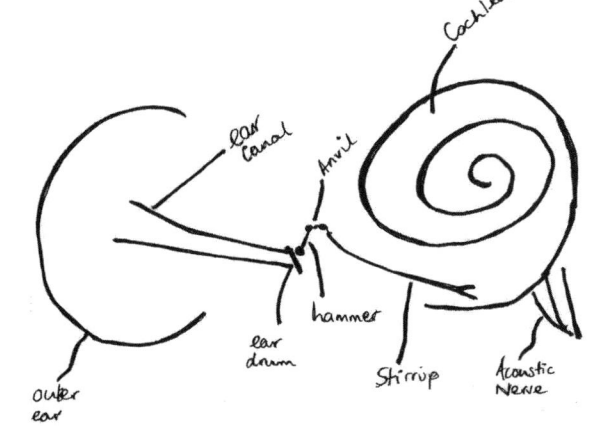   Figure 9-4: The ear (hand drawn).   Source: ACT.

Excessive noise over long periods of time can cause damage to the hairs (nerves) in the cochlea of the ear. This results in **noise induced hearing loss (deafness)**, which can be of a temporary or permanent nature. Also, a single high pressure event can damage the ear by dislocation of a bone or rupturing the ear drum. It has been shown that high levels of noise can cause, or increase the onset of, **tinnitus** ('ringing in the ears').

Meaning of terms commonly used in the measurement of sound

SOUND POWER AND PRESSURE

For noise to occur power must be available. It is the sound power of a source (measured in Watts) which causes the sound pressure (measured in Pascals) to occur at a specific point.

INTENSITY AND FREQUENCY

The amplitude of a sound wave represents the intensity of the sound pressure. When measuring the **amplitude** of sound there are two main parameters of interest - *as shown in Figure 9-5.* One is related to the energy in the sound pressure wave and is known as the 'root mean square' (rms) value, and the other is the 'peak' level. We use the rms sound pressure for the majority of noise measurements, apart from some impulsive types of noise when the peak value is also measured.

Sound (noise) waves travel through air at the *'speed of sound'* which is approximately equal to 344 m/s. A sound can have a *'frequency'* or *'pitch'*, which is measured in cycles per second (Hz).

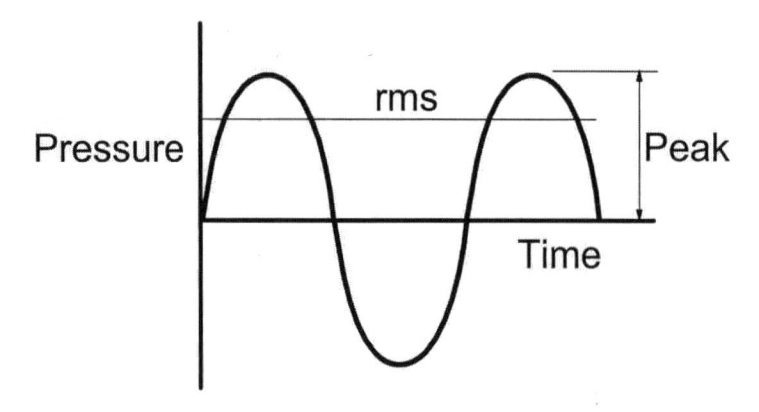

Figure 9-5: Rms and peak levels of a sound wave.   Source: ACT.

THE DECIBEL SCALE

The ear can detect pressures over a very wide range, from 20 µPa to 20 Pa (Pascals). To help deal with this wide range, the **deciBel (dB)** is used to measure noise. A decibel is a unit of sound pressure (intensity) measured on a logarithmic scale from a base level taken to be the threshold of hearing (0dB). Typical noise levels include:

Source	dB	Source	dB
Disco	110	Radio in average room	70
Smoke detector at 1 metre	105	Library	30
Machine Shop	90	Threshold of Hearing	0

A problem with decibels is that they are based on a logarithmic scale and cannot be added together in the conventional way, for example:

   2 dB + 2 dB = 5 dB   (deciBel Arithmetic) and
   85 dB + 85 dB = 88 dB   (deciBel Arithmetic)

WEIGHTING SCALES - THE TERMS DB(A) AND DB(C)

The human ear can hear sound over a range of frequencies, from 20 Hz up to approximately 20,000 Hz (20 kHz). However, the ear does not hear the same at all frequencies; it naturally reduces (attenuates) low frequencies and very high frequencies. To take account of the response of the human ear sound level meters use weighting scales or filters. The most widely used sound level filter is the A scale. Using this filter, the sound level meter is thus less sensitive to very high and very low frequencies. Measurements made on this scale are expressed as dB(A) or referred to as *'A weighted'*. The majority of measurements are made in terms of dB(A), although there are other weightings that are used in some circumstances. One of these is the C scale which is suitable for subjective measurements only for very high sound levels. Measurements made on this scale are expressed as dB(C). There is also a (rarely used) B weighting scale, intermediate between A and C.

The range of frequencies that we encounter is often divided into **Octave Bands**. A noise can be measured in each octave band and these levels can be used when assessing the attenuation of hearing protectors, or when diagnosing noise problems.

Other noise units

In most situations the noise level varies with time. When measuring noise we need to determine the average, or 'equivalent continuous level', over a period of time. This is known as the **Leq**. Not all noise meters include a **Leq** function. Other noise units commonly encountered are also listed below:

L_{eq} the average, or 'equivalent continuous level'.

$L_{EP,d}$ daily personal exposure level, dB(A). This is equivalent to the L_{eq} over an 8-hour working day. The $L_{EP,d}$ is directly related to the risk of hearing damage.

L_{peak} peak pressure - pascals or dB (C).

Action and limit values

ACTION VALUES

Regulation 2 of The Control of Noise at Work Regulations (CNWR) 2005 sets out the definition of 'daily average noise exposure' as the time weighted average of the levels of noise to which a worker is exposed over an 8 hour working day, taking account of levels of noise and duration of exposure and including impulsive noises. Weekly noise exposure level means the average of daily noise exposure levels over a week and normalised to five working days.

	Lower exposure action values	Upper exposure action values	Exposure limit values
Daily or weekly personal noise exposure (A-weighted)	80 dB	85 dB	87 dB
Peak sound pressure (C-weighted).	135 dB	137 dB	140 dB

Under regulation 4 of CNWR 2005 if the noise levels in the workplace vary greatly, then the employer can choose to use weekly noise exposure levels instead of daily noise exposure levels. The exposure can take into account personal hearing protection provided to the employee.

Lower exposure action value

Where the daily or weekly exposure level of 80dB(A) or a peak sound pressure level of 135 dB(C) is likely to be exceeded the employer must make hearing protection available upon request and provide the employees and their representatives with suitable and sufficient information, instruction and training. This shall include:

- Nature of risks from exposure to noise.
- Organisational and technical measures taken in order to comply.
- Exposure limit values and upper and lower exposure action values.
- Significant findings of the risk assessment, including any measurements taken, with an explanation of those findings.
- Availability and provision of personal hearing protectors and their correct use.
- Why and how to detect and report signs of hearing damage.
- Entitlement to health surveillance.
- Safe working practices to minimise exposure to noise.
- The collective results of any health surveillance in a form calculated to prevent those results from being identified as relating to a particular person.

Figure 9-6: Noise hazard sign. Source: ACT.

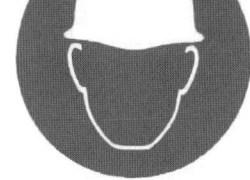

Figure 9-7: Mandatory signs. Source: Stocksigns.

Upper exposure action value

Where the daily or weekly exposure level of 85dB(A) or a peak sound pressure level of 137 dB(C) is likely to be exceeded the employer shall:

- Provide employees with hearing protection. In addition the employer will:
  - Ensure that the area is designated a hearing protection zone, fitted with mandatory hearing protection signs.
  - Ensure access to the area is restricted where practicable.
  - So far as reasonably practicable, ensure those employees entering the area wear hearing protection.

The employer must ensure that workers are not exposed to levels above an exposure limit value or if one is exceeded immediately reduce exposure below that level, investigate the reasons and modify measures to prevent a reoccurrence.

Simple noise measurement techniques

REGULATION REQUIREMENTS FOR NOISE ASSESSMENT

Regulation 5 of CNWR 2005 states that any employer that carries out work which is likely to expose any employees to noise must make a suitable and sufficient assessment of the risk to health and safety created by noise at the workplace. In conducting the risk assessment the employer should assess the level of noise the workers are exposed to by:

- Observation.
- Reference to information on expected levels for work conditions and equipment.
- If necessary by measurement of the level of noise to which his employees may be exposed.

The risk assessment shall include consideration of:

- Level, type and duration of exposure, including any exposure to peak sound pressure.
- Effects of exposure to *noise* on employees or groups of employees whose health is at particular risk from such exposure.
- So far as is practicable, any effects on the health and safety of employees resulting from the interaction between *noise* and the use of toxic substances at *work*, or between *noise* and vibration.

- Indirect effects on the health and safety of employees resulting from the interaction between *noise* and audible warning signals or other sounds that need to be audible in order to reduce risk at *work*.
- Information provided by the manufacturers of *work* equipment.
- Availability of alternative equipment designed to reduce the emission of *noise*.
- Any extension of exposure to *noise* at the workplace beyond normal *working* hours, including exposure in rest facilities supervised by the employer.
- Appropriate information obtained following health surveillance, including, where possible, published information.
- Availability of personal hearing protectors with adequate attenuation characteristics.

Employees or their representatives must be consulted, significant findings and measures taken or planned to comply with the regulations have to be recorded.

MEASUREMENT TECHNIQUES

Noise is measured using a sound level meter, which works in simple terms by converting pressure variations into an electric signal. This is achieved by capturing the sound with a microphone, pre-amplification of the resultant voltage signal and then processing the signal into the information required dependent on the type of meter (e.g. 'A' weighting, integrating levels, fast or slow response). The microphone is the most important component within the meter as its sensitivity and accuracy will determine the accuracy of the final reading. Meters can be set to fast or slow response depending on the characteristics of the noise level. Where levels are rapidly fluctuating, rapid measurements are required and the meter should be set to fast time weighting.

Sound level meters should be calibrated using a portable acoustic calibrator and batteries checked before, during and after each measurement session. Laboratory calibration should be carried out annually or according to the manufacturer's instructions. Meters are used to measure the:

- Sound pressure level (L_p) - the intensity of sound at a given moment in time at a given position (i.e. the instantaneous level): an unweighted linear measurement dB (L_{in}).
- Equivalent continuous sound level (L_{eq}) - an average measure of intensity of sound over a reference period, usually the period of time over which the measurement was taken. Measured in dB(A). As the intensity and spacing of the noise levels usually vary with time, an integrating meter is used. This meter automatically calculates the L_{eq} by summing or integrating the sound level over the measurement period.
- Peak pressure level - some sound level meters produce peak pressure values for impulsive noise or where a fast time weighting reading exceeds 125 dB(A).

The expense and time consuming nature of personal dosimetry means that they should only be used when other techniques are unsuitable. It is used in situations where the task of the worker involves movement around the workplace and exposure is likely to vary.

Basic noise control techniques

Requirements for noise control set out in Regulation 6 of CNWR 2005 follow the general principles of prevention set out in the MHSWR 1999. Employers must ensure that risk from the exposure of his employees to noise is either eliminated at source or, where this is not reasonably practicable, reduced to as low as is reasonably practicable. Consideration should be made to:

- Other *working* methods which reduce exposure to *noise*.
- Choice of appropriate *work* equipment emitting the least possible *noise*, taking account of the *work* to be done.
- Design and layout of workplaces, *work* stations and rest facilities.
- Suitable and sufficient information and training for employees, such that *work* equipment may be used correctly, in order to minimise their exposure to *noise*.
- Reduction of *noise* by technical means.
- Appropriate maintenance programmes for *work* equipment, the workplace and workplace systems.
- Limitation of the duration and intensity of exposure to *noise*.
- Appropriate *work* schedules with adequate rest periods.

The employer has to take care that noise levels in rest facilities are suitable for their purpose. The employer must adapt measures provided to suit a group or individual employee whose health is likely to be of particular risk from exposure to noise at work. Employees or their representatives must be consulted on the measures used.

NOISE CONTROL TECHNIQUES

Noise can be controlled at different points in the following 'chain':

1) The source (e.g., a noisy machine).

2) The path (e.g., through the air).

3) The receiver (e.g., the operator of a machine).

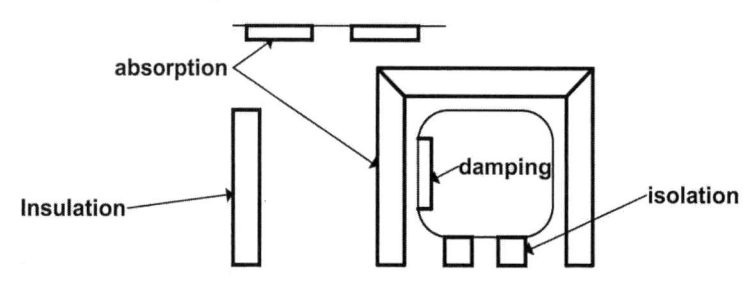

Figure 9-8: Basic layout of the main control methods.

Source: ACT.

The main methods of noise control are listed below:

Isolation — Positioning an elastic element (e.g. rubber mount etc.) in the path of vibration can isolate a noise radiating area from a vibration input.

Absorption — When noise passes through porous materials (e.g. foam, mineral, wool etc.) some of its energy is absorbed.

Insulation — Imposing a barrier (e.g. a brick wall, lead sheet etc.) between the noise source and the receivers will provide noise insulation.

Damping — Mechanical vibration can be converted into heat by damping materials (e.g. metal/plastic/metal panels).

Silencing — Pipe/boxes can be designed to reduce air/gas noise (e.g. engine exhaust silencers, duct silencers, etc.).

Other specialist control methods (NOT examinable):

Force Reduction - Reduce impacts by using rubber pads or lower drop heights.

Air exhaust and jet silencers - Proprietary silencers can be used.

Active - Equal but opposite phase noise can cancel a problem noise.

In addition to controlling the amplitude of noise the **exposure level** can be reduced by minimising the amount of time an employee is exposed to noise, for example, by job rotation. Increasing the distance between noisy equipment and a work location can reduce the noise to which an employee is exposed. When buying new plant and equipment employers should adopt a purchasing policy which results in the quietest machines being bought.

Figure 9-9: Silenced diesel welder. Source: Speedy Hire Plc.

PERSONAL HEARING PROTECTION

All types of personal ear protector should carry a CE marking.

Purpose

The purpose of personal hearing protection is to protect the user from the adverse effects on hearing caused by exposure to high levels of noise. All hearing protection must be capable of reducing exposure to below the second level or upper exposure action value as per the CNWR 2005 regulations. (85dB over 8 hours).

Application and limitations of various types

Earmuffs:
1) Banded.
2) Helmet mounted.
3) Communication muffs.

Advantages:
- Worn on the outside of the ear so less chance of infection.
- Clearly visible therefore easy to monitor.
- Can be integrated into other forms of PPE e.g. head protection.

Limitations:
- Can be uncomfortable when worn for long periods.
- Incompatibility with other forms of PPE.
- Effectiveness may be compromised by e.g. long hair, spectacles etc.
- Requires correct storage facilities and regular maintenance.

Ear plugs:
1) Pre-moulded.
2) User formable.
3) Custom moulded.
4) Banded plugs.

Advantages:
- Easy to use and store - but must be inserted correctly.
- Available in many materials and designs, disposable.
- Relatively lightweight and comfortable. Can be worn for long periods.

Limitations:
- They are subject to hygiene problems unless care is taken to keep them clean.
- Correct size may be required. Should be determined by a competent person.
- Interferes with communication.
- Worn inside the ear, difficult to monitor.

Selection

When selecting personal hearing protectors employers must take into consideration several factors, including:
- Provision of information and training.
- Readily available.
- Comfort and personal choice.
- Issue to visitors.
- Care and maintenance.
- Noise reduction.

Use

All PPE should be used in accordance with employer's instructions, which should be based on manufacturer's instructions for use. PPE should only be used after adequate training has been given. Also, adequate supervision must be provided to ensure that training and instructions are being followed. Personal ear protection may not provide adequate protection due to any of the following reasons:

a) Long hair, spectacles, earrings etc, may cause a poor seal to occur.
b) Ear protectors are damaged, e.g. cracked.

c) Not fitted properly - due to lack of training.
d) Not wearing ear protectors all of the time.
e) Specification of protectors does not provide sufficient attenuation.

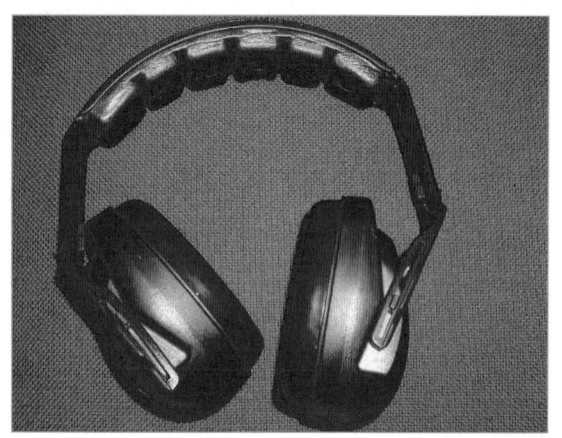

Figure 9-10: Ear defenders.   Source: ACT.

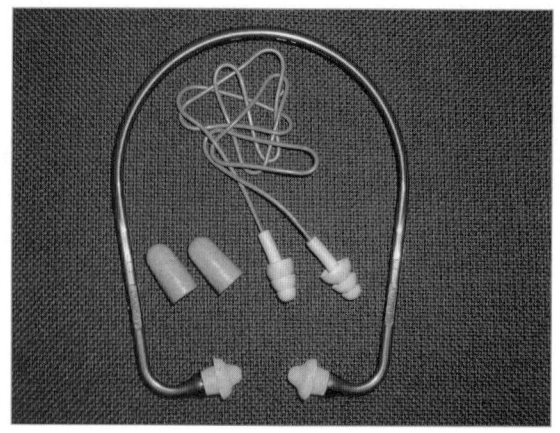

Figure 9-11: Disposable ear plugs.   Source: ACT.

Maintenance

Employers have a legal duty to ensure that any PPE is maintained in an efficient state, efficient working order and good repair. Simple maintenance can be carried out by the trained wearer, but more intricate repairs should only be done by specialist personnel.

Attenuation factors

The attenuation (noise reduction) associated with personal ear protectors must be supplied with the product. The information required is in terms of:

1) Octave band mean attenuation and the standard deviation.   **2)** HML (High, Medium and Low) values.   **3)** SNR (Single Number Rating) values.

Health surveillance

Regulation 9 of the CNWR 2005 states that if a risk assessment indicates a risk to the health and safety of employees who are, or are liable to be, exposed to noise, then they must be put under suitable health surveillance (including testing of their hearing). The employer must keep and maintain a suitable health record. The employer will, providing reasonable notice is provided, allow the employee access to their health record.

Where, as a result of health surveillance, an employee is found to have identifiable hearing damage the employer shall ensure that the employee is examined by a doctor. If the doctor, or any specialist to whom the doctor considers it necessary to refer the employee, considers that the damage is likely to be the result of exposure to *noise*, the employer shall:

- Ensure that a suitably qualified person informs the employee accordingly.
- Review the risk assessment.
- Review any measure taken to comply with the regulations.
- Consider assigning the employee to alternative *work.*
- Ensure continued health surveillance.
- Provide for a review of the health of any other employee who has been similarly exposed.

Employees must, when required by the employer and at the cost of the employer, present themselves during *working* hours for health surveillance procedures.

9.3 - Vibration

The effects on the body of exposure to vibration

HARM TO HEALTH

Occupational exposure to vibration may arise in a number of ways, often reaching workers at intensity levels disturbing to comfort, efficiency and health and safety. Long-term, regular exposure to vibration is known to lead to permanent and debilitating health effects such as vibration white finger, loss of sensation, pain, and numbness in the hands, arms, spine and joints. These effects are collectively known as hand-arm or whole body vibration syndrome.

WHOLE BODY VIBRATION (WBV)

In the case of whole body vibration (WBV) it is transmitted to the worker through a contacting or supporting structure which is itself vibrating, e.g. a ship's deck, the seat or floor of a vehicle (tractor or tank), or a whole structure shaken by machinery (e.g. in the processing of coal, iron ore or concrete), where the vibration is intentionally generated for impacting.

The most widely reported WBV injury is back pain. Prolonged exposure can lead to considerable pain and time off work and may result in permanent injury and having to give up work. High-risk activities include driving site vehicles (e.g. dumper trucks) and the prolonged use of compactors.

HAND-ARM VIBRATION (HAV)

Prolonged intense vibration transmitted to the hands and arms by vibrating tools and equipment can lead to a condition known as *hand-arm vibration syndrome (HAVs).* These are a range of conditions relating to long term damage to the circulatory system, nerves, soft tissues, bones and joints. Probably the best known of these conditions is known as vibration white finger (VWF). Here the fingers go white and numb (known as **Raynaud's phenomenon**), leading to 'pins and needles' and an often painful deep red flush.

Figure 9-12: Use of road drill - vibration.   *Source: ACT.* 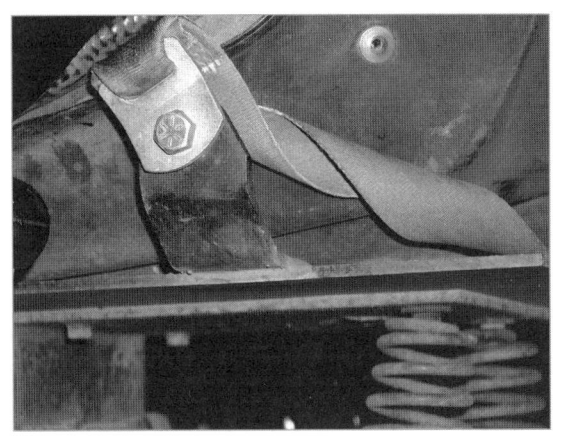   Figure 9-13: Dumper truck seat.   *Source: ACT.*

This seems to occur in response to a change in metabolic demand in the fingers induced, for example, by temperature change. It seems that the blood vessels are unable to dilate either at all or rapidly enough because of the thickened tissues that then become anoxic (lacking in oxygen).

CONTRIBUTORY FACTORS

As with all work-related ill health there are a number of factors which when combined result in the problem occurring. These include:-

- Vibration frequency - frequencies ranging from 2- 1,500 Hz are potentially damaging but the most serious is the 5-20 Hz range.
- Duration of exposure - this is the length of time the individual is exposed to the vibration.
- Contact Force - this is the amount of grip or push used to guide or apply the tools or work piece. The tighter the grip the greater the vibration to the hand.
- Factors affecting circulation - including temperature and smoking.
- Individual susceptibility.

EXAMPLES OF RISK ACTIVITIES

- The use of hand-held chain saws in forestry.
- The use of hand-held rotary tools in grinding or in the sanding or polishing of metal, or the holding of material being ground, or metal being sanded or polished by rotary tools.
- The use of hand-held percussive metal-working tools, or the holding of metal being worked upon by percussive tools in riveting, caulking, chipping, hammering, fettling or swaging.
- The use of hand-held powered percussive drills or hand-held powered percussive hammers in demolition, or on roads or footpaths, including road construction.

The medical effects are in the main more serious and permanent and are summarised below:

a) Vascular changes in the blood vessels of the fingers.
b) Neurological changes in the peripheral nerves.
c) Muscle and tendon damage in the fingers, hands, wrists and forearms.
d) Suspected bone and joint changes.
e) Damage to the autonomic centres of the central nervous system in the brain influencing the endocrine, cardiac, vestibular and cochlear functions (not proven).

Assessment of exposure, including limit and action values

LIMITS AND ACTION LEVELS

Regulation 4 of the Control of Vibration at Work Regulations (CVWR) 2005 states the personal daily exposure limits and daily exposure action values, normalised over an 8-hour reference period.

	Daily exposure action values	Daily exposure limits
Hand arm vibration	2.5 m/s^2	5 m/s^2
Whole body vibration	0.5 m/s^2	1.15 m/s^2

RISK ASSESSMENT

Regulation 5 of CVWR 2005 requires the employer to make a suitable and sufficient assessment of the risk created by work that is liable to expose employees to risk from vibration. The assessment must observe work practices, make reference to information regarding the magnitude of vibration from equipment and, if necessary, measurement of the magnitude of the vibration.

Consideration must also be given to the type, duration, effects of exposure, exposures limit / action values, effects on employees at particular risk, the effects of vibration on equipment and the ability to use it, manufacturers' information, availability of replacement equipment, and extension of exposure at the workplace (e.g. rest facilities), temperature and information on health surveillance. The risk assessment should be recorded as soon as is practicable after the risk assessment is made and reviewed regularly.

Basic vibration control measures

Regulation 6 of CVWR 2005 states that the employer must seek to eliminate the risk of vibration at source or, if not reasonably practicable, reduce it to as low a level as is reasonably practicable. Where the personal daily exposure limit is exceeded the employer must reduce exposure by implementing a programme of organisational and technical measures. Measures include the use of other methods of work, ergonomics, maintenance of equipment, design and layout, rest facilities, information, instruction and training, limitation by schedules and breaks and the provision of personal protective equipment to protect from cold and damp.

Measures must be adapted to take account of any group or individual employee whose health may be of particular risk from exposure to vibration.

Protective measures are the only means of protecting people who work with vibrating machinery. The following controls should be considered.

CHOICE OF EQUIPMENT

The choice of equipment is the most important consideration when controlling vibration. It is important to consider if the task could be done without the interface between human beings and machinery, thereby eliminating the vibratory factors totally e.g. hand-held pneumatic drill replaced with excavator. Where this is not possible, the equipment should be assessed, evaluated and compared with manufacturers data, preferably prior to purchase, so that the best possible equipment is sourced which give the least vibration.

MAINTENANCE

Equipment should be maintained and inspected on a regular basis, so that any deterioration in the equipment e.g. vibration absorbing pads/grips or dampers are detected early, thereby reducing any potential risks to the user. A proactive approach to maintenance should be adopted with faulty equipment being withdrawn from use and replaced preferably with newer less harmful equipment.

LIMITING EXPOSURE

Exposure should be limited to a minimum where possible, thereby decreasing the possible risk of injury. This can be done by job or task rotation/sharing.

Duration and magnitude

Length of exposure to vibration and the magnitude (force) impacts greatly on the time the user can safely use the equipment before there are any signs of injury/damage. Equipment should be replaced with lesser vibratory impact machinery.

Work schedules and rest periods

Work schedules and rest periods should be designed and adopted to give adequate periods of rest from equipment.

Clothing to protect against cold etc

It is important that the circulation is not decreased due to cold working conditions or due to adverse weather, as this can magnify the vibratory effects on the hands or body. Insulated clothing e.g. gloves/jackets/trousers should be issued, making sure these are appropriate for the working environment.

SUMMARY OF PREVENTIVE AND PRECAUTIONARY MEASURES

Prevention

- The need for such machinery should be reviewed so as to eliminate unnecessary operations.
- Consideration should be given to the automation of processes.
- Wearing gloves is recommended for safety and for retaining heat. They will not absorb a significant fraction of the vibration energy which lies within the 30-300Hz range. Care needs to be taken to select appropriate gloves, as the absorbent material in some gloves for thermal insulation may introduce a resonance frequency which may increase the total energy input to the hands (early work, Bednall, Health and Safety Executive).
- Many manufacturers claim to use composite materials that, when moulded into hand-grips and fitted onto vibrating power tools, reduce vibration by up to 45%.
- The greater the coupling (hand and tool interface), the more energy enters the hand. Increasing grip force increases the coupling. There are working techniques for all tools and the expertise developed over time justifies an initial training period for new starters.
- Operators with established HAVS should avoid exposure to cold and thus minimise the number of blanching attacks. Operators with advanced HAVS who are deteriorating (as measured by annual medical checks) should be removed from further exposure. The medical priority is to prevent finger tip ulceration (tissue necrosis).

Precautionary

- The vibration characteristics of the hand tools should be assessed and reference made to the BSI and ISO Guidelines.
- The work schedule should be examined to reduce vibration exposure either by alternating with non-vibration work or avoiding continuous vibration by, for example, scheduling ten minute breaks every hour.
- Carry out a detailed ergonomic assessment of hazardous tasks (e.g. breaking asphalt with a road breaker). This should include duration and frequency of the task.
- Development of a purchasing policy to include consideration of vibration and, where necessary, vibration isolating devices.
- Training of all exposed employees on the proper use of tools and the minimisation of exposure.
- Establish a routine health surveillance programme. Operators of vibrating equipment should be trained to recognise the early symptoms of HAVS and WBV and how to report them.
- Tools should be maintained to their optimum performance thereby reducing vibration to a minimum (e.g. the bearings of grinders).
- A continuous review with regard to the redesigning of tools, rescheduling work methods, or automating the process until such time as the risks associated with vibration are under control.

- As with any management system, the controls in place for vibration should include audit and review.

Regulation 8 of CVWR 2005 states that employers must provide information, instruction and training to all employees who are exposed to risk from vibration and their representatives. This includes any organisational and technical measures taken, exposure limits and values, risk assessment findings, why and how to detect injury, entitlement to and collective results of health surveillance and safe working practices. Information, instruction and training shall be updated to take account of changes in the employer's work or methods. The employer shall ensure all persons, whether or not an employees, who carries out work in connection with the employer's duties have been provided with information, instruction and training.

Health surveillance

Regulation 7 of CVWR 2005 states that health surveillance must be carried out if there is a risk to the health of employees liable to be exposed to vibration. This is in order to prevent or diagnose any health effect linked with exposure to vibration. A record of health shall be kept of any employee who undergoes health surveillance. The employer shall, providing reasonable notice is given, provide the employee with access to their health records and provide copies to an enforcing officer on request.

If health surveillance identifies a disease or adverse health effect, considered by a doctor or other occupational health professional to be a result of exposure to vibration, the employer shall ensure that a qualified person informs the employee and provides information and advice. The employer must ensure they are kept informed of any significant findings from health surveillance, taking into account any medical confidentiality. In addition the employer must also:

- Review risk assessments.
- Review the measures taken to comply.
- Consider assigning the employee to other work.
- Review the health of any other employee who has been similarly exposed and consider alternative work.

9.4 - Heat and radiation

Temperature

The body generates heat energy by the conversion of foodstuffs; energy is generated through muscle action. At rest, typically 80 watts of energy is produced, whereas during heavy physical exercise perhaps 500 watts is produced. The body loses (exchanges) heat energy by the process of sweat evaporation, conduction contact of the feet with the floor and by radiation (infra red energy loss).

EXTREMES OF TEMPERATURE

Exposure to the effects of cold temperature relies on high calorie diet, physical exercise and suitable protective clothing. Clothing should have a high tog rating of 20 - 25 tog, and prevent absorption of water and be suitably fastened to reduce the effects of wind chill.

The feet should be insulated to avoid loss through conduction. The head should be covered to the maximum extent to avoid excessive heat loss. Clothing should be light and white in colour to prevent heat loss through radiation.

Exposure to the effects of heat may be minimised by suitable clothing, such as light and loose or reflective clothing if working with very hot sources of heat. Issues such as conduction from hot surfaces and movement of heat will need to be considered. Consideration will need to be given to humidity levels and workload

Figure 9-14: Workplace temperature. *Source: ACT.*

EFFECTS OF EXPOSURE

People working outside their thermal comfort range can suffer a dramatic loss of efficiency e.g. hot metal process working, working in refrigerated warehouses, working outdoors. The precise effects will depend upon the type of work being carried out, the rate of air movement (wind chill) and temperature and humidity. The main effects of working at high and low temperatures are outlined as follows:

General effects

Cold
- Loss of concentration in mental work.
- Reduced manipulative powers in manual work.
- Discomfort caused by shivering.

Hot
- Loss of concentration.
- Reduced activity rate.
- Discomfort caused by sweating.

Heat stress

Heat syncope	-	fainting due to vasodilatation.
Heat rash or 'prickly heat'	-	skin disorder.
Heat exhaustion	-	fatigue, nausea, headache, giddiness.
Anhidrotic heat exhaustion	-	insufficient moisture to sweat.
Heat cramps	-	painful spasms of muscles - insufficient salt.
Heat stroke	-	breakdown of control mechanisms, body temperatures soar, immediate cooling of body temperature required, otherwise death ensues.

Cold

- Hypothermia.
- Frost bite.
- Trench foot.
- Violent shivering.

RELEVANT FACTORS

One of the fundamental mechanisms by which the body regulates its temperature is by perspiration. Key factors which aid or hinder this process are airflow and humidity. Humidity relates to the moisture content in the air. Air with a relatively high humidity has little capacity to cool the body by 'wicking' away sweat whereas low relative humidity can cause dry skin and has been identified as a possible factor in facial dermatitis (occasional itching or reddened skin) reported by some Display Screen Equipment users. Industries and occupations particularly susceptible to extremes of temperature include foundries, cold stores, those who carry out hot work (e.g. burning and welding) or work in confined spaces where temperatures are often uncomfortably high. Likewise, those who work outdoors can be subject to extreme weather conditions. In winter the strength of the wind can significantly affect the temperature (wind-chill).

PREVENTIVE MEASURES

Steps that employers should consider to reduce the effects of extremes of temperature should include:

- Regular work breaks with fluid intake.
- Improved ventilation and humidity control, screening, suitable clothing.
- In the case of cold stores, removal of ice, improved lighting and the provision of anti-locking devices.

Ionising and non-ionising radiation

IONISING RADIATION

Radiation is emitted by a wide range of sources and appliances used throughout industry, medicine and research. It is also a naturally occurring part of the environment.

All matter is composed of **atoms**. Different atomic structures give rise to unique **elements**. Examples of common elements, which form the basic structure of life, are hydrogen, oxygen and carbon.

Atoms form the building blocks of nature and cannot be further sub divided by chemical means. The centre of the atom is called the **nucleus**, which consists of **protons** and **neutrons**. Electrons take up orbit around the nucleus.

Protons - Have a unit of mass and carry a positive electrical charge.

Neutrons - These also have mass but no charge.

Electrons - Have a mass about 2,000 times less than that of protons and carry a negative charge.

In an electrically neutral atom the number of electrons equals the number of protons (the positive and negative charges cancel out each other). If the atom loses an electron then a positively charged atom is created. The process of losing or gaining electrons is called **ionisation**. If the matter which is ionised is a human cell, the cell chemistry will change and this will lead to functional changes in the body tissue. Some cells can repair radiation damage, others cannot. The cell's sensitivity to radiation is directly proportional to its reproductive function; bone marrow, and reproductive organs are the most vulnerable.

"Ionising radiation is that radiation which has sufficient energy to produce ions by interacting with matter".

Figure 9-15: Ionising radiation. Source: ACT.

Ionising radiation found in industry are alpha, beta and gamma, and X-rays. Whilst X-rays may occur in nature generally they are created in the work place either with knowledge, e.g. X-ray machines or sometimes without knowledge from high voltage equipment. The human body absorbs radiation readily from a wide variety of sources, mostly with adverse effects.

Types of ionising radiation

(**Note**. For the purpose of the NEBOSH National Certificate in Construction you do not need to understand the differences between types of ionising radiation.)

There are a number of different types of ionising radiation each with their different powers of penetration and effects on the body. Therefore, the type of radiation will determine the type and level of protection.

Alpha particles

Are comparatively large. Alpha particles travel short distances in dense materials, and can only just penetrate the skin. The principal risk is through ingestion or inhalation of a source e.g. radon of alpha particles which might place the material close to vulnerable tissue; when this happens the high localised energy effect will destroy tissue of the organ/s affected.

Beta particles

Are much faster moving than alpha particles. They are smaller in mass than alpha particles, but have longer range, so they can damage and penetrate the skin. Whilst they have greater penetrating power than alpha particles, beta particles are less ionising and take longer to effect the same degree of damage.

Gamma rays

Have great penetrating power. Gamma radiation passing through a normal atom will sometimes force the loss of an electron, leaving the atom positively charged; this is called an **ion**.

X-rays

Are very similar in their effects to gamma rays. X-rays are produced by sudden acceleration or deceleration of a charged particle, usually when high-speed electrons strike a suitable target under controlled conditions. The electrical potential required to accelerate electrons to speeds where X-ray production will occur is a minimum of **15,000 volts**. X-rays and gamma rays have **high energy**, and **high penetration** power through fairly dense material. In low density substances, including air, they may travel long distances.

Potential health effects

The effects on the body of exposure to ionising radiation will depend on the type of radiation, the frequency and duration of exposure. Acute effects will include nausea, vomiting, diarrhoea and burns (either superficial skin burns or deep, penetrating burns causing cell damage). Long term (chronic) effects such as dermatitis, skin ulcers, cataracts and cancers can also be expected.

NON IONISING RADIATION

Generally, non-ionising radiation does not possess sufficient energy to cause the ionisation of matter. Radiation of this type includes ultraviolet, visible, infra-red, micro and radio waves. Artificially produced laser beams are a special case.

Types of non-ionising radiation

Ultraviolet

Possible sources. There are many possible sources of Ultra Violet (UV) radiation to which people may be exposed at work:

- The sun.
- Electric arc welding.
- Insect killers.
- Sunbeds and sunlamps.
- Crack detection equipment.
- Tanning and curing equipment.
- Forgery detectors.
- Some lasers.
- Mercury vapour lamps.
- Tungsten halogen lamps

Potential health effects.

Much of the natural ultraviolet in the atmosphere is filtered out by the ozone layer. Sufficient penetrates to cause sunburn and even blindness.

Its effect is thermal and photochemical, producing burns and skin thickening, and eventually skin cancer. Electric arcs and ultraviolet lamps can produce an effect by absorption on the conjunctiva of the eyes, resulting in "arc-eye" and cataract formation.

Visible light (including lasers)

Possible sources.

Any high intensity source of visible light can cause problems. Lasers are an obvious danger but so are light beams, powerful light bulbs and the sun. The danger is always due to direct or reflected radiation.

Potential health effects.

Light in the visible frequency range can cause damage if it is present in sufficiently intense form. The eyes are particularly vulnerable but skin tissue may also be damaged. Indirect danger may also be created by employees being temporarily dazzled.

Figure 9-16: UV - from welding. *Source: Speedy Hire Plc.*

Infra-red

Possible sources.
Anything that glows is likely to be a source of IR radiation, for example:

- Furnaces or fires.
- Molten metal or glass.
- Burning or welding.
- Heat lamps.
- Some lasers.
- The sun.

Potential health effects.

Exposure results in a thermal effect such as skin burning and loss of body fluids (heat exhaustion and dehydration). The eyes can be damaged in the cornea and lens which may become opaque (cataract). Retinal damage may also occur if the radiation is focused.

RADIO-FREQUENCY AND MICROWAVES

Possible sources.

This type of radiation is produced by radio/television transmitters. It is used industrially for induction heating of metals and is often found in intruder detectors.

Potential health effects.

Figure 9-17: Radio mast. *Source: ACT.*

Burns can be caused if persons using this type of equipment allow parts of the body which carry jewellery to enter the radio frequency field. Intense fields at the source of transmitters will damage the body and particular precautions need to be taken to isolate radio/television transmitters to protect maintenance workers. Microwaves can produce the same deep heating effect in live tissue as they can produce in cooking.

Typical occupational sources of ionising and non-ionising radiation

SOURCES OF IONISING RADIATION

The most familiar examples of ionising radiation in the workplace are in hospitals, dentist surgeries and veterinary surgeries where X-rays are used extensively. X-ray machines are used for security purposes at baggage handling points in airports. In addition, Gamma rays are used in non-destructive testing of metals, for example, site radiography of welds in pipelines.

In other industries ionising radiation is used for measurement, for example, in the paper industry for measuring the thickness of paper, and in the food processing industry for measuring the contents of sealed tins.

SOURCES OF NON-IONISING RADIATION

- Ultra-violet.
  - The sun.
  - Arc welding and cutting.
  - Adhesive curing processes.
  - Water treatment.
- Microwave.
  - Telecommunications.
  - Cooking equipment.
- Visible radiation.
  - Lasers, for example, in surveying or level alignment equipment.
  - Other high intensity lights such as photocopiers and printers.
- Radio frequency.
  - Overhead power lines.
  - Plastic welding.
  - High powered transmitters.

The basic means of controlling exposures to ionising and non-ionising radiation

CONTROLS FOR IONISING RADIATION

Preventive measures

Reduced time

Reducing the duration of exposure through redesigning work patterns. Giving consideration to shift working, job rotation etc. The dose received will also depend upon the time of the exposure. These factors must be taken into account when devising suitable operator controls.

Increased distance

Radiation intensity is subject to the inverse square law. Energy received *(dose)* is inversely proportional to the square of the distance from the source.

Shielding

The type of shielding required to give adequate protection will depend on the penetration power of the radiation involved. For example, it may vary from thin sheets of silver paper to protect from Beta particles through to several centimetres of concrete and lead for protection against Gamma or X-rays. In addition to the previous specific controls, the following general principles must be observed:

- Radiation should only be introduced to the work place if there is a positive benefit.
- Safety information must be obtained from suppliers about the type(s) of radiation emitted or likely to be emitted by their equipment.
- Safety procedures must be reviewed regularly.
- Protective equipment provided must be suitable and appropriate, as required by relevant Regulations. It must be checked and maintained regularly.
- Emergency plans must cover the potential radiation emergency.
- Written authorisation by permit should be used to account for all purchase/use, storage, transport and disposal of radioactive substances.

CONTROLS FOR NON-IONISING RADIATION

Ultra-violet

Protection is relatively simple; sunbathers may use simple barrier creams. That emitted from industrial processes can be isolated by physical shielding such as partitions or plastic curtains; some plastic materials differ in their absorption abilities and care needs to be taken in selection. Users of emitting equipment, such as welders, can protect themselves by the use of goggles and protective clothing - the latter to avoid "sunburn". Assistants often fail to appreciate the extent of their own exposure, and require similar protection.

Visible light

Is detected by the eye which has two protective control mechanisms of its own, the eyelids and the iris. These are normally sufficient, as the eyelid has a reaction of 150 milliseconds. There are numerous sources of high-intensity light which could produce damage or damaging distraction, and sustained glare may also cause eye fatigue and headaches. Basic precautions include confinement of high-intensity sources, matt finishes to nearby paint-work, and provision of optically-correct protective glasses for outdoor workers in snow, sand or near large bodies of water.

Infra-red

Radiation problems derive from thermal effects and include skin burning, sweating and loss of body salts leading to cramps, exhaustion and heat stroke. Clothing and gloves will protect the skin, but the hazard should be recognised so that effects can be minimised without recourse to personal protective equipment.

Radio-frequency and microwaves

Radiation can usually be shielded to protect the users. If size and function prohibits this, restrictions on entry and working near an energised microwave device will be needed. Metals, tools, flammable and explosive materials should not be left in the electromagnetic field generated by microwave equipment. Appropriate warning devices should be part of the controls for each such appliance.

Basic radiation protection strategies

Basic radiation protection strategies include the application of the principles of time, distance and shielding. Exposure should be limited to as few as possible and those individuals should be monitored and exposure levels maintained within limits. Where possible only sealed sources should be used and a system developed to minimise dose levels to individuals. This work must be under the control of the radiation protection advisor.

RADIATION PROTECTION SUPERVISOR

A radiation employer is required to appoint one or more Radiation Protection Supervisors for the purpose of securing compliance with the Regulations in respect of work carried out in any area subject to 'local rules for work in controlled or supervised areas'. Their area of work needs to be defined and they must be trained so that they understand the requirements of legislation and local rules insofar as they affect their area of work. They also need to understand the reasons for the precautions that need to be taken in their area of work, and they should command the respect of those they supervise.

RADIATION PROTECTION ADVISERS (RPA)

With the exception of the operations specified in Schedule 1 of the IRR 1999, at least one radiation protection adviser (RPA) must be appointed in writing by employers using ionising radiation. The numbers of RPA appointed must be appropriate to the risk and the areas where advice is needed is to be stated. Employers must consult the RPA on:

- The implementation of controlled and supervised areas.
- The prior examination of plans for installations and the acceptance into service of new or modified sources of ionising radiation in relation to any engineering controls, design features, safety features and warning devices provided to restrict exposure to ionising radiation.
- The regular calibration of equipment provided for monitoring levels of ionising radiation and the regular checking that such equipment is serviceable and correctly used.
- The periodic examination and testing of engineering controls, design features, safety features and warning devices and regular checking of systems of work provided to restrict exposure to ionising radiation.

Adequate information and facilities must be provided by the employer to the RPA in order to allow them to fulfil their functions.

CLASSIFIED WORKERS

Persons entering a controlled area should either be classified or be entering in accordance with 'written arrangements' designed to ensure that doses will not exceed, in cases of persons over 18, levels which would otherwise require the persons to be classified. In the case of other persons the relevant dose limit is applicable.

Figure 9-18: Personal dose monitor.   Source: ACT.

Figure 9-19: Contamination monitoring.   Source: ACT.

9.5 - Stress

When individuals experience too much work load without the opportunity to recover they start to experience stress. Employers have a duty to assess the risk to their employees from work-related stress to protect their health, safety and welfare.

Causes

Six key risk factors that can be the causes of work related stress have been identified. Dealing with each factor forms the basis of management standards introduced to help employers devise prevention strategies.

Demand

This includes issues like workload and work patterns - where an individual cannot cope with the demands of the job, and the work environment itself. Typical environmental stressors are:

- Bodily injury.
- Noise.
- Extremes of temperature.
- Poor lighting.

Control

If an individual has little control over the pace and manner they work this can create stress. In particular, undertaking new or difficult work without first achieving the appropriate skills to complete successfully or safely first can be significant.

Support

If an individual perceives a lack of encouragement, sponsorship or resources provided by the organisation, line management and colleagues, a feeling of remoteness can be created.

Relationships

This includes issues with conflict and unacceptable behaviour between individuals, such as bullying at work or harassment.

Role

If individuals do not understand their role within the organisation or have been allocated conflicting roles then this can increase the potential for stress.

Change

If the management of organisational change in an organisation is not conducted or communicated well, individuals can be confused.

Effects of stress

Being exposed to stressful situations brings about changes in behaviour and also physical well being.

Physical effects

- Increased heart rate.
- Increased sweating.
- Headache.
- Dizziness.
- Blurred vision.
- Aching neck and shoulders.
- Skin rashes.
- Lowered resistance to infection.

Behavioural effects

- Increased anxiety.
- Irritability.
- Increased alcohol intake.
- Increased smoking.
- Erratic sleep patterns.
- Poor concentration.
- Feeling of inability to cope with everyday tasks.

This can result in

- Lack of motivation.
- Lack of commitment.
- Poor timekeeping.
- Increase in mistakes.
- Increase in sickness absence.
- Poor decision making.
- Poor planning.

Stress is reflected in relationships at work as

- Tension between colleagues/supervisors.
- Poor service to clients.
- Deterioration in industrial relations.
- Increase in disciplinary problems.

Prevention strategies

GENERAL MANAGEMENT AND CULTURE

The organisation should ensure:

- Employees are provided with adequate and achievable demands in relation to the hours of work and breaks.
- Employees are consulted over their work patterns.
- Employees concerns about their work environment are addressed.
- Where deficient, employees are encouraged to develop their skills.
- Policies and procedures to adequately support employees.
- Employees are aware of the probable impact of any changes to their jobs and if necessary, employees are given training to support any changes in their jobs.

Job design

The organisation should ensure:

- Jobs are designed to be within the capabilities of employees.
- Individual skills, abilities and capabilities are matched to the job demands.
- Employees know how to access the required resources to do their job.

Relationships at work

The organisation should ensure that:

- Positive behaviour at work is promoted to avoid conflict and ensure fairness.
- Employees share information relevant to their work.
- Policies and procedures to prevent or resolve unacceptable behaviour are in place.
- Different requirements it places upon employees are compatible.

9.6 - Violence and drugs at work

Risk factors relating to violence at work

People who deal directly with the public may face aggressive or violent behaviour. They may be sworn at, threatened or even attacked. In addition, it is necessary to consider possible violence between employees. Construction activities can carry quite a lot of pressure to conduct work within strict, often pressured, timetables. This can lead to a good deal of tension that might result in violence.

> "any incident in which a person is abused, threatened or assaulted in circumstances relating to their work".

Figure 9-20: Definition of work related violence. *Source: HSE.*

Verbal abuse and threats are the most common types of incident. Physical attacks are comparatively rare. Those most at risk are engaged in caring, education, cash handling, representing authority.

Find out if you have a problem

- Ask staff informally through managers and safety representatives.
- Keep detailed records.
- Classify all incidents according to their severity of outcome.
- Try to predict what might happen.

CONTROL MEASURES

Decide what action to take

- Decide who might be harmed and how. Who is most vulnerable? Where appropriate identify potentially violent people in advance.
- Evaluate the risk. Check existing arrangements. Train your employees to recognise early signs of violence.
- Provide information - case histories, etc.
- Improve the environment - better seating, lighting, etc.
- Improve security - video cameras, coded locks, wider counters.
- Redesign the job - use credit cards rather than cash, bank money more frequently, check arrangements for lone workers.
- Arrange safe transport or secure car parking for people who work late at night.

Take action

The policy for dealing with violence should be written into the safety policy statement so that all employees are aware of it. This will encourage employees to cooperate with the policy and report further incidents.

Check what you have done

Check regularly to see if the arrangements are working by consulting employees and safety representatives. If violence is still a problem, go back to stages one and two.

What about the victims

If there is a violent incident involving your workplace you might like to consider the following:

- Debriefing - victims might need to talk through their experience as soon as possible.
- Time off work - individuals may need differing times to recover. In some cases they might need counselling.
- Legal help - legal assistance may be appropriate in serious cases.
- Other employees - may need guidance or counselling to help them react appropriately.

Source: HSE INDG69 (rev).

Effects on health and safety of alcohol and drugs

Drugs and alcohol are becoming increasingly commonplace in society. People who start consuming alcohol or drugs usually have a nil or low dependency and do so for recreational reasons. This however can escalate quickly into abuse when larger quantities of alcohol are consumed more frequently and become habitual. The effects of alcohol or drugs can vary dependant upon the individual's state of health and fitness, and resilience to the chemicals. Alcohol and drugs (prescribed and controlled) can remain in the body for a considerable time after consumption and its effects still be present the next day when at work. Effects on health and safety include:

- Poor co-ordination and balance.
- Perception ability reduced.
- Overall state of poor health including fatigue, poor concentration and stress.
- Poor attitude, lack of adherence to rules, violence to fellow workers.

CONTROL MEASURES

The use of alcohol and drugs is a personal choice over which employers usually have little or no control. However employers should have a policy to deal with the issue should it start to impact on the employees' performance at work.

Control strategies often start with the identification of safety critical work, where the influence of drugs and alcohol would have a significant effect. It is usual that strategies do not presume use or non-use of drugs and alcohol for those that conduct safety critical work, treating them all equally. In a simple approach all workers that come on to a construction site might be considered to be in safety critical work. All would work to the same rules banning them being under the influence while at work and offering them opportunities to talk to someone about how this affects them, coupled with carrying out random drugs and alcohol tests. When accidents occur it is common to consider drugs and alcohol as factors. It may not always be possible to test an injured party for causing their own accident by being under the influence of drugs and alcohol, but it may be possible to test a driver of a dumper truck that ran into someone for example.

Element 10

Working at height - hazards and control

Learning outcomes

On completion of this element, candidates should be able to demonstrate understanding of the content through the application of knowledge to familiar and unfamiliar situations. In particular they should be able to:

10.1 Describe the hazards and the risks of working at height and outline the general requirements necessary to control them.

10.2 Describe safe working practices for access equipment and roofwork.

10.3 Identify the appropriate control measures necessary to protect other persons not involved in the work at height.

10.4 Outline the particular appropriate control measures to ensure safety when working over water.

Content

10.1 - Working at height hazards and risks	179
Work activities involving a risk of injury from falling from height	179
Basic hazards and factors affecting the risk from working at height	179
Methods of avoiding working at height	181
Main precautions necessary to prevent falls and falling materials	181
Requirements for head protection	182
Inspection requirements for work equipment	182
10.2 - Safe working practices for access equipment and roofwork	182
Scaffolding	182
Ladders	190
Other techniques for working at height	192
Fall arrest equipment	193
Roofwork	194
10.3 - Protection of others	194
10.4 - Working over or near water	195
Prevention of drowning	195
Additional control measures	196

Sources of reference

A Guide to the Construction (Head Protection) Regulations (L102), HSE Books ISBN 0-7176-1478-6
Essentials of health and safety at work, HSE Books ISBN 0-7176-0716-X
Health and safety in roofwork (HSG33), HSE Books ISBN 0-7176-1425-5
Protecting the public: Your next move (HSG151), HSE Books ISBN 0-7176-1148-5
Safe use of work equipment (ACoP) (L22), HSE Books ISBN 0-7176-1626-6

Relevant statutory provisions

The Construction (Design and Management) Regulations (CDM) 2007
The Construction (Head Protection) Regulations (CHPR) 1989
The Personal Protective Equipment at Work Regulations (PPER) 1992
The Provision and Use of Work Equipment Regulations (PUWER) 1998
The Work at Height Regulations (WAH) 2005

10.1 - Working at height hazards and risks

Work activities involving a risk of injury from falling from height

Falls are the most common cause of fatal injuries in the construction industry. They account for more than half of those accidentally killed each year. Much of the work carried out on a construction site is done above ground at heights of more than two metres. Typical activities that involve working at height are:

- Steel erecting.
- Fixing of cladding, roof work.
- Painting and decorating.
- Demolition and dismantling.
- Bricklaying.
- Scaffold erection.
- Electrical installation and maintenance.
- Bridge construction repairs.

The main injuries sustained as a result of falls from height are broken bones or permanent damage to the human body, leading to lack of mobility or even death.

The risks of falls from height are substantial, however long or short the work. Risks related to work activities at height are increased by the presence of fragile roofs, roof lights, voids, deteriorating materials and the weather. Some jobs rarely involve the average worker needing to work above ground level, such as welding and machinery maintenance. This means that workers with little or no experience of work at height find themselves exposed to the dangers of working above ground level when carrying out their usual job in a construction setting.

Basic hazards and factors affecting the risk from working at height

It is important that the work / task is correctly planned, implemented and risk assessed prior to the commencement of work in accordance with **Regulation 4 of the Work at Height Regulations (WAH) 2005**. Regular site meetings should take place to communicate the daily work/tasks to be completed, with special attention paid to new or inexperienced employees (these should be supervised by a competent person). This should include managers, employees and sub-contractors. Slips and trips from ladders, scaffolding or roofing are some of the more obvious hazards, although incorrect use of fitted PPE e.g. fall arrest harness, could play a significant hazard leading to injuries.

VERTICAL DISTANCE

Though some construction work involves work activities to be carried out at a significant height, for example on a roof or scaffold, it should not be assumed that work at less significant heights is without risk. Major injuries can occur if a fall results whilst carrying out tasks at height of less than 2 metres, for example fitting false ceilings or installing utilities inside buildings. This should not give the impression that people are not injured by falls from heights less than 2 metres. This remains a significant risk and many injuries result each year. Legislation, the Work at Height Regulations (WAH) 2005, reflects this risk and requires controls to be in place to manage the risk of falling, whatever the height. This legislation applies to workplaces in general, and therefore includes construction activities. Under these regulations the interpretation of 'work at height' includes any place of work at, above, or below ground level that a person could fall a distance which would be liable to cause personal injury; including places for obtaining access or egress, except by staircase in a permanent workplace.

WAH 2005 Regulation 6 states that work at height must only be carried out when it is not reasonably practicable to carry out the work otherwise. If work at height does take place, suitable and sufficient measures must be taken to prevent a fall of any distance, to minimise the distance and the consequences of any fall liable to cause injury. Employers must also make a risk assessment, as required by regulation 3 of the Management of Health and Safety at Work Regulations (MHSWR) 1999.

ROOFS

Working at height and on roofs carries a high risk of accidents, unless proper procedures and precautions are taken. The danger of people or materials falling affects the safety of those working at height and those working beneath.

Particular danger arises from two types of roof - fragile roofs and sloping roofs.

Fragile roofs

Fragile roofs can cause a hidden hazard, as it is not always obvious that there is potential problem. Skylights can be hidden under debris or moss, slates or roof supports may have unseen damage or may have become brittle which can lead to failure or collapse.

Materials such as asbestos, cement, glass or plastic are likely to be unable to bear the weight of a person. Asbestos sheet deteriorates over time leaving the remaining material in a particularly fragile state. Though the sheet looks intact it will only have a small fraction of its original strength. In a similar way plastic roof material, such as may be used in roof lights, will be affected by exposure to sunlight leaving it brittle. It should not be assumed that it is safe to walk on newly installed roof material. Though the material may have some strength it may not be enough to bear the weight of a worker. All fragile roofs and/or access routes to them should be marked with an appropriate warning sign.

The WAH 2005 Regulation 9 states that every employer shall ensure that suitable and sufficient steps are taken to prevent any person at work falling through any fragile surface; and that no work may pass across or near, or work on, from or near, fragile surfaces when it is reasonably practicable to carry out work without doing so. If work has to be from a fragile roof then suitable and sufficient means of support must be provided that can sustain foreseeable loads. No person at work should be allowed to pass or work near a fragile surface unless suitable and sufficient guard rails and other means of fall protection is in place. Signs must be situated at a prominent place at or near to work involving fragile surfaces, or persons must be made aware of the fragile roof by other means.

Sloping roofs

Sloping roofs are those with a pitch greater than 10 degrees. Falls from the edge of sloping roofs can cause serious injury even when the eaves are relatively low. The hazard of sloping roofs is less obvious when the pitch is small causing people to underestimate the possibility of workers sliding off the edge. The material and therefore the surface of the roof have a significant influence on the hazard, for example a smooth sheet metal surface can present a significant hazard even when the pitch is small.

The chances of an accident are increased when working on roofs that are wet or covered in moss growth and in extreme weather conditions such as high winds. The other significant influencing issue is the footwear used by the worker, smooth flat soled footwear may seem suitable in dry conditions but may not provide sufficient grip and deal with surface water in wet conditions. A build up of dry particles or grit on a roof can present a surface that leads to a high risk of slipping as the particles become free to move and form a mobile layer between the roof and the worker's foot.

VOIDS

Voids in groundworks e.g. cellars, drains or old mine shafts could remain undetected which could lead to major hazards. A site survey should be completed prior to commencing any work to identify these hazards. Excavations, incomplete scaffolding/boards or guard rails, ladders should be inspected / checked on a daily basis for damage or unauthorised alterations to reduce any potential hazards. A variety of voids will be created during the construction phase of a multi storey building; these include holes in floors for services, spaces for stairwells and lifts. It is important at the planning stage to make provision for fall protection to include guard rails for stairwells and lift shafts, and hand rails on stairs; fixing covers over other holes in floors; providing adequate levels of lighting; and ensuring a good standard of housekeeping and a high level of supervision and control.

DETERIORATION OF MATERIALS

The condition of the structure on which people are working can deteriorate with time. The rate of deterioration will accelerate if the structure is exposed to adverse weather conditions (including extremes of temperature) or attack by chemicals, animals, insects etc. It may be too late before the evidence of deterioration is noticed. Asbestos cement, fibreglass and plastic deteriorate with age and become more fragile. Similarly, steel sheets may rust or may not be supported properly. This presents a serious risk to workers who work on these materials without means to prevent falls.

Accidental damage may have also occurred to structural parts of the building during the construction phase. There should be a formal way of reporting these incidents.

UNPROTECTED EDGES

Roofs, scaffolds, unfinished steel work and access platforms may sometimes have open sides. This increases the likelihood of someone or something falling, particularly if people have to approach them, work at them or pass by them repeatedly. It is very easy in these circumstances to lose perception of the hazard and forget that it is there. Errors, such as stepping back over an edge, overreaching, or being pushed over the edge whilst manoeuvring materials can easily lead to fatal falls.

UNSTABLE / POORLY MAINTAINED ACCESS EQUIPMENT

An employer, having committed to providing access to height by the provision of work equipment, needs to understand that employees using it are at risk from basic hazards relating to its stability and maintenance. Working with mobile elevated work platforms (MEWPs), ladders and scaffolds have their own specific stability and maintenance issues, the hazard of falling from height whilst using them being the common theme. Each is influenced by the problem of the stability of the ground conditions they are placed on and the height they are used at compared to their stability base. **See also - Mobile Elevating Work Platforms - later in this element.**

All equipment, access equipment being no exception, can fail if not properly maintained. Cracks may occur in the sides of ladders and loose rungs can lead to failure. They may warp or rot if left exposed to the elements. Defects in ladders may be hidden if they are painted or covered in plaster.

The effective working of the hydraulics of a MEWP is critical and failure to maintain this could lead to a sudden and catastrophic failure of the MEWP whilst it is extended. Scaffolds need periodic maintenance to ensure load bearing parts are still secured and those critical items such as brakes on mobile scaffolds are in place and effective. Failure to maintain them can quickly undermine the strength, integrity and stability of the scaffold leading to collapse or overturning.

WEATHER

Adverse weather can have a significant effect on the safety of those working at height. Rain, snow and ice increase the risk of slips and falling from a roof. When handling large objects, such as roof panels, then high wind can be a serious problem and may cause the person to be blown off the roof. Extremely cold temperatures can increase the likelihood of brittle failure of materials and therefore increase the likelihood of failure of roof supports, scaffold components and plastic roof lights.

In addition, moisture can freeze, increasing the slipperiness of surfaces and on many occasions the presence of ice is not easily visible. Workers exposed to the cold can lose their dexterity and when hot, sweat may cause them to lose their grip.

FALLING MATERIALS

Caused by:

- Poor housekeeping of people working above.
- Absence of toe boards or edge protection.
- Incorrect hooking and slinging.
- Incorrect assembly of gin wheels for raising materials.
- Surplus materials incorrectly stacked.
- Open, unprotected edges.
- Deterioration of structures causing crumbling masonry.

Figure 10-1: Working above ground level. *Source: ACT.*

The risk of falling materials causing injury should be minimised by keeping platforms clear of loose materials. In addition, methods provided should prevent materials or other objects rolling, or being kicked off the edges of platforms. This may be done with toe boards, solid barriers, brick guards, or similar being positioned at open edges.

If working in a public place, nets, fans or covered walkways may be needed to give extra protection for people who may be passing below. High-visibility barrier netting is not suitable for use as a fall prevention device.

Materials such as old slates, tiles, etc. should not be thrown from the roof or scaffold - passers-by may be at risk of being injured. Enclosed debris chutes should be used or debris should be lowered in containers.

Methods of avoiding working at height

Where possible, work at height should be avoided by conducting the work at ground level. This could be achieved by using different equipment or method of work, for example the pre-assembly of roof trusses, either before delivery or on the ground on site, instead of assembly at height.

Good planning arrangements, considering how fixtures / fittings, plant and services can be designed or installed can be utilised to avoid the need to work at height both during construction and in ongoing cleaning or maintenance.

Main precautions necessary to prevent falls and falling materials

PROPER PLANNING AND SUPERVISION OF WORK

Fall of people

Regulation 4 of the **Work at Height Regulations (WAH) 2005** states that all work at height must be properly planned, supervised and be carried out so far as is reasonably practicable safely. Planning must include the selection of suitable equipment, take account of emergencies and give consideration to weather conditions impacting on safety.

WAH 2005 Regulation 5 states that those engaged in any activity in relation to work at height must be competent; and, if under training, be supervised by a competent person.

WAH 2005 Regulation 6 states that work at height must only be carried out when it is not reasonably practicable to carry out the work otherwise. If work at height does take place, suitable and sufficient measures must be taken to prevent a fall of any distance, to minimise the distance and the consequences of any fall liable to cause injury. Employers must also make a risk assessment, as required by regulation 3 of the Management of Health and Safety at Work Regulations (MHSWR) 1999.

This means that organisations should review work done to determine a response to the above requirements. This may affect those that fill equipment hoppers located at height manually, requiring consideration of bulk delivery and automatic feed systems. Where workers have to lubricate or adjust equipment set at height by hand, options to automate or route the lubrication/adjustment mechanisms to ground level should be considered. If materials are pre-painted or pre-drilled this can greatly reduce the work needed to be done at height. Long reach handling devices can be used to allow cleaning or other tasks to be conducted from the ground. Where equipment, such as light units, requires maintenance an option may be to lower it sufficiently to enable bulbs to be changed and cleaning to be conducted from the ground.

Fall of materials

WAH 2005 Regulation 10 states that every employer shall take reasonably practicable steps to prevent injury to any person from the fall of any material or object; and where it is not reasonably practicable to do so, to take similar steps to prevent any person being struck by any falling material or object which is liable to cause personal injury. Also, that no material is thrown or tipped from height in circumstances where it is liable to cause injury to any person. Materials and objects must be stored in such a way as to prevent risk to any person arising from the collapse, overturning or unintended movement of the materials or objects.

WAH 2005 Regulation 11 states that every employer shall ensure that where an area presents a risk of falling from height or being struck from an item falling at height that the area is equipped with devices preventing unauthorised persons from entering such areas and the area is clearly indicated.

AVOIDING WORKING IN ADVERSE WEATHER CONDITIONS

Adverse weather can include wind, rain, sun, cold, snow and ice. Each of these conditions, particularly in extreme cases, can present a significant hazard to construction work. When long term projects are planned methods are often adjusted to minimise the effects. For example, road and walk routes that could quickly be affected by rain are made up into formal structures by the use of hardcore, concrete and tarmac. Work areas can be covered over at an early stage to enable work to be conducted in relative comfort. In some cases it may be that work is organised in an order that predicts expected adverse weather, allowing tasks to be adjusted until short term weather conditions improve. In some cases adverse weather must be considered formally and work may have to cease until conditions improve, for example, work on a roof in icy conditions or high winds. Similar approaches may have to be taken for operating a mobile elevating work platform (MEWP) in windy conditions or entering a sewer during a rain storm.

EMERGENCY RESCUE

Where an individual has fallen from height but has been protected by personal fall arrest equipment such as a harness, significant health effects known as suspension trauma may be experienced if they are not rescued quickly. This is mainly due to blood pooling in the legs, reducing the amount circulating through the rest of the body which has consequential effects for vital organs such as the brain, heart and kidneys. Unless the individual is rescued very quickly the lack of oxygenated blood to vital organs can be fatal. Therefore a rescue procedure and equipment must be available and practiced. The procedure should also take into account that a sudden transition from a vertical to a horizontal position when rescued and laid down, can lead to a massive amount of deoxygenated blood entering the heart, causing cardiac arrest. Steps must be taken to minimise the risk of injury due to the fall or contact with the safeguard. Even a short fall onto a net or other fall arresting safeguard could cause minor injuries or fractures. This should be anticipated and workers taught how to minimise the likelihood of injury.

Requirements for head protection

The Construction (Head Protection) Regulations (CHPR) 1989 make specific requirements about hard hats. *See also - Relevant statutory provisions section.* Hard hats are required where there is a foreseeable risk of injury to the head other than by falling e.g. struck by falling materials or where people might hit their heads.

Hazards to consider:

- Loose material kicked into an excavation.
- Material falling from a scaffold platform.
- Material falling off a load being lifted by a crane or goods hoist or carried on a site dumper or truck.
- Dropping a fitting while erecting or dismantling a scaffold.

Decide on which areas of the site where hats have to be worn. Make site rules and tell everyone in the area. Provide employees with hard hats. Make sure hats are worn and worn correctly. A wide range of hats is available. Let employees try a few and decide which is most suitable for the job and for them. Some hats have extra features including a sweatband for the forehead and a soft, or webbing harness. Although these hats are slightly more expensive, they are much more comfortable and therefore more likely to be worn.

Inspection requirements for work equipment

Inspection requirements for work equipment specified for use for work at height are set out in regulation 12 of the WAH 2005. Requirements are:

- Where safety depends on how it is installed or assembled in any position - before used in that position.
- Where exposed to conditions causing deterioration which is liable to result in dangerous situations, to ensure that health and safety conditions are maintained and that any deterioration can be detected and remedied in good time - at suitable intervals and each time that exceptional circumstances which are liable to jeopardise the safety of the work equipment have occurred.
- Work platforms used for construction work in which a person could fall 2 metres or more - inspected in position, or if a mobile work platform inspected on the site, within the previous 7 days.

Result of an inspection must be recorded and kept until the next inspection. An inspection report containing the particulars set out below must be prepared before the end of the working period within which the inspection is completed and, within 24 hours of completing the inspection, be provided to the person it was carried out for. The report must be kept at the site where the inspection was carried out until the construction work is completed and afterwards at an office of the person it was carried out for, for 3 months.

Reports on inspections must include the following particulars:

1) Name and address of person for whom the inspection is carried out.
2) Location of the work equipment.
3) Description of the work equipment.
4) Date and time of inspection.
5) Details of any matter identified that could give rise to a risk to the health and safety of any person.
6) Details of any action taken as a result of 5 above.
7) Details of any further action considered necessary.
8) Name and position of the person making the report.

10.2 - Safe working practices for access equipment and roofwork

Scaffolding

DESIGN FEATURES OF SCAFFOLDING

Independent tied

This type of scaffold typically uses two sets of standards; one near to the structure and the other set at the width of the work platform. It is erected so that it is independent from the structure and does not rely on it for its primary stability. However, as the name suggests, it is usual to tie the scaffold to the structure in order to prevent the scaffold falling towards or away from the structure.

Figure 10-2: Independent tied scaffold. Source: ACT.

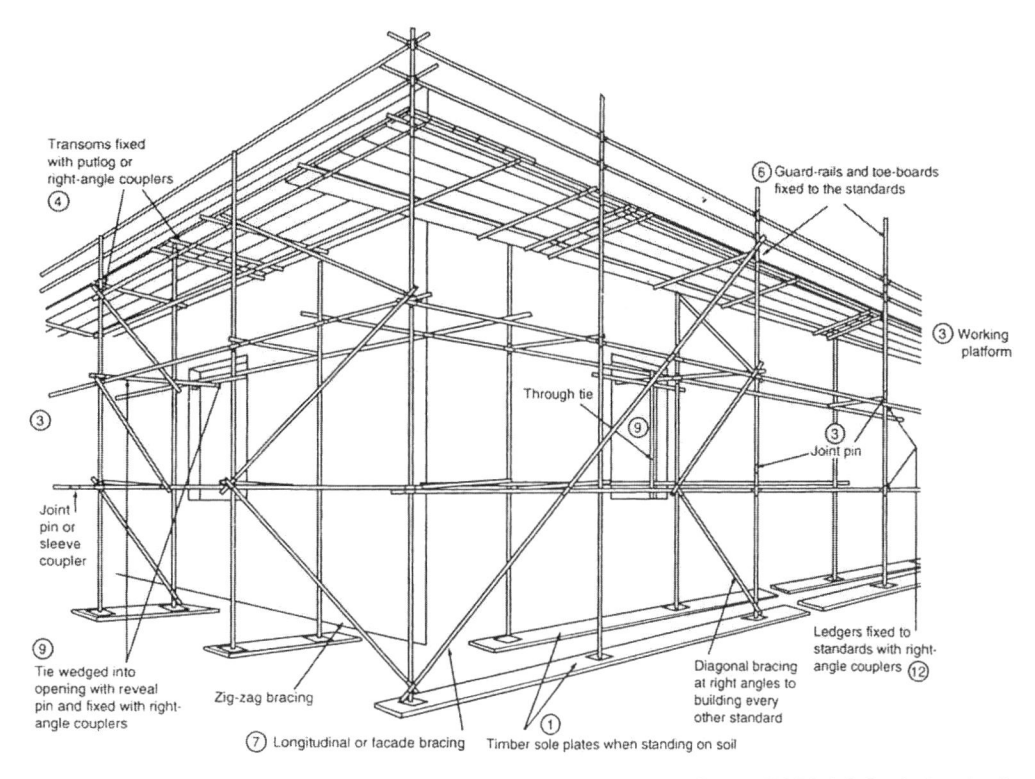

Figure 10-3: Independent tied scaffold.   *Source: HSG150 Safety in Construction.*

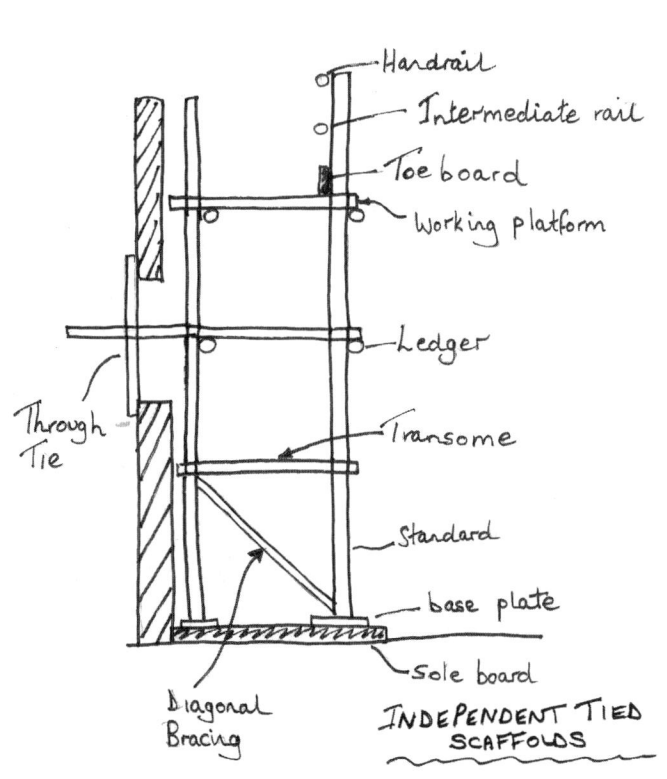

Figure 10-4: Independent tied scaffold (hand drawn example).   *Source: ACT.*

Figure 10-5: Independent tied scaffold.   *Source: ACT.*

Figure 10-6: Tie through window.   *Source: ACT.*

Putlog

This type of scaffold has a single set of standards erected at the width required for the work platform. The transoms have a flat end that is inserted into the mortar gap in the wall. The structure effectively provides the inner support for the work platform and therefore an inner set of standards is not needed.

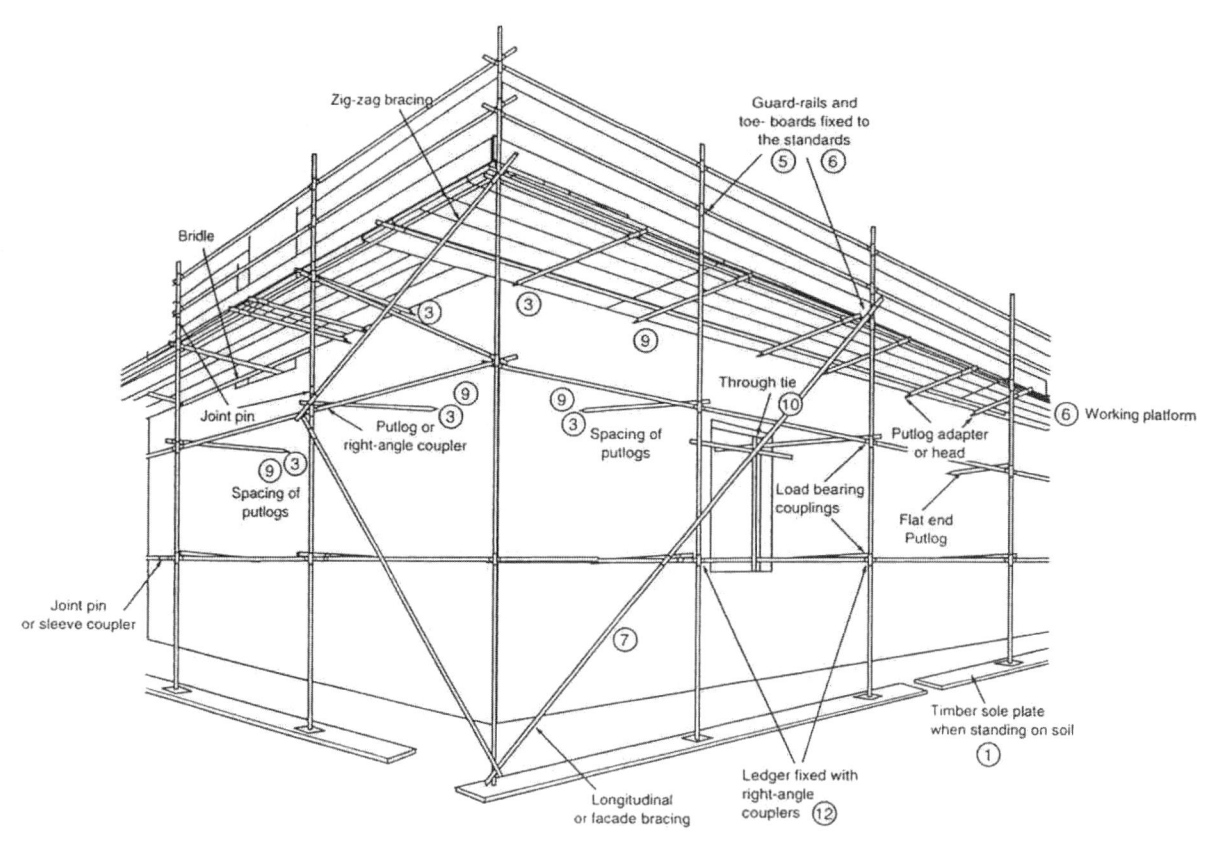

Figure 10-7: Putlog scaffold. *Source: HSG150 Safety in Construction.*

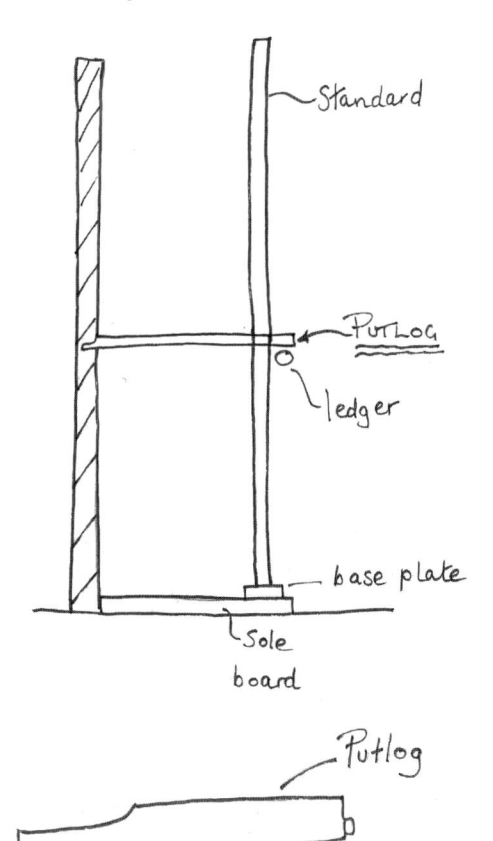

Figure 10-8: Putlog (hand drawn example). *Source: ACT.*

Figure 10-9: Putlog scaffold. *Source: ACT.*

Figure 10-10: Putlog scaffold. *Source: ACT.*

Fan

Fans are scaffold boards fixed on scaffold tubes set at an upward angle out from a scaffold in order to catch debris that may fall from the scaffold. They may be provided at the entrances to buildings to protect persons entering and leaving the building that the scaffold is erected against. They are also used where a scaffold is erected alongside a pedestrian walkway where there is a need to have an increased confidence that materials that might fall cannot contact people below. In some cases it may be necessary for horizontal barriers to be erected to direct pedestrians under the fan.

Cantilevered

A cantilever scaffold is assembled in the normal way then continued outwards by erecting a cantilever section from the inner vertical columns. Care must be taken to ensure the structure remains safe and stable. Adding stabilisers to the main scaffold or tying-in to the building are normally essential safety precautions. The use of adjustable bases either under the main scaffold or cantilever or both is usually helpful in ensuring the cantilever section rests firmly on the building.

Figure 10-11: Fans. Source: ACT.

Mobile tower scaffolds

Mobile scaffold towers are widely used as they are convenient for work which involves frequent access to height over a short period of time in a number of locations that are spaced apart. However, they are often incorrectly erected or misused and accidents occur due to people / materials falling or the tower overturning / collapsing. They must be erected and dismantled by trained, competent personnel, strictly in accordance with the supplier's instructions. All parts must be sound and from the same manufacturer.

- The height of an untied, independent tower must never exceed the manufacturer's recommendations. A 'rule of thumb' may be:
  - Outdoor use - 3 times the minimum base width.
  - Indoor use - 3.5 times the minimum base width.

Figure 10-12: Wheels with brakes. Source: ACT.

- If the height of the tower is to exceed these maximum figures then the scaffold MUST be secured (tied) to the structure or outriggers used.
- Working platforms must only be accessed by safe means. Use internal stairs or fixed ladders only and never climb on the outside.
- Before climbing a tower the wheels must be turned outwards, the wheel brakes "on", locked and kept locked.
- Never move a tower unless the platform is clear of people, materials, tools etc.
- Towers must only be moved by pushing them at base level. Instruct operators not to pull the tower along whilst on it. Pay careful attention to obstructions at base level and overhead.
- Never use a tower near live overhead power lines or cables.
- Working platforms must always be fully boarded out. Guard rails and toe boards must be fitted if there is a risk of a fall of more than two metres. Inspections must be carried out by a competent person - before first use, after substantial alteration and after any event likely to have affected its stability.

Figure 10-13: Mobile tower scaffold. Source: ACT.

Figure 10-14: Mobile tower scaffold. Source: ACT.

SAFETY FEATURES

Base plates & Sole boards
- A base plate must be used under every standard - it spreads the load and helps to keep the standard vertical.
- Sole boards are used to spread the weight of the scaffold and to provide a firm surface on which to erect a scaffold, particularly on soft ground. Sole boards must be sound and sufficient, and should run under at least two standards at a time.

Figure 10-15: Base plates and sole boards.   Source: Lincsafe.

Figure 10-16: Base plate and protection.   Source: ACT.

Figure 10-17: Scaffold boards - some defective.   Source: ACT.

Figure 10-18: Ladder access.   Source: ACT.

Toe boards

These are scaffold boards placed against the standards at right angles to the surface of the working platform. They help prevent materials from falling from the scaffold and people slipping under rails.

- The toe boards should be fixed to the inside of the standards with toe board clips.
- Minimum height of 150 mm.
- Joints must be as near as possible to a standard.
- Continuous around the platform where a guard-rail is required.
- Any toe board which is removed temporarily for access or for any other reason must be replaced as soon as possible.

Guardrails

These are horizontal scaffold tubes which help to prevent people falling from a scaffold.

- They must be fitted to any working platform which is two metres or more above ground level.
- They must be fixed to the *inside* of the standards, at least 910 mm from the platform.
- An intermediate guard rail must be no more than 470 mm between the top guardrail and the toe boards.
- Guardrails must always be fitted with load-bearing couplers.
- Joints in guardrails must be near to a standard.
- Must be secured with sleeve couplers.
- Guardrail must go all round the work platform.
- If the gap between the structures is 300 mm or more, then a guardrail must be fitted to the inside of the working platform as well as the outside.
- Guardrails must always be carried round the end of a scaffold, to make a "stop end".

Boarding

Boards provide the working platform of a scaffold and landings for access ladders. Boards supported by transoms or putlogs must be close fitting, free from cracks or splits or large knots, and must not be damaged in any way which could cause weakness.

Brick guards

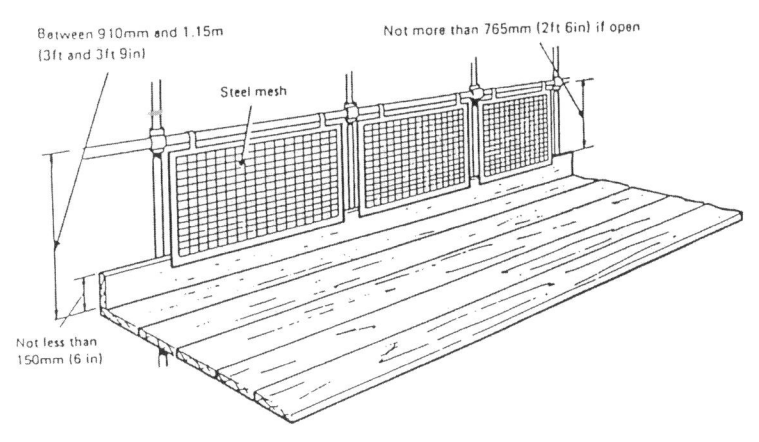

Figure 10-19: Brick guards. *Source: HSG150 Safety in Construction.*

Debris netting

Debris netting is often fixed to the sides of a scaffold to limit the amount of debris escaping from the scaffold that may come from work being done on it. It provides a tough, durable and inexpensive method of helping to provide protection from the danger of falling debris and windblown waste. It allows good light transmission and reduces the effects of adverse weather. Debris netting may also be slung underneath steelwork or where roof work is being conducted to catch items that may fall. In this situation it should not be assumed that the debris netting is sufficient to hold the weight of a person who might fall.

Figure 10-20: Nets and sheets. *Source: ACT.*

Figure 10-21: Nets. *Source: ACT.*

REQUIREMENTS FOR SCAFFOLD ERECTORS

Scaffold erectors must erect and dismantle scaffold in a way that minimises the risk of falling. Where practicable they should erect intermediate platforms, with guard rails and toe boards, to enable them to build the next scaffold 'lift' safely. If a platform is not practicable falls must be prevented (or their effects minimised) by other means, such as the use of a safety harness or similar fall arrest equipment.

MEANS OF ACCESS

> "So far as is reasonably practicable as regards any place of work under the employer's control, the maintenance of it in a condition that is safe and without risks to health and the provision and maintenance of means of access to and egress from it that are safe and without such risks"
> *Health and Safety at Work Act (HASAWA) 1974 S2(2)(d).*

General access must not be allowed to any scaffold until its erection has been fully completed. Access must be prevented to any subsequent sections of scaffold that are not completed and a "scaffold incomplete" sign displayed. Ladders often provide access and egress to and from scaffolds where stairs cannot be provided. Factors to be considered in the safe use of ladders for access include:

- They should be free from defect and not painted.
- The correct length used to reduce manual handling risks, flexing in use.
- Placed on a firm footing, with each stile equally supported.
- Positioned so that there is sufficient space at each rung to give an adequate foothold.
- Positioned approximately at an angle of 75^0 (1 unit horizontally to 4 units vertically).
- Extended to a height of 1 metre above the working platform (unless there is another adequate hand hold).
- When more than 3 metres in length, must be securely tied at the top or footed at the bottom to prevent slipping.
- Not be so long that it extends excessively past the stepping off point as this can cause the ladder to pivot around the tie/stepping off point and cause the user to fall.
- Positioned so that the vertical height of the ladder running between landings does not exceed 9 metres.
- Both hands should be free when climbing a ladder.

DESIGN OF LOADING PLATFORMS

Scaffold platforms that are used for loading of materials or equipment will need to be designed to take into account any concentration of heavy loads that will be placed upon them (e.g. bricks, blocks, mortar or timber). A loading platform is designed to withstand a weight that would be excessive on the normal working area of a scaffold. Often this will be a separate scaffold structure, assembled adjacent to the main working scaffold, tied to both the building and the main scaffold and will consist of additional braces and sections to provide extra support. The platform must be correctly signed as a loading area with a safe working load specified. Workers must not be allowed to access the area directly below the platform where the loading and unloading will take place.

SCAFFOLD HOISTS (PERSONS, MATERIALS)

The hoist should be protected by a substantial enclosure to prevent anyone from being struck by any moving part of the hoist or material falling down the hoist way. Gates must be provided at all access landings, including at ground level. The gates must be kept shut, except when the platform is at the landing. The controls should be arranged so that the hoist can be operated from one position only. All hoist operators must be trained and competent. The hoist's safe working load must be clearly marked. If the hoist is for materials only there should be a prominent warning notice on the platform or cage to stop people riding on it. The hoist should be inspected weekly, and thoroughly examined every six months by a competent person and the results of inspection recorded.

Inclined hoists are often used to transport materials. Inclined hoists should be erected and used by competent personnel. Additionally, there would need to be arrangements for its inspection, testing and regular maintenance and for ensuring the guarding of dangerous parts of the machinery and the integrity of any electrical installation. Protection would need to be provided at the base and top of the hoist and means provided to ensure the security of the load as it travels to the roof. Relocation and or dismantling should only be carried out by competent persons.

ENSURING STABILITY

Effects of materials

Scaffold systems are a means of providing safe access when work at height cannot be avoided. They are not designed for storage of materials for long periods. It is however, acceptable to situate materials on scaffolds in small quantities to reflect the usage rate of the materials by the people using the scaffold. Provided the safe working load specified for the scaffold is not exceeded materials may be distributed evenly on the working platform. Care should be taken to ensure the working platform is not reduced to a width that compromises access around the scaffold, the materials are distributed evenly and the safe working load specified for the scaffold is not exceeded.

Materials (bricks, mortar, timber, etc) when placed on scaffold systems tend to be placed on the outer edge of the scaffold, creating an uneven balance and placing greater forces on the mechanical joints. These factors can contribute to failure of the joints, or buckling of the tube sections which may ultimately lead to a full or partial collapse of the structure. If this occurs, a host of other hazards become present (falls from height, falling materials).

All loading of scaffolds with materials should be well planned to prevent uneven loading and carried out under supervision. The scaffold should be checked to ensure the safe working load is adhered to at all times.

Weather

Adverse weather conditions not only affect the condition of structures and equipment but can also present dangers to those people who are exposed to them (cold weather can affect dexterity, awareness and morale). These need to be anticipated and suitable precautions taken. Rain, sleet or snow can make surfaces very slippery and in winter freeze to create ice or frost. Heavy rainfall can lead to soil being washed away from the base of the scaffold or the soil can subside leading to the scaffold becoming unstable. Scaffolds should always be inspected prior to work starting. If conditions have changed, checks should be made on whether it is safe to continue working.

A sudden gust of wind can cause loss of balance. This is usually exaggerated when working at height and/ or handling large sheets of materials. In extreme circumstances, work should be stopped during windy weather as people can easily be thrown off balance while carrying out their work. When deciding whether to continue or suspend work consider:

- Wind speed.
- The measures which have already been taken to prevent falls from the scaffold.
- The position and height of the scaffold and the work being carried out.
- The relationship of the work to other large structures as wind may be tunnelled and amplified at certain points.

Sheeting

Sheeting can be used on the outside of scaffold systems as a means of preventing materials, dust and other debris being blown from the working areas of the scaffold onto the construction site or possibly a public area, and it can also provide a means of restricting and controlling access. It is not a means of fall protection.

Whilst sheeting is relatively light and causes little stress on the scaffold system, the additional forces created by wind, rain or snow spread over the surface of the sheeting could cause sufficient force to affect the safe stability of the scaffold. It is also important that sheeting is securely fixed to the structure and not allowed to flail loosely as this could be snagged on site mobile plant resulting in the scaffold being pulled and causing it to collapse.

Protection from impact of vehicles

Construction sites quite often involve numerous types of vehicles of varying size and weight all presenting hazards to other people carrying out work within the site. Protection from impact should be applied to all aspects of work carried out, not just to scaffold structures in particular. Measures that may be implemented in order to maintain a safe environment in relation to vehicles and scaffolds may include:

- Clear lighting provided around the scaffold perimeter.
- Signs warning of scaffold, high visibility tape or sheath around scaffold standards.
- Ensuring adequate road width for the size of vehicle accessing the site.

- Provision of one-way systems around sites or turning points (away from scaffold) to minimise the need for reversing.
- Reversing vehicles properly controlled by trained banksmen. Competent drivers correctly trained.
- Concrete impact blocks strategically placed around scaffold perimeter to limit proximity.

Figure 10-22: 'Scaftag'. Source: ACT.

Figure 10-23: Lighting. Source: ACT.

Inspection requirements

Inspection requirements for scaffolds are set out in the CDM 2007, LOLER 1998 and WAH 2005 Regulations. All scaffolds used must be inspected by a competent person before being taken into use for the first time, after any substantial addition, dismantling or other alteration, after any event likely to have affected its strength or stability and at regular intervals not exceeding 7 days since the last inspection.

Reports on inspections to include the following details:

1) Location of the place of work inspected.
2) Description of the place of work or part of that place inspected (including any plant and equipment and materials, if any).
3) Date and time of inspection.
4) Details of any matter identified that could give rise to a risk to the health and safety of any person.
5) Details of any action taken as a result of 4) above.
6) Details of any further action considered necessary.
7) Name and position of the person making the report.

MOBILE ELEVATING WORK PLATFORMS

A mobile elevating work platform (MEWP) is, as the name suggests, a means of providing a work platform at height. The equipment is designed to be movable, under its own power or by being towed, so that it can easily be set up in a location where it is needed. Various mechanical and hydraulic means are used to elevate the work platform to the desired height, including telescopic arms and scissor lifts. The versatility of this equipment, enabling the easy placement of a platform at height, makes it a popular piece of access equipment. Often, to do similar work by other means would take a lot of time or be very difficult. They are now widely available and, like other equipment such as fork lift trucks there is a tendency for people to oversimplify their use and allow people to operate them without prior training and experience. This places users and others at high risk of serious injury.

Some MEWPs can be used on rough terrain. This usually means that they are safe to use on uneven or undulating ground. Always check their limitations in the manufacturer's handbook before moving on to unprepared or sloping ground and operate within the defined stability working area. Wearing a harness with a lanyard attached to the platform provides extra protection against falls especially when the platform is being raised or lowered.

Use of Mobile Elevating Work Platforms

Mobile Elevating Work Platforms (MEWPs) can provide excellent safe access to high level work. When using a MEWP make sure:

- Whoever is operating it is fully trained and competent.
- The work platform is fitted with guard rails and toe boards.
- It is used on suitable firm and level ground. The ground may have to be prepared in advance.
- Tyres are properly inflated.
- The work area is cordoned off to prevent access below the work platform.
- That it is well lit if being used on a public highway in poor lighting.
- Outriggers are extended and chocked as necessary before raising the platform.
- All involved know what to do if the machine fails with the platform in the raised position.

Figure 10-24: Mobile elevated work platform (MEWPs). Source: ACT.

Figure 10-25: Mobile elevated work platform (MEWPs). *Source: ACT.*

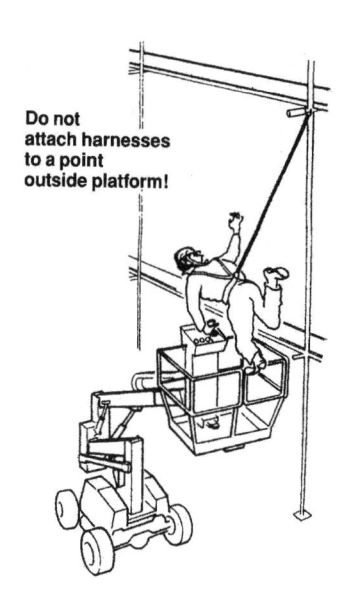

Figure 10-26: Use of harness with a MEWP. *Source: HSG150.*

Figure 10-28: Scissor lift. *Source: ACT.*

Do not
- Operate MEWPs close to overhead cables or dangerous machinery.
- Allow a knuckle, or elbow, of the arm to protrude into a traffic route when working near vehicles.
- Move the equipment with the platform in the raised position unless the equipment is especially designed to allow this to be done safely (check the manufacturer's instructions).
- Overload or overreach from the platform.

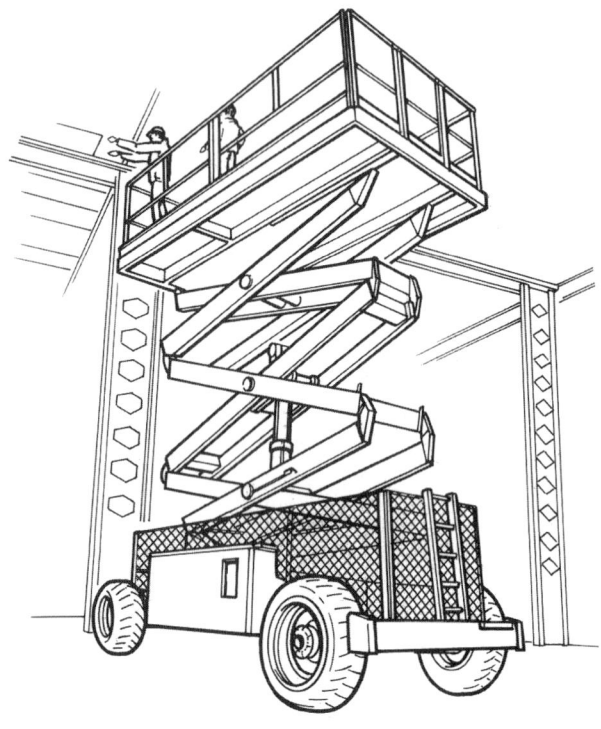

Figure 10-27: Scissor lift. *Source: HSG150, HSE.*

Ladders

USE OF LADDERS

Ladders are primarily a means of vertical access to a workplace. However, they are often used to carry out work and this frequently results in accidents. Many accidents involving ladders happen during work lasting 30 minutes or less. Ladders are often used for short jobs when it would be safer to use other equipment, e.g. mobile scaffold towers or MEWPs. Generally, ladders should be considered as access equipment and use of a ladder as a work platform should be discouraged. There are situations when working from a ladder would be inappropriate, for example:

- When two hands are needed or the work area is large.
- Where the equipment or materials used are large or awkward.
- Excessive height.
- Work of long duration.
- Where the ladder cannot be secured or made stable.
- Where the ladder cannot be protected from vehicles etc.
- Adverse weather conditions.

Figure 10-29: Ladder as access and workplace. Source: ACT.

Figure 10-30: Improper use. Source: ACT.

Before using a ladder to work from, consider whether it is the right equipment for the job. Ladders are only suitable as a workplace for light work of short duration, and for a large majority of activities a scaffold, mobile tower or MEWP is likely to be more suitable and safer.

- Pre-use inspection. Make sure the ladder is in good condition. Check the rungs and stiles for warping, cracking or splintering, the condition of the feet, and for any other defects. Do not use defective or painted ladders.
- Position the ladder properly for safe access and out of the way of vehicles.
- Ladders must stand on a firm, level base, be positioned approximately at an angle of 75^0 (1 unit horizontally to 4 units vertically) and extend about 1 metre above the landing place. Do not rest ladders against fragile surfaces.
- Ladders must be properly tied near the top, even if only in use for a short time. If not tied, ladders must be secured near the bottom, footed or weighted. Footing is not considered effective on ladders longer than five metres. While being tied, a ladder must be footed.
- Keep both hands free to grip the ladder when climbing or descending, with only one person on the ladder at any time. Beware of wet, greasy or icy rungs and make sure soles of footwear are clean.

Figure 10-31: Poor storage. Source: Lincsafe.

Figure 10-32: Use of roof ladders. Source: HSG150, HSE.

STEP LADDERS

Stepladders require careful use. They are subject to the same general health and safety rules as ladders.

However, in addition, they will not withstand any degree of side loading and overturn very easily.

Over-reaching is to be avoided at all costs.

The top step of a stepladder should not be used as a working platform unless it has been specifically designed for that purpose. Ladder stays must be 'locked out' properly before use.

UNIT NCC1 - ELEMENT 10 - WORKING AT HEIGHT - HAZARDS AND CONTROL

TRESTLES

Trestles are pre-fabricated steel, aluminium or wood supports, of approximately 500 mm - 1 metre width, that may be of fixed height or may be height adjustable by means of sliding struts with varying fixing points (pin method) or various cross bars to suit the height required. They are used to span scaffold boards from one to the other in order to make a work platform. *These can only be used where work cannot be carried out from the ground but where a scaffold would be impracticable.* A good example would be a plasterer who is installing and plastering a new ceiling. Typical working heights when using a trestle system ranges from 300 mm to 1 metre but can be up to above 4 metres. Edge protection should be fitted wherever practical. As with any work carried out above ground level, a risk assessment, as required by the Management of Health and Safety at Work Regulations (MHSWR) 1999, should be carried out and consideration given to the application of the WAH Regulations 2005 and/or the Construction (Design and Management) Regulations (CDM) 2007 and/or the Workplace (Health, Safety and Welfare) Regulations (WHSWR) 1992.

STAGING PLATFORMS

Staging platforms can be made of metal alloy or wood and are often used for linking trestle systems or tower scaffolds together safely. They also provide a safe work platform for work on fragile roofs. They are produced in various lengths. The same rules apply for edge protection as with other scaffold platforms.

LEADING EDGE PROTECTION SYSTEMS

Leading edges are created as new roof sheets are laid, or old ones are removed. Falls from a leading edge need to be prevented.

Figure 10-33: Stepladder. Source: ACT.

Work at the leading edge requires careful planning to develop a safe system of work. Nets are the preferred method for reducing the risk of injury from falls at the leading edge, as they provide protection to everyone on the roof. Nets should be erected by trained riggers and be strong enough to take the weight of people. Debris nets are only rigged to trap light weight debris - therefore it is important to know which type is in use at a workplace.

Staging platforms fitted with guard rails or suitable barriers and toe boards, in advance of the leading edge, can provide protection in some circumstances. But these will need to be used in conjunction with harnesses attached to a suitable fixing. Close supervision of this system of work will be needed as it is difficult for the harness to remain safely clipped at all times throughout the work activity.

Other techniques for working at height

Where it is not possible to work from the existing structure and the use of a scaffold working platform is not appropriate, a range of mobile access equipment including boatswain's chairs or seats, suspended cradles, rope access equipment and mobile elevating work platforms (MEWPs) can be used.

Those using this type of equipment should be trained and competent to operate it. They should learn emergency and evacuation procedures so that they know what to do if for example the power to the platform fails or fire breaks out in the building being worked on. With many pieces of equipment, more than one person will be needed to ensure safe operation.

BOATSWAIN'S CHAIR

Boatswain's chairs and seats can be used for light, short-term work. They should only be used where it is not practicable to provide a working platform.

Safety checklist

Before use
- Installation and use of boatswain's chair to be supervised by trained, experienced and competent person.
- Chair and associated equipment carefully examined for defects.
- Confirm test / examination certificates are valid. Establish safe working load.
- Check that user is both trained and competent in the use of the chair.
- Warning notice displayed and notification of intention to carry out work given.
- Prohibit access to the area below the chair in case materials fall.

In use
- Free of material or articles which could interfere with user's hand-hold.
- The fall rope must be properly tied off in use and always under or around a cleat to act as a brake.

After use
- Chairs and rope should be left in a safe condition:
  - Top rope secured.
  - Chair and rope secured to prevent swing.

- Raised when out of use or for overnight storage.
- Inspected for defects.
- Ropes (and chair, if timber) dried before storage.

CRADLES (INCLUDING SUSPENSION FROM CRADLES)

Before work starts, check that:

- Equipment is installed, modified and dismantled only by competent specialists.
- There is a current report of thorough examination for the equipment.
- A handover certificate is provided by the installer. The certificate should cover how to deal with emergencies, operate, check and maintain the equipment, and state its safe working load.
- Areas of the site where people may be struck by the cradle or falling materials have been fenced off or similar. Debris fans or covered walkways may also be required.
- Systems are in place to prevent people within the building being struck by the cradle as it rises or descends and prevent the cradle coming into contact with open windows or similar obstructions which could cause it to tip.
- Supports are protected from damage (for example, by being struck by passing vehicles or by interference from vandals).
- The equipment should not be used in adverse weather. High winds will create instability. Establish a maximum safe wind speed for operation. Storms and snow falls can also damage platforms, so they should be inspected before use after severe weather.
- Only trained personnel are to operate.

At the end of each day, check that:

- All power has been switched off and, where appropriate, power cables have been secured and made dead.
- The equipment is secured where it will not be accessible to vandals or trespassers.
- Notices are attached to the equipment warning that it is out of service and must not be used.
- Check the shift report for warnings of malfunction.

ROPE ACCESS

Often known as abseiling, this technique is usually used for inspection work rather than construction work. Like a boatswain's chair, it should only be used when a working platform cannot be provided. If rope access is necessary, then check that:

- A competent person has installed the equipment.
- The user is fully trained.
- There is more than one point securing the equipment.
- Tools and equipment are securely attached or the area below cordoned off.
- The main rope and safety rope are attached to separate points.

Figure 10-34: Personal suspension equipment.   Source: ACT.

Fall arrest equipment

HARNESSES

There may be circumstances in which it is not practicable for guard rails etc to be provided, for example, where guard rails are taken down for short periods to land materials. In this situation if people approach an open edge from which they would be liable to fall two metres or more, a suitably attached harness and temporary horizontal lifeline could allow safe working. When using harnesses and temporary horizontal lifelines, remember:

- The harness and lanyards are made of man-made fibres and as such are prone to degradation by sunlight, chemicals etc. It is important to carry out tactile pre-use checks daily, in good light, before taking harnesses and lanyards into use. If there is the slightest doubt about a harness or the lanyard, do not use it. Faults can be noticed by discolouration, little tears, nicks and grittiness to touch.
- A harness will not prevent a fall - it can only minimise the injury if there is a fall. The person who falls may be injured by the impact load to the body when the line goes tight or when they strike against parts of the structure during the fall. An energy absorber fitted to the energy-absorbing lanyard can reduce the risk of injury from impact loads.
- Where possible the energy-absorbing lanyard should be attached above the wearer to reduce the fall distance. Extra free movement can be provided by running temporary horizontal lifelines or inertia reels. Any attachment point must be capable of withstanding the impact load in the event of a fall. Consider how to recover anyone who does fall.
- Anyone who needs to attach themselves should be able to do so from a safe position. They need to be able to attach themselves before they move into a position where they are relying on the protection provided by the harness.
- To ensure that there is an adequate fall height to allow the system to operate and arrest the fall.
- A twin lanyard may be necessary in some cases where the wearer needs to move about. A twin lanyard allows the wearer to clip on one lanyard in a different position before unclipping the other lanyard.
- Installation of equipment to which harnesses will be fixed, e.g. a suitable anchor, must be inspected regularly.
- Everyone who uses a harness must be instructed in how to check, wear and adjust it before use and how to connect themselves to the structure or safety line as appropriate.
- They should be thoroughly examined at intervals of no more than every six months.

SAFETY NETS

Safety nets are used in a variety of applications where other forms of protection are not reasonably practicable - such as steel erecting and roof work where site personnel are at risk of falling through fragile roofs onto solid surfaces or structures (steel work) below. Safety nets will arrest the fall of an individual preventing an impact that may cause injury or death. Safety nets must be installed beneath the work area, as a minimum, and consideration should be given to an extension of the protection to allow for people working outside the planned area. Safety nets are only to be installed under supervision by competent installers and are to be inspected weekly and checked daily. It should be remembered that nets are also used to collect debris that may fall. This may be rigged to take a lesser weight than that for protection of people. It is important to identify which type of net is in use in a workplace as reliance on the wrong type may have fatal consequences.

Figure 10-35: Safety nets. Source: ACT.

SOFT LANDING SYSTEMS

These normally consist of inflatable air bags or bean bags which are placed, prior to work commencing, under the work area.

CRASH DECKS

These are normally scaffold structures erected to protect the general public or employees from debris e.g. over public walkways or adjacent to roads. They are described as a semi-permanent and fully boarded or metal sheeted protection deck over a pavement.

EMERGENCY PROCEDURES INCLUDING RESCUE

It is essential that risk assessments are completed and they should include planned emergency procedures. Employees should be trained and competent in procedures. These procedures should be rehearsed, so that in the event of an actual incident, employees are competent.

Roofwork

MEANS OF ACCESS

This is usually by ladder. A ladder should extend at least 1.05 metres above the edge of the roof, and it should be securely lashed in position, preferably with wire bond or a safety tie.

EDGE AND LEADING EDGE PROTECTION

Guard rails and toe boards or suitable barriers erected at the edge or eaves level of a roof are usually needed to stop people and materials from falling off.

See also the section - leading edge protection - earlier in this element.

CRAWLING BOARDS

On any fragile or angled roof (greater than 30^0) or on any roof which is considered hazardous because of its condition or because of the weather, suitable crawling boards must be used. They must be correctly positioned and secure. If it is obvious that the job requires a progression along the roof, extra crawling boards must be provided and no fewer than two such boards shall be taken on any job.

Figure 10-36: Edge protection and boards. Source: ACT.

FALL ARREST EQUIPMENT

See also the section - Harnesses - earlier in this element.

10.3 - Protection of others

DEMARCATION

When working at height is being carried out it is important to protect others from the hazards of items or objects falling onto them. A simple way of doing this is to identify hazardous zones with hazard tape and barriers. Inform those that may be affected by the work that is being undertaken and warn of the possible dangers that may arise within the demarcated area.

Clear demarcation of areas where construction work is being undertaken and where it is not will assist those not involved in the work to keep out of the area and avoid exposure to hazards. The area should be demarcated at a distance that relates to the hazards, such as materials or tools falling. A safety margin should always be built into the demarcation to ensure risks are controlled.

BARRIERS

Barriers are a physical means of preventing access to an area that is required to be restricted. As such they are particularly appropriate if people, such as the public, might stray past an area marked only with hazard tape. These can be situated at a proximity that is relative to the hazards associated with the work being carried out. If necessary to ensure a demarcation zone the barriers may be 2 metre high fencing.

TUNNELS

Tunnels can be used to 'isolate' others from any surrounding hazards by enclosing an area (i.e. walkway) and thus preventing any contact with likely hazards until through the danger area. An example of this could be the ground level of a scaffold on a shop front in a busy high street, being enclosed to form a tunnel that allows the public to pass through the works safely whilst allowing the work to continue above.

Figure 10-37: Nets / sheeting.   Source: ACT.

Figure 10-38: Marking.   Source: ACT.

SIGNS

Safety signs are used to provide people with information relating to the works being carried out, to control or divert people and most importantly of any dangers or hazards. Signs may be situated at a location in advance of the work area to give prior warning in addition to the works perimeter and actual work location.

MARKING

Where equipment used to gain access to height may be collided with it should carry hazard marking. For example, the standards of a scaffold at ground level on a street may be marked with hazard tape. **See also the sections - Demarcation and Signs - above in this element.**

LIGHTING

Suitable and adequate lighting should be provided to allow the works being carried out and any possible hazards to be seen clearly in advance and allow people to take the required actions to avoid interference with the site. Scaffolds located near roads may be fitted with lighting to warn traffic of its presence. MEWPs and similar equipment used in poor lighting conditions on or near roads and walkways must use standard vehicle lighting.

SHEETING, NETTING AND FANS

Sheeting can protect others by preventing dust, materials or tools being ejected from working at height. **See also "sheeting" in the section - Ensuring Stability - earlier in this element.**

HEAD PROTECTION

Head protection, such as hard hats, provide the user with limited protection from objects falling from height. Hard hats are made from toughened plastic and have an approximate life of 3 years. There is a need and legal duty to wear head protection where there is a risk of injury from falling materials; typically this includes working around people working at height.

10.4 - Working over or near water

Prevention of drowning

The CDM Regulations Part 4 Duties Relating to Health and Safety on Construction Sites, Regulation 35,state that "if there is a risk of persons falling into water and drowning, suitable steps should be taken to prevent a person from falling, and to ensure that suitable rescue equipment is provided". This means that prior to work above water being undertaken, a full risk assessment must be made that takes into account the conditions of the water being worked over or near (tidal, depth, temperature, fast flowing) and suitable control measures identified and implemented including emergency rescue plans and procedures.

Where possible and practicable, a scaffold system is the best method of safe working over water. Working above water brings an extra dimension to workplace safety and where the water is fast flowing additional risks need to be considered. Safety precautions will include protection for river traffic (advance warnings, lighting of obstructions and consultation with river authorities) and the need for the protection against the possibility of the structure being struck by such traffic. There may also be the need for additional guardrails to working platforms or fall arrest equipment such as safety nets or harnesses; the provision of rescue equipment such as life belts and the availability of a rescue boat under the control of a competent person, should someone fall into the water. Scaffolds must be erected and inspected by competent persons with inspections required weekly. Workers who are required to work near to or over water are required to be properly trained with a provision made so that any person who does fall into water is able to float - **see also the section - Buoyancy Aids - below in this element** and be recovered as quickly as possible. Additional means of preventing fall into water may include floating stages, safety nets, safety harnesses and barriers.

Additional control measures

BUOYANCY AIDS

Buoyancy aids must be provided and their use enforced when working on or near water. However, a distinction between buoyancy aids and lifejackets needs to be noted. Both lifejackets and buoyancy aids are designed to keep the wearer afloat with the main difference that a buoyancy aid will provide sufficient buoyancy to keep a conscious person afloat in a reasonable flotation position. A lifejacket will support an unconscious person in a face upright flotation position, therefore reducing the likelihood of the wearer drowning.

Buoyancy aids and lifejackets can be used with safety harnesses so long as the items do not interfere with each other and reduce effectiveness. It is possible to obtain a combined piece of equipment. All staff that are required to use this equipment must be properly trained in its use and be fully aware of its functions and limitations.

Management systems must be in place that considers the use, inspection and storage of lifejackets and buoyancy aids.

The majority of drowning occurs close to the bank or waters edge, and this should be taken into account at the planning stage. Other methods of equipment available to assist someone to remain afloat are life buoys or rescue lines. Life buoys are normally attached to approximately 30 metres of lifeline but can only be thrown a short distance of 6 - 8 metres. Rescue lines are available in various forms with life lines ranging from 25 to 40 metres in length. Rescue lines work by throwing a bag or capsule to the person in the water and the line deploying as the bag / capsule goes further out. The line, bag and capsule all stay afloat and allow the person in the water to grab the line and be pulled to safety. Care must be taken that the person deploying the line is secure at the bank and unable to be pulled into the water.

In fast flowing channels that have no water borne traffic, then 'safety nets' or 'safety lines' may be stretched across the width of the channel to allow the person in the water to hang on and wait for rescue. This is only effective if the person in the water remains conscious.

SAFETY BOATS

Where works are being carried out on fast flowing, or tidal waters then a rescue boat should be made available. Requirements state that it must have a reliable engine, carry oars, and the person that is operating the boat must be competent and experienced at handling small boats on flowing water. It must be fitted with grab lines for persons who have fallen into the water and if any work is carried out in the hours of darkness, then the boat will be required to be fitted with high efficiency lighting. It may be a requirement to have two-way radio installed on the boat for communication between boat and shore.

Element 11

Excavation work and confined spaces - hazards and control

Learning outcomes

On completion of this element, candidates should be able to demonstrate understanding of the content through the application of knowledge to familiar and unfamiliar situations. In particular they should be able to:

11.1 Describe the hazards and risks of excavation work.

11.2 Describe the appropriate control measures for excavation work.

11.3 Define a confined space and describe the hazards and risks associated with confined space working.

11.4 Describe the appropriate control measures for confined space working.

Content

11.1 - Excavations hazards and assessment	199
The hazards of work in and around excavations	199
Risk assessment	200
11.2 - Control measures for excavation work	201
Controls	201
Particular requirements for contaminated ground	205
Inspection requirements for excavation support	206
11.3 - Confined spaces hazards and risks	206
Definition of a 'confined space'	206
Typical confined spaces found during construction activities	206
Hazards and risks associated with confined spaces	207
11.4 - Control measures for confined space working	208
Precautions for safe entry	208
Monitoring arrangements	210
Emergency arrangements	210

Sources of reference

A guide to the Construction (Head Protection) Regulations (L102), HSE Books ISBN 0-7176-1478-6
Avoiding danger from underground services (HSG47), HSE Books ISBN 0-7176-1744-0
Essentials of health and safety at work, HSE Books ISBN 0-7176-0716-X
Health and safety in excavations: Be safe and shore (HSG185), HSE Books ISBN 0-7176-1563-4
Protecting the public: Your next move (HSG151), HSE Books ISBN 0-7176-1148-5
Safe work in confined spaces (ACOP) (L101), HSE Books ISBN 0-7176-1405-0

Relevant statutory provisions

The Confined Spaces Regulations (CSR) 1997
The Construction (Design and Management) Regulations (CDM) 2007
The Construction (Head Protection) Regulations (CHPR) 1989
The Personal Protective Equipment at Work Regulations (PPER) 1992
The Work at Height Regulations (WAH) 2005

11.1 - Excavations hazards and assessment

The hazards of work in and around excavations

Work in excavations and trenches, basements, underground tanks, sewers, manholes etc., can involve high risks and each year construction workers are killed with some buried alive or asphyxiated.

Figure 11-1: Buried services. *Source: ACT.*

Figure 11-2: Excavation hazards. *Source: ACT.*

BURIED SERVICES

Although electricity cables provide the most obvious risk, gas pipes, water mains, drains and sewers can all release dangerous substances. Gas is particularly dangerous if there is a potential ignition source close by. Fibre-optic cables may not produce a health and safety risk but are very expensive to repair.

Buried services (electricity, gas, water, etc.) are not obvious upon site survey and so the likelihood of striking a service when excavating, drilling or piling is increased. The results of striking an underground service are varied, and the potential to cause injury or fatality is high. As with overhead power lines, any underground service should be treated as live until confirmed dead by an authority. Incidents can include shock, electrocution, explosion and burns from power cables, explosion, burns or unconsciousness from gas or power cables, impact injury from dislodged stones or flooding from ruptured water mains.

FALLS OF PERSONS/EQUIPMENT/MATERIAL INTO THE EXCAVATION

When people are working below ground in excavations, the problems are very similar to those faced when people are working at a height - falls and falling objects. Particular problems arise when:

- Materials, including spoil, are stored too close to the edge of the excavation.
- The excavation is close to another building and the foundations may be undermined.
- The edge of the excavation is not clear, especially if the excavation is in a public area.
- Absence of barriers or lighting.
- Poor positioning or the absence of access ladders allowing people to fall.
- Absence of organized crossing points.
- Badly constructed ramps for vehicle access which can cause the vehicle to topple.
- No stop blocks for back filling.
- Routing of vehicles too close to the excavation.

COLLAPSE OF SIDES

Often, the soil and earth that make up the sides of the excavation cannot be relied upon to support their own weight, leading to the possibility of collapse. The risk can be made worse if:

- The soil structure is loose or made unstable by water logging.
- Heavy plant or materials are too close to the edge of the excavation.
- Machinery or vehicles cause vibration.
- There is inadequate support for the sides.

The consequences of even a minor collapse can be very serious. A minor fall of earth can happen at high speed and bring with it anything (plant and machinery) that may be at the edge. Even if the arms and head of a person are not trapped in the soil, the material pressing on the person can lead to severe crush injuries to the lower body and asphyxiation due to restriction of movement of the chest.

COLLAPSE OF ADJACENT STRUCTURES

Excavations that are carried out within close proximity to existing buildings or structures may result in their foundations becoming undermined and create the potential for significant settling damage to occur or worse still, collapse. Consideration should be given to the effects that excavation work might have on foundations of neighbouring buildings or structures, and control measures implemented to ensure that foundations are not disturbed or undermined. Building foundations that are at a distance of less than twice the excavation depth from the face of the excavation are more likely to be affected by ground movement; underpinning or shoring of such structures may be required to prevent structural damage.

UNIT NCC1 - ELEMENT 11 - EXCAVATION WORK AND CONFINED SPACES - HAZARDS AND CONTROL

WATER INGRESS

Unless a major watercourse is breached, leading to a massive ingress of water, drowning is not likely to be an issue. However, heavy rainfall, breaking into drains and digging below the natural water table can all lead to flooding. In deep excavations, where access is not readily available, the combined effect of water and mud could lead to difficulty in escape and risk of drowning. In addition, this can lead to the sides of the trench becoming soft and the integrity of the supports can be undermined.

CONTAMINATED GROUND

Digging may uncover buried materials that have the potential to be hazardous to health. The history of the site should be examined to try to identify if substances have been buried on the site during its previous use. Sites that once were used as steel works may contain arsenic and cyanide dating back many years; farmyards may have been used as graves for animals and to dispose of pesticides and organo-phosphates. There is always the presence of vermin to consider - this can increase the risk of diseases such as leptospirosis.

TOXIC AND ASPHYXIATING ATMOSPHERES

Excavations can under different circumstances be subject to toxic, asphyxiating or explosive atmospheres. Chalk or limestone deposits when in contact with acidic groundwater can release carbon dioxide, and gases such as methane or hydrogen sulphide can seep into excavations from contaminated ground or damaged services in built-up areas. These atmospheres can accumulate at the bottom of an excavation and result in asphyxiation, poisoning, explosion or potential fatalities.

Excavations should be treated with similar caution to that applied to confined spaces, and an assessment should be carried out prior to work commencing in excavations to identify the risk of toxic gas, oxygen deficiency, and fire or explosion.

It should also identify the appropriate risk control measures required, such as:

- Type of gas monitoring equipment to be provided.
- Testing of the atmosphere before entry into the excavation.
- Provision of suitable ventilation equipment.
- Training of employees.
- Use of a sufficient number of people, including one at ground level.
- Procedures and equipment needed for an emergency rescue.

MECHANICAL HAZARDS

Figure 11-3: Water in excavation. Source: ACT.

Large pieces of mobile plant and equipment that are commonly used on construction sites have the potential to cause serious harm to site workers and members of the public. To keep people and vehicles apart, the following need to be considered:

- Exclusion zones identified by barriers.
- Warning signs and lights.
- Excavator cabs should have good visibility.
- Operators properly trained and close supervision provided.

Risk assessment

FACTORS TO CONSIDER

The depth of the excavation

Risks increase with the depth of excavation, risks from materials falling increase with the height they may fall and there is an increased risk of collapse at greater depths as the amount of material to support (comprising the excavation wall) increases. A collapse of an excavation deeper than the head height of a worker carries a high risk of suffocation. It should be remembered that a worker may have to work low down in an excavation so a shallow excavation can present serious risks, depending on the work being carried out in it.

The type of soil being excavated

Clay presents specific risks of collapse due to it drying out or becoming more fluid when wet. If the soil is not compacted, for example because of a previous excavation near by, its strength may not be as higher as if it has had chance to settle and become compacted. Soil changes its strength significantly when it becomes wet; presenting an added risk that water may make its way into the excavation and cause flooding. If the soil is chalky carbon dioxide may be liberated as part of the excavation process, similarly if it is in contaminated land there may be toxic substances and risks from methane.

The type of work being undertaken

If the work to be done to create and work in the excavation is to be done manually or mechanically the risks vary significantly. The task being conducted can increase the risks, for example, pipe jointing operations carried out manually will usually bring the head of the worker below the top of the excavation for a significant time. Additional risks may also be created by hot working or work in a confined space.

The use of mechanical equipment

Though this can reduce the risk to workers by not requiring them to enter the excavation to dig it they carry risks of their own. Where people work alongside this equipment there is a risk of contact or collision and as it carries a considerable amount of momentum major injuries or death would not be uncommon if contact was made.

Proximity of roadways and structures etc

Where excavations are within close proximity of roadways and structures, vehicles should be segregated and excluded from excavation areas wherever possible. Brightly painted baulks or barriers and or fencing should be used where necessary to protect and clearly identify the excavation area. If vehicles have to unload materials into excavations, then the use of stop blocks to prevent such vehicles falling into the excavation as a result of over-running is recommended. Special consideration should be given to the reinforcement of the sides of the excavation, which may need extra support, especially when adjacent to busy roads.

Excavations should not be allowed to affect the footings of scaffolds or the foundations of nearby structures. Walls especially in older properties may have very shallow foundations, which could be undermined by small trenches, therefore some structures may need temporary support even before digging can commence. It is always best practice to conduct surveys of the foundations and gain the advice of a structural engineer in such cases.

Presence of public

Excavations in public areas should be fenced off, fitted with toe boards and stop block type barriers to prevent pedestrians and vehicles falling into them. Where children or trespassers might inadvertently get access to a site out of hours then certain precautions should be considered such as backfilling or securely covering excavations to reduce the potential of such people being injured. The excavation should have suitable and sufficient identification and signage, with any pedestrian routes or detours clearly marked, fenced off and lit (if appropriate).

Weather

Heavy rain or fast melting snow may undermine the stability of the ground and therefore of the supports or wall sides. Hence careful consideration should be given to the type of shoring used depending on the site and sub-soils.

Services

The presence or likelihood of services in the area of an excavation carries high risks of a different type. For example, contact with an electrical service may be immediately fatal to a worker or damage to a gas service may cause a risk of major explosion.

Material and vehicles

If materials are placed too close to excavations or vehicles pass near by there is an increased risk of collapse or fall of materials/vehicle.

Required support equipment that may be needed

The risks from excavations may be reduced by using the correct support equipment. Care has to be taken to ensure that the right type and quantity is used if the risk is to be reduced effectively. For example, there may be a need to provide close shoring of the sides of an excavation to control a particular soil condition or where the effects of water are likely.

11.2 - Control measures for excavation work

Controls

> "All practicable steps should be taken, where necessary, to prevent danger to any person, including, where necessary, the provision of supports or battering, to ensure that;
>
> (a) any excavation or part of an excavation does not collapse;
>
> (b) no material from a side or roof of, or adjacent to, any excavation is dislodged or falls; and
>
> (c) no person is buried or trapped in an excavation by material which is dislodged or falls.
>
> Regulation 31 of CDM 2007

IDENTIFICATION AND MARKING OF BURIED SERVICES

Excavation operations should not begin until all available service location drawings have been identified and thoroughly examined. Record plans and location drawings should not be considered as totally accurate but serve only as an indication of the likelihood of the presence of services, their location and depth. It is possible for the position of an electricity supply cable to alter if previous works have been carried out in the location due to the flexibility of the cable and movement of surrounding features since original installation of the cable. In addition, plans often show a proposed position for the services that does not translate to the ground, such that services are placed in position only approximately where the plan says.

It is important that 'service location devices' such as a cable avoidance tool (CAT) are used by competent, trained operatives to assist in the identification and marking of the actual location and position of buried services. When identified it is essential that physical markings be placed on the ground to show where these services are location.

Figure 11-4: Marking of services.   Source: ACT.

SAFE DIGGING METHODS

Safe digging methods should be implemented within 0.5 metres of a buried service. This involves the use of insulated hand tools such as a spade or shovel with curved edges (to be used with light force and not sudden blows). Mechanical, probing or piercing tools and equipment such as excavator's, forks, picks or drills should *NOT* be used when in the vicinity of buried services, as these may cause damage to any service if they strike it. Careful hand digging using a spade or shovel should be used instead.

Example of a permit to dig

Contract: .... Contract No: ....

Principal Contractor: .... Sub Contractor: ....

Permit No: .... Date: ....

1. Location: ....

2. Size, detail and depth of excavation: ....
   ....

3. Are Service Plans on site ?   YES / NO
   Comments: ....

4. Has cable locating equipment been used to identify services ?   YES / NO
   Comments: ....

5. Are all known services marked out ? (site inspection by relevant statutory bodies)   YES / NO
   Comments: ....

6. Are trial holes required ?   YES / NO
   Comments: ....

7. Have precautions been taken to prevent contact if overhead lines are in the vicinity of the operation or near approach to the operation?   YES / NO

8. Additional precautions, i.e. Shoring/Fencing/Access/Storage/Fumes/Record of setting out points to re-establish services routes

   Comments: ....

9. Sketch details or attach copy of plans

10. Date and time of excavation: ....

    Signed: ....   Accepted by: ....
    For and on behalf of issuing party   (Work shall not commence unless all persons involved are aware of the safe systems of work)

    A new permit will be required for any further excavations. This permit is for guidance only.
    Persons carrying out work must take reasonable precautions when working around services.

Figure 11-5: Permit to dig.   *Source: Reproduced by kind permission of Lincsafe.*

METHODS OF SUPPORTING EXCAVATIONS

"Suitable and sufficient steps shall be taken to prevent any person, work equipment, or any accumulation of material from falling into any excavation."

Regulation 31 of CDM 2007

Precautions must be taken to prevent collapse. The methods of supporting (shoring) the sides of excavations vary widely in design depending on:

- The nature of the subsoil - for example wet may require close shoring with sheets.
- Projected life of the excavation - a trench box may give ready made access where it is only needed for short duration.
- Work to be undertaken, including equipment used - for example the use of a trench box for shoring where pipe joints are made.
- The possibility of flooding from ground water and heavy rain - close shoring would be required.
- The depth of the excavation - a shallow excavation may use battering instead of shoring, particularly where shoring may impede access.
- The number of people using the excavation at any one time - a lot of space may be required so cantilever sheet piling may be preferred.

In order to ensure satisfactory support for excavations:

- Prevent collapse by battering the sides to a safe angle or supporting them with sheeting or proprietary support systems.
- Use experienced people for the erection and dismantling of timbering and other supports.
- Adequate material must be used to prevent danger from falls or falling objects.

Figure 11-6: Battering. *Source: ACT.*

Figure 11-7: Trench box - for shoring. *Source: ACT.*

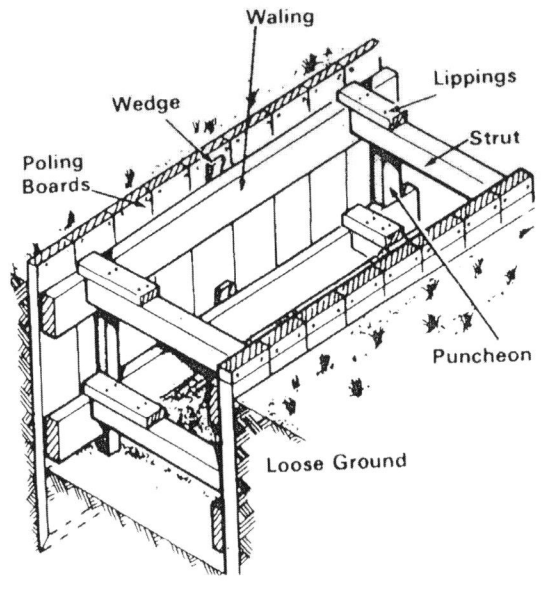

Figure 11-8: Close boarded excavation. *Source: BS6031.*

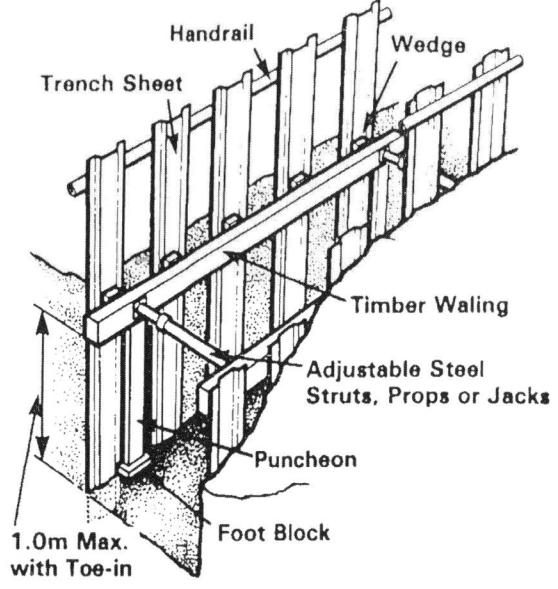

Figure 11-9: Open sheeting. *Source: BS6031.*

Figure 11-10: Close sheeting. *Source: ACT.*

Figure 11-11: Open sheeting. *Source: ACT.*

MEANS OF ACCESS

Ladders are the usual means of access and egress to excavations. They must be properly secured, in good condition and inspected regularly. The ladder should extend about one metre or three rungs above ground level to give a good handhold.

CROSSING POINTS

Crossing excavations should only be allowed at predetermined points. The crossing point should be able to withstand the maximum foreseeable load and be provided with guard rails and toe boards. The spacing or location of crossing points should be such that workers and others are encouraged to use them, rather than to attempt other means of crossing the excavation.

BARRIERS, LIGHTING AND SIGNS

Where people or materials can fall a distance of more than two metres, edge protection must be provided. It is also sensible to cover shallow trenches when they are left unattended. Guardrails must meet the same standards as those provided for working platforms. Concrete or wooden blocks (usually old railway sleepers) are placed some distance from the edge to prevent vehicles from getting too close, particularly when the excavation is being 'back filled'. In this case the wooden blocks provide a 'stop block'.

Signs that comply with The Health and Safety (Signs and Signals) Regulations (SSSR) 1996 should be displayed to warn people of the excavation and any special measures to be taken. If working on a public highway, the police or the local authority must be consulted over the positioning of traffic lights. Appropriate lighting should be provided; it must provide sufficient illumination for those at work but should not create glare or other distractions for passers by, especially motorists. Battery operated headlamps (to avoid trailing cables) may be considered for individual use. If excavations are present in dark conditions they must be suitably lit to prevent vehicles or people colliding or falling into them.

SAFE STORAGE OF SPOIL

Excavated material (spoil), other materials, plant and vehicles should never be stored or parked close to the sides of any excavation. The additional pressure distributed on the ground from spoil, vehicles, etc significantly increases the likelihood of collapse occurring at the sides of the excavation. Though it will depend on the weight of the material it would normally be kept a minimum of 1 metre from the edge of the excavation. In addition, spoil heaps consist of loose materials that have the risk of spilling into the excavation. A means of preventing spillage of spoil into an excavation is by positioning scaffold boards as toe boards, fixed along the outside of trench sheets. This provides additional protection to combat the risk of loose materials spilling into the excavation. An alternative to this is to allow boards or sheeting to protrude above the top of the excavation sufficient to act as toe boards and prevent materials falling.

Unless sufficient control is implemented, workers can suffer injury from spoil or stored materials falling from ground level into an excavation. Head protection must be worn and this will provide protection for those working in the excavation from small pieces of materials falling either from above or from the sides of the excavation. If stored at a suitable distance away from an excavation and at a suitable height, spoil heaps can form an effective barrier against vehicles travelling around the construction site and assist in preventing falls of vehicles and plant into an excavation and onto workers.

Figure 11-12: Materials storage. *Source: ACT.*

Figure 11-13: Preventing water ingress. *Source: ACT.*

DE-WATERING AND USE OF FREEZING EQUIPMENT

Ingress of water may occur through rainfall, flood (river, sea) or when an excavation continues below the natural groundwater level. Consideration must be given to the likelihood of water entering the excavation and the measures to be implemented in order to control water entering the excavation and water levels between it. Usually water is abstracted from excavations and pumped to sumps for settlement from where it can be pumped out for disposal. When an excavation is liable to water ingress the stability of walls can be undermined; this will influence the choice of shoring, for example, close sheeting rather than open sheeting.

It is permissible to distribute pumped groundwater from within an excavation over grassy areas where any silt deposits can be absorbed and not have a detrimental effect on the environment. However, when works are within close proximity to a watercourse, i.e. within 10 metres, then advice should be sought on the disposal of groundwater and a 'Consent for Works Affecting Watercourses' should be obtained from the Environment Agency.

Pipe freezing equipment is used for stopping the flow of liquid in a pipe. It is an easy method, which permits repairs and installation without draining the entire piping system. Liquid nitrogen is used in the freezing process. Only competent trained personnel should use pipe freezing equipment.

POSITIONING AND ROUTING OF VEHICLES, PLANT AND EQUIPMENT

To prevent objects falling into excavations, the following precautions should be taken:

- Spoil and building materials must not be stacked near to the edge.
- The weight of stacks should not be enough to cause the sides to collapse.
- Designated operating areas for vehicles and machinery must be routed away from the excavation.
- Where vehicles have to approach, stop blocks must be provided to prevent overrunning.

PERSONAL PROTECTIVE EQUIPMENT

As well as the need for hard hats to limit the risks from falling materials, other personal protective equipment (PPE) may be necessary, such as:

- Breathing apparatus.
- Safety harnesses.
- Hearing protection.
- Clothing to protect from the rays of the sun.
- Masks and respirators.
- Face masks and gloves for welding and grinding.
- Footwear.

Particular requirements for contaminated ground

Contaminated ground can give rise to various health hazards, including biological and chemical hazards. Exposure to the hazards can vary depending on the work to be carried out and assessments should be made to determine which controls are required.

Site preparation work which involves the removal of topsoil from land known to be contaminated with heavy metals will require specific arrangements in relation to personal protective equipment required and practices to be carried out. The work is likely to require the provision of gloves, overalls, eye protection and respirators. Additionally, the work will require campaigns of awareness training to ensure good levels of personal hygiene are maintained, with emphasis on ensuring that open cuts are covered with waterproof dressings whenever required. Consideration will need to be given to specific welfare facilities provision, for example a decontamination unit. There should be arrangements in place in order to prevent contamination when eating and smoking. First-aid and emergency decontamination facilities should be made available located near to the place of work.

SOIL TESTING

Surveys should be undertaken, and a soil-testing programme implemented prior to works beginning. As each site is different and may involve various contaminant types, the methods of testing and analysis used should be suitable to the particular local needs of each site.

Usually, specialist contractors are used to carry out this type of work. Historical information such as land deeds, maps, building plans and any other information relating to the site provide useful assistance. Contaminants will usually be found in the top 0.5 - 1m layer (strata) of ground and soil samples should be at least to the greatest depth of any excavation, remembering that contamination may seep from one part of a site to another. As a minimum precaution, any proposed control measures chosen should adequately protect against the highest concentrations of contaminant found on site.

WELFARE FACILITIES

Ensuring good hygiene standards is one of the more important elements of protective measures to be taken when working on construction sites and in particular with contaminated ground. Whilst the level of risk that is identified will establish the range of measures that are to be provided, the principles outlined should always be followed when working on a contaminated site.

Installation of a sufficiently ventilated and lit hygiene facility must be provided. This may be purpose built or a smaller standard unit may be sufficient depending upon the number of personnel involved at the site. The installation of the hygiene/decontamination unit should be situated at the most convenient point to or from the dirty zone.

The hygiene/decontamination facility should generally be in three stages but prior to entering the unit, a boot wash point should be provided that includes running water and fixed or hand brushes for removing contaminated matter. The hygiene facility should then be arranged in its three stages as follows:

Stage 1   Should provide storage for ordinary clothing not used whilst at work.

Stage 2   A high standard washing facility. This includes the provision of hot and cold water with taps preferably operated by the elbow or foot, detergent, nail brushes and disposable towels. In certain circumstances (toxic or corrosive contamination) showers may be the necessary means of cleansing. Both men and women may use showers (at separate times) provided that it is in a separate room with a lock on the inside of the door.

Stage 3   Should provide storage for contaminated work wear such as overalls, boots, etc.

In addition to the hygiene facility, toilets should be provided. The location of toilet units on contaminated sites must be situated so workers are directed through the hygiene facility prior to reaching the toilet for use. Daily cleaning and decontamination must be carried out on toilet facilities. Everyone who works on construction sites must have access to adequate toilet and washing facilities, a place for warming up and a clean room set aside for taking meals and refreshment. Secure storage for clothing and facilities for drying wet clothing. First Aid facilities should also be provided.

HEALTH SURVEILLANCE

The employer should decide about the need for health surveillance as part of the Control of Substances Hazardous to Health Regulations (COSHH) 2002 assessment. Health surveillance is appropriate where a disease or adverse effect may be related to exposure; and It is likely that this could arise in the circumstances of the work; and there are valid techniques for detecting the disease or effect. For example, work with cadmium, phenol, or arsenic, will normally need health surveillance including biological monitoring of workers.

Inspection requirements for excavation support

The CDM 2007 Regulations require inspections and reports to be carried out for excavations.

A competent person must inspect excavations:

- At the start of each shift in which the work is to be carried out.
- After any event likely to have affected the strength or stability of the excavation.
- After any material unintentionally falls or is dislodged and the person who carried out the inspection is satisfied that the work can be carried out there safely.

The competent person must:

- Where the person who carried out the inspection has informed the person on whose behalf the inspection was carried out of any matter about which he or she is not satisfied, work shall not be carried out in the excavation until the matters have been satisfactorily remedied.
- Prepare a report and shall within 24 hours of completing the inspection to which the report relates, provide the report or a copy of it to the person on whose behalf the inspection was carried out.
- Where the person owing a duty is an employee or works under the control of another, his employer or, or as the case may be, the person under whose control he works shall ensure that he performs the duty.

The inspection report record must include the following information:

- Name and address of person on whose behalf the inspection was carried out.
- Location of the workplace inspected.
- Description of workplace or part of workplace inspected (including any plant and equipment and materials, if any).
- Date and time of inspection.
- Details of any matter identified that could lead to a risk to the health and safety of anyone.
- Details of any action taken as a result of any matter identified in the last point.
- Details of any more action considered necessary.
- The name and position of the person making the report.

11.3 - Confined spaces hazards and risks

A failure to appreciate the dangers associated with confined spaces has led not only to the deaths of many workers, but also to the demise of some of those who have attempted to rescue them.

Definition of a 'confined space'

A confined space is a space which is substantially enclosed and where there will be a reasonably foreseeable risk of serious injury from substances or conditions. This therefore means not only a space which is small and difficult to enter, exit or work in but one with limited or restricted access; or it can also be a space which is badly ventilated e.g. a tank or a large tunnel.

Typical confined spaces found during construction activities

The Confined Spaces Regulations (CSR) 1997 defines a confined space as any place, including:

Chamber	e.g. cellar, tunnel, chamber for a pump, oven or similar space in process machinery.
Tank	e.g. storage tanks or solid or liquid chemical.
Vat	e.g. process vessel which may be open, but by its depth confines a person.
Silo	e.g. may be an above the ground structure for storing cereal, crops.
Pit	e.g. excavations or trenches.
Pipe	e.g. concrete, plastic steel etc, fabrication used to carry liquids or gases.
Sewer	e.g. brick or concrete structure for the carrying of liquid waste.
Flue	e.g. exhaust chimney for disposal of waste gases.
Well	e.g. deep source of water.
Cellar	e.g. an enclosed low level room or space below ground level usually found in old buildings or public houses.
Trench	e.g. a relatively shallow narrow excavation usually dug for some utility laying provision or drainage facility.

Or other similar space, in which, by virtue of its enclosed nature, there is a foreseeable risk of a 'specified occurrence'.

Figure 11-14: Confined space - chamber. Source: ACT.

Figure 11-15: Confined space - sewer. Source: ACT.

A "SPECIFIED OCCURRENCE" IS DEFINED AS:
- Fire or explosion.
- Loss of consciousness or asphyxiation of any person at work arising from gas, fumes, vapour or lack of oxygen.
- Drowning of any person at work.
- Asphyxiation of any person at work arising from a free flowing solid.
- Loss of consciousness of any person arising from a high ambient temperature.

Figure 11-16: Confined space - Cement Silo. Source: ACT.

Figure 11-17: Confined space - open tank. Source: ACT.

Hazards and risks associated with confined spaces

EXPOSURE TO TOXIC, EXPLOSIVE AND OXYGEN DEFICIENT ATMOSPHERES

Air in the confined space is made unbreathable either by toxic gases, fumes or by lack of oxygen. There is not enough natural ventilation to keep the air fit to breathe. In some cases the gases may be flammable, so there may also be a fire or explosion risk.

Some confined spaces are naturally dangerous, for example, because of:
- Gas build-up in sewers and manholes and pits connected to them.
- Gases leaking into trenches and pits in contaminated land such as old refuse tips and old gas works.
- Rust inside tanks and vessels which eats up the oxygen.
- Liquids and slurries which can suddenly fill the space or release gases into it when disturbed.
- Chemical reaction between some soils and air causing oxygen depletion or the action of ground water on chalk and limestone producing carbon dioxide.

Some places are made dangerous by vapours from the work done in them. Where possible, it is important to keep hazards out of confined spaces, for example, do not use petrol or diesel engines in or near to confined spaces, because exhaust gases can cause asphyxiation. Because paints and glues used in construction work processes may give off hazardous vapours it is essential to ensure the confined space has enough ventilation to make the air fit to breathe; mechanical ventilation might be needed.

HEAT

Confined spaces have limited natural ventilation and depending on the tasks being undertaken within the area may become hot and uncomfortable to work in. In extreme cases this may cause heat exhaustion which may lead to loss of consciousness. It may be necessary to implement a forced ventilation system to refresh and cool the air within the confined space.

WATER

Many confined spaces do not allow for ease of exit. If a large volume of water were to enter a confined space the consequences could be the drowning of workers due to the restrictions on space preventing rapid exit.

FREE-FLOWING SOLIDS

The term "free flowing solid" means any substance consisting of solid particles and which is of, or is capable of being in, a flowing or running consistency. This includes flour, grain, sugar, sand or other similar material. These materials are usually stored in silos (enclosed tank) that are classed as a confined space. Asphyxiation can result as a consequence of falling into a free flowing solid such as grain, due to sinking into the material as it becomes displaced as weight is applied. Because the material can appear firm, possibly because a crust of material has formed, someone may be tempted to access and walk on the crust in order to dislodge it. It is common for such a crust to break up without warning causing the person to fall into the free-flowing solid.

Silos are increasingly used on construction sites to store cement or mortar and they need to be maintained regularly. Hazards associated with maintaining this type of plant include: the residues of content (cement); working at height; difficulty of access and egress; oxygen deficiency and poor lighting levels and that there are potential hazards connected with incoming services.

RESTRICTED SPACE

Working space may be restricted, bringing workers into close contact with other hazards such as moving machinery, electricity or steam vents and pipes. The entrance to a confined space, for example a small access hole, may make escape or rescue in an emergency more difficult.

11.4 - Control measures for confined space working

Precautions for safe entry

AVOIDANCE WHERE POSSIBLE

Employers have a duty to prevent employees, or others who are to any extent within the employer's control, such as contractors, from entering or working inside a confined space where it is reasonably practicable to undertake the work without entering the space. Similarly, the self-employed should not enter or work inside a confined space where it is reasonably practicable to undertake the work without entering it.

In every situation, the employer or the self-employed must consider what measures can be taken to enable the work to be carried out without the need to enter the confined space. The measures might involve modifying the confined space itself to avoid the need for entry, or to enable the work to be undertaken from outside the space. In many cases it will involve modifying working practices.

The following are examples of modified working practices avoiding the need for entry:

- It is usually possible to test the atmosphere or sample the contents of confined spaces from outside.
- Using appropriate long tools and probes to do work.
- In some cases you can clean a confined space, or remove residues from it, from the outside using water jetting, steam or chemical cleaning, long-handled tools, or in-place cleaning systems.
- Blockages can be cleared in silos where grain or other flowing solids can 'bridge' or where voids can form by the use of remotely-operated rotating flail devices, vibrators and air purgers which avoid the need to enter the space.
- In some cases it is possible to see what is happening inside without going in by looking in through a porthole, sight glass, grille or hole. If a sight glass tends to become blocked, it can be cleaned with a wiper and washer. Lighting can be provided inside or by shining in through a window. The use of closed circuit television (CCTV) systems may be appropriate in some cases.

RISK ASSESSMENT AND PLANNING

There should be a safe system of work for operations inside confined spaces, and everyone should know and follow the system. A permit-to-work system may be required.

If entry is essential:

- Identify what work must be done in the confined space and the hazards involved.
- Consider if the space could be altered to make it permanently safe or if the work could be changed to make entry to the dangerous area unnecessary.
- Make sure workers have been trained in the dangers and precautions, including rescue procedures.
- Make sure the entrance to the space is big enough to allow workers wearing all the necessary equipment to climb in and out easily.
- Before entry, ventilate the space as much as possible, test the air inside the space and only enter if the test shows it is safe.
- After entry, continue to test the air for toxic substances, flammable gases and oxygen deficiency as necessary.
- If there is a flammable risk, the space must be ventilated until it is safe. When selecting equipment, remember heat or sparks from electrical or other equipment could ignite flammable vapours, so air-powered tools may be required. The risk from flammable vapours is very high when work is carried out on the tanks of petrol service stations and similar sites. This is work which may be safer left to a specialist contractor.
- Disturbing deposits and slurries in pipes and tanks may produce extra vapour, resulting in a greater risk, so clear deposits before entry where possible.
- If the air inside the space cannot be made fit to breath because of the presence of a toxic risk or lack of oxygen, workers must wear breathing apparatus.
- Never try to 'sweeten' the air in a confined space with oxygen as this can produce a fire and explosion risk.
- Workers inside the confined space should wear rescue harnesses, with lifelines attached, which run back to a point outside the confined spaces.
- Someone should be outside to keep watch and to communicate with anyone inside, raise the alarm in an emergency and take charge of rescue procedures if it becomes necessary. It is essential those outside the space know what to do in an emergency. They need to know how to use breathing apparatus if they are to effect a rescue. *See also - Emergency Arrangements - later in this element.*

PERMIT TO WORK PROCEDURES AND REQUIREMENTS

A permit-to-work system is a formal written system and is usually required where there is a reasonably foreseeable risk of serious injury in entering or working in the confined space. The permit-to-work procedure is an extension of the safe system to work, not a replacement for it. The use of a permit-to-work system does not, by itself, make the job safe. It supports the safe system, providing a ready means of recording findings and authorisations required to proceed with the entry. It also contains information, for example, time limits on entry, results of the gas testing, and other information that may be required during an emergency and which, when the job is completed, can also provide historical information on original entry conditions. A permit-to-work system is appropriate, for example:

- To ensure that the people working in the confined space are aware of the hazards involved and the identity, nature and extent of the work to be carried out.
- To ensure there is a formal check undertaken confirming elements of a safe system of work are in place. This needs to take place before people are allowed to enter or work in the confined space.
- Where there is a need to coordinate or exclude, using controlled and formal procedures, other people and their activities where they could affect work or conditions in the confined space.
- If the work requires the authorisation of more than one person, or there is a time-limit on entry. It may also be needed if communications with the outside are other than by direct speech, or if particular respiratory protective and/or personal protective equipment is required.

A permit-to-work should be cancelled once the operations to which it applies have finished.

LOCK-OFF

Where there are distinct hazards presented by stored energy such as plant and machinery or civil utilities which would need to be disconnected and isolated in order for work to be conducted safely, then a lock off tag out regime should be in place. For example, if there could be residual energy or potential of harm from electrical systems, gas mains, high pressure water mains, heat or chemical carrying lines, then it would be essential that these hazardous sources of danger should be locked off at distribution boxes, control valves and supply lines. An ideal safe system would be to have a multiple hasp type configuration with all key responsible personnel controlling or managing the work in the hazardous area to have a padlock and attach it to the hasp which would restrict the controlling member such as a distribution box isolator, control valve or distribution point therefore a unified decision would have to be made in order to reinstate these various hazardous supplies. Along with the lock off there would also be identification in the form of a tag notifying that the main control points have been isolated and by whom. Lock off and tagging procedures are usually fundamental and included with both safe systems of work and permits to work.

TRAINING AND THE USE OF COMPETENT PERSONS

To be competent to work safely in confined spaces, adequate training and experience in the particular work involved is essential. Training standards must be appropriate to the task, and to the individual's roles and responsibilities, so that work can be carried out safely. Where the risk assessment indicates that properly trained individuals can work for periods without supervision, you will need to check that they are competent to follow the established safe system of work and have been provided with adequate information and instruction about the work to be done. It is important that those that issue and work under a permit to work for entry into confined spaces are trained and competent to do so in general and that consideration is given to whether this training is sufficient for a specific confined space being worked in. If necessary, because of special features of the confined space, further training may be required. Anyone providing emergency rescue must be trained and competent to do so.

It is likely that general training will need to cover:

- Awareness of the Confined Spaces Regulations (CSR) 1997.
- An understanding of the work to be done, the hazards and the necessary precautions.
- An understanding of safe systems of work and permits to work, where appropriate.
- How emergencies arise and the dangers, and prepared emergency arrangements.

Specific training will relate to the type of equipment used and the circumstances of use. Refresher training should be planned and conducted in order to maintain knowledge and skill.

ATMOSPHERIC TESTING

Testing of the atmosphere may be needed where the atmosphere might be contaminated or abnormal. The appropriate choice of testing equipment will depend on particular circumstances. For example, when testing for toxic atmospheres, chemical detector tubes or portable atmospheric monitoring equipment is appropriate. However there may be cases requiring monitoring equipment specifically designed to measure for flammable atmospheres.

Only persons experienced and competent in the practice should carry out testing and records should be kept.

MEANS OF ACCESS

- Openings need to be sufficiently large and free from obstruction to allow the passage of persons wearing the necessary protective clothing and equipment and to allow access and egress for rescue purposes.
- Practice drills will help to check that the size of openings and entry procedures are satisfactory.
- Where entry to a confined space is necessary, employers will need to ensure that the necessary safety features are provided. For example, alongside openings which allow for safe access these might include a safety sign warning against unauthorised entry and platforms to enable safe working within the confined space.

Figure 11-18: Entrance to a confined space.   Source: ACT.

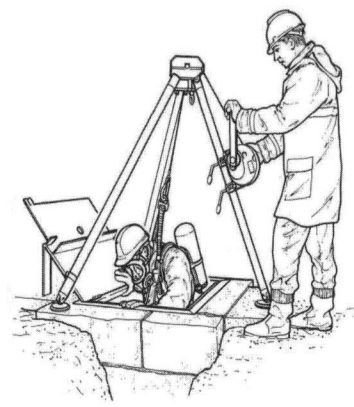

Figure 11-19: Confined space.   Source: HSG150, HSE.

PERSONAL PROTECTIVE EQUIPMENT

So far as is reasonably practicable, it should be ensured that a confined space is safe to work in without the need for personal protective equipment (PPE) and respiratory protective equipment (RPE) which should be a last resort, except for rescue work (including the work of the emergency services). Use of PPE and RPE may be identified as necessary in your risk assessment, in which case it needs to be suitable and should be provided and used by those entering and working in confined spaces. Such equipment is in addition to engineering controls and safe systems of work. The type of PPE provided will depend on the hazards identified but might include safety lines, harnesses and suitable breathing apparatus. Take account of foreseeable hazards that might arise, and the need for emergency evacuation

Wearing respiratory protective equipment and personal protective equipment can contribute to heat stress. In extreme situations cooling air may be required for protective suits.

Monitoring arrangements

The system of work must be monitored to ensure health and safety. This will include checking the permit to work and the practical precautions related to it. It is important that the atmosphere be monitored to ensure it stays breathable; this can be done by using specific sampler equipment or personal sampler equipment. Personal gas detectors should be worn whenever appropriate to take account of the hazard of local pockets of contaminant.

The use of personal communication equipment or a communication line will assist with monitoring the progress of the activities within the confined space and the condition of the workers. This can help decide suitable breaks, the need to stop tasks or the need to instigate emergency rescue.

It is every employer's duty to ensure that any personal protective equipment provided to his employees is maintained (including replaced or cleaned as appropriate) in an efficient state, in efficient working order and in good repair. Arrangements should be in place to ensure that any PPE issued for confined spaces working is inspected, maintained and all findings recorded.

Emergency arrangements

The CSR prohibit any person to enter or carry out work in a confined space unless there are suitable and sufficient rescue arrangements in place. Emergency arrangements shall be suitable and sufficient provided they:

- Require the provision and maintenance of resuscitation equipment.
- Require the provision and maintenance of such equipment as is necessary to enable the emergency rescue to be carried out effectively.
- Restrict, so far as is reasonably practicable, the risks to health and safety of any rescuer.
- Shall immediately be put into operation when circumstances arise requiring a rescue.

The arrangements for emergency rescue will depend on the nature of the confined space, the risks identified and consequently the likely nature of an emergency rescue.

The arrangements might need to cover:

- Rescue and resuscitation equipment.
- Special arrangements with local hospitals (e.g. for foreseeable poisoning).
- Raising the alarm and rescue.
- Safeguarding the rescuers.
- Safeguarding the third parties.
- Fire fighting.
- Control of plant.
- First aid.
- Public emergency services.

Element 12

Demolition - hazards and controls

Learning outcomes

On completion of this element, candidates should be able to demonstrate understanding of the content through the application of knowledge to familiar and unfamiliar situations. In particular they should be able to:

12.1 Identify the main hazards of demolition work.

12.2 Outline the appropriate control measures for demolition work, identify the purpose and scope of a pre-demolition survey, outline the main appropriate control measures that a demolition method statement should consider.

Content

12.1 - Demolition hazards	213
Basic hazards and factors relating to demolition	213
12.2 - Demolition appropriate control measures	215
General appropriate control measures for demolition work	215
Pre-demolition investigation / survey	216
Demolition method statement	218

UNIT NCC1 - ELEMENT 12 - DEMOLITION - HAZARDS AND CONTROLS

Sources of reference

A Guide to the Construction (Head Protection) Regulations (L102), HSE Books ISBN 0-7176-1478-6
British Standard Code of practice for demolition (BS 6187), British Standards Institution ISBN 0-5803-3206-3
Protecting the public: Your next move (HSG151), HSE Books ISBN 0-7176-1148-5

Relevant statutory provisions

The Construction (Design and Management) Regulations (CDM) 2007
The Environmental Protection Act (EPA) 1990
The Personal Protective Equipment at Work Regulations (PPER) 1992
The Provision and Use of Work Equipment Regulations (PUWER) 1998

12.1 - Demolition hazards

Basic hazards and factors relating to demolition

PREMATURE COLLAPSE

If a building selected for demolition comprises decaying materials and is unstable it may present an intrinsic hazard of premature collapse. In addition the process of demolition can create a hazard of premature collapse or increase the risk if it is already there. Removal of part of a supporting wall could be sufficient to release cast concrete floor slabs to drop from one level to another, and the resultant kinetic energy can lead to the further collapse of floors below. The likelihood of premature collapse is a particular consideration when using the wrecking ball method or carrying out partial demolition. In some cases the façade of a building may be left intact for renovation and the rest of the structure removed. In these circumstances great care must be taken to avoid freestanding walls and in order to provide adequate support to the structure. When carrying out wrecking ball demolition the impact of the ball is designed to weaken the structure; if it is not used in a planned and careful manner the wrong parts of the structure or too much of it may be weakened leading to premature collapse.

Premature collapse can also be caused when carrying out systematic demolition by hand, particularly when load bearing parts of the structure, such as beams, lintels, load bearing walls and roof supports are removed. Premature collapse can occur in a similar way when carrying out building/structure undermining or dismantling.

FALLS AND FALLING MATERIALS

Depending on the type of building and method of demolition, workers may be expected to work at a significant height, for example when demolishing a brick built structure by hand, and this can present a fall hazard. In the case of hand demolition it would be usual to remove parts of the structure in essentially the reverse order that it was erected. As such the same hazard of falling would exist as would be the case when constructing such a building. Fall hazards can often occur in the demolition process by the action of removing material, such as floors and stairs, or when access doors are not secured when part of the structure is removed. Part of the process of demolition may mean the removal of equipment built into the structure to prevent falls when in normal use, thus exposing hazards, such as a rail and barrier around an atrium walkway. As with other construction work there is a risk of a worker falling outside the framework of a scaffold erected as part of the demolition process, particularly where workers over-reach. If the site is not well controlled there is a possibility of unauthorised people gaining access to the area, and in so doing they could be exposed to the risk of falling.

The process of demolition involves the movement of large quantities of material to ground level. If this is not done in an organised way and material is allowed to fall it may expose workers and passers by to the hazard. This is particularly the case where workers are carrying out demolition above other workers or near to access routes. In addition, mechanical or explosive demolition may eject material which could fall significant distances from the demolition process. Even small items of material represent a significant hazard when they are allowed to fall from a great height. In demolition processes, depending on how well they are conducted, material may fall in significant quantities and unexpectedly.

Figure 12-1: Risk of falling or premature collapse. *Source: ACT.*

Figure 12-2: Falling materials. *Source: ACT.*

PLANT, VEHICLES AND OTHER EQUIPMENT OVERTURNING

Demolition processes create large quantities of material that accumulate at low level. As this builds up, demolition equipment may be working on top of it to gain access to part of a structure. This can cause the centre of gravity of the equipment to be moved towards the edge of or outside its stability base. Sudden movement or an unexpected heavy load can cause it to overbalance and overturn. Other ways in which the hazard of overturning may present itself are:

1. Weak ground support, e.g. cellars, sump covers, soft ground, causing one side of the equipment to be lower than another.
2. Operating outside the machine's capability, e.g. too large a load at too great a distance.
3. Striking or getting caught up in fixed obstructions.

MANUAL HANDLING

In demolition processes there are large quantities of a wide variety of materials to be moved. This presents a potential manual handling hazard, though, in many cases, much of the manual handling hazards have been removed by the use of mechanical handling equipment. In situations where demolition is done by hand there is usually a lot of debris to move which may be done also by hand as the structure is reduced. In some cases the distance debris is moved is limited by the provision of chutes. Where material is being salvaged this can mean an increase in manual handling is necessary in order to safeguard the condition of the material.

DUST AND FUME

Dust can be a nuisance and a risk to health to the public as well as to the workers. It may contain fungal and bacterial matter, which is pathogenic to humans, or asbestos. Structures that are being demolished may contain materials used in the construction of the structure which present a hazard as a dust or fume, for example asbestos as fire insulation, lead as a protective paint for metalwork. In addition, the use of the structure may lead to the presence of chemical deposits in the form of contaminated dusts; this may include toxic substances such as arsenic. As structures fall out of use it is not uncommon for pigeons to take up residence; their droppings contain a biological hazard that can lead to a lung disease called cyticosis if the dust from the droppings are breathed in. The process of demolition may liberate these materials such that they are present in the air where people are working or the public is passing by. If the process is conducted in dry conditions and windy conditions the dust may be more mobile and therefore presents more of a risk. Workers may carry out demolition work that creates large quantities of dust which may be considered a nuisance in the open air, such as brick dust, but when encountered in a confined area may be a hazard because of the quantity of dust in the air.

Carbon monoxide fumes present a chemical asphyxiant hazard and may be given off by equipment used to support the demolition process, e.g. demolition plant or generators used to provide temporary power supply.

Figure 12-3: Noise and dust.   Source: Rollaston Council.

Figure 12-4: Siting of plant.   Source: ACT.

NOISE AND VIBRATION

Much of the equipment used in the demolition process can present a noise hazard. Not surprisingly explosive charges present a noise hazard, as does impact equipment such as wrecking ball plant. Crusher and manipulation equipment can also present a noise hazard as the hydraulic system draws its power from the equipment's engine. Debris crusher plant can emit a large amount of noise as debris such as bricks is reduced. Hand demolition may be supplemented by the use of electric or pneumatic chisels which emit high noise levels. On a busy demolition site this cumulative noise can have an effect on workers and people nearby. Neighbours or other residents of an adjoining property may be affected by demolition work in the form of ground borne vibration, surface shock wave, or air overpressure from demolition work.

The use of hammer drills, pneumatic chisels, hammers and other similar equipment presents a vibration hazard that could lead to a work related upper limb disorder (WRULD). The operation of demolition equipment such as manipulation and bucket equipment can expose the operator to whole body vibration hazards.

EXISTENCE OF SERVICES SUCH AS GAS, ELECTRICITY AND WATER

Services that may be encountered during demolition present different hazards. Electricity may be still present in a building's mains supply because it had not been isolated and present a risk of electric shock. Sometimes there is a belief that mains circuits have been isolated but because it is fed from more than one route only part of the supply has been dealt with. Some buildings have backup systems in the form of batteries and/or capacitors which can present an unexpected electrical hazard when encountered. High voltage power supplies may pass underground or overhead, and these will present a significant hazard if not isolated before work commences.

Gas supplies routed into or under a building, if not isolated, may carry a risk of fire or explosion if they are disrupted. Residual quantities of gas left in isolated services within a building can present a lesser hazard but should not be ignored.

Water supplies that are damaged can present an indirect hazard in that they can lead to flooding of lower areas of a building where workers may be present. In addition, it may undermine part of the structure leading to premature collapse, increase the risk of slips trips and falls or aggravate a risk of electric shock.

HAZARDOUS SUBSTANCES

Hazardous substances may be present on the demolition site because they are left over from prior use. In industrial buildings this may mean such things as cadmium, arsenic, mercury, acids, alkalis and fuel oils and solvents (some of which may be prohibited by current good practices). In laboratory or hospital buildings that are to be demolished biological hazards may be present. Asbestos has been commonly used in buildings for many years and when the substance is broken up and fibres get into the air it can present a significant health risk. Asbestos fibres may get into the lungs and it can take many years (sometimes up to 40 years) before the symptoms of illnesses, like mesothelioma (cancer of the membrane lining the lungs), become apparent. The asbestos fibres may also be released into the air and contaminate clothing which may pose an additional risk of harm to other workers and the public in the vicinity.

During demolition sewers may become exposed and present a risk of biological contamination from substances within them. In addition hazardous substances from the site could contaminate sewers. Where vehicles are being used to transport the demolition waste material to a disposal site, they may inadvertently carry hazardous substances that may come off their wheels or drop off when travelling. Demolition work also possesses the potential to generate waste substances, such as oils, which can leak away into the soil.

12.2 - Demolition appropriate control measures

General appropriate control measures for demolition work

The Construction (Design and Management) Regulations (CDM) 2007 - Part 2 applies to all construction projects, of which demolition is a part. This focuses on management duties such as competence, co-operation, co-ordination, principles of prevention and duties of those involved in the project. In addition CDM Part 4 sets out duties related to health and safety on construction sites, including - good order and site security, stability of structures, demolition and dismantling, explosives, excavations, energy distribution installations, traffic routes and vehicles.

AVOIDANCE OF PREMATURE COLLAPSE

Irrespective of which demolition process is used it is important that the demolition be conducted in a systematic way that prevents premature collapse of the structure. This will mean working with a good understanding of the building's strong and weak points. It is important that the demolition process does not leave unsupported walls or parts of a structure. Those controlling the demolition process should have a good understanding of building structure and mechanics, to avoid removing parts of the structure that can place an excessive load on other fragile parts. Modern machines can be fitted with scissor jaws that can break down a wall in small pieces. The use of this process reduces the likelihood of major structural damage or premature collapse. When the wrecking ball method or partial demolition is conducted, as these processes often leave free standing structures, it is important that a careful demolition plan is adhered to. As part of this plan it is important to leave the structure in its most stable condition when not working on it. This may mean not starting a phase of demolition because it cannot be completed before the end of the day or providing shoring to the structure that is left. If a part of a building, such as a façade is to be left intact for renovation it is important to provide adequate longer term support.

PROTECTION FROM FALLS AND FALLING MATERIAL

The technical advances in mechanical plant have considerably reduced the risk to demolition workers of working at a height. Modern equipment enables a lot of demolition to be conducted by agile high reach equipment. Where it is necessary for people to work at height the same standards of protection from falls must be provided to demolition workers as are provided to other construction workers. This will include provision of safe work platforms, use of mechanical elevating work platforms (MEWPs), nets and fall arrest equipment.

In order to prevent debris falling on to passers-by, protective screens, and where appropriate fans, should be set up around scaffolds erected around buildings undergoing demolition. In addition, brick guards, debris nets and sheeting will help to contain falling materials and prevent them falling outside the framework of a scaffold erected as part of the demolition process. Areas of a structure under demolition that present a risk from falling material must be clearly demarcated from other areas. Where buildings are being demolished by hand a safe access route to the workplace must be maintained, which may include demarcated routes and temporary erection of covered areas. The use of audible and visual warnings will assist in removing people from hazard areas at times that they are at risk from a particular demolition task. Head protection is an essential last line of defence for workers in this environment.

SITING AND USE OF PLANT, VEHICLES AND OTHER EQUIPMENT

Access to the site should be established to enable the large plant and appliances to be taken or driven there safely. It may also be necessary to get permission to close roads or pathways for the duration of the work.

Any plant and equipment if used in the manner for which it was designed should not fall over and injure any person at work. In order to prevent overturning care should be taken to:

1. Identify weak ground conditions.
2. Avoid operating outside the machine's capability.
3. Create space sufficient to manoeuvre to avoid striking obstructions.
4. Maintain safe access to work areas by the prompt removal of demolition debris.

The key to preventing plant overturning is planning and control. The appointment of a competent person to organise the operation of the plant, vehicles and machinery is essential. Care with siting of plant is essential in order to prevent accidental contact with nearby structures, the building being demolished, power lines or other overhead obstructions. In restricted areas tight control of the use of plant and vehicles is essential; this may include physical barriers to restrict movement, where practicable.

It is important to restrict access to plant, vehicles and other machinery to prevent unauthorised use, by, for example, children. This will include securing plant in compounds, locking doors and securing keys effectively. Taking steps to prevent unauthorised access to the demolition site by using barriers, fencing, and increased security is the responsibility of the principal contractor.

DUST AND FUME

Large volumes of dust can be dissipated when demolition work is conducted. This can be in the form of brick dust asbestos or cement based materials. Asbestos is a special case, and the substance should be identified and removed by specialists who are authorised and registered by the Health and Safety Executive (HSE) to remove asbestos material. All asbestos should be removed before any demolition work takes place. The liberation of other dusts can be limited and restricted by the amount of demolition activities conducted at any one time. Consideration of when to demolish and dismantle is also a key factor as wind direction can play a significant role, affecting the direction of travel of dust and materials. Exclusion of workers while a dust producing activity is conducted and subsequent clean up processes can also control the exposure of workers to dust.

The build up of fume emissions from equipment can be reduced by limiting the amount of plant and machinery activities conducted at any one time. This can be combined with control measures or restrictions imposed to segregate plant and machinery from any person who is likely to come into contact with such fume emissions. The use of modern plant and machinery significantly reduces the level of emissions as they possess more efficient engines with reduced output and cleaner exhaust systems, such as larger scale versions of catalytic converters.

UNIT NCC1 - ELEMENT 12 - DEMOLITION - HAZARDS AND CONTROLS

Where fume may be emitted form the actual demolition process, for example when demolishing some form of storage vessel such as in a chemical plant or hospital, then potential emission should be restricted by draining any system or vessel holding fume producing substances in a controlled and planned manner.

MANUAL HANDLING

Most of the demolition process should, where possible, be done by using mechanical equipment to prevent or reduce any potential manual handling hazards. Shoots and conveyers should be used to transport debris from the upper floors of the building into skips, thereby eliminating any manual handling between floors.

NOISE AND VIBRATION

Noise and vibration can be a major cause of harm to workers; therefore it is important that suitable and sufficient risk assessments are produced. Exposure to noise and vibration should be minimised by the careful selection and maintenance of equipment such that levels emitted are kept to a minimum. For example, vibration damped seats for cab operated equipment, vibration mats for areas where workers stand to operate crusher plant, and vibration damped handles for power tools.

Exposure levels can be controlled by the careful use of task rotation such that those exposed to high noise and vibration levels are periodically moved to tasks that have low exposure levels. Where levels of noise are above the action values hearing protection must be made available or provided, as appropriate and it is the duty of the employer to enforce and ensure that such protection is worn. A noise protected refuge may be required in order to allow workers to move out of noisy areas to limit their exposure during rest breaks.

PROTECTION OF THE ENVIRONMENT

Where vehicles are being used to transport the demolition waste material to a disposal site, then provision should be made for wheel washes and the cleaning of the highway by a road sweeper. Waste substances, such as oils, must not be allowed to leak away into the soil and must be disposed of in a controlled manner. During demolition sewers may become exposed and be at risk of contamination from substances, so care should be taken to identify and protect them from entry of such materials. In the same way it may be necessary to establish interceptor pits to control water run off into water courses and/or fit temporary pressure drain covers.

COMPETENCE OF WORKFORCE

It is the client's responsibility to check the competence of the principal contractor. In turn, the principal contractor must ensure the competence of contractors appointed to conduct demolition and dismantling. Competence checks can include taking up references on past work and reviewing contractor's health and safety policies and procedures. It is important to recognise that demolition contractors may not be competent to act as principal contractors on larger or more complex projects. It is important that demolition work is controlled by someone with an understanding of buildings/structures and in turn that workers understand the effects on the building or structure that their work will make. In this way premature collapse may be prevented. Operators of plant and equipment must be competent to operate the specific items they use, in demolition circumstances. Operation in demolition work can be quite different to operation in other building work and is particularly affected by the terrain of the demolition work area.

Figure 12-5: Doubtful competence of workers. *Source: Lincsafe.*

Figure 12-6: Use of demolition equipment. *Source: ACT.*

Pre-demolition investigation / survey

PURPOSE OF PRE-DEMOLITION INVESTIGATION / SURVEY

Before any demolition work begins a survey is carried out to ensure that the demolition can go ahead safely and that property surrounding the site is protected from the demolition work as it progresses. The survey should give special consideration to the location of the intended demolition work, for example if it is near a place of worship, school, hospital, shopping area, leisure centre, or housing estate then the survey may identify the need for extra provisions to control risks to members of the public. It is important to know the previous use of the building/structure; it may still contain toxic or flammable materials, biological hazards or even radioactive materials or sources.

It is the client's responsibility to ensure that any building/structure to be demolished is adequately surveyed.

TYPE OF STRUCTURE

The survey should clearly identify the type of structure to be worked on e.g. high rise office blocks, chimneys or old buildings, as this will have a considerable impact on the method of demolition, the hazards present and the precautions to be taken.

METHOD OF CONSTRUCTION

The method of construction will also have a similar effect. The method of construction will particularly influence the method and order of demolition. Where buildings/structures contain pre-stressed or post-stressed concrete beams, this must be identified in the survey. These buildings/structures have beams containing steel rods held under tension, which helps to bind the building/structure together. If part of the structure is demolished this may release the forces under tension and cause premature collapse.

Figure 12-7: Building structure. *Source: ACT.*

Figure 12-8: Structural condition and substances. *Source: ACT.*

STRUCTURAL CONDITION

The structural condition of the building/structure should be surveyed in order to identify any degradation of materials that might influence the method and order of demolition. The structural condition might present such risks that it is not safe to carry out demolition by entering inside the building/structure and other means, such as the use of mechanical demolition equipment, may be required. When demolition work is done by hand it involves the demolition worker moving about at height on materials that may have degraded and are not able to sustain their weight. In this type of operation full scaffolding and other platforms should be provided and the building demolished in the reverse order of erection.

PRESENCE OF CELLARS

Basements, cellars, wells or storage tanks need to be identified in order to apply control measures to the risks they create. Workers may fall through into underground areas, while tanks pose a special risk if they have held or still hold toxic or flammable materials.

IDENTIFICATION OF SERVICES

Details and location of all the public utility services must be identified in order to identify the hazards they present and to take action to isolate, divert or otherwise protect them. This will involve the examination of service location drawings held by the utility service organisations. Most of these will be buried services, including gas pipes, electricity cables, water pipes and sewerage. This will be supported by visual examination, test equipment and, in some cases, test digging to establish the specific location and status of the services.

Figure 12-9: Hazardous substances. *Source: Stocksigns.*

Figure 12-10: Proximity of other structures. *Source: D Hitchen.*

PRESENCE OF HAZARDOUS SUBSTANCES

There may be health hazards present which could affect the demolition worker or others, e.g. Weil's disease from rats, breathing difficulties from the dust of pigeon droppings or chemicals from the previous use of the building. A particular health hazard that should be identified at time of survey is possible exposure to asbestos, which can present a significant risk, especially if workers are unaware of its presence and no precautions have been taken. Asbestos may be present in lagging of boilers and pipe work, fire proofing of structures and roofing materials. It is important to obtain details of any prior survey conducted on the building/structure by the owner/occupier, for consideration as part of the pre-demolition survey.

PROXIMITY AND CONDITION OF OTHER STRUCTURES AND ROADWAYS

The survey should seek to identify the proximity and condition of other structures to determine the influence they may have on the demolition process.

UNIT NCC1 - ELEMENT 12 - DEMOLITION - HAZARDS AND CONTROLS

If a structure is close to the building/structure to be demolished and is in poor condition it may be necessary to shore it up and route demolition plant and equipment away from it. The proximity and condition of roads to a demolition site is an essential item to survey. If roads are good, and wide enough to take plant transport vehicles and debris vehicles, this will have a positive influence on the safety of the demolition activity. If restrictions exist it may be necessary to obtain police co-operation to clear roads and time delivery of plant. A new, dedicated access may be necessary to avoid using a small road and provide access to a larger road near by. This may influence the order of demolition as part of the building/structure may need to be demolished to create better access. Early identification of risk and nuisance to adjoining land, buildings or road users will enable early notification to those affected.

Demolition method statement

The Construction (Design and Management) Regulations (CDM) 2007 - Regulation 22 requires planning of construction projects, including demolition activities. Part of the planning work for any project should include the development of method statements. These should consider all or some of the following issues where necessary.

TYPE AND SEQUENCE OF DEMOLITION

Piecemeal

Piecemeal demolition is done by hand using hand held tools and is sometimes a preliminary to other methods. It can be completed or begun by machines. For example, when demolishing a tall chimney with occupied buildings in close proximity, the job may commence with the painstaking task of dismantling by hand - brick by brick. When the structure has been reduced to about 10 metres, then conventional heavy equipment can be used.

Controlled collapse and pre-weakening

Deliberate controlled collapse involves the pre-weakening of the structure or building. This involves removing key structural members so the remaining structure collapses under its own weight.

There are several problems associated with this method of demolition:

- The structure may collapse to a greater extent than was anticipated.
- The planned collapse may only be a partial collapse and could leave the structure hazardous and insecure.
- The resultant debris may be projected over a wider area than anticipated.
- The pile of debris that is left after the collapse of the structure may be in a dangerous condition, presenting a serious risk to those who remove it.

One method of removing the key structural members is overturning by wire rope pulling. Wires are attached to the main supports, which are pulled away using a heavy tracked vehicle or a winch to provide the motive power. The area must be cleared of workers for this operation and there must be enough clearance for the vehicle to move the distance required to pull out the structural supports.

Problems associated with this method arise when the wire becomes overstressed. If it breaks, then whiplash can occur which can have sufficient force to slice through the human body. The forces applied may be enough to overturn the winch or the tracked vehicle. Another problem can occur when the action of pulling has begun and there is inadequate power to complete it.

Use of explosives - the use of explosives requires the expertise of an experienced explosives engineer. Also, the Health and Safety Executive (HSE) should be consulted to ensure compliance with The Control of Explosives Regulations 1991. There are a number of factors to be considered for safe demolition with the use of explosives, which include:

- The local and structural conditions must be considered when fixing the size of the charges. The structure to be blasted can be divided into a number of sections and suitable charges applied to each section.
- Shot holes should be drilled electrically. Drilling pneumatically could cause vibration, which could result in premature collapse.
- Charges should not be placed near cast iron as it easily shatters into shrapnel.
- The area around the structure being demolished and the firing point should be barricaded and unauthorised persons not allowed to enter.
- The demolition engineer must be satisfied that no dangerous situation or condition has been left or created. The danger zone must be barricaded until rendered safe.

Figure 12-11: Hydraulic demolition jaws. *Source: ACT.*

Figure 12-12: Hydraulic demolition grapple. *Source: ACT.*

ISOLATION OR DIVERSION OF SERVICES

It is important to isolate services at the furthest point practicable from the structure to be demolished, for example, at the site boundary. This may include gas or water services isolated in the pavement outside the demolition site. This will help to remove the hazard at source and is preferable to local isolation of the services within the building. It should be remembered that some systems will store energy from services and should not be presumed safe merely by isolating the service. This includes electricity stored in capacitors and batteries, stored water in tanks, and compressed oils / air in pressure systems.

EQUIPMENT TO BE USED

The method statement should specify the type and capacity of equipment to be used at different stages in the demolition process, in order that it can be used within its capability and for the right purpose. The equipment specified should match the factors identified at time of survey. Due to the dangerous nature of demolition work all equipment should only be used by trained, competent and authorised workers. The method statement should take account of this and the availability of suitable operators at the demolition site.

PROTECTION OF PUBLIC AND OTHERS

The method statement should specify the measures to remove and prevent people accessing the building/structure, such as children, persons sleeping rough and those who wish to salvage materials, as well as people who are just passing by. The boundaries of the demolition site need to provide an effective barrier to persons not involved with the work, typically 2.5 metres high fencing with warning signs posted around it. Fencing must be maintained to a good standard and checks must be made at the end of each day to ensure it is in place and up to standard. Where the demolition process is close to where the public may pass they should be protected from falling materials by the use of sheets, brick guards, nets, fans and covered areas. In some cases demolition work in such an area may take place at a specified time and the public prevented from accessing the area.

Figure 12-13: Protection of public.   Source: ACT.

Figure 12-14: Disposal of waste.   Source: ACT.

SITE ACCESS AND SECURITY

Unauthorised access to sites should be controlled. Single access points are easier to control, but some larger sites may have several, each point should be controlled and monitored. The site should have clearly identified physical boundaries; these may take the form of fences or barriers. Signage should also be posted on the perimeter; access points should be clearly indicated. Site rules and regulations should be posted at all access points. Good lighting can be added to assist security measures and deter unauthorised access. Security is paramount due to the dangerous nature of the work, and some sites employ external security companies to control unauthorised access. There should be a site register for all visitors. It may be a requirement, due to the dangerous nature of the work, that visitors are accompanied in the whole or part of the site.

ACCESS AND EGRESS

The method statement should give consideration to the movement of vehicles and people on and around the site. Arrangements for access and egress for loading and unloading materials should be considered. Segregation of vehicle and pedestrian traffic should be specified. Access and egress routes should be kept clear of any obstructions, with traffic and pedestrian routes clearly marked and signed. Emergency routes may have unique signage. All routes should be inspected on a regular basis for compliance. Where possible, it is good practice to operate a one way traffic management system.

TRAINING AND WELFARE ARRANGEMENTS

Adequate training and information must be provided to visitors, new workers, transferred employees from another site and contractors. This should take the form of an induction course and include the following: outline of the project; site rules; key personnel and line managers; sites health and safety risks - transport, any site contamination, hazardous substances and manual handling; safe systems of work, permits to work systems; security arrangements; hearing protection zones; personal protective equipment (PPE) provision, storage and cleaning stations; housekeeping and material storage; first-aid arrangements; reporting of accidents or incidents; emergency procedures; welfare arrangements e.g. personal clothing storage, drying facilities, showers/toilets and rest areas.

The method statement should set out details of welfare facilities suitable for the demolition activity. This may include specialist decontamination facilities for workers dealing with contaminated materials or asbestos.

NAMED RESPONSIBLE PERSONS

The client has the ultimate responsibility for the demolition project. The Principal Contractor should appoint a named individual or agent to act on their behalf.

CO-ORDINATION OF WORK ACTIVITIES ON SITE

The method statement should specify measures for co-operation and co-ordination between people involved in the demolition project, for example, CDM Co-ordinator, Principal Contractor and contractors. The site manager or agent of the Principal Contractor has overall control and co-ordination of the demolition process. The demolition process should follow the approved plan produced in conjunction with the Client, CDM Co-ordinator and the Principal Contractor. The site manager or agent co-ordinates and controls the demolition process; taking into account any changes or new hazards identified, they liaise with employees or sub-contractors and update any health and safety requirements.

SEPARATION AND DISPOSAL OF WASTE

Taking into account the size of the site, waste material must not be allowed to accumulate. This means controlling build up of waste at local points around the site, particularly where they impede access and egress, as well as any major accumulation points. The disposal of building materials must be controlled by consignment certificates and taken to a recognised licensed landfill site. Care must also be taken of hazardous waste such as asbestos.

EMERGENCY PROCEDURES

The method statement should set out emergency procedures and arrangements. These should be sufficient for dealing with foreseeable emergencies e.g. fire, explosions, chemical leaks, premature collapse of the structure. Fire detection, fire alarms, fire-fighting equipment, first-aid provisions, site evacuation, and rescue plans should form part of these arrangements. The method statement should specify necessary training in the use of emergency techniques and equipment.

Relevant statutory provisions

Content

Chemicals (Hazard Information and Packaging for Supply) Regulations (CHIP 3) 2002.................................. 222
Chemicals (Hazard Information and Packaging for Supply) (Amendment) Regulations 2005......................... 224
Confined Spaces Regulations (CSR) 1997... 224
Construction (Design and Management) Regulations (CDM) 2007 225
Construction (Head Protection) Regulations (CHPR) 1989.. 234
Control of Asbestos Regulations (CAR) 2006... 235
Control of Noise at Work Regulations (CNWR) 2005 237
Control of Substances Hazardous to Health Regulations (COSHH) 2002 239
Control of Substances Hazardous to Health (Amendment) Regulations 2004... 243
Control of Vibration at Work Regulations (CVWR) 2005 243
Dangerous Substances and Explosive Atmospheres Regulations (DSEAR) 2002.. 244
Electricity at Work Regulations (EWR) 1989 246
Environmental Protection Act (EPA) 1990 248
Fire (Scotland) Act 2005 249
Hazardous Waste Regulations (HWR) 2005 251
Health and Safety (Display Screen Equipment) Regulations (DSE) 1992 254
Health and Safety (First-Aid) Regulations (FAR) 1981 254
Health and Safety (Safety Signs and Signals) Regulations (SSSR) 1996 255
Health and Safety at Work etc. Act (HASAWA) 1974 255
Ionising Radiations Regulations (IRR) 1999... 258
Lifting Operations and Lifting Equipment Regulations (LOLER) 1998 260
Management of Health and Safety at Work Regulations (MHSWR) 1999 260
Management of Health and Safety at Work & Fire Precautions (Workplace) (Amendment) Regulations 2003 264
Manual Handling Operations Regulations (MHOR) 1992... 265
New Roads and Street Works Act 1991 266
Personal Protective Equipment at Work Regulations (PPER) 1992... 268
Provision and Use of Work Equipment Regulations (PUWER) 1998 269
Regulatory Reform (Fire Safety) Order (RRFSO) 2005.. 271
Reporting of Injuries, Diseases and Dangerous Occurrences Regulations (RIDDOR) 1995.......................... 273
Supply of Machinery (Safety) Regulations (SMSR) 1992... 275
Work at Height Regulations (WAH) 2005 277
Work at Height (Amendment) Regulations 2007 278

RELEVANT STATUTORY PROVISIONS

Chemicals (Hazard Information and Packaging for Supply) Regulations (CHIP 3) 2002

Arrangement of regulations

1) Citation and commencement.
2) Interpretation.
3) Application of these Regulations.
4) Meaning of the approved supply list.
5) Classification of substances and preparations dangerous for supply.
6) Safety data sheets for substances and preparations dangerous for supply.
7) Advertisements for substances dangerous for supply.
8) Packaging of substances and preparations dangerous for supply.
9) Labelling of substances and preparations dangerous for supply.
10) Particular labelling requirements for certain preparations.
11) Methods of marking or labelling packages.
12) Child resistant fastenings and tactile warning devices.
13) Retention of classification data for substances and preparations dangerous for supply.
14) Notification of the constituents of certain preparations dangerous for supply to the poisons advisory centre.
15) Exemption certificates.
16) Enforcement, civil liability and defence.
17) Transitional provisions.
18) Extension outside Great Britain.
19) Revocations and modifications.

Schedule 1   Classification of substances and preparations dangerous for supply.
Schedule 2   Indications of danger and symbols for substances and preparations dangerous for supply.
Schedule 3   Classification provisions for preparations dangerous for supply.
Schedule 4   Classification provisions for preparations intended to be used as pesticides.
Schedule 5   Headings under which particulars are to be provided in safety data sheets.
Schedule 6   Particulars to be shown on labels for substances and preparations dangerous for supply and certain other preparations.
Schedule 7   British and International Standards relating to child resistant fastenings and tactile warning devices.
Schedule 8   Modifications to certain enactments relating to the flashpoint of flammable liquids.

The Chemicals (Hazard Information and Packaging for Supply) Regulations (CHIP 3) 2002 apply to those who supply dangerous chemicals. They are based on European Directives, which apply to all EU and European Economic Area (EEA) Countries. The Directives are constantly reviewed and changed when necessary. When changes do occur to the Directives, CHIP is changed as well (about once a year). CHIP may be changed by amending Regulations or if there are major changes, the principal Regulations are revised.

The Regulations are designed to protect people's health and the environment by:

- Identification of the hazardous properties of materials (classification).
- Provision of health and safety information to users (safety data sheet and label).
- Packaging of materials safely.

CHIP introduces a new scheme to classify products based upon a calculation method.

Outline of key points

REGULATION 6 (1)

'The supplier of a substance or preparation dangerous for supply **shall** provide the recipient of that substance or preparation with a safety data sheet containing information under the headings specified in Schedule 5 to enable the recipient of that substance or preparation to take the necessary measures relating to the protection of health and safety at work and relating to the protection of the environment and the safety data sheet shall clearly show its date of first publication or latest revision as the case may be.'

The test of adequacy of the information provided in a safety data sheet is whether the information enables the recipient to take the necessary measures relating to the protection of health and safety at work and relating to the protection of the environment.

This does not mean that the safety data sheet will take the place of a risk assessment which would require specific detail of the circumstances in which the chemical is to be used.

GUIDANCE ON THE CONTENTS OF SAFETY DATA SHEETS

The headings shown here are those specified in Schedule 5 of CHIP 3. However, information given here is indicative of the issues to be addressed by the person compiling the safety data sheet and do not impose an absolute requirement for action or controls.

Identification of the substance/preparation and the company
- Name of the substance.
- Name, address and telephone number (including emergency number) of supplier.

Composition/information on ingredients
- Sufficient information to allow the recipient to identify readily the associated risks.

Hazards identification
- Important hazards to man and the environment.
- Adverse health effects and symptoms.

First-aid measures
- Whether immediate attention is required.
- Symptoms and effects including delayed effects.
- Specific information according to routes of entry.
- Whether professional advice is advisable.

Fire fighting measures
- Suitable extinguishing media.
- Extinguishing media that must not be used.
- Hazards that may arise from combustion e.g., gases, fumes etc.
- Special protective equipment for fire fighters.

Accidental release measures
- Personal precautions such as removal of ignition sources, provision of ventilation, avoid eye/skin contact etc.
- Environmental precautions such as keep away from drains, need to alert neighbours etc.
- Methods for cleaning up e.g. absorbent materials. Also, "Never use…."

Handling and storage
- Advice on technical measures such as local and general ventilation.
- Measures to prevent aerosol, dust, fire etc.
- Design requirements for specialised storage rooms.
- Incompatible materials.
- Special requirements for packaging/containers.

Exposure controls/personal protection
- Engineering measures taken in preference to personal protective equipment (PPE) 1992.
- Where PPE is required, type of equipment necessary e.g. type of gloves, goggles, barrier cream etc.

Physical and chemical properties
- Appearance, e.g. solid, liquid, powder, etc.
- Odour (if perceptible).
- Boiling point, flash point, explosive properties, solubility etc.

Stability and reactivity
- Conditions to avoid such as temperature, pressure, light, etc.
- Materials to avoid such as water, acids, alkalis, etc.
- Hazardous by-products given off on decomposition.

Toxicological information
- Toxicological effects if the substance comes into contact with a person.
- Carcinogenic, mutagenic, toxic for reproduction etc.
- Acute and chronic effects.

Ecological information
- Effects, behaviour and environmental fate that can reasonably be foreseen.
- Short and long term effects on the environment.

Disposal considerations
- Appropriate methods of disposal e.g. land-fill, incineration etc.

Transport information
- Special precautions in connection with transport or carriage.
- Additional information as detailed in the Carriage of Dangerous Goods by Road Regs (CPL) 1994 may also be given.

Regulatory information
- Health and safety information on the label as required by CHIP 3.
- Reference might also be made to Health and Safety at Work etc Act (HASAWA) 1974 and Control of Substances Hazardous to Health Regulations (COSHH) 2002.

Other information
- Training advice.
- Recommended uses and restrictions.
- Sources of key data used to compile the data sheet.

RELEVANT STATUTORY PROVISIONS

RISK PHRASES AND SAFETY PHRASES

More useful information to help ensure the safe use of dangerous substances comes in the form of risk phrases and safety phrases. These are often displayed either on the container label or in the safety data sheet. There are currently 48 risk phrases and 53 safety phrases. Some examples are given below and detailed information can be found in the ACOP to (CHIP) 2.

Risk Phrase		*Safety Phrase*	
R3	Risk of explosion by shock, friction, fire or other sources of ignition.	S2	Keep out of reach of children.
R20	Harmful by inhalation.	S20	When using do not eat or drink.
R30	Can become highly flammable in use.	S25	Avoid contact with eyes.
R45	May cause cancer.	S36	Wear suitable protective clothing.
R47	May cause birth defects.	S41	In case of fire and/or explosion do not breathe fumes.

Absence of hazard symbols or risk and safety advice does not mean the item is harmless.

Chemicals (Hazard Information and Packaging for Supply) (Amendment) Regulations 2005

These Regulations came into force on the 31st October 2005.

The principal Regulations shall be amended as follows.

(2) In regulation 2(1) -

(a) for the definition of "the approved supply list" substitute -

"the approved supply list" means the document entitled "Information Approved for the Classification and Labelling of Dangerous Substances and Dangerous Preparations (Eighth Edition)" approved by the Health and Safety Commission on 26 July 2005;"; - (updated from April 2002).

(b) Omit the definition of "the CDGCPL Regulations".

(3) In regulation 5(12)(a), for "and" substitute "or" - *this changes the meaning of the term "supply".*

(4) In regulation 7(3)(a), for the words "the CDGCPL Regulations" substitute "the Carriage of Dangerous Goods and Use of Transportable Pressure Equipment Regulations 2004".

(5) In regulation 8(1), for the words "Subject to regulations 9 and 10 of the CDGCPL Regulations (which allow combined carriage and supply labelling in certain circumstances) and paragraphs (8) to (12)" substitute "Subject to regulation 8A and paragraphs (8) to (12)".

(6) In regulation 9(2), for the words "regulations 9 and 10 of the CDGCPL Regulations (which allow combined carriage and supply labelling in certain circumstances)" substitute "regulation 8A".

(7) Omit regulations 13 and 18(2).

(8) In Part II of Schedule 3, in Table VIA, in line 1 for "0.%" substitute "0.1%" - *reclassification of gaseous substances or preparations to be assigned R45 or R49.*

(9) In Part I of Schedule 5 -

(a) In paragraph 2(4), for "22(1)" substitute "6".

(b) In paragraph 3(5), for "(2)" substitute "(3)".

Confined Spaces Regulations (CSR) 1997

Arrangement of regulations

1) Citation, commencement and interpretation.
2) Disapplication of regulations.
3) Duties.
4) Work in confined spaces.
5) Emergency arrangements.
6) Exemption certificates.
7) Defence in proceedings.
8) Extension outside Great Britain.
9) Repeal and revocations.

Outline of key points

The Confined Spaces Regulations (CSR) 1997 repeal and replace earlier provisions contained in s.30 of the Factories Act 1961.

A failure to appreciate the dangers associated with confined spaces has led not only to the deaths of many workers, but also to the demise of some of those who have attempted to rescue them.

A confined space is not only a space which is small and difficult to enter, exit or work in; it can also be a large space, but with limited/restricted access. It can also be a space which is badly ventilated e.g. a tank or a large tunnel.

The Confined Spaces Regulations (CSR) 1997, define a confined space as any place, including any chamber, tank, vat, silo, pit, pipe, sewer, flue, well, or other similar space, in which, by virtue of its enclosed nature, there is a foreseeable risk of a 'specified occurrence'.

Construction (Design and Management) Regulations (CDM) 2007

Revisions to the Construction (Design and Management) (CDM) Regulations (1994) (CDM 94) came into force on 6th April 2007.

Construction remains a disproportionately dangerous industry where improvements in health and safety are urgently needed. The improvements require significant and permanent changes in duty holder attitudes and behaviour. Since CDM 94 was introduced in 1995, concerns have been raised that their complexity, and the bureaucratic approach of many duty holders, frustrate the Regulations' underlying health and safety objectives. These views were supported by an industry-wide consultation in 2002, resulting in the Health and Safety Commission's (HSC) decision to revise the Regulations.

The new, simplified CDM Regulations revise and bring together the existing CDM 1994 and the Construction (Health Safety and Welfare) (CHSWR) Regulations 1996 into a single regulatory package. They are supported by an Approved Code of Practice (ACoP) and industry-approved guidance.

To give construction and design professionals time to plan and prepare for the regulatory changes, the ACoP was made available in February 2007, two months before the regulations came into force.

The new CDM regulations offer an opportunity for a step change in health and safety performance and will be used to re-emphasise the health, safety and broader business benefits of a well-managed and co-ordinated approach to the management of health and safety in construction.

Arrangement of regulations

Part 1 - Introduction

1. Citation and commencement.
2. Interpretation.
3. Application.

Part 2 - General management duties applying to construction projects

4. Competence.
5. Co-operation.
6. Co-ordination.
7. General principles of prevention.
8. Election by clients.
9. The client's duty in relation to arrangements for managing projects.
10. Client's duty in relation to information.
11. Duties of designers.
12. Designs prepared or modified outside Great Britain.
13. Duties of contractors.

Part 3 - Additional duties where project is notifiable

14. Appointments by the client.
15. Client's duty in relation to information.
16. The client's duty in relation to the start of construction phase.
17. The client's duty in relation to the health and safety file.
18. Additional duties of designers.
19. Additional duties of contractors.
20. General duties of CDM co-ordinators.
21. Notification of project by CDM co-ordinator.
22. Duties of the principal contractor.
23. Principal contractor's duties in relation to the construction phase plan.
24. Principal contractor's duties in relation to co-operation and consultation with workers.

Part 4 - Duties relating to health and safety on construction sites

25. Application of regulations 26-44.
26. Safe places of work.
27. Good order and site security.
28. Stability of structures.
29. Demolition or dismantling.
30. Explosives.

RELEVANT STATUTORY PROVISIONS

31. Excavations.
32. Cofferdams and caissons.
33. Reports of inspections.
34. Energy distribution installations.
35. Prevention of drowning.
36. Traffic routes.
37. Vehicles.
38. Prevention of risk from fire etc.
39. Emergency procedures.
40. Emergency routes and exits.
41. Fire detection and fire-fighting.
42. Fresh air.
43. Temperature and weather protection.
44. Lighting.

Part 5 - General

45. Civil liability.
46. Enforcement in respect of fire.
47. Transitional provision.
48. Revocation and amendments.

SCHEDULES

Schedule 1 (regulation 21(1), (2) and (4)) - Particulars to be notified to the Executive

Schedule 2 (regulation 11, 16(l)(b)and 19(4)) - Welfare facilities

1. Sanitary conveniences.
2. Washing facilities.
3. Drinking water.
4. Changing rooms and lockers.
5. Facilities for rest.

Schedule 3 (regulation 33(1)(b)) - Particulars to be included in a report of inspection

Schedule 4 (regulation 48(1)) - Revocation of instruments

Schedule 5 (regulation 48(2)) - Amendments

OUTLINE OF KEY POINTS - PART 2 - GENERAL MANAGEMENT DUTIES

Competence

4(1) No person on whom these regulations place a duty shall:

    (a) Appoint or engage a co-ordinator, designer, principal contractor or contractor unless he has taken reasonable steps to ensure that he is competent.

    (b) Accept such appointment or engagement unless he is competent.

    (c) Arrange for or instruct a worker to carry out or manage design or construction work unless he is -

        (i) Competent.

        (ii) Under the supervision of a competent person.

Co-operation

5(1) Every person concerned in a project on whom a duty is placed by these regulations, including paragraph (2), shall:

    (a) Co-operate with any other person concerned in any project involving construction work at the same or an adjoining site so far as is necessary to enable the latter to perform any duty or function under these regulations.

    (b) Seek the co-operation of any other person concerned in any project involving construction work at the same or an adjoining site so far as is necessary to enable the former to perform any duty or function under these regulations.

(2) Every person concerned in a project who is working under the control of another person shall report to him anything which he is aware is likely to endanger the health or safety of himself or others.

Co-ordination

6   All persons shall coordinate their activities with one another in a manner which ensures, so far as is reasonably practicable, the health and safety of persons affected by the work.

General principles of prevention

7   Every person on whom a duty is placed by these regulations in relation to the design, planning and preparation of a project shall take account of the general principles of prevention in the performance of those duties during all the stages of the project.

Election by clients

8.   If, in relation to a project, one or more clients elect in writing to be treated for the purposes of these regulations as the only clients, other clients who have agreed in writing to such election shall not be subject to any duty owed by a client under these regulations after such election and consent, save the duties in regulations 5(1)(a), 10(1) so far as it relates to information in his possession, and 12(1).

The client's arrangements for managing projects

9(1)   The client shall take reasonable steps to ensure that arrangements are made, and maintained throughout the project, for managing it which are suitable to ensure:

   (a)   that -

   (i) the construction work can be carried out; and

   (ii) any structure to which the construction work relates, and which is designed for use as a place of work, can be used,

   without risk to health or safety; and

   (b)   the welfare of the persons carrying out the construction work.

(2)   The arrangements referred to in paragraph (1) shall include:

   (a)   the allocation of resources (including time) to:

   (i) the design of a structure;

   (ii) planning and preparation for construction work; and

   (iii) the construction work itself,

   which are, so far as the client in question can reasonably determine, adequate; and

(b)   arrangements for:

   (i) review and revision of the arrangements;

   (ii) review of the suitability and compatibility of designs and for any modification;

   (iii) ensuring that persons arc appointed under regulation 8 or engaged as designers or contractors in a suitable sequence and in good time;

   (iv) the planning for and monitoring of construction work; (v) ensuring that the duties in regulations 5 and 16 are performed; and

   (vi) communication.

Client's duty in relation to information

10(1)   The client shall ensure that the persons specified in regulation 13(l)(f)(i) to (iii) are promptly provided by the co-ordinator with all the information in the client's possession, or prepared by the co-ordinator, or which is reasonably obtainable (or with such of the information as is relevant to the person to whom the co-ordinator provides it), including:

   (a)   any such information in a health and safety file;

   (b)   any such further information about or affecting the site or the construction work;

   (c)   information provided by a designer under regulation 14(5);

   (d)   the minimum notice which will be allowed to the principal contractor, and the contractors directly appointed by the client, for planning and preparation for construction work, which is relevant to the purposes specified in paragraph (2).

(2)   The purposes referred to in paragraph (1) are:

   (a)   to secure so far as is reasonably practicable the health, safety of persons engaged in the construction work and the health and safety of persons liable to be affected by the way in which it is carried out;

   (b)   without prejudice to sub-paragraph (a), to assist the persons to whom information is provided under this regulation

   (i) to perform their duties and functions under these regulations; and

RELEVANT STATUTORY PROVISIONS

(ii) to determine the adequacy of the resources referred to in regulation 7(2) to be allocated by them.

Duties of designers

11   No designer shall commence work in relation to a project unless any client for the project is aware of his duties under these regulations.

Every designer shall in preparing or modifying a design which may be used in construction work in Great Britain avoid foreseeable risks to the health and safety of any person liable to be affected by such construction work;

In discharging these duties, the designer shall -

- Eliminate hazards which may give rise to risks.
- Reduce risks from any remaining hazards, and in so doing shall give collective measures priority over individual measures.

In designing any structure for use as a workplace the designer shall take account of the provisions of the Workplace (Health, Safety and Welfare) Regulations 1992 which relate to the design of, and materials used in, the structure.

The designer shall take all reasonable steps to provide with his design sufficient information about aspects of the design of the structure or its construction or maintenance as will adequately assist -

- Clients.
- Other designers.
- Contractors.

to comply with their duties under these Regulations.

Designs prepared or modified outside Great Britain

12.   Where a design is prepared or modified outside Great Britain for use in construction work to which these Regulations apply:

    (a)   the person who commissions it, if he is established within Great Britain; or

    (b)   if that person is not so established, the client, shall ensure that Regulation 14 is complied with.

Duties of contractors

13   No contractor shall carry out construction work in relation to a project unless any client for the project is aware of his duties under these Regulations.

Every contractor shall ensure that any contractor whom he appoints or engages in his turn in connection with a project is informed of the minimum amount of time which will be allowed to him for planning and preparation before he begins construction work

Every contractor shall provide every worker carrying out the construction work under his control with any information and training which he needs for the particular work to be carried out safely and without risk to health.

No contractor shall begin work on a construction site unless reasonable steps have been taken to prevent access by unauthorised persons to that site.

OUTLINE OF KEY POINTS - PART 3 - ADDITIONAL DUTIES FOR NOTIFIABLE PROJECTS

Appointments by the client

14(1)   The client shall:

    (a)   appoint a person ("the co-ordinator"), before design work, or planning or other preparation for construction work is begun, to perform the functions specified in regulation 13(1); and

    (b)   ensure so far as is reasonably practicable that the functions are performed.

(2)   The client shall appoint one person (in these Regulations called "the principal contractor") as soon as is practicable after the client knows enough about the project to be able to select a suitable person for such appointment, to perform the functions specified in regulations 16 to 18.

(3)   The client shall ensure that appointments under paragraphs (1) and (2) are changed or renewed as necessary to ensure that there are at all times until the end of the construction phase -

    (a)   a co-ordinator; and

    (b)   a principal contractor, filling them.

(4)   The client shall:

    (a)   be deemed for the purposes of these Regulations, save paragraphs (1) and (2) and regulations 14(l)(b) and 19(1)(b), to have been appointed as the co-ordinator or principal contractor for any period for which no person (including himself) has been so appointed; and

    (b)   accordingly be subject to the duty imposed by regulation 13(2) on a co-ordinator or, as the case may be, the duties imposed by regulations 16 to 18 on a principal contractor.

(5)   Any reference in this regulation to appointment is to appointment in writing.

Client's duty in relation to information where a project is notifiable

15. Where the project is notifiable, the client shall provide the CDM co-ordinator with pre-construction information consisting of -
    - Any information about or affecting the site or the construction work.
    - Any information concerning the proposed use of the structure as a workplace.
    - The minimum amount of time before the construction phase which will be allowed to the contractors appointed by the client for planning and preparation for construction work.
    - Any information in any existing health and safety file.

The client's duty in relation to the start of construction phase

16. The client shall ensure that the construction phase does not start unless:

    (a) the principal contractor has prepared a construction phase plan which is sufficient to enable the construction work to start without undue risk to health or safety; and

    (b) the requirements of Schedule 2 are complied with.

The client's duty in relation to the health and safety file

17(1) The client shall ensure that the co-ordinator is provided with all the health and safety information likely to be needed during any subsequent works for inclusion in a record ("the health and safety file").

(1) Where a single health and safety file relates to more than one project, site or structure, or where it includes other related information the client shall ensure that the information relating to each site or structure can be easily identified.

(2) The client shall take reasonable steps to ensure that after the construction phase the information in the health and safety file:

   (a) is kept available for inspection by any person who may need it to comply with the relevant statutory provisions; and

   (b) is revised as often as may be appropriate to incorporate any relevant new information, including information specified in regulation 4(9)(c) of the Control of Asbestos at Work Regulations 2002(d) *(see S.I. 2002/2675.)*

(3) It shall be sufficient compliance with paragraph (3)(a) by a client who disposes of his entire interest in the site if he delivers the health and safety file to the person who acquires his interest in it and ensures that he is aware of the nature and purpose of the file.

Additional duties of designers

18(1) No designer shall commence work in relation to a project unless:

   (a) the client is aware of his duties under these Regulations;

   (b) a co-ordinator has been appointed for the project; and

   (c) notice of the project has been given to the Executive under regulation 9.

(2) The duties in paragraphs (3) and (4) shall be performed so far as is reasonably practicable, taking due account of other relevant design considerations.

(3) Every designer shall in preparing or modifying a design which may be used in construction work in the United Kingdom avoid risks to the health and safety of any person:

   (a) carrying out construction work;

   (b) cleaning or maintaining the permanent fixtures and fittings of a structure;

   (c) using a structure designed as a place of work; or

   (d) liable to be affected by such construction work.

(4) In discharging the duty in paragraph (3), the designer shall:

   (a) eliminate hazards which may give rise to risks; and

   (b) reduce risks from any remaining hazards, and in doing so shall give collective measures priority over individual measures.

(5) The designer shall provide with the design sufficient information about aspects of the design of a structure or its construction or maintenance as will adequately assist:

   (a) other designers to comply with their duties under this regulation;

   (b) contractors to comply with their duties under regulation 19.

Additional duties of contractors

19 Where a project is notifiable, no contractor shall carry out construction work in relation to the project unless -
   - He has been provided with the names of the CDM co-ordinator and principal contractor.
   - He has been given access to such part of the construction phase plan as is relevant to the work to be performed by him, containing sufficient detail in relation to such work.
   - Notice of the project has been given to the Executive.

RELEVANT STATUTORY PROVISIONS

Every contractor shall -

- Provide the principal contractor with any information (including any relevant part of any risk assessment in his possession or control) which -
- Might affect the health or safety of any person carrying out the construction work or of any person who may be affected by it.
- Might justify a review of the construction phase plan.
- Which has been identified for inclusion in the health and safety file in pursuance of regulation 22(1)(j).
- Identify any contractor whom he appoints or engages in his turn in connection with the project to the principal contractor.
- Comply with -
- Any directions of the principal contractor given to him under regulation 22(1)(e).
- Any site rules.
- Provide the principal contractor with the information in relation to any death, injury, condition or dangerous occurrence which the contractor is required to notify or report under the Reporting of Injuries, Diseases and Dangerous Occurrences Regulations 1995.

Every contractor shall -

- Take all reasonable steps to ensure that the construction work is carried out in accordance with the construction phase plan.
- Notify the principal contractor of any significant finding which requires the construction phase plan to be altered or added to.

General duties of CDM co-ordinators

20(1) The functions of a co-ordinator, referred to in regulation 8(l)(a), are to:

(a) advise and assist the client in undertaking the measures he needs to take to comply with these Regulations (including in particular, in assisting the client in complying with regulations 9 and 16);

(b) identify and extract the information specified in regulation 10;

(c) advise on the suitability and compatibility of designs and on any need for modification;

(d) co-ordinate design work, planning and other preparation;

(e) liaise with the principal contractor in relation to any design or change to a design requiring a review of the construction phase plan, during the construction phase;

(f) promptly provide, in a convenient form, to:

(i) every person designing the structure;

(ii) the principal contractor; and

(iii) every contractor who has been or is likely to be appointed by the client, the information specified in regulation 10 (or such of it as is relevant to him);

(g) prepare, where none exists, and otherwise review and update the health and safety file;

(h) at the end of the construction phase, pass the health and safety file to the client.

(2) A co-ordinator shall so far as is reasonably practicable perform any function specified in paragraph (1) for which he is appointed.

Notification of the project by the CDM co-ordinator

21 The CDM co-ordinator shall as soon as is practicable after his appointment ensure that notice is given to the Executive containing such of the particulars specified in Schedule 1 as are available.

Duties of the principal contractor

22 The principal contractor for a project shall -

- Plan, manage and monitor the construction phase in a way which ensures that, so far as is reasonably practicable, it is carried out without risks to health or safety, including facilitating -

(i) Co-operation and co-ordination between persons concerned in the project in pursuance of regulations 5 and 6; and

(ii) The application of the general principles of prevention in pursuance of regulation 7.

- Liaise with the CDM co-ordinator in performing his duties in regulation 20(2)(d) during the construction phase in relation to any design or change to a design.
- Ensure that sufficient welfare facilities are provided.
- Draw up rules which are appropriate to the construction site and the activities on it.
- Give reasonable directions to any contractor.
- Ensure that every contractor is informed of the minimum amount of time which will be allowed to him.
- Consult a contractor before finalising such part of the construction phase plan as is relevant to the work to be performed by him.
- Ensure that every contractor is given, access to such part of the construction phase plan as is relevant to the work to be performed by him.
- Ensure that every contractor is given, such further information as he needs to carry out the work to be performed by him without risk.

- Identify to each contractor the information relating to the contractor's activity which is likely to be required by the CDM co-ordinator for inclusion in the health and safety file.
- Ensure that the particulars required to be in the notice are displayed in a readable condition in a position where they can be read by any worker.
- Take reasonable steps to prevent access by unauthorised persons to the construction site.

The principal contractor shall take all reasonable steps to ensure that every worker carrying out the construction work is provided with -

- A suitable site induction.
- Any further information and training which he needs for the particular work to be carried out without undue risk to health or safety.

The principal contractor's duty in relation to the construction phase plan

The principal contractor shall -

- Prepare a construction phase plan.
- Update, review, revise and refine the construction phase plan.
- Arrange for the construction phase plan to be implemented in a way which will ensure so far as is reasonably practicable the health and safety of all persons carrying out construction work and all persons who may be affected by the work.

The principal contractor's duty in relation to co-operation and consultation with workers

The principal contractor shall -

- Consult those workers or their representatives on matters connected with the project which may affect their health, safety or welfare.
- Ensure that such workers or their representatives can inspect and take copies of any information except any information—
  - The disclosure of which would be against the interests of national security.
  - Which he could not disclose without contravening a prohibition imposed by or under an enactment.
  - Relating specifically to an individual, unless he has consented to its being disclosed.
  - The disclosure of which would, for reasons other than its effect on health, safety or welfare at work, cause substantial injury to his undertaking or, where the information was supplied to him by some other person, to the undertaking of that other person.
  - Obtained by him for the purpose of bringing, prosecuting or defending any legal proceedings.

Principal contractor's duties in relation to the construction phase plan

23(1) the principal contractor shall

(a) before the start of the construction phase, prepare a sufficient health and safety plan to allow the construction phase to start, so far as is reasonably practicable, without risk to health and safety

(b) review, update, revise and refine the plan as necessary

(c) arrange for the construction phase to be implemented in such a way as to ensure, so far as is reasonably practicable, the health and safety of people carrying out the construction work

(2) take reasonable steps to ensure that the construction phase plan identifies all the risks arising from the construction phase.

Principal contractor's duties in relation to co-operation and consultation with workers

24 the principal contractor shall

(a) make and maintain arrangements to ensure that workers co-operate in promoting and developing measures to ensure the health, safety and welfare of workers.

(b) consult with workers or their representatives in good time on matters that may affect their health, safety or welfare.

(c) ensure that relevant information is available to workers except any information which is specified in the Health and Safety (Consultation with Employees) Regulations 1996.

OUTLINE OF KEY POINTS - PART 4 - DUTIES RELATING TO HEALTH AND SAFETY ON CONSTRUCTION SITES

A general duty to ensure a safe place of work and safe means of access to and from that place of work, this Regulation sets out a general requirement which applies to all construction work. It applies equally to places of work in the ground, at ground level and at height. In essence it requires that 'reasonably practicable' steps should be taken to provide for safety and to ensure risks to health are minimised. This means that action to be taken should be proportionate to the risk involved.

Work on structures (regulations 28, 29 and 30)

- Prevent accidental collapse of new or existing structures or those under construction.
- Make sure any dismantling or demolition of any structure is planned and carried out in a safe manner under the supervision of a competent person.
- Only fire explosive charges after steps have been taken to ensure that no one is exposed to risk or injury from the explosion.

Every year there are structural collapses which have the potential to cause serious accidents. The CHSW 1996 set a high standard to prevent collapses which involves taking into account the hazard during the planning stage. Demolition or dismantling are recognised as high risk activities. In any cases where this work presents a risk of danger to anyone, it should be planned and carried out under the direct supervision of a competent person.

RELEVANT STATUTORY PROVISIONS

Excavations, cofferdams and caissons (regulations 31 and 32)

- Prevent collapse of ground both in and above excavations.
- Identify and prevent risk from underground cables and other services.
- Ensure cofferdams and caissons are properly designed, constructed and maintained.

From the outset, and as work progresses, any excavation which has the potential to collapse unless supported, should have suitable equipment immediately available to provide such support. Underground cables and services can also be a source of danger. These should be identified before work starts and positive action taken to prevent injury.

Energy distribution installations (regulation 34)

- Where necessary to prevent danger, energy distribution installations shall be suitably located, checked and clearly indicated.
- Where there is a risk from electric power cables: they shall be directed away from the area of risk; or the power shall be cut off; or if it is not reasonably practicable to comply with these requirements:
  - Suitable warning notices.
  - Barriers suitable for excluding work equipment which is not needed.
  - Where vehicles need to pass beneath the cables, suspended protections.
  - In either case, measures providing an equivalent level of safety, shall be provided or (in the case of measures) taken.
- No construction work which is liable to create a risk to health or safety from an underground service, or from damage to or disturbance of it, shall be carried out unless suitable and sufficient steps (including any steps required by this regulation) have been taken to prevent such risk, so far as is reasonably practicable.

Prevention or avoidance of drowning (regulation 35)

- Take steps to prevent people from falling into water or other liquid so far as is reasonably practicable.
- Ensure that personal protective and rescue equipment is immediately available for use and maintained, in the event of a fall.
- Make sure safe transport by water is under the control of a competent person.

Traffic routes and vehicles (regulations 36 and 37)

- Ensure construction sites are organised so that pedestrians and vehicles can both move safely and without risks to health.
- Make sure routes are suitable and sufficient for the people or vehicles using them.
- Prevent or control the unintended movement of any vehicle.
- Make arrangements for giving a warning of any possible dangerous movement, e.g. reversing vehicles.
- Ensure safe operation of vehicles including prohibition of riding or remaining in unsafe positions.
- Make sure doors and gates which could present danger, e.g. trapping risk of powered doors, have suitable safeguards.

Prevention and control of emergencies (regulations 38, 39, 40 and 41)

- Prevent risk from fire, explosion, flooding and asphyxiation.
- Provide emergency routes and exits.
- Make arrangements for dealing with emergencies, including procedures for evacuating the site.
- Where necessary, provide fire-fighting equipment, fire detectors and alarm systems.

These Regulations require the prevention of risk as far as it is reasonably practicable to achieve. However, there are times when emergencies do arise and planning is needed to ensure, for example, that emergency routes are provided and evacuation procedures are in place. These particular Regulations (as well as those on traffic routes, welfare, cleanliness and signing of sites) apply to construction work which is carried out on construction sites. However, the rest of the Regulations apply to all construction work.

The HSE continues to be responsible for inspection of means of escape and fire-fighting for most sites. However, fire authorities have enforcement responsibility in many premises which remain in normal use during construction work. This continues the sensible arrangement which ensures that the most appropriate advice is given.

Site-wide issues (regulations 27, 42, 43, and 44)

- Ensure sufficient fresh or purified air is available at every workplace, and associated plant is capable of giving visible or audible warning of failure.
- Make sure a reasonable working temperature is maintained at indoor work places during working hours.
- Provide facilities for protection against adverse weather conditions.
- Make sure suitable and sufficient emergency lighting is available.
- Make sure suitable and sufficient lighting is available, including providing secondary lighting where there would be a risk to health or safety if primary or artificial lighting failed.
- Keep construction sites in good order and in a reasonable state of cleanliness.
- Ensure the perimeter of a construction site to which people, other than those working on the site could gain access, is marked by suitable signs so that its extent can be easily identified.

Reports of inspections (regulation 33)

- The person who carries out an inspection under regulations 31 or 32 must:
  - Inform the person for whom the inspection was carried out if he is not satisfied that the construction work can be carried out safely at the place inspected.
  - Prepare a report which includes the particulars set out in Schedule 3 and within 24 hours of completion of the inspection, to which the report relates, provide a copy to the person for whom the inspection was carried out.
- The inspector's employer, or the person under whose control he works, shall ensure that the inspector performs his duty.

- The person for whom the inspection was carried out must keep the report or a copy of it available for inspection at the site of the place of work until that work is completed, and after that for 3 months, and send out extracts from or copies of it as required by an inspector appointed under section 19 of The Health and Safety at Work etc. Act 1974.
- No further inspection reports required within a 7 day period.

OUTLINE OF KEY POINTS - SCHEDULE 2 (REGULATIONS 9(1)(B), 13(7) AND 22(1)(C))
WELFARE FACILITIES
SANITARY CONVENIENCES

1. Suitable and sufficient sanitary conveniences shall be provided or made available at readily accessible places. So far as is reasonably practicable, rooms containing sanitary conveniences shall be adequately ventilated and lit.

2. So far as is reasonably practicable, sanitary conveniences and the rooms containing them shall be kept in a clean and orderly condition.

3. Separate rooms containing sanitary conveniences shall be provided for men and women, except where and so far as each convenience is in a separate room the door of which is capable of being secured from the inside.

Washing facilities

4. Suitable and sufficient washing facilities, including showers if required by the nature of the work or for health reasons, shall so far as is reasonably practicable be provided or made available at readily accessible places.

5. Washing facilities shall be provided:
   (a) in the immediate vicinity of every sanitary convenience, whether or not provided elsewhere; and
   (b) in the vicinity of any changing rooms required by paragraph 15 whether or not provided elsewhere.

6. Washing facilities shall include:
   (a) a supply of clean hot and cold, or warm, water (which shall be running water so far as is reasonably practicable); and
   (b) soap or other suitable means of cleaning; and
   (c) towels or other suitable means of drying.

7. Rooms containing washing facilities shall be sufficiently ventilated and lit.

8. Washing facilities and the rooms containing them shall be kept in a clean and orderly condition.

9. Subject to paragraph 10 below, separate washing facilities shall be provided for men and women, except where and so far as they are provided in a room the door of which is capable of being secured from inside and the facilities in each such room arc intended to be used by only one person at a time.

10. Paragraph 9 above shall not apply to facilities which are provided for washing hands, forearms and face only.

Drinking water

11. An adequate supply of wholesome drinking water shall be provided or made available at readily accessible and suitable places.

12. Every supply of drinking water shall be conspicuously marked by an appropriate sign where necessary for reasons of health and safety.

13. Where a supply of drinking water is provided, there shall also be provided a sufficient number of suitable cups or other drinking vessels unless the supply of drinking water is in a jet from which persons can drink easily.

Changing rooms and lockers

14(1) Suitable and sufficient changing rooms shall be provided or made available at readily accessible places if:
   (a) a worker has to wear special clothing for the purposes of his work; and
   (b) he cannot, for reasons of health or propriety, be expected to change elsewhere, being separate rooms for, or separate use of rooms by, men and women where necessary for reasons of propriety.

(2) Changing rooms shall:
   (a) be provided with seating;
   (b) include, where necessary, facilities to enable a person to dry any such special clothing and his own clothing and personal effects.

(3) Suitable and sufficient facilities shall, where necessary, be provided or made available at readily accessible places to enable persons to lock away:
   (a) any such special clothing which is not taken home;
   (b) their own clothing which is not worn during working hours; and

Facilities for rest

15(1) Suitable and sufficient rest rooms or rest areas shall be provided or made available at readily accessible places.

(1) Rest rooms and rest areas shall:

- (a) include suitable arrangements to protect non-smokers from discomfort caused by tobacco smoke;
- (b) be equipped with an adequate number of tables and adequate seating with backs for the number of persons at work likely to use them at any one time;
- (c) where necessary, include suitable facilities for any person at work who is a pregnant woman or nursing mother to rest lying down;
- (d) include suitable arrangements to ensure that meals can be prepared and eaten; and
- (e) include the means for boiling water.

Construction (Head Protection) Regulations (CHPR) 1989

Arrangement of regulations

1) Citation, commencement and interpretation.
2) Application of these Regulations.
3) Provision, maintenance and replacement of suitable head protection.
4) Ensuring suitable head protection is worn.
5) Rules and directions.
6) Wearing of suitable head protection.
7) Reporting the loss of, or defect in, suitable head protection.
8) Extension outside Great Britain.
9) Exemption certificates.

Outline of key points

ENSURING SUITABLE HEAD PROTECTION IS WORN

Reg. 4(1) Every employer shall ensure so far as is reasonably practicable that each of his employees who is at work on operations or works to which these Regulations apply wears suitable head protection, unless there is no foreseeable risk to injury to his head other than by his falling.

4(2) Every employer, self-employed person or employee who has control over any other person who is at work on operations or works to which these Regulations apply shall ensure so far as is reasonably practicable that each such other person wears suitable head protection, unless there is no foreseeable risk of injury to that other person's head other than by his falling.

RULES AND DIRECTIONS

Reg.5(1) The person for the time being having control of a site where operations or works to which these Regulations apply are being carried out may, so far as is necessary to comply with regulation 4 of these Regulations, make rules regulating the wearing of suitable head protection on that site by persons at work on those operations or works.

5(2) Rules made in accordance with paragraph (1) of this regulation shall be in writing and shall be brought to the notice of persons who may be affected by them.

5(3) An employer may, so far as is necessary to comply with regulation 4(1) of these Regulations, give directions requiring his employees to wear suitable head protection.

5(4) An employer, self-employed person or employee who has control over any other self-employed person may, so far as is necessary to comply with regulation 4(2) of these Regulations, give directions requiring each such other self-employed person to wear suitable head protection.

WEARING OF SUITABLE HEAD PROTECTION

Reg.6(1) Every employee who has been provided with suitable head protection shall wear that head protection when required to do so by rules made or directions given under regulation 5 of these Regulations.

6(2) Every self-employed person shall wear suitable head protection when required to do so by rules made or directions given under regulation 5 of these Regulations.

6(3) Every self-employed person who is at work on operations or works to which these Regulations apply, but who is not under the control of another employer or self-employed person or of an employee, shall wear suitable head protection unless there is no foreseeable risk of injury to his head other than by his falling.

6(4) Every employee or self-employed person who is required to wear suitable head protection by or under these Regulations shall do so properly.

REPORTING THE LOSS OF, OR DEFECT IN, SUITABLE HEAD PROTECTION

Reg. 7 Every employee who has been provided with suitable head protection by his employer shall take reasonable care of it and shall forthwith report to his employer any loss of, or obvious defect in, that head protection.

Control of Asbestos Regulations (CAR) 2006

Arrangement of regulations

PART 1 - PRELIMINARY
1) Citation and commencement.
2) Interpretation.
3) Application of these Regulations.

PART 2 - GENERAL REQUIREMENTS
4) Duty to manage asbestos in non-domestic premises.
5) Identification of the presence of asbestos.
6) Assessment of work which exposes employees to asbestos.
7) Plans of work.
8) Licensing of work with asbestos.
9) Notification of work with asbestos.
10) Information, instruction and training.
11) Prevention or reduction of exposure to asbestos.
12) Use of control measures etc.
13) Maintenance of control measures etc.
14) Provision and cleaning of protective clothing.
15) Arrangements to deal with accidents, incidents and emergencies.
16) Duty to prevent or reduce the spread of asbestos.
17) Cleanliness of premises and plant.
18) Designated Areas.
19) Air Monitoring.
20) Standards for air testing and site clearance certification.
21) Standards for analysis.
22) Health records and medical surveillance.
23) Washing and changing facilities.
24) Storage, distribution and labelling of raw asbestos and asbestos waste.

PART 3 - PROHIBITIONS AND RELATED PROVISIONS
25) Interpretation of prohibitions.
26) Prohibitions of exposure to asbestos.
27) Prohibition of the importation of asbestos.
28) Prohibition of the supply of asbestos.
29) Prohibition of the use of asbestos.
30) Labelling of products containing asbestos.
31) Additional provisions in the case of exceptions and exemptions.

PART 4 - MISCELLANEOUS
32) Exemption certificates.
33) Exemptions relating to the Ministry of Defence.
34) Extension outside Great Britain.
35) Existing licences and exemption certificates.
36) Revocations, amendments and savings.
37) Defence

SCHEDULES
Schedule 1 - particulars to be included in a notification.
Schedule 2 - the labelling of raw asbestos, asbestos waste and products containing asbestos.
Schedule 3 - exceptions to the prohibitions on the importation, supply and use of chrysotile.
Schedule 4 - revocations.
Schedule 5 - amendments.

RELEVANT STATUTORY PROVISIONS

Outline of key points

SUMMARY

The Control of Asbestos Regulations 2006 came into force on 13 November 2006 (Asbestos Regulations - SI 2006/2737). These Regulations bring together the three previous sets of Regulations covering the prohibition of asbestos, the control of asbestos at work and asbestos licensing:

- Asbestos (Licensing) Regulations (ASLIC) 1983 (and as amended).
- Asbestos (Prohibitions) Regulations 1992 (and as amended).
- Control of Asbestos at Work Regulations (CAWR) 2002.

The Regulations prohibit the importation, supply and use of all forms of asbestos. They continue the ban introduced for blue and brown asbestos 1985 and for white asbestos in 1999. They also continue the ban the second-hand use of asbestos products such as asbestos cement sheets and asbestos boards and tiles; including panels which have been covered with paint or textured plaster containing asbestos.

REMEMBER: The ban applies to new use of asbestos. If existing asbestos containing materials are in good condition, they may be left in place, their condition monitored and managed to ensure they are not disturbed.

Duty to manage asbestos in non-domestic premises (regulation 4)

The Asbestos Regulations also include the 'duty to manage asbestos' in non-domestic premises. Guidance on the duty to manage asbestos can be found in the 'Approved Code of Practice, The Management of Asbestos in Non-Domestic Premises', L27, ISBN 0 7176 6209 8.

Information, instruction and training (regulation 10)

The Regulations require mandatory training for anyone liable to be exposed to asbestos fibres at work. This includes maintenance workers and others who may come into contact with or who may disturb asbestos (e.g. cable installers) as well as those involved in asbestos removal work.

Prevention or reduction of exposure to asbestos (regulation 11)

When work with asbestos or which may disturb asbestos is being carried out, the Asbestos Regulations require employers and the self-employed to prevent exposure to asbestos fibres. Where this is not reasonably practicable, they must make sure that exposure is kept as low as reasonably practicable by measures other than the use of respiratory protective equipment. The spread of asbestos must be prevented. The Regulations specify the work methods and controls that should be used to prevent exposure and spread.

Control limits

Worker exposure must be below the airborne exposure limit (Control Limit). The Asbestos Regulations have a single Control Limit for all types of asbestos of 0.1 fibres per cm^3. A Control Limit is a maximum concentration of asbestos fibres in the air (averaged over any continuous 4 hour period) that must not be exceeded.

In addition, short term exposures must be strictly controlled and worker exposure should not exceed 0.6 fibres per cm^3 of air averaged over any continuous 10 minute period using respiratory protective equipment if exposure cannot be reduced sufficiently using other means.

Respiratory protective equipment

Respiratory protective equipment is an important part of the control regime but it must not be the sole measure used to reduce exposure and should only be used to supplement other measures. Work methods that control the release of fibres such as those detailed in the **Asbestos Essentials task sheets** (available on the HSE website) for non-licensed work should be used. Respiratory protective equipment must be suitable, must fit properly and must ensure that worker exposure is reduced as low as is reasonably practicable.

Asbestos removal work undertaken by a licensed contractor

Most asbestos removal work must be undertaken by a licensed contractor but any decision on whether particular work is licensable is based on the risk. Work is only exempt from licensing if:

- The exposure of employees to asbestos fibres is sporadic and of low intensity (but exposure cannot be considered to be sporadic and of low intensity if the concentration of asbestos in the air is liable to exceed 0.6 fibres per cm3 measured over 10 minutes); and
- It is clear from the risk assessment that the exposure of any employee to asbestos will not exceed the control limit; and
- The work involves:
  - Short, non-continuous maintenance activities. Work can only be considered as short, non-continuous maintenance activities if any one person carries out work with these materials for less than one hour in a seven-day period. The total time spent by all workers on the work should not exceed a total of two hours*.
  - Removal of materials in which the asbestos fibres are firmly linked in a matrix. Such materials include: asbestos cement; textured decorative coatings and paints which contain asbestos; articles of bitumen, plastic, resin or rubber which contain asbestos where their thermal or acoustic properties are incidental to their main purpose (e.g. vinyl floor tiles, electric cables, roofing felt) and other insulation products which may be used at high temperatures but have no insulation purposes, for example gaskets, washers, ropes and seals.
  - Encapsulation or sealing of asbestos-containing materials which are in good condition, or
  - Air monitoring and control, and the collection and analysis of samples to find out if a specific material contains asbestos.

*It is important that the amount of time you or your employees spend working with asbestos insulation, asbestos coatings or asbestos insulating board (AIB) is managed to make sure that these time limits are not exceeded. This includes the time for activities such as building enclosures and cleaning.

Under the Asbestos Regulations, anyone carrying out work on asbestos insulation, asbestos coating or AIB needs a licence issued by HSE unless they meet one of the exemptions above.

REMEMBER: Although you may not need a licence to carry out a particular job, you still need to comply with the rest of the requirements of the Asbestos Regulations.

Licensable work - additional duties

If the work is licensable you have a number of additional duties. You need to:

- Notify the enforcing authority responsible for the site where you are working (for example HSE or the local authority).
- Designate the work area (see regulation 18 for details).
- Prepare specific asbestos emergency procedures.
- Pay for your employees to undergo medical surveillance.

Air monitoring (regulation 19)

The Asbestos Regulations require any analysis of the concentration of asbestos in the air to be measured in accordance with the 1997 WHO recommended method.

Standards for air testing and site clearance certification (regulation 20)

From 06 April 2007, a clearance certificate for re-occupation may only be issued by a body accredited to do so. At the moment, such accreditation can only be provided by the United Kingdom Accreditation Service (UKAS).

You can find more details of how to undertake work with asbestos containing materials, the type of controls necessary, what training is required and analytical methods in the following HSE publications:

- Approved Code of Practice Work with Materials containing Asbestos, L143, ISBN 0 7176 6206 3.
- Asbestos: the Licensed Contractors Guide, HSG 247, ISBN 0 7176 2874 4.
- Asbestos: The analysts' guide for sampling, analysis and clearance procedures, HSG 248, ISBN 0 7176 2875 2.
- Asbestos Essentials, HSG 210, ISBN 0 71761887 0. (See also the 'Asbestos Essentials task sheets' available on the HSE website).

REMEMBER: You must also comply with other health and safety legislation.

Source: HSE Website: www.hse.gov.uk.

Control of Noise at Work Regulations (CNWR) 2005

The Noise at Work Regulations were established in 1989 and have had a significant effect on the reduction of exposure to workplace noise. The implementation of the European Physical Agents (Noise) Directive as the Control of Noise at Work Regulations 2005 came into force on 06 April 2006. These regulations replace the Noise at Work Regulations 1989. The main changes are the reduction by 5dB of the exposure levels at which action has to be taken, and the introduction of a new exposure limit value and a specific requirement on health surveillance. In practice this means that there is now a requirement to ensure that noise exposure levels are reduced to meet the new regulations.

Arrangement of regulations

1) Citation and commencement.
2) Interpretation.
3) Application and transition.
4) Exposure limit values and action values.
5) Assessment of the risk to health created by exposure to noise at the workplace.
6) Elimination or control of exposure to noise at the workplace.
7) Hearing protection.
8) Maintenance and use of equipment.
9) Health surveillance.
10) Information, instruction and training.
11) Exemption certificates from hearing protection.
12) Exemption certificates for emergency services.
13) Exemption relating to the Ministry of Defence etc.
14) Extension outside Great Britain.
15) Revocations, amendment and savings.

Outline of key points

Changes to the action levels (regulation 4)

The values of the actions levels associated with noise at work have been lowered and their names have been changed. The first action level is reduced from **85 dB(A) down to 80 dB(A)** and will be known as the *lower exposure action value.* Meanwhile, the

RELEVANT STATUTORY PROVISIONS

section level is reduced from **90 dB(A) down to 85 dB(A)** and will be known as the **upper exposure action value**. The Regulations also allow the employer to average out the exposure to noise over a one week period instead of the previous normal eight hour period, in situations where the noise exposure varies on a day-to-day basis. When determining noise levels for the purposes of determining exposure action levels, the noise exposure reducing effects of hearing protection may not be taken in to account.

Where exposure is at, or above, the **lower exposure action value** (80 dB(A)) the employer has a duty to provide hearing protection to those employees that request it. The employer also has a duty to information, instruction and training on the risks posed by exposure to noise and the control measures to be used.

Where the exposure it at, or above, the **upper exposure action value** (85 dB(A)) the employer is also required to introduce a formal programme of control measures. The measures to be taken as part of this programme of control measures will depend on the findings of the noise risk assessment (see below).

The Control of Noise at Work Regulations 2005 also introduces a new value known as the **exposure limit value**. When evaluating the risks to employees from noise, the employer needs to take account of the exposure limit values. These are limits set both in terms of daily (or weekly) personal noise exposure (LEP,d of 87 dB) and in terms of peak noise ($LCpeak$ of 140 dB). The exposure action values, take account of the protection provided by personal hearing protection (unlike the two exposure action values). *If an employee is exposed to noise at or above the exposure limit value, then the employer must take immediate action to bring the exposure down below this level.*

Summary of exposure limit values and action values

The lower exposure action values are: A daily or weekly personal noise exposure of 80 dB (A-weighted).
                                         A peak sound pressure of 135 dB (C-weighted).

The upper exposure action values are: A daily or weekly personal noise exposure of 85 dB (A-weighted).
                                         A peak sound pressure of 137 dB (C-weighted).

The exposure limit values are: A daily or weekly personal exposure of 87 dB (A-weighted).
                                         A peak sound pressure of 140 db (C-weighted).

Noise risk assessment and control measures (regulations 5 and 6)

The requirement for a noise risk assessment carries through from the Noise at Work Regulations 1989 into the Control of Noise at Work Regulations 2005. Employers are required (in accordance with the general risk assessment and control measure hierarchy contained in Schedule 1 to the Management of Health and Safety at Work Regulation 1999) to ensure that the risks associated with employees' exposure to noise are eliminated where this is reasonably practicable. Where elimination is not reasonably practicable, then the employer must reduce the risks down to as low a level as is reasonably practicable.

Regulation 6(2) of the proposed Control of Noise at Work Regulations 2005 introduces the requirement for a formal programme of control measures and states:

If any employee is likely to be exposed to noise at or above an upper exposure action value, the employer shall reduce exposure to a minimum by establishing and implementing a programme of organisational and technical measures, excluding the provision of personal hearing protectors, which is appropriate to the activity and consistent with the risk assessment, and shall include consideration of:

(a)   Other working methods which eliminate or reduce exposure to noise.
(b)   Choice of appropriate work equipment emitting the least possible noise, taking account of the work to be done.
(c)   The design and layout of workplaces, work stations and rest facilities.
(d)   Suitable and sufficient information and training for employees, such that work equipment may be used correctly, in order to minimise their exposure to noise.
(e)   Reduction of noise by technical means including:
   (i)   In the case of airborne noise the use of shields, enclosures, and sound-absorbent coverings.
   (ii)   In the case of structure-borne noise by damping and isolation.
(f)   Appropriate maintenance programmes for work equipment, the workplace and workplace systems.
(g)   Limitation of the duration and intensity of exposure to noise.
(h)   Appropriate work schedules with adequate rest periods.

If the risk assessment indicates an employee is likely to be exposed to noise at or above an upper exposure action value, the employer shall ensure that

- The area is designated a Hearing Protection Zone.
- The area is demarcated and identified by means of the sign specified for the purpose of indicating "ear protection must be worn" (to be consistent with the Health and Safety (Safety Signs and Signals) Regulations 1996).
- The sign shall be accompanied by text that indicates that the area is a Hearing Protection Zone and that employees must wear personal hearing protectors while in that area.
- Access to the area is restricted where this is technically feasible and the risk of exposure justifies it and shall make every effort to ensure that no employee enters that area unless they are wearing personal hearing protectors.

Maintenance and use of equipment (regulation 8)

There is a duty on the employer to maintain the control introduced to protect employees. This will include maintenance of acoustic enclosures, etc as well as the maintenance of machinery (as required under the Provision and Use of Work Equipment Regulations 1998) to control noise at source.

Health surveillance (regulation 9)

Under the Control of Noise at Work Regulations 2005, employees who are regularly exposed to noise levels of 85 dB(A) or higher must be subject to health surveillance, including audiometric testing. This constitutes a big change from the previous Regulations that only required an employer to carry out health surveillance where the employee was subject to noise levels of 95 dB(A) or higher. Where exposure is between 80 dB and 85 dB, or where employees are only occasionally exposed above the upper exposure action values, health surveillance will only be required if information comes to light that an individual may be particularly sensitive to noise induced hearing loss.

Summary

The Control of Noise at Work Regulations 2005 became part of UK health and safety law in April 2006. They introduce levels for employees to control exposure down to, including a new exposure limit value, above which employers are obliged to take immediate action to reduce exposure. These new lower limits mean that about a further million workers will be afforded protection by these new Regulations. The requirements for risk assessments, control measures and health surveillance have been updated, but are broadly similar to previous requirements.

(Source: www.lrbconsulting com & www.hse.gov.uk).

Control of Substances Hazardous to Health Regulations (COSHH) 2002

Arrangement of regulations

1) Citation and commencement.
2) Interpretation.
3) Duties under these Regulations.
4) Prohibitions on substances.
5) Application of regulations 6 to 13.
6) Assessment of health risks created by work involving substances hazardous to health.
7) Control of exposure.
8) Use of control measures etc.
9) Maintenance of control measures.
10) Monitoring exposure.
11) Health surveillance.
12) Information etc.
13) Arrangements to deal with accidents, incidents and emergencies.
14) Exemption certificates.
15) Extension outside Great Britain.
16) Defence in proceedings for contravention of these Regulations.
17) Exemptions relating to the Ministry of Defence etc.
18) Revocations, amendments and savings.
19) Extension of meaning of "work".
20) Modification of section 3(2) of the Health and Safety at Work etc Act (HASAWA) 1974.

Schedule 1	Other substances and processes to which the definition of "carcinogen" relates.
Schedule 2	Prohibition of certain substances hazardous to health for certain purposes.
Schedule 3	Special provisions relating to biological agents.
Schedule 4	Frequency of thorough examination and test of local exhaust ventilation plant used in certain processes.
Schedule 5	Specific substances and processes for which monitoring is required.
Schedule 6	Medical surveillance.
Schedule 7	Legislation concerned with the labelling of containers and pipes.
Schedule 8	Fumigations excepted from regulation 14.
Schedule 9	Notification of certain fumigations.
Appendix 1	Control of carcinogenic substances.
Annex 1	Background note on occupational cancer.
Annex 2	Special considerations that apply to the control of exposure to vinyl chloride.
Appendix 2	Additional provisions relating to work with biological agents.
Appendix 3	Control of substances that cause occupational asthma.

NOTE the main impact to the latest version of the COSHH Regs concern the control of substances that cause occupational asthma.

Outline of key points

REGULATIONS

Reg. 2 **Interpretation**

RELEVANT STATUTORY PROVISIONS

"Substance hazardous to health" includes:

1) Substances which under The Chemicals (Hazard Information and Packaging) Regulations (CHIP 3) 2002 are in categories of very toxic, toxic, harmful, corrosive or irritant.
2) A substance listed in Schedule 1 to the Regs or for which the HSC have approved a maximum exposure limit or an occupational exposure standard.
3) A biological agent.
4) Dust in a concentration in air equal to or greater than:
   - 10 mg/m3 inhalable dust as an 8hr TWA.
   - 4mg/m3 respirable dust as an 8hr TWA.
5) Any other substance which creates a health hazard comparable with the hazards of the substances in the other categories above.

Reg. 3 Duties

Are on employer to protect:

Employees

Any other person who may be affected, except:

- Duties for health surveillance do not extend to non-employees.
- Duties to give information may extend to non-employees if they work on the premises.

Reg. 4 Prohibitions on substances

Certain substances are prohibited from being used in some applications. These are detailed in Schedule 2 to Regs.

Reg. 5 Application of regulations 6 - 13

Regs. 6 - 13 are made to protect a person's health from risks arising from exposure. They do not apply if:

The following Regs already apply:

- The Control of Lead at Work Regulations (CLAW) 2002.
- The Control of Asbestos at Work Regulations (CAWR) 2002.

The hazard arises from one of the following properties of the substance:

- Radioactivity, explosive, flammable, high or low temperature, high pressure.
- Exposure is for medical treatment.
- Exposure is in a mine.

Reg. 6 Assessment

Employer must not carry out work which will expose employees to substances hazardous to health unless he has made an assessment of the risks to health and the steps that need to be taken to meet the requirements of the Regs. The assessment must be reviewed if there are changes in the work and at least once every 5 years.

A suitable and sufficient assessment should include:

- An assessment of the risks to health.
- The practicability of preventing exposure.
- Steps needed to achieve adequate control.

An assessment of the risks should involve:

- Types of substance including biological agents.
- Where the substances are present and in what form.
- Effects on the body.
- Who might be affected?
- Existing control measures.

Reg. 7 Control of exposure

1) Employer shall ensure that the exposure of employees to substances hazardous to health is either prevented or, where this is not reasonably practicable, adequately controlled.
2) So far as is reasonably practicable (1) above except to a carcinogen or biological agent shall be by measures other than personal protective equipment (PPE).
3) Where not reasonably practicable to prevent exposure to a carcinogen by using an alternative substance or process, the following measure shall apply:

- Total enclosure of process.
- Use of plant, process and systems which minimise generation of, or suppress and contain, spills, leaks, dust, fumes and vapours of carcinogens.
- Limitation of quantities of a carcinogen at work.
- Keeping of numbers exposed to a minimum.
- Prohibition of eating, drinking and smoking in areas liable to contamination.
- Provision of hygiene measures including adequate washing facilities and regular cleaning of walls and surfaces.
- Designation of areas/installations liable to contamination and use of suitable and sufficient warning signs.
- Safe storage, handling and disposal of carcinogens and use of closed and clearly-labelled containers.

RELEVANT STATUTORY PROVISIONS

4) If adequate control is not achieved, then employer shall provide suitable PPE to employees in addition to taking control measures.

5) PPE provided shall comply with The Personal Protective Equipment at Work Regulations (PPER), 2002 (dealing with the supply of PPE).

6&7) For substances which have a maximum exposure limit (MEL), control of that substance shall, so far as inhalation is concerned, only be treated if the level of exposure is reduced as far as is reasonably practicable and in any case below the MEL.

Where a substance has an occupational exposure standard (OES), control of that substance shall, so far as inhalation is concerned, only be treated as adequate if the OES is not exceeded or if it is, steps are taken to remedy the situation as soon as reasonably practicable.

8) Respiratory protection must be suitable and of a type or conforming to a standard approved by the HSE.

9) In the event of failure of a control measure which may result in the escape of carcinogens, the employer shall ensure:

- Only those who are responsible for repair and maintenance work are permitted in the affected area and are provided with PPE.
- Employees and other persons who may be affected are informed of the failure forthwith.

Reg. 8 Employer shall take all reasonable steps to ensure control measures, PPE, etc. are properly used/applied.

Employee shall make full and proper use of control measures, PPE etc. and shall report defects to employer.

Reg. 9 **Maintenance of control measures**

Employer providing control measures to comply with Reg.7 shall ensure that it is maintained in an efficient state, in efficient working order and in good repair and in the case of PPE in a clean condition, properly stored in a well-defined place checked at suitable intervals and when discovered to be defective repaired or replaced before further use.

- Contaminated PPE should be kept apart and cleaned, decontaminated or, if necessary destroyed.
- Engineering controls - employer shall ensure thorough examination and tests.
- Local exhaust ventilation (LEV) - Once every 14 months unless process specified in Schedule 4.
- Others - At suitable intervals.
- Respiratory protective equipment - employer shall ensure thorough examination and tests at suitable intervals.
- Records of all examinations, tests and repairs kept for 5 years.

Reg. 10 **Monitoring exposure**

Employer shall ensure exposure is monitored if
- Needed to ensure maintenance of adequate control.
- Otherwise needed to protect health of employees.
- Substance/process specified in Schedule 5.

Records kept if:
- There is an identified exposure of identifiable employee - 40 years.
- Otherwise - 5 years.

Reg. 11 **Health surveillance**

1) Where appropriate for protection of health of employees exposed or liable to be exposed, employer shall ensure suitable health surveillance.

2) Health surveillance is appropriate if:
- Employee exposed to substance/process specified in Schedule 6.
- Exposure to substance is such that an identifiable disease or adverse health effect can result, there is a reasonable likelihood of it occurring and a valid technique exists for detecting the indications of the disease or effect.

3) Health records kept for at least 40 years.

4) If employer ceases business, HSE notified and health records offered to HSE.

5) If employee exposed to substance specified in Schedule 6, then health surveillance shall include medical surveillance, under Employment Medical Adviser (EMA) at 12 monthly intervals - or more frequently if specified by EMA.

6) EMA can forbid employee to work in process, or specify certain conditions for him to be employed in a process.

7) EMA can specify that health surveillance is to continue after exposure has ceased. Employer must ensure.

8) Employees to have access to their own health record.

9) Employee must attend for health/medical surveillance and give information to EMA.

10) EMA entitled to inspect workplace.

11) Where EMA suspends employee from work exposing him to substances hazardous to health, employer of employee can apply to HSE in writing within 28 days for that decision to be reviewed.

RELEVANT STATUTORY PROVISIONS

Reg. 12 Information etc.

Employer shall provide suitable and sufficient information, instruction and training for him to know:
- Risks to health.
- Precautions to be taken.

This should include information on:
- Results of monitoring of exposure at workplace.
- Results of collective health surveillance.

If the substances have been assigned a maximum exposure limit, then the employee/Safety Representative must be notified forthwith if the MEL has been exceeded.

Reg. 13 Arrangements to deal with accidents, incidents and emergencies.

To protect the health of employees from accidents, incidents and emergencies, the employer shall ensure that:
- Procedures are in place for first aid and safety drills (tested regularly).
- Information on emergency arrangements is available.
- Warning, communication systems, remedial action and rescue actions are available.
- Information made available to emergency services: external and internal.
- Steps taken to mitigate effects, restore situation to normal and inform employees.
- Only essential persons allowed in area.

These duties do not apply where the risks to health are slight or measures in place Reg 7(1) are sufficient to control the risk.

The employee must report any accident or incident which has or may have resulted in the release of a biological agent which could cause severe human disease.

NOTE the main impact to the latest version of the COSHH Regs concern the control of substances that cause occupational asthma.

APPENDIX 3 CONTROL OF SUBSTANCES THAT CAUSE OCCUPATIONAL ASTHMA

This relates certain regulations specifically to substances with the potential to cause asthma.
- Regulation 6 - assessment of risk to health created by work involving substances hazardous to health, (i.e. substances that may cause asthma).
- Regulation 7 - prevention or control of exposure to substances hazardous to health, (i.e. substances that may cause occupational asthma).
- Regulation 11 - health surveillance, (for employees who are or may be exposed to substances that may cause occupational asthma).
- Regulation 12 - information, instruction and training for persons who may be exposed to substances hazardous to health, to include: typical symptoms of asthma, substances that may cause it, the permanency of asthma and what happens with subsequent exposures, the need to report symptoms immediately and the reporting procedures.

Training should be given, including induction training before they start the job.

SCHEDULE 3 ADDITIONAL PROVISIONS RELATING TO WORK WITH BIOLOGICAL AGENTS

Regulation 7(10)

Part I Provision of general application to biological agents

1 Interpretation.

2 Classification of biological agents.

The HSC shall approve and publish a "Categorisation of Biological Agents according to hazard and categories of containment" which may be revised or re-issued.

Where no approved classification exists, the employer shall assign the agent to one of four groups according to the level of risk of infection.

Group 1 - unlikely to cause human disease.

Group 2 - can cause human disease.

Group 3 - can cause severe disease and spread to community.

Group 4 - can cause severe disease, spread to community and there is no effective treatment.

3 **Special control measures for laboratories, animal rooms and industrial processes**

Every employer engaged in research, development, teaching or diagnostic work involving Group 2, 3 or 4 biological agents; keeping or handling laboratory animals deliberately or naturally infected with those agents, or industrial processes involving those agents, shall control them with the most suitable containment.

4 **List of employees exposed to certain biological agents**

The employer shall keep a list of employees exposed to Group 3 or 4 biological agents for at least 10 years. If there is a long latency period then the list should be kept for 40 years.

5 **Notification of the use of biological agents**

Employers shall inform the HSE at least 20 days in advance of first time use or storage of Group 2, 3 or 4 biological hazards. Consequent substantial changes in procedure or process shall also be reported.

6 **Notification of the consignment of biological agents**

The HSE must be informed 30 days before certain biological agents are consigned.

Part II Containment measures for health and veterinary care facilities, laboratories and animal rooms.

Part III Containment measures for industrial processes.

Part IV Biohazard sign.

The biohazard sign required by regulation 7(6) (a) shall be in the form shown.

Part V Biological agents whose use is to be notified in accordance with paragraph 5(2) of Part I of this Schedule

- Any Group 3 or 4 agent.
- Certain named Group 2 agents.

Figure RSP-1: Biohazard sign.
Source: COSHH 2002.

Control of Substances Hazardous to Health (Amendment) Regulations 2004

These Regulations make minor amendments to The Control of Substances Hazardous to Health Regulations (COSHH) 2002 and came into force on 17th January 2005 and 6th April 2005.

Arrangement of regulations

1) Citation and commencement.
2) Amendments of the Control of Substances Hazardous to Health (Amendment) Regulations 2004.
3) Amendment of the Chemicals (Hazard Information and Packaging for Supply) Regulations 2002.
4) Amendments of the Control of Lead at Work Regulations 2002.

Outline of key points

The main change is that maximum exposure limits (MELs) and occupational exposure standards (OESs) have been replaced by the new workplace exposure limits (WELs).

Control of Vibration at Work Regulations (CVWR) 2005

Hand-arm vibration (HAV) and whole body vibration (WBV) are caused by the use of work equipment and work processes that transmit vibration into the hands, arms and bodies of employees in many industries and occupations. Long-term, regular exposure to vibration is known to lead to permanent and debilitating health effects such as vibration white finger, loss of sensation, pain, and numbness in the hands, arms, spine and joints. These effects are collectively known as hand-arm or whole body vibration syndrome. These Regulations introduce controls, which aim substantially to reduce ill health caused by exposure to vibration. These Regulations came into force on 06 July 2005.

Arrangement of regulations

1) Citation and commencement.
2) Interpretation.
3) Application and transition.
4) Exposure limit values and action values.
5) Assessment of the risk to health created by vibration at the workplace.
6) Elimination or control of exposure to vibration at the workplace.
7) Health surveillance.
8) Information, instruction and training for persons who may be exposed to risk from vibration.
9) Exemption certificates for emergency services.
10) Exemption certificates for air transport.
11) Exemption relating to the Ministry of Defence etc.
12) Extension outside Great Britain.
13) Amendment.

Outline of key points

Regulation 3 makes provision for transition arrangements affecting equipment provided for use before 06 July 2007 and does not permit compliance with the exposure limits, taking into account technical advances and organisational measures to respond to the

RELEVANT STATUTORY PROVISIONS

regulations, the regulations shall not apply until 06 July 2010. Duties under most of these regulations extend not only to employees but to others, whether or not at work, that may be affected. The duty does not include regulation 7 (health surveillance) or regulation 8 (information instruction and training), these are limited to employees.

Regulation 4 states the personal daily exposure limits and daily exposure action values, normalised over an 8-hour reference period.

	Daily exposure action values	*Daily exposure limits*
Hand arm vibration	2.5 m/s^2	5 m/s^2
Whole body vibration	0.5 m/s^2	1.15 m/s^2

Regulation 5 requires the employer to make a suitable and sufficient assessment of the risk created by work that is liable to expose employees to risk from vibration. The assessment must observe work practices, make reference to information regarding the magnitude of vibration from equipment and if necessary measurement of the magnitude of the vibration.

Consideration must also be given to the type, duration, effects of exposure, exposures limit / action values, effects on employees at particular risk, the effects of vibration on equipment and the ability to use it, manufacturers' information, availability of replacement equipment, and extension of exposure at the workplace (e.g. rest facilities), temperature and information on health surveillance. The risk assessment should be recorded as soon as is practicable after the risk assessment is made and reviewed regularly.

Regulation 6 states that the employer must seek to eliminate the risk of vibration at source or, if not reasonably practicable, reduce it to as low a level as is reasonably practicable. Where the personal daily exposure limit is exceeded the employer must reduce exposure by implementing a programme of organisational and technical measures. Measures include the use of other methods of work, ergonomics, maintenance of equipment, design and layout, rest facilities, information, instruction and training, limitation by schedules and breaks and the provision of personal protective equipment to protect from cold and damp.

Measures must be adapted to take account of any group or individual employee whose health may be of particular risk from exposure to vibration.

Regulation 7 states that health surveillance must be carried out if there is a risk to the health of employees liable to be exposed to vibration. This is in order to prevent or diagnose any health effect linked with exposure to vibration. A record of health shall be kept of any employee who undergoes health surveillance. The employer shall, providing reasonable notice is given, provide the employee with access to their health records and provide copies to an enforcing officer on request. If health surveillance identifies a disease or adverse health effect, considered by a doctor or other occupational health professional to be a result of exposure to vibration, the employer shall ensure that a qualified person informs the employee and provides information and advice. The employer must ensure they are kept informed of any significant findings from health surveillance, taking into account any medical confidentiality. In addition the employer must also:

- Review risk assessments.
- Review the measures taken to comply.
- Consider assigning the employee to other work.
- Review the health of any other employee who has been similarly exposed and consider alternative work.

Regulation 8 states that employers must provide information, instruction and training to all employees who are exposed to risk from vibration and their representatives. This includes any organisational and technical measures taken, exposure limits and values, risk assessment findings, why and how to detect injury, entitlement to and collective results of health surveillance and safe working practices. Information instruction and training shall be updated to take account of changes in the employers work or methods. The employer shall ensure all persons, whether or not an employee, who carries out work in connection with the employer's duties has been provided with information, instruction and training.

Dangerous Substances and Explosive Atmospheres Regulations (DSEAR) 2002

Arrangement of regulations

1) Citation and commencement.
2) Interpretation.
3) Application.
4) Duties under these Regulations.
5) Risk assessment.
6) Elimination or reduction of risks from dangerous substances.
7) Places where explosive atmospheres may occur.
8) Arrangements to deal with accidents, incidents and emergencies.
9) Information, instruction and training.
10) Identification of hazardous contents of containers and pipes.
11) Duty of co-ordination.
12) Extension outside Great Britain.
13) Exemption certificates.
14) Exemptions for Ministry of Defence etc.
15) Amendments.
16) Repeals and revocations.
17) Transitional provisions.

Schedule 1. General safety measures.
Schedule 2. Classification of places where explosive atmospheres may occur.
Schedule 3. Criteria for the selection of equipment and protective systems.
Schedule 4. Warning sign for places where explosive atmospheres may occur.
Schedule 5. Legislation concerned with the marking of containers and pipes.
Schedule 6. Amendments.
Schedule 7. Repeal and revocation.

Outline of key points

These new regulations aim to protect against risks from fire, explosion and similar events arising from dangerous substances that are present in the workplace.

DANGEROUS SUBSTANCES

These are any substances or preparations that due to their properties or the way in which they are being used could cause harm to people from fires and explosions. They may include petrol, liquefied petroleum gases, paints, varnishes, solvents and dusts.

APPLICATION

DSEAR applies in most workplaces where a dangerous substance is present. There are a few exceptions where only certain parts of the regulations apply, for example:

- Ships.
- Medical treatment areas.
- Explosives/chemically unstable substances.
- Mines.
- Quarries.
- Boreholes.
- Offshore installations.
- Means of transport.

MAIN REQUIREMENTS

You must:

- Conduct a risk assessment of work activities involving dangerous substances.
- Provide measures to eliminate or reduce risks.
- Provide equipment and procedures to deal with accidents and emergencies.
- Provide information and training for employees.
- Classify places into zones and mark zones where necessary (to be phased in) -

    Workplace in use by July 2003   -   Meet requirements by July 2006
    Workplace modified before July 2006 -   Meet requirements at time of modifications
    New workplace after 30 June 2003   -   Meet requirements from start.

The risk assessment should include:

- The hazardous properties of substance.
- The way they are used or stored.
- Possibility of hazardous explosive atmosphere occurring.
- Potential ignition sources.
- Details of zoned areas (July 2003).
- Co-ordination between employers (July 2003).

SAFETY MEASURES

Where possible eliminate safety risks from dangerous substances or, if not reasonably practicable to do this, control risks and reduce the harmful effects of any fire, explosion or similar event.

Substitution - Replace with totally safe or safer substance (best solution).

Control measures - If risk cannot be eliminated apply the following control measures in the following order:

- Reduce quantity.
- Avoid or minimise releases.
- Control releases at source.
- Prevent formation of explosive atmosphere.
- Collect, contain and remove any release to a safe place e.g. ventilation.
- Avoid ignition sources.
- Avoid adverse conditions e.g. exceeding temperature limits.
- Keep incompatible substances apart.

Mitigation measures - Apply measures to mitigate the effects of any situation.

- Prevent fire and explosions from spreading to other plant, equipment or other parts of the workplace.
- Reduce number of employees exposed.
- Provide process plant that can contain or suppress an explosion, or vent it to a safe place.

RELEVANT STATUTORY PROVISIONS

ZONED AREAS

In workplaces where explosive atmospheres may occur, areas should be classified into zones based on the likelihood of an explosive atmosphere occurring. Any equipment in these areas should ideally meet the requirements of the Equipment and Protective Systems Intended for Use in Potentially Explosive Atmospheres Regulations (ATEX) 1996. However equipment in use before July 2003 can continue to be used providing that the risk assessment says that it is safe to do so. Areas may need to be marked with an 'Ex' warning sign at their entry points. Employees may need to be provided with appropriate clothing e.g. anti static overalls. Before use for the first time, a person competent in the field of explosion protection must confirm hazardous areas as being safe.

ACCIDENTS, INCIDENTS AND EMERGENCIES

DSEAR builds on existing requirements for emergency procedures, which are contained in other regulations. These may need to be supplemented if you assess that a fire, explosion or significant spillage could occur, due to the quantities of dangerous substances present in the workplace. You may need to arrange for:

- Suitable warning systems.
- Escape facilities.
- Emergency procedures.
- Equipment and clothing for essential personnel who may need to deal with the situation.
- Practice drills.
- Make information, instruction and training available to employees and if necessary liaise with the emergency services.

Electricity at Work Regulations (EWR) 1989

Arrangement of regulations

PART I - INTRODUCTION

1) Citation and commencement.
2) Interpretation.
3) Persons on whom duties are imposed by these Regulations.

PART II - GENERAL

4) Systems, work activities and protective equipment.
5) Strength and capability of electrical equipment.
6) Adverse or hazardous environments.
7) Insulation, protection and placing of conductors.
8) Earthing or other suitable precautions.
9) Integrity of referenced conductors.
10) Connections.
11) Means for protecting from excess of current.
12) Means for cutting off the supply and for isolation.
13) Precautions for work on equipment made dead.
14) Work on or near live conductors.
15) Working space, access and lighting.
16) Persons to be competent to prevent danger and injury.

PART III - REGULATIONS APPLYING TO MINES ONLY

17) Provisions applying to mines only.
18) Introduction of electrical equipment.
19) Restriction of equipment in certain zones below ground.
20) Cutting off electricity or making safe where firedamp is found either below ground or at the surface.
21) Approval of certain equipment for use in safety-lamp mines.
22) Means of cutting off electricity to circuits below ground.
23) Oil-filled equipment.
24) Records and information.
25) Electric shock notices.
26) Introduction of battery-powered locomotives and vehicles into safety-lamp mines.
27) Storage, charging and transfer of electrical storage batteries.
28) Disapplication of section 157 of the Mines and Quarries Act 1954.

PART IV - MISCELLANEOUS AND GENERAL

29) Defence.
30) Exemption certificates.
31) Extension outside Great Britain.
32) Disapplication of duties.
33) Revocations and modifications.

Schedule 1. Provisions applying to mines only and having effect in particular in relation to the use below ground in coal mines of film lighting circuits.

Schedule 2. Revocations and modifications.

Outline of key points

SYSTEMS, WORK ACTIVITIES AND PROTECTIVE EQUIPMENT (REGULATION 4)

The system and the equipment comprising it must be designed and installed to take account of all reasonably foreseeable conditions of use.

- The system must be maintained so as to prevent danger.
- All work activities must be carried out in such a manner as to not give rise to danger.
- Equipment provided to protect people working on live equipment must be suitable and maintained.

STRENGTH AND CAPABILITY OF ELECTRICAL EQUIPMENT (REGULATION 5)

Strength and capability refers to the equipment's ability to withstand the effects of its load current and any transient overloads or pulses of current.

ADVERSE OR HAZARDOUS ENVIRONMENTS (REGULATION 6)

This regulation requires that electrical equipment is suitable for the environment and conditions that might be reasonably foreseen. In particular, attention should be paid to:

- *Mechanical damage* caused by for example; vehicles, people, vibration, etc.
- Weather, natural hazards, temperature or pressure. Ice, snow, lightning, bird droppings, etc.
- *Wet, dirty, dusty or corrosive conditions.* Conductors, moving parts, insulators and other materials may be affected by the corrosive nature of water, chemicals and solvents. The presence of explosive dusts must be given special consideration.
- *Flammable or explosive substances.* Electrical equipment may be a source of ignition for liquids, gases, vapours etc.

INSULATION, PROTECTION AND PLACING OF CONDUCTORS (REGULATION 7)

The purpose of this regulation is to prevent danger from direct contact. Therefore, if none exists, no action is needed. Conductors though will normally need to be insulated and also have some other protection to prevent mechanical damage.

EARTHING OR OTHER SUITABLE PRECAUTIONS (REGULATION 8)

The purpose of this regulation is to prevent danger from indirect contact. Conductors such as metal casings may become live through fault conditions. The likelihood of danger arising from these circumstances must be prevented by using the techniques described earlier in this section i.e. earthing, double insulation, reduced voltages etc.

INTEGRITY OF REFERENCED CONDUCTORS (REGULATION 9)

In many circumstances the reference point is earthed because the majority of power distribution installations are referenced by a deliberate connection to earth at the generators or distribution transformers. The purpose of this regulation is to ensure that electrical continuity is never broken.

CONNECTIONS (REGULATION 10)

As well as having suitable insulation and conductance, connections must have adequate mechanical protection and strength. Plugs and sockets must conform to recognised standards as must connections between cables. Special attention should be paid to the quality of connections on portable appliances.

MEANS FOR PROTECTING FROM EXCESS CURRENT (REGULATION 11)

Faults or overloads can occur in electrical systems and protection must be provided against their effects. The type of protection depends on several factors but usually rests between fuses and circuit breakers.

MEANS FOR CUTTING OFF THE SUPPLY AND FOR ISOLATION (REGULATION 12)

Means must be provided to switch off electrical supplies together with a means of isolation so as to prevent inadvertent reconnection.

PRECAUTIONS FOR WORK ON EQUIPMENT MADE DEAD (REGULATION 13)

Working dead should be the norm. This regulation requires that precautions be taken to ensure that the system remains dead and to protect those at work on the system. Any or all of the following steps should be considered:

- Identify the circuit. Never assume that the labelling is correct.
- Disconnection and isolation. These are the most common methods: isolation switches, fuse removal and plug removal.
- Notices and barriers.
- Proving dead. The test device itself must also be tested before and after testing.
- Earthing.
- Permits to work.

WORK ON OR NEAR LIVE CONDUCTORS (REGULATION 14)

Live work must only be done if it is unreasonable for it to be done dead. If live work must be carried out then any or all of the following precautions should be taken:

- Competent staff (see reg. 16).
- Adequate information.
- Suitable tools. Insulated tools, protective clothing.
- Barriers or screens.

RELEVANT STATUTORY PROVISIONS

- Instruments and test probes. To identify what is live and what is dead.
- Accompaniment.
- Designated test areas.

WORKING SPACE, ACCESS AND LIGHTING (REGULATION 15)

Space. Where there are dangerous live exposed conductors, space should be adequate to:

- Allow persons to pull back from the hazard.
- Allow persons to pass each other.

Lighting. The first preference is for natural lighting then for permanent artificial lighting.

PERSONS TO BE COMPETENT TO PREVENT DANGER AND INJURY (REGULATION 16)

The object of this regulation is to 'ensure that persons are not placed at risk due to a lack of skills on the part of themselves or others in dealing with electrical equipment'.

In order to meet the requirements of this regulation a competent person would need:

- An understanding of the concepts of electricity and the risks involved in work associated with it.
- Knowledge of electrical work and some suitable qualification in electrical principles.
- Experience of the type of system to be worked on with an understanding of the hazards and risks involved.
- Knowledge of the systems of work to be employed and the ability to recognise hazards and risks.
- Physical attributes to be able to recognise elements of the system e.g. colour blindness and wiring.

Advice and queries regarding qualifications and training can be directed to the IEE - Institute of Electrical Engineers, London.

DEFENCE (REGULATION 29)

In any Regulation where the absolute duty applies, a defence in any criminal proceedings shall exist where a person can show that: *"He took all reasonable steps and exercised due diligence to avoid the commission of the offence."*

Is there a prepared procedure (steps), is the procedure being followed (diligence) and do you have the records or witness to prove it retrospectively?

Environmental Protection Act (EPA) 1990

Outline of key points

"An Act to make provision for the improved control of pollution arising from certain industrial and other processes;

to re-enact the provisions of the Control of Pollution Act 1974 relating to waste on land with modifications as respects the functions of the regulatory and other authorities concerned in the collection and disposal of waste and to make further provision in relation to such waste;

to restate the law defining statutory nuisances and improve the summary procedures for dealing with them, to provide for the termination of the existing controls over offensive trades or businesses and to provide for the extension of the Clean Air Acts to prescribed gases;

to amend the law relating to litter and make further provision imposing or conferring powers to impose duties to keep public places clear of litter and clean;

to make provision conferring powers in relation to trolley abandoned on land in the open air; to amend the Radioactive Substances Act 1960;

to make provision for the control of genetically modified organisms; to make provision for the abolition of the Nature Conservancy Council and for the creation of councils to replace it and discharge the functions of that Council and, as respects Wales, of the Countryside Commission; to make further provision for the control of the importation, exportation, use, supply or storage of prescribed substances and articles and the importation, exportation, use, supply or storage of prescribed substances and articles and the importation or exportation of prescribed descriptions of waste; to confer powers to obtain information about potentially hazardous substances; to amend the law relating to the control of hazardous substances on, over or under land;

to amend section 107(6) of the Water Act 1989 and sections 31 (7)(a), 31 A(2) (c)(i) and 32(7)(a) of the Control of Pollution Act 1974;

to amend the provisions of the Food and Environmental Protection Act 1985 as regards the dumping of waste at sea;

to make further provision as respects the prevention of oil pollution from ships; to make provision for and in connection with the identification and control of dogs;

to confer powers to control the burning of crop residues;

to make provision in relation to financial or other assistance for purposes connected with the environment;

to make provision in relation to financial or other assistance for purposes connected with the environment;

to make provision as respects superannuation of employees of the groundwork Foundation and for remunerating the chairman of the Inland Waterways Amenity Advisory Council; and

for purposes connected with those purposes." [1st November 1990].

The EPA 1990 has 9 main Parts plus 16 Schedules.

MAIN PARTS

Part I   Integrated Pollution Control and Air Pollution Control by Local Authorities.
Part II   Waste on Land.
Part III Statutory Nuisances and Clean Air.
Part IV   Litter etc. (provisions relating to litter and abandoned trolleys).

RELEVANT STATUTORY PROVISIONS

Part V Amendment of the Radioactive Substances Act 1960.
Part VI Genetically Modified Organisms.
Part VII Nature Conservation in Great Britain and Countryside Matters in Wales
Part VIII Miscellaneous (Other controls on substances, articles or waste, Pollution at sea, Control of dogs, Straw and stubble burning and Environmental expenditure)
Part IX General

SCHEDULES

Schedule 1 Authorisations for Processes: Supplementary Provisions.
    Part I Grant of Authorisations.
    Part II Variation of Authorisations.
Schedule 2 Waste Disposal Authorities and Companies.
    Part I Transition to Companies.
    Part II Provisions regulating Waste Disposal Authorities and Companies.
Schedule 3 Statutory Nuisances: Supplementary Provisions.
Schedule 4 Abandoned Shopping and Luggage Trolleys.
Schedule 5 Further Amendments of the Radioactive Substances Act 1960.
    Part I Miscellaneous and Consequential Amendments.
    Part I Amendments relating to Scotland and Northern Ireland.
Schedule 6 The Nature Conservancy Councils for England and Scotland and the Countryside Council for Wales: Constitution.
Schedule 7 The Joint Nature Conservation Committee.
Schedule 8 Amendment of Enactments relating to Countryside Matters.
Schedule 9 Amendment of Enactments conferring Nature Conservancy Functions.
Schedule 10 Transfer Schemes and Staff of Existing Councils.
    Part I Transfer Schemes: Nature Conservancy Council.
    Part II Transfer Schemes: The Countryside Commission.
    Part III Employment of staff of Existing Bodies.
Schedule 11 Transitional Provisions and Savings for Part VII
    Part I Countryside Functions.
    Part II Nature Conservation Functions.
    Part III Supplementary.
Schedule 12 Injurious or Hazardous Substances: Advisory Committee.
Schedule 13 Amendments of Hazardous Substances Legislation.
    Part I England and Wales.
    Part II Scotland.
Schedule 14 Amendments of the Prevention of Oil Pollution Act 1971.
Schedule 15 Consequential and Minor Amendments of Enactments.
Schedule 16 Repeals.
    Part I Enactments relating to Processes.
    Part II Enactments relating to Waste on Land.
    Part III Enactments relating to Statutory Nuisances.
    Part IV Enactments relating to Litter.
    Part V Enactments relating to Radioactive Substances.
    Part VI Enactments relating to Nature Conservation and Countryside Matters.
    Part VII Enactments relating to Hazardous Substances.
    Part VII Enactments relating to Deposits at Sea.
    Part IX Miscellaneous Enactments.

Fire (Scotland) Act 2005

Arrangement of regulations

PART 1 - FIRE AND RESCUE AUTHORITIES

Fire and rescue authorities
Joint fire and rescue boards
Meaning of "relevant authority"

PART 2 - FIRE AND RESCUE SERVICES

Chapter 1 Appointment of chief officer.
Chapter 2 Principal fire and rescue functions.
Chapter 3 Ancillary functions.

© ACT

RELEVANT STATUTORY PROVISIONS

Chapter 4	Water supply.
Chapter 5	Powers of employees and constables.
Chapter 6	Mutual assistance etc.
Chapter 7	Assaulting or impeding employees and others.
Chapter 8	Central supervision and support.
Chapter 9	Employment.
Chapter 10	Interpretation.

PART 3 - FIRE SAFETY

Chapter 1	Fire safety duties.
Chapter 2	Enforcement.
Chapter 3	Miscellaneous.
Chapter 4	Offences.
Chapter 5	General.

PART 4 - MISCELLANEOUS

Inquiries
Consultation requirements

Pre-commencement consultation
Advisory bodies

Payments in respect of advisory bodies
Abolition of Scottish Central Fire Brigades Advisory Council

False alarms

Disposal of land

PART 5 - GENERAL

Ancillary provision
Orders and regulations
Minor and consequential amendments and repeals
Commencement
Short title

Schedule 1	Joint fire and rescue boards: supplementary provision
Schedule 2	Fire safety measures
Schedule 3	Minor and consequential amendments
Schedule 4	Repeals

Outline of key points

The Act is targeted at reducing the number of workplace fires by imposing far reaching responsibilities on all employers, as well as those who have control to any extent of non-domestic premises, to assess and reduce the risks from fire.

Fire certificates are abolished under the Act and have been replaced by a new fire safety regime based upon the principles of risk assessment and the requirement to take steps to mitigate the detrimental effects of a fire on relevant premises.

Who does it apply to?

The new regime applies to all employers as well as to anyone who has control of non-domestic premises to any extent including building owners, tenants, occupiers and factors.

What are the new duties?

The overriding duty is to ensure, so far as is reasonably practicable, safety in respect of harm caused by fire in the workplace.

The overriding duty is supplemented by a number of prescriptive duties:

- To carry out a fire safety risk assessment of the premises. If you have 5 or more employees, the risk assessment must be recorded in writing.
- Not to employ a young person (a person under 18) unless an assessment of the risks of fire to young persons has been undertaking.
- To appoint a competent person to assist with the discharge of fire safety duties.
- To identify the fire safety measures necessary.
- To put in place arrangements for the planning, organisation, control, monitoring and review of the fire safety measures that are put in place.
- To implement these fire safety measures using risk reduction principles.
- To inform employees of the fire safety risks and provide fire safety training.
- To co-ordinate and co-operate with other duty holders in the same premises.
- To review the risk assessment.

Hazardous Waste Regulations (HWR) 2005

INTRODUCTION

These regulations replace the existing Special Waste Regulations 1996 (as amended); the regulations came into force from 16 July 2005.

Outline of key points

1. The term "special waste" has been replaced by "hazardous waste".
2. The European Waste Catalogue (EWC) and the Hazardous Waste List (part of the EWC) have been formally transposed into UK legislation. All wastes need to be characterised by their EWC code.
3. Some wastes which were not classified as special waste will now be classified as hazardous waste by virtue of their EWC code, as a result more waste will need to be consigned.
4. Hazardous waste movements will continue to require a consignment note. However, additional information will be required.
5. 200 additional wastes have been added to the Hazardous Waste List. Among them are everyday items such as fluorescent tubes, fridges, TVs, computer monitors and end of life vehicles. There are new requirements on hazardous waste producers (registration, inspections, consignment notes, record keeping):
   - All producers of hazardous waste are required to annually register each of their sites with the Environment Agency, for which there is a fee.
   - Some sites will be exempt from registration such as those producing less than 200kg of hazardous waste per annum.
   - The requirement to pre-notify the Environment Agency for every consignment of hazardous waste will be abolished, as will the consignment note charge.
   - Consignees (Disposal/Transfer Sites) are required to provide quarterly returns that will form the basis of the new consignment charge.
7. Mixing of hazardous wastes with other hazardous wastes and with non-hazardous wastes is not permitted, except under license.
8. Fixed penalty charges of £300.00 for minor offences.

All Hazardous Waste producers must be registered; it will be an offence for companies to move the waste if the producers are not registered.

From 16 July 2005 all treated hazardous waste accepted into hazardous or special 'cells' of a non-hazardous landfill site must comply with the full Waste Acceptance Criteria (WAC), as required by the Landfill Regulations 2002.

EXCLUSIONS

The only hazardous waste type excluded from the regulations will be 'domestic wastes', arising from households.

THE NEED TO REGISTER WITH THE ENVIRONMENT AGENCY AS A HAZARDOUS WASTE PRODUCER

If hazardous waste is produced (as defined in the Hazardous Waste List of the EWC) the production site will be classed as a producer of hazardous waste. Each hazardous waste production site must be registered annually with the Environment Agency.

Registration applies to sites where separately collected fractions of domestic waste are bulked up (CA site, transfer station, etc).

These sites are classed as sites of production with appropriate notification fees.

THE RULES FOR NOTIFICATION AND RECORD KEEPING

1. Consignment Notes are used as before under the Special Waste Regulations, but a 72 hour pre-notification to the Environment Agency will be required before hazardous waste is moved.
2. Quarterly consignee returns have replaced the system of the consignee copying each Consignment Note to the Environment Agency. Electronic transfer is encouraged.
3. Sites exempt from waste management licensing need to send quarterly returns to the Environment Agency.
4. The consignee must send returns to waste producers notifying them of the receipt of their wastes. It is an offence to collect hazardous waste from non-notified premises if the producer is not exempt.

HOW THE CHANGES AFFECT THE COLLECTION OF WASTE

Waste producers cannot mix different categories of hazardous waste or mix hazardous waste with non-hazardous waste, except under license.

If multiple hazardous waste streams from industrial or commercial premises are deposited within a single container, all the individual EWC codes must accompany the consignment note, which must contain the relevant EWC codes.

Both individual and multiple collections of hazardous wastes can be arranged. There is one consignment note for multiple collections with space in an annex for the details of individual loads rather than completely separate consignment notes for each collection.

For waste collections using multi-lift vehicles and single compartment tankers, a transfer note will exist for each waste producer. Differences in the contents of the individual containers must be recorded in the individual written descriptions.

DUTIES RELATING TO THE WASTE ACCEPTANCE CRITERIA

From 16 July 2005 all hazardous and non hazardous wastes destined for disposal in landfill have to meet the WAC before they can be deposited. WAC contain the 'quality standards' wastes have to comply with before they are allowed to be placed in inert, non hazardous or hazardous landfills.

RELEVANT STATUTORY PROVISIONS

The waste producer is under a duty of care to ensure the characterisation of the waste to establish its key characteristics as specified in the Regulations. That is, to assess the physical and chemical properties to identify if they classify as hazardous, non hazardous or inert waste. In particular, details of the chemical composition and leaching behaviour of the waste are required. The flow chart below illustrates the procedure.

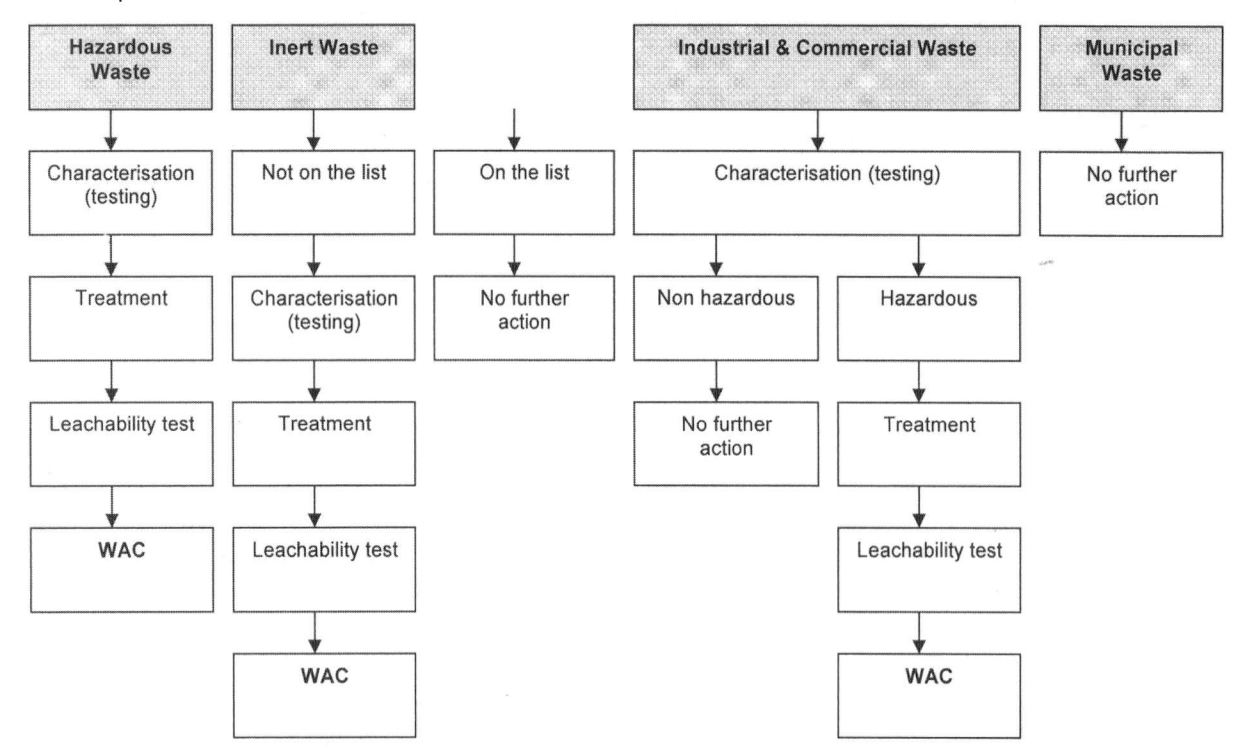

Figure RSP-2: Flowchart - characterisation of waste.
Source: SITA.

This assessment takes the form of sample testing, whereby a representative sample of waste arisings is sent away for scientific analysis.

THE INSPECTION REGIME

The Environment Agency will periodically inspect hazardous waste producing premises and assess the following:

a. Does the site produce hazardous waste?
b. Has the site been notified (i.e. registered)?
c. Is mixing carried out?
d. Are the Consignment Note records complete?
e. Is the waste moved by a registered carrier …
f. … and taken to a permitted consignee?
g. If going to landfill how are the Waste Acceptance Criteria being met?

The Environment Agency issues fixed penalties (spot fines) for:

- Failing to notify premises.
- Failing to complete consignment notes.
- Failing to apply for review of existing permit.

Source: www.sita.co.uk. Document code M141, Review of the Hazardous Waste (England) Regulations 2005 and the introduction of the Waste Acceptance Criteria.

List of Wastes (England) Regulations (LoWR) 2005

OUTLINE OF KEY POINTS

Includes the European Waste Catalogue (EWC) and the Hazardous Waste List (part of the EWC); all wastes need to be characterised by their EWC code.

These regulations include Chapters of the List numbered 01-20. The Chapters are broken down into specific materials or substances which are further identified as 'wastes' or 'hazardous wastes'; **a waste marked with an asterisk in the List of Wastes is considered listed as a hazardous waste**, whereas those without an asterisk are considered as a waste.

The different types of wastes in the List of Wastes are fully defined by the six-digit code for the waste and the respective two-digit and four-digit chapter headings, and accordingly, for purposes connected with the regulation of waste or hazardous waste -

(a)   Any reference to a waste by its six-digit code as specified in the List of Wastes is to be treated as a reference to that waste.

(b)   A reference to wastes by the respective two-digit or four-digit chapter heading is a reference to the wastes listed in the List of Wastes under that chapter heading.

The following steps should be taken to identify a waste in the list:

1. Identify the source generating the waste in chapters 01 to 12 or 17 to 20 and identify the appropriate six-digit code of the waste (excluding codes ending with 99 of these chapters). A specific production unit may need to classify its activities in several chapters. For instance, a car manufacturer may find its wastes listed in chapters 12 (wastes from shaping and surface treatment of metals), 11 (inorganic wastes containing metals from metal treatment and the coating of metals) and 08 (wastes from the use of coatings), depending on the different process steps. Note: separately collected packaging waste (including mixtures of different packaging materials) shall be classified in 15 01, not in 20 01.
2. If no appropriate waste code can be found in chapters 01 to 12 or 17 to 20, the chapters 13, 14 and 15 must be examined to identify the waste.
3. If none of these waste codes apply, the waste must be identified according to chapter 16.
4. If the waste is not in chapter 16 either, the 99 code (wastes not otherwise specified) must be used in the section of the list corresponding to the activity identified in step one.

See the Regulations for specific details.

Source: The List of Wastes (England) Regulations 2005.

Hazardous properties

Wastes on the List of Wastes are hazardous if they have one or more of the following hazardous properties:

H1	***Explosive:*** substances and preparations which may explode under the effect of flame or which are more sensitive to shocks or friction than dinitrobenzene.
H2	***Oxidizing:*** substances and preparations which exhibit highly exothermic reactions when in contact with other substances, particularly flammable substances.
H3A	***Highly flammable:*** ■ Liquid substances and preparations having a flash point below 21C (including extremely flammable liquids). ■ Substances and preparations which may become hot and finally catch fire in contact with air at ambient temperature without any application of energy. ■ Solid substances and preparations which may readily catch fire after brief contact with a source of ignition and which continue to burn or to be consumed after removal of the source of ignition. ■ Gaseous substances and preparations which are flammable in air at normal pressure. ■ Substances and preparations which, in contact with water or damp air, evolve highly flammable gases in dangerous quantities.
H3B	***Flammable:*** liquid substances and preparations having a flash point equal to or greater than 21°C and less than or equal to 55°C.
H4	***Irritant:*** non-corrosive substances and preparations which, through immediate, prolonged or repeated contact with the skin or mucous membrane, can cause inflammation.
H5	***Harmful:*** substances and preparations which, if they are inhaled or ingested or if they penetrate the skin, may involve limited health risks.
H6	***Toxic:*** substances and preparations (including very toxic substances and preparations) which, if they are inhaled or ingested or if they penetrate the skin, may involve serious, acute or chronic health risks and even death.
H7	***Carcinogenic:*** substances and preparations which, if they are inhaled or ingested or if they penetrate the skin, may induce cancer or increase its incidence.
H8	***Corrosive:*** substances and preparations which may destroy living tissue on contacts.
H9	***Infectious:*** substances containing viable micro-organisms or their toxins which are known or reliably believed to cause disease in man or other living organisms.
H10	***Teratogenic:*** substances and preparations which, if they are inhaled or ingested or if they penetrate the skin, may induce non-hereditary congenital malformations or increase their incidence.
H11	***Mutagenic:*** substances and preparations which, if they are inhaled or ingested or if they penetrate the skin, may induce hereditary genetic defects or increase their incidence.
H12	Substances and preparations which release toxic or very toxic gases in contact with water, air or an acid.
H13	Substances and preparations capable by any means, after disposal, of yielding another substance, e.g. a leachate, which possesses any of the characteristics listed above.
H14	***Ecotoxic:*** substances and preparations which present or may present immediate or delayed risks for one or more sectors of the environment.

Figure RSP-3: Hazardous properties.

Source: Environment Agency, HWR01, What is a Hazardous Waste?

RELEVANT STATUTORY PROVISIONS

Health and Safety (Display Screen Equipment) Regulations (DSE) 1992

Arrangement of regulations

2) Every employer shall carry out suitable and sufficient analysis of workstations.
3) Employers shall ensure that equipment provided meets the requirements of the schedule laid down in these Regulations.
4) Employers shall plan activities and provide such breaks or changes in work activity to reduce employees' workload on that equipment.
5) For display screen equipment (DSE) users, the employer shall provide, on request, an eyesight test carried out by a competent person.
6 & 7) Provision of information and training.

Outline of key points

WORKSTATION ASSESSMENTS (REG 2)

Should take account of:

- Screen   - positioning, character definition, character stability etc.
- Keyboard   - tilt able, character legibility etc.
- Desk   - size, matt surface etc.
- Chair   - adjustable back and height, footrest available etc.
- Environment   - noise, lighting, space etc.
- Software   - easy to use, work rate not governed by software.

INFORMATION AND TRAINING (REGS 6 & 7)

Should include:

- Risks to health.
- Precautions in place (e.g. the need for regular breaks).
- How to recognise problems.
- How to report problems.

Health and Safety (First-Aid) Regulations (FAR) 1981

Arrangement of regulations

1) Citation and commencement.
2) Interpretation.
3) Duty of employer to make provision for first-aid.
4) Duty of employer to inform his employees of the arrangements.
5) Duty of self-employed person to provide first-aid equipment.
6) Power to grant exemptions.
7) Cases where these Regulations do not apply.
8) Application to mines.
9) Application offshore.
10) Repeals, revocations and modification.
Schedule 1   Repeals.
Schedule 1   Revocations.

Outline of key points

2) Regulation 2 defines first aid as: '…treatment for the purpose of preserving life and minimising the consequences of injury or illness until medical (doctor or nurse) help can be obtained. Also, it provides treatment of minor injuries which would otherwise receive no treatment, or which do not need the help of a medical practitioner or nurse.'
3) Requires that every employer must provide equipment and facilities which are adequate and appropriate in the circumstances for administering first-aid to his employees.
4) An employer must inform his employees about the first-aid arrangements, including the location of equipment, facilities and identification of trained personnel.
5) Self-employed people must ensure that adequate and suitable provision is made for administering first-aid while at work.

Health and Safety (Safety Signs and Signals) Regulations (SSSR) 1996

Arrangement of regulations

1) Citation and commencement.
2) Interpretation.
3) Application.
4) Provision and maintenance of safety signs.
5) Information, instruction and training.
6) Transitional provisions.
7) Enforcement.
8) Revocations and amendments.

Outline of key points

The Regulations require employers to provide specific safety signs whenever there is a risk which has not been avoided or controlled by other means, e.g. by engineering controls and safe systems of work. Where a safety sign would not help to reduce that risk, or where the sign is not significant, there is no need to provide a sign.

They require, where necessary, the use of road traffic signs within workplaces to regulate road traffic.

They also require employers to:

- Maintain the safety signs which are provided by them.
- Explain unfamiliar signs to their employees and tell them what they need to do when they see a safety sign.

Regulations cover 4 main areas of signs:

1) **PROHIBITION** - circular signs, prime colours red and white. e.g. no pedestrian access.
2) **WARNING** - triangular signs, prime colours black on yellow. e.g. overhead electrics.
3) **MANDATORY** - circular signs, prime colours blue and white e.g. safety helmets must be worn.
4) **SAFE CONDITION** - oblong/square signs, prime colours green and white e.g. fire exit, first aid etc.

Supplementary signs provide additional information.

Supplementary signs with yellow/black or red/white diagonal stripes can be used to highlight a hazard, but must not substitute for signs as defined above.

Fire fighting, rescue equipment and emergency exit signs have to comply with a separate British Standard.

Health and Safety at Work etc. Act (HASAWA) 1974

Arrangement of Act

PRELIMINARY

1) Preliminary.

GENERAL DUTIES

2) General duties of employers to the employees.
3) General duties of employers and self-employed to persons other than their employees.
4) General duties of persons concerned with premises to persons other than their employees.
5) [repealed].
6) General duties of manufacturers etc. as regards articles and substances for use at work.
7) General duties of employees at work.
8) Duty not to interfere with or misuse things provided pursuant to certain provisions.
9) Duty not to charge employees for things done or provided pursuant to certain specific requirements.

THE HEALTH AND SAFETY COMMISSION AND THE HEALTH AND SAFETY EXECUTIVE

10) Establishment of the Commission and the Executive.
11) General functions of the Commission and the Executive.
12) Control of the Commission by the Secretary of State.
13) Other powers of the Commission.
14) Power of the Commission to direct investigations and Inquiries.

HEALTH AND SAFETY REGULATIONS AND APPROVED CODES OF PRACTICE

15) Health and safety regulations.
16) Approval of codes of practice by the Commission.
17) Use of approved codes of practice in criminal proceedings.

RELEVANT STATUTORY PROVISIONS

ENFORCEMENT
18) Authorities responsible for enforcement of the relevant statutory provisions.
19) Appointment of inspectors.
20) Powers of inspectors.
21) Improvement notices.
22) Prohibition notices.
23) Provisions supplementary toss. 21 and 22.
24) Appeal against improvement or prohibition notice.
25) Power to deal with cause of imminent danger.
26) Power of enforcing authorities to indemnify their inspectors.

OBTAINING AND DISCLOSURE OF INFORMATION
27) Obtaining of information by the Commission, the Executive, enforcing authorities etc.
28) Restrictions on disclosure of information.

SPECIAL PROVISIONS RELATING TO AGRICULTURE
29-32) [repealed].

PROVISIONS AS TO OFFENCES
33) Offences.
34) Extension of time for bringing summary proceedings.
35) Venue.
36) Offences due to fault of other person.
37) Offences by bodies corporate.
38) Restriction on institution of proceedings in England and Wales.
39) Prosecutions by inspectors.
40) Onus of proving limits of what is practicable etc.
41) Evidence.
42) Power of court to order cause of offence to be remedied or, in certain cases, forfeiture.

FINANCIAL PROVISION
43) Financial provisions.

MISCELLANEOUS AND SUPPLEMENTARY
44) Appeals in connection with licensing provisions in the relevant statutory provisions.
45) Default powers.
46) Service of notices.
47) Civil liability.
48) Application to Crown.
49) Adaptation of enactments to metric units or appropriate metric units.
50) Regulations under the relevant statutory provisions.
51) Exclusion of application to domestic employment.
52) Meaning of work and at work.
53) General interpretation of Part I.
54) Application of Part I to Isles of Scilly.

Outline of key points

AIMS
1) To protect people.
2) To protect the public from risks which may arise from work activities.

THE MAIN PROVISIONS - SECTION 1
a) Securing the health, safety and welfare of people at work.
b) Protecting others against risks arising from workplace activities.
c) Controlling the obtaining, keeping, and use of explosive and highly flammable substances.
d) Controlling emissions into the atmosphere of noxious or offensive substances.

Duties imposed on:
a) The employer.
b) The self employed.
c) Employees.
d) Contractors and subcontractors.
e) Designers, manufacturers, suppliers, importers and installers.

f) Specialists - architects, surveyors, engineers, personnel managers, health and safety specialists, and many more.

EMPLOYER'S DUTIES - [TO EMPLOYEES]

Section 2(1)

To ensure, so far as *reasonably practicable*, the health, safety and welfare at work of employees.

Section 2(2)

Ensuring health, safety and welfare at work through:
- Safe plant and systems of work e.g. provision of guards on machines.
- Safe use, handling, storage and transport of goods and materials e.g. good manual handling of boxes.
- Provision of information, instruction, training and supervision e.g. provision of induction training.
- Safe place of work including means of access and egress e.g. aisles kept clear.
- Safe and healthy working environment e.g. good lighting.

Further duties are placed on the employer by:

Section 2(3)

Prepare and keep up to date a written safety policy supported by information on the organisation and arrangements for carrying out the policy. The safety policy has to be brought to the notice of employees. If there are fewer than five employees, this section does not apply.

Section 2(4)

Recognised Trade Unions have the right to appoint safety representatives to represent the employees in consultations with the employer about health and safety matters.

Section 2(6)

Employers must consult with any safety representatives appointed by recognised Trade Unions.

Section 2(7)

To establish a safety committee if requested by two or more safety representatives.

EMPLOYER'S DUTIES - [TO PERSONS NOT HIS EMPLOYEES]

Section 3

a) Not to expose them to risk to their heath and safety e.g. contractor work barriered off.
b) To give information about risks which may affect them e.g. location induction for contractors.

SELF EMPLOYED DUTIES

Section 3

a) Not to expose themselves to risks to their health and safety e.g. wear personal protection.
b) Not to expose other persons to risks to their health and safety e.g. keep shared work area tidy.

Some of the practical steps that an organisation might take in order to ensure the safety of visitors to its premises are:
- Identify visitors by signing in, badges etc.
- Provide information regarding the risks present and the site rules and procedures to be followed, particularly in emergencies.
- Provide escorts to supervise visitors throughout the site.
- Restrict access to certain areas.

PEOPLE IN CONTROL OF PREMISES

Section 4

This section places duties on anyone who has control to any extent of non-domestic premises used by people who are not their employees. The duty extends to the provision of safe premises, plant and substances, e.g. maintenance of a boiler in rented out property.

MANUFACTURERS, DESIGNERS, SUPPLIERS, IMPORTERS, INSTALLERS

Section 6

This section places specific duties on those who can ensure that articles and substances are as safe and without risks as is reasonably practicable. The section covers:
- Safe design, installation and testing of equipment (including fairground equipment).
- Safe substances tested for risks.
- Provision of information on safe use and conditions essential to health and safety.
- Research to minimise risks.

RELEVANT STATUTORY PROVISIONS

EMPLOYEES' DUTIES

Section 7

a) To take reasonable care for themselves and others that may be affected by their acts / omissions e.g. wear eye protection, not obstruct a fire exit.

b) To co-operate with the employer or other to enable them to carry out their duty and/or statutory requirements e.g. report hazards or defects in controls, attend training, provide medical samples.

Additional duties created by the Management of Health and Safety at Work Regulations employees' duties:

- Every employee shall use any equipment, material or substance provided to them in accordance with any training and instruction.
- Every employee shall inform (via supervisory staff) their employer of any (a) risk situation or (b) shortcoming in the employer's protection arrangements.

OTHER DUTIES

Section 8

No person to interfere with or misuse anything provided to secure health and safety - e.g. wedge fire door open, remove first aid equipment without authority, breach lock off systems.

Section 9

Employees cannot be charged for anything done or provided to comply with a specific legal obligation e.g. personal protective equipment, health surveillance or welfare facilities.

OFFENCES COMMITTED BY OTHER PERSONS

Section 36

- Where the commission by any person of the breach of legislation is due to the act or default of some other person, that other person shall be guilty of the offence and may be charged with and convicted of the offence whether or not proceedings are taken against the first mentioned person.
- Case law indicates that 'other person' refers to persons lower down the corporate tree than mentioned in section 37, e.g. middle managers, safety advisors, training officers; and may extend to people working on contract e.g. architects, consultants or a planning supervisor.

OFFENCES COMMITTED BY THE BODY CORPORATE

Section 37

Where there has been a breach of legislation on the part of a body corporate (limited company or local authority) and the offence can be proved to have been committed with the consent or connivance of or to be attributable to any neglect on the part of any director, manager, secretary or similar officer of the body corporate, he, as well as the body corporate, can be found guilty and punished accordingly.

ONUS OF PROOF

Section 40

In any proceedings for an offence under any of the relevant statutory involving a failure to comply with a duty or requirement:

- To do something so far as is practicable.
- To do something so far as is reasonably practicable.
- It shall be for the accused to prove that the requirements were met rather than for the prosecution to prove that the requirements were not met.

Ionising Radiations Regulations (IRR) 1999

Arrangement of regulations

PART I - INTERPRETATION AND GENERAL

1. Citation and commencement.
2. Interpretation.
3. Application.
4. Duties under the Regulations.

PART II - GENERAL PRINCIPLES AND PROCEDURES

5. Authorisation of specified practices.
6. Notification of specified work.
7. Prior risk assessment etc.
8. Restriction of exposure.
9. Personal protective equipment.

10. Maintenance and examination of engineering controls etc. and personal protective equipment.
11. Dose limitation.
12. Contingency plans.

PART III - ARRANGEMENTS FOR THE MANAGEMENT OF RADIATION PROTECTION

13. Radiation protection adviser.
14. Information, instruction and training.
15. Co-operation between employers.

PART IV - DESIGNATED AREAS

16. Designation of controlled or supervised areas.
17. Local rules and radiation protection supervisors.
18. Additional requirements for designated areas.
19. Monitoring of designated areas.

PART V - CLASSIFICATION AND MONITORING OF PERSONS

20. Designation of classified persons.
21. Dose assessment and recording.
22. Estimated doses and special entries.
23. Dosimetry for accidents etc.
24. Medical surveillance.
25. Investigation and notification of overexposure.
26. Dose limitation for overexposed employees.

PART VI - ARRANGEMENTS FOR THE CONTROL OF RADIOACTIVE SUBSTANCES, ARTICLES AND EQUIPMENT

27. Sealed sources and articles containing or embodying radioactive substances.
28. Accounting for radioactive substances.
29. Keeping and moving of radioactive substances.
30. Notification of certain occurrences.
31. Duties of manufacturers etc. of articles for use in work with ionising radiation.
32. Equipment used for medical exposure.
33. Misuse of or interference with sources of ionising radiation.

PART VII - DUTIES OF EMPLOYEES AND MISCELLANEOUS

34. Duties of employees.
35. Approval of dosimetry services.
36. Defence on contravention.
37. Exemption certificates.
38. Extension outside Great Britain.
39. Transitional provisions.
40. Modifications relating to the Ministry of Defence.
41. Modification, revocation and saving.

SCHEDULES

Schedule 1. Work not required to be notified under regulation 6.
Schedule 2. Particulars to be provided in a notification under regulation 6(2).
Schedule 3. Additional particulars that the Executive may require.
Schedule 4. Dose limits.
Schedule 5. Matters in respect of which radiation protection adviser must be consulted by a radiation employer.
Schedule 6. Particulars to be entered in the radiation passbook.
Schedule 7. Particulars to be contained in a health record.
Schedule 8. Quantities and concentrations of radionuclides.
Schedule 9. Modifications.

Outline of key points

These Regulations supersede and consolidate the Ionising Radiations Regulations 1985 and the Ionising Radiation (Outside Workers) Regulations 1993.

The Regulations impose duties on employers to protect employees and other persons against ionising radiation arising from work with radioactive substances and other sources of ionising radiation and also impose certain duties on employees.

The Regulations are divided into 7 Parts.

RELEVANT STATUTORY PROVISIONS

Lifting Operations and Lifting Equipment Regulations (LOLER) 1998

Arrangements of regulations

1) Citation and commencement.
2) Interpretation.
3) Application.
4) Strength and stability.
5) Lifting equipment for lifting persons.
6) Positioning and installation.
7) Marking of lifting equipment.
8) Organisation of lifting operations.
9) Thorough examination and inspection.
10) Reports and defects.
11) Keeping of information.
12) Exemption for the armed forces.
13) Amendment of the Shipbuilding and Ship-repairing Regulations 1960.
14) Amendment of the Docks Regulation 1988.
15) Repeal of provisions of the Factories Act 1961.
16) Repeal of section 85 of the Mines and Quarries Act 1954.
17) Revocation of instruments.
Schedule 1. Information to be contained in a report of a thorough examination.
Schedule 2. Revocation of instruments.

Outline of key points

The Lifting Operations and Lifting Equipment Regulations (LOLER) 1998 impose health and safety requirements with respect to lifting equipment (as defined in regulation 2(1)). They are not industry specific and apply to almost all lifting operations.

The Regulations place duties on employers, the self-employed, and certain persons having control of lifting equipment (of persons at work who use or supervise or manage its use, or of the way it is used, to the extent of their control (regulation 3(3) to (5)).

The Regulations make provision with respect to:

- The strength and stability of lifting equipment (regulation 4).
- The safety of lifting equipment for lifting persons (regulation 5).
- The way lifting equipment is positioned and installed (regulation 6).
- The marking of machinery and accessories for lifting, and lifting equipment which is designed for lifting persons or which might so be used in error (regulation 7).
- The organisation of lifting operations (regulation 8).
- The thorough examination (defined in (regulation 2(1)) and inspection of lifting equipment in specified circumstances, (regulation 9(1) to (3)).
- The evidence of examination to accompany it outside the undertaking (regulation 9(4)).
- The exception for winding apparatus at mines from regulation 9 (regulation 9(5)).
- Transitional arrangements relating to regulation 9 (regulation 9(6) and (7)).
- The making of reports of thorough examinations and records of inspections (regulation 10 and Schedule 1).
- The keeping of information in the reports and records (regulation 11).

Management of Health and Safety at Work Regulations (MHSWR) 1999

Arrangement of regulations

1) Citation, commencement and interpretation.
2) Disapplication of these Regulations.
3) Risk assessment.
4) Principles of prevention to be applied.
5) Health and safety arrangements.
6) Health surveillance.
7) Health and safety assistance.
8) Procedures for serious and imminent danger and for danger areas.
9) Contacts with external services.
10) Information for employees.
11) Co-operation and co-ordination.
12) Persons working in host employers' or self-employed persons' undertakings.

13) Capabilities and training.
14) Employees' duties.
15) Temporary workers.
16) Risk assessment in respect of new or expectant mothers.
17) Certificate from a registered medical practitioner in respect of new or expectant mothers.
18) Notification by new or expectant mothers.
19) Protection of young persons.
20) Exemption certificates.
21) Provisions as to liability.
22) Exclusion of civil liability.
23) Extension outside Great Britain.
24) Amendment of the Health and Safety (First-Aid) Regulations 1981.
25) Amendment of the Offshore Installations and Pipeline Works (First-Aid) Regulations 1989.
26) Amendment of the Mines Miscellaneous Health and Safety Provisions Regulations 1995.
27) Amendment of the Construction (Health, Safety and Welfare) Regulations 1996.
28) Regulations to have effect as health and safety regulations.
29) Revocations and consequential amendments.
30) Transitional provision.

Schedule 1. General principles of prevention.
Schedule 2. Consequential amendments.

Outline of key points

Management of Health and Safety at Work Regulations (MHSWR) 1999 set out some broad general duties which apply to almost all kinds of work. They are aimed mainly at improving health and safety management. You may already be familiar with broad health and safety law of this kind - as it is the form taken by the Health and Safety at Work Act (HASAWA) 1974. The Regulations work in a similar way, and in fact they can be seen as a way of fleshing out what is already in the HASAWA 1974. The 1999 Regulations replace the Management of Health and Safety at Work Regulations 1992, the Management of Health and Safety at Work (Amendment) Regulations 1994, the Health and Safety (Young Persons) Regulations 1997 and Part III of the Fire Precautions (Workplace) Regulations 1997. The Principal Regulations are discussed below.

RISK ASSESSMENT (REGULATION 3)

The regulations require employers (and the self-employed) to assess the risk to the health and safety of their employees and to anyone else who may be affected by their work activity. This is necessary to ensure that the preventive and protective steps can be identified to control hazards in the workplace.

A *hazard* is defined as something with the potential to cause harm and may include machinery, substances or a work practice.

A *risk* is defined as the likelihood that a particular hazard will cause harm. Consideration must be given to the population, i.e. the number of persons who might be exposed to harm and the consequence of such exposure.

Where an employer is employing or about to employ young persons (under 18 years of age) he must carry out a risk assessment which takes particular account of:

- The inexperience, lack of awareness of risks and immaturity of young persons.
- The layout of the workplace and workstations.
- Exposure to physical, biological and chemical agents.
- Work equipment and the way in which it is handled.
- The extent of health and safety training to be provided.
- Risks from agents, processes and work listed in the Annex to Council Directive 94/33/EC on the protection of young people at work.

Where 5 or more employees are employed, the significant findings of risk assessments must be recorded in writing (the same threshold that is used in respect of having a written safety policy). This record must include details of any employees being identified as being especially at risk.

PRINCIPLES OF PREVENTION TO BE APPLIED (REGULATION 4)

Regulation 4 requires an employer to implement preventive and protective measures on the basis of general principles of prevention specified in Schedule 1 to the Regulations. These are:

1) Avoiding risks.
2) Evaluating the risks which cannot be avoided.
3) Combating the risks at source.
4) Adapting the work to the individual, especially as regards the design of workplaces, the choice of work equipment and the choice of working and production methods, with a view, in particular, to alleviating monotonous work and work at a predetermined work-rate and to reducing their effect on health.
5) Adapting to technical progress.
6) Replacing the dangerous by the non-dangerous or the less dangerous.
7) Developing a coherent overall prevention policy which covers technology, organisation of work, working conditions, social relationships and the influence of factors relating to the working environment.
8) Giving collective protective measures priority over individual protective measures.

RELEVANT STATUTORY PROVISIONS

9) Giving appropriate instructions to employees.

HEALTH AND SAFETY ARRANGEMENTS (REGULATION 5)

Appropriate arrangements must be made for the effective planning, organisation, control, monitoring and review of preventative and protective measures (in other words, for the management of health and safety). Again, employers with five or more employees must have their arrangements in writing.

HEALTH SURVEILLANCE (REGULATION 6)

In addition to the requirements of specific regulations such as Control of Substances Hazardous to Health (COSHH) 2002 and Asbestos regulations, consideration must be given to carry out health surveillance of employees where there is a disease or adverse health condition identified in risk assessments.

HEALTH AND SAFETY ASSISTANCE (REGULATION 7)

The employer must appoint one or more competent persons to assist him in complying with the legal obligations imposed on the undertaking (including Part II of the Fire Precautions (Workplace) Regulations (FPWR) 1997). The number of persons appointed should reflect the number of employees and the type of hazards in the workplace.

If more than one competent person is appointed, then arrangements must be made for ensuring adequate co-operation between them. The Competent person(s) must be given the necessary time and resources to fulfil their functions. This will depend on the size the undertaking, the risks to which employees are exposed and the distribution of those risks throughout the undertaking.

The employer must ensure that competent person(s) who are not employees are informed of the factors known (or suspected) to affect the health and safety of anyone affected by business activities.

Competent people are defined as those who have sufficient training and experience or knowledge and other qualities to enable them to perform their functions.

Persons may be selected from among existing employees or from outside. Where there is a suitable person in the employer's employment, that person shall be appointed as the 'competent person' in preference to a non-employee.

PROCEDURES FOR SERIOUS AND IMMINENT DANGER AND FOR DANGER AREAS (REGULATION 8)

Employers are required to set up emergency procedures and appoint **competent persons** to ensure compliance with identified arrangements, to devise control strategies as appropriate and to limit access to areas of risk to ensure that only those persons with adequate health and safety knowledge and instruction are admitted.

The factors to be considered when preparing a procedure to deal with workplace emergencies such as fire, explosion, bomb scare, chemical leakage or other dangerous occurrence should include:

- The identification and training requirements of persons with specific responsibilities.
- The layout of the premises in relation to escape routes etc.
- The number of persons affected.
- Assessment of special needs (disabled persons, children etc.).
- Warning systems.
- Emergency lighting.
- Location of shut-off valves, isolation switches, hydrants etc.
- Equipment required to deal with the emergency.
- Location of assembly points.
- Communication with emergency services.
- Training and/or information to be given to employees, visitors, local residents and anyone else who might be affected.

CONTACTS WITH EXTERNAL SERVICES (REGULATION 9)

Employers must ensure that, where necessary, contacts are made with external services. This particularly applies with regard to first-aid, emergency medical care and rescue work.

INFORMATION FOR EMPLOYEES (REGULATION 10)

Employees must be provided with relevant information about hazards to their health and safety arising from risks identified by the assessments. Clear instruction must be provided concerning any preventative or protective control measures including those relating to serious and imminent danger and fire assessments. Details of any competent persons nominated to discharge specific duties in accordance with the regulations must also be communicated as should risks arising from contact with other employer's activities (see Regulation 11).

Before employing a child (a person who is not over compulsory school age) the employer must provide those with parental responsibility for the child with information on the risks that have been identified and preventative and protective measures to be taken.

CO-OPERATION AND CO-ORDINATION (REGULATION 11)

Employers who work together in a common workplace have a duty to co-operate to discharge their duties under relevant statutory provisions. They must also take all reasonable steps to inform their respective employees of risks to their health or safety which may arise out of their work. Specific arrangements must be made to ensure compliance with fire legislation (i.e. the Fire Precautions (Workplace) Regulations (FPWR) 1997).

PERSONS WORKING IN HOST EMPLOYERS' OR SELF EMPLOYED PERSONS' UNDERTAKINGS (REGULATION 12)

This regulation extends the requirements of regulation 11 to include employees working as sole occupiers of a workplace under the control of another employer. Such employees would include those working under a service of contract and employees in temporary employment businesses under the control of the first employer.

CAPABILITIES AND TRAINING (REGULATION 13)

Employers need to take into account the capabilities of their employees before entrusting tasks. This is necessary to ensure that they have adequate health and safety training and are capable enough at their jobs to avoid risk. To this end consideration must be given to recruitment including job orientation when transferring between jobs and work departments. Training must also be provided when other factors such as the introduction of new technology and new systems of work or work equipment arise.

Training must:

- Be repeated periodically where appropriate.
- Be adapted to take account of any new or changed risks to the health and safety of the employees concerned.
- Take place during working hours.

EMPLOYEES' DUTIES (REGULATION 14)

Employees are required to follow health and safety instructions by using machinery, substances, transport etc. in accordance with the instructions and training that they have received.

They must also inform their employer (and other employers) of any dangers or shortcoming in the health and safety arrangements, even if there is no risk of imminent danger.

TEMPORARY WORKERS (REGULATION 15)

Consideration is given to the special needs of temporary workers. In particular to the provision of particular health and safety information such as qualifications required to perform the task safely or any special arrangements such as the need to provide health screening.

RISKS ASSESSMENT IN RESPECT OF NEW OR EXPECTANT MOTHERS (REGULATION 16)

Where the work is of a kind which would involve risk to a new or expectant mother or her baby, then the assessment required by regulation 3 should take this into account.

If the risk cannot be avoided, then the employer should take reasonable steps to:

- Adjust the hours worked.
- Offer alternative work.
- Give paid leave for as long as is necessary.

CERTIFICATE FROM A REGISTERED MEDICAL PRACTITIONER IN RESPECT OF NEW OR EXPECTANT MOTHERS (REGULATION 17)

Where the woman is a night shift worker and has a medical certificate identifying night shift work as a risk then the employer must put her on day shift or give paid leave for as long as is necessary.

NOTIFICATION BY NEW OR EXPECTANT MOTHERS (REGULATION 18)

The employer need take no action until he is notified in writing by the woman that she is pregnant, has given birth in the last six months, or is breastfeeding.

PROTECTION OF YOUNG PERSONS (REGULATION 19)

Employers of young persons shall ensure that they are not exposed to risk as a consequence of their lack of experience, lack of awareness or lack of maturity.

No employer shall employ young people for work which:

- Is beyond his physical or psychological capacity.
- Involves exposure to agents which chronically affect human health.
- Involves harmful exposure to radiation.
- Involves a risk to health from extremes of temperature, noise or vibration.
- Involves risks which could not be reasonably foreseen by young persons.

This regulation does not prevent the employment of a young person who is no longer a child for work:

- Where it is necessary for his training.
- Where the young person will be supervised by a competent person.
- Where any risk will be reduced to the lowest level that is reasonably practicable.

(Note: Two HSE publications give guidance on the changes. HSG122 - New and expectant mothers at work: a guide for employers and HSG165 - Young people at work: a guide for employers.)

EXEMPTION CERTIFICATES (REGULATION 20)

The Secretary of State for Defence may, in the interests of national security, by a certificate in writing exempt the armed forces, any visiting force or any headquarters from certain obligations imposed by the Regulations.

PROVISIONS AS TO LIABILITY (REGULATION 21)

Employers cannot submit a defence in criminal proceedings that contravention was caused by the act or default either of an employee or the competent person appointed under Regulation 7.

EXCLUSION OF CIVIL LIABILITY (REGULATION 22)

Breach of a duty imposed by these Regulations shall not confer a right of action in any civil proceedings for those other than employees.

REVOCATIONS AND AMENDMENTS (REGULATIONS 24-29)

The Regulations:

- Revoke regulation 6 of the Health and Safety (First-Aid) Regulations (FAR) 1981 which confers power on the Health and Safety Executive to grant exemptions from those Regulations.
- Amend the Offshore Installations and Pipeline Works (First-Aid) Regulations 1989.
- Amend the Mines Miscellaneous Health and Safety Provisions Regulations 1995.
- Amend the Construction (Health, Safety and Welfare) Regulations (CHSW) 1996.

The Regulations provide that, with some exceptions, the Fire Precautions (Workplace) Regulations (FPWR) 1997 are to be considered as health and safety regulations within the meaning of the Health and Safety at Work etc Act (HASAWA) 1974. The Regulations also make amendments to the statutory instruments as specified in Schedule 2.

TRANSITIONAL PROVISION (REGULATION 30)

The Regulations contain a transitional provision (regulation 30). The substitution of provisions in the 1999 Regulations for provisions of the Management of Health and Safety at Work Regulations (MHSWR) 1992 shall not affect the continuity of the law; and accordingly anything done under or for the purposes of such provision of the 1992 Regulations shall have effect as if done under or for the purposes of any corresponding provision of these Regulations.

Management of Health and Safety at Work and Fire Precautions (Workplace) (Amendment) Regulations 2003

Fire Precautions (Workplace) Regulations 1997 have now been repealed by the Regulatory Reform (Fire Safety) Order 2005.

See also - Management of Health and Safety at Work Regulations (MHSWR) 1999.

Arrangement of regulations

1) Citation and commencement.
2-6) Amendments to the Management of Health and Safety at Work Regulations 1999.
7-13) Amendments to the Fire Precautions (Workplace) Regulations 1997.

Outline of key points

AMENDMENTS TO MANAGEMENT OF HEALTH AND SAFETY AT WORK REGULATIONS 1999

2. The Management of Health and Safety at Work Regulations 1999[5] shall be amended in accordance with regulations 3 to 6 of these Regulations and any reference in those provisions to any specified provision shall, unless the context requires otherwise, be taken to be a reference to the provision so specified of the Management of Health and Safety at Work Regulations 1999.

3. For regulation 2 there shall be substituted the following regulation -

    " Disapplication of these Regulations 2. -

    (1) These Regulations shall not apply to or in relation to the master or crew of a ship, or to the employer of such persons, in respect of the normal ship-board activities of a ship's crew which are carried out solely by the crew under the direction of the master.

    (2) Regulations 3(4), (5), 10(2) and 19 shall not apply to occasional work or short-term work involving work regarded as not being harmful, damaging or dangerous to young people in a family undertaking.

    (3) In this regulation -

    "normal ship-board activities" include -

    (a) the construction, reconstruction or conversion of a ship outside, but not inside, Great Britain; and
    (b) the repair of a ship save repair when carried out in dry dock; "ship" includes every description of vessel used in navigation, other than a ship belonging to Her Majesty which forms part of Her Majesty's Navy.".

4. In regulation 3(3) the words "and where" to the end shall follow and not appear in subparagraph (b).
5. Regulation 19(4) shall be omitted.
6. For regulation 22 there shall be substituted the following regulation - " Restriction of civil liability for breach of statutory duty 22. Breach of a duty imposed on an employer by these Regulations shall not confer a right of action in any civil proceedings insofar as that duty applies for the protection of persons not in his employment."

Manual Handling Operations Regulations (MHOR) 1992

Arrangement of regulations

1) Citation and commencement.
2) Interpretation.
3) Disapplication of Regulations.
4) Duties of employers.
5) Duty of employees.
6) Exemption certificates.
7) Extension outside Great Britain.
8) Repeals and revocations.

Outline of key points

CITATION AND COMMENCEMENT (1)

INTERPRETATION (2)

"Injury" does not include injury caused by toxic or corrosive substances which:
- Have leaked/spilled from load.
- Are present on the surface but not leaked/spilled from it.
- Are a constituent part of the load.

"Load" includes any person or animal.

"Manual Handling Operations" means transporting or supporting a load including:
- Lifting and putting down.
- Pushing, pulling or moving by hand or bodily force.
- Shall as far as is reasonably practicable.

DISAPPLICATION OF REGULATIONS (3)

DUTIES OF EMPLOYERS (4)

AVOIDANCE OF MANUAL HANDLING (4) (1)(A)

The employer's duty is to avoid the need for manual handling operations which involve a risk of their employees being injured - as far as is reasonably practicable.

REDUCING THE RISK OF INJURY (4) (1)(B)(II)

Take appropriate steps to reduce the risk of injury to the lowest level reasonably practicable.

THE LOAD - ADDITIONAL INFORMATION (4) (1)(B)(III)

Employers shall provide information on general indications or where reasonably practicable precise information on:
- The weight of each load.
- The heaviest side of any load whose centre of gravity is not central.

REVIEWING THE ASSESSMENT (4) (2)

Assessment review:
- Where there is reason to believe the assessment is no longer valid.
- There is sufficient change in manual handling operations.

DUTY OF EMPLOYEES (5)

Employees shall make full and proper use of any system of work provided for his use by his employer.

EXEMPTION CERTIFICATES (6)

EXTENSION OUTSIDE GREAT BRITAIN (7)

REPEALS AND REVOCATIONS (8)

SCHEDULES

Schedule 1 - Factors to which the employer must have regard and questions he must consider when making an assessment of manual handling operations.

Schedule 2 - Repeals and revocations.

Appendix 1 - Numerical guidelines for assessment.

Appendix 2 - Example of an assessment checklist.

Thus the Regulations establish a clear hierarchy of measures:

1. Avoid hazardous manual handling operations so far as is reasonably practicable.
2. Make a suitable and sufficient assessment of any hazardous manual handling operations that cannot be avoided.
3. Reduce the risk of injury so far as is reasonably practicable.

RELEVANT STATUTORY PROVISIONS

New Roads and Street Works Act 1991

Arrangement of regulations

PART I
New Roads in England and Wales
Concession agreements
Toll orders
Further provisions with respect to tolls
Annual report
Miscellaneous
General

PART II
New Roads in Scotland
Toll Roads
Further provision with respect to tolls
Report
Supplementary provisions

PART III
Street works in England and Wales
Introductory provisions
The street works register
Notice and co-ordination of works
Streets subject to special controls
General requirements as to execution of street works
Reinstatement
Charges, fees and contributions payable by undertakers
Duties and liabilities of undertakers with respect to apparatus
Apparatus affected by highway, bridge or transport works
Provisions with respect to particular authorities and undertakings
Power of street authority or district council to undertake street works
Supplementary provisions

PART IV
Road works in Scotland
Introductory provisions
The road works register
Notice and co-ordination of works
Roads subject to special controls
General requirements as to execution of road works
Reinstatement
Charges, fees and contributions payable by undertakers
Duties and liabilities of undertakers with respect to apparatus
Apparatus affected by road, bridge or transport works
Provisions with respect to particular authorities and undertakings
Power of road works authority or district council to undertake road works
Supplementary provisions

PART V
General

Schedule 1	Supplementary provisions as to termination of concession.
Schedule 2	Procedure in connection with toll orders.
Schedule 3	Street works licences.
Schedule 4	Streets with special engineering difficulties.
Schedule 5	Procedure for making certain orders under Part III.
Schedule 6	Roads with special engineering difficulties.

Schedule 7	Procedure for making certain orders under Part IV.
Schedule 8	Minor and consequential amendments.
Part I	Amendments of the Highways Act 1980.
Part II	Amendments of the Road Traffic Regulation Act 1984.
Part III	Amendments of the Roads (Scotland) Act 1984.
Part IV	Amendments of other enactments.
Schedule 9	Repeals.

Outline of key points

1. One of the most important elements of the street works legislation is the duty on street authorities to co-ordinate all works in the highway. As important is the parallel duty on undertakers to co-operate in this process. It is essential that both street authorities and undertakers take these responsibilities seriously. This Code of Practice is intended to help them do so.

2. The New Roads and Street Works Act 1991 ("the Act") spells out the objectives of the co-ordination function. They are:

    - To ensure safety.

    - To minimise inconvenience to people using a street, including a specific reference to people with a disability.

    - To protect the structure of the street and apparatus in it.

    It is essential that these objectives are taken into account by everyone responsible for planning and carrying out works in the highway.

3. The legislative and regulatory provisions explained in the Code are perhaps best viewed as three pillars of the co-ordination framework:

    - The notice system - the notices themselves provide vital information to aid the co-ordination process, while the notice periods provide time within which appropriate steps can be taken. The best method of exchanging notices is electronically.

    - Streets subject to special controls - these designation procedures provide a mechanism by which attention can be focused on particularly sensitive streets. Particularly important in this context are traffic-sensitive streets.

    - The co-ordination tools - the legislation provides a range of tools to facilitate the co-ordination process. These include: the power to direct the timing of street works; the power to restrict street works following substantial road works; and the requirement on undertakers to avoid unnecessary delay and obstruction.

4. There are three key principles to which undertakers and street authorities must adhere if this aspect of the legislation is to be effective. They are:

    - The need to balance the potentially conflicting interests of road users and undertakers' customers. All concerned must remember that the motorists and pedestrians who suffer as a result of works of all kinds in the street are the same people who benefit from and depend on a reliable service from the undertakers.

    - The importance of close co-operation and liaison between street authorities and undertakers. Good communication is central to the co-ordination process.

    - An acknowledgement on all sides of the fact that works programmes and practices may have to be adjusted in order to ensure that the statutory objectives of the co-ordination provisions are achieved.

5. The Code of Practice explains how these principles can be implemented in practice. Particularly significant elements of the guidance are:

    - The fact that the notice periods specified in the legislation and Regulations are minimum periods: wherever possible longer periods of notice should be given and information contained in notices should be updated whenever appropriate.

    - The central role played by local liaison meetings between street authorities, undertakers and other interested parties.

    - The importance of the designation of streets subject to special controls. Street authorities should ensure that designation is confined to those cases where it is strictly necessary. Undertakers must respect the objectives of designation when planning and carrying out works in such streets.

6. In carrying out their responsibilities under the legislation, street authorities and undertakers should endeavour to ensure that their works are planned in such a way as to minimise inconvenience to all road users including disability groups. This has implications for: the timing of works, the way in which they are carried out, and programming of undertakers' and street authorities' medium- and long-term works planning. Inevitably, in all but the quietest situations, works in the street must interfere with traffic to some extent; the aim should, however, be to ensure that only in exceptional circumstances will:

    - Serious traffic disruption be caused by street works.

    - Recently resurfaced or reconstructed streets be affected by street works.

    - One undertaker carry out planned street works in a street within a short time of earlier works being carried out.

    The street authority is generally the first point of contact for public complaints. In order to ensure the public is aware who is responsible for the works, it is therefore important that the promoting undertaker gives advance information and warning to affected frontagers not only about any disruption to their services, but also if their access is to be affected for any length of time. Details of alternative access arrangements, or any other form of mitigating action to be taken by the promoting undertaker, should be supplied.

7. In no provision is the crucial balance between highway and utility interests better illustrated than the execution of urgent works on traffic-sensitive streets. The concept of urgent works reflects the crucial importance of some types of street works which fall short of emergencies as defined in the Act. Traffic-sensitive streets are those on which street works are most likely to cause traffic disruption.

RELEVANT STATUTORY PROVISIONS

8. It is important that, in this area in particular, authorities and undertakers work closely together. If they do not the urgent works provisions will fall into disrepute and the credibility of the legislation and the two key players in its implementation will be undermined.

9. Street authorities must pay particular attention to the need to minimise the impact of works on people with disabilities. Similarly, undertakers must take full account of the interests of people with disabilities when planning and implementing their works.

Source: http://www.dft.gov.uk/consultations/archive/2000/codpcs/codeofpracticeforthecoordina1185?page=2.

Personal Protective Equipment at Work Regulations (PPER) 1992

Arrangement of regulations

1) Citation and commencement.
2) Interpretation.
3) Disapplication of these Regulations.
4) Provision of personal protective equipment.
5) Compatibility of personal protective equipment.
6) Assessment of personal protective equipment.
7) Maintenance and replacement of personal protective equipment.
8) Accommodation for personal protective equipment.
9) Information, instruction and training.
10) Use of personal protective equipment.
11) Reporting loss or defect.
12) Exemption certificates.
13) Extension outside Great Britain.
14) Modifications, repeal and revocations directive.

Schedule 1	Relevant Community.
Schedule 2	Modifications.
Part I	Factories Act 1961.
Part II	The Coal and Other Mines (Fire and Rescue) Order 1956.
Part III	The Shipbuilding and Ship-Repairing Regulations 1960.
Part IV	The Coal Mines (Respirable Dust) Regulations 1975.
Part V	The Control of Lead at Work Regulations 1980.
Part VI	The Ionising Radiations Regulations 1985.
Part VII	The Control of Asbestos at Work Regulations 1987.
Part VIII	The Control of Substances Hazardous to Health Regulations 1988.
Part IX	The Noise at Work Regulations 1989.
Part X	The Construction (Head Protection) Regulations 1989.
Schedule 3	Revocations.

Outline of key points

2) Personal protective equipment (PPE) means all equipment (including clothing provided for protection against adverse weather) which is intended to be worn or held by a person at work and which protects him against risks to his health or safety.

3) These Regulations do not apply to:
   - Ordinary working clothes / uniforms.
   - Offensive weapons.
   - Portable detectors which signal risk.
   - Equipment used whilst playing competitive sports.
   - Equipment provided for travelling on a road.

   The Regulations do not apply to situations already controlled by other Regulations i.e.
   - Control of Lead at Work Regulations 1998.
   - Ionising Radiation Regulations 1999.
   - Control of Asbestos at Work Regulations 1987 (and as amended 1999).
   - CoSHH Regulations 1999.
   - Noise at Work Regulations 1989.
   - Construction (Head Protection) Regulations 1989.

4) Suitable PPE must be provided when risks cannot be adequately controlled by other means. Reg. 4 shall ensure suitable PPE:
   - Appropriate for the risk and conditions.
   - Ergonomic requirements.
   - State of health of users.
   - Correctly fitting and adjustable.

- Complies with EEC directives.

5) Equipment must be compatible with any other PPE which has to be worn.

6) Before issuing PPE, the employer must carry out a risk assessment to ensure that the equipment is suitable.
   - Assess risks not avoided by other means.
   - Define characteristics of PPE and of the risk of the equipment itself.
   - Compare characteristics of PPE to defined requirement.
   - Repeat assessment when no longer valid, or significant change has taken place.

7) PPE must be maintained.
   - In an efficient state.
   - In efficient working order.
   - In good repair.

8) Accommodation must be provided for equipment when it is not being used.

9) Information, instruction and training must be given on:
   - The risks PPE will eliminate or limit.
   - Why the PPE is to be used.
   - How the PPE is to be used.
   - How to maintain the PPE.
   - Information and instruction must be comprehensible to the wearer/user.

10) Employers shall take reasonable steps to ensure PPE is worn.
    - Every employee shall use PPE that has been provided.
    - Every employee shall take reasonable steps to return PPE to storage.

11) Employees must report any loss or defect.

The Guidance on the Regulations points out:

"Whatever PPE is chosen, it should be remembered that, although some types of equipment do provide very high levels of protection, none provides 100%"

PPE includes the following when worn for health and safety reasons at work:

- Aprons.
- Adverse weather gear.
- High visibility clothing.
- Gloves.
- Safety footwear.
- Safety helmets.
- Eye protection.
- Life-jackets.
- Respirators.
- Safety harness.
- Underwater breathing gear.

Provision and Use of Work Equipment Regulations (PUWER) 1998

Arrangement of regulations

PART I - INTRODUCTION
1) Citation and commencement.
2) Interpretation.
3) Application.

PART II - GENERAL
4) Suitability of work equipment.
5) Maintenance.
6) Inspection.
7) Specific risks.
8) Information and instructions.
9) Training.
10) Conformity with Community requirements.
11) Dangerous parts of machinery.
12) Protection against specified hazards.
13) High or very low temperature.
14) Controls for starting or making a significant change in operating conditions.
15) Stop controls.
16) Emergency stop controls.
17) Controls.
18) Control systems.
19) Isolation from sources of energy.
20) Stability.
21) Lighting.

RELEVANT STATUTORY PROVISIONS

22) Maintenance operations.
23) Markings.
24) Warnings.

PART III - MOBILE WORK EQUIPMENT
25) Employees carried on mobile work equipment.
26) Rolling over of mobile work equipment.
27) Overturning of fork-lift trucks.
28) Self-propelled work equipment.
29) Remote-controlled self-propelled work equipment.
30) Drive shafts.

PART IV - POWER PRESSES
31) Power presses to which Part IV does not apply.
32) Thorough examination of power presses, guards and protection devices.
33) Inspection of guards and protection devices.
34) Reports.
35) Keeping of information.

PART V - MISCELLANEOUS
36) Exemption for the armed forces.
37) Transitional provision.
38) Repeal of enactment.
39) Revocation of instruments.

Schedule 1   Instruments which give effect to Community directives concerning the safety of products.
Schedule 2   Power presses to which regulations 32 to 35 do not apply.
Schedule 3   Information to be contained in a report of a thorough examination of a power press, guard or protection device.
Schedule 4   Revocation of instruments.

Outline of key points

These Regulations impose health and safety requirements with respect to the provision and use of work equipment, which is defined as 'any machinery, appliance, apparatus, tool or installation for use at work (whether exclusively or not)'. These regulations:

- Place general duties on employers.
- Certain persons having control of work equipment, of persons at work who use or supervise or manage its use or of the way it is used, to the extent of their control.
- List minimum requirements for work equipment to deal with selected hazards whatever the industry.
- 'Use' includes any activity involving work equipment and includes starting, stopping, programming, setting, transporting, repairing, modifying, maintaining, servicing and cleaning.

The general duties require you to:

- Make sure that equipment is suitable for the use that will be made of it.
- Take into account the working conditions and hazards in the workplace when selecting equipment.
- Ensure equipment is used only for operations for which, and under conditions for which, it is suitable.
- Ensure that equipment is maintained in an efficient state, in efficient working order and in good repair.
- Ensure the inspection of work equipment in specified circumstances by a competent person; keep a record of the result for specified periods; and ensure that evidence of the last inspection accompany work equipment used outside the undertaking.
- Give adequate information, instruction and training.
- Provide equipment that conforms with EU product safety directives.

Specific requirements cover
- Guarding of dangerous parts of machinery.
- Protection against specified hazards i.e. falling/ejected articles and substances, rupture/disintegration of work equipment parts, equipment catching fire or overheating, unintended or premature discharge of articles and substances, explosion.
- Work equipment parts and substances at high or very low temperatures.
- Control systems and control devices.
- Isolation of equipment from sources of energy.
- Stability of equipment.
- Lighting.
- Maintenance operations.
- Warnings and markings.

Mobile work equipment must have provision as to:
- Its suitability for carrying persons and its safety features.
- Means to minimise the risk to safety from its rolling over.
- Means to reduce the risk to safety from the rolling over of a fork-lift truck.
- The safety of self-propelled work equipment and remote-controlled self propelled work equipment.
- The drive shafts of mobile work equipment.

This did not apply to existing mobile work equipment (in use before 5 Dec 1998) until 5 Dec 2002 for existing mobile work equipment.

Puwer also applies to certain power presses

The Regulations provide for:

- The thorough examination (defined in regulation 2(1)) of power presses and their guards and protection devices (regulation 32).
- Their inspection after setting, re-setting or adjustment of their tools, and every working period (regulation 33).
- The making (regulation 34 and Schedule 3) and keeping (regulation 35) of reports.
- The regulations implement an EC directive aimed at the protection of workers. There are other directives setting out conditions which much new equipment (especially machinery) will have to satisfy before it can be sold in EC member states.

Regulatory Reform (Fire Safety) Order (RRFSO) 2005

Introduction

The amount of legislation covering the risk of fire has grown considerably over time. The situation was identified as unwieldy with many different regulations, often with conflicting definitions and requirements. In order to simply this and remove confusion the Regulatory Reform (Fire Safety) Order 2005 was introduced.

There were 4 principal pieces of legislation that covered fire safety in the workplace, which have been affected by the RRFSO:

- Fire Precautions Act (FPA).
- Fire Precautions (Workplace) Regulations (FPWR).
- Management of Health and Safety at Work Regulations (MHSWR).
- Dangerous Substances & Explosive Atmosphere Regulations (DSEAR).

FIRE PRECAUTIONS ACT

This legislation is has been repealed by the RRFSO 2005.

FIRE PRECAUTIONS WORKPLACE REGULATIONS

This regulation outlined the fire safety measures that need to be achieved via the risk assessment of fire and management of fire safety within a workplace. These regulations have been repealed by the implementation of the RRFSO, however they have been incorporated within the RRFSO 2005.

MANAGEMENT OF HEALTH AND SAFETY AT WORK REGULATIONS

It is this regulation that makes the legal requirement for risk assessments. In addition, it made various requirements for the management of fire safety within workplaces. This regulation will continue as a stand alone health and safety regulation as the relevant fire aspects of this regulation have been incorporated within the RRFSO 2005.

DANGEROUS SUBSTANCES & EXPLOSIVE ATMOSPHERE REGULATIONS

This regulation outlines the safety and control measures that need to be taken if dangerous or flammable / explosive substances are present. This regulation will continue as a stand alone health and safety regulation. Again the relevant fire aspects of this regulation have been incorporated within the RRFSO 2005.

REGULATORY REFORM (FIRE SAFETY) ORDER 2005

This is a new, all encompassing, fire safety order came into force 01 October 2006. As shown above it has many aspects of other fire related legislation within it and has been compiled in such a way as to present a single reference point for fire safety legislation.

The order is split into 5 parts:

- Part 1   General.
- Part 2   Fire Safety Duties.
- Part 3   Enforcement.
- Part 4   Offences and appeals.
- Part 5   Miscellaneous.

Each part is then subdivided into the individual points or articles as they are called in the order.

Arrangement of Order

Part 1 - general

1) Citation, commencement and extent.
2) Interpretation.
3) Meaning of "responsible person".
4) Meaning of "general fire precautions".
5) Duties under this Order.
6) Application to premises.
7) Disapplication of certain provisions.

Part 2 - fire safety duties

8) Duty to take general fire precautions.
9) Risk assessment.
10) Principles of prevention to be applied.
11) Fire safety arrangements.

RELEVANT STATUTORY PROVISIONS

12) Elimination or reduction of risks from dangerous substances.
13) Fire-fighting and fire detection.
14) Emergency routes and exits.
15) Procedures for serious and imminent danger and for danger areas.
16) Additional emergency measures in respect of dangerous substances.
17) Maintenance.
18) Safety assistance.
19) Provision of information to employees.
20) Provision of information to employers of self-employed from outside undertakings.
21) Training.
22) Co-operation and co-ordination.
23) General duties of employees at work.
24) Power to make regulations about fire precautions.

Part 3 - enforcement

25) Enforcing authorities.
26) Enforcement of Order.
27) Powers of inspectors.
28) Exercise on behalf of fire inspectors etc of their powers by officers of fire brigades.
29) Alterations notices.
30) Enforcement notices.
31) Prohibition notices.

Part 4 - offences and appeals

32) Offences.
33) Defence.
34) Onus of proving limits of what is practicable or reasonably practicable.
35) Appeals.
36) Determination of dispute by Secretary of State.

Part 5 - miscellaneous

37) Fire-fighters' switches for luminous tube signs etc.
38) Maintenance of measures provided for protection of fire-fighters.
39) Civil liability for breach of statutory duty.
40) Duty not to charge employees for things done or provided.
41) Duty to consult employees.
42) Special provisions in respect of licensed etc. premises.
43) Suspension of terms and conditions of licences dealing with same matters as this Order.
44) Suspension of byelaws dealing with same matters as this Order.
45) Duty to consult enforcing authority before passing plans.
46) Other consultation by authorities.
47) Disapplication of the Health and Safety at Work etc. Act 1974 in relation to fire precautions.
48) Service of notices etc.
49) Application to the Crown and to the Houses of Parliament.
50) Guidance.
51) Application to visiting forces etc.
52) Subordinate provisions.
53) Repeals, revocations, amendments and transitional provisions.

Schedule 1

Part 1   Matters to be considered in risk assessment in respect of dangerous substances.
Part 2   Matters to be considered in risk assessment in respect of young persons.
Part 3   Principles of prevention.
Part 4   Measures to be taken in respect of dangerous substances.

Schedule 2   Amendments of primary legislation.

Schedule 3   Amendments of subordinate legislation.

Schedule 4   Repeals.

Schedule 5   Revocations.

Outline of key points

PART 1 - GENERAL

This part covers various issues such as the interpretation of terminology used, definition of responsible person, definition of general fire precautions, duties under the order, and its application.

PART 2 - FIRE SAFETY DUTIES

This part imposes a duty on the responsible person to carry out a fire risk assessment to identify what the necessary general fire precautions should be. It also outlines the principles of prevention that should be applied and the necessary arrangements for the management of fire safety.

The following areas are also covered:

- Fire-fighting and fire detection.
- Emergency routes and exits.
- Procedures for serious and imminent danger and for danger areas.
- Additional emergency measures re dangerous substances.
- Maintenance.
- Safety assistance.
- Provision of information to employees, employers and self employed.
- Capabilities and training.
- Co-operation and co-ordination.
- General duties of employees.

PART 3 - ENFORCEMENT

This part details who the enforcing authority is, (which in the main is the Fire Authority), and it states they must enforce the order. It also details the powers of inspectors. It also details the different types of enforcement that can be taken:

- Alterations notice.
- Enforcement notice.
- Prohibition notice.

PART 4 - OFFENCES AND APPEALS

This part details the 13 offences that may occur and the subsequent punishments and appeals procedure. It also explains that the legal onus for proving that an offence was not committed is on the accused. A new disputes procedure is also outlined within this part.

PART 5 - MISCELLANEOUS

Various matters are covered within this part the principal points being:

- 'Fire-fighters switches' for luminous tube signs etc.
- Maintenance of measures provided for the protection of fire-fighters.
- Civil liability.
- Duty to consult employees.
- Special provisions for licensed premises.
- Application to crown premises.

There is then a schedule that covers the risk assessment process, plus details of the various legislation that will be repealed or amended.

This regulation is very comprehensive, encompassing all of the general requirements for fire safety in premises into one document. The onus of responsibility is moved totally to the 'responsible person' to ascertain the control measures that are needed.

Reporting of Injuries, Diseases and Dangerous Occurrences Regulations (RIDDOR) 1995

Arrangement of regulations

1) Citation and commencement.
2) Interpretation.
3) Notification and reporting of injuries and dangerous occurrences.
4) Reporting of the death of an employee.
5) Reporting of cases of disease.
6) Reporting of gas incidents.
7) Records.
8) Additional provisions relating to mines and quarries.
9) Additional provisions relating to offshore workplaces.
10) Restrictions on the application of regulations 3, 4 and 5.
11) Defence in proceedings for an offence contravening these Regulations.
12) Extension outside Great Britain.
13) Certificates of exemption.

RELEVANT STATUTORY PROVISIONS

14) Repeal and amendment of provisions in the Regulation of Railways Act 1871, the Railway Employment (Prevention of Accidents) Act 1900 and the Transport and Works Act 1992.
15) Revocations, amendments and savings.

Schedule 1	Major Injuries.
Schedule 2	Dangerous Occurrences.
Schedule 3	Reportable Diseases.
Schedule 4	Records.
Schedule 5	Additional provisions relating to mines and quarries.
Schedule 6	Additional provisions relating to offshore workplaces.
Schedule 7	Enactments or instruments requiring the notification of events which are not required to be notified or reported under these Regulations.
Schedule 8	Revocations and amendments.

Outline of key points

The Reporting of Injuries, Diseases and Dangerous Occurrences Regulations (RIDDOR) 1995 cover the requirement to report certain categories of injury and disease sustained at work, along with specified dangerous occurrences and gas incidents, to the relevant enforcing authority. These reports are used to compile statistics to show trends and to highlight problem areas in particular industries or companies.

REPORTING

1) When a person **dies or suffers any serious condition** specified in Schedule 1 *(Reporting of Injuries)* and Schedule 2 *(Reporting of Dangerous Occurrences)* a responsible person is to notify by the quickest possible means (usually by telephone) the enforcing authorities and must send them a written report within 10 days (F2508).

2) In cases of diseases which are linked to work activities listed in Schedule 3 *(Reporting of Diseases)* a responsible person is required to notify by the quickest possible means (usually by telephone) the enforcing authorities and must send them a written report forthwith (F2508A).

3) If personal injury results in **more than 3 days incapacity** from work off from normal duties, but does not fall in the category of "major", the written report alone is required. The day of the accident is not counted.

4) The enforcing authority is either the Health and Safety Executive or the Local Authority. The approved form for reporting is F2508 for injuries and dangerous occurrences and F2508A for diseases.

"Accident" includes:
- An act of non-consensual physical violence done to a person at work.
- An act of suicide which occurs on or in the course of the operation of a relevant transport system.

ROAD TRAFFIC ACCIDENTS

Road traffic accidents only have to be reported if:
- Death or injury results from exposure to a substance being conveyed by a vehicle.
- Death or injury results from the activities of another person engaged in the loading or unloading of an article or substance.
- Death or injury results from the activities of another person involving work on or alongside a road.
- Death or injury results from an accident involving a train.

NON EMPLOYEE

The responsible person must not only report non-employee deaths, but also cases that involve major injury or hospitalisation.

RECORDING

In the case of an accident at work, the following details must be recorded:
- Date.
- Name.
- Nature of injury.
- Brief description of the event.
- Time.
- Occupation.
- Place of accident.

Copies of F2508 or suitable alternative records must be kept for at least 3 years. This may be held electronically provided it is printable.

DEFENCES

A person must prove that he was not aware of the event and that he had taken all reasonable steps to have such events brought to his notice.

Typical examples of major injuries, diseases and dangerous occurrences

MAJOR INJURIES (RIDDOR - SCHEDULE 1)

The list of major injuries includes:
- Any fracture, other than the finger or thumbs or toes.
- Any amputation.

- Dislocation of the shoulder, hip, knee or spine.
- Permanent or temporary loss of sight.
- Chemical, hot metal or penetrating eye injury.
- Electrical shock, electrical burn leading to unconsciousness or resuscitation or admittance to hospital for more than 24 hours.
- Loss of consciousness caused by asphyxia or exposure to a harmful substance or biological agent.
- Acute illness or loss of consciousness requiring medical attention due to any entry of substance by inhalation, ingestion or through the skin.
- Acute illness where there is a reason to believe that this resulted from exposure to a biological agent or its toxins or infected material.
- Any other injury leading to hypothermia, heat-induced illness or unconsciousness requiring resuscitation, hospitalisation greater than 24 hours.

DISEASES (RIDDOR - SCHEDULE 3)

Conditions due to physical agents and the physical demands of work
- Inflammation, ulceration or malignant disease of the skin due to ionising radiation.
- Decompression illness.
- Subcutaneous cellulitis of the hand (beat hand).
- Carpal tunnel syndrome.
- Hand-arm vibration syndrome.

Infections due to biological agents
- Anthrax.
- Hepatitis.
- Legionellosis.
- Leptospirosis.
- Tetanus.

Conditions due to chemicals and other substances
- Arsenic poisoning.
- Ethylene Oxide poisoning.
- Cancer of a bronchus or lung.
- Folliculitis.
- Acne.
- Pneumoconiosis.
- Asbestosis.
- Occupational dermatitis.

DANGEROUS OCCURRENCES (RIDDOR - SCHEDULE 2)

Dangerous occurrences are events that have the potential to cause death or serious injury and so must be reported whether anyone is injured or not. Examples of dangerous occurrences that must be reported are:

- The failure of any load bearing part of any lift, hoist, crane or derrick etc.
- The failure of any pressurised closed vessel.
- The failure of any freight container in any of its load bearing parts.
- Any unintentional incident in which plant or equipment either comes into contact with an uninsulated overhead electric line causes an electrical discharge from such an electric line by coming into close proximity to it.
- Electrical short circuit or overload attended by fire or explosion which results in the stoppage of the plant involved for more than 24 hours.

Note: This information is a brief summary only. For full details consult HSE document L73 A Guide to RIDDOR 95.

Supply of Machinery (Safety) Regulations (SMSR) 1992

Outline of key points

GENERAL ADVICE

The Supply of Machinery (Safety) Regulations (SMSR) 1992 came into force on 1 January 1993 and implement the EC Machinery Directive (89/392/EEC) and its first amendment (91/368/EEC). Duties are placed upon those who supply machinery. 'Supply' is given a broad definition and those covered by the Regulations include manufacturers, importers and others in the supply chain. There is a transitional period from January 1993 to January 1995, during which time suppliers can either meet the users' national laws in force before 1993 or these Regulations. Machinery first supplied after 1 January 1995 must comply with these Regulations. These Regulations are being mirrored in other EC countries and also those not in the EC but within the European Economic Area (EEA) (EC and EFTA countries except Switzerland), so that there will eventually be uniformity in legislation, and legal barriers to trade within the EEA will be removed. The machinery covered is very wide ranging. There are some exclusions, however, such as most manually powered machines, machinery for medical use and most means of transport (see Schedule 5 of the Regulations). Machinery whose risks are mainly electrical are also excluded.

AMENDING REGULATIONS

In 1994 the Supply of Machinery (Safety) Regulations were extended so as to implement two more recent European Directives. The principal effect of this has been to apply the above requirements, as from 1 January 1995, to safety components, as defined, and widens the scope to include a greater range of lifting machines (but not classical passenger lifts and other specified exclusions).

RELEVANT STATUTORY PROVISIONS

There is a further two year transitional period from January 1995, during which time compliance with the new requirements is optional with certain conditions.

MEETING THE REQUIREMENTS

The duty to meet the requirements mainly falls to the 'responsible person' who is defined as the manufacturer or the manufacturer's representative. If the manufacturer is not established in the EEA, the person who first supplies the machinery in the EEA may be the responsible person, which can be a user who manufactures or imports a machine for his/her own use.

There are basically three steps to dealing with the requirements.

Step 1 - Conformity assessment

The responsible person should ensure that machinery and safety components satisfy the essential health and safety requirements (EHSRs), and that appropriate conformity assessment procedures have been carried out. The EHSRs are laid out in the Directive and repeated in the Regulations (Schedule 3). This can be done either by reference directly to these requirements or to a relevant transposed harmonised standard where one exists. Harmonised standards are currently being prepared by the European Standards Organisations, CEN and CENELEC, before formal adoption by the European Commission. Harmonised standards will be available for a wide range of industrial machinery, including agricultural, textiles, engineering, construction, machinery. In addition, the responsible person must draw up a technical file (see below).

For certain classes if dangerous machine and safety component, a more rigorous procedure is required. Such products are listed in Annex 4 of the Directive and reproduced in Schedule 4 of the Regulations. In additional to the above requirements, the responsible person must arrange for type-examination of these produces by an approved body if there are no harmonised standards formally adopted by the EC for them, or if they are not manufactured to such standards. The Department of Trade and Industry (DTI) has appointed approved bodies in the UK for this purpose. Details are available from: DTI, Technology and Innovation Policy Division, 151 Buckingham Palace Road, London SW1W 9SS (Tel: 0171 215 5000).

Step 2 - Declaration procedure

The responsible person must issue one of two forms of declaration.

Declaration of conformity

This declaration should be issued with the finished product so that it is available to the user. It will contain various details such as the manufacturer's address, the machinery type and serial number, and Harmonised European or other Standards used in design.

Declaration of Incorporation

Where machinery is intended for incorporation into other machinery, the responsible person can draw up a declaration of incorporation. This should state that the machinery must not be put into service until the machinery into which it is to be incorporated has been given a Declaration of Conformity. A CE mark is not affixed at this intermediate stage.

Step 3 - Marking

When the first two steps have been satisfactorily completed, the responsible person or the person assembling the final product should affix the EC mark.

ENFORCEMENT

In this country the Health and Safety Executive is responsible for enforcing these Regulations in relation to machinery designed for use at work. Trading Standards Officers are responsible for enforcing these Regulations in relation to consumer goods. *After 01 January 1995 it is an offence for the responsible person to supply machinery which does not comply with these requirements. It is also an offence for any supplier to supply machinery which is not safe (and which was not first supplied before 01 January 1995).*

Detailed advice for the designer and manufacturer.

TECHNICAL FILE CONTENTS

The responsible person (defined above) is required to draw up a technical file for all machinery and safety components covered by these Regulations. The file or documents should comprise:

a) An overall drawing of the product together with the drawings of the control circuits.
b) Full detailed drawings, accompanied by any calculation notes, test results etc. required to check the conformity of the product with the essential health and safety requirements.
c) A list of the essential health and safety requirements, transposed harmonised standards, national standards and other technical specifications which were used when the product was designed.
d) A description of methods adopted to eliminate hazards presented by the machinery or safety component.
e) If the responsible person so desires, any technical report or certificate obtained from a component body or laboratory.
f) If the responsible person declares conformity with a transposed harmonised standard, any technical report giving the results of tests.
g) A copy of the instructions for the product.

For series manufacture, the responsible person must also have available documentation on the necessary administrative measures that the manufacturer will take to ensure that the product meets requirements.

TECHNICAL FILE PROCEDURE

The technical file document need not be on a permanent file, but it should be possible to assemble and make them available to an enforcement authority. The technical file documents should be retained and kept available for at least ten years following the date of manufacture of the product or of the last unit produced, in the case of a series manufacture. If the technical file documents are drawn up in the United Kingdom, they should be in English unless they are to be submitted to an Approved/Notified Body in another Member

State, in which case they should be in a language acceptable to that approved Body. In all cases the instructions for the machinery should be in accordance with the language requirements of the EHSRs.

Work at Height Regulations (WAH) 2005

Introduction

Falls from height at work are the most common cause of fatality and the second most common cause of major injury to workers and during the period between 2001/2002 resulted in 68 fatalities and approximately 4,000 serious injuries.

Health and Safety Commission (HSC) consultation on these regulations ended in April 2004, resulting in the production of a draft regulation. An additional consultative document was also issued concerning retention of the above 'two metre rule'; consultation on this ended in December 2004. The final version of the regulations designated the **Work at Height Regulations (WAH) 2005** came into force 06 April 2005.

Under these regulations the interpretation of 'work at height' includes any place of work at ground level, above or below ground level that a person could fall a distance liable to cause personal injury and includes places for obtaining access or egress, except by staircase in a permanent workplace.

Arrangement of regulations

1) Citation and commencement.
2) Interpretation.
3) Application.
4) Organisation and planning.
5) Competence.
6) Avoidance of risks from work at height.
7) Selection of work equipment for work at height.
8) Requirements for particular work equipment.
9) Fragile surfaces.
10) Falling objects.
11) Danger areas.
12) Inspection of work equipment.
13) Inspection of places of work at height.
14) Duties of persons at work.
15) Exemption by the Health and Safety Executive.
16) Exemption for the Armed Forces.
17) Amendment to the Provision and Use of Work Equipment Regulations (PUWER) 1998.
18) Repeal of section 24 of the Factories Act 1961.
19) Revocation of instruments.

SCHEDULES

Schedule 1   Requirements for existing places of work and means of access or egress at height.
Schedule 2   Requirements for guard-rails, toe-boards, barriers and similar collective means of protection.
Schedule 3   Requirements for working platforms.
    Part 1   Requirements for all working platforms
    Part 2   Additional requirements for scaffolding
Schedule 4   Requirements for collective safeguards for arresting falls.
Schedule 5   Requirements for personal fall protection systems.
    Part 1   Requirements for all personal fall protection systems.
    Part 2   Additional requirements for work positioning systems.
    Part 3   Additional requirements for rope access and positioning techniques.
    Part 4   Additional requirements for fall arrest systems.
    Part 5   Additional requirements for work restraint systems.
Schedule 6   Requirements for ladders.
Schedule 7   Particulars to be included in a report of inspection.
Schedule 8   Revocation of instruments.

Amendments to other regulations as a result of the Work at Height Regulations 2005

These regulations make an amendment to the Provision and Use of Work Equipment Regulations 1998; they also replace certain regulations in the Workplace (Health and Safety) Regulations; and amend definitions in the Construction (Health, Safety and Welfare) Regulations -

Regulation 17 - amendment of the Provision and Use of Work Equipment Regulations (PUWER) 1998. There shall be added to regulation 6(5) of the Provision and Use of Work Equipment Regulations 1998 the following sub-paragraph -

RELEVANT STATUTORY PROVISIONS

(f) "work equipment to which regulation 12 of the Work at Height Regulations 2005 applies".

Schedule 8 - revocation of instruments

Workplace (Health and Safety) Regulations 1992 - extent of revocation: regulation 13(1) to (4).

Construction (Health, Safety and Welfare) Regulations 1996 - extent of revocation: in regulation 2(1), the definitions of "fragile material", "personal suspension equipment" and "working platform"; regulations 6 to 8; in regulation 29(2) the word "scaffold" in both instances; regulation 30(5) and (6)(a); Schedules 1 to 5; and the entry first mentioned in columns 1 and 2 of Schedule 7.

Outline of key points

Regulation 4 states that all work at height must be properly planned, supervised and be carried out so far as is reasonably practicable safe. Planning must include the selection of suitable equipment, take account of emergencies and give consideration to weather conditions impacting on safety.

Regulation 5 states that those engaged in any activity in relation to work at height must be competent; and, if under training, be supervised by a competent person.

Regulation 6 states that work at height must only be carried out when it is not reasonably practicable to carry out the work otherwise. If work at height does take place, suitable and sufficient measures must be taken to prevent a fall of any distance, to minimise the distance and the consequences of any fall liable to cause injury. Employers must also make a risk assessment, as required by regulation 3 of the Management of Health and Safety at Work Regulations.

Regulation 7 states that when selecting equipment for use in work at height the employer shall take account of working conditions and any risk to persons in connection with the place where the equipment is to be used. The selection of work equipment must have regard in particular to the purposes specified in regulation 6.

Regulation 8 sets out requirements for particular equipment to conform to standards expressed in schedules to the regulations. It includes guard-rails, toe-boards, working platforms, nets, airbags, personal fall arrest equipment rope access and ladders.

Regulation 9 states that every employer shall ensure that suitable and sufficient steps are taken to prevent any person at work falling through any fragile surface; and that no work may pass across or near, or work on, from or near, fragile surfaces when it is reasonably practicable to carry out work without doing so. If work has to be from a fragile roof then suitable and sufficient means of support must be provided that can sustain foreseeable loads. No person at work should be allowed to pass or work near a fragile surface unless suitable and sufficient guard rails and other means of fall protection is in place. Signs must be situated at a prominent place at or near to works involving fragile surfaces, or persons are made aware of the fragile roof by other means.

Regulation 10 states that every employer shall take reasonably practicable steps to prevent injury to any person from the fall of any material or object; and where it is not reasonably practicable to do so, to take similar steps to prevent any person being struck by any falling material or object which is liable to cause personal injury. Also, that no material is thrown or tipped from height in circumstances where it is liable to cause injury to any person. Materials and objects must be stored in such a way as to prevent risk to any person arising from the collapse, overturning or unintended movement of the materials or objects.

Regulation 11 states that every employer shall ensure that where an area presents a risk of falling from height or being struck from an item falling at height that the area is equipped with devices preventing unauthorised persons from entering such areas and the area is clearly indicated.

Regulation 12 states that every employer shall ensure that, where the safety of work equipment depends on how it is installed or assembled, it is not used after installation or assembly in any position unless it has been inspected in that position. Also, that work equipment is inspected at suitable intervals and each time that exceptional circumstances which are liable to jeopardise the safety of the work equipment occur. Specific requirements exist for periodic (every 7 days) inspection of a working platform where someone could fall 2 metres or more.

Regulation 13 states that every employer shall ensure that fall protection measures of every place of work at height are visually inspected before use.

Regulation 14 states the duties of persons at work to report defects and use equipment in accordance with training / instruction.

Work at Height (Amendment) Regulations 2007

These Regulations make minor amendments to The Work at Height Regulations 2005 and came into force on 6th April 2007.

Arrangement of regulations

1) Citation and commencement.
2) Amendment of the Work at Height Regulations 2005.

Outline of key points

The amendment inserts a new paragraph (14A) concerning the provision of instruction or leadership to one or more persons in connection with their engagement in caving or climbing by way of sport, recreation, team building or similar activities. "Caving" includes the exploration of parts of mines which are no longer worked; "climbing" means climbing, traversing, abseiling or scrambling over natural terrain or man-made structures.

Where this paragraph applies, an employer, self-employed person or other person shall be taken to have complied with the "caving and climbing requirements" (detailed in regulation 8(d)(ii) of the Work at Height Regulations), if he maintains a level of safety equivalent to that required by those requirements.

Assessment

Content

Written assessments - Papers NGC1 and NCC1	280
NEBOSH sample questions	281
Construction health and safety practical application (NCC2)	285
Aims	285
Procedure	285
Sample practical application (NCC2)	286
NEBOSH sample questions - answers	295

ASSESSMENT

Written assessments - Papers NGC1 and NCC1

At every examination a number of candidates - including some good ones - perform less well than they might because of poor examination technique. It is essential that candidates practice answering both essay-type and short answer questions and learn to budget their time according to the number of marks allocated to questions (and parts of questions) as shown on the paper.

Those who undertake a full course of study for the NEBOSH National Certificate in Construction Health and Safety will need to attend examinations for paper NGC1 and paper NCC1 and complete the practical assessment NCC2. Others who have already achieved the NEBOSH National General Certificate (paper NGC1) within the last 5 years are all exempt from Unit NGC1 of the NEBOSH National Certificate in Construction Health and Safety; therefore such candidates would not have to sit the NGC1 examination paper again but will need to attend the examination for paper NCC1 and complete the practical assessment NCC2.

Each written paper (NGC1 and NCC1) is 2 hours duration and contains 2 sections:

Section 1 has one question carrying 20 marks requiring quite an 'in-depth' answer. This question should be allocated 30 minutes in total. If time (e.g. 5 minutes) is given to reading, planning and checking, the time available for writing is 25 minutes. Two pages are allowed for this answer; candidates should produce approximately 1½ sides for an average answer.

Section 2 has 10 questions each carrying 8 marks. If time (e.g. 10 minutes) is allowed for reading, planning and checking then there are 8 minutes to answer each question. One page is allowed for each of these answers, candidates should produce approximately ½ a side for an average answer.

A common fault is that candidates may fail to pay attention to the 'action verb' in each question. To help to emphasize their importance "action verbs" are highlighted in **bold** type on certificate examination question papers. The most common "action verbs" used in examination questions are:

define	provide a generally recognised or accepted definition
state	a less demanding form of 'define', or where there is no generally recognised definition
sketch	provide a simple line drawing using labels to call attention to specific features
explain	give a clear account of, or reasons for
describe	give a word picture
outline	give the most important features of (less depth than either 'explain' or 'describe', but more depth than 'list'.)
list	provide a list without explanation
give	provide without explanation (used normally with the instruction 'give an example [or examples] of…')
identify	select and name

Other questions may start with 'what, when, how' etc. In such cases the examiners are expecting candidates to give their own explanations.

NEBOSH questions will progressively change to reflect practical issues that need to be managed in the workplace. Questions will increasingly reflect more than one element of knowledge, for example "electrical fires" which could require an understanding of Element 6 and Element 7 to answer adequately.

It is essential for candidates to pay proper attention to the 'action verb'. Candidates will lose available marks if the question asks for an 'outline' and only a list is given. Equally, if a 'list' is required, candidates who write out an explanation will be consuming valuable time that could be spent more profitably elsewhere on the paper.

The need to understand the meaning of the 'action verb' and to read the question carefully is emphasised in the comments below which are taken from some recent examiner's reports:

"… many answers were too brief to satisfy the requirement for an outline or description. Points made should have been supported by sufficient reasoning to show their relevance to the question."

"Some candidates, even though they identified many of the relevant factors, could not be awarded the full range of marks available because they produced a truncated list that did not properly outline the relationship between each factor and the corresponding risks."

"It was disappointing to note that some candidates again misread the question and provided outlines of the duties of employers rather than employees."

"While answers to this question were generally to a reasonable standard, many were too brief to attract all the marks that were available."

"In answering questions on Paper NCC1, practical issues should be addressed. It is not sufficient in questions such as this merely to refer to generic issues such as risk assessment and safe systems of work without providing further detail of the controls that a risk assessment might show to be necessary or the elements of a safe system of work."

"Weaker answers tended to be those that provided insufficient detail - for example, mention of "PPE" or "edge protection" should have been accompanied by some examples of what might be required and reference to the purpose that they serve."

"Some answers were extremely brief and candidates should remember that one-fifth of the marks for the entire paper are available for answers to this question (question 1). Answers are expected to be proportionate to the marks available."

NEBOSH sample questions

NCC1 - Managing and controlling hazards in construction activities

ELEMENT 1

1. **Outline** the principal duties of a client under the Construction (Design and Management) Regulations 2007. (8)

   Dec 2006 Paper 1 Question 3

2. **Outline** the requirements of the Construction (Design and Management) Regulations 2007 relating to sanitary and washing facilities on construction sites. (8)

   Based on Dec 2005 Paper 2 Question 8

3. **Outline** the main factors to be considered when assessing the health and safety competence of a sub-contractor. (8)

   Based on Dec 2000 Paper 2 Question 15

ELEMENT 2

1. Site preparation work involves the removal of topsoil from land known to be contaminated with heavy metals. **Outline** the specific requirements for this work in relation to:

   (i) Personal protective equipment and practices. (4)

   (ii) Welfare facilities. (4)

   Dec 2000 Section 2 Question 7

2. **Identify** the factors that should be considered when assessing the adequacy of first-aid arrangements on a site. (8)

   Dec 2003 Paper 1 Question 3

3. A site manager has been tasked to provide site induction training to the employees of a contractor about to start work on site.

   List SIXTEEN items that should be addressed in the session. (8)

   Dec 2003 Paper 1 Question 11

ELEMENT 3

1. A significant number of the accidents associated with work on construction sites is associated with plant and vehicle movement.

   Outline the control measures that should be adopted to prevent such accidents occurring. (8)

   Dec 2006 Paper 2 Question 2

2. **Outline** a hierarchy of measures to minimise the risks from reversing vehicles on a construction site. (8)

   Jun 2006 Paper 2 Question 4

3. Approximately one quarter of all accidents on construction sites are associated with plant, machinery and vehicles.

   Outline the elements of a strategy designed to prevent such accidents. (8)

   Jun 2005 Paper 2 Question 7

ELEMENT 4

1. **Identify** the main items to be checked by the person appointed to have overall control of a lifting operation which is to be carried out with the use of a crane hired for the purpose. (8)

   Dec 2006 Paper 2 Question 4

2. **Outline** the factors that might cause a mobile crane to overturn during use. (8)

   Jun 2006 Paper 2 Question 3

3. A rolled steel joist (RSJ) is to be used in the support of the second floor of a town house that is being refurbished. It is thought that the layout of the house and the arrangement of the supports are such that mechanical means cannot be used either to transport the RSJ from the ground floor or to lift it into its final position.

   Outline the factors that would need to be considered when undertaking a manual handling assessment of the task.

© ACT

281

ASSESSMENT

(8)

Jun 2005 Paper 2 Question 5

ELEMENT 5

1. The Provision and Use of Work Equipment Regulations 1998 require that work equipment used in hostile environments is inspected at suitable intervals.

    Identify the items on a small dumper truck that should be the subject of such an inspection. (8)

    Dec 2005 Paper 2 Question 10

2. It is necessary for maintenance purposes to enter a large cement silo situated on a construction site.

    (i) **Identify** the likely hazards. (5)

    (ii) **Outline** the precautions to be taken to reduce the risks to personnel entering the silo. (15)

    Jun 2006 Paper 2 Question 1

3. **Identify** the main items to be checked by the person appointed to have overall control of a lifting operation which is to be carried out with the use of a crane hired for the purpose. (8)

    Dec 2006 Paper 2 Question 4

ELEMENT 6

1. HSG85 Electricity at Work-Safe Working Practices gives guidance on the frequency of inspection for such equipment.

    State frequencies for the inspection and testing of electrical hand tools and associated equipment used on a construction site and support your answers with appropriate examples. (8)

    Dec 2006 Paper 2 Question 3

2. Ground works are about to commence on a site crossed by high voltage overhead power lines. The work will involve the use of excavators and tipper lorries to remove spoil from the site.

    Outline a management strategy for the avoidance of accidents involving accidental contact with the overhead power lines. (8)

    Dec 2005 Paper 2 Question 4

3. **Outline** the measures to be taken to minimise the risk of shock from the use of electric hand tools. (8)

    Jun 2004 Paper 2 Question 3

ELEMENT 7

1. (a) **Outline** the practical measures that should be adopted to prevent fires and explosions during welding operations on a construction site. (6)

    (b) **Identify TWO** types of radiation associated with welding activities. (2)

    Jun 2006 Paper 2 Question 10

2. Timber sections are stored in an enclosed compound.

    (i) **Describe** the precautions that should be taken to prevent a fire occurring. (4)

    (ii) **Identify** the extinguishing media that may be used for dealing with a fire in such a situation, and **explain** how each works to extinguish the fire. (4)

    Jun 2004 Paper 2 Question 4

3. A major hazard on a refurbishment project is fire.

    (i) **Identify THREE** activities that represent an increased fire risk in such a situation. (3)

    (ii) **Outline** the precautions that may be taken to prevent a fire from occurring. (5)

    Jun 2005 Paper 2 Question 6

ASSESSMENT

ELEMENT 8

1. (a) **Describe** the typical symptoms of occupational dermatitis. (2)

   (b) **Identify** the factors that will influence the likelihood of dermatitis occurring amongst site operatives handling wet cement. (6)

   Jun 2006 Paper 2 Question 2

2. **Outline** a system for the management and disposal of waste from a construction site. (8)

   Jun 2006 Paper 2 Question 5

3. **List** the information that should be included in a manufacturer's safety data sheet for a hazardous substance used on a construction site. (8)

   Dec 2005 Paper 2 Question 11

ELEMENT 9

1. **Outline** the actions that site management might consider in order to reduce levels of occupational stress amongst workers on site. (8)

   Jun 2005 Paper 2 Question 7

2. **Outline**, with reasons, the particular health issues that should be addressed during routine health surveillance examinations for construction workers. (8)

   Dec 2005 Paper 2 Question 3

ELEMENT 10

1. **Describe** the specific measures that may be necessary to ensure safety when work is to be carried out from a scaffold that overhangs a fast flowing river. (8)

   Jun 2006 Paper 2 Question 8

2. **Outline** the measures to be taken to prevent falls associated with stairwells and other holes in floors during the construction of a multi storey building. (8)

   Dec 2005 Paper 2 Question 9

3. **Outline** the requirements of the Construction (Head Protection) Regulations 1989.

   Dec 2004 Paper 2 Question 8

ELEMENT 11

1. **Sketch** a labelled diagram of a steel trench support system that clearly shows ait the main components and features, (8)

   Dec 2004 Paper 2 Question7

2. **Identify**:

   (i) **FOUR** specific hazards associated with work in a confined space. (4)

   (ii) **FOUR** examples of a confined space that may be encountered on a construction site. (4)

   Dec 2005 Paper 2 Question 8

3. A project involves shallow excavations in land previously used as a landfill site.

   Outline the welfare facilities that should be provided for such work. (8)

   Dec 2006 Paper 2 Question 6

ELEMENT 12

1. A three-storey office block is to be demolished. **Outline** the likely hazards to the environment caused by the work together with the actions needed to control them. (8)

   Dec 2003 Paper 2 Question 5

2. **Outline** the main areas to be addressed in a demolition method statement. (8)

   Jun 2006 Paper 2 Question 7

ASSESSMENT

3. A large industrial site has been closed recently. The owners of the site are to have the buildings demolished before selling the site for redevelopment.

   Outline the issues the principal demolition contractor should address as part of the health and safety plan. (20)

   Dec 2005 Paper 2 Question 1

QUESTIONS REQUIRING KNOWLEDGE FROM MORE THAN ONE ELEMENT

1. On a long-term contract, joiners are working with medium density fibreboard using hand-held circular saws and portable electric planers in a temporary site unit. **Explain** how you would ensure that the joiners' health is not put at risk during this activity. (8)

   Jun 2006 Paper 2 Question 9

PLEASE REFER TO BACK OF THIS SECTION FOR ANSWERS

Construction health and safety practical application (NCC2)

The practical assessment must be carried out under the control of the accredited centre and will normally be carried out on a working construction site identified by the practical assessor. The assessment must take place within 14 days of (before or after) the date of the written papers (date of the examination). Please make sure you are clear about when you will carry out the assessment and that your assessment invigilator has set the time aside.

Aims

The aim of the practical assessment is to test a candidate's ability to complete a health and safety assessment of a construction site. In particular, the assessment requires candidates to:

- Carry out unaided a health and safety inspection of a construction site (or part of a site), identifying the more common hazards, deciding whether they are adequately controlled and, where necessary, suggesting appropriate and cost effective remedial action.
- Prepare a report that persuasively urges site management to take appropriate action, explaining why such action is needed (including reference to possible breaches of legislation) and identifying, with due consideration of reasonable practicability, the remedial measures that should be taken.

Procedure

A report form / observation sheet should be used during your inspection. There are four columns on the form; observations, priority / risk, timescales; and brief notes on actions. The forms must be completed during the inspection and must be included with your covering management report for marking by the assessor.

The maximum time allocated to the practical assessment is 2 hours. You should spend 45 minutes making an assessment of the site, covering as wide a range of hazards as possible. The remaining time should be allocated to write a report to management in your own handwriting.

You are expected to recognise physical, health and environmental hazards - good, as well as bad, work practices. While only short notes on each hazard are required, it is important that the assessor is able to subsequently identify the following:

- Where the hazard was located.
- The nature of the hazard.
- In what way, if any, the hazard is being controlled.
- The remedial action, where appropriate.
- Preventative action required.

You should, however, note that the assessment is not intended to be a pure hazard spotting exercise and consideration should be given to other matters such as:

- Availability and standard of washing and toilet facilities.
- Adequacy of heating, lighting and ventilation.
- General condition of floors and gangways.
- Cleanliness of structures.
- If staff are present, are they aware of the actions to take in the event of an emergency?

On completion of the inspection, you should use lined paper to produce a report, consulting your own (and only your own) notes made during the inspection. The report should be in your own handwriting. The marking sheet will be used by the assessor when marking your paper, it is not confidential and you should bear it in mind when you are writing your report.

ASSESSMENT

Sample practical application (NCC2)

NEBOSH NATIONAL CERTIFICATE IN CONSTRUCTION HEALTH AND SAFETY   **FORM C**

Candidate's observation sheet No _1_ of _6_

Candidate's Name: _J. Bloggs_   and number: _F_

Place inspected: _Store in Tamworth_   Date of Inspection: _XX/XX/200X_

Observations — List hazards, unsafe practices and good practices	Priority / risk (H,M,L)	Actions to be taken (if any) — List any immediate *and* longer-term actions required	Timescale (immediate, 1 week, etc.)
1, Risk of fire control, e.g. Fire Plan, Fire points, emergency lighting and fire alarm systems. One exit partially blocked – three others available.	L	Remove items partially blocking fire exit	I
		Provide proper storage for 12V batteries and herras fence bases	M
		Daily checks on exits – weekly checks on systems	L
2, Risk of poor welfare controlled by site cabins with hot / cold water, kettle, toaster and microwave. Facilities for storing clothes and PPE	L	No immediate actions	I
		Weekly checks on condition of facilities	M
		Ensure confirmed provision of washing up liquids, clean tea towels, enough storage	L
3, Risk of poor welfare controlled by provision of toilet block – clean soap, hot and cold water	L	Clean facilities – no immediate action	I
		Provide ample supplies of toilet paper	M
		Weekly inspection and daily cleaning schedule.	L
4, Risk of poor welfare due to no barrier cream, moisturising cream or towels	M	Provide barrier and moisturizing creams & towels	I
		Weekly inspection to ensure adequate supplies	M
		Regular tool box talks about dermatitis hazards	L

ASSESSMENT

NEBOSH NATIONAL CERTIFICATE IN CONSTRUCTION HEALTH AND SAFETY — **FORM C**

Candidate's observation sheet No 2 of 6

Candidate's Name: J. Bloggs and number: F

Place inspected: Store in Tamworth Date of Inspection: XX/XX/200X

Observations — List hazards, unsafe practices and good practices	Priority / risk (H,M,L)	Actions to be taken (if any) — List any immediate *and* longer-term actions required	Timescale (immediate, 1 week, etc.)
5. Risk of fire from propane bottles, controlled by storage in mesh cage in yard, but due to cage too close to building	M	Move cage away from building to reduce risk of explosion in case of fire	I
		Ensure bottles are stored in cage at the end of each shift / day	M
		Use electric fork lift truck	L
6. Risk of trips / falls due to strapping from bundles of materials left on floor in yard	M	Clear yard	I
		Daily / weekly site inspections to check housekeeping	M
		Tool box talks on housekeeping – skips emptied regularly	L
7. Risk of electric shock from bare wires (conductors) trailing by main distribution board	H	Electrician to make safe / remove cables	I
		Instruct strip out electricians to strip cables back	M
		H&S Plan under CDM to cover this risk?	L
8. Risk of fall from height into unguarded lift shaft at ground level (deep pit)	H	Guard entrance to lift shaft	I
		Daily checks on guarding	M
		Lift installers to devise safe method of guarding lift shaft while installing the lift	L

ASSESSMENT

NEBOSH NATIONAL CERTIFICATE IN CONSTRUCTION HEALTH AND SAFETY — FORM C

Candidate's observation sheet No 3 of 6

Candidate's Name: J. Bloggs and number: F
Place inspected: Store in Tamworth Date of Inspection: XX/XX/200X

Observations List hazards, unsafe practices and good practices	Priority / risk (H,M,L)	Actions to be taken (if any) List any immediate *and* longer-term actions required	Timescale (immediate, 1 week, etc.)
9. Risk of fall from height from unguarded mezzanine edge at goods loading point.	H	Work stopped straight away	I
		Install edge protection along mezzanine edge	M
		Provide 'pallet gate' or similar at loading point	L
10. Risk of being struck by falling mezzanine floor boards as area under leading edge not barricaded	H	Work under leading edge stopped	I
		Barricade area under the leading edge	M
		Control access under the edge as the mezzanine is built	L
11. Risk of falling while accessing / egressing the mezzanine as no proper access. Only incorrectly assembled tower scaffold.	H	Work on mezzanine stopped	I
		Provide suitably tied ladder	M
		Provide temporary stairs until permanent stairs installed	L
12. Risk of tower scaffold overturning as tower being pushed with man on top landing.	H	Stopped this taking place	I
		Toolbox talks on use of tower scaffolds	M
		Provide mobile scissor lift to mezzanine floor erectors	L

NEBOSH NATIONAL CERTIFICATE IN CONSTRUCTION HEALTH AND SAFETY **FORM C**

Candidate's observation sheet No 4 of 6

Candidate's Name: J. Bloggs and number: F
Place inspected: Store in Tamworth Date of Inspection: XX/XX/200X

Observations — List hazards, unsafe practices and good practices	Priority / risk (H,M,L)	Actions to be taken (if any) — List any immediate *and* longer-term actions required	Timescale (immediate, 1 week, etc.)
13, -Risk of dermatitis from cement while mixing mortar. No PPE in use	M	Provide suitable gloves to operative	I
		Tool box talks on risks from cement	M
		Inspect and monitor use of gloves	L
14, Risk of health problems whilst using disc cutter on lift shaft blocks. No dust mask used	M	Provide dust mask to operative	I
		Information /Instruction and supervision re Hazards	M
		Look at different cutting methods e.g. wet or dust collection	L
15, Risk of fire from 5 gallon jerry can of petrol for disc cutter in the building	H	Remove petrol can from building to yard store	I
		Control filling of cutter to outside the building	M
		Provide electrically powered tools	L
16, Risk of injury from saw bench as emergency stop button damaged and will not operate immediately	H	Take saw out of use	I
		Ensure daily /weekly inspections done and faults reported / recorded	M
		Repair faulty equipment	L

ASSESSMENT

NEBOSH NATIONAL CERTIFICATE IN CONSTRUCTION HEALTH AND SAFETY — FORM C

Candidate's observation sheet No 5 of 6

Candidate's Name: J. Bloggs and number: F
Place inspected: Store in Tamworth Date of Inspection: XX/XX/200X

Observations List hazards, unsafe practices and good practices	Priority / risk (H,M,L)	Actions to be taken (if any) List any immediate *and* longer-term actions required	Timescale (immediate, 1 week, etc.)
17, Risk of noise induced hearing loss whilst using portable tools to bolt portions into place. Only operative using tool has hearing protection	M	Provide all operatives in the immediate area with hearing protection.	I
		Carry out regular checks to ensure hearing protection is worn	M
		Information / instruction / supervision – tool box talks / posters	L
18, Risk of electric shock from portable tools. Not labelled and no PAT Test on angle grinder and electric drill.	H	Take tools out of use.	I
		Have them tested	M
		Set up labelling, testing, inspection, and recording system for PAT	L
19, Risk of severe cuts from petrol driven disc cutter that continues to run whilst not in use.	H	Stop using this cutter	I
		Provide electrical cutter with a 'dead mans switch'	M
		Inspect / test / maintain the equipment	L
20, Risk from handling of cement and sand. Controlled by delivery in IBC for sand and pallet for cement.	L	No immediate action	I
		Continue to order bulk materials in containers that can be moved by a FLT	M
		Regular checks to maintain the system	L

ASSESSMENT

NEBOSH NATIONAL CERTIFICATE IN CONSTRUCTION HEALTH AND SAFETY   **FORM C**

Candidate's observation sheet No 6 of 6

Candidate's Name: J. Bloggs   and number: F

Place inspected: Store in Tamworth   Date of Inspection: XX/XX/200X

Observations — List hazards, unsafe practices and good practices	Priority / risk (H,M,L)	Actions to be taken (if any) — List any immediate *and* longer-term actions required	Timescale (immediate, 1 week, etc.)
21. Risk of collision of fork lift truck with people and plant / building as keys left in ignition	H	Instruct steel erectors to remove ignition key	I
		Instruction / Information / supervision in hazards of FLT	M
		Daily checks on use of FLT and competent driver	L
22. Risk of hand / arm vibration from floor scabbler and angle grinder. No PPE in use.	M	Provide suitable gloves for operative	I
		Plan work so that equipment used short term or intermittently	M
		Source equipment which provides lower vibration levels	L
23. Risk of slips / trips due to site rubbish	M	Clean site	I
		Schedule for daily site cleaning	M
		Inspections and tool box talks to operatives	L
24. Risk of fall into escalator pit as poorly boarded with gaps and bowing boards	H	Replace wooden boarding with metal plates	I
		Signs for danger of falling into pit	M
		Provide secure fence around pit	L

© ACT

Site Inspection Report for _____ Store

Introduction

This report looks at the building site area of the ___ Store in Tamworth. The work covers the construction of a full cover mezzanine with lifts, escalators and associated services. The purpose of the report is to identify hazards and good practice with the aim of preventing accidents and identifying areas for continuous improvement. The inspection sheets (attached in appendix) and report were completed by J. Bloggs, Health and Safety Manager.

Summary

I was particularly pleased to see very good fire precautions in place with high quality temporary systems and knowledgeable operatives. Equally pleasing was the high standard of the welfare facilities provided.

However, there were some high risks areas that were unacceptable and needed immediate action. These concerned the building of the mezzanine which seems to be unplanned. There was a risk of operatives falling, heavy boards being dropped onto operatives below and no proper access to the mezzanine. There was also risk of electric shock from untested tools and exposed bare wires.

Main Findings

Please not that the numbered observations relate to the numbered hazards on the inspection sheets.

Hazard 8,
The lift shaft pit was unguarded which could have resulted in operatives falling into it. This could lead to major injuries or even fatalities. This shaft should be guarded, which could be done with strong plywood boards (8 x 4 ft) at a cost of £50-£100. It is a breach of the Health and Safety at Work act 1974 and the Working at Height Regs 2005 to allow falls from a height.

Hazard 9,

The goods loading area on the mezzanine floor was unguarded with operatives working on the mezzanine close to the edge. The chance of a fatality if someone was to fall is high. The loading area should have toe boards, top and intermediate guard rails when it is not in use. Alternatively an 'up and over' pallet gate could be installed. Guard rails would cost £100-£200 while a pallet gate (much the preferred option) could cost up to £750. Breach of legislation here comes under the Health and safety at Work Act 1974 and the Construction, Design and Management Regs 2007 (no suitable health and safety plan).

The whole mezzanine installation was poor – see hazards 10 and 11.

Hazard 12,

The operative bolting the partitions to the mezzanine was being pushed while on top of a tower scaffold. This was to allow him to bolt both ends of the portion without climbing down. The tower scaffold could easily overturn resulting in a major injury or fatality. This action was stopped immediately and information and instructions must be given to operatives through tool box talks. Provision of a suitable mobile / scissor lift would prevent this problem. Ongoing hire of a scissor lift would only be in the low hundreds of pounds. Legislation breached here includes the Working at Height Regs 2005, The Health & Safety at Work Act 1974 and the Provision and Use of Work Equipment Regs 1998.

Hazard 15,

There was a 5 gallon jerry can of petrol stored inside the building for the disc cutter. Petrol is highly flammable and so increases the risk of fire dramatically. The can was removed to stores outside the building. Supervisory controls to ensure the cutter is filled outside the building costs nothing. Renting an electrically operated cutter would be less than £100 per week. Legislation breached here includes the Dangerous Substances and Explosive Atmospheres Regs 2002 and the Health and Safety at Work Act 1974.

Hazard 18,

Portable tools were found with no unique identification on them. This means there was no way of checking if they had been PAT tested (portable appliance testing). Electrical equipment that is not maintained, inspected or tested can develop faults that can lead to electrocution and death. All portable tools should have a unique number, be inspected and tested at regular intervals. The results of the testing should be entered into a log. The frequency of testing depends on usage / environment. Costs of setting up this system are initially high in terms of time but become less when ongoing. The Electricity at Work Regs 1989 where breached here.

ASSESSMENT

<u>Conclusion</u>

The site is clean and well maintained, however there are a number of items which require urgent management attention. I have only highlighted a few hazards (as listed above), but management should also pay attention to the other hazards identified in the attached appendix.

Apart from the moral aspect, to protect our fellow workers, we have legal duties under Acts of Parliament and Regulations. Breaches of these duties can and will lead to criminal prosecution, followed by fines and / or imprisonment. This applies to the company (senior management), site managers and individual employees. Further breaches could lead to civil claims with high damages being awarded.

Financially, lack of safety can be very costly with high absenteeism, staff turnover, potential damage to the company image and reputation through adverse publicity should also be considered. Not only could the company be fined, but repairs for damage to property and increased insurance premiums should also be accounted for.

It is clear from the observations that the company has failed to implement an effective health and safety management system. The priority should be to meet the requirements of current legislation highlighted within this report and to comply with the CDM Regulations 2007.

ASSESSMENT

NEBOSH sample questions - answers

NCC1 - Managing and controlling hazards in construction activities

ELEMENT 1

1. **Outline** the principal duties of a client under the Construction (Design and Management) Regulations 2007. (8)

Dec 2006 Paper 1 Question 3

Candidates are expected to recognise that the client has duties:
- *To appoint a CDM Co-ordinator and a principal contractor; to ensure the competence of the persons appointed (including the project designer if the designer has been appointed by the client).*
- *To ensure that they possess adequate resources to carry out the requirements placed on them by the Regulations.*
- *To provide the CDM Co-ordinator with relevant health and safety information about existing structures and the site.*
- *To ensure a health and safety plan is prepared before the project starts.*
- *To provide information for the plan, and to retain the health and safety file after completion of the project and make it available for inspection when required.*

2. **Outline** the requirements of the Construction (Design and Management) Regulations 2007 relating to sanitary and washing facilities on construction sites. (8)

Based on Dec 2005 Paper 2 Question 8

Candidates with a good knowledge of the Construction (Design and Management) Regulations 2007 should have had little difficulty in answering this question. Where practicable, toilets that may be flushed should be provided, with separate facilities for men and women unless they are in a room, intended for one person, where the door may be locked from the inside. Washing facilities should include a supply of hot and cold (or warm) running water, soap or other cleansing agent and means of drying. If the nature of the work demands, showers should also be provided.

3. **Outline** the main factors to be considered when assessing the health and safety competence of a sub-contractor. (8)

Based on Dec 2000 Paper 2 Question 15

There is a requirement under the Construction (Design and Management) Regulations 2007 for principal contractors to ensure that any contractors they engage are suitable and competent, as far as their management of health and safety is concerned, to undertake the work that they are required to carry out.

Most candidates should be able to outline several important indicators of a sub-contractor's health and safety competence, with health and safety policy, quality of risk assessments, suitability of method statements, previous work and accident history, and the level of training of staff featuring highly.

ELEMENT 2

1. Site preparation work involves the removal of topsoil from land known to be contaminated with heavy metals.
   Outline the specific requirements for this work in relation to:
   (i) Personal protective equipment and practices. (4)
   (ii) Welfare facilities. (4)

Dec 2000 Section 2 Question 7

For part (i), candidates need to think of the potential effects of contaminated ground on the health of construction workers and outline the types of personal protective equipment that would be necessary to minimise the risk. Reference should be made to the need to provide gloves, overalls, eye protection and respirators. Additionally, good levels of personal hygiene and ensuring that open cuts are covered with waterproof dressings would be required.

For part (ii) what is required is an outline of the welfare facilities that should be provided on site. Candidates should identify that a decontamination unit is needed which has a dirty area where contaminated clothing can be removed after work, an area with a shower or other means of washing and a clean area where normal clothes can be kept while employees are working on site. Additionally, there should be arrangements in place in order to prevent contamination when eating and smoking, and first-aid and emergency decontamination facilities should be made available.

2. **Identify** the factors that should be considered when assessing the adequacy of first-aid arrangements on a site. (8)

Dec 2003 Paper 1 Question 3

Most candidates should identify the key factors of the number of trained first-aiders and the first-aid facilities provided (in terms of the number and content of first-aid boxes, first-aid rooms, etc) and then relate these to the distribution, composition and size of the workforce, and the types of hazard and level of risk present on site. Better answers should also refer to the proximity to emergency medical services and to the ability to provide continued cover over different work patterns and for sickness, leave and other absences.

3. A site manager has been tasked to provide site induction training to the employees of a contractor about to start work on site.

ASSESSMENT

List SIXTEEN items that should be addressed in the session. (8)

Dec 2003 Paper 1 Question 11

Candidates should show an understanding of the purpose of induction training - namely, to provide information to new employees (either to the job or, more particularly in this case, to the site) on organisational systems and work procedures. Issues to be covered during the training would include site-specific hazards (the risks they pose and the precautions required to be taken by employees), site rules (on PPE, smoking, etc) and method statements.

Other relevant issues include:
- *Emergency procedures.*
- *Details of the welfare and first-aid arrangements.*
- *The system for obtaining PPE.*
- *Reporting procedures in the case of accidents, incidents, unsafe conditions, etc.*
- *The procedures for signing in and out.*

Better answers would be by providing a few examples of the types of safety issue that would typically be addressed - such as electricity, plant and equipment hazards, hazardous substances, manual handling and so on.

ELEMENT 3

1. A significant number of the accidents associated with work on construction sites is associated with plant and vehicle movement.

   Outline the control measures that should be adopted to prevent such accidents occurring. (8)

   Dec 2006 Paper 2 Question 2

Candidates should identify and outline control measures such as: site planning and maintenance of traffic routes to segregate pedestrians and vehicles; imposing site speed restrictions in respect of vehicles and preventing the unauthorised use or movement of plant; compliance with the general safety requirements in respect of all plant and machinery such as the proper selection of equipment for the task in hand, the need to ensure that dangerous parts of machines were properly guarded, and that a regime of planned inspections and maintenance and procedures for reporting defects was put in place and finally ensuring that all operators were competent to perform the tasks allotted to them.

2. **Outline** a hierarchy of measures to minimise the risks from reversing vehicles on a construction site. (8)

   Jun 2006 Paper 2 Question 4

One of the first measures to be considered is to eliminate or reduce the need for reversing by introducing a one-way system and providing turning circles or loading / unloading areas. In circumstances where this might not be possible, it would be necessary to ensure that safe systems of work are in place and followed.

Such systems would include:
- *The exclusion of pedestrians from site traffic areas.*
- *The use of banksmen.*
- *The provision of information, instructions and training for site personnel.*
- *The mandatory wearing of hi-visibility clothing.*

Finally the vehicles need to be fitted with audible/visual reversing warning devices and features such as CCTV and Fresnel lens and mirrors to ensure adequate driver visibility.

Candidates should structure their answers as a hierarchy as required by the question.

3. Approximately one quarter of all accidents on construction sites are associated with plant, machinery and vehicles.

   Outline the elements of a strategy designed to prevent such accidents. (8)

   Jun 2005 Paper 2 Question 7

In answering this question candidates should identify and outline elements such as:
- *Site planning and maintenance of traffic routes to segregate pedestrians and vehicles.*
- *Imposing site speed restrictions in respect of vehicles and preventing the unauthorised use or movement of plant.*
- *Compliance with the general safety requirements in respect of all plant and machinery such as the proper selection of equipment for the task in hand, the need to ensure that dangerous parts of machines are properly guarded, and that a regime of planned inspections and maintenance and procedures for reporting defects is put in place.*
- *Ensuring that all operators are competent to perform the tasks allotted to them.*

ELEMENT 4

1. **Identify** the main items to be checked by the person appointed to have overall control of a lifting operation which is to be carried out with the use of a crane hired for the purpose. (8)

Dec 2006 Paper 2 Question 4

It is important that the use of lifting equipment on sites is properly controlled and this question tests candidates' knowledge of the checks that should be carried out by a person appointed to have overall control of a lifting operation.

Answers should include reference to items such as:
- *The need to carry out an overall assessment of the operation to take account of the ground conditions for the proposed site of the crane and the presence of any overhead obstructions such as power lines.*
- *The suitability of the lifting appliance and associated equipment selected with particular reference to their safe working loads.*
- *The documentary evidence to prove that the required examinations, inspections and maintenance has been carried out*
- *The competence of all personnel involved in the operation such as the crane driver, slinger and banksman and their familiarity with the hand signals or other means of communication that are to be used.*

2. **Outline** the factors that might cause a mobile crane to overturn during use. (8)

Jun 2006 Paper 2 Question 3

This question probes candidates' knowledge of situations that might cause a mobile crane to overturn. Factors such as the failure to set the crane on a level footing, siting it on poor and unstable ground and failing to distribute the weight of the crane by providing adequate timber beneath outriggers would be likely to cause it to overturn. Additional factors affecting stability would be overloading, incorrect slinging resulting in an unstable load, operating when winds were too strong and driver error such as slewing too quickly or causing an abrupt movement of the jib, both of which could have a detrimental effect on stability.

3. A rolled steel joist (RSJ) is to be used in the support of the second floor of a town house that is being refurbished. It is thought that the layout of the house and the arrangement of the supports are such that mechanical means cannot be used either to transport the RSJ from the ground floor or to lift it into its final position.

    Outline the factors that would need to be considered when undertaking a manual handling assessment of the task. (8)

Jun 2005 Paper 2 Question 5

In some situations, particularly on refurbishment projects, it is not practicable to lift heavy beams by mechanical means. This question is designed to test candidates' understanding of the factors that would need to be considered when carrying out a manual handling assessment of this sort of task.

In carrying out the assessment, consideration would need to be given to the weight and length of the beam, how far it needed to be carried and how high it had to be lifted onto its final resting place. Other factors related to the space available to work in and the condition of the floors and stairs over which the beam had to be carried.

ELEMENT 5

1. The Provision and Use of Work Equipment Regulations 1998 require that work equipment used in hostile environments is inspected at suitable intervals.

    Identify the items on a small dumper truck that should be the subject of such an inspection. (8)

Dec 2005 Paper 2 Question 10

Such items should include:
- *The provision and condition of roll over protection and driver restraints (eg seat belts).*
- *The condition of the bodywork and seat.*
- *The condition of the tyres; the effectiveness of the braking system, steering and warning devices.*
- *The performance of the bucket release and tilt mechanisms.*
- *The integrity of fuel, oil and hydraulic systems.*
- *The legibility of labels and signs.*

2. It is necessary for maintenance purposes to enter a large cement silo situated on a construction site.

    (i) **Identify** the likely hazards. (5)

    (ii) **Outline** the precautions to be taken to reduce the risks to personnel entering the silo. (15)

Jun 2006 Paper 2 Question 1

ASSESSMENT

Silos are increasingly used on construction sites to store cement or mortar and these need to be maintained at times. Part (i) of the question requires candidates to identify the hazards in entering one of these silos whilst in part (ii) they are asked to outline the precautions to be taken to reduce the risks to those entering.

Hazards associated with maintaining this type of plant include: the residues of content (cement); working at height; difficulty of access and egress; oxygen deficiency and poor lighting levels. Marks are also available for recognising that the inside of the silo is a confined space and that there are potential hazards connected with incoming services.

In part (ii), Examiners expect precautions to be outlined such as: the use of personal protective equipment (helmets, gloves, boots and hearing protection); the introduction of a permit-to-work system; atmospheric testing; the provision of adequate lighting; the isolation and locking-off of services and the use of competent and experienced workers.

Candidates who structure their answer by relating answers in part (ii) to the hazards identified in part (i) in a logical sequence do best.

3. **Identify** the main items to be checked by the person appointed to have overall control of a lifting operation which is to be carried out with the use of a crane hired for the purpose. (8)

Dec 2006 Paper 2 Question 4

It is important that the use of lifting equipment on sites is properly controlled and this question tests candidates' knowledge of the checks that should be carried out by a person appointed to have overall control of a lifting operation.

Answers include reference to items such as:

- *The need to carry out an overall assessment of the operation to take account of the ground conditions for the proposed site of the crane and the presence of any overhead obstructions such as power lines.*
- *The suitability of the lifting appliance and associated equipment selected with particular reference to their safe working loads.*
- *The documentary evidence to prove that the required examinations, inspections and maintenance had been carried out.*
- *The competence of all personnel involved in the operation such as the crane driver, slinger and banksman and their familiarity with the hand signals or other means of communication that were to be used.*

ELEMENT 6

1. HSG85 Electricity at Work-Safe Working Practices gives guidance on the frequency of inspection for such equipment.

   State frequencies for the inspection and testing of electrical hand tools and associated equipment used on a construction site and support your answers with appropriate examples. (8)

Dec 2006 Paper 2 Question 3

Users of electrical hand tools need to inspect them before use and that the parts of equipment whose condition should be checked include cables, cord grips, casings and plugs. In addition the recommended frequencies for carrying out inspection and testing are:

- *For 230 volt equipment, a test should be carried out before first use and then at monthly intervals while a formal weekly inspection would also be required.*
- *Equipment operated at 110 volts should be tested before first use and at three monthly intervals with a formal inspection every month.*
- *As for extension leads, the guidance suggests an initial test before first use followed by one at monthly intervals coupled with a daily user check and a formal weekly inspection.*
- *Marks are also available for recognising that a record should be kept of the tests carried out and that equipment should be provided with a label indicating when the next test is due.*

2. Ground works are about to commence on a site crossed by high voltage overhead power lines. The work will involve the use of excavators and tipper lorries to remove spoil from the site.

   Outline a management strategy for the avoidance of accidents involving accidental contact with the overhead power lines. (8)

Dec 2005 Paper 2 Question 4

HSE Guidance Note GS6 identifies the need, when working in the vicinity of overhead power lines, to consult the electricity supply company and to make the lines dead where possible. Other precautions are the erection of goalpost barriers and warning signs. Better answers would also include reference to fitting plant with height restrictors, the use of competent banksmen, communicating the safety precautions to the operatives and having emergency procedures in place.

3. **Outline** the measures to be taken to minimise the risk of shock from the use of electric hand tools. (8)

Jun 2004 Paper 2 Question 3

The most common technique for minimising the effect of shock from electrical equipment on construction sites is the use of reduced low voltage through a transformer centre-tapped to earth together with the use of residual current devices or earth leakage protection.

Other measures include:

- *The protection and safe positioning of supply cables, using double-insulated or cordless (battery-operated) equipment.*
- *Ensuring the correct rating of fuses and introducing a system for the routine visual inspection.*
- *Testing of cables and equipment.*

ELEMENT 7

1. (a) **Outline** the practical measures that should be adopted to prevent fires and explosions during welding operations on a construction site. (6)

   (b) **Identify TWO** types of radiation associated with welding activities. (2)

   Jun 2006 Paper 2 Question 10

Various types of welding are common on construction sites and this question seeks to probe candidates' knowledge of practical ways of preventing fires and explosion.

In answering part (a), measures that should be adopted for electric arc welding include cleaning and securing electrical connections, ensuring the proper earthing of equipment and the work piece, and the maintenance and testing of transformers and other equipment. In the case of gas welding, reference should be made to the fitting of flashback arrestors, the storage and transportation of cylinders and the visual inspection of hoses and connections prior to use. General measures to prevent fires are the removal of combustible material in the welding area and the purging of vessels prior to welding. Reference to the provision of fire extinguishers may be mentioned although they may help to reduce or prevent the spread of fire, they do nothing to prevent the fire occurring.

In part (b), identify that visible light, infra-red, and ultra-violet radiation are associated with welding activities.

2. Timber sections are stored in an enclosed compound.

   (i) **Describe** the precautions that should be taken to prevent a fire occurring. (4)

   (ii) **Identify** the extinguishing media that may be used for dealing with a fire in such a situation, and **explain** how each works to extinguish the fire. (4)

   Jun 2004 Paper 2 Question 4

For part (i) of the question, candidates are expected to describe precautions such as ensuring that the storage area is secure (thereby reducing the risk of arson or accidental fires), separating the stored timber from flammable materials, keeping the area clear of paper and other rubbish and vegetation, and prohibiting smoking or operations involving hot work near to the compound.

For part (ii), candidates should identify the use of water to cool the fire and dampen adjacent timber, and foam to exclude oxygen. Other extinguishing media include sand or carbon dioxide.

3. A major hazard on a refurbishment project is fire.

   (i) **Identify THREE** activities that represent an increased fire risk in such a situation. (3)

   (ii) **Outline** the precautions that may be taken to prevent a fire from occurring. (5)

   Jun 2005 Paper 2 Question 6

For part (i) answers include cutting and welding, the use of flammable or highly flammable materials, electrical work, individuals smoking and burning rubbish on site.

In part (ii), candidate should outline precautions such as the inspection and testing of electrical systems, hot work permit systems, inspection of the work area after the completion of hot work, regular clearing away of accumulated rubbish, the proper storage of flammable and combustible materials, the control of smoking and the prohibition of bonfires.

ELEMENT 8

1. (a) **Describe** the typical symptoms of occupational dermatitis. (2)

   (b) **Identify** the factors that will influence the likelihood of dermatitis occurring amongst site operatives handling wet cement. (6)

   Jun 2006 Paper 2 Question 2

Dermatitis is quite common among construction workers and this question probes candidates' understanding of the problems. Good descriptions of symptoms are reddening, blistering and cracking of skin, leading to ulceration and infection in severe cases.

For part (b), the influencing factors include: duration, frequency and extent of contact with wet cement; existing skin conditions such as cuts and abrasions; failure to use personal protective equipment such as gloves and overalls and a lack of welfare facilities. Additional factors to include are individual sensitivity and personal hygiene practices.

2. **Outline** a system for the management and disposal of waste from a construction site. (8)

ASSESSMENT

Jun 2006 Paper 2 Question 5

Do not restrict responses to only the management and disposal of asbestos waste. All construction waste, if not categorised as hazardous waste (e.g. asbestos) falls into the category of controlled waste.

Candidates should identify matters such as: separating the waste into similar types (rubble, timber, plasterboard, adhesives, etc) and ensuring it is properly contained; the need to describe the waste accurately on transfer notes; the use of licensed contractors to remove the waste from site and additionally making the necessary checks to ensure that the waste is transferred by the carrier to a licensed tip or transfer station. Marks are also available for referring to the use of minimising or recycling techniques and for recognising that burning is an inappropriate disposal method.

3. **List** the information that should be included in a manufacturer's safety data sheet for a hazardous substance used on a construction site. (8)

Dec 2005 Paper 2 Question 11

The information that must be provided on a manufacturer's data sheet is specified in schedule 4 to the Chemicals (Hazard Information and Packaging for Supply) Regulations 2002 and includes: the name of the substance; composition/information on ingredients; the nature of the hazards presented; first-aid measures; fire-fighting measures; accidental release measures; precautions to be taken in its handling and storage; exposure controls and personal protection; physical and chemical properties of the substance; information on its stability and reactivity; toxicological information (e.g. health effects); ecological information; disposal considerations; transport information and regulatory information.

ELEMENT 9

1. **Outline** the actions that site management might consider in order to reduce levels of occupational stress amongst workers on site. (8)

Jun 2005 Paper 2 Question 7

Options that are available to management to reduce stress levels amongst their employees include those related to the environment and those associated with organisational, job and individual stress factors. In the former category, actions include reduction in noise levels, provision of adequate levels of lighting and the maintenance of high levels of housekeeping while for the latter, actions might be those related to work/life balance (such as discouraging the working of excessively long hours and introducing flexible working arrangements); introducing job rotation and increasing work variety; drawing up clear job descriptions and taking steps to match individuals to the descriptions; seeking the views of employees and involving them in decisions; introducing and implementing policies to cover harassment, discrimination, violence and the investigation of complaints and ensuring adequate levels of supervision with supervisors trained to recognise the symptoms of stress so that ameliorative action can be taken or, in extreme cases, so that those affected might be offered counselling.

2. **Outline**, with reasons, the particular health issues that should be addressed during routine health surveillance examinations for construction workers. (8)

Dec 2005 Paper 2 Question 3

Construction work may have a long term affect upon the health of workers and this question is designed to test candidates' understanding of these effects including their causes and detection. Refer to effects on the lungs caused by exposure to chemicals such as silica or isocyanates; musculoskeletal problems arising from manual handling; dermatitis following contact with cement or solvents; hearing loss caused by exposure to high levels of noise and hand arm vibration syndrome following the use of vibrating or percussive tools. The intention of routine health surveillance is to identify early signs of such conditions so that corrective action can be taken. Health surveillance typically also includes checks on general health issues such as sight, blood pressure and general well-being in order to assess a person's fitness to work.

ELEMENT 10

1. **Describe** the specific measures that may be necessary to ensure safety when work is to be carried out from a scaffold that overhangs a fast flowing river. (8)

Jun 2006 Paper 2 Question 8

Working above water brings an extra dimension to workplace safety and where the water is fast flowing additional risks are to be expected. Descriptions of safety measures should include: protection for river traffic (advance warnings, lighting of obstructions and consultation with river authorities); the provision of means of preventing falls, such as additional guardrails to working platforms or fall arrest equipment such as safety nets or harnesses; the provision of rescue equipment such as life belts and the availability of a rescue boat under the control of a competent person, should someone fall into the water. Marks are also available for recognising that the scaffold needs protection against the possibility of being struck by river traffic.

2. **Outline** the measures to be taken to prevent falls associated with stairwells and other holes in floors during the construction of a multi storey building. (8)

Dec 2005 Paper 2 Question 9

Most serious injuries on construction sites are as a result of falls. The risk of falls from a height is present on almost all sites at some stage. It is important, therefore, that those with responsibilities for safety have a good understanding of the measures needed to minimise this particular risk.

Good answers should refer to:
- *The provision of guard rails for stairwells and lift shafts, and hand rails on stairs.*
- *Fixing covers over other holes in floors.*
- *Providing adequate levels of lighting.*
- *Ensuring a good standard of housekeeping and a high level of supervision and control.*

3. **Outline** the requirements of the Construction (Head Protection) Regulations 1989.

Dec 2004 Paper 2 Question 8

This question is designed to test candidates' knowledge of the stated Regulations. The main requirements that are expected to be outlined are the obligations on employers to provide suitable head protection for their employees, to ensure that it is stored, maintained and replaced when necessary, and to enforce the wearing of the protection provided unless there is no foreseeable risk of head injury. Similarly, there is an obligation on employees to wear the head protection when required and to report defects.

ELEMENT 11

1. **Sketch** a labelled diagram of a steel trench support system that clearly shows ait the main components and features, (8)

Dec 2004 Paper 2 Question 7

Candidates can choose to sketch either a sheet or a box system, providing that the components and features relevant to the chosen method are identified.

For the box system sketches should show interlocking trench sheets (toed in at the bottom of the trench and rising above the top), walers, wedges, struts, edge protection and means of access to the trench via a protected area.

For a support box system, sketches should depict, as well as the elements in common with the sheet system, the correct installation of rams, the presence of lifting eyes and weight indicators.

2. **Identify**:
    (i) **FOUR** specific hazards associated with work in a confined space. (4)
    (ii) **FOUR** examples of a confined space that may be encountered on a construction site. (4)

Dec 2005 Paper 2 Question 8

Work in confined spaces is quite common in construction. For part (a), a range of possible hazards include the presence of toxic, flammable or explosive fumes and vapours, lack of oxygen, oxygen enrichment, ingress of fluids, falls of materials, the possibility of injury, particularly to the head, due to restricted space, and claustrophobic effects.

For part (b) provide examples of a confined space such as manholes, sewers, tunnels, excavations, tanks, chambers and pits and unventilated rooms.

3. A project involves shallow excavations in land previously used as a landfill site.

    Outline the welfare facilities that should be provided for such work. (8)

Dec 2006 Paper 2 Question 6

Welfare facilities that should be provided for operatives excavating through a landfill site include:
- *Hot and cold or warm running water with soap and towels made available;.*
- *Showers.*
- *A sufficient number of toilets and the provision of changing rooms with separate storage for contaminated and clean clothing.*
- *Facilities for drying clothing.*
- *A room set aside for taking meals and refreshment, equipped with means of boiling water and heating food.*
- *First aid facilities.*

ELEMENT 12

1. A three-storey office block is to be demolished. **Outline** the likely hazards to the environment caused by the work together with the actions needed to control them. (8)

Dec 2003 Paper 2 Question 5

Refer to hazards such as noise, dust, silt affecting drainage systems, and mud and debris being deposited on adjacent roads.

Appropriate control measures include: damping down the structure to reduce the production of dust, sheeting of disposal vehicles, noise controls (such as barriers), fitting filters or stoppers to site drain gullies and bunding of fuel tanks.

ASSESSMENT

2. **Outline** the main areas to be addressed in a demolition method statement. (8)

Jun 2006 Paper 2 Question 7

This question is intended to probe candidates' understanding of the various factors that need to be considered when drawing up a method statement for a demolition project. The method statement essentially sets out the sequence of work and the methods to be employed for each part of the work. In this case, particular emphasis needs to be placed on preparation work (such as pre-weakening, temporary propping, and isolation of existing services), protection of the public, control of noise and dust, and the removal of waste from the site. The statement would additionally need to address issues such as dealing with hazardous materials, the provision of temporary services, emergency procedures, control and co-ordination on site, and the competencies of the personnel involved in the demolition work.

3. A large industrial site has been closed recently. The owners of the site are to have the buildings demolished before selling the site for redevelopment.

    Outline the issues the principal demolition contractor should address as part of the health and safety plan. (20)

Dec 2005 Paper 2 Question 1

Issues that the principal demolition contractor will have to address as part of the health and safety plan include:
- *Arrangements for the coordination of all contractors on site.*
- *Risk assessments (including specific assessments under the Control of Substances Hazardous to Health Regulations and for noise).*
- *The sequence of work.*
- *Demolition method statements.*
- *Procedures for evaluating the competency of sub-contractors*
- *Arrangements for liaising with the client and planning supervisor.*

Issues connected with the more practical aspects of the work include:
- *The control of noise and dust (and particularly asbestos if found to be present).*
- *The prevention of water course contamination.*
- *Isolation of existing services.*
- *The need for the introduction of permit to work systems.*
- *The common use of plant and access equipment.*
- *Traffic management systems including pedestrian segregation and access and egress to and from the site.*
- *The control and disposal of waste.*

Marks are also awarded to candidates who identify additional issues to be addressed such as welfare and first aid arrangements; procedures for the reporting of accidents to the enforcing authority; the provision of information and training and importantly arrangements for the regular monitoring of compliance with health and safety standards and procedures on site.

QUESTIONS REQUIRING KNOWLEDGE FROM MORE THAN ONE ELEMENT

1. On a long-term contract, joiners are working with medium density fibreboard using hand-held circular saws and portable electric planers in a temporary site unit. **Explain** how you would ensure that the joiners' health is not put at risk during this activity. (8)

Jun 2006 Paper 2 Question 9

Work of this nature produces dust, vibration and noise all of which have the potential to affect joiners' health.

Identify measures that include:
- *Assessments of the levels of dust, noise and vibration.*
- *The provision of efficient dust extraction equipment or respirators with the appropriate protection factor.*
- *The provision of hearing protection.*
- *The need to manage vibration by the use of lower vibration tools or job rotation.*

Index

A
Accidents, 30, 41, 96, 110
Acute chronic health effects, 143
Agents
    biological, 131
    chemical, 131
    forms, 131
Alarm systems for fire, 120
Alteration of existing premises, 3
Arrangements
    emergency, 211
Asbestos, 152, 153
    identification, 152
    requirements for removal, 154
Assessment initial site, 17
Avoiding premature collapse, 214

B
Base plates, 188
Basic electricity circuitry, 92
Biological agents, 131
Brick guards, 189
British standards, 11
'Building works', 3

C
Causes
    common for fires, 95
    fires during construction work, 110
CDM co-ordinators duties, 7
CE marking, 69
Cellars, 218
Chemical agents, 131
Chemicals (Hazard Information and Packaging for Supply) Regulations (CHIP 3) 2002, 222
Chronic health effects, 143
'Civil engineering', 3
Classification
    fires, 110
Cleaning, 4
Client duties, 6
Combustible materials, 115
Confined spaces, 207
    hazards associated with, 208
Confined Spaces Regulations (CSR) 1997, 224
Construction (Design and Management) Regs. (CDM) 2007, 7, 225
Construction (Head Protection) Regulations (CHPR) 1989, 234
Contact with overhead power lines, 104
Contaminated ground, 17, 201, 206
Content of the pre-construction information pack, 9
Contractors duties, 8
Control measures, 20
    dust, 33, 151
    electricity, 92
    enclosure, 144
    health surveillance, 150, 168, 171, 207
    ignition sources, 115
    lifting operations, 56
    local exhaust ventilation, 144
    other protective equipment and clothing, 148
    pedestrian hazards, 30
    personal hygiene and protection regimes, 149
    process changes, 144
    reduced time exposure, 144
    respiratory protective equipment, 146
    use and limitations of dilution ventilation, 146
    vehicle operations, 37
Control of Asbestos Regulations (CAR) 2006, 235
Control of Noise at Work Regulations (CNWR) 2005, 237
Control of Substances Hazardous to Health Regulations (COSHH) 2002, 239
Controlled collapse and pre-weakening demolition, 200
Conveyors, 55, 58
Cranes, 187
Crawling boards, 196

D
Dangerous Substances & Explosive Atmospheres Regulations. (DSEAR) 2002, 244
Decoration, 4
Defective equipment, 72, 78, 111
Definition
    fire, 109
Demolition, 3
    avoidance of premature collapse, 214, 216
    cellars, 218
    competence of workforce, 217
    disposal of waste, 221
    dust, 33, 133, 140, 151, 215
    environment, 217
    falling materials, 214
    hazardous substances, 215
    investigation /survey, 217
    method of construction, 218
    method statement, 219
    noise, 215
    plant and machinery, 216
    proximity of other structures, 218
Demolition and dismantling, 3
Designer duties, 7
    structural condition, 218
    type of structure, 217
Detection of fire, 112, 120
Double insulation, 102
Drugs and alcohol, 177
Dumper trucks, 34, 52
Duration rate, 17, 93
Duty of care, employer's, 158

E
Earthing, 100
Electricity
    protective systems, 99
    basic circuitry, 92
    burns, 95
    control measures, 97
    fires, 95
    hazards, 93, 96
    inspection and maintenance, 102
    overhead power lines, 102
    portable electrical equipment, 96
    principles, 92
    secondary hazards, 96
    selection and suitability of equipment, 97
    shock and its effect on the body, 93
    site electrical systems, 98
Electricity at Work Regulations (EWR) 1989, 246
Elimination or substitution, 143
Emergency
    Arrangements, 183
Employer's
    duty of care, 158
Enclosure, 144
Ensuring competence of workforce, 217
Environmental
    effluent and atmospheric pollution control, 155
    issues, 155
    protection, 155
    waste disposal, 158
Environmental Protection Act (EPA) 1990, 155, 248
Equipment
    procedures for defects, 78
Ergonomics, 161
European standards, 11
Evacuation procedures, 125
Examination of work equipment, 63, 72
Excavations, 4, 200, 203
    contaminated ground, 207
    hazards, 36, 200
Excavators, 52
External agencies, 12
Extinguishing media, 122

INDEX

F
Fabrication, 4
Falls of persons, 200
Fans, 197
Fire
    alarm systems, 120
    basic principles, 109
    causes during construction work, 110
    classification of fires, 110
    common causes, 110
    control measures, 110
    detection systems, 120
    drills, 126
    evacuation procedures, 125
    extinguishing media, 122
    good housekeeping, 118
    means of escape, 124
    portable fire fighting equipment, 120
    precautions, 109
    provision for disabled, 126
    risk assessment, 112
    spread of fire and smoke, 120
    systems of work, 116
First aid, 23, 25, 94
Flammable and combustible materials
    fire, 120
    storage, 115, 120
    gases in cylinders, 120
Forklift trucks, 51
Format of the pre-construction information pack, 9
Forms of agents, 131

G
General requirements for work equipment, 68
Good housekeeping and fire, 118
Gradients, 35
Ground consolidation equipment, 85, 90
Ground level barriers, 105
Guard rails, 86, 87, 88
Guards and safety devices,
Guidelines for assessment of manual handling operations, 47

H
Hand tools, 76
Hazard
    confined spaces, 207
    excavations, 200
    machinery, 79
    manual handling, 215
    electricity, 92
    pedestrians, 28
    site vehicle, 34
    to the public from street works, 29
Hazardous substances in demolition, 215
Health and safety
    moral, legal and financial argument, 6
    sources of information, 12
Health and Safety (Display Screen Equipment) Regulations (DSE) 1992, 254
Health and Safety (First-Aid) Regulations (FAR) 1981, 254
Health and Safety (Safety Signs and Signals) Regulations (SSSR) 1996, 255
Health and Safety at Work etc. Act (HASAWA) 1974, 255
Hierarchy of measures
    machinery, 86
Highly flammable or flammable liquids, 119
Hoists, 54, 57, 190
HSE and HSC publications, 11

I
Ignition sources, 115
Information
    pre-construction, 9
    provision of, 11
    to be included by the supplier, 137
    providing hazard, 137
    limitations, 138
    training, 163
Information, instruction, training and supervision, 49, 89
Inspection and examination, 72
    excavations, 207
    work equipment, 184
Inspection, 103
    frequency, 103
    records, 104
    requirements, 146, 191
Installation, removal and maintenance of services, 4
International standards, 11
Ionising Radiations Regulations (IRR) 1999, 258
Isolation of services, 100, 220
IT sources, 11

J
Joint occupation
    co-operation and co-ordination, 23
    premises, 23

K
Keyboard operation, 162

L
Ladders, 192
Landscaping, 4
Legislation, 11
Lifting equipment, 63
Lifting operations and lifting equipment, 51, 56
    accessories, 58
    control of lifting operations, 60
    cranes, 56, 58
    special requirements, 63
Lifting Operations and Lifting Equipment Regulations (LOLER) 1998, 260
Lifting techniques for manual handling, 50
Liquefied petroleum and other gases in cylinders, 118
Loading, unloading and storage of materials, 4
Local exhaust ventilation, 144

M
Machinery guards
    fixed guards, 86
    self adjusting, 88
    fixed, 29, 34
    guards and safety devices, 86, 87, 88, 91, 189
    hierarchy of measures, 86
    mechanical hazards, 79
    non-mechanical hazards, 81
    trip device, 87
Maintenance, 102, 121, 148, 168, 170
Maintenance of existing premises, 3
Management of Health and Safety at Work Regulations (MHSWR) 1999, 76, 260
Management systems for driver competence, 42
Manual handling, 46, 214, 217, 265
    hazards, 46
    means of minimising the risks from, 49
    risks assessment, 46, 49
Manual Handling operations Regulations (MHOR) 1992, 265
Manually operated load moving equipment, 53, 57
Manufacturers' data, 11
Maximum exposure limits, 142
Means of escape, 124
Mechanical handling
    dumper trucks, 52, 57
    equipment operators, 56
    excavators, 52, 57
    forklift trucks, 51, 56
    hoists, 54, 57
    manually operated load moving equipment, 53, 57
    telehandlers, 52, 57
Mechanical hazards, 79, 82, 201
Method of construction, 218
Minimising
    manual handling risks, 49
    pollution from waste, 159
Mobile tower scaffolding, 187

N
Nets, 189, 196, 197
New Roads and Street Works Act 1991, 266
Noise, 163
    action levels, 169
    control techniques, 166
    environmental, 33
    hearing, 163
    measurement techniques, 165
    personal hearing protection, 167
Non-english speaking workers, 5
Non-mechanical hazards, 79
Notification of projects, 8

O
Objective of machinery guarding, 85
Office machinery, 83, 90
Operation and emergency controls, 74
Organic solvents, 133
Oxygen meters, 140

INDEX

P

Particular construction issues, 4
Pedestrians
    hazards, 28
    measures for no segregation from vehicles, 38
    segregating from vehicles, 34
Personal hygiene, 149
Personal protective equipment and clothing, 89, 148, 154, 206, 211
Personal Protective Equipment at Work Regulations (PPER) 1992, 268
Piecemeal demolition, 219
Poor levels of numeracy and literacy of workers, 5
Portable
    electrical equipment, 96
    fire fighting equipment, 121
    power tools, 76
Power tools, 76
Practicable, 143
Precautions
    excavations, 36
    safe entry confined spaces, 207, 208
Pre-construction information, 8
Preparation of the health and safety file, 10
Preparation of the health and safety plan, 8
Prime concerns, priorities and targets of the regulator, 5
Principles
    fire, 109
    heat transmission and fire spread, 110
    electricity, 92
Principle contractors duties, 7
Procedural
    defective equipment, 72
Process changes, 144
Protection
    environment, 217
    falling materials, 38
    machinery hazards, 79
    others working at height, 194
    public and others, 220
Provision and Use of Work Equipment Regulations (PUWER) 1998, 68, 69, 70, 71, 72, 74, 75, 85, 91, 269
Proximity of other structures, 202, 218
Putlog scaffolding, 185

R

Radiation, 120, 171
    ionising, 172
    means of controlling exposures, 174
    non-ionising, 173
    typical occupational sources, 174
Reasonably practicable, 143
Reasons why fires spread, 111
Reduced time exposure, 144
Reduced voltage, 100
Renovation of existing premises, 3
Reporting of Injuries, Diseases and Dangerous Occurrences Regulations (RIDDOR) 1995, 273
Residual current device, 101
Respiratory protective equipment, 146
Risk assessment
    fire, 112
    hazard, 201
    confined spaces, 209
Risk
    drugs, 177
    falling, 181
    heights, 181
Roof work, 196
Routes of entry, 134

S

Safety devices and guards, 86
Scaffolding, 184
    base plates, 188
    brick guards, 188
    fans, 187
    guard rails, 188
    independent tied scaffolding, 184
    inspection, 191
    mobile tower scaffolding, 187
    nets, 196
    putlog scaffolding, 185
    sheeting, 190
    sole boards, 188
    toe boards, 188
Scope and application of the Construction (Design and Management) Regulations 2007, 6
Scope of work equipment, 68
Selection
    drivers, 41
    electrical equipment, 97
Services, 202,

Severity rate, 93
Sheeting, 190, 197
Signs, 21, 40, 124, 197
Site
    arrangements with client/occupier of premises, 23
    assessment, 17
    clearance, 3
    controls and facilities, 20
    electrical systems, 98
    movements, 4
    planning, 20
    preparation for specialist activities, 21
    rules, 23, 41
    security and means of protecting the public, 22
Smoke control, 120
Sole boards, 188
Statutory restrictions of work equipment, 70
Storage of flammable and combustible materials, 115
Street works
    hazards to the public, 29
    public vehicle hazards during, 36
    traffic safety measures and signs, 42
Stress, 176
Structural condition, 218
Suitability of work equipment, 68
Supply of Machinery (Safety) Regulations (SMSR) 1992, 275
Surveys for health risks, 138

T

Telehandlers, 52
Temperature, 171
Temporary nature of construction activities and the constantly changing workplace, 4
The legal, moral and financial consequences of failing to manage health and safety within the construction industry, 5
The particular duties under the Construction (Design and Management) Regulations (CDM) 2007
The size of the construction health and safety 'problem' in terms of numbers of work related fatalities and incidents of ill health, 5
Time pressures from clients, 5
Toe boards, 188
Tools, 76
    hand tools, 76
    portable power tools, 76
    procedures for defective equipment, 78
Tower scaffolding, 187
Trade organisations, 11
Traffic safety measures and signs for street works, 42
Training,
    mechanical handling, 56
    cranes, 59
    work equipment, 70
    fire equipment, 122
Transitory nature of workers, 4
Type of structure, 217

U

Use and limitations of dilution ventilation, 14
Use of flammable and combustible materials, 115

V

Vehicle operations, 34
    protective measures for people and structures on site, 40
    public vehicles hazards during public highway works, 36
    selection and training of drivers, 41
    site rules, 23
    site vehicle hazards, 34
    traffic safety measures and signs for street works, 42
    vehicle safety requirements, 40
Vehicles
    hazards, 34
    measures when segregation is not practicable, 39
    safety requirements, 40
    segregating pedestrians, 38
Vibration, 168
    effects of exposure, 168
    preventive and precautionary measures, 170
    risk activities, 169
Violence, 177
    risk factors, 177

INDEX

W

Weather conditions, 5
Welfare, 24, 206, 220
Who are contractors and the self employed, 8
Who is the CDM co-ordinator, 7
Who is the principle contractor, 7
Work equipment
    inspection requirements for, 184
    general requirements for, 68
Working at height
    base plates, 188
    brick guards, 189
    fall arrest equipment, 195, 196
    fans, 197
    guard rails, 188
    hazards and risks, 181
    independent tied scaffolding, 184
    ladders, 192
    mobile elevating work platforms (MEWP), 191
    mobile tower scaffolding, 187
    nets, 189, 196
    other techniques for working at a height, 194
    protection of others, 196
    putlog scaffolding, 185
    roof work, 196
    scaffolding, 184
    sheeting, 190
    sole boards, 188
    toe boards, 188
    working over water, 197
Working over water, 197
Workplace (Health, Safety and Welfare) Regulations (WHSWR) 1992, 76
Work-related ill-health, 6
'Works of engineering construction', 3
Workstation design, 161
    ergonomics, 161
    ill-health effects, 162
    preventative and precautionary measures, 163
    risk activities, 162